Labor Law and Legislation

Fifth Edition

A. Howard Myers A.B., M.A., Ph.D.

Visiting Professor of Labor Relations
College of Business and Public Administration
Florida Atlantic University

David P. Twomey B.S., M.B.A., J.D.

Associate Professor of Law
School of Management
Boston College

Published by

L97   **SOUTH-WESTERN PUBLISHING CO.**

CINCINNATI   WEST CHICAGO, III.   DALLAS   PELHAM MANOR, N.Y.
PALO ALTO, CALIF.   BRIGHTON, ENGLAND

ISBN: 0-538-12970-0

Library of Congress Catalog Card Number: 74-78643

345Ki987

Printed in the United States of America

Preface

This Fifth Edition of *Labor Law and Legislation* retains the objective of previous editions: presenting a "coherent picture of labor law and legislation in its present social setting as conditioned by landmarks of the historical past." To achieve this continuing objective, many older cases have been removed or reduced to textual reference, making room for cases and materials of more current significance.

The evolving labor law concepts are presented in both case and essay form in order to help the student gain a fuller understanding of problems of labor relations in the United States, the legislative foundations of our labor laws, and the legal processes and institutions that infuse our labor law with its effectiveness. Case and chapter questions are utilized to further assist the student in reaching an understanding of the materials.

Our book is designed primarily for use by students not in law school. Keeping this in mind, we strove at all times to achieve clarity and conciseness of presentation without sacrificing completeness and research of a professional quality. If we succeeded, this book will be useful as well to lawyers and those in law school.

We, the authors, wish to express appreciation to all those who have helped to make this book possible; especially Stephen J. Mueller, who was sole author of the original edition and co-author of the second edition.

A. H. M.

Boca Raton, Florida
Squantum, Massachusetts

D. P. T.

Contents

Chapter 5/ Bargaining Units and Representation

Chapter 6/ Employer Unfair Labor Practices

Chapter 7/ Union Unfair Labor Practices

Chapter 8/ Picket and Boycott Activity

Chapter 9/ Legality of Strikes

Chapter 10/ Dispute Settlement Law

Chapter 11/ Regulating Internal Union Conduct

Chapter 12/ Fair Employment Practices

Chapter 13/ Public Employment and Labor Law

Appendix

Table of Cases

NOTE: The majority of the footnotes in the cases have been omitted. The remaining footnotes in the cases have been renumbered to conform with the chapter numbering.

Chapter 1

Labor Law—Sources and Doctrines

SECTION I / THE LAW AND LABOR

The law can be defined as a body of rules for guiding our conduct or as an instrument for social control. In our democratic system law provides a framework for group relations and an orderly method of change. With established procedures and rules, the law gives the stability of conservative methods to the governing authorities and to the individuals and interest groups that are governed. With the continuing development of new needs and changed conditions, the law affords us a flexible means of adaptation to a dynamic economy and an evolving society.

Public law regulates groups and classes in their relationships to each other; and in the total community interest, it protects their rights as indicated by public interest considerations. Thus, the seeds of labor law began to develop when the majority of the people in Western Europe ceased to be serfs or vassals with the ending of feudalism, and as wage earners depended upon property owners for their terms of employment. In early America the supply and demand of a local market were soon affected by spontaneous self-help efforts of working groups and the start of trade unions. The courts were asked to intervene on occasion to determine the rights of owners, laborers, and the public. What we call common or judge-made law thus evolved in the employment relationships, individual and collective, with rights defined from conflict-of-interest situations.

Our American constitutional form of government divides the responsibility for the law and its evolutionary change. The division of authority between the federal government and the state governments is defined by constitutional standards. Jurisdictional lines are themselves subject to interpretation and modification by both judicial and legislative action. The substance of the labor-management law itself has evolved through legislation, judicial decisions, administrative rulings, and executive enforcement as a joint product of the three branches of government. These all interact upon one another, and from this interaction labor law has evolved.

As we shall see, the influence of the courts for over a century was directed primarily at protecting the right of contract, property, and the freedom of the market, which frequently left the worker with little opportunity or market power to match the employer's superior position, his bargaining power, and his economic security. In the past fifty years, however, the neglect of human rights and the support of property rights in the "free" market has been corrected, mostly by legislation. That reversal in recent decades has caused a revolution of labor standards and union relations. The evolving public policy and its case-by-case application to specific areas of management and labor activity provide the subject matter of the ensuing chapters.

Notwithstanding the sensitivity of labor law in its process of adjustment to the unending needs of a competitive economic system, or the fact that its rules do not lend themselves to definite cataloguing, it will be well to remember that any area of law is essentially effect and not cause. Labor law, too, cannot be subjected to meaningful scrutiny apart from its cause—the social setting in which particular rules of law arise, are modified, or are rescinded. The legal controls on conduct of management and labor become coherent only in this broader view.

Thus, at the outset, two broad questions are presented. First, what are the sources of current American labor law? Second, what early doctrines and historical landmarks have influenced the course that labor law and legislation has subsequently taken? It should be apparent that little more than a survey treatment can be accorded these questions.

SECTION 2 / SOURCES OF LABOR LAW

Labor law is a heterogeneous body of regulations which slices through and draws upon other established fields for much of its procedure and substance. When, for example, a labor union enters into a collective agreement with an employer, that agreement becomes subject to the law of contract as to its validity and construction. If it is breached by one of the parties, the law of evidence is resorted to in proving the agreement and its breach, while the law of damages may determine the compensation to be rendered the aggrieved party. In the course of the breach of a contract, assuming that a trespass to person or property has been committed as an incident of strike or picketing activity, the rules peculiar to tort law are brought into play. If an injunction is requested, the law of equity is invoked. In defense of picketing activity, the labor union may attempt to hold itself blameless under rules of agency or may seek to show that it was merely exercising rights guaranteed by the Constitution under the First, Fifth, or Fourteenth Amendments. This will serve to illustrate the complexity of our first source, namely, the rules of law drawn from other fields.

A second major source of American labor law is found in our heritage from the English as to their common law and their statutory enactments.

A third source of our labor law, the most important, is the authority to be found in the Federal Constitution. Legislation such as the National Labor Relations Act and the Railway Labor Act have been enacted by Congress under the delegated powers in the Constitution, principally under the commerce power. Not only is the Constitution important because it is the source of all Congressional authority, but also in the labor area because of certain rights that it guarantees to all citizens. Such concepts as freedom of speech and press have been the nexus of extended litigation involving permissible strike, picket, and boycott activity by labor unions.

The following sections of the Constitution are reprinted here because they embrace the principal powers and rights mentioned above and are repeatedly referred to in many of the cases included in this series.

1. Article I. Section 8. "The Congress shall have Power. . . . To regulate Commerce with foreign Nations, and among the several States, and with the Indian Tribes. . . ."
2. First Amendment. "Congress shall make no law respecting an establishment of religion, or prohibiting the free exercise thereof; or abridging the freedom of speech, or of the press; or the right of the people peaceably to assemble, and to petition the Government for a redress of grievances."
3. Fifth Amendment. "No person shall . . . be deprived of life, liberty, or property, without due process of law. . . ."
4. Fourteenth Amendment. Section 1. ". . . No State shall make or enforce any law which shall abridge the privileges or immunities of citizens of the United States; nor shall any State deprive any person of life, liberty, or property, without due process of law; nor deny to any person within its jurisdiction the equal protection of the laws."

The federal government has only a limited police power, that is, power to burden property and contract rights in the interest of the general welfare. It has only such police power as is required to effectuate its express and implied powers under the Constitution. The bulk of police power thus resides in the several states, never having been delegated by them to the national government. Under their police power, state legislatures have enacted legislation covering workmen's compensation, minimum wages, and general laws touching upon the safety, health, or morals of constituents. Some of the cases herein included treat of the thorny problem facing the Supreme Court when it is called upon to decide a conflict between the state's reserved police power and the constitutional rights of due process and equal protection of laws guaranteed to federal citizens by the Fifth and Fourteenth Amendments.

State constitutions are another source of labor law. They are of prime importance at present because of the vast body of state labor legislation that is subjected to scrutiny in the state courts. It should be noted, however, that, in case of ultimate conflict between the state constitution and the Federal Constitution, the latter prevails; but, as a point of initial inquiry, in cases in the state courts the state constitution is controlling.

Next to be considered are the legislative enactments of federal and state bodies. Federal laws such as the National Labor Relations Act, the Fair Labor Standards Act, and the Federal Anti-Injunction Act find their counterparts in state legislation, such as laws governing the limits of permissible strike, picket, and boycott activity. Included are statutes protecting employee and employer in individual dealings and in collective bargaining relations, laws as to dispute handling, and labor standards laws restraining the effects of competition in the labor market. A state act may be concurrent with federal legislation or may exist in the absence of similar federal legislation. If state and federal acts in the same area are inconsistent, then the federal law prevails.

Court decisions, or case law, contribute an important segment to the law of this field. Under some statutes, such as the National Labor Relations Act, only the federal courts have complete jurisdiction; as to others, state courts have jurisdiction concurrent with the federal. On the other hand, if jurisdictional requirements are met, such as diversity of citizenship or presentment of a federal question, the federal courts may be a forum concurrent with those of the state, even as to the interpretation of a state legislative enactment or the application of a state common-law rule. Case law is a term roughly synonymous with the term "common law." In a more accurate sense, however, a common-law rule is one developed by a court decision in the absence of a statute governing the issue.

Final contribution to the mass of labor law comes from a relatively new source, namely, administrative law. Thousands of rules and decisions are promulgated annually by such agencies as the National Labor Relations Board and the Wage and Hour Administrator of the Fair Labor Standards Act; an example on the state side is the Wisconsin Employment Relations Board, which interprets and carries out the provisions of Wisconsin's Employment Relations Act. These are quasi-legislative and judicial agencies set up to administer those labor laws that require continuing application and interpretation. The courts have been divested of some of their powers in this area because as purely judicial bodies, relatively inexpert and slow in decision, they are not effective for the expeditious settlement of labor controversies; hence, legislatures have more and more delegated interpretative and policing powers to administrative agencies.

The courts, nevertheless, have not been completely divested of their control over the results since administrative decisions and rulings are subjected to court review in the enforcement process. Therefore, court decisions for the most part appear in subsequent chapters as the conclusive authority.

Thus, labor law can be described as stable but not static, being determined by the justices' check on the conduct of administrators. They still exercise the right of review as to matters of law; matters of fact that are decided by the agency below, if supported by evidence, are generally not disturbed by the courts. The amended National Labor Relations Act provides that the validity of a factual determination by the National Labor Relations Board depends upon whether it is supported, not by some evidence as under the 1935 Act, but by substantial evidence. Thus, the powers of evidentiary review by the federal courts have seemingly been expanded by the amendment of 1947 although the Act does not provide for a trial *de novo* in the courts, but only for a review as to points of law.

SECTION 3 / SECONDARY SOURCES

Secondary sources of labor law, such as the reports of legislative committees, debates, and hearings, may be turned to by administrative bodies or by the courts in connection with the application or the interpretation of legislation that is vague or unclear as to language or as to objective. If the intent is ambiguous, boards or the courts can search the legislative record of discussions leading to the enactment of the statute to determine what the drafters intended to accomplish.

Another secondary source of labor law arises from the conduct of the participants in collective bargaining. Thus, management-union agreements provide a body of rules and procedures, including arbitration of differences as to what shall be included in new agreements or over grievances arising under existing agreements. This contractual law has been called "industrial jurisprudence."

As has been stated already, much of labor law reflects social and economic developments and changes in community thinking. Thus are expressed the values and social judgments of the people as to individual rights and equity, as to class conflict, intergroup friction, and power relations. The church, the family, and the schools are among the influences on people's attitudes and moral values, thus affecting judicial and legislative opinion. The content of labor law, as revised over the years, has been, therefore, a reflection of the community thinking as the ultimate source of public standards in our democratic system.

With this brief review of sources, we turn to a consideration of early doctrines in labor law as a prelude to our study for a better understanding of modern legislative and judicial standards.

SECTION 4 / **ENGLISH BACKGROUND**

Because of the inarticulate position of the slave in the Egyptian and Roman civilizations, those periods allowed no urgent labor problem as such. The slave was a mere chattel subject to purchase, usage, and sale at the will of the privileged overlord. Since the slave possessed no rights, no legal remedies were developed. For our purposes, any extended treatment of slave labor forms would seem superfluous.

Much the same can be said of the serf's status under the feudal system of the Middle Ages; however, in comparison to the social and legal position of the slave, we can begin to detect the emergence of limited rights. "The serf occupied a position in rural society which it is difficult for us to understand. He was not a slave . . . because he was free to work for himself at least part of the time; he could not be sold to another master; and he could not be deprived of the right to cultivate land for his own benefit. He was not a hired man, for he received no wages. And he was not a tenant farmer, inasmuch as he was attached to the soil . . . unless he succeeded in running away or in purchasing complete freedom, in which case he would cease to be a serf and would become a freeman." [1]

Feudalism as a social system in England did not disintegrate rapidly nor for any single reason. Four major causes, concurrently operating, served to weaken, and eventually to destroy, this planned and ordered society based upon the tenure system of land holding and centering about the manor as the economic, political, and military unit.

1. The Crusades, ending in the thirteenth century, which decimated the ruling caste from which the feudal leaders were drawn.
2. The sweeping of western Europe by the bubonic plague, which caused an acute labor shortage.
3. The defection of the serfs and villeins from the manors to the towns and cities.
4. The reopening of international trade routes to the East, with its consequent emphasis upon commerce rather than land as a source of wealth.

A true system of labor jurisprudence thus followed the disintegration of feudalism, for it then became necessary to develop new rules of law to govern labor relationships.

---

[1] Hayes, *A Political and Cultural History of Modern Europe* (New York: Macmillan, 1936), I, 49.

Mercantilism, extending roughly from the years 1350 to 1776, superseded feudalism. Its philosophy centered about the objective of securing a favorable balance of foreign trade, which would bring in gold; it was to be attained by securing foreign monopolies, supported by an expanded merchant fleet and strengthened agriculture and manufacture. English mercantilism represents a rather illuminating corollary with present-day societies based upon minute governmental regulation of production and distribution factors, for it too was predicated upon the same foundation. It is to this era that we must turn to trace the source of such modern economic forms as the trade union and the employer association. These are but modified outgrowths of the craft and merchant guilds that early saw the economic advantage arising from monopolistic competition and collective action.

One of the major effects of the Black Death, the growth of urban centers, the freeing of serfs, and the infusion of life into international commercial channels was the creation of an acute labor shortage, which, given free expression in a price and profit economy, caused the price of labor to ricochet upward. Alarmed at this turn of events, the landed gentry and the merchants, who were now dependent upon hired laborers and who alone were represented in Parliament, secured the passage of restrictive labor legislation and the assistance of the judiciary in counteracting the all-too-favorable position of labor.

The earliest restrictive labor legislation is found in 1351 in the Statute of Laborers (25 Edw. 3, St. 1), in which a broad, national attempt was made to reduce labor's bargaining power by requiring able-bodied persons to work, by fixing the price of labor, by controlling the freedom of labor to contract, and by providing criminal punishment for the violation of its mandates.

Over two hundred years later, Parliament issued in 1562 a superseding Statute of Laborers (5 Eliz. C. 4), which was perhaps more embracive than the Act of 1351 had been. It defined the elements inhering in the master-and-servant relationship, established rules limiting the mobility of labor to stop the exodus of labor from rural to urban centers, outlined product quality and price standards to control craft and merchant guilds, and fixed by law the price of labor.

Governing the commercial activity of this mercantile era, we find the permissible labor contract delineated by the statute and common law, and the area of governmental regulation extended also over manufacture and merchandising. Both Statutes of Laborers incorporated limits to permissible employer activity as it touched his labor and marketing relations. Business combinations of this period, more properly termed merchant and craft guilds, engaged in considerable self-imposed regulation, in the interest of promoting monopoly and of maintaining prices, quality, and output standards. The merchant and craft guilds were, however, basically concerned with the problem of limiting outside competition.

Trade unions, as distinguished from labor or industrial unions, found their inception in the decline of the guild system, which was accelerated by the Industrial Revolution of the 18th Century. With the substitution of capital equipment for labor, necessitated by the technological advancement of the Revolution, many journeymen found themselves unable to enter the master ranks because their finances were inadequate to the heavier fixed and working capital requirements. As a corollary, many erstwhile masters were forced back into the journeyman ranks for the same reason. An amalgamation of these two disenfranchised groups culminated in the formation of the earliest true trade unions, which were utilized to nullify the monopolistic bargaining advantage of the fewer remaining masters, who were banded together in powerful employer groups and, by now, could be classified as manufacturers rather than artisans. It was these early trade unions that were made the subject of the mercantile period's labor law.

SECTION 5 / THE CRIMINAL CONSPIRACY DOCTRINE

Concurrent with statutory control, the English common law developed what is known as the doctrine of *criminal conspiracy,* which made unlawful concerted action by workers in making demands upon merchant or manufacturer. The case of the *King against the Journeymen-Taylors of Cambridge,* decided in England in 1721, illustrates the criminal conspiracy idea applied to labor under statute and common law. There it was held that, while the action against the combination of tailors might not lie because the prosecutor's indictment did not bring the action within the prohibition of the criminal conspiracy statute of 1720 (7 Geo. 1, C. 13), yet the conviction of the defendant tailors would stand because a labor combination was a criminal conspiracy at common law and could be punished independent of whether the procedural requirements of the statute were met.

Following the rule of the *Journeymen-Taylors of Cambridge* case there was the case of the *Journeymen Cordwainers,* decided in New York in 1809 and reported by Yates, a court reporter, who summarized the gist of the case in longhand, since shorthand verbatim reporting was then unknown to court reporting. The decision reflects the influence of our heritage of English common law, which, almost a century later, led us to hold labor combinations to be violative of the criminal law of New York State. The common law doctrine of criminal conspiracy is not presently followed, except in the modified form of the Sherman Act of 1890, which outlaws as criminal certain conspiracies in restraint of trade. Consideration of the present status of the criminal conspiracy doctrine is deferred for subsequent detailed consideration under the heading of criminal syndicalism and the antitrust laws.

SECTION 6 / LABOR'S ENDS AND MEANS

Analogy can be drawn as to the common-law doctrines in England and America that were directed at the outlawry of labor organization formation and activity. The concept of a free and open market, however, was gradually modified in the 19th century, as applied to both capital and labor. In the face of permissible monopolistic competitive practices by large-scale employer groups, some liberal thinking began to concede to labor a correlative right to combine for the purpose of securing a more equitable distribution of the gains of economic progress.

The landmark American decision in this transition period covering the basic legality of labor combination, when utilized for proper purposes, is *Commonwealth* v. *Hunt,* reprinted immediately below. Since the rendition of this decision, the right of American labor to organize has not been seriously questioned by either the courts or legislatures.

Under some state laws, conspiring together for any illegal purpose makes the additional charge of conspiracy possible; in some cases this doctrine has been followed against labor organizations. A relatively recent decision of the Supreme Court expressed that body's view on applications of conspiracy charges to a labor union. Reversing a damages award against the United Mine Workers of America which had been allowed by the Kentucky courts in a tort case, the decision of the Supreme Court made this comment as to the conspiracy doctrine:

> "The tort claimed was in essence a conspiracy to interfere with Gibbs' contractual relations. The tort of conspiracy is poorly defined and susceptible to judicial expansion; its relatively brief history is colored by use as a weapon against the developing labor movement." [2]

Commonwealth v. Hunt

Supreme Court of Massachusetts, 1842. 4 Metcalf 111, 38 Am. Dec. 346

SHAW, C. J. . . . The general rule of the common law is that it is a criminal and indictable offense for two or more to confederate and combine together, by concerted means, to do that which is unlawful or criminal, to the injury of the public, or portions or classes of the community, or even to the rights of an individual. This rule of law may be equally in force as a rule of the common law, in England and in this commonwealth; and yet it must depend upon the local laws of each country to determine whether the purpose to be accomplished by the combination, or the concerted means of accomplishing it, be unlawful or criminal in the respective countries. . . . Without attempting to review and reconcile all the cases, we are of opinion, that as a general description, though perhaps not a precise and accurate definition, a conspiracy must be a combination of two or more persons, by some concerted action, to accomplish some criminal or unlawful purpose, or to accomplish some purpose, not in itself criminal or unlawful, by criminal or unlawful means.

The first count set forth that the defendants, with divers others unknown, on the day and at the place named being workmen and journeymen in the art and occupation of bootmakers, unlawfully, perniciously, and deceitfully designing and intending to continue, keep up, form and unite themselves into an unlawful club, society, and combination, and make unlawful bylaws, rules, and orders among themselves, and thereby govern themselves and other workmen in the said art, and unlawfully and unjustly to extort great sums of money by means thereof, did unlawfully assemble and meet together, and being so assembled, did unjustly and corruptly conspire, combine, confederate, and agree together that none of them should thereafter work for any master or person whatsoever, in the said art, mystery, and occupation, who should

---

[2] *United Mine Workers* v. *Gibbs,* 383 U.S. 715 (1966).

employ any workman or journeyman, or other person in the said art, who was not a member of said club, society, or combination, after notice given him to discharge such workman from the employ of such master; to the great damage and oppression, etc. . . .

Stripped, then, of these introductory recitals and alleged injurious consequences, and of the qualifying epithets attached to the facts, the averment is this: that the defendants and others formed themselves into a society and agreed not to work for any person who should employ any journeyman or other person not a member of such society after notice given him to discharge such workman.

The manifest intent of the association is to induce all those engaged in the same occupation to become members of it. Such a purpose is not unlawful. It would give them a power which might be exerted for useful and honorable purposes, or for dangerous and pernicious ones. If the latter were the real and actual object, and susceptible of proof, it should have been specially charged. Such an association might be used to afford each other assistance in times of poverty, sickness, and distress; or to raise their intellectual, moral, and social condition; or to make improvement in their art; or for other proper purposes. Or the association might be designed for purposes of oppression and injustice. But in order to charge all those who become members of an association with the guilt of a criminal conspiracy, it must be averred and proved that the actual, if not the avowed object of the association was criminal. An association may be formed, the declared objects of which are innocent and laudable, and yet they may have secret articles, or an agreement communicated only to the members, by which they are banded together for purposes injurious to the peace of society or the rights of its members. Such would undoubtedly be a criminal conspiracy, on proof of the fact, however meritorious and praiseworthy the declared objects might be. The law is not to be hoodwinked by colorable pretenses. It looks at truth and reality, through whatever disguise it may assume. But to make such an association, ostensibly innocent, the subject of prosecution as a criminal conspiracy, the secret agreement which makes it so, is to be averred and proved as the gist of the offense. But when an association is formed for purposes actually innocent, and afterward its powers are abused by those who have the control and management of it, to purposes of oppression and injustice, it will be criminal in those who thus misuse it, or give consent thereto, but not in the other members of the association. In this case, no such secret agreement, varying the objects of the association from those avowed, is set forth in this count of the indictment.

Nor can we perceive that the objects of this association, whatever they may have been, were to be attained by criminal means. The means which they proposed to employ, as averred in this count, and which, as we are not to presume, were established by the proof, were, that they would not work for a person, who, after due notice, should employ a journeyman not a member of their society. Supposing the object of the association to be laudable and lawful, or at least not unlawful, are these means criminal? The case supposes that these persons are not bound by contract, but free to work for whom they please, or not to work, if they so prefer. In this state of things, we can not perceive that it is criminal for men to agree together to exercise their own acknowledged rights, in such a manner as best to subserve their own interests. One way to test this is to consider the effect of such an agreement, where the object of the association is acknowledged on all hands to be a laudable one. Suppose a class of workmen, impressed with the manifold evils of intemperance, should agree with each other not to work in a shop in which ardent spirit was furnished, or not to work in a shop in which any one used it, or not to work for an employer who should, after notice, employ a journeyman who habitually used it. The consequences might be the same. A workman who should still persist in the use of ardent spirit, would find it more difficult to get employment; a master employing such an one might, at times, experience inconvenience in his work, in losing the services of a skillful but intemperate workman. Still it seems to us, that as the object would be lawful, and the means not unlawful, such an agreement could not be pronounced a criminal conspiracy. . . .

We think, therefore, that associations may be entered into, the object of which is to adopt measures that may have a tendency to impoverish another, that is, to diminish his gains and profits, and yet so far from being criminal or unlawful, the object may be highly meritorious and public-spirited. The legality of such an association will therefore depend upon the means to be used for its accomplishment. If it is to be carried into effect by fair or honorable and lawful means, it is, to say the least, innocent; if by falsehood or force, it may be stamped with the character of conspiracy. . . .

Several other exceptions were taken, and have been argued; but this decision on the main question has rendered it unnecessary to consider them.

CASE **QUESTIONS**	**1.** What was the "manifest intent" of the labor organization in the parent case? **2.** How does the court define a criminal conspiracy? **3.** State the rule of law developed by the court.

SECTION 7 / **THE CIVIL CONSPIRACY DOCTRINE**

With the approach of the 19th Century, heralding the advent of the Industrial Revolution, we find strong and powerful influences working to overthrow the restrictive legislation that was hamstringing business and labor. The reaction was crystallized by the publication of Adam Smith's *Wealth of Nations* (1776) in which the new *laissez-faire* doctrine was epitomized. Contending that the least regulation is the best regulation, and that the public interest would best be served by resort to economic, rather than statute, law in matters of supply, demand, and price, Smith found popular favor with the articulate public. Acceptance of this doctrine, at least as applied to nonlabor groups, became the guiding rule of *laissez-faire* capitalism, ushered in in 1776.

As applied to labor, however, governmental control appeared to remain as the most desirable alternative. In 1799 and 1800, Parliament passed the Combination Acts (39 Geo. 3, C. 81 and 40 Geo. 3, C. 106), which made ". . . void . . . all contracts . . . entered into by or between . . . workmen for obtaining an advance of wages . . . for lessening or altering . . . usual hours or time of working, or for decreasing the quantity of work, or for preventing or hindering any person or persons from employing whomsoever he . . . think proper to employ in his business. . . ." The Act also made it a criminal offense to picket or boycott an employer or to refuse to work with a nonunion workman. In 1875, the Conspiracy and Protection Act (38 and 39 Vict. C. 86) removed labor union action from the ban of criminal conspiracy and broadened greatly the allowable limits of peaceful picketing. The result of this act was the invalidation of most of the adverse English labor legislation of the preceding century.

This liberality on the English labor scene, however, was obscured by the *Quinn* v. *Leathem* case (1901, A.C. 495), in which the Court, conceding the outlawry of the *criminal* conspiracy doctrine by the Act of 1875, nevertheless found the union liable under its newly created *civil* conspiracy doctrine, which, when combined with the ruling in the *Taff Vale Railway Company* case (1901, A.C. 426) holding unions liable as an entity for members' torts, confronted labor with another hurdle to surmount.

SECTION 8 / THE CONTRACTUAL INTERFERENCE DOCTRINE

A third doctrine limiting the permissible activities of labor combinations is that of tortious interference with contractual or work relationships. In a legal sense, the doctrine may be confusing, as the right to be free of interference arises in contract while the remedy is pursued in tort. The theory that interference with a contract relation was an actionable tort arose first in the case of *Lumley* v. *Gye,* an English decision of 1853. Although a labor union was not involved in *Lumley* v. *Gye,* the rule developed in that case was accepted both in England and America in labor cases arising at later dates. An English example of the rule being applied occurred in the 1905 case of *South Wales Miners' Federation* v. *Glamorgan Coal Co., Ltd.,* House of Lords, A.C. 239. The miners' federation, a labor union, apprehensive of wage reductions, called for "stop" days on which most of the miners failed to report for work. Glamorgan, and other coal companies, sued the federation "claiming damages for wrongfully . . . inducing workmen . . . to break their contract of service. . . ." The federation was found liable.

The influence of the *Lumley* and *South Wales* cases on the courts in America is revealed by the *Vegelahn* and *Hitchman* decisions, which are overruled classics in American labor law. The reader's attention is directed to the dissenting opinion in the *Vegelahn* case of Justice Holmes, then on the Massachusetts bench, insofar as it reveals the anticipatory vision of that great jurist.

The doctrine of illegal interference with contractual employment conditions was extended by the Supreme Court to legislative prohibitions of antiunion or yellow-dog employment agreements. First, the Court ruled unconstitutional a provision of the 1898 Erdman Act prohibiting such antiunion contracts. It found the law conflicting with the Fifth Amendment, Justice Holmes dissenting.[3] A similar prohibition in a state law was held to be "repugnant to the due process

---

[3] *Adair* v. *United States,* 208 U.S. 161 (1908).

clause of the Fourteenth Amendment, and therefore void." Again Justice Holmes dissented.[4]

At present, yellow-dog contracts containing the provision that employees will not join a union without surrendering their employment are outlawed by Section 2(5) of the Railway Labor Act and Section 3 of the Federal Anti-Injunction Act and implicitly outlawed in the Labor Management Relations Act. The present rule is that interference with a contractual or work relationship by a labor union is permissible as long as the purpose is proper and the means employed to effectuate the end are peaceful and within permissible bounds.

Vegelahn v. Guntner

Supreme Judicial Court of Massachusetts, 1896. 167 Mass. 92, 44 N.E. 1077

ALLEN, J. The principal question in this case is whether the defendants should be enjoined against maintaining the patrol. The report shows that, following upon a strike of the plaintiff's workmen, the defendants conspired to prevent him from getting workmen and thereby to prevent him from carrying on his business, unless and until he should adopt a certain schedule of prices. The means adopted were persuasion and social pressure, threats of personal injury or unlawful harm conveyed to persons employed or seeking employment, and a patrol of two men in front of the plaintiff's factory, maintained from half past 6 in the morning till half past 5 in the afternoon, on one of the busiest streets of Boston. The number of men was greater at times, and at times showed some little disposition to stop at the plaintiff's door. The patrol proper at times went further than simple advice not obtruded beyond the point where the other person was willing to listen; and it was found that the patrol would probably be continued if not enjoined. There was also some evidence of persuasion to break existing contracts. The patrol was maintained as one of the means of carrying out the defendants' plan, and it was used in combination with social pressure, threats of personal injury or unlawful harm, and persuasion to break existing contracts. It was thus one means of intimidation, indirectly to the plaintiff, and directly to persons actually employed, or seeking to be employed, by the plaintiff, and of rendering such employment unpleasant or intolerable to such persons.

Such an act is an unlawful interference with the rights both of the employer and of the employed. An employer has a right to engage all persons who are willing to work for him, at such prices as may be mutually agreed upon, and persons employed or seeking employment have a corresponding right to enter into or remain in the employment of any person or corporation willing to employ them. These rights are secured by the constitution itself. . . .

The defendants contend that these acts were justifiable because they were only seeking to secure better wages for themselves by compelling the plaintiff to accept their schedule of wages. This motive or purpose does not justify

---

[4] *Coppage* v. *Kansas,* 236 U.S. 1 (1915).

maintaining a patrol in front of the plaintiff's premises, as a means of carrying out their conspiracy. A combination among persons merely to regulate their own conduct is within allowable competition, and is lawful, although others may be indirectly affected thereby. But a combination to do injurious acts expressly directed to another, by way of intimidation or constraint, either of himself or of persons employed or seeking to be employed by him, is outside of allowable competition, and is unlawful. . . .

Nor does the fact that the defendants' acts might subject them to an indictment prevent a court of equity from issuing an injunction. It is true that, ordinarily, a court of equity will decline to issue an injunction to restrain the commission of a crime; but a continuing injury to property or business may be enjoined, although it may also be punishable as a nuisance or other crime. . . .

A question is also presented whether the court should enjoin such interference with persons in the employment of the plaintiff who are not bound by contract to remain with him, or with persons who are not under any existing contract, but who are seeking or intending to enter into his employment. A conspiracy to interfere with the plaintiff's business by means of threats and intimidation, and by maintaining a patrol in front of his premises, in order to prevent persons who are in his employment from continuing therein, is unlawful, even though such persons are not bound by contract to enter into or continue in his employment; and the injunction should not be so limited as to relate only to persons who are bound by existing contracts. We therefore think that the injunction should be in the form originally issued. So ordered.

HOLMES, J. (dissenting). . . . One of the eternal conflicts out of which life is made up is that between the efforts of every man to get the most he can for his services, and that of society, disguised under the name of capital, to get his services for the least possible return. Combination on the one side is patent and powerful. Combination on the other is the necessary and desirable counterpart, if the battle is to be carried on in a fair and equal way. . . .

If it be true that workingmen may combine with a view, among other things, to getting as much as they can for their labor, just as capital may combine with a view to getting the greatest possible return, it must be true that, when combined, they have the same liberty that combined capital has, to support their interests by argument, persuasion, and the bestowal or refusal of those advantages which they otherwise lawfully control. I can remember when many thought that, apart from violence or breach of contract, strikes were wicked, as organized refusals to work. I suppose that intelligent economists and legislators have given up that notion today. I feel pretty confident that they equally will abandon the idea that an organized refusal by workmen of social intercourse with a man who shall enter their antagonist's employ is unlawful, if it is disassociated from any threat of violence, and is made for the sole object of prevailing, if possible, in a contest with their employer about the rate of wages. The fact that the immediate object of the act by which the benefit to themselves is to be gained is to injure their antagonist does not necessarily make it unlawful, any more than when a great house lowers the price of goods for the purpose and with the effect of driving a smaller antagonist from the business. . . .

CASE
QUESTIONS

1. Was the picketing peaceful or tainted with violence?
2. Will an equity court ordinarily enjoin the commission of a crime?
3. What was the scope of the court's injunction?
4. In his classic dissent, how does Justice Holmes justify the infliction of injury by a labor organization?

Hitchman Coal & Coke Co. v. Mitchell

Supreme Court of the United States, 1917. 245 U.S. 229

PITNEY, J. This was a suit in equity, commenced October 24, 1907, in the United States Circuit (afterwards District) Court for the Northern District of West Virginia, by the Hitchman Coal & Coke Company, a corporation organized under the laws of the state of West Virginia, against certain citizens of the state of Ohio, sued individually and also as officers of the United Mine Workers of America. Other non-citizens of plaintiff's state were named as defendants but not served with process. . . .

Plaintiff owns about 5,000 acres of coal lands situate at or near Benwood, in Marshall county, West Virginia, and within what is known as the "Panhandle District" of that state, and operates a coal mine thereon employing between 200 and 300 men, and having an annual output, in and before 1907, of about 300,000 tons. At the time of the filing of the bill, and for a considerable time before and ever since, it operated its mine "nonunion," under an agreement with its men to the effect that the mine should be run on a nonunion basis, that the employees should not become connected with the union while employed by plaintiff, and that if they joined it their employment with plaintiff should cease. . . .

. . . The general object of the bill was to obtain an injunction to restrain defendants from interfering with the relations existing between plaintiff and its employees in order to compel plaintiff to "unionize" the mine. . . .

. . . On April 15, 1906, defendant Zelenka, vice-president of the subdistrict, visited the mine, called a meeting of the miners, and addressed them in a foreign tongue, as a result of which they went on strike the next day, and the mine was shut down until the 12th of June, when it resumed as a "nonunion" mine, so far as relations with the U.M.W.A. were concerned.

During this strike plaintiff was subjected to heavy losses and extraordinary expenses with respect to its business, of the same kind that had befallen it during the previous strikes.

About the 1st of June a self-appointed committee of employees called upon plaintiff's president, stated in substance that they could not remain longer on strike because they were not receiving benefits from the union, and asked upon what terms they could return to work. They were told that they could come back, but not as members of the United Mine Workers of America; that thenceforward the mine would be run nonunion, and the company would deal with each man individually. They assented to this, and returned to work on a nonunion basis. Mr. Pickett, the mine superintendent, had charge of employing the men, then and afterwards, and to each one who applied for employment he explained the conditions which were that while the company paid the wages demanded by the union and as much as anybody else, the mine was run nonunion and would continue so to run; that the company would not recognize the United Mine Workers of America; that if any man wanted to become a member of that union he was at liberty to do so; but he could not be a member of it and remain in the employ of the Hitchman Company; that if he worked for the company he would have to work as a nonunion man. To this each man employed gave his assent, understanding that while he worked for the company he must keep out of the union.

Since January, 1908 (after the commencement of the suit), in addition to having this verbal understanding, each man has been required to sign an employment card expressing in substance the same terms. This has neither enlarged nor diminished plaintiff's rights, the agreement not being such as is required by law to be in writing. Under this arrangement as to the terms of employment, plaintiff operated its mine from June 12, 1906, until the commencement of the suit in the fall of the following year.

During the same period a precisely similar method of employment obtained, at the Glendale mine, a property consisting of about 200 acres of coal land adjoining the Hitchman property on the south, and operated by a company having the same stockholders and the same management as the Hitchman; the office of the Glendale mine being at the Hitchman Coal & Coke Company's office. Another mine in the Panhandle, known as Richland, a few miles north of the Hitchman, likewise was run "nonunion."

In fact, all coal mines in the Panhandle and elsewhere in West Virginia, except in a small district known as the Kanawha field, were run "nonunion" while the entire industry in Ohio, Indiana, and Illinois was operated on the "closed shop" basis, so that no man could hold a job about the mines unless he was a member of the United Mine Workers of America. Pennsylvania occupied a middle ground, only a part of it being under the jurisdiction of the union. Other states need not be particularly mentioned.

The unorganized condition of the mines in the Panhandle and some other districts was recognized as a serious interference with the purposes of the union in the Central Competitive Field, particularly as it tended to keep the cost of production low, and, through competition with coal produced in the organized field, rendered it more difficult for the operators there to maintain prices high enough to induce them to grant certain concessions demanded by the Union. . . .

What are the legal consequences of the facts that have been detailed?

That the plaintiff was acting within its lawful rights in employing its men only upon terms of continuing nonmembership in the United Mine Workers of America is not open to question. Plaintiff's repeated costly experience of strikes and other interferences while attempting to "run union" were a sufficient explanation of its resolve to run "nonunion," if any were needed. But neither explanation nor justification is needed. Whatever may be the advantages of "collective bargaining" it is not bargaining at all, in any just sense, unless it is voluntary on both sides. . . . . This court repeatedly has held that the employer is as free to make nonmembership in a union a condition of employment, as the working man is free to join the union, and that this is part of the constitutional rights of personal liberty and private property, not to be taken away even by legislation, unless through some proper exercise of the paramount police power. . . .

Defendants set up, by way of justification or excuse, the right of workingmen to form unions, and to enlarge their membership by inviting other workingmen to join. The right is freely conceded, provided the objects of the union be proper and legitimate, which we assume to be true, in a general sense, with respect to the union here in question. *Gompers* v. *Bucks Stove & Range Co.,* 221 U.S. 418, 439, 31 Sup. Ct. 492, 55 L. Ed. 797, 34 L.R.A. (N.S.) 874. The cardinal error of defendants' position lies in the assumption that the right is so absolute that it may be exercised under any circumstances and without any qualification; whereas in truth, like other rights that exist in civilized society, it must always be exercised with reasonable regard for the conflicting rights of others. *Brennan* v. *United Hatters,* 73 N.J. Law, 729, 749, 65 Atl. 165, 9 L.R.A. (N.S.) 254, 118 Am. St. Rep. 727, 9 Ann. Cas. 698. . . .

In any aspect of the matter, it cannot be said that defendants were pursuing their object by lawful means. The question of their intentions—of their bona fides—cannot be ignored. It enters into the question of malice. As Bowen, L. J., justly said, in the *Mogul Steamship Case,* 23 Q.B. Div. 613:

> Intentionally to do that which is calculated in the ordinary course of events to damage, and which does, in fact, damage another in that other person's property or trade, is actionable if done without just cause or excuse.

Another fundamental error in defendants' position consists in the assumption that all measures that may be resorted to are lawful if they are "peaceable"—that is, if they stop short of physical violence, or coercion through fear of it. In our opinion, any violation of plaintiff's legal rights contrived by defendants for the purpose of inflicting damage, or having that as its necessary effect, is as plainly inhibited by the law as if it involved a breach of the peace. A combination to procure concerted breaches of contract by plaintiff's employees constitutes such a violation. . . .

Upon all the facts, we are constrained to hold that the purpose entertained by defendants to bring about a strike at plaintiff's mine in order to compel plaintiff, through fear of financial loss, to consent to the unionization of the mine as the lesser evil, was an unlawful purpose, and that the methods resorted to by Hughes—the inducing of employees to unite with the union in an effort to subvert the system of employment at the mine by concerted breaches of the contracts of employment known to be in force there, not to mention misrepresentation, deceptive statements, and threats of pecuniary loss communicated by Hughes to the men—were unlawful and malicious methods, and not to be justified as a fair exercise of the right to increase the membership of the union. . . .

That the damage resulting from a strike would be irremediable at law is too plain for discussion.

As against the answering defendants, plaintiff's right to an injunction is clear; as to the others named as defendants, but not served with process, the decree is erroneous, as already stated. . . .

The decree of the Circuit Court of Appeals is reversed, and the decree of the District Court is modified as above stated. . . .

CASE QUESTIONS

1. What agreement did the Hitchman Company ask its employees to abide by?
2. At the time of this case, what states were mining coal on a closed-shop basis?
3. What is a closed shop?
4. Were the organizing efforts of the U.M.W. peaceful? Was this a good defense?
5. Did the court concede that workers had the right to form and join labor organizations?
6. Did the court uphold the yellow-dog contract?

QUESTIONS ON CHAPTER 1

1. What are the sources of American labor law?
2. Explain the role of administrative law as a source of labor law.
3. What right of review can a court exercise over the rulings of an administrative agency?
4. List the secondary sources of labor law.
5. What were the mercantilistic counterparts of the modern trade union and employers' association?
6. What three early common-law doctrines were applied to labor organizations?
7. What is the present status of the so-called yellow-dog contract?

Antitrust and Anti-Injunction Acts

SECTION 9 / EARLY APPLICATIONS OF THE SHERMAN ACT

We have seen earlier, in Sections 5 and 7, the application of the criminal and civil conspiracy doctrines to labor union activity that tended to restrain trade. Restraint of trade was the early common-law doctrine applied to contracts, agreements, and combinations diminishing the flow of goods or services to the market in an effort to control their prices, although not every interference with a free and open market constituted an unlawful restraint.

Whenever the issue was posed in the courts, two questions arose. First, was the restraint justifiable; and second, were noncoercive methods employed to effectuate the restraint? If a negative answer ensued, the result was the application of the criminal or civil conspiracy rules. Hence, a consideration of both ends and means was vital to the issue. If the end purpose of a strike or a picket was to maliciously injure another, without any direct benefit to those causing injury, the strike or picket activity was considered illegal. On the other hand, if the activity causing injury was devoid of malice and promised direct benefit to the participants, but force or intimidation was employed to secure the lawful end, this latter element of coercion again brought into play the proscriptive ban of the law.

In the present era, the common-law doctrines of civil and criminal conspiracy and restraint of trade have been embodied in, or modified by, statutory enactments commencing with the Sherman Act of 1890. It has been long debated whether Congress intended the Sherman Act's prohibitions to extend to the actions of labor combinations in view of the undoubted proposition that the enactment was in response to public pressure for the control of monopolistic practices by big business combinations such as the Standard Oil and American Tobacco companies. Notwithstanding the authorities pro and con—and a strong case can be mustered for either view—the federal courts, under the verbiage of Section 1, construed the Sherman Act as applying with equal vigor to *all* combinations, labor or otherwise.

The passage of the Clayton Act of 1914 followed the political efforts of labor in order to secure relief from the restrictions of the Sherman Act. In spite of the express language of the Clayton Act's Section 6, the courts construed the Act as being merely declaratory of what had been lawful or unlawful theretofore. On the whole, the Clayton Act left labor in a more exposed position than formerly. The Sherman Act still applied as fully, and, in addition, the Clayton Act enabled employers to sue in their own right for restraining orders and injunctions under the Sherman Act, a right formerly had only by the federal authorities.

Litigation under the Sherman Act may be grounded in equity under Section 4 if an injunction or restraining order is desired, at law if for treble damages under Section 7, or it may be a criminal prosecution pursued by the government under Section 1. As such, the procedural and evidentiary requirements will vary as found in the decided cases, making observance of the form of action significant, for the evidentiary requirements are much stricter to support a criminal, rather than a civil, prosecution.

The portions of the four sections of the Sherman Act of 1890 that relate to the problems discussed in this book are as follows:

Sec. 1. Every contract, combination in the form of trust or otherwise, or conspiracy, in restraint of trade or commerce among the several States, or with foreign nations, is hereby declared to be illegal. Every person who shall make any such contract or engage in any such combination or conspiracy, shall be deemed guilty of a misdemeanor, and, on conviction thereof, shall be punished by fine not exceeding five thousand dollars, or by imprisonment not exceeding one year, or by both said punishments, in the discretion of the court.

Sec. 4. The several circuit courts of the United States are hereby invested with jurisdiction to prevent and restrain violations of this act; and it shall be the duty of the several district attorneys of the United States, in their respective districts, under the direction of the Attorney-General, to institute proceedings in equity to prevent and restrain such violations. Such proceedings may be by way of petition setting forth the case and praying that such violation shall be enjoined or otherwise prohibited. When the parties complained of shall have been duly notified of such petition the court shall proceed, as soon as may be, to the hearing and determination of the case; and pending such petition and before final decree, the court may at any time make such temporary restraining order or prohibition as shall be deemed just in the premises.

Sec. 7. Any person who shall be injured in his business or property by any other person or corporation by reason of anything forbidden or declared to be unlawful by this act, may sue therefor in any circuit court of the United States in the district in which the defendant resides or is found, without respect to the amount in controversy, and shall recover three fold the damages by him sustained, and the costs of suit, including a reasonable attorney's fee.

Sec. 8. That the word "person," or "persons," wherever used in this act shall be deemed to include corporations and associations existing under or authorized by the laws of either the United States, the laws of any of the Territories, the laws of any State, or the laws of any foreign country.

Lawlor v. Loewe

Supreme Court of the United States, 1915. 235 U.S. 522

HOLMES, J. This is an action under the act of July 2, 1890, C. 647, Sec. 7, 26 Stat. 209, 210, 15 U.S.C.A. Sec. 15 note, for a combination and conspiracy in restraint of commerce among the States, specifically directed against the plaintiffs (defendants in error), among others, and effectively carried out with the infliction of great damage. The declaration was held good on demurrer in *Loewe* v. *Lawlor,* 208 U.S. 274, 28 S. Ct. 301, 52 L. Ed. 488, 13 Ann. Cas. 815, where it will be found set forth at length. The substance of the charge is that the plaintiffs were hat manufacturers who employed nonunion labor; that the defendants were members of the United Hatters of North America and also of the American Federation of Labor; that in pursuance of a general scheme to unionize the labor employed by manufacturers of fur hats (a purpose previously made effective against all but a few manufacturers), the defendants and other members of the United Hatters caused the American Federation of Labor to declare a boycott against the plaintiffs and against all hats sold by the plaintiffs to dealers in other States and against dealers who should deal in them; and that they carried out their plan with such success that they have restrained or destroyed the plaintiff's commerce with other States. The case now has been tried, the plaintiffs have got a verdict and the judgment of the District Court has been affirmed by the Circuit Court of Appeals. 209 F. 721, 126 C.C.A. 445.

The grounds for discussion under the statute that were not cut away by the decision upon the demurrer have been narrowed still further since the trial by the case of *Eastern States Retail Lumber Dealers' Ass'n* v. *United States,* 234 U.S. 600, 34 S. Ct. 951, 58 L. Ed. 1490, L.R.A. 1915A, 788. Whatever may be the law otherwise, that case establishes that, irrespective of compulsion or even agreement to observe its intimation, the circulation of a list of "unfair dealers," manifestly intended to put the ban upon those whose names appear therein, among an important body of possible customers combined with a view to joint action and in anticipation of such reports, is within the prohibitions of the Sherman Act if it is intended to restrain and restrains commerce among the States.

It requires more than the blindness of justice not to see that many branches of the United Hatters and the Federation of Labor, to both of which the defendants belonged, in pursuance of a plan emanating from headquarters made use of such lists, and of the primary and secondary boycott in their effort to subdue the plaintiffs to their demands. The union label was used and a strike of the plaintiffs' employees was ordered and carried out to the same end, and the purpose to break up the plaintiffs' commerce affected the quality of the acts. *Loewe* v. *Lawlor,* 208 U.S. 274, 299, 28 S. Ct. 301, 52 L. Ed. 488, 13 Ann. Cas. 815. We agree with the Circuit Court of Appeals that a combination and conspiracy forbidden by the statute were proved, and that the question is narrowed to the responsibility of the defendants for what was done by the sanction and procurement of the societies above named.

The court in substance instructed the jury that if these members paid their dues and continued to delegate authority to their officers unlawfully to interfere with the plaintiffs' interstate commerce in such circumstances that they knew or ought to have known, and such officers were warranted in the belief that they were acting in the matters within their delegated authority, then such members were jointly liable, and no others. It seems to us that this instruction sufficiently guarded the defendants' rights, and that the defendants got all that they were entitled to ask in not being held chargeable with knowledge as matter of law. It is a tax on credulity to ask anyone to believe that members of labor unions at that time did not know that the primary and secondary boycott and the use of the "We don't patronize" or "Unfair" list were means expected to be employed in the effort to unionize shops. Very possibly they were thought to be lawful. See *Gompers* v. *United States,* 233 U.S. 604, 34 S. Ct. 693, 58 L. Ed. 1115. By the Constitution of the United Hatters the directors are to use "all the means in their power" to bring shops "not under our jurisdiction" "into the trade." The bylaws provide a separate fund to be kept for strikes, lockouts, and agitation for the union label. Members are forbidden to sell nonunion hats. The Federation of Labor with which the Hatters were affiliated had organization of labor for one of its objects, helped affiliated unions in trade disputes, and to that end, before the present trouble, had provided in its constitution for prosecuting and had prosecuted many what it called legal boycotts. Their conduct in this and former cases was made public especially among the members in every possible way. If the words of the documents on their face and without explanation did not authorize what was done, the evidence of what was done publicly and habitually showed their meaning and how they were interpreted. The jury could not but find that by the usage of the unions the acts complained of were authorized, and authorized without regard to their interference with commerce among the States. We think it unnecessary to repeat the evidence of the publicity of this particular struggle in the common newspapers and union prints, evidence that made it almost inconceivable that the defendants, all living in the neighborhood of the plaintiffs, did not know what was done in the specific case. If they did not know that, they were bound to know the constitution of their societies, and at least well might be found to have known how the words of those constitutions had been construed in the act. . . .

Judgment affirmed.[1]

<table>
<tr><td>**CASE**
QUESTIONS</td><td>**1.** What purpose was pursued by the United Hatters?
2. What pressure methods did the American Federation of Labor and the Hatters exert?
3. State the rule of the case.</td></tr>
</table>

SECTION 10 / **INJUNCTIONS AND THE CLAYTON ACT**

The earliest recorded issuance of a court injunction in a labor dispute dates from the 1880's. After 1894 when a federal court enjoined the American Railway Union and its officers from strike activities against the Pullman Palace Car Company, the authority of the courts was applied increasingly and with greater restrictions against organizing and strike conduct. One authority has found records, in state and federal courts, from 1890 to 1931 of 1,872 labor injunctions

---

[1] By Section 301(b) of the National Labor Relations Act of 1947, money judgments are enforceable only against the union as an entity "and shall not be enforceable against any individual member or his assets."

granted at employers' requests and 223 cases in which such applications for relief were denied.[2] Section 11, which follows in this volume, contains a discussion of the limitations imposed on the federal courts by Congress in the Anti-Injunction Act of 1932 to correct this use of equity power to restrain collective activity of labor.

Understanding of the statutory and case materials in this chapter requires a preliminary statement about the injunctive process. An injunction may be defined as a mandatory or prohibitory writ issued by a court of equity, alternately known as a court of chancery. It is one of the extraordinary remedies within the inherent powers of courts of equity, and it was provided to give relief to an aggrieved party in those cases where the remedy of money damages at law was inadequate. Courts of law are limited in remedial power to the giving of money damages; they may not issue injunctions. Nor may a court of equity generally give the remedy of damages, unless it does so as an incident of equitable relief.

The injunction is used primarily as a device to protect property or property rights by preventing injury thereto as the result of continued trespass or nuisance. An injunctive writ is *prohibitory* if it orders the defendant to refrain from specified conduct; it is *mandatory* if it requires performance of an affirmative act. A single injunction, however, may have both prohibitory and mandatory aspects at the same time, as when a union is concurrently ordered to refrain from violence in picketing and to bargain in good faith with the employer. In a further sense, an injunction may be *preliminary* or *final.* The former enjoins commission of the disputed acts during the time of suit and while the case is being adjudicated on its merits. The latter is issued after a hearing on the merits, or the preliminary injunction is made final by court order.

We have stated that the injunction is used generally to protect against the unlawful invasion of property or property rights. As applied to trespasses by labor, the employer found the injunction a keen and effective tool for the following reasons:

1. Speed of action was secured, since affidavit proof was admitted to issue a preliminary restraining order.
2. Delay between issuance of the preliminary and the final injunction was often so prolonged as to ensure defeat of the strikers or picketers, notwithstanding eventual victory of the union in securing dissolution of the restraining order.
3. The employer had a choice of tribunal to which he would direct his plea and could select an antilabor forum.
4. Lack of a jury trial in equity reduced labor's chances of winning an injunction case.
5. Blanket and obscure language in the wording of some injunctions intimidated unionists because of their inability to separate legal from illegal acts, as well as their inability to determine exactly what conduct was permissible and what was forbidden.

The case of *In re Debs,* decided in 1895, 158 U.S. 164, popularized the usage of the injunction in labor cases in America. Over the ensuing years, labor carried on a relentless running battle to secure a narrowing of judicial injunctive power in labor cases. The first fruit of this agitation was the Clayton Antitrust Act of

---

[2] E. E. Witte, *The Government in Labor Disputes,* (New York: McGraw-Hill Book Company, 1932), p. 64.

1914 (38 Stat. 730). Congress here sought to substantially reenact the Sherman Antitrust Act of 1890 (26 Stat. 209), but, at the same time, to withdraw the applicability of that Act to labor combinations and to divest the courts of their wide injunctive powers in labor dispute cases. Sec. 6 provided "That the labor of a human being is not a commodity or article of commerce . . . nor shall such (labor) organizations, or the members thereof, be held or construed to be illegal combinations or conspiracies in restraint of trade, under the antitrust laws."

Sec. 20 imposes a statutory restriction on injunctive relief by providing that no injunction would issue in a labor dispute between employers and employees unless irreparable injury to property or property rights was threatened for which the law remedy of damages was inadequate. Narrow interpretations of the Clayton Act emasculated the edicts of Secs. 6 and 20 as is shown by the *Duplex* v. *Deering* and the *American Steel Foundries* decisions of 1921, reported in this section. The courts found a path around the Act by making the exception the rule under various theories, among them that the Act did not change preexisting law, did not apply in boycott cases, did not protect "outsiders" such as union organizers, did not apply where the union objective was recognition, did not apply where yellow-dog contracts were in effect, and finally, did not protect strikers since they were no longer employees.

The injunction device to counteract labor militancy was even more popular after passage of the Clayton Act, since an employer could now bring the action in a federal court as a party plaintiff, whereas, under the Sherman Act, only the government had that power. Disappointed by the Supreme Court's adverse construction of the Clayton Act in the *Duplex* and *American Steel Foundries* cases, labor intensified its political pressure in both state and federal areas, securing, in 1932, passage of the Federal Anti-Injunction Act (Norris-LaGuardia Act), 47 Stat. 70. This legislation effectively divested the federal courts of their equity power to issue injunctions at the behest of private parties in those situations where a bona fide labor dispute was in existence. The jurisdictional requirements set out in Section 7 furnished an almost insurmountable barrier to injunctive action when coupled with Section 13, which very broadly defined the term "labor dispute" as to include controversies without regard to whether the proximate relation of employer and employee existed.

The case of *Truax* v. *Corrigan* cast considerable doubt upon the constitutionality of proposed anti-injunction legislation, but these doubts were favorably resolved for labor by the Supreme Court in the 1937 case of *Senn* v. *Tile Layers Protective Union,* 301 U.S. 468.

Employers were thus placed in a difficult position, the legislative and judicial tenor having taken a complete turnabout. They turned for assistance to the state courts, only to find that here, too, many states had barred the door with anti-injunction legislation patterned after the Norris-LaGuardia Act. With the enactment of the Labor Management Relations Act of 1947, reflecting the ever-changing public temper, the immunities afforded labor from injunctive interdiction by the Anti-Injunction Act have been substantially narrowed by Sec. 10 (1), which provides that, as to strike and boycott activity outlawed by Sec. 8(b) (4), the National Labor Relations Board may secure a federal court injunction against unions without inhibition of the Federal Anti-Injunction Act. The reader should observe that the employer is not granted this remedy, being limited to his right to sue for damages under Sections 301 and 303 of the Labor Management Relations Act of 1947, unless he can satisfy the jurisdictional requirements of Sec. 7 of the Anti-Injunction Act.

We have already considered the text of the Clayton Act's labor provisions. In two Supreme Court decisions construing them, the reader should pay special note to Sec. 20, for, contrary to popular belief, this section does not completely immunize labor organizations from the injunction as an employer weapon. The immunity is qualified as revealed by the words "unless necessary to prevent irreparable injury to property, or to a property right, of the party making the application. . . ." Relying on this sentence of Section 20, the Supreme Court, in the *American Steel Foundries* decision, found that the Clayton Act did not materially change preexisting law as to the issuance of injunctions in those cases where strike and picket activity was unlawful in object or method.

The sections of the Clayton Act of 1914 that have application to labor controversies are quoted in the footnote on page 27 of this chapter.

Duplex Printing Press Company v. Deering

Supreme Court of the United States, 1921. 254 U.S. 443

PITNEY, J. This was a suit in equity brought by appellant in the District Court for the Southern District of New York for an injunction to restrain a course of conduct carried on by defendants in that District and vicinity in maintaining a boycott against the products of complainant's factory, in furtherance of a conspiracy to injure and destroy its good will, trade, and business —especially to obstruct and destroy its interstate trade. There was also a prayer for damages, but this has not been pressed and calls for no further mention. Complainant is a Michigan corporation and manufactures printing presses at a factory in Battle Creek, in that State, employing about 200 machinists in the factory in addition to 50 office employees, traveling salesmen, and expert machinists or road men who supervise the erection of the presses for complainant's customers at their various places of business. The defendants who were brought into court and answered the bill are Emil J. Deering and William Bramley, sued individually and as business agents and representatives of District No. 15 of the International Association of Machinists, and Michael T. Neyland, sued individually and as business agent and representative of Local Lodge No. 328 of the same association. . . .

. . . Complainant conducts its business on the "open shop" policy, without discrimination against either union or nonunion men. The individual defendants and the local organizations of which they are the representatives are affiliated with the International Association of Machinists, an unincorporated association having a membership of more than 60,000; and are united in a combination, to which the International Association also is a party, having the object of compelling complainant to unionize its factory and enforce the "closed shop," the eight-hour day, and the union scale of wages, by means of interfering with and restraining its interstate trade in the products of the factory. Complainant's principal manufacture is newspaper presses of large size and complicated mechanism, varying in weight from 10,000 to 100,000 pounds, and requiring a considerable force of labor and a considerable expenditure of time—a week or more—to handle, haul and erect them at the point of delivery. These presses are sold throughout the United States and in foreign countries; and, as they are especially designed for the production of daily papers, there is a large market for them in and about the City of New York. They are delivered there in the ordinary course of interstate commerce, the handling, hauling and installation work at destination being done by employees of the purchaser under the supervision of a specially skilled machinist supplied by complainant. The acts complained of and sought to be restrained have nothing to do with the conduct or management of the factory in Michigan, but solely with the installation and operation of the presses by complainant's customers. None of the defendants is or ever was an employee of complainant, and complainant at no time has had relations with either of the organizations that they represent. In August, 1913 (eight months before the filing of the bill), the International Association called a strike at complainant's factory in Battle Creek, as a result of which union machinists to the number of about eleven in the factory and three who supervised the erection of presses in the field left complainant's employ. But the defection of so small a number did not materially interfere with the operation of the factory, and sales and shipments in interstate commerce continued. The acts complained of made up the details of an elaborate programme adopted and carried out by defendants and their organizations in and about the City of New York as part of a country-wide programme adopted by the International Association, for the purpose of enforcing a boycott of complainant's product. The acts embraced the following, with others: warning customers that it would be better for them not to purchase, or having purchased not to install, presses made by complainant, and threatening them with loss should they do so; threatening customers with sympathetic strikes in other trades; notifying a trucking company usually employed by customers to haul the presses not to do so, and threatening it with trouble if it should; inciting employees of the trucking company, and other men employed by customers of complainant, to strike against their respective employers in order to interfere with the hauling and installation of presses, and thus bring pressure to bear upon the customers; notifying repair shops not to do repair work on Duplex presses; coercing union men by threatening them with loss of union cards and with being blacklisted as "scabs" if they assisted in installing the presses; threatening an exposition company with a strike if it permitted complainant's presses to be exhibited;. and resorting to a variety of other modes of preventing the sale of presses of complainant's manufacture in or about New York City, and delivery of them in interstate commerce, such as injuring and threatening to injure complainant's customers and prospective customers, and persons concerned in hauling, handling, or installing the presses. In some cases the threats were undisguised, in other cases polite in form but none the less sinister in purpose and effect. All the judges of the Circuit Court of Appeals concurred in the view that defendants' conduct consisted essentially of efforts to render it impossible for complainant to carry on any commerce in printing presses between Michigan and New York; and that defendants had agreed to do and were endeavoring to accomplish the very thing pronounced unlawful by this court in *Loewe* v. *Lawlor,* 208 U.S. 274, 235 U.S. 522. The judges also agreed that the interference with interstate commerce was such as ought to be enjoined, unless the Clayton Act of October 15, 1914, forbade such injunction.

That act was passed after the beginning of the suit but more than two years before it was brought to hearing. We are clear that the courts below were right in giving effect to it; the real question being, whether they gave it the proper effect. In so far as the act (a) provided for relief by injunction to private suitors, (b) imposed conditions upon granting such relief under particular circumstances, and (c) otherwise modified the Sherman Act, it was effective from the time of its passage, and applicable to pending suits for injunction. . . .

The Clayton Act, in Sec. 1, includes the Sherman Act in a definition of "antitrust laws," and, in Sec. 16 (38 Stat. 737), gives to private parties a right to relief by injunction in any court of the United States against threatened loss or damage by a violation of the antitrust laws, under the conditions and principles regulating the granting of such relief by courts of equity.

As we shall see, the recognized distinction between a primary and a secondary boycott is material to be considered upon the question of the proper construction of the Clayton Act. But, in determining the right to an injunction under that and the Sherman Act, it is of minor consequence whether either kind of boycott is lawful or unlawful at common law or under the statutes of particular States. Those acts, passed in the exercise of the power of Congress to regulate commerce among the States, are of paramount authority, and their prohibitions must be given full effect irrespective of whether the things prohibited are lawful or unlawful at common law or under local statutes.

In *Loewe* v. *Lawlor,* 208 U.S. 274, where there was an effort to compel plaintiffs to unionize their factory by preventing them from manufacturing articles intended for transportation beyond the State, and also by preventing vendees from reselling articles purchased from plaintiffs and negotiating with plaintiffs for further purchases, by means of a boycott of plaintiffs' products and of dealers who handled them, this court held that there was a conspiracy in restraint of trade actionable under Sec. 7 of the Sherman Act, and in that connection said (p. 293): "The act prohibits any combination whatever to secure action which essentially obstructs the free flow of commerce between the States, or restricts, in that regard, the liberty of a trader to engage in business. The combination charged falls within the class of restraints of trade aimed at compelling third parties and strangers involuntarily not to engage in the course of trade except on conditions that the combination imposes." And when the case came before the court a second time, 235 U.S. 522, 534, it was held that the use of the primary and secondary boycott and the circulation of a list of "unfair dealers," intended to influence customers of plaintiffs and thus subdue the latter to the demands of the defendants, and having the effect of interfering with plaintiffs' interstate trade, was actionable.

In *Eastern States Retail Lumber Dealers' Association* v. *United States,* 234 U.S. 600, wholesale dealers were subjected to coercion merely through the circulation among retailers, who were members of the association, of information in the form of a kind of "black list," intended to influence the retailers to refrain from dealing with the listed wholesalers, and it was held that this constituted a violation of the Sherman Act. Referring to this decision, the court said, in *Lawlor* v. *Loewe,* 235 U.S. 522, 534: "That case established that, irrespective of compulsion or even agreement to observe its intimation, the circulation of a list of 'unfair dealers,' manifestly intended to put the ban upon those whose names appear therein, among an important body of possible customers combined with a view to joint action and in anticipation of such reports, is within the prohibitions of the Sherman Act if it is intended to restrain and restrains commerce among the States."

It is settled by these decisions that such a restraint produced by peaceable persuasion is as much within the prohibition as one accomplished by force or threats of force; and it is not to be justified by the fact that the participants in the combination or conspiracy may have some object beneficial to themselves or their associates which possibly they might have been at liberty to pursue in the absence of the statute.

Upon the question whether the provisions of the Clayton Act forbade the grant of an injunction under the circumstances of the present case, the Circuit Court of Appeals was divided; the majority holding that under Sec. 20, "perhaps in conjunction with Section 6," there could be no injunction. These sections are set forth in the margin.[3]

Defendants seek to derive from them some authority for their conduct. As to Sec. 6, it seems to us its principal importance in this discussion is for what it does not authorize, and for the limit it sets to the immunity conferred. The section assumes the normal objects of a labor organization to be legitimate, and declares that nothing in the antitrust laws shall be construed to forbid the existence and operation of such organizations or to forbid their

---

[3] "Sec. 6. That the labor of a human being is not a commodity or article of commerce. Nothing contained in the antitrust laws shall be construed to forbid the existence and operation of labor, agricultural, or horticultural organizations, instituted for the purposes of mutual help, and not having capital stock or conducted for profit, or to forbid or restrain individual members of such organizations from lawfully carrying out the legitimate objects thereof; nor shall such organizations, or the members thereof, be held or construed to be illegal combinations or conspiracies in restraint of trade, under the antitrust laws."

"Sec. 20. That no restraining order or injunction shall be granted by any court of the United States, or a judge or the judges thereof, in any case between an employer and employees, or between employers and employees, or between employees, or between persons employed and persons seeking employment, involving or growing out of, a dispute concerning terms or conditions of employment, unless necessary to prevent irreparable injury to property, or to a property right, of the party making the application, for which injury there is no adequate remedy at law, and such property or property right must be described with particularity in the application, which must be in writing and sworn to by the applicant or by his agent or attorney.

"And no such restraining order or injunction shall prohibit any person or persons, whether singly or in concert, from terminating any relation of employment, or from ceasing to perform any work or labor, or from recommending, advising, or persuading others by peaceful means so to do; or from attending at any place where any such person or persons may lawfully be, for the purpose of peacefully obtaining or communicating information, or from peacefully persuading any person to work or to abstain from working; or from ceasing to patronize or to employ any party to such dispute, or from recommending, advising, or persuading others by peaceful and lawful means so to do; or from paying or giving to, or withholding from, any person engaged in such dispute, any strike benefits or other moneys or things of value; or from peaceably assembling in a lawful manner, and for lawful purposes; or from doing any act or thing which might lawfully be done in the absence of such dispute by any party thereto; nor shall any of the acts specified in this paragraph be considered or held to be violations of any law of the United States."

members from lawfully carrying out their legitimate objects; and that such an organization shall not be held in itself—merely because of its existence and operation—to be an illegal combination or conspiracy in restraint of trade. But there is nothing in the section to exempt such an organization or its members from accountability where it or they depart from its normal and legitimate objects and engage in an actual combination or conspiracy in restraint of trade. And by no fair or permissible construction can it be taken as authorizing any activity otherwise unlawful, or enabling a normally lawful organization to become a cloak for an illegal combination or conspiracy in restraint of trade as defined by the antitrust laws.

The principal reliance is upon Sec. 20. This regulates the granting of restraining orders and injunctions by the courts of the United States in a designated class of cases, with respect to (a) the terms and conditions of the relief and the practice to be pursued, and (b) the character of acts that are to be exempted from the restraint; and in the concluding words it declares (c) that none of the acts specified shall be held to be violations of any law of the United States. All its provisions are subject to a general qualification respecting the nature of the controversy and the parties affected. It is to be a "case between an employer and employees, or between employers and employees, or between employees, or between persons employed and persons seeking employment, involving, or growing out of, a dispute concerning terms or conditions of employment."

The first paragraph merely puts into statutory form familiar restrictions upon the granting of injunctions already established and of general application in the equity practice of the courts of the United States. It is but declaratory of the law as it stood before. The second paragraph declares that "no *such* restraining order or injunction" shall prohibit certain conduct specified—manifestly still referring to a "case between an employer and employees . . . involving, or growing out of, a dispute concerning terms or conditions of employment," as designated in the first paragraph. It is very clear that the restriction upon the use of the injunction is in favor only of those concerned as parties to such a dispute as is described. The words defining the permitted conduct include particular qualifications consistent with the general one respecting the nature of the case and dispute intended; and the concluding words, "nor shall any of the acts specified in this paragraph be considered or held to be violations of any law of the United States," are to be read in the light of the context, and mean only that those acts are not to be held so when committed by parties concerned in "a dispute concerning terms or conditions of employment." If the qualifying words are to have any effect, they must operate to confine the restriction upon the granting of injunctions, and also the relaxation of the provisions of the antitrust and other laws of the United States, to parties standing in proximate relation to a controversy such as is particularly described.

The majority of the Circuit Court of Appeals appear to have entertained the view that the words "employers and employees," as used in Sec. 20, should be treated as referring to "the business class or clan to which the parties litigant respectively belong"; and that, as there had been a dispute at complainant's factory in Michigan concerning the conditions of employment there—a dispute created, it is said, if it did not exist before, by the act of the Machinists' Union in calling a strike at the factory—Sec. 20 operated to permit members of the Machinists' Union elsewhere—some 60,000 in number—although standing in no relation of employment under complainant, past, present, or prospective, to make that dispute their own and proceed to instigate sympathetic strikes, picketing, and boycotting against employers wholly unconnected with complainant's factory and having relations with the ordinary course of interstate commerce—and this where there was no dispute between such employers and their employees respecting terms or conditions of employment.

We deem this construction altogether inadmissible. Section 20 must be given full effect according to its terms as an expresssion of the purpose of Congress; but it must be borne in mind that the section imposes an exceptional and extraordinary restriction upon the equity powers of the courts of the United States and upon the general operation of the antitrust laws, a restriction in the nature of a special privilege or immunity to a particular class, with corresponding detriment to the general public; and it would violate rules of statutory construction having general application and far-reaching importance to enlarge that special privilege by resorting to a loose construction of the section, not to speak of ignoring or slighting the qualifying words that are found in it.

Nor can Sec. 20 be regarded as bringing in all members of a labor organization as parties to a "dispute concerning terms or conditions of employment" which proximately affects only a few of them, with the result of conferring upon any and all members—no matter how many thousands there may be, nor how remote from the actual conflict—those exemptions which Congress in terms conferred only upon parties to the dispute. That would enlarge by construction the provisions of Sec. 20, which contains no mention of labor organizations, so as to produce an inconsistency with Sec. 6, which deals specifically with the subject and must be deemed to express the measure and limit of the immunity intended by Congress to be incident to mere membership in such an organization. At the same time it would virtually repeal by implication the prohibition of the Sherman Act, so far as labor organizations are concerned, notwithstanding repeals by implication are not favored; and in effect, as was noted in *Loewe* v. *Lawlor,* 208 U.S. 274, 303–304, would confer upon voluntary associations of individuals formed within the States a control over commerce among the States that is denied to the governments of the States themselves.

The qualifying effect of the words descriptive of the nature of the dispute and the parties concerned is further borne out by the phrases defining the conduct that is not to be subjected to injunction or treated as a violation of the laws of United States, that is to say: (a) "terminating any relation of employment . . . or persuading others by peaceful and lawful means so to do"; (b) "attending at any place where any such person or persons may lawfully be, for the purpose of peacefully obtaining or communicating information, or from peacefully persuading any person to work or to abstain from working"; (c) "ceasing to patronize or to employ any party to such dispute, or . . . recommending, advising, or persuading others by peaceful and lawful means so to do"; (d) "paying or giving to, or withholding from, any person engaged in such dispute, any strike benefits . . ."; (e) "doing any act or thing which might lawfully be done in the absence of such dispute by any party thereto." The emphasis placed on the words "lawful" and "lawfully," "peaceful" and "peacefully," and the references to the dispute and the parties to it, strongly rebut a legislative intent to confer a general immunity for conduct violative of the antitrust laws, or otherwise unlawful. The subject of the boycott is dealt with specifically in the "ceasing to patronize" provision, and by the clear force of the language employed the exemption is limited to pressure exerted upon a "party to such dispute" by means of "peaceful and *lawful*" influence upon neutrals. There is nothing here to justify defendants or the organizations they represent in using either threats or persuasion to bring about strikes or a cessation of work on the part of employees of complainant's customers or prospective customers, or of the trucking company employed by the customers, with the object of compelling such customers to withdraw or refrain from commercial relations with complainant, and of thereby constraining complainant to yield the matter in dispute. To instigate a sympathetic strike in aid of a secondary boycott cannot be deemed "peaceful and lawful" persuasion. In essence it is a threat to inflict damage upon the immediate employer, between whom and his employees no dispute exists, in order to bring him against his will into a concerted plan to inflict damage upon another employer who is in dispute with his employees. . . .

Reaching the conclusion, as we do, that complainant has a clear right to an injunction under the Sherman Act as amended by the Clayton Act, it becomes unnecessary to consider whether a like result would follow under the common law or local statutes; there being no suggestion that relief thereunder could be broader than that to which complainant is entitled under the acts of Congress.

There should be an injunction against defendants and the associations represented by them, and all members of those associations, restraining them, according to the prayer of the bill, from interfering or attempting to interfere with the sale, transportation, or delivery in interstate commerce of any printing press or presses manufactured by complainant, or the transportation, carting, installation, use, operation, exhibition, display, or repairing of any such press or presses, or the performance of any contract or contracts made by complainant respecting the sale, transportation, delivery, or installation of any such press or presses, by causing or threatening to cause loss, damage, trouble, or inconvenience to any person, firm, or corporation concerned in the purchase, transportation, carting, installation, use, operation, exhibition, display, or repairing of any such press or presses, or the performance of any such contract or contracts; and also and especially from using any force, threats, command, direction, or even persuasion with the object or having the effect of causing any person or persons to decline employment, cease employment, or not seek employment, or to refrain from work or cease working under any person, firm, or corporation being a purchaser or prospective purchaser of any printing press or presses from complainant, or engaged in hauling, carting, delivering, installing, handling, using, operating, or repairing any such press or presses for any customer of complainant. Other threatened conduct by defendants or the associations they represent, or the members of such associations, in furtherance of the secondary boycott should be included in the injunction according to the proofs.

Complainant is entitled to its costs in this court and in both courts below.

Decree reversed, and the cause remanded to the District Court for further proceedings in conformity with this opinion.

CASE **QUESTIONS**	1. What demands did the International Association of Machinists seek to enforce upon their employer? 2. How are the newspaper presses installed? 3. What acts did the union engage in to enforce their demands? 4. How does the Supreme Court circumvent the language of Section 6 of the Clayton Act? 5. How does the Supreme Court handle Section 20 of the Clayton Act? 6. Does the Clayton Act make secondary boycotts lawful according to the Supreme Court? Why? 7. What view did the Circuit Court of Appeals take upon the secondary boycott question of the Clayton Act? Why?

American Steel Foundries v. Tri-City Central Trades Council

(SUPPLEMENTAL CASE DIGEST—THE CLAYTON ACT)
Supreme Court of the United States, 1921. 527 U.S. 184

The Central Trades Council, a labor organization composed of 37 craft units, invoked a strike for higher wages and for recognition against the American Steel Foundries. Picketing of the plant, though essentially orderly, was marked by a few cases of assaults upon nonstrikers seeking employment. An injunction was issued against the union restraining all picketing activity by the union. This appeal was taken to determine the applicability and effect of the labor clauses of the Clayton Act, 38 Stat. 738, especially Sec. 20 thereof, in divesting the courts of their injunctive powers in labor disputes. As finally ordered by the court, picketing activity was restricted to one representative at each point of ingress or egress in the plant. Chief Justice Taft, speaking for the court, laid down the following interpretation.

"The first question in the case is whether Section 20 of the Clayton Act of 1914 is to be applied to this case.

"It has been determined by this court that the irreparable injury to property or to a property right, in the first paragraph of Section 20, includes injury to the business of an employer, and that the second paragraph applies only in cases growing out of a dispute concerning terms or conditions of employment, between an employer and employee, between employers and employees, or between employees, or between persons employed and persons seeking employment, and not to such dispute between an employer and persons who are neither ex-employees nor seeking employment. *Duplex Printing Press Co.* v. *Deering,* 254 U.S. 443, 41 S. Ct. 172, 65 L. Ed. 349, 16 A.L.R. 196. Only two of the defendants, Cook and Churchill, who left at the time of the strike, can invoke in their behalf Section 20. We must, therefore, first consider the propriety of the decree as against them, and then as against the other defendants.

"The prohibitions of Section 20, material here, are those which forbid an injunction against, first, recommending, advising or persuading others by peaceful means to cease employment and labor; second, attending at any place where such person or persons may lawfully be for the purpose of peacefully obtaining or communicating information, or peacefully persuading any person to work or to abstain from working; third, peaceably assembling in a lawful manner and for lawful purposes. This court has already called attention in the *Duplex* case to the emphasis upon the words 'peaceable' and 'lawful' in this section. 254 U.S. 443, 473, 41 S. Ct. 172, 65 L. Ed. 349, 16 A.L.R. 196. It is clear that Congress wished to forbid the use by the federal courts of their equity arm to prevent peaceable persuasion by employees, discharged or expectant, in promotion of their side of the dispute, and to secure them against judicial restraint in obtaining or communicating information in any place where they might lawfully be. This introduces no new principle into the equity jurisprudence of those courts. It is merely declaratory of what was the best practice always. Congress thought it wise to stabilize this rule of action and render it uniform.

"The object and problem of Congress in Section 20, and indeed of courts of equity before its enactment, was to reconcile the rights of the employer in his business and in the access of his employees to his place of business and egress therefrom without intimidation or obstruction, on the one hand, and the right of the employees, recent or expectant, to use peaceable and lawful means to induce present employees and would-be employees to join their ranks, on the other. If in their attempts at persuasion or communication with those whom they would enlist with them, those of the labor side adopt methods which however lawful in their announced purpose inevitably lead to intimidation and obstruction, then it is the court's duty, which the terms of Section 20 do not modify, so to limit what the propagandists do as to time, manner and place as shall prevent infractions of the law and violations of the right of the employees, and of the employer for whom they wish to work.

"How far may men go in persuasion and communication and still not violate the right of those whom they would influence? In going to and from work, men have a right to as free a passage without obstruction as the streets afford, consistent with the right of others to enjoy the same privilege. We are a social people and the accosting by one of another in an inoffensive way and an offer by one to communicate and discuss information with a view to influencing the other's action are not regarded as aggression or a violation of that other's rights. If, however, the offer is declined, as it may rightfully be, then persistence, importunity, following and dogging become unjustifiable annoyance and obstruction which is likely soon to savor of intimidation. From all of this the person sought to be influenced has a right to be free and his employer has a right to have him free."

CASE **1.** Upon what theory did the union base its appeal?
QUESTIONS **2.** How does the court reason around the prohibition of Section 20 of the Clayton Act?
3. Would the Supreme Court's decision have been the same if the picketing were unmarked by violence?

SECTION 11 / **THE NORRIS-LAGUARDIA ACT**

In response to labor pressure, Congress in 1932 passed the Federal Anti-Injunction Act, otherwise known for its principal sponsors. The Act reflects legislative disapproval of Supreme Court construction of the Clayton Act, which largely nullified the Congressional intent that was manifested, but not too explicitly stated, in Sections 6 and 20. The text of the Federal Anti-Injunction Act merits analysis as to those provisions that throw substantial safeguards around legitimate union activity, in protecting the same from private injunctive process in the federal courts.[4] Many states enacted anti-injunction statutes patterned after the federal law, thus placing the employer in a somewhat difficult position in all forums.

Analysis of the principal provisions of the Norris-LaGuardia Act follows:

a. Section 1 divests federal courts of injunctive powers in cases growing out of a labor dispute, except as provided by Section 7.

b. Section 2 states that the policy of the Act is to foster labor's right to form labor organizations without interference by the employer.

c. Section 3 outlaws yellow-dog contracts.

d. Section 4 reiterates the worker's right to strike, assemble and peacefully picket, and identifies nine specific situations protected from injunctive process.

e. Section 6 lays down a very stringent rule of agency liability, requiring, before liability for unlawful acts of others may attach to an officer or agent of any organization, in a labor dispute case, that there be proof of actual participation, actual authorization, or ratification after actual knowledge of the commission of unlawful acts.

f. Section 7 provides that the complainant in a labor dispute case will be denied relief unless he can prove, in open court, under adverse cross-examination, a case incorporating the following elements:

1. Unlawful acts have been threatened or committed.

2. Injury to property will follow therefrom.

3. Injury to complainant will be greater than injury to defendant unless the unlawful acts are enjoined.

4. Complainant has no adequate remedy at law.

5. Police are unable or unwilling to furnish adequate protection to complainant's property.

g. Section 8 adds the further jurisdictional requirement that complainant must come in with clean hands, having made reasonable efforts to negotiate the differences existing.

h. Section 9 requires the injunction to enjoin only specific acts complained of, eliminating the omnibus type of injunction.

i. Section 10 provides for expeditious appeal.

---

[4] It should be noted that this act does not apply when the NLRB or the federal government is a party.

  j. Section 11 allows a jury trial in contempt cases not committed in the court's presence or near thereto.
  k. Section 13(c) provides a broad definition of a labor dispute and that the disputants need not "stand in the proximate relation of employer and employee."

Significant changes in the common law and in the use of injunctions issued by federal courts were accomplished by the statute's provisions: By Sections 2 and 3 the judges were deprived of all discretion regarding legal rights of employees to organize for collective bargaining; the illegality of any type of interference or restraint or coercion by employers was established and also removed from the jurisdiction of the courts. Any and all forms of antiunion contracts or restrictions in employment conditions were outlawed. Federal courts were explicitly deprived by Sections 4 and 5 of all jurisdiction to restrain or to find as an unlawful combination or conspiracy conduct by persons participating or even interested in a labor dispute. A dispute as broadly defined by Section 13 now included all those who are disputants in any labor controversy regardless of employer-employee relationship. Thus nonemployee supporters of labor or union agents, singly or collectively, as well as the employees were protected against the issuance of federal court orders prohibiting the following:

  a. Ceasing or refusing to perform any work or to remain in any relation of employment;
  b. Becoming or remaining a member of any labor organization or of any employer organization, regardless of any such undertaking or promise as is described in Section 3 of this Act;
  c. Paying or giving to, or withholding from, any person participating or interested in such labor dispute, any strike or unemployment benefits or insurance, or other moneys or things of value;
  d. By all lawful means aiding any person participating or interested in any labor dispute who is being proceeded against in, or is prosecuting, any action or suit in any court of the United States or of any State;
  e. Giving publicity to the existence of, or the facts involved in, any labor dispute, whether by advertising, speaking, patrolling, or by any other method not involving fraud or violence;
  f. Assembling peaceably to act or to organize to act in promotion of their interests in a labor dispute;
  g. Advising or notifying any person of an intention to do any of the acts heretofore specified;
  h. Agreeing with other persons to do or not to do any of the acts heretofore specified; and
  i. Advising, urging, or otherwise causing or inducing without fraud or violence the acts heretofore specified, regardless of any such undertaking or promise as is described in Section 3 of this Act.

As further prohibition it is stated in Sections 6 and 7 that no officer or member of any association or organization, and no association or organization participating or interested in a labor dispute shall be held responsible or liable for the unlawful acts of individual officers, members, or agents, except upon clear proof of actual participation in, or actual authorization of, or of ratification of such acts after actual knowledge. Moreover, a temporary or permanent injunction may not be issued in a labor dispute, except after hearing the testimony of witnesses in open court (with opportunity for cross-examination) in support of the allegations of a complaint made under oath, and testimony in opposition and except after findings of fact by the court, to the effect—

(a) That unlawful acts have been threatened and will be committed unless restrained or have been committed and will be continued unless restrained, but no injunction or temporary restraining order shall be issued on account of any threat or unlawful act excepting against the person or persons, association, or organization making the threat or committing the unlawful act or actually authorizing or ratifying the same after actual knowledge thereof;

(b) That substantial and irreparable injury to complainant's property will follow;

(c) That as to each item of relief granted greater injury will be inflicted upon complainant by the denial of relief than will be inflicted upon defendants by the granting of relief;

(d) That complaint has no adequate remedy at law; and

(e) That the public officers charged with the duty to protect complainant's property are unable or unwilling to furnish adequate protection.

It is further provided that no restraining order or injunctive relief shall be granted to any complainant who has failed to comply with any obligations imposed by law which is involved in a labor dispute in question, or who has failed to make every reasonable effort to settle such dispute either by negotiation or with the aid of any available governmental machinery of mediation or voluntary arbitration.

These provisions were to reverse much of the common law if a labor dispute sought the improvement of labor conditions or bargaining power. Not all union conduct was immune, however, as can be seen from some cases that follow in this chapter. In later chapters the relation of the Anti-Injunction Act to the Railway Labor Act and subsequent labor legislation will be presented.

New Negro Alliance v. Sanitary Grocery Co., Inc.

Supreme Court of the United States, 1938. 303 U.S. 552

The matter in controversy is whether the case made by the pleadings involves or grows out of a labor dispute within the meaning of Section 13 of the Norris-LaGuardia Act. . . .

The case, then, as it stood for judgment, was this: The petitioners requested the respondent to adopt a policy of employing Negro clerks in certain of its stores in the course of personnel changes; the respondent ignored the request and the petitioners caused one person to patrol in front of one of the respondent's stores on one day carrying a placard which said: "Do Your Part! Buy Where You Can Work! No Negroes Employed Here!" and caused or threatened a similar patrol of two other stores of respondent. The information borne by the placard was true.

The patrolling did not coerce or intimidate respondent's customers; did not physically obstruct, interfere with, or harass persons desiring to enter the store, the picket acted in an orderly manner, and his conduct did not cause crowds to gather in front of the store.

The trial judge was of the view that the laws relating to labor disputes had no application to the case. He entered a decree enjoining the petitioners and their agents and employees from picketing or patrolling any of the respondent's stores, boycotting or urging others to boycott respondent; restraining them, whether by inducements, threats, intimidation or actual or threatened physical force from hindering any person entering respondent's places of business, from destroying or damaging or threatening to destroy or damage respondent's property and from aiding or abetting others in doing any of the prohibited things. The Court of Appeals thought that the dispute was not a labor dispute within the Norris-LaGuardia Act because it did not involve terms and conditions of employment such as wages, hours, unionization or betterment of working conditions, and that the trial court, therefore, had jurisdiction to issue the injunction. We think the conclusion that the dispute was not a labor dispute within the meaning of the Act because it did not involve terms and conditions of employment in the sense of wages, hours, unionization or betterment of working conditions is erroneous.

Subsection (a) of Section 13 provides: "A case shall be held to involve or to grow out of a labor dispute when the case involves persons who are engaged in the same industry, trade, craft, or occupation, or have direct or indirect interests therein; . . . or when the case involves any conflicting or competing interests in a 'labor dispute' (as hereinafter defined) of 'persons participating or interested' therein (as hereinafter defined)." Subsection (b) characterizes a person or association as participating or interested in a labor dispute "if relief is sought against him or it and if he or it . . . has a direct or indirect interest therein, . . ."

Subsection (c) defines the term "labor dispute" as including "any controversy concerning terms or conditions of employment, . . . regardless of whether or not the disputants stand in the proximate relation of employer and employee." These definitions plainly embrace the controversy which gave rise to the instant suit and classify it as one arising out of a dispute defined as a labor dispute. They leave no doubt that The New Negro Alliance and the individual petitioners are, in contemplation of the Act, persons interested in the dispute.

In quoting the clauses of Section 13 we have omitted those that deal with disputes between employers and employees and disputes between associations of persons engaged in a particular trade or craft, and employers in the same industry. It is to be noted, however, that the inclusion in the definitions of such disputes, and the persons interested in them, serves to emphasize the fact that the quoted portions were intended to embrace controversies other than those between employers and employees; between labor unions seeking to represent employees and employers; and between persons seeking employment and employers.

The Act does not concern itself with the background or the motives of the dispute. The desire for fair and equitable conditions of employment on the part of persons of any race, color, or persuasion, and the removal of discriminations against them by reason of their race or religious belief is quite as important to those concerned as fairness and equity in terms and conditions of employment can be to trade or craft unions or any form of labor organization or association. Race discrimination by an employer may reasonably be deemed more unfair and less excusable than discrimination against workers on the ground of union affiliation. There is no justification in the apparent purposes or the express terms of the Act for limiting its definition of labor disputes and cases arising therefrom by excluding those which arise with respect to discrimination in terms and condition of employment based upon differences of race or color.

The purpose and policy of the Act respecting the jurisdiction of the federal courts is set forth in Sections 4 and 7. The former deprives those courts of jurisdiction to issue an injunction against, *inter alia,* giving publicity to the existence of, or the facts involved in, any labor dispute, whether by advertising, speaking, patrolling, or by any other method not involving fraud or violence; against assembling peaceably to act or to organize to act in promotion of their interests in a labor dispute; against advising or notifying any person of an intention to do any of the acts specified; against agreeing with other persons to do any of the acts specified.

The legislative history of the Act demonstrates that it was the purpose of the Congress further to extend the prohibitions of the Clayton Act respecting the exercise of jurisdiction by federal courts and to obviate the results of the judicial construction of that Act. It was intended that peaceful and orderly dissemination of information by those defined as persons interested in a labor dispute concerning "terms and conditions of employment" in an industry or a plant or a place of business should be lawful; that, short of fraud, breach of the peace, violence, or conduct otherwise unlawful, those having a direct or indirect interest in such terms and conditions of employment should be at liberty to advertise and disseminate facts and information with respect to terms and conditions of employment, and peacefully to persuade others to concur in their views respecting an employer's practices. The District Court erred in not complying with the provisions of the Act.

The decree must be reversed and the cause remanded to the District Court for further proceedings in conformity with this opinion.

So ordered.

Mr. Justice MCREYNOLDS, dissenting: Mr. Justice BUTLER and I cannot accept the view that a "labor dispute" emerges whenever an employer fails to respond to a communication from A, B, and C—irrespective of their race, character, reputation, fitness, previous or present employment—suggesting displeasure because of his choice of employees and their expectation that in the future he will not fail to select men of their complexion.

It seems unbelievable that, in all such circumstances, Congress intended to inhibit courts from extending protection long guaranteed by law and thus, in effect, encourage mobbish interference with the individual's liberty of action. Under the tortured meaning now attributed to the words, "labor dispute," no employer—merchant, manufacturer, builder, cobbler, housekeeper or what-not—who prefers helpers of one color or class can find adequate safeguard against intolerable violations of his freedom if members of some other class, religion, race or color demand that he give them precedence.

Design thus to promote strife, encourage trespass and stimulate intimidation, ought not to be admitted where, as here, not plainly avowed. The ultimate result of the view now approved to the very people whom present petitioners claim to represent, it may be, is prefigured by the grievous plight of minorities in lands where the law has become a mere political instrument.

CASE **QUESTIONS**	1. What provisions of the Norris-LaGuardia Act were concerned in the case? Why? 2. Why did the Trial Court grant relief? 3. What was the Circuit Court's reasoning? 4. How did the minority opinion differ from the Supreme Court majority ruling?

SECTION 12 / NORRIS-LAGUARDIA AND NO-STRIKE INJUNCTIONS

Section 4 of the Norris-LaGuardia Act, with a limited exception not pertinent here, prohibits federal court injunctions in labor disputes. Section 301 of the Labor Management Relations Act provides that employers and unions may sue each other whenever a breach of a collective bargaining contract takes place. Section 301, however, does not include any statutory provision insulating cases brought under Section 301 from the prohibition against injunctions in the Norris-LaGuardia Act. Are federal courts then allowed to use the injunction as a remedy in breach of collective bargaining agreement (Section 301) cases? We must analyze the Supreme Court decisions that have construed these statutes for our answer.

In *Textile Workers Union* v. *Lincoln Mills* [5] the United States Supreme Court allowed the use of an injunction to compel an employer to fulfill his obligation to arbitrate under an existing collective bargaining agreement. However, in *Sinclair Refining Company* v. *Atkinson* [6] the Court refused to enjoin a strike by a union, even though the collective bargaining agreement in effect at the time of the strike contained a no-strike clause and an arbitration clause. In *Sinclair,* Mr. Justice Black wrote for the majority that Section 301 did not modify the Norris-LaGuardia Act insofar as the statute prohibited injunctions in labor disputes, and that federal district courts were without jurisdiction to order injunctive relief. In *Avco Corporation* v. *Aero Lodge* [7] the Supreme Court in effect negated the employers' right to seek injunctive relief to enforce a no-strike clause in a state court (remember, Norris-LaGuardia prohibitions against the use of injunctions apply only to federal courts) by allowing the union to remove the case from the state court to a federal court. *The Boys Markets* decision, reported in this section, overruled *Sinclair.* In it, the Supreme Court held that there must be an accomodation between the seemingly absolute terms of the Norris-LaGuardia Act and the policy considerations underlying Section 301. The Court concluded that the federal courts do have limited injunctive powers in Section 301 cases. The Court does caution that this decision is "a narrow one"; and only under certain limited

---

[5] 353 U.S. 448 (1957).
[6] 370 U.S. 195 (1962).
[7] 390 U.S. 557 (1968).

circumstances may a court enjoin a strike in violation of a contractual no-strike clause.

Boys Markets, Inc. v. Retail Clerks Union, Local 770

Supreme Court of the United States, 1970. 398 U.S. 235

BRENNAN, J.: In this case we re-examine the holding of *Sinclair Refining Co.* v. *Atkinson,* 370 U.S. 195 (1962), that the anti-injunction provisions of the Norris-LaGuardia Act preclude a federal district court from enjoining a strike in breach of a no-strike obligation under a collective bargaining agreement, even though that agreement contains provisions, enforceable under § 301(a) of the Labor-Management Relations Act for binding arbitration of the grievance dispute concerning which the strike was called. The Court of Appeals for the Ninth Circuit, considering itself bound by *Sinclair,* reversed the grant by the District Court for the Central District of California of petitioner's prayer for injunctive relief. 416 F.2d 368 (1969). We granted certiorari. 396 U.S. 1000 (1970). Having concluded that *Sinclair* was erroneously decided and that subsequent events have undermined its continuing validity, we overrule that decision and reverse the judgment of the Court of Appeals.

In February 1969, at the time of the incidents that produced this litigation, petitioner and respondent were parties to a collective bargaining agreement which provided, *inter alia,* that all controversies concerning its interpretation or application should be resolved by adjustment and arbitration procedures set forth therein and that, during the life of the contract, there should be "no cessation or stoppage of work, lock-out, picketing or boycotts. . . ." The dispute arose when petitioner's frozen foods supervisor and certain members of his crew who were not members of the bargaining unit began to rearrange merchandise in the frozen food cases of one of petitioner's supermarkets. A union representative insisted that the food cases be stripped of all merchandise and be restocked by union personnel. When petitioner did not accede to the union's demand, a strike was called and the union began to picket petitioner's establishment. Thereupon petitioner demanded that the union cease the work stoppage and picketing and sought to invoke the grievance and arbitration procedures specified in the contract.

The following day, since the strike had not been terminated, petitioner filed a complaint in California Superior Court seeking a temporary restraining order, a preliminary and permanent injunction, and specific performance of the contractual arbitration provision. The state court issued a temporary restraining order forbidding continuation of the strike and also an order to show cause why a preliminary injunction should not be granted. Shortly thereafter, the union removed the case to the federal district court and there made a motion to quash the state court's temporary restraining order. In opposition, petitioner moved for an order compelling arbitration and enjoining continuation of the strike. Concluding that the dispute was subject to arbitration under the collective bargaining agreement and that the strike was in violation of the contract, the District Court ordered the parties to arbitrate the underlying dispute and simultaneously enjoined the strike, all picketing in the vicinity of petitioner's supermarket, and any attempts by the union to induce the employees to strike or to refuse to perform their services.

At the outset, we are met with respondent's contention that *Sinclair* ought not to be disturbed because the decision turned on a question of statutory construction which Congress can alter at any time. Since Congress has not modified our conclusions in *Sinclair,* even though it has been urged to do so, respondent argues that principles of *stare decisis* should govern the present case.

We do not agree that the doctrine of *stare decisis* bars a re-examination of *Sinclair* in the circumstances of this case. We fully recognize that important policy considerations militate in favor of continuity and predictability in the law. Nevertheless, as Mr. Justice Frankfurter wrote for the Court, "[*S*]*tare decisis* is a principle of policy and not a mechanical formula of adherence to the latest decision, however recent and questionable, when such adherence involves collision with a prior doctrine more embracing in its scope, intrinsically sounder, and verified by experience." *Helvering* v. *Hallock,* 309 U.S. 106, 119 (1940). See *Swift & Co.* v. *Wickham,* 382 U.S. 111, 116 (1965). It is precisely because *Sinclair* stands as a significant departure from our otherwise consistent emphasis upon the congressional policy to promote the peaceful settlement of labor disputes through arbitration and our efforts to accommodate and harmonize this policy with those underlying the anti-injunction provisions of the Norris-LaGuardia Act that we believe *Sinclair* should be reconsidered. Furthermore, in light of developments subsequent to *Sinclair,* in particular our decision in *Avco Corp.* v. *Aero Lodge 735,* 390 U.S. 557 (1968), it has become clear that the *Sinclair* decision does not further but rather frustrates realization of an important goal of our national labor policy.

Nor can we agree that conclusive weight should be accorded to the failure of Congress to respond to *Sinclair* on the theory that congressional silence should be interpreted as acceptance of the decision. The Court has cautioned that "[i]t is at best treacherous to find in congressional silence alone the adoption of a controlling rule of law." *Girouard* v. *United States,* 328 U.S. 61, 69 (1946). Therefore, in the absence of any persuasive circumstances evidencing a clear design that congressional inaction be taken as acceptance of *Sinclair,* the mere silence of Congress is not a sufficient reason for refusing to reconsider the decision. *Helvering* v. *Hallock,* supra, at 119–120. . . .

An additional reason for not resolving the existing dilemma by extending *Sinclair* to the States is the devastating implications for the enforceability of arbitration agreements and their accompanying no-strike obligations if equitable remedies were not available. As we have previously indicated, a no-strike obligation, express or implied, is the *quid pro quo* for an undertaking by the employer to submit grievance disputes to the process of arbitration. . . . Any incentive for employers to enter into such an arrangement is necessarily dissipated if the principal and most expeditious method by which the no-strike obligation can be enforced is eliminated. While it is of course true, as respondent contends, that other avenues of redress, such as an action for damages, would remain open to an aggrieved employer, an award of damages after a dispute has been settled is no substitute for an immediate halt to an illegal strike. Furthermore, an action for damages prosecuted during or after a labor dispute would only tend to aggravate industrial strife and delay an early resolution of the difficulties between employer and union.

Even if management is not encouraged by the unavailability of the injunction remedy to resist arbitration agreements, the fact remains that the effectiveness of such agreements would be greatly reduced if injunctive relief were withheld. Indeed, the very purpose of arbitration procedures is to provide a mechanism for the expeditious settlement of industrial disputes without resort to strikes, lock-outs, or other self-help measures. This basic purpose is obviously largely undercut if there is no immediate, effective remedy for those very tactics which arbitration is designed to obviate. Thus, because *Sinclair,* in the aftermath of *Avco,* casts serious doubt upon the effective enforcement of a vital element of stable labor-management relations—arbitration agreements with their attendant no-strike obligations—we conclude that *Sinclair* does not make a viable contribution to federal labor policy.

We have also determined that the dissenting opinion in *Sinclair* states the correct principles concerning the accommodation necessary between the seemingly absolute terms of the Norris-LaGuardia Act and the policy considerations underlying § 301(a). 370 U.S., at 215. Although we need not repeat all that was there said, a few points should be emphasized at this time.

The literal terms of § 4 of the Norris-LaGuardia Act must be accommodated to the subsequently enacted provisions of § 301(a) of the Labor-Management Relations Act and the purposes of arbitration. Statutory interpretation requires more than concentration upon isolated words; rather, consideration must be given to the total corpus of pertinent law and the policies which inspired ostensibly inconsistent provisions. See *Richards* v. *United States,* 369 U.S. 1, 11 (1962). . . .

The Norris-LaGuardia Act was responsive to a situation totally different from that which exists today. In the early part of this century, the federal courts generally were regarded as allies of management in its attempt to prevent the organization and strengthening of labor unions; and in this industrial struggle the injunction became a potent weapon which was wielded against the activities of labor groups. The result was a large number of sweeping decrees, often issued *ex parte,* drawn on an *ad hoc* basis without regard to any systematic elaboration of national labor policy. See *Drivers' Union* v. *Lake Valley Co.,* 311 U.S. 91, 102 (1940).

In 1932 Congress attempted to bring some order out of the industrial chaos that had developed and to correct the abuses which had resulted from the interjection of the federal judiciary into union-management disputes on the behalf of management. See Declaration of Public Policy, Norris-LaGuardia Act, § 2, 47 Stat. 70 (1932). Congress, therefore, determined initially to limit severely the power of the federal courts to issue injunctions "in any case involving or growing out of any labor dispute. . . ." 47 Stat. 70. Even as initially enacted, however, the prohibition against federal injunctions was by no means absolute. See Norris-LaGuardia Act, §§ 7, 8, 9, 47 Stat. 70 (1932). Shortly thereafter Congress passed the Wagner Act, designed to curb various management activities which tended to discourage employee participation in collective action.

As labor organizations grew in strength and developed toward maturity, congressional emphasis shifted from protection of the nascent labor movement to the encouragement of collective bargaining and to administrative techniques for the peaceful resolution of industrial disputes. This shift in emphasis was accomplished, however, without extensive revision of many of the older enactments, including the anti-injunction section of the Norris-LaGuardia Act. Thus it became the task of the courts to accommodate, to reconcile the older statutes with the more recent ones.

A leading example of this accommodation process is *Brotherhood of R. R. Trainmen* v. *Chicago River & Ind. R. R.,* 353 U.S. 30 (1957). There we were confronted with a peaceful strike which violated the statutory duty to arbitrate imposed by the Railway Labor Act. The Court concluded that a strike in violation of a statutory arbitration duty was not the type of situation to which the Norris-LaGuardia Act was responsive, that an important federal policy was involved in the peaceful settlement of disputes through the statutorily-mandated arbitration procedure, that this important policy was imperiled if equitable remedies were not available to implement it, and hence that Norris-LaGuardia's policy of nonintervention by the federal courts should yield to the overriding interest in the successful implementation of the arbitration process.

The principles elaborated in *Chicago River* are equally applicable to the present case. To be sure, *Chicago River* involved arbitration procedures established by statute. However, we have frequently noted, in such cases as *Lincoln Mills,* the *Steelworkers Trilogy,* and *Lucas Flour,* the importance which Congress has attached generally to the voluntary settlement of labor disputes without resort to self-help and more particularly to arbitration as a means to this end. Indeed, it has been stated that *Lincoln Mills,* in its exposition of § 301(a), "went a long way towards making arbitration the central institution in the administration of collective bargaining contracts."

The *Sinclair* decision, however, seriously undermined the effectiveness of the arbitration technique as a method peacefully to resolve industrial disputes without resort to strikes, lockouts, and similar devices. Clearly employers will be wary of assuming obligations to arbitrate specifically enforceable against them when no similarly efficacious remedy is available to enforce the concomitant undertaking of the union to refrain from striking. On the other hand, the central purpose of the Norris-LaGuardia Act to foster the growth and viability of labor organizations is hardly retarded—if anything, this goal is advanced—by a remedial device which merely enforces the obligation that the union freely undertook under a specifically enforceable agreement to submit disputes to arbitration. We conclude, therefore, that the unavailability of equitable relief in the arbitration context presents a serious impediment to the congressional policy favoring the voluntary establishment of a mechanism for the peaceful resolution of labor disputes, that the core purpose of the Norris-LaGuardia Act is not sacrificed by the limited use of equitable remedies to further this important policy, and consequently that the Norris-LaGuardia Act does not bar the granting of injunctive relief in the circumstances of the instant case.

Our holding in the present case is a narrow one. We do not undermine the vitality of the Norris-LaGuardia Act. We deal only with the situation in which a collective bargaining contract contains a mandatory grievance adjustment or arbitration procedure. Nor does it follow from what we have said that injunctive relief is appropriate as a matter of course in every case of a strike over an arbitrable grievance. The dissenting opinion in *Sinclair* suggested the following principles for the guidance of the district courts in determining whether to grant injunctive relief—principles which we now adopt:

> "A District Court entertaining an action under § 301 may not grant injunctive relief against concerted activity unless and until it decides that the case is one in which an injunction would be appropriate despite the Norris-LaGuardia Act. When a strike is sought to be enjoined because it is over a grievance which both parties are contractually bound to arbitrate, the District Court may issue no injunctive order until it first holds that the contract *does* have that effect; and the employer should be ordered to arbitrate, as a condition of his obtaining an injunction against the strike. Beyond this, the District Court must, of course, consider whether issuance of an injunction would be warranted under ordinary principles of equity— whether breaches are occurring and will continue, or have been threatened and will be committed; whether they have caused or will cause irreparable injury to the employer; and whether the employer will suffer more from the denial of an injunction than will the union from its issuance." 370 U.S., at 228. (Emphasis in original.)

In the present case there is no dispute that the grievance in question was subject to adjustment and arbitration under the collective bargaining agreement and that the petitioner was ready to proceed with arbitration at the time an injunction against the strike was sought and obtained. The District Court also concluded that, by reason of respondent's violations of its no-strike obligation, petitioner "has suffered irreparable injury and will continue to suffer irreparable injury." Since we now overrule *Sinclair*, the holding of the Court of Appeals in reliance on *Sinclair* must be reversed. Accordingly, we reverse the judgment of the Court of Appeals and remand the case with directions to enter a judgment affirming the order of the District Court.

It is so ordered.

Mr. Justice MARSHALL took no part in the decision of this case.

STEWART, J., concurring: When *Sinclair Refining Co.* v. *Atkinson,* 370 U.S. 195, was decided in 1962, I subscribed to the opinion of the Court. Before six years had passed I had reached the conclusion that the *Sinclair* holding should be reconsidered, and said so in *Avco Corp.* v. *Aero Lodge No. 735,* 390 U.S. 557, at 562 (concurring opinion). Today I join the Court in concluding "that *Sinclair* was erroneously decided and that subsequent events have undermined its continuing validity. . . ."

In these circumstances the temptation is strong to embark upon a lengthy personal *apologia.* But since Mr. Justice BRENNAN has so clearly stated my present views in his opinion for the Court today, I simply join in that opinion and in the Court's judgment. An aphorism of Mr. Justice FRANKFURTER provides me refuge: "Wisdom too often never comes, and so one ought not to reject it merely because it comes late." *Henslee* v. *Union Planters Bank,* 335 U.S. 595, at 600 (dissenting opinion).

WHITE dissents for the reasons stated in the majority opinion in *Sinclair Refining Co.* v. *Atkinson,* 370 U.S. 195 (1962). . . .

BLACK, J. dissenting: . . . Although Congress has been urged to overrule our holding in *Sinclair,* it has steadfastly refused to do so. Nothing in the language or history of the two Acts has changed. Nothing at all has changed, in fact, except the membership of the Court and the personal views of one Justice. I remain of the opinion that *Sinclair* was correctly decided, and, moreover, that the prohibition of the Norris-LaGuardia Act is close to the heart of the entire federal system of labor regulation. In my view *Sinclair* should control the disposition of this case. . . .

When the Court implies that the doctrine called *stare decisis* rests solely on "important policy considerations . . . in favor of continuity and predictability in the law," it does not tell the whole story. Such considerations are present and, in a field as delicate as labor relations, extremely important. Justice Brandeis said, dissenting in *Burnet* v. *Coronado Oil & Gas Co.,* 285 U.S. 393, 406 (1932):

> "*Stare decisis* is usually the wise policy, because in most matters it is more important that the applicable rule of law be settled than that it be settled right. . . ."

. . . When the law has been settled by an earlier case then any subsequent "reinterpretation" of the statute is gratituous and neither more nor less than an amendment: it is no different in effect from a judicial alteration of language that Congress itself placed in the statute.

Altering the important provisions of a statute is a legislative function. And the Constitution states simply and unequivocally: "All legislative Powers herein granted shall be vested in a Congress of the United States. . . ." U.S. Const. Art. I. It is the Congress, not this Court, that responds to the pressures of political groups, pressures entirely proper in a free society. . . .

CASE QUESTIONS

1. How did the labor dispute that led to this litigation arise?
2. What are the issues before the Supreme Court?
3. Does the majority believe that the doctrine of *stare decisis* bars a re-examination of the *Sinclair* decision handed down in 1962?
4. What is Mr. Justice Black's dissenting position on the role of *stare decisis?*
5. The Union argued to the Court that the employer had other avenues of redress besides seeking injunctive relief. What was the Court's response?
6. What are the guiding principles adopted by the Court to be utilized by district courts in determining whether or not to grant injunctive relief?

SECTION 13 / INTERLACED CONSTRUCTION OF THE ACTS

The two decisions of the Supreme Court presented here show that after 1932 the early application of antitrust law to union activity became only of historical value. The dynamic change in legal application indicated by the cases in this section is due to a series of causes that found their inception in the late thirties, among them being: the presence of a liberal Supreme Court; the enactment of the Norris-LaGuardia Anti-Injunction, and Wagner Acts, reflecting a change in Congressional policy; and finally, federal sponsorship of labor organization.

Apex Hosiery Co. v. Leader

Supreme Court of the United States, 1940. 310 U.S. 469

STONE, J. Petitioner, a Pennsylvania corporation, is engaged in the manufacture, at its factory in Philadelphia, of hosiery, a substantial part of which is shipped in interstate commerce. It brought the present suit in the Federal District Court for Eastern Pennsylvania against respondent Federation, a labor organization, and its officers, to recover treble the amount of damage inflicted on it by respondents in conducting a strike at petitioner's factory alleged to be a conspiracy in violation of the Sherman Antitrust Act. 26 Stat. 209, 15 U.S.C. Sec. 1. The trial to a jury resulted in a verdict for petitioner in the sum of $237,310, respondents saving by proper motions and exceptions the question whether the evidence was sufficient to establish a violation of the Sherman Act. The trial judge trebled the verdict to $711,-932.55, in conformity to the provision of the Sherman Act as amended by Sec. 4 of the Clayton Act, 1914, 38 Stat. 731, 15 U.S.C. Sec. 15, and gave judgment accordingly. The Court of Appeals for the Third Circuit reversed, 108 F.(2d) 71, on the ground that the interstate commerce restrained or affected by respondents' acts was unsubstantial, the total shipment of merchandise from petitioner's factory being less than three percent of the total value of the output in the entire industry of the country, and on the further ground that the evidence failed to show an intent on the part of respondents to restrain interstate commerce. We granted certiorari, 309 U.S. 644, the questions presented being of importance in the administration of the Sherman Act.

The facts are undisputed. There was evidence from which the jury could have found as follows. Petitioner employs at its Philadelphia factory about twenty-five hundred persons in the manufacture of hosiery, and manufactures annually merchandise of the value of about $5,000,000. Its principal raw materials are silk and cotton, which are shipped to it from points outside the state. It ships interstate more than 80 percent of its finished product, and in the last eight months of 1937 it shipped in all 274,791 dozen pairs of stockings. In April, 1937, petitioner was operating a nonunion shop. A demand of the respondent Federation at that time for a closed-shop agreement came to nothing. On May 4, 1937, when only eight of petitioner's employees were members of the Federation, it ordered a strike. Shortly after midday on May 6, 1937, when petitioner's factory was shut down, members of the union, employed by other factories in Philadelphia who had stopped work, gathered at petitioner's plant. Respondent Leader, president of the Federation, then made a further demand for a closed-shop agreement. When this was refused Leader declared a "sit-down strike." Immediately, acts of violence against petitioner's plant and the employees in charge of it were committed by the assembled mob. It forcibly seized the plant, whereupon, under union leadership, its members were organized to maintain themselves as sit-down strikers in possession of the plant, and it remained in possession until June 23, 1937, when the strikers were forcibly ejected pursuant to an injunction ordered by the Court of Appeals for the Third Circuit in *Apex Hosiery Co.* v. *Leader,* 90 F.2d 155, 159; reversed and dismissal ordered as moot in *Leader* v. *Apex Hosiery Co.,* 302 U.S. 656.

The locks on all gates and entrances of petitioner's plant were changed; only strikers were given keys. No others were allowed to leave or enter the plant without permission of the strikers. During the period of their occupancy, the union supplied them with food, blankets, cots, medical care, and paid them strike benefits. While occupying the factory, the strikers wilfully wrecked machinery of great value, and did extensive damage to other property and equipment of the company. All manufacturing operations by petitioner ceased on May 6th. As the result of the destruction of the company's machinery and plant, it did not resume even partial manufacturing operations until August 19, 1937. The record discloses a lawless invasion of petitioner's plant and destruction of its property by force and violence of the most brutal and wanton character, under leadership and direction of respondents, and without interference by the local authorities.

For more than three months, by reason of respondents' acts, manufacture was suspended at petitioner's plant and the flow of petitioner's product into interstate commerce was stopped. When the plant was seized, there were on hand 130,000 dozen pairs of finished hosiery, of a value of about $800,000 ready for shipment on unfilled orders, 80 percent of which were to be shipped to points outside the state. Shipment was prevented by the occupation of the factory by the strikers. Three times in the course of the strike respondents refused requests made by petitioner to be allowed to remove the merchandise for the purpose of shipment in filling the orders.

Section 1 of the Sherman Act provides: "Every contract, combination in the form of trust or otherwise, or conspiracy, in restraint of trade or commerce among the several States, or with foreign nations, is hereby declared to be illegal." Only a single question is presented by the record for our decision, whether the evidence which we have detailed, whose verity must be taken to be established by the jury's verdict, establishes a restraint of trade or commerce which the Sherman Act condemns. . . .

A point strongly urged in behalf of respondents in brief and argument before us is that Congress intended to exclude labor organizations and their activities wholly from the operation of the Sherman Act. To this the short answer must be made that for the thirty-two years which have elapsed since the decision of *Loewe* v. *Lawlor,* 208 U.S. 274, this Court, in its efforts to determine the true meaning and application of the Sherman Act has repeatedly held that the words of the act, "Every contract, combination . . . or conspiracy in restraint of trade or commerce" do embrace to some extent and in some circumstances labor unions and their activities; and that during that period Congress, although often asked to do so, has passed no act purporting to exclude labor unions wholly from the operation of the Act. On the contrary Congress has repeatedly enacted laws restricting or purporting to curtail the application of the Act to labor organizations and their activities, thus recognizing that to some extent not defined they remain subject to it. . . .

. . . In 1890 when the Sherman Act was adopted there were only a few federal statutes imposing penalties for obstructing or misusing interstate transportation. With an expanding commerce, many others have since been enacted safeguarding transportation in interstate commerce as the need was seen, including statutes declaring conspiracies to interfere or actual interference with interstate commerce by violence or threats of violence to be felonies. It was another and quite a different evil at which the Sherman Act was aimed. It was enacted in the era of "trusts" and of "combinations" of business and of capital organized and directed to control of the market by suppression of competition in the marketing of goods and services, the monopolistic tendency of which had become a matter of public concern. The end sought was the prevention of restraints to free competition in business and commercial transactions which tended to restrict production, raise prices or otherwise control the goods and services, all of which had come to be regarded as a special form of public injury. . . .

. . . In the cases considered by this Court since the Standard Oil case in 1911 some form of restraint of commercial competition has been the *sine qua non* to the condemnation of contracts, combinations or conspiracies under the Sherman Act, and in general, restraints upon competition have been condemned only when their purpose or effect was to raise or fix the market price. It is in this sense that it is said that the restraints, actual or intended, prohibited by the Sherman Act are only those which are so substantial as to affect market prices. Restraints on competition or on the course of trade in the merchandising of articles moving in interstate commerce is not enough, unless the restraint is shown to have or is intended to have an effect upon prices in the market or otherwise to deprive purchasers or consumers of the advantages which they derive from free competition. . . .

The question remains whether the effect of the combination or conspiracy among respondents was a restraint of trade within the meaning of the Sherman Act. This is not a case of a labor organization being used by combinations of those engaged in an industry as the means or instrument for suppressing competition or fixing prices. See *United States* v. *Brims,* 272 U.S. 549; *Local 167* v. *United States,* 291 U.S. 293. Here it is plain that the combination or conspiracy did not have as its purpose restraint upon competition in the market for petitioner's product. Its object was to compel petitioner to acceed to the union's demands and an effect of it, in consequence of the strikers' tortious acts, was the prevention of the removal of petitioner's product for interstate shipment. So far as appears the delay of these shipments was not intended to have and had no effect on prices of hosiery in the market, and so was in that respect no more a restraint forbidden by the Sherman Act than the restriction upon competition and the course of trade held lawful in *Appalachian Coals* v. *United States,* because, notwithstanding its effect upon the marketing of the coal, it nevertheless was not intended to, and did not, affect market price.

A combination of employees necessarily restrains competition among themselves in the sale of their services to the employer; yet such a combination was not considered an illegal restraint of trade at common law when the Sherman Act was adopted, either because it was not thought to be unreasonable or because it was not deemed a "restraint of trade." Since the enactment of the declaration in Sec. 6 of the Clayton Act that "the labor of a human being is not a commodity or article of commerce . . . nor shall such (labor) organizations, or the members thereof, be held or construed to be illegal combinations or conspiracies in the restraint of trade under the antitrust laws," it would seem plain that restraints on the sale of the employee's services to the employer, however much they curtail the competition among employees, are not in themselves combinations or conspiracies in restraint of trade or commerce under the Sherman Act.

Strikes or agreements not to work, entered into by laborers to compel employers to yield to their demands, may restrict to some extent the power of employers who are parties to the dispute to compete in the market with those not subject to such demands. But under the doctrine applied to nonlabor cases, the mere fact of such restrictions on competition does not in itself bring the parties to the agreement within the condemnation of the Sherman Act. *Appalachian Coals* v. *United States, supra,* 360. Furthermore, successful union activity, as for example consummation of a wage agreement with employers, may have some influence on price competition by eliminating that part of such competition which is based on differences in labor standards. Since, in order to render a labor combination effective it must eliminate the competition from nonunion made goods, see *American Steel Foundries* v. *Tri-City Central Trades Council,* 257 U.S. 184, 209, an elimination of price competition based on differences in labor standards is the objective of any national labor organization. But this effect on competition has not been considered to be the kind of curtailment of price competition prohibited by the Sherman Act. . . .

This Court first applied the Sherman Act to a labor organization in *Loewe* v. *Lawlor,* 208 U.S. 274, in 1908, holding that the trial court had erroneously sustained a demurrer to the declaration in a suit for damages for violation of the Sherman Act on the ground that the combination alleged was not within the Act. The combination or conspiracy charged was that of a nationwide labor organization to force all manufacturers of fur hats in the United States to organize their workers by maintaining a boycott against the purchase of the product of nonunion manufacturers shipped in interstate commerce. The restraint alleged was not a strike or refusal to work in the complainants' plant, but a secondary boycott by which, through threats to the manufacturer's wholesale customers and their customers, the Union sought to compel or induce them not to deal in the product of the complainants, and to purchase the competing products of other unionized manufacturers. This Court pointed out that the restraint was precisely like that in *Eastern States Retail Lumber Dealers Co.* v. *United States,* 234 U.S. 600, 610, 614, in which a conspiracy to circulate a "blacklist," intended to persuade retailers not to deal with specified wholesalers, was held to violate the Act because of its restraint upon competition with unlisted wholesalers. The Court in the *Loewe* case held that the boycott operated as a restraint of trade or commerce within the meaning of the Sherman Act, and that the language of the Act, "every combination, etc.," was broad enough to include a labor union imposing such a restraint.

Like problems found a like solution in *Duplex Printing Press Co.* v. *Deering,* 254 U.S. 443, and in *Bedford Cut Stone Co.* v. *Journeymen Stone Cutters Assn.,* 274 U.S. 37; where, in the one case, a secondary boycott, and in the other, the refusal of the union to work on a product in the hands of the purchaser, were carried on on a countrywide scale by a national labor organization, in order to induce the purchasers of a manufactured product shipped in interstate commerce to withdraw their patronage from the producer. In both, as in the *Loewe* case, the effort of the union was to compel unionization of an employer's factory, not by a strike in his factory but by restraining, by the boycott or refusal to work on the manufactured product, purchases of his product in interstate commerce in competition with the like product of union shops.

In the *Bedford Stone* case it was pointed out that, as in the *Duplex Printing Press Co.* case, the strike was directed against the use of the manufactured product by consumers "with the immediate purpose and effect of restraining future sales and shipments in interstate commerce" and "with the plain design of suppressing or narrowing the interstate market," and that in this respect the case differed from those in which a factory strike, directed at the prevention of production with consequent cessation of interstate shipments, had been held not to be a violation of the Sherman law. See *First Coronado* case, 259 U.S. 344; *Leather Workers* case, 285 U.S. 457; cf. *Second Coronado* case, 268 U.S. 295, 310.

It will be observed that in each of these cases where the Act was held applicable to labor unions, the activities affecting interstate commerce were directed at control of the market and were so widespread as substantially to affect it. There was thus a suppression of competition in the market by methods which were deemed analogous to those found to be violations in the nonlabor cases. . . . That the objective of the restraint in the boycott cases was the strengthening of the bargaining position of the union and not the elimination of business competition—which was the end in the nonlabor cases—was thought to be immaterial because the Court viewed the restraint itself, in contrast to the interference with shipments caused by a local factory strike, to be of a kind regarded as offensive at common law because of its effect in curtailing a free market and it was held to offend against the Sherman Act because it effected and was aimed at suppression of competition with union made goods in the interstate market. . . .

These cases show that activities of labor organizations not immunized by the Clayton Act are not necessarily violations of the Sherman Act. Underlying and implicit in all of them is recognition that the Sherman Act was not enacted to police interstate transportation, or to afford a remedy for wrongs, which are actionable under state law, and result from combinations and conspiracies which fall short, both in their purpose and effect, of any form of market control of a commodity, such as to "monopolize the supply, control its price, or discriminate between its would-be purchasers." These elements of restraint of trade, found to be present in the *Second Coronado* case and alone to distinguish it from the *First Coronado* case and the *Leather Workers* case, are wholly lacking here. We do not hold that conspiracies to obstruct or prevent transportation in interstate commerce can in no circumstances be violations of the Sherman Act. Apart from the Clayton Act it makes no distinction between labor and nonlabor cases. We only hold now, as we have previously held both in labor and nonlabor cases, that such restraints are not within the Sherman Act unless they are intended to have, or in fact have, the effects on the market on which the Court relied to establish violation in the *Second Coronado* case. Unless the principle of these cases is now to be discarded, an impartial application of the Sherman Act to the activities of industry and labor alike would seem to require that the Act be held inapplicable to the activities of respondents which had an even less substantial effect on the competitive conditions in the industry than the combination of producers upheld in the *Appalachian Coals* case and in others on which it relied.

If, without such effects on the market, we were to hold that a local factory strike, stopping production and shipment of its product interstate, violates the Sherman law, practically every strike in modern industry would be brought within the jurisdiction of the federal courts, under the Sherman Act, to remedy local law violations. The Act was plainly not intended to reach such a result, its language does not require it, and the course of our decision precludes it. The maintenance in our federal system of a proper distribution between state and national governments of police authority and of remedies private and public for public wrongs is of far-reaching importance. An intention to disturb the balance is not lightly to be imputed to Congress. The Sherman Act is concerned with the character of the prohibited restraints and with their effect on interstate commerce. It draws no distinction between the restraints effected by violence and those achieved by peaceful but oftentimes quite as effective means. Restraints not within the Act, when achieved by peaceful means, are not brought within its sweep merely because, without other differences, they are attended by violence.

Affirmed.

CASE QUESTIONS

1. What was the verdict in the District Court? In the Circuit Court? In the Supreme Court?
2. State the controlling facts about the employer's business.
3. What was the Union's demand? How did it seek to enforce it? Was the method of enforcement legal?
4. What is the "single question" presented by the record for decision by the Supreme Court?
5. Does this Supreme Court feel that labor combinations were intended to be entirely excluded from operation of the Sherman Act by Congress?
6. What type of restraints does the Supreme Court feel is prohibited by the Sherman Act?
7. Did the delay in hosiery shipments have an effect upon market price?
8. What does the Court say as to the legality of "elimination of price competition based on differences in labor standards"?
9. How does the Supreme Court distinguish the *Apex* from the *Loewe, Bedford,* and *Duplex* cases? Does it overrule them?

10. What does the Court mean when it says the Sherman Act "draws no distinction between the restraints effected by violence and those achieved by peaceful . . . means"?
11. What illogical result does the Supreme Court feel would follow if it declared the present case to be within the Sherman Act?

United States v. Hutcheson

Supreme Court of the United States, 1941. 312 U.S. 219

FRANKFURTER, J. Whether the use of conventional, peaceful activities by a union in controversy with a rival union over certain jobs is a violation of the Sherman Law, Act of July 2, 1890, 26 Stat. 209, as amended, 15 U.S.C. Sec. 1, is the question. It is sharply presented in this case because it arises in a criminal prosecution. Concededly an injunction either at the suit of the Government or of the employer could not issue.

Summarizing the long indictment, these are the facts. Anheuser-Busch, Inc., operating a large plant in St. Louis, contracted with Borsari Tank Corporation for the erection of an additional facility. The Gaylord Container Corporation, a lessee of adjacent property from Anheuser-Busch, made a similar contract for a new building with the Stocker Company. Anheuser-Busch obtained the materials for its brewing and other operations and sold its finished products largely through interstate shipments. The Gaylord Corporation was equally dependent on interstate commerce for marketing its goods, as were the construction companies for their building materials. Among the employees of Anheuser-Busch were members of the United Brotherhood of Carpenters and Joiners of America and of the International Association of Machinists. The conflicting claims of these two organizations, affiliated with the American Federation of Labor, in regard to the erection and dismantling of machinery had long been a source of controversy between them. Anheuser-Busch had had agreements with both organizations whereby the Machinists were given the disputed jobs and the Carpenters agreed to submit all disputes to arbitration. But in 1939 the president of the Carpenters, their general representative, and two officials of the Carpenters' local organization, the four men under indictment, stood on the claims of the Carpenters for the jobs. Rejection by the employer of the Carpenters' demand and the refusal of the latter to submit to arbitration were followed by a strike of the Carpenters, called by the defendants against Anheuser-Busch beer.

These activities on behalf of the Carpenters formed the charge of the indictment as a criminal combination and conspiracy in violation of the Sherman Law. Demurrers denying that what was charged constituted a violation of the laws of the United States were sustained, 32 F. Supp. 600, and the case came here under the Criminal Appeals Act. . . .

Section 1 of the Sherman Law on which the indictment rested is as follows: "Every contract, combination in the form of trust or otherwise, or conspiracy, in restraint of trade or commerce among the several States, or with foreign nations, is hereby declared to be illegal." The controversies engendered by its application to trade union activities and the efforts to secure legislative relief from its consequences are familiar history. The Clayton Act of 1914 was the result. Act of October 15, 1914, 38 Stat. 730. "This statute was the fruit of unceasing agitation, which extended over more than twenty years and was designed to equalize before the law the position of workingmen and employer as industrial combatants." *Duplex Co.* v. *Deering,* 254 U.S. 443, 484. Section 20 of that Act, withdrew from the general interdict of the Sherman Law specifically enumerated practices of labor unions by prohibiting injunctions against them—since the use of the injunction had been the major source of dissatisfaction—and also relieved such practices of all illegal taint by the catch-all provision, "nor shall any of the acts specified in this paragraph be considered or held to be violations of any law of the United States." The Clayton Act gave rise to new litigation and to renewed controversy in and out of Congress regarding the status of trade unions. By the generality of its terms the Sherman Law had necessarily compelled the courts to work out its meaning from case to case. It was widely believed that into the Clayton Act courts read the very beliefs which that Act was designed to remove. Specifically the courts restricted the scope of Sec. 20 to trade union activities directed against an employer by his own employees. *Duplex Co.* v. *Deering, supra.* Such a view, it was urged, both by powerful judicial dissents and informed lay opinion, misconceived the area of economic conflict that had best be left to economic forces and the pressure of public opinion and not subjected to the judgment of courts. *Ibid,* pp. 485–486. Agitation again led to legislation and in 1932 Congress wrote the Norris-LaGuardia Act. Act of March 23, 1932, 47 Stat. 70, 29 U.S.C. Secs. 101–115.

The Norris-LaGuardia Act removed the fetters upon trade union activities, which, according to judicial construction, Sec. 20 of the Clayton Act had left untouched, by still further narrowing the circumstances under which the federal courts could grant injunctions in labor disputes. More especially, the Act explicitly formulated the "public policy of the United States" in regard to the industrial conflict, and by its light established that the allowable area of union activity was not to be restricted, as it had been in the *Duplex* case, to an immediate employer-employee relation. Therefore, whether trade union conduct constitutes a violation of the Sherman Law is to be determined only by reading the Sherman Law and Sec. 20 of the Clayton Act and the Norris-LaGuardia Act as a harmonizing text of outlawry of labor conduct.

Were, then, the acts charged against the defendants prohibited, or permitted, by these three interlacing statutes? If the facts laid in the indictment come within the conduct enumerated in Sec. 20 of the Clayton Act they do not constitute a crime within the general terms of the Sherman Law because of the explicit command of that section that such conduct shall not be "considered or held to be violations of any law of the United States." So long as a union acts in its self-interest and does not combine with nonlabor groups, the licit and the illicit under Sec. 20 are not to be distinguished by any judgment regarding the wisdom or unwisdom, the rightness or wrongness, the selfishness or unselfishness of the end of which the particular union activities are the means. There is nothing remotely within the terms of Sec. 20 that differentiates between trade union conduct directed against an employer because of a controversy arising in the relation between employer and employee, as such, and conduct similarly directed but ultimately due to an internecine struggle between two unions seeking the favor of the same employer. Such strife between competing unions has been an obdurate conflict in the evolution of so-called craft unionism and has undoubtedly been one of the potent forces in the modern development of industrial unions. These conflicts have intensified industrial tension but there is not the slightest warrant for saying that Congress has made Sec. 20 inapplicable to trade union conduct resulting from them.

In so far as the Clayton Act is concerned, we must therefore dispose of this case as though we had before us precisely the same conduct on the part of the defendants in pressing claims against Anheuser-Busch for increased wages, or shorter hours, or other elements of what are called working conditions. The fact that what was done in a competition for jobs against the Machinists rather than against, let us say, a company union is a differentiation which Congress has not put into the federal legislation and which therefore we cannot write into it.

It is at once apparent that the acts with which the defendants are charged are the kinds of acts protected by Sec. 20 of the Clayton Act. The refusal of the Carpenters to work for Anheuser-Busch or on construction work being done for it and its adjoining tenant, and the peaceful attempt to get members of other unions similarly to refuse to work, are plainly within the free scope accorded to workers by Sec. 20 for "terminating any relation of employment," or "ceasing to perform any work or labor," or "recommending, advising, or persuading others by peaceful means so to do." The picketing of Anheuser-Busch premises with signs to indicate that Anheuser-Busch was unfair to organized labor, a familiar practice in these situations, comes within the language "attending at any place where any such person or persons may lawfully be, for the purpose of peacefully obtaining or communicating information, or from peacefully persuading any person to work or to abstain from working." Finally, the recommendation to union members and their friends not to buy or use the product of Anheuser-Busch is explicitly covered by "ceasing to patronize . . . any party to such dispute, or from recommending, advising, or persuading others by peaceful and lawful means so to do."

Clearly, then, the facts here charged constitute lawful conduct under the Clayton Act unless the defendants cannot invoke that Act because outsiders to the immediate dispute also shared in the conduct. But we need not determine whether the conduct is legal within the restrictions which *Duplex Co.* v. *Deering* gave to the immunities of Sec. 20 of the Clayton Act. Congress in the Norris-LaGuardia Act has expressed the public policy of the United States and defined its conception of a "labor dispute" in terms that no longer leave room for doubt. *Milk Wagon Drivers' Union* v. *Lake Valley Farm Products,* 311 U.S. 91. This was done, as we recently said, in order to "obviate the results of the judicial construction" theretofore given the Clayton Act. *New Negro Alliance* v. *Sanitary Grocery Co.,* 303 U.S. 552, 562; see *Apex Hosiery Co.* v. *Leader,* 310 U.S. 469, 507, n. 26. Such a dispute, Sec. 13(c) provides, "includes any controversy concerning terms or conditions of employment, or concerning the association or representation of persons in negotiating, fixing, maintaining, changing, or seeking to arrange terms or conditions of employment, regardless of whether or not the disputants stand in the proximate relation of employer and employee." And under Sec. 13(b) a person is "participating or interested in a labor dispute" if he "is engaged in the same industry, trade, craft, or occupation, in which such dispute occurs, or has a direct or indirect interest therein, or is a member, officer, or agent of any association composed in whole or in part of employers or employees engaged in such industry, trade, craft, or occupation."

To be sure, Congress expressed this national policy and determined the bounds of a labor dispute in an act explicitly dealing with the further with-drawal of injunctions in labor controversies. But to argue, as it was urged before us, that the Duplex case still governs for purposes of a criminal prosecu-tion is to say that that which on the equity side of the court is allowable conduct may in a criminal proceeding become the road to prison. It would be strange indeed that although neither the Government nor Anheuser-Busch could have sought an injunction against the acts here challenged, the elaborate efforts to permit such conduct failed to prevent criminal liability punishable with imprisonment and heavy fines. That is not the way to read the will of Congress, particularly when expressed by a statute which, as we have already indicated, is practically and historically one of a series of enactments touching one of the most sensitive national problems. Such legislation must not be read in a spirit of mutilating narrowness. . . .

The relation of the Norris-LaGuardia Act to the Clayton Act is not that of a tightly drawn amendment to a technically phrased tax provision. The underlying aim of the Norris-LaGuardia Act was to restore the broad purpose which Congress thought it had formulated in the Clayton Act but which was frustrated, so Congress believed, by unduly restrictive judicial construction. This was authoritatively stated by the House Committee on the Judiciary. "The purpose of the bill is to protect the rights of labor in the same manner the Congress intended when it enacted the Clayton Act, October 15, 1914 (38 Stat. L. 738), which act, by reason of its construction and application by the Federal courts, is ineffectual in accomplishing the congressional intent." H. Rep. No. 669, 72d Congress, 1st Session, p. 3. The Norris-LaGuardia Act was a disapproval of *Duplex Printing Press Co.* v. *Deering, supra,* and *Bedford Cut Stone Co.* v. *Journeymen Stone Cutters' Assn.,* 274 U.S. 37, as the authoritative interpretation of Sec. 20 of the Clayton Act, for Congress now placed its own meaning upon that section. The Norris-LaGuardia Act reasserted the original purpose of the Clayton Act by infusing into it the immunized trade union activities as redefined by the later Act. In this light Sec. 20 removes all such allowable conduct from the taint of being a "violation of any law of the United States," including the Sherman Law.

There is no profit in discussing those cases under the Clayton Act which were decided before the courts were furnished the light shed by the Norris-LaGuardia Act on the nature of the industrial conflict. And since the facts in the indictment are made lawful by the Clayton Act in so far as "any law of the United States" is concerned, it would be idle to consider the Sherman Law apart from the Clayton Act as interpreted by Congress. Cf. *Apex Hosiery*

Co. v. *Leader,* 310 U.S. 469. It was precisely in order to minimize the difficulties to which the general language of the Sherman Law in its application to workers had given rise, that Congress cut through all the tangled verbalisms and enumerated concretely the types of activities which had become familiar incidents of union procedure.

Affirmed.

CASE **QUESTIONS**	1. State the facts of this case. 2. According to this court, how can it be determined whether trade union conduct constitutes a violation of the Sherman Law? 3. What does the Court say about jurisdictional disputes and Section 20 of the Clayton Act? 4. What does Section 8(b)(4)(D) of the National Labor Relations Act of 1947 say about jurisdictional disputes? (See text of Act in the Appendix.) 5. In the instant case, is the Norris-LaGuardia Act important to the decision? Why?

SECTION 14 / CONCERT WITH EMPLOYERS

It is not to be concluded that the Sherman Act has been stripped of all impact upon labor organizations. There remains an area, somewhat narrow in scope, across which the antitrust laws still raise a limiting barrier. The nature of that barrier is exemplified in the following *Allen Bradley, Pennington, Jewel Tea* and *Musicians* decisions. These decisions show the interaction of antitrust, anti-injunction, labor relations, and other legislation.

Allen Bradley Co. v. Local Union No. 3

Supreme Court of the United States, 1945. 325 U.S. 797

BLACK, J. The question presented is whether it is a violation of the Sherman Anti-Trust Act for labor unions and their members, prompted by a desire to get and hold jobs for themselves at good wages and under high working standards, to combine with employers and with manufacturers of goods to restrain competition in, and to monopolize the marketing of, such goods.

Upon the complaint of petitioners and after a lengthy hearing the District Court held that such a combination did violate the Sherman Act, entered a declaratory judgment to that effect, and entered an injunction restraining respondents from engaging in a wide range of specified activities. 41 F. Supp. 727, 51 F. Supp. 36. The Circuit Court of Appeals reversed the decision and dismissed the cause, holding that combinations of unions and business men which restrained trade and tended to monopoly were not in violation of the Act where the bona fide purpose of the unions was to raise wages, provide better working conditions, and bring about better conditions of employment for their members. 145 F.2d 215. The Ninth Circuit Court of Appeals having reached a contrary conclusion in a similar case, 144 F.2d 546, we granted certiorari in both cases.

The facts were sufficiently set out in the opinions below and need not be detailed again. The following summary will suffice for our purposes.

Petitioners are manufacturers of electrical equipment. Their places of manufacture are outside of New York City, and most of them are outside of New York State as well. They have brought this action because of their desire to sell their products in New York City, a market area that has been closed to them through the activities of respondents and others.

Respondents are a labor union, its officials and its members. The union, Local No. 3 of the International Brotherhood of Electrical Workers, has jurisdiction only over the metropolitan area of New York City. It is therefore impossible for the union to enter into a collective bargaining agreement with petitioners. Some of the petitioners do have collective bargaining agreements with other unions, and in some cases even with other locals of the I.B.E.W.

Some of the members of respondent union work for manufacturers who produce electrical equipment similar to that made by petitioners; other members of respondent union are employed by contractors and work on the installation of electrical equipment, rather than in its production.

The union's consistent aim for many years has been to expand its membership, to obtain shorter hours and increased wages, and to enlarge employment opportunities for its members. To achieve this latter goal—that is, to make more work for its own members—the union realized that local manufacturers, employers of the local members, must have the widest possible outlets for their product. The union therefore waged aggressive campaigns to obtain closed-shop agreements with all local electrical equipment manufacturers and contractors. Using conventional labor union methods, such as strikes and boycotts, it gradually obtained more and more closed-shop agreements in New York City area. Under these agreements, contractors were obligated to purchase equipment from none but local manufacturers who also had closed-shop agreements with Local No. 3; manufacturers obligated themselves to confine their New York City sales to contractors employing the Local's members. In the course of time, this type of individual employer-employee agreement expanded into industry-wide understandings, looking not merely to terms and conditions of employment but also to price and market control. Agencies were set up composed of representatives of all three groups to boycott recalcitrant local contractors and manufacturers and to bar from the area equipment manufactured outside its boundaries. The combination among the three groups, union, contractors, and manufacturers, became highly successful from the standpoint of all of them. . . .

Quite obviously, this combination of business men has violated both Secs. 1 and 2 of the Sherman Act, unless its conduct is immunized by the participation of the union. For it intended to and did restrain trade in and monopolize the supply of electrical equipment in the New York City area to the exclusion of equipment manufactured in and shipped from other states, and did also control its price and discriminate between its would-be customers. *Apex Ho-*

siery Co. v. *Leader,* 310 U.S. 469, 512–513. Our problem in this case is therefore a very narrow one—do labor unions violate the Sherman Act when, in order to further their own interests as wage earners, they aid and abet business men to do the precise things which that Act prohibits?

The Sherman Act as originally passed contained no language expressly exempting any labor union activities. Sharp controversy soon arose as to whether the Act applied to unions. One viewpoint was that the only evil at which Congress had aimed was high consumer prices achieved through combinations looking to control of markets by powerful groups; that those who would have a great incentive for such combinations would be the business men who would be the direct beneficiaries of them; therefore, the argument proceeded, Congress drafted its law to apply only to business combinations, particularly the large trusts, and not to labor unions or any of their activities as such. Involved in this viewpoint were the following contentions: that the Sherman Act is a law to regulate trade, not labor, a law to prescribe the rules governing barter and sale, and not the personal relations of employers and employees; that good wages and working conditions helped and did not hinder trade, even though increased labor costs might be reflected in the cost of products; that labor was not a commodity; that laborers had an inherent right to accept or terminate employment at their own will, either separately or in concert; that to enforce their claims for better wages and working conditions, they had a right to refuse to buy goods from their employer or anybody else; that what they could do to aid their cause, they had a right to persuade others to do; and that the antitrust laws designed to regulate trading were unsuitable to regulate employer-employee relations and controversies. The claim was that the history of the legislation supported this line of argument.

The contrary viewpoint was that the Act covered all classes of people and all types of combinations, including unions, if their activities even physically interrupted the free flow of trade or tended to create business monopolies, and that a combination of laborers to obtain a raise in wages was itself a prohibited monopoly. Federal courts adopted the latter view and soon applied the law to unions in a number of cases. Injunctions were used to enforce the Act against unions. At the same time, employers invoked injunctions to restrain labor union activities even where no violation of the Sherman Act was charged.

Vigorous protests arose from employee groups. The unions urged congressional relief from what they considered to be two separate, but partially overlapping evils—application of the Sherman Act to unions, and issuance of injunctions against strikes, boycotts and other labor union weapons. Numerous bills to curb injunctions were offered. Other proposed legislation was intended to take labor unions wholly outside any possible application of the Sherman Act. All of this is a part of the well-known history of the era between 1890 and 1914.

To amend, supplement, and strengthen the Sherman Act against monopolistic business practices, and in response to the complaints of the unions against injunctions and application of the Act to them, Congress in 1914 passed the Clayton Act. Elimination of those "trade practices" which injuriously affected competition was its first objective. Each section of the measure prohibiting such trade practices contained language peculiarly appropriate to commercial transactions as distinguished from labor union activities, but there is no record indication in anything that was said or done in its passage which indicates that those engaged in business could escape its or the Sherman Act's prohibitions by obtaining the help of labor unions or others. That this bill was intended to make it all the more certain that competition should be the rule in all commercial transactions is clear from its language and history.

In its treatment of labor unions and their activities, the Clayton Act pointed in an opposite direction. Congress in that Act responded to the prolonged complaints concerning application of the Sherman law to labor groups by adopting Sec. 6; for this purpose, and also drastically to restrict the general power of federal courts to issue labor injunctions, Sec. 20 was adopted. Section 6 declared that labor was neither a commodity nor an article of commerce, and that the Sherman Act should not be "construed to forbid the existence and operation of labor, agricultural, or horticultural organizations, instituted for the purposes of mutual help. . . ." Section 20 limited the power of courts to issue injunctions in a case "involving or growing out of a labor dispute over terms or conditions of employment. . . ." It declared that no restraining order or injunction should prohibit certain specified acts, and further declared that no one of these specified acts should be "held to be violations of any law of the United States." This Act was broadly proclaimed by many as labor's "Magna Carta," wholly exempting labor from any possible inclusion in the antitrust legislation; others, however, strongly denied this.

This Court later declined to interpret the Clayton Act as manifesting a congressional purpose wholly to exempt labor unions from the Sherman Act. *Duplex Co.* v. *Deering,* 254 U.S. 443; *Bedford Cut Stone Co.* v. *Journeymen Stone Cutters' Assn.,* 274 U.S. 37. In those cases labor unions had engaged in a secondary boycott; they had boycotted dealers, by whom the union members were not employed, because those dealers insisted on selling goods produced by the employers with whom the unions had an existing controversy over terms and conditions of employment. This court held that the Clayton Act exempted labor union activities only in so far as those activities were directed against the employees' immediate employers and that controversies over the sale of goods by other dealers did not constitute "labor disputes" within the meaning of the Clayton Act.

Again the unions went to Congress. They protested against this Court's interpretation, repeating the arguments they had made against application of the Sherman Act to them. Congress adopted their viewpoint, at least in large part, and in order to escape the effect of the *Duplex* and *Bedford* decisions, passed the Norris-LaGuardia Act, 47 Stat. 70. That Act greatly broadened the meaning this Court had attributed to the words "labor dispute," further restricted the use of injunctions in such a dispute, and emphasized the public importance under modern economic conditions of protecting the rights of "concerted activities for the purpose of collective bargaining or other mutual aid or protection." This congressional purpose found further expression in the Wagner Act, 49 Stat. 449.

We said in *Apex Hosiery Co.* v. *Leader, supra,* 488, that labor unions are still subject to the Sherman Act to "some extent not defined." The opinion in that case, however, went on to explain that the Sherman Act "was enacted in the era of 'trusts' and of 'combinations' of businesses and of capital organized and directed to control of the market by suppression of competition in the marketing of goods and services, the monopolistic tendency of which had become a matter of public concern"; that its purpose was to protect consumers from monopoly prices, and not to serve as a comprehensive code to regulate and police all kinds and types of interruptions and obstructions to the flow of trade. This was a recognition of the fact that Congress had accepted the arguments made continuously since 1890 by groups opposing application of the Sherman Act to unions. It was an interpretation commanded by a fair consideration of the full history of anti-trust and labor legislation.

United States v. *Hutcheson,* 312 U.S. 219, declared that the Sherman, Clayton and Norris-LaGuardia Acts must be jointly considered in arriving at a conclusion as to whether labor union activities run counter to the anti-trust legislation. Conduct which they permit is not to be declared a violation of federal law. That decision held that the doctrine of the *Duplex* and *Bedford* cases was inconsistent with the congressional policy set out in the three "interlacing statutes."

The result of all this is that we have two declared congressional policies which it is our responsibility to try to reconcile. The one seeks to preserve a competitive business economy; the other to preserve the rights of labor to organize to better its conditions through the agency of collective bargaining. We must determine here how far Congress intended activities under one of these policies to neutralize the results envisioned by the other.

Aside from the fact that the labor union here acted in combination with the contractors and manufacturers, the means it adopted to contribute to the combination's purpose fall squarely within the "specified acts" declared by Sec. 20 not to be violations of federal law. For the union's contribution to the trade boycott was accomplished through threats that unless their employers bought their goods from local manufacturers the union laborers would terminate the "relation of employment" with them and cease to perform "work or labor" for them; and through their "recommending, advising, or persuading others by peaceful and lawful means" not to "patronize" sellers of the boycotted electrical equipment. Consequently, under our holdings in the Hutcheson case and other cases which followed it, had there been no union-contractor-manufacturer combination, the union's actions here, coming as they did within the exemptions of the Clayton and Norris-LaGuardia Acts, would not have been violations of the Sherman Act. We pass to the question of whether unions can with impunity aid and abet business men who are violating the Act.

On two occasions this Court has held that the Sherman Act was violated by a combination of labor unions and business men to restrain trade. In neither of them was the Court's attention sharply called to the crucial questions here presented. Furthermore, both were decided before the passage of the Norris-LaGuardia Act and prior to our holding in the Hutcheson case. It is correctly argued by respondents that these factors greatly detract from the weight which the two cases might otherwise have in the instant case. See *United States* v. *Hutcheson, supra,* 236. Without regard to these cases, however, we think

Congress never intended that unions could, consistently with the Sherman Act, aid nonlabor groups to create business monopolies and to control the marketing of goods and services.

Section 6 of the Clayton Act declares that the Sherman Act must not be so construed as to forbid the "existence and operation of labor, agricultural, or horticultural organizations, instituted for the purposes of mutual help. . . ." But "the purpose of mutual help" can hardly be thought to cover activities for the purpose of "employer-help" in controlling markets and prices. And in an analogous situation where an agricultural association joined with other groups to control the agricultural market, we said:

"The right of these agricultural producers thus to unite in preparing for market and in marketing their products, and to make the contracts which are necessary for that collaboration, cannot be deemed to authorize any combination or conspiracy *with other persons* in restraint of trade that these producers may see fit to devise." *United States* v. *Borden Co.,* 308 U.S. 188, 204–205. (Italics supplied.)

We have been pointed to no language in any act of Congress or in its reports or debates, nor have we found any, which indicates that it was ever suggested, considered, or legislatively determined that labor unions should be granted an immunity such as is sought in the present case. It has been argued that this immunity can be inferred from a union's right to make bargaining agreements with its employer. Since union members can, without violating the Sherman Act strike to enforce a union boycott of goods, it is said they may settle the strike by getting their employers to agree to refuse to buy the goods. Employers and the union did here make bargaining agreements in which the employers agreed not to buy goods manufactured by companies which did not employ the members of Local No. 3. We may assume that such an agreement standing alone would not have violated the Sherman Act. But it did not stand alone. It was but one element in a far larger program in which contractors and manufacturers united with one another to monopolize all the business in New York City, to bar all other business men from that area, and to charge the public prices above a competitive level. It is true that victory of the union in its disputes, even had the union acted alone, might have added to the cost of goods, or might have resulted in individual refusals of all of their employers to buy electrical equipment not made by Local No. 3. So far as the union might have achieved this result acting alone, it would have been the natural consequence of labor union activities exempted by the Clayton Act from the coverage of the Sherman Act. *Apex Hosiery Co.* v. *Leader, supra,* 503. But when the unions participated with a combination of business men who had complete power to eliminate all competition among themselves and to prevent all competition from others, a situation was created not included within the exemptions of the Clayton and Norris-LaGuardia Acts.

It must be remembered that the exemptions granted the unions were special exceptions to a general legislative plan. The primary objective of all the anti-trust legislation has been to preserve business competition and to proscribe business monopoly. It would be a surprising thing if Congress, in order to prevent a misapplication of that legislation to labor unions, had bestowed upon such unions complete and unreviewable authority to aid business groups to frustrate its primary objective. For if business groups, by combining with labor unions, can fix prices and divide up markets, it was little more than a futile gesture for Congress to prohibit price fixing by business groups themselves. Seldom, if ever, has it been claimed before, that by permitting labor unions to carry on their own activities, Congress intended completely to abdicate its constitutional power to regulate interstate commerce and to empower interested business groups to shift our society from a competitive to a monopolistic economy. Finding no purpose of Congress to immunize labor unions who aid and abet manufacturers and traders in violating the Sherman Act, we hold that the district court correctly concluded that the respondents had violated the Act.

Our holding means that the same labor union activities may or may not be in violation of the Sherman Act, dependent upon whether the union acts alone or in combination with business groups. This, it is argued, brings about a wholly undesirable result—one which leaves labor unions free to engage in conduct which restrains trade. But the desirability of such an exemption of labor unions is a question for the determination of Congress. *Apex Hosiery Co.* v. *Leader, supra.* It is true that many labor union activities do substantially interrupt the course of trade and that these activities, lifted out of the prohibitions of the Sherman Act, include substantially all, if not all, of the normal peaceful activities of labor unions. It is also true that the Sherman Act "draws no distinction between the restraints effected by violence and those achieved by peaceful . . . means," *Apex Hosiery Co.* v. *Leader, supra,* 513, and that a union's exemption from the Sherman Act is not to be determined by a judicial "judgment regarding the wisdom or unwisdom, the rightness or wrongness, the selfishness or unselfishness of the end of which the particular union activities are the means." *United States* v. *Hutcheson, supra,* 232. Thus, these congressionally permitted union activities may restrain trade in and of themselves. There is no denying the fact that many of them do so, both directly and indirectly. Congress evidently concluded, however, that the chief objective of anti-trust legislation, preservation of business competition, could be accomplished by applying the legislation primarily only to those business groups which are directly interested in destroying competition. The difficulty of drawing legislation primarily aimed at trusts and monopolies so that it could also be applied to labor organizations without impairing the collective bargaining and related rights of those organizations has been emphasized both by congressional and judicial attempts to draw lines between permissible and prohibited union activities. There is, however, one line which we can draw with assurance that we follow the congressional purpose. We know that Congress feared the concentrated power of business organizations to dominate markets and prices. It intended to outlaw business monopolies. A business monopoly is no less such because a union participates, and such participation is a violation of the Act.

The judgment of the Circuit Court of Appeals ordering the action dismissed is accordingly reversed and the cause is remanded to the district court for modification and clarification of the judgment and injunction, consistent with this opinion.

Reversed and remanded.

CASE QUESTIONS

1. Discuss the triangular nature of the agreement to exercise price and market control in this situation.
2. State the problem of the case in the words of the court.
3. State the line of argument employed by those who contend that the Sherman Act was intended for application only against employer combinations and not labor combinations.
4. Reiterate the provisions of Sections 6 and 20 of the Clayton Act.
5. Discuss the history of the Norris-LaGuardia Act.
6. Would it have been a violation of the Sherman Act if the employers agreed with the union not to purchase goods by companies not employing members of Local No. 3?
7. Did the agreement go further than that stated in Question 6?
8. State the major rule of law developed by the case.

United Mine Workers of America v. James A. Pennington

Supreme Court of the United States, 1965. 381 U.S. 657

WHITE, J.: This action began as a suit by the trustees of the United Mine Workers of America Welfare and Retirement Fund against the respondents, individually and as owners of Phillips Brothers Coal Company, a partnership, seeking to recover some $55,000 in royalty payments alleged to be due and payable under the trust provisions of the National Bituminous Coal Wage Agreement of 1950, as amended, September 29, 1952, executed by Phillips and United Mine Workers of America on or about October 1, 1953, and reexecuted with amendments on or about September 8, 1955, and October 22, 1956. Phillips filed an answer and a cross claim against UMW, alleging in both that the trustees, the UMW, and certain large coal operators had conspired to restrain and to monopolize interstate commerce in violation of Paragraphs 1 and 2 of the Sherman Antitrust Act, 15 U.S.C. Par. 1, 2 (1958 ed.). Actual damages in the amount of $100,000 were claimed for the period beginning February 14, 1954, and ending December 31, 1958.

The allegations of the cross claim were essentially as follows: Prior to the 1950 Wage Agreement between the operators and the union, severe controversy had existed in the industry, particularly over wages, the welfare fund and the union's efforts to control the working time of its members. Since 1950, however, relative peace has existed in the industry, all as the result of the 1950 wage agreement and its amendments and the additional understandings entered into between UMW and the large operators. Allegedly the parties considered overproduction to be the critical problem of the coal industry. The agreed solution was to be the elimination of the smaller companies, thereby controlling the market. More specifically, the union abandoned its efforts to control the working time of the miners, agreed not to oppose the rapid mechanization of the mines which would substantially reduce mine employment, agreed to help finance such mechanization, and agreed to impose the terms of the 1950 agreement on all operators without regard for their ability to pay. The benefit to the union was to be increased wages as productivity increased with mechanization, these increases to be demanded of the smaller companies whether mechanized or not. Royalty payments into the welfare fund were to be increased also, and the union was to have effective control over the Fund's use. The union and large companies agreed upon other steps to exclude the marketing, production, and sale of nonunion coal. Thus the companies agreed not to lease coal lands to nonunion operators, and in 1958 agreed not to sell or buy coal from such companies. The companies and the union jointly and successfully approached the Secretary of Labor to obtain establishment under the Walsh-Healey Act, 41 U.S.C. Par. 35 *et seq.* (1958 ed.), of a minimum wage for employees of contractors selling coal to the TVA, such minimum wage being much higher than in other industries and making it difficult for small companies to compete in the TVA term contract market. At a later time, at a meeting attended by both union and company representatives, the TVA was urged to curtail its spot market purchases, a substantial portion of which were exempt from the Walsh-Healey order. Thereafter four of the larger companies waged a destructive and collusive price-cutting campaign in the TVA spot market for coal, two of the companies, West Kentucky Coal Co. and its subsidiary Nashville Coal Co., being those in which the union had large investments and over which it was in position to exercise control.

The complaint survived motions to dismiss and after a five-week trial before a jury, a verdict was returned in favor of Phillips and against the trustees and the union, the damages against the union being fixed in the amount of $90,000, to be trebled under 15 U.S.C. Par. 15 (1958 ed.). The trial court set aside the verdict against the trustees but overruled the union's motion for judgment notwithstanding the verdict or in the alternative for a new trial. The Court of Appeals affirmed. 325 F.2d 804. It ruled that the union was not exempt from liability under the Sherman Act on the facts of the case, considered the instructions adequate, and found the evidence generally sufficient to support the verdict. We reverse and remand the case for proceedings consistent with this opinion.

We first consider UMW's contention that the trial court erred in denying its motion for directed verdict and for judgment notwithstanding the verdict, since a determination in UMW's favor on this issue would finally resolve the controversy. The question presented by this phase of the case is whether in the circumstances of this case the union is exempt from liability under the antitrust laws. We think the answer is clearly in the negative and that the union's motions were correctly denied.

The antitrust laws do not bar the existence and operation of labor unions as such. Moreover, Par. 20 of the Clayton Act and Par. 4 of the Norris-LaGuardia Act permit a union, acting alone, to engage in the conduct therein specified without violating the Sherman Act. *United States* v. *Hutcheson,* 312 U.S. 219; *United States* v. *International Hod Carriers Council,* 313 U.S. 539, affirming per curiam, 37 F. Supp. 191 (D.C.N.D. Ill. 1941); *United States* v. *American Federation of Musicians,* 318 U.S. 741, affirming *per curiam,* 47 F. Supp. 304 (D.C.N.D. Ill. 1942).

But neither Par. 20 nor Par. 4 expressly deals with arrangements or agreements between unions and employers. Neither section tells us whether any or all such arrangements or agreements are barred or permitted by the antitrust laws. Thus *Hutcheson* itself stated:

"So long as a union acts in its self-interest *and does not combine with nonlabor groups,* the licit and illicit under Par. 20 are not to be distinguished by any judgment regarding the wisdom or unwisdom, the rightness or wrongness, the selfishness or unselfishness of the end of which the particular union activities are the means." 312 U.S., at 232 (Italic added.)

And in *Allen-Bradley* v. *Local Union No. 3,* IBEW, 325 U.S. 797, this Court made explicit what had been merely a qualifying expression in *Hutcheson* and held that "when the unions participated with a combination of businessmen who had complete power to eliminate all competition among themselves and to prevent all competition from others, a situation was created not included within the exemptions of the Clayton and Norris-LaGuardia Acts." *Id.,* at 809. See also *United Brotherhood of Carpenters* v. *United States,* 330 U.S. 395, 398–400; *United States* v. *Employing Plasterers Assn.,* 347 U.S. 186, 190. Subsequent cases have applied the Allen-Bradley doctrine to such combinations without regard to whether they found expression in a collective bargaining agreement, *United Brotherhood of Carpenters* v. *United States, supra;* see *Teamsters Union* v. *Oliver,* 358 U.S. 283, 296, and even though the mechanism for effectuating the purpose of the combination was an agreement on wages, see *Adams Dairy Co.* v. *St. Louis Dairy Co.,* 260 F.2d 46 (C.A. 8th Cir. 1958), or on hours of work, *Philadelphia Record Co.* v. *Manufacturing Photo-Engravers Assn.,* 155 F.2d 799 (C.A. 3d Cir. 1946).

If the UMW in this case, in order to protect its wage scale by maintaining employer income, had presented a set of prices at which the mine operators would be required to sell their coal, the union and the employers who happened to agree could not successfully defend this contract provision if it were challenged under the antitrust laws by the United States or by some party injured by the arrangement. Cf. *Allen-Bradley* v. *Local Union No. 3, IBEW,* 325 U.S. 797; *United States* v. *Borden Co.,* 308 U.S. 188, 203–205; *Lumber Prods. Assn* v. *United States,* 144 F.2d 546, 548 (C.A. 9th Cir. 1944), aff'd on this issue *sub nom. Brotherhood of Carpenters* v. *United States,* 330 U.S. 395, 398–400; *Las Vegas Merchant Plumbers Assn.* v. *United States,* 210 F.2d 732 (C.A. 9th Cir. 1954), cert. denied, 348 U.S. 817; *Local 175, IBEW* v. *United States,* 219 F.2d 431 (C.A. 6th Cir. 1955), cert. denied, 349 U.S. 917. In such a case, the restraint on the product market is direct and immediate, is of the type characteristically deemed unreasonable under the Sherman Act and the union gets from the promise nothing more concrete than a hope for better wages to come.

Likewise, if as is alleged in this case, the union became a party to a collusive bidding arrangement designed to drive Phillips and others from the TVA spot market, we think any claim to exemption from antitrust liability would be frivolous at best. For this reason alone the motions of the unions were properly denied.

A major part of Phillips' case, however, was that the union entered into a conspiracy with the large operators to impose the agreed-upon wage and royalty scales upon the smaller, nonunion operators, regardless of their ability to pay and regardless of whether or not the union represented the employees of these companies, all for the purpose of eliminating them from the industry, limiting production and preempting the market for the large, unionized operators. The UMW urges that since such an agreement concerned wage standards, it is exempt from the antitrust laws.

It is true that wages lie at the very heart of those subjects about which employers and unions must bargain and the law contemplates agreements on wages, not only between individual employers and a union but agreements between the union and employers in a multi-employer bargaining unit. *Labor Board* v. *Truck Drivers Union,* 353 U.S. 87, 94–96. The union benefit from the wage scale agreed upon is direct and concrete and the effect on the product market, though clearly present, results from the elimination of competition based on wages among the employers in the bargaining unit, which is not the kind of restraint Congress intended the Sherman Act to proscribe. *Apex Hosiery* v. *Leader,* 310 U.S. 469, 503–504; see *Adams Dairy Co.* v. *St. Louis Dairy Co.,* 260 F.2d 46 (C.A. 8th Cir. 1958). We think it beyond question that a union may conclude a wage agreement for the multi-employer bargaining unit without violating the antitrust laws and that it may as a matter of its own policy, and not by agreement with all or part of the employers of that unit, seek the same wages from other employers.

This is not to say that an agreement resulting from union-employer negotiations is automatically exempt from Sherman Act scrutiny simply because the negotiations involve a compulsory subject of bargaining, regardless of the subject or the form and content of the agreement. Unquestionably the Board's demarcation of the bounds of the duty to bargain has great relevance to any consideration of the sweep of labor's antitrust immunity, for we are concerned here with harmonizing the Sherman Act with the national policy expressed in the National Labor Relations Act of promoting "the peaceful settlement of industrial disputes by subjecting labor-management controversies to the mediatory influence of negotiation," *Fibreboard Paper Prods. Corp.* v. *Labor Board,* 379 U.S. 203, 211. But there are limits to what a union or an employer may offer or extract in the name of wages, and because they must bargain does not mean that the agreement reached may disregard other laws. *Teamsters Union* v. *Oliver,* 358 U.S. 283, 296; *Brotherhood of Carpenters* v. *United States,* 330 U.S. 395, 399–400.

We have said that a union may make wage agreements with a multi-employer bargaining unit and may in pursuance of its own union interests seek to obtain the same terms from other employers. No case under the antitrust laws could be made out on evidence limited to such union behavior.[8] But we think a union forfeits its exemption from the antitrust laws when it is clearly shown that it has agreed with one set of employers to impose a certain wage

---

[8] Unilaterally, and without agreement with any employer group to do so, a union may adopt a uniform wage policy and seek vigorously to implement it even though it may suspect that some employers cannot effectively compete if they are required to pay the wage scale demanded by the union. The union need not gear its wage demands to those which the weakest units in the industry can afford to pay. Such union conduct is not alone sufficient evidence to maintain a union-employer conspiracy charge under the Sherman Act. There must be additional direct or indirect evidence of the conspiracy. There was, of course, other evidence in this case, but we indicate no opinion as to its sufficiency.

scale on other bargaining units. One group of employers may not conspire to eliminate competitors from the industry and the union is liable with the employers if it becomes a party to the conspiracy. This is true even though the union's part in the scheme is an undertaking to secure the same wages, hours, or other conditions of employment from the remaining employers in the industry.

We do not find anything in the national labor policy that conflicts with this conclusion. This Court has recognized that a legitimate aim of any national labor organization is to obtain uniformity of labor standards and that a consequence of such union activity may be to eliminate competition based on differences in such standards. *Apex Hosiery* v. *Leader,* 310 U.S. 469, 503. But there is nothing in the labor policy indicating that the union and the employers in one bargaining unit are free to bargain about the wages, hours, and working conditions of other bargaining units or to attempt to settle these matters for the entire industry. On the contrary, the duty to bargain unit by unit leads to a quite different conclusion. The union's obligation to its members would seem best served if the union retained the ability to respond to each bargaining situation as the individual circumstances might warrant, without being straitjacketed by some prior agreement with the favored employers.

So far as the employer is concerned it has long been the Board's view that an employer may not condition the signing of a collective agreement on the union's organization of a majority of the industry. *American Range Lines, Inc.,* 13 N.L.R.B. 147 (1939); *Samuel Youlin,* 22 N.L.R.B. 879, 885 (1940); *Newton Chevrolet, Inc.,* 37 N.L.R.B. 334, 341 (1941); See *Labor Board* v. *George P. Pilling & Son Co.,* 119 F.2d 32, 38 (C.A. 3d Cir. 1941). In such cases the obvious interest of the employer is to ensure that acceptance of the union's wage demands will not adversely affect his competitive position. In *American Range Lines, Inc. supra,* the Board rejected that employer interest as a justification for the demand. "(A)n employer cannot lawfully deny his employees the right to bargain collectively through their designated representative in an appropriate unit because he envisons competitive disadvantages accruing from such bargaining." 13 N.L.R.B., at 147. Such an employer condition, if upheld, would clearly reduce the extent of collective bargaining. Thus, in *Newton Chevrolet, Inc., supra,* where it was held a refusal to bargain for the employer to insist on a provision that the agreed contract terms would not become effective until five competitors had signed substantially similar contracts, the Board stated that "(t)here is nothing in the Act to justify the imposition of a duty upon an exclusive bargaining representative to secure an agreement from a majority of an employer's competitors as a condition precedent to the negotiation of an agreement with the employer. To permit individual employers to refuse to bargain collectively until some or all of their competitors had done so clearly would lead to frustration of the fundamental purpose of the Act to encourage the practice of collective bargaining." 37 N.L.R.B., at 341. Permitting insistence on an agreement by the union to attempt to impose a restraining influence on the extent of collective bargaining, for the union could avoid impasse only by surrendering its freedom to act in its own interest *vis-a-vis* other employers, something it will be unwilling to do in many instances. Once again, the employer's interest is a competitive interest rather than an interest in regulating its own labor relations, and the effect on the union of such an agreement would be to limit the free exercise of the employees' right to engage in concerted activities according to their own views of their self-interest. In sum, we cannot conclude that the national labor policy provides any support for such agreements.

On the other hand, the policy of the antitrust laws is clearly set against employer-union agreements seeking to prescribe labor standards outside the bargaining unit. One could hardly contend, for example, that one group of employers could lawfully demand that the union impose on other employers wages that were significantly higher than those paid by the requesting employers, or a system of computing wages that, because of differences in methods of production, would be more costly to one set of employers than to another. The anticompetitive potential of such a combination is obvious, but is little more severe than what is alleged to have been the purpose and effect of the conspiracy in this case to establish wages at a level that marginal producers could not pay so that they would be driven from the industry. And if the conspiracy presently under attack were declared exempt it would hardly be possible to deny exemption to such avowedly discriminatory schemes.

From the viewpoint of antitrust policy, moreover, all such agreements between a group of employers and a union that the union will seek specified labor standards outside the bargaining unit suffer from a more basic defect, without regard to predatory intention or effect in the particular case. For the salient characteristic of such agreements is that the union surrenders its freedom of action with respect to its bargaining policy. Prior to the agreement the union might seek uniform standards in its own self-interest but would be required to assess in each case the probable costs and gains of a strike or other collective action to that end and thus might conclude that the objective of uniform standards should temporarily give way. After the agreement, the union's interest would be bound in each case to that of the favored employer group. It is just such restraints upon the freedom of economic units to act according to their own choice and discretion that run counter to antitrust policy. See, *e.g., Associated Press* v. *United States,* 326 U.S. 1, 19; *Fashion Originators' Guild* v. *Federal Trade Comm'n,* 312 U.S. 457, 465; *Anderson* v. *Shipowners Assn.,* 272 U.S. 359, 364–365.

Thus the relevant labor and antitrust policies compel us to conclude that the alleged agreement between UMW and the large operators to secure uniform labor standards throughout the industry, if proved, was not exempt from the antitrust laws. . . .

GOLDBERG, HARLAN, and STEWART, J. J., dissenting:

Stripped of all the pejorative adjectives and reduced to their essential facts, both *Pennington* and *Jewel Tea* represent refusals by judges to give full effect to congressional action designed to prohibit judicial intervention via the antitrust route in legitimate collective bargaining. The history of these cases furnishes fresh evidence of the observation that in this area, necessarily involving a determination of "what public policy in regard to the industrial struggle demands," *Duplex Co.* v. *Deering,* 254 U.S. 479, 485 (dissenting opinion of Mr. Justice Brandeis), "courts have neither the aptitude nor the criteria for reaching sound decisions." Cox, *Labor and Antitrust Laws—A Preliminary Analysis,* 104 U. Pa. L. Rev. 252, 269–270 (1955); see Winter, *Collective Bargaining and Competition: The Application of Antitrust Standards to Union Activities,* 73 Yale L.J. 14 (1963).

Pennington presents a case of a union negotiating with the employers in the industry for wages, fringe benefits, and working conditions. Despite allegations of conspiracy, which connotes clandestine activities, it is no secret that the United Mine Workers, acting to further what it considers to be the best interests of its members, espouses a philosophy of achieving uniform high wages, fringe benefits, and good working conditions. As the *quid pro quo* for this, the Union is willing to accept the burdens and consequences of automation. Further, it acts upon the view that the existence of marginal operators who cannot afford these high wages, fringe benefits, and good working conditions does not serve the best interests of the working miner but, on the contrary, depresses wage standards and perpetuates undesirable conditions. This has been the articulated policy of the Union since 1933. See Baratz, *The Union and the Coal Industry,* 62–74 (1955). The Mine Workers has openly stated its preference, if need be, for a reduced working force in the industry, with those employed working at high wages, rather than for greater total employment at lesser wage rates. *Ibid.* See also Folliard, *Roar of John L. Lewis Subdued at 85,* The Washington Post, Feb. 14, 1965, Par. E. p. 3; Hearings before a Subcommittee of the Senate Committee on Labor and Public Welfare on S. Res. 274, 81st Cong., 1st Sess., 1 Proceedings of Forty-Second Consecutive Constitutional Convention of the United Mine Workers of America, 9–14 (1956). Consistent with this view, the Union welcomes automation, insisting only that the workers participate in its benefits. . . .

The Court's holding in *Pennington* today flies in the face of *Apex* and *Hutcheson* and restrains collective bargaining in the same way as did the holding of the majority in *Duplex*—a holding which Congress has expressly repudiated in favor of Mr. Justice Brandeis' dissenting views. It represents contemporary manifestations of the reluctance of judges to give full effect to congressional purpose in this area and the substitution of judges' views for those of Congress as to how free collective bargaining should operate. . . .

CASE QUESTIONS

1. What is the nature of the agreement involved in the antitrust action?
2. Does the court find uniform wages a proper industry-wide basis of agreement here? Why or why not may a union seek this end?
3. How does the policy of the antitrust laws limit collective agreements, according to the majority opinion?
4. Why does the dissent find fault with the opinion of the majority?

Amalgamated Meat Cutters, Local 189 v. Jewel Tea Co., Inc.

(SUPPLEMENTAL CASE DIGEST—CONCERT WITH EMPLOYERS)
United States Supreme Court, 1965. 381 U.S. 676

WHITE, J.: Like No. 48, *United Mine Workers* v. *Pennington,* decided today, *ante,* this case presents questions regarding the application of Paragraphs 1 and 2 of the Sherman Antitrust Act. . . .

This litigation arose out of the 1957 contract negotiations between the representatives of 9,000 Chicago retailers of fresh meat and the seven union petitioners, who are local affiliates of the Amalgamated Meat Cutters and Butcher Workmen of North America, AFL-CIO, representing virtually all butchers in the Chicago area. During the 1957 bargaining sessions the employer group presented several requests for union consent to a relaxation of the existing contract restriction on marketing hours for fresh meat. The unions rejected all such suggestions, and their own proposal retaining the marketing hours restriction was ultimately accepted at the final bargaining session by all but two of the employers, National Tea Co. and Jewel Tea Co. (hereinafter "Jewel"). Associated Food Retailers of Greater Chicago, a trade association having about 1,000 individual and independent merchants as members and representing some 300 meat dealers in the negotiations, was among those who accepted. Jewel, however, asked the union negotiators to present to their membership, on behalf of it and National Tea, a counteroffer that included provision for Friday night operations. At the same time Jewel voiced its belief, as it had midway through the negotiations, that any marketing hours restriction was illegal. On the recommendation of the union negotiators, the Jewel offer was rejected by the union membership, and a strike was authorized. Under the duress of the strike vote, Jewel decided to sign the contract previously approved by the rest of the industry.

In July, 1958, Jewel brought suit against the unions, certain of their officers, Associated, and Charles H. Bromann, Secretary-Treasurer of Associated, seeking invalidation under §§ 1 and 2 of the Sherman Act of the contract provision that prohibited night meat market operations. The gist of the complaint was that the defendants and others had conspired together to prevent the retail sale of fresh meat before 9 a.m. and after 6 p.m. As evidence of the conspiracy Jewel relied in part on the events during the 1957 contract negotiations—the acceptance by Associated of the market hours restriction and the unions' imposition of the restriction on Jewel through a strike threat. . . .

. . . The prohibition of night meat marketing, it was alleged, unlawfully impeded Jewel in the use of its property and adversely affected the general public in that many persons find it inconvenient to shop during the day. An injunction, treble damages, and attorney's fees were demanded. . . .

We pointed out in *Pennington* that exemption for union-employer agreements is very much a matter of accommodating the coverage of the Sherman Act to the policy of the labor laws. Employers and unions are required to bargain about wages, hours and working conditions, and this fact weighs heavily in favor of antitrust exemption for agreements on these subjects. But neither party need bargain about other matters and either party commits an unfair labor practice if it conditions its bargaining upon discussions of a nonmandatory subject. *Labor Board* v. *Borg-Warner Corp.*, 356 U.S. 342. Jewel, for example, need not have bargained about or agreed to a schedule of prices at which its meat would be sold and the union could not legally have insisted that it do so. But if the union had made such a demand, Jewel had agreed and the United States or an injured party had challenged the agreement under the antitrust laws, we seriously doubt that either the union or Jewel could claim immunity by reason of the labor exemption, whatever substantive questions of violation there might be.

Thus the issue in this case is whether the marketing-hours restriction, like wages, and unlike prices, is so intimately related to wages, hours, and working conditions that the unions' successful attempt to obtain that provision through bona fide, arms-length bargaining in pursuit of its own labor union policies, and not at the behest of or in combination with nonlabor groups, falls within the protection of the national labor policy and is therefore exempt from the Sherman Act. We think that it is.

Contrary to the Court of Appeals, we think that the particular hours of the day and the particular days of the week during which employees shall be required to work are subjects well within the realm of "wages, hours, and other terms and conditions of employment" about which employers and unions must bargain. . . . *Reversed.*

DOUGLAS, J., with whom BLACK and CLARK, JJ., concur, dissenting: If we followed *Allen-Bradley Co.* v. *Union,* we would hold with the Court of Appeals that this multi-employer agreement with the union not to sell meat between 6 p.m. and 9 a.m. was not immunized from the antitrust laws and that respondent's evidence made out a prima facie case that it was in fact a violation of the Sherman Act. . . .

In saying that there was no conspiracy, the District Court failed to give any weight to the collective agreement itself as evidence of a conspiracy and to the context in which it was written. This Court makes the same mistake. We said in *Allen-Bradley Co.* v. *Union, supra,* at 808, ". . . we think Congress never intended that unions could, consistently with the Sherman Act, aid nonlabor groups to create business monopolies and to control the marketing of goods and services." Here the contract of the unions with a large number of employers shows it was planned and designed not merely to control but entirely to prohibit "the marketing of goods and services" from 6 p.m. until 9 a.m. the next day. Some merchants relied chiefly on price competition to draw trade; others employed courtesy, quick service, and keeping their doors open long hours to meet the convenience of customers. The unions here induced a large group of merchants to use their collective strength to hurt others who wanted the competitive advantage of selling meat after 6 p.m. . . .

CASE **QUESTIONS**	**1.** What is the basis of this antitrust charge? **2.** Why does the Court find the agreement exempt from the antitrust laws?

3. Why would the dissenting opinion sustain Jewel Tea's charge?

4. Compare the dissenting judges' reasoning with the majority opinion in the *Pennington* case.

American Federation of Musicians v. Carroll

(SUPPLEMENTAL CASE DIGEST—CONCERT WITH EMPLOYERS)
Supreme Court of the United States, 1968. 391 U.S. 99

BRENNAN, J.: This action for injunctive relief and treble damages alleging violations of the Sherman Act, 15 U.S.C. §§ 1 and 2, was brought in the District Court for the Southern District of New York against the petitioners American Federation of Musicians and its Local 802. The question is whether union practices of the petitioners affecting orchestra leaders violate the Sherman Act as activities in combination with a "non-labor" group, or are exempted by the Norris-LaGuardia Act as activities affecting a "labor" group which is party to a "labor dispute." After a five-week trial without a jury the District Court dismissed the action on the merits, holding that all of the petitioners' practices brought in question "come within the definition of the term 'labor dispute'. . . . and are exempt from the antitrust laws." 241 F. Supp. 865, 894. The Court of Appeals for the Second Circuit reversed on the issue of alleged pricefixing, but in all other respects affirmed the dismissal. 372 F. 2d 155. Both parties sought certiorari. . . . We granted both petitions, 389 U.S. 817. We hold that the District Court properly dismissed the action on the merits, and that the Court of Appeals should have affirmed the District Court judgment in its entirety.

The petitioners are labor unions of professional musicians. The union practices questioned here are mainly those applied to "club-date" engagements of union members. These are one-time engagements of orchestras to provide music, usually for only a few hours, at such social events as weddings, fashion shows, commencements, and the like. . . .

The four respondents were members of the petitioner Federation and Local 802 when this suit was filed. Virtually all musicians in the United States and the great majority of the orchestra leaders are union members. There are no collective bargaining agreements in the club-date field. Club-date engagements are rigidly regulated by unilaterally adopted union bylaws and regulations. Under these bylaws and regulations

(1) Petitioners enforce a closed shop and exert various pressures upon orchestra leaders to become union members.

(2) Orchestra leaders must engage a minimum number of sidemen for club-date engagements.

(3) Orchestra leaders must charge purchasers of music minimum prices prescribed in a "Price List Booklet." The prices are the total of (a) the minimum wage scales for sidemen, (b) a "leader's fee" which is double the sideman's scale when four or more musicians comprise the orchestra and (c) an additional 8% to cover social security, unemployment insurance, and other

expenses. When the leader does not personally appear at an engagement, but designates a subleader and four or more musicians perform, the leader must pay the subleader one and one-half the wage scale out of his "leader's fee." . . .

The criterion applied by the District Court in determining that the orchestra leaders were a "labor" group and parties to a "labor dispute" was the "presence of a job or wage competition or some other economic interrelationship affecting legitimate union interests between the union members and the independent contractors. If such a relationship existed the independent contractors were a 'labor group' and party to a labor dispute under the Norris-LaGuardia Act." 241 F. Supp., at 887. The Court of Appeals held, and we agree, that this is a correct statement of the applicable principles. The Norris-LaGuardia Act took all "labor disputes" as therein defined outside the reach of the Sherman Act and established that the allowable area of union activity was not to be restricted to an immediate employer-employee relation. . . .

The District Court also sustained the legality of the "Price List" stating, "In view of the competition between leaders and sidemen and subleaders which underlies the finding that the leaders are a labor group, the union has a legitimate interest in fixing minimum fees for a participating leader and minimum engagement prices equal to the total minimum wages of the sidemen and the participating leader." 241 F. Supp., at 890. The Court of Appeals, one judge dissenting, disagreed that the "Price List" was within the labor exemption, stating that "the unions' establishment of price floors on orchestral engagements constitutes a per se violation of the Sherman Act." 372 F.2d, at 165. The premise of the majority's conclusion was that the "Price List" was disqualified for the exemption because its concern is "prices" and not "wages." But this overlooks the necessity of inquiry beyond the form. Mr. Justice WHITE's opinion in *Meat Cutters* v. *Jewel Tea,* 381 U.S. 676, 690, n. 5, emphasized that "[t]he crucial determinant is not the form of the agreement—*e.g.,* prices or wages—but its relative impact on the product market and the interests of union members." It is therefore not dispositive of the question that petitioners' regulation in form establishes price floors. The critical inquiry is whether the price floors in actuality operate to protect the wages of the subleader and sidemen. The District Court found that the price floors were expressly designed to and did function as a protection of sidemen's and subleaders' wage scales against the job and wage competition of the leaders. . . .

The reasons which entitle the Price List to the exemption embrace the provision fixing the minimum price for a club-date engagement when the orchestra leader does not perform, and does not displace an employee-musician. That regulation is also justified as a means of preserving the scale of the sidemen and subleaders. There was evidence that when the leader does not collect from the purchaser of the music an amount sufficient to make up the total of his out-of-pocket expenses, including the sum of his wage-scale wages and the scale wages of the sidemen, he will, in fact, not pay the sidemen the prescribed scale. . . . In other words, the price of the product—here the price for an orchestra for a club-date—represents almost entirely the scale wages of the sidemen and the leader. Unlike most industries, except for the 8%

charge, there are no other costs contributing to the price. Therefore, if leaders cut prices, inevitably wages must be cut. . . .

The judgment of the Court of Appeals is vacated and the case is remanded with direction to enter a judgment affirming the judgment of the District Court in its entirety.

It is so ordered.

The Chief Justice and Mr. Justice MARSHALL took no part in the consideration or decision of these cases.

Mr. Justice WHITE, joined by Mr. Justice BLACK, dissented.

CASE QUESTIONS	**1.** Why did the Court of Appeals hold that the price floors constituted a per se violation of the Sherman Act?
	2. What rationale did the Supreme Court accept for allowing the Union to continue its "Price List" practices?

SECTION 15 / BURDEN OF PROOF IN ANTITRUST CASES

The plaintiff has the burden of proof or persuasion regarding the facts on which he relies to establish his right to recovery. The defendant has the burden of proof with respect to any affirmative defenses or counterclaims upon which he may rely. How heavy a burden the proponent carries depends on the subject matter of the controversy. In the ordinary civil action, the person having the burden of proof must prove his or her case by a "preponderance of the evidence": this requires that the trier of the facts find the evidence of the person having the burden of proof to be more credible and convincing than the contrary evidence. Civil cases involving allegations of moral turpitude frequently require a higher degree of proof than the ordinary case. The standard used when fraud is alleged may be "clear and convincing evidence" or "clear proof." In criminal cases, the state is required to prove the essential facts "beyond a reasonable doubt."

If the "preponderance of the evidence" rather than "clear proof" standard were to be required of plaintiffs in antitrust suits against labor unions, the plaintiffs would have a lesser burden; and the effect would be to make unions more vulnerable to liability under the antitrust laws for conduct that is beyond the scope of their statutory immunity.

In the case of *Ramsey* v. *United Mine Workers,* 401 U.S. 302 (1971), an antitrust suit brought as a result of the *Pennington* decision reported in the previous section and with similar factual averments, the union asserted that Section 6 of the Norris-LaGuardia Act required a plaintiff to show by "clear proof" that the alleged agreement by large coal producers and the union to impose wage demands on all producers regardless of their ability to pay occurred, that they amounted to a conspiracy, and that the plaintiff was injured thereby. Section 6 of the Norris-LaGuardia Act provides:

> No officer or member of any association or organization and no association or organization participating or interested in a labor dispute, shall be held responsible or liable in any court of the United States for the unlawful acts of individual officers, members,

or agents, except upon clear proof of actual participation in, or actual authorization of, such acts, or of ratification of such acts after actual knowledge thereof.

The district court that tried the case agreed that the proof of the conspiracy was not the usual "preponderance of the evidence" rule but the "clear proof" required by Section 6 of the Norris-LaGuardia Act, a stricter standard than the ordinary proof required in civil conspiracy cases. Judging by this stricter standard, the court found the sufficiency of the proof of a conspiracy to be lacking (the judge said a different result could have been reached if the applicable standard of proof were the preponderance of the evidence standard). The Sixth Circuit heard the case *en banc* and affirmed the district court by an even division on the issue.

The Supreme Court reversed and remanded the case in a five to four decision. Mr. Justice White, speaking for the Court, said that the courts below had read too much into Section 6. "Nothing in the words of this section suggests that a new standard of proof was being prescribed for all issues in actions against a union, its members or its officers involved in a labor dispute." Section 6 merely says that "when illegal acts of any individual are charged against one of the major antagonists in a labor dispute—whether employers or union—the evidence must clearly prove that the individual's acts were authorized or ratified." Section 6 does not provide "any basis for . . . fashioning a new standard of proof applicable in antitrust actions against labor unions." Thus the rule is that the ordinary preponderance of the evidence standard is applicable against a union except with respect to proving the authority of individual members, officers and agents to perform on behalf of the union the acts complained of where the "clear proof" standard applies.

Justice Douglas, with whom Justices Black, Harlan and Marshall concurred, dissented. The dissent took the position that the Court was drastically rewriting Section 6. Justice Douglas argued that the proper interpretation of Section 6 requires clear proof that the unions had "full complicity in the scheme."

The ambiguity of the "clear proof" issue is amply evidenced by the fact that the eighteen judges and justices who considered the case, from the district court, through the court of appeals to the Supreme Court, divided evenly in their interpretation of Section 6.

QUESTIONS ON CHAPTER 2

1. How did the Anti-Injunction Act change the position of labor in the federal courts?
2. To what extent did it allow the application of injunctions to labor?
3. What is the present situation as to union violations of the antitrust laws?
4. Compare the *Allen Bradley* ruling with: (a) the *Jewel Tea* majority view; (b) the *Jewel Tea* minority view.
5. What standard of proof is applicable against a union in an antitrust suit?

Chapter 3

The Railway Labor Act

SECTION 16 / HISTORY, PURPOSE, CONSTITUTIONALITY

Because of their immediate impact upon interstate commerce and their economic character as a public utility, American interstate railways were early recognized as an appropriate and necessary object of federal legislative intervention in the public interest. This necessity gradually became more manifest in its labor relations aspect as employees of the carriers, in the 1860's, began to form and join the nucleus of the Big Four Brotherhoods.[1] By 1880, railroad workers sought to exercise their latent strength by engaging in a series of prolonged and costly strikes.

As a result of this early flareup in the ranks of organized railway labor, Congress enacted the first in a series of legislative enactments designed to promote the peaceful settlement of controversies and to forestall employment of the strike weapon in so vital an industry. This Arbitration Act of 1888 provided for voluntary arbitration between the parties and for the creation of investigatory boards in work stoppage situations. However, these boards, which were appointed by the President as need arose, lacked power other than the power of publicity to enforce their conclusions upon the merits of a labor dispute. The arbitration provisions were rarely used, and the investigatory powers were invoked only in connection with the Pullman strike of 1894.

This Act was permitted to atrophy for ten years. Congress finally decided to supplant the Act of 1888 with the Erdman Act of 1898. This later legislation strengthened the voluntary arbitration provisions of its predecessor, introduced the method of federal mediation and conciliation to further peaceful settlement efforts, and rendered illegal employer discrimination for the reason of union membership. Some resort was had to the arbitration features of the Act, but because of the resistance or apathy of the carriers, little benefit was secured from its mediation provisions. The Supreme Court, in *Adair* v. *U.S.*, 208 U.S. 161, decided in 1908, invalidated the penal antidiscrimination portion of the Act, leaving it likewise useless; and setting a precedent for the *Hitchman Coal* decision, discussed in Chapter 1.

---

[1] Locomotive Engineers Union, 1863; Railroad Conductors Brotherhood, 1818; Locomotive Firemen and Enginemen, 1873; and the Railway Trainmen, 1883.

Upon failure of hoped-for results from the Erdman Act, Congress passed the Newlands Act of 1913, which established a permanent three-member Board of Mediation but retained almost intact the voluntary arbitration features of the Erdman Act. The Newlands Act met its nemesis in 1916 when the four railroad brotherhoods began agitation for the 8-hour day. A strike loomed imminent as the Brotherhood of Firemen and Engineers flatly rejected arbitration of this issue; it was prevented only upon passage of the Adamson Act of 1916, which established the 8-hour day for railway employees.

For the next three years little labor difficulty was encountered, as the carriers were operated by the government and labor had girded itself to the war effort. A general order of the Director General of Railroads served to protect from discrimination those railway workers who sought to form and join labor organizations. In retrospect, these war years were marked by a placid labor front and the flourishing of the principle of collective bargaining. The government entered into trade agreements with authorized bargaining agents; any disputes arising from diverse interpretations of these agreements were required to be ultimately referred to boards of adjustment for final settlement. Strikes were implicitly outlawed by this mandatory settlement procedure.

As the carriers were returned to private operation, Congress revised the Newlands Act in the form of the Transportation Act of 1920. This act created a Railway Labor Board of three members, the carrier, the employees, and the public securing one representative each. The Board was empowered to publish its decisions upon investigation of the facts of a dispute; sole reliance was to be placed upon the force of public opinion. While arbitration was fostered by the Act of 1920, mediation was completely neglected as being ineffective. More significantly, the immediate postwar period gave rise to a concerted push by employers in the direction of company-dominated labor organizations.

The conspicuous failing of the Transportation Act, as was true also of its predecessors, was the inability of the Labor Board to compel injunctive compliance on the part of the party adversely affected by an award. While public opinion did give rise to some influential pressure, generally it was not an effective force of telling impact in most disputes.

In enacting the Railway Labor Act of 1926, Congress drew heavily upon the experience it had accumulated in railroad labor legislation and disputes since 1888. We are not to infer, however, that this permeating policy was to be fundamentally changed. Now, more than ever, the machinery for peaceful arbitration and mediation was strengthened; and emphasis continued to rest upon the voluntary settlement procedure rather than upon the compulsive provisions of the Act, though the latter were available if required. Criminal penalties, however, were not attached for noncompliance with the 1926 Act.

The purpose of this enactment was to avoid work stoppages by employees and lockouts by employers through establishing a legal basis for negotiation, mediation, and arbitration procedure, effectuated by the legislative sanction that previously was lacking. The principle of mediation, which had been discarded by the Act of 1920, again was to play a principal role. Major power of administration was vested in a nonpartisan Board of Mediation appointed by the President. Disputes were to be settled as follows:

1. In the event of a labor dispute, the Mediation Board was called upon to attempt to get the parties to *negotiate* their differences.
2. Failing in this, the next step was to induce them to submit the difficulty to *arbitration.* If arbitration was agreed to, the awards accruing therefrom became binding and legally enforceable. The parties could not be compelled to submit their controversy to arbitration. Arbitration was, and remains, voluntary.
3. If arbitration is refused by one or both parties, the Board of Mediation, in its discretion, was to recommend that the President create an emergency board of investigation. (a) If the President created such an emergency board, the latter was required to submit a report to the President on the controversy within 30 days. The disputants were required by law to maintain the *status quo* in effect until the board submitted its report and 30 days thereafter. At the expiration, then, of a maximum of 60 days, if the parties still are at variance and do not agree to abide by the findings of the emergency board, they are free to engage in a strike or a lockout. (b) If the President does not appoint an emergency board as recommended by the Board of Mediation, the disputants are required to maintain the *status quo* for 30 days. It can be seen that the effect of either alternative is to *delay* precipitate action on the part of the disputants in the hope that, in the interim, their dispute will satisfactorily be settled either by way of negotiation or arbitration. Labor is not deprived of its right to strike under the Act, nor is the employer deprived of the lockout; however, these rights may be exercised only upon compliance with the dilatory features of the Act. Further, while labor continues to have the right to strike under the Act, it should be noted that the government in recent years has consistently intervened to prohibit national or widespread work stoppages in the railroad industry by the use of emergency *ad hoc* legislation.[2]

The Railway Labor Act was amended in important respects in 1934, 1936, 1951 and 1966. At this point, only one matter of significance need be developed. That is the provision in the Act which gives both parties the right to designate representatives without the "interference, influence, or coercion" of the other (Sec. 2, third subdivision). The *Texas and New Orleans* pronouncement of the Supreme Court in 1930, 281 U.S. 548, is the landmark decision on the 1926 Railway Labor Act. Not only does the decision handle the constitutional questions raised by the Texas & New Orleans Railroad Company, but it also interprets the major procedural and substantive provisions of the Act, including the controverted Sec. 2, Third.

In brief, The Brotherhood of Railway Clerks brought suit against the railway company in the District Court for an injunction to restrain the carrier from interfering with collective action by its workers. The action was predicated upon Sec. 2, Third which had not, as yet, been approved by the Supreme Court. The Brotherhood also asked the court to disestablish an existing union which was company dominated. The District Court granted the requested injunction, the Circuit Court affirmed, and the company appealed the adverse result to the Supreme Court on constitutional grounds. The high court ruled that the Act of 1926 was a valid exercise of the federal commerce power and that the right of labor to organize without employer impediment could also be constitutionally

---

[2] Congress enacted special legislation for the settlement of deadlocked railway labor disputes endangering the national interest in 1963, 1967 and 1970. For an example of special legislation prohibiting unilateral action while a voluntary solution was pursued see S.J. Res. 59, signed by President Nixon on Feb. 9, 1973, which delayed for 90 days a strike by the UTU against the Penn Central Transportation Company over the issue of reduction of train crew size.

protected. "As the carriers subject to the Act have no constitutional right to interfere with the freedom of employees to make their selections, they cannot complain of the statute on constitutional grounds." The decision had important statutory results, as it gave workers in the railway field the right to be free of the employer's interference, as judicially enforceable; made illegal company-dominated unions, also enforceable; made compliance with arbitration awards enforceable though submission to arbitration is voluntary; imposed a delay of 60 days upon the strike or lockout; and sanctioned amicable settlement of conflicts through the fostering of mediation and arbitration.

SECTION 17 / EXPANDING INTERVENTION

After watching the Railway Labor Act of 1926 in operation for nearly a decade, Congress, though gratified with the successful operation that attended the Act, sought to fill in the loopholes that by then had become apparent. In 1934, 1936, 1951 and 1966 the Railway Labor Act was amended. The 1966 amendments are discussed in the next section of the chapter. The major particulars of the three previous amendments are as follows:

1. Criminal penalties were added by Sec. 2, Tenth, for violations by unions, carriers and their officers of certain of the Act's provisions. The provisions carrying strong misdemeanor sanction are 2, Third, Fourth, Fifth, Seventh, and Eighth.
   a. Sec. 2, Third, provides that "Representatives . . . shall be designated without interference, influence, or coercion by either party over the designation of representatives by the other. . . ."
   b. Sec. 2, Fourth, grants employees "the right to organize and bargain collectively through representatives of their own choosing."
   c. Sec. 2, Fifth, stipulates "No carrier . . . shall require any person seeking employment to sign any contract or agreement promising to join or not to join a labor organization. . . ." This outlawed not only the yellow-dog contract, but also any form of compulsory unionism in the interest of union security. The Railway Labor Act was more stringent than the National Labor Relations Act of 1947 which does permit limited forms of union security arrangements, but the RLA in 1951 was made to conform in this respect to the NLRA.
   d. Sec. 2, Seventh, reads "No carrier . . . shall change the rates of pay, rules, or working conditions of its employees as a class as embodied in agreements except in the manner prescribed in such agreements or in Section 6 of this Act." This section, as can be seen, forces the parties to arbitrate their differences if they would avoid the stringent penal sanction imposed by Sec. 2, Tenth.
   e. Sec. 2, Eighth, requires carriers to notify its employees through printed notices, "and in such notices there shall be printed verbatim, in large type, the third, fourth, and fifth paragraphs of this section. The provisions of said paragraphs are hereby made a part of the contract of employment between the carrier and each employee . . . regardless of any other express or implied agreements between them." Thus is impressed on both parties the public character of the rights and duties created.
2. The duty to recognize and bargain with the designated representative was vastly strengthened by the addition of Sec. 2, Ninth, which provides a method for the designation of bargaining representatives by certification procedure and commands that "Upon receipt of such certification the carrier shall treat with the representative

so certified as the representative of the craft or class for the purposes of this Act." It should be noted that Sec. 2, Ninth, above merely strengthens Sec. 2, First, which provides "It shall be the duty of all carriers . . . and employees to exert every reasonable effort to make and maintain agreements concerning rates of pay, rules, and working conditions, and to settle all disputes . . . to avoid any interruption to commerce. . . ." While these two paragraphs do not provide the remedy of equitable enforcement in so many words, the Supreme Court held, in the *Virginian* case, reprinted in this section, that the *duty to bargain* was made so strong by the Act's language as to require the courts to impose injunctive pressure on the party refusing to bargain in good faith; and as is true under the National Labor Relations Act, the duty to treat with a bargaining representative does not make it mandatory for the parties to reach an accord, but requires only good-faith negotiation and the reduction of any agreements reached to writing.

3. The third major change introduced by the Railway Labor Act of 1934 was to create the National Railroad Adjustment Board and to reconstitute the Board of Mediation with new powers as the National Mediation Board. The details of this change are discussed in Section 18 of this chapter.
4. Another amendment to the Railway Labor Act was added in 1936 when coverage of the Act was extended to include common air carriers in interstate or foreign commerce or the transportation of United States mail.
5. The original Act declared illegal any form of compulsory unionism, but Sec. 2, Eleventh, added in 1951, now permits rail and airline employees to bargain for certain union security measures, namely, the *union shop* and the *checkoff* of union dues, initiation fees, and assessments. These provisions closely parallel those found in the amended National Labor Relations Act.

In the *Virginian Railway Co.* case we find the Supreme Court giving to the 1934 Act the vitality lacking in all its predecessors, by permitting judicial enforcement of the duty to bargain. An excellent historical summary of the weaknesses of the forerunners of the 1934 enactment is also embodied in this decision.

Virginian Railway Co. v. System Federation No. 40

Supreme Court of the United States, 1937. 300 U.S. 515

STONE, J. This case presents questions as to the constitutional validity of certain provisions of the Railway Labor Act of May 20, 1926, as amended by the Act of June 21, 1934, and as to the nature and extent of the relief which courts are authorized by the Act to give.

Respondents are System Federation No. 40, which will be referred to as the Federation, a labor organization affiliated with the American Federation of Labor and representing shop craft employees of petitioner railway, and certain individuals who are officers and members of the System Federation. They brought the present suit in equity in the District Court for Eastern Virginia, to compel petitioner, an interstate rail carrier, to recognize and treat with respondent Federation, as the duly accredited representative of the mechanical department employees of petitioner, and to restrain petitioner from in any way interfering with, influencing or coercing its shop craft employees in their free choice of representatives, for the purpose of contracting with petitioner with respect to rules, rates of pay and working conditions, and for the purpose of considering and settling disputes between petitioner and such employees. . . .

In 1927 the American Federation of Labor formed a local organization, which, in 1934, demanded recognition by petitioner of its authority to represent the shop craft employees, and invoked the aid of the National Mediation Board, constituted under the Railway Labor Act as amended, to establish its authority. The Board, pursuant to agreement between the petitioner, the Federation, and the Association, and in conformity to the statute, held an election by petitioner's shop craft employees, to choose representatives for the purpose of collective bargaining with petitioner. As the result of the election, the Board certified that the Federation was the duly accredited representative of petitioner's employees in the six shop crafts.

Upon this and other evidence, not now necessary to be detailed, the trial court found that the Federation was the duly authorized representative of the mechanical department employees of petitioner, except the carmen and coach cleaners; that the petitioner, in violation of Sec. 2 of the Railway Labor Act, had failed to treat with the Federation as the duly accredited representative of petitioner's employees; that petitioner had sought to influence its employees against any affiliation with labor organizations other than an association maintained by petitioner, and to prevent its employees from exercising their right to choose their own representative; that for that purpose, following the certification by the National Mediation Board, of the Federation, as the duly authorized representative of petitioner's mechanical department employees, petitioner had organized the Independent Shop Craft Association of its shop craft employees, and had sought to induce its employees to join the independent association, and to put it forward as the authorized representative of petitioner's employees.

Upon the basis of these findings the trial court gave its decree applicable to petitioner's mechanical department employees except the carmen and coach cleaners. It directed petitioner to "treat with" the Federation and to "exert every reasonable effort to make and maintain agreements concerning rates of pay, rules and working conditions, and to settle all disputes, whether arising out of the application of such agreements or otherwise. . . ." It restrained petitioner from "entering into any contract, undertaking or agreement of whatsoever kind concerning rules, rates of pay or working conditions affecting its Mechanical Department employees . . . except . . . with the Federation," and from "interfering with, influencing or coercing" its employees with respect to their free choice of representatives "for the purpose of making and maintaining contracts" with petitioner "relating to rules, rates of pay, and working conditions or for the purpose of considering and deciding disputes between the Mechanical Department employees" and petitioner. The decree further restrained the petitioner from organizing or fostering any union of its mechanical department employees for the purpose of interfering with the Federation as the accredited representative of such employees. 11 F. Supp. 621.

On appeal the Court of Appeals for the Fourth Circuit approved and adopted the findings of the District Court and affirmed its decree. 84 F.(2d) 641. This Court granted certiorari to review the cause as one of public importance.

Petitioner here, as below, makes two main contentions: First, with respect to the relief granted, it maintains that Sec. 2, Ninth, of the Railway Labor Act, which provides that a carrier shall treat with those certified by the Mediation Board to be the representatives of a craft or class, imposes no legally enforcible obligation upon the carrier to negotiate with the representative so certified, and that in any case the statute imposes no obligation to treat or negotiate which can be appropriately enforced by a court of equity. Second, that Sec. 2, Ninth, in so far as it attempts to regulate labor relations between petitioner and its "back shop" employees, is not a regulation of interstate commerce authorized by the commerce clause because, as it asserts, they are engaged solely in intrastate activities; and that so far as it imposes on the carrier any obligation to negotiate with a labor union authorized to represent its employees, and restrains it from making agreements with any other labor organization, it is a denial of due process guaranteed by the Fifth Amendment. Other minor objections to the decree, so far as relevant to our decision, will be referred to later in the course of this opinion. . . .

First. The Obligation Imposed by the Statute. By Title III of the Transportation Act of February 28, 1920, C. 91, 41 Stat. 456, 469, Congress set up the Railroad Labor Board as a means for the peaceful settlement, by agreement or by arbitration, of labor controversies between interstate carriers and their employees. It sought "to encourage settlement without strikes, first by conference between the parties; failing that, by reference to adjustment boards of the parties' own choosing, and if this is ineffective, by a full hearing before a National Board. . . ." *Pennsylvania R. Co.* v. *Railroad Labor Board,* 261 U.S. 72, 79. The decisions of the Board were supported by no legal sanctions. The disputants were not "in any way to be forced into compliance with the statute or with the judgments pronounced by the Labor Board, except through the effect of adverse public opinion." *Pennsylvania Federation* v. *Pennsylvania R. Co.,* 267 U.S. 203, 216.

In 1926 Congress, aware of the impotence of the Board, and of the fact that its authority was generally not recognized or respected by the railroads or their employees, made a fresh start towards the peaceful settlement of labor disputes affecting railroads, by the repeal of the 1920 Act and the adoption of the Railway Labor Act. Report, Senate Committee on Interstate Commerce, No. 222, 69th Cong., 1st Sess. *Texas & N. O. R. Co.* v. *Brotherhood of Railway & S.S. Clerks,* 281 U.S. 548, 563. By the new measure Congress continued its policy of encouraging the amicable adjustment of labor disputes by their voluntary submission to arbitration before an impartial board, but it supported that policy by the imposition of legal obligations. It provided means for enforcing the award obtained by arbitration between the parties to labor disputes. Sec. 9. In certain circumstances it prohibited any change in conditions, by the parties to an unadjusted labor dispute, for a period of thirty days, except by agreement. Sec. 10. It recognized their right to designate representatives for the purposes of the Act "without interference, influence or coercion exercised by either party over the self-organization or designation of representatives by the other." Sec. 2, Third. Under the last-mentioned provision this Court held, in the Railway Clerks case, *supra,* that employees were free to organize and to make choice of their representatives without the "coercive interference" and "pressure" of a company union organized and maintained by the employer; and that the statute protected the freedom of choice of representatives, which was an essential of the statutory scheme, with a legal sanction which it was the duty of courts to enforce by appropriate decree.

The prohibition against such interference was continued and made more explicit by the amendment of 1934. Petitioner does not challenge that part of the decree which enjoins any interference by it with the free choice of representatives by its employees, and the fostering, in the circumstances of this case, of the company union. That contention is not open to it in view of our decision in the *Railway Clerks* case, *supra,* and of the unambiguous language of Sec. 2, Third and Fourth of the Act, as amended.

But petitioner insists that the statute affords no legal sanction for so much of the decree as directs petitioner to "treat with" respondent Federation "and exert every reasonable effort to make and maintain agreements concerning rates of pay, rules and working conditions, and to settle all disputes whether arising out of the application of such agreements or otherwise." It points out that the requirement for reasonable effort to reach an agreement is couched in the very words of Sec. 2, First, which was taken from Sec. 301 of the Transportation Act, and which were held to be without legal sanction in that Act. *Pennsylvania Federation* v. *Pennsylvania R. Co., supra,* 215. It is argued that they cannot now be given greater force as reenacted in the Railway Labor Act of 1926, and continued in the 1934 amendment. But these words no longer stand alone and unaided by mandatory provision of the statute as they did when first enacted. The amendment of the Railway Labor Act added new provisions in Sec. 2, Ninth, which makes it the duty of the Mediation Board, when any dispute arises among the carrier's employees, "as to who are the representatives of such employees," to investigate the dispute and to certify, as was done in this case, the name of the organization authorized to represent the employees. It commands that "Upon receipt of such certification the carrier shall treat with the representative so certified as the representative of the craft or class for the purposes of this Act."

It is, we think, not open to doubt that Congress intended that this requirement be mandatory upon the railroad employer, and that its command, in a proper case, be enforced by the courts. The policy of the Transportation Act of encouraging voluntary adjustment of labor disputes, made manifest by those provisions of the Act which clearly contemplated the moral force of public opinion as affording its ultimate sanction, was, as we have seen, abandoned by the enactment of the Railway Labor Act. Neither the purposes of the later Act, as amended, nor its provisions when read, as they must be, in the light of our decision in the *Railway Clerks* case, *supra,* lend support to the contention that its enactments, which are mandatory in form and capable of enforcement by judicial process, were intended to be without legal sanction. . . .

Petitioner argues that the phrase "treat with" must be taken as meaning "regard" or "act towards," so that compliance with its mandate requires the employer to meet the authorized representative of the employees only if and when he shall elect to negotiate with them. This suggestion disregards the words of the section, and ignores the plain purpose made manifest throughout the numerous provisions of the Act. Its major objective is the avoidance of industrial strife, by conference between the authorized representatives of employer and employee. The command to the employer to "treat with" the authorized representative of the employees adds nothing to the 1926 Act, unless it requires some affirmative act on the part of the employer. Compare the *Railway Clerks* case, *supra.* As we cannot assume that its addition to the statute was purposeless, we must take its meaning to be that which the words suggest, which alone would add something to the statute as it was before amendment, and which alone would tend to effect the purpose of the legislation. The statute does not undertake to compel agreement between the employer and employees, but it does command those preliminary steps without which no agreement can be reached. It at least requires the employer to meet and confer with the authorized representative of its employees, to listen to their complaints, to make reasonable effort to compose differences—in short, to enter into a negotiation for the settlement of labor disputes such as is contemplated by Sec. 2, First.

Petitioner's insistence that the statute does not warrant so much of the decree as forbids it to enter into contracts of employment with its individual employees is based upon a misconstruction of the decree. Both the statute and the decree are aimed at securing settlement of labor disputes by inducing collective bargaining with the true representative of the employees and by preventing such bargaining with any who do not represent them. . . .

Second. Constitutionality of Sec. 2 of the Railway Labor Act. (A) Validity Under the Commerce Clause. The power of Congress over interstate commerce extends to such regulations of the relations of rail carriers to their employees as are reasonably calculated to prevent the interruption of interstate commerce by strikes and their attendant disorders. *Wilson* v. *New,* 243 U.S. 332, 347–348. The Railway Labor Act, Sec. 2, declares that its purposes, among others, are "To avoid any interruption to commerce or to the operation of any carrier engaged therein," and "to provide for the prompt and orderly settlement of all disputes concerning rates of pay, rules or working conditions." The provisions of the Act and its history, to which reference has been made, establish that such are its purposes, and that the latter is in aid of the former. What has been said indicates clearly that its provisions are aimed at the settlement of industrial disputes by the promotion of collective bargaining between employers and the authorized representative of their employees, and by mediation and arbitration when such bargaining does not result in agreement. It was for Congress to make the choice of the means by which its objective of securing the uninterrupted service of interstate railroads was to be secured, and its judgment, supported as it is by our long experience with industrial disputes, and the history of railroad labor relations, to which we have referred, is not open to review here. The means chosen are appropriate to the end sought and hence are within the congressional power. See *Railway Clerks* case, *supra,* 570; *Railroad Retirement Board* v. *Alton R. Co.,* 295 U.S. 330, 369.

But petitioner insists that the Act as applied to its "back shop" employees is not within the commerce power since their duties have no direct relationship to interstate transportation. Of the 824 employees in the six shop crafts eligible to vote for a choice of representatives, 322 work in petitioner's "back shops" at Princeton, West Virginia. They are there engaged in making classified repairs, which consist of heavy repairs on locomotives and cars withdrawn from service for that purpose for long periods (an average of 105 days for locomotives and 109 days for cars). The repair work is upon the equipment used by petitioner in its transportation service, 97% of which is interstate. At times a continuous stream of engines and cars passes through the "back shops" for such repairs. When not engaged in repair work, the back shop employees perform "store order work," the manufacture of material such as rivets and repair parts, to be placed in railroad stores for use at the Princeton shop and other points on the line.

The activities in which these employees are engaged have such a relation to the other confessedly interstate activities of the petitioner that they are to be regarded as a part of them. All taken together fall within the power of Congress over interstate commerce. *Baltimore & Ohio R. Co.* v. *Interstate Commerce Comm'n,* 221 U.S. 612, 619; Cf. *Pedersen* v. *Delaware, L. & W. R. Co.,* 229 U.S. 146, 151. Both courts below have found that interruption by strikes of the back shop employees, if more than temporary, would seriously cripple petitioner's interstate transportation. The relation of the back shop to transportation is such that a strike of petitioner's employees there, quite apart from the likelihood of its spreading to the operating department, would subject petitioner to the danger, substantial, though possibly indefinable in its extent, of interruption of the transportation service. The cause is not remote from the effect. The relation between them is not tenuous. The effect on commerce cannot be regarded as negligible. . . .

Affirmed.

CASE QUESTIONS

1. What questions does the Court say are presented for decision?
2. What was the purpose of the suit originally brought by System Federation?
3. State the facts giving rise to the dispute.
4. State the decision of the District Court.
5. Outline the two defenses imposed by the petitioner Railway Co.
6. How does the court dispose of the defenses of the Railway Co.?
7. Discuss the "back shop" question raised in this case.

QUESTIONS ON SECTIONS 16 AND 17

1. What was the effect of the Arbitration Act of 1888, the Erdman Act of 1898, and the Newlands Act of 1913?
2. Discuss the salient features of the Transportation Act of 1920.
3. Were there any beneficial results from the Railway Labor Act of 1926 as to labor?
4. What are some of the major provisions of the Railway Labor Act as to its current status?
5. State the latest change made by Congress in the Act.

SECTION 18 / ADMINISTRATION, REMEDY, ENFORCEMENT

Three major agencies are invoked by the Railway Labor Act to effectuate its administrative aspects, the National Mediation Board, the National Railroad Adjustment Board, and the Interstate Commerce Commission. Least important of these three is the Interstate Commerce Commission, so its duty under this Act will be disposed of initially.

Coverage of the Railway Labor Act extends over all railroads in interstate commerce, including express companies, Pullmans, bridges, lighters, ferries, terminal facilities, refrigeration, storage and delivery service, but not trucking service. The Act does not apply to any street, interurban, or suburban electric railway unless such railway is operating as part of a general railroad system. The Interstate Commerce Commission has power to investigate and decide whether any railway operated by electric power comes under the sweep of the Act. As mentioned in the previous section, the Act was amended in 1936 to extend its coverage to the airline industry. At this point it is well to reiterate that the coverage of the Railway Labor Act and the National Labor Relations Act is mutually exclusive.

It is significant that with the 1934 amendments, the Railway Labor Act included more functions and powers than Congress included in the later Wagner Act of 1935. Both Acts provided for certifying bargaining representatives and for the freedom of employees from employer interference or influence in organizing, but the Wagner Act imposed no duties or restrictions on unions until amended in 1947. Also, fact-finding and conciliation of disputes over wages or other new contract terms were covered in the RLA but not in the Wagner Act.

Establishment of government boards for settling grievances and contract interpretation differences was not included in the 1947 Taft-Hartley Act, although this became a well-used part of the RLA machinery, so much so that difficulties arose over long delays in deciding cases which often ran into a matter of several years.

The National Mediation Board

The most important agency created by the Railway Labor Act is the National Mediation Board. It is composed of three impartial members appointed by the President, no more than two of whom can be of the same political party. Their term extends for three years. Its powers and duties may be classified into four categories:

1. Representation questions under Sec. 2, Ninth.
2. Mediation questions under Sec. 5 of the Act. These concern the reconciliation of differences between the carrier and the labor organization at the time they are negotiating *new* agreements with references to wages, hours, and working conditions. Note that the Mediation Board has no power to dictate conditions to be incorporated or to require that new agreements be reached upon the expiration of existing agreements. It is merely an intermediary having the duty to bring the parties into negotiation.

3. Questions concerning the interpretation of agreements entered into between the parties through the mediation efforts of the Board. If the parties have reached an agreement and an interpretation question later arises out of the agreement, the National Railroad Adjustment Board has sole interpretative jurisdiction. Sec. 5, Second.

4. In some instances, labor disputes may reach a critical stage upon failure of *negotiation* between the parties. If *mediation* is ineffective, the Mediation Board is bound to propose *arbitration* under Sec. 5, First. If arbitration is spurned, the Mediation Board, in its discretion, may certify the dispute to the President, who then may create an *emergency board* of investigation.

The National Railroad Adjustment Board

We have observed that the National Railroad Adjustment Board was created by the 1934 amendment to interpret questions "growing out of *grievances* or out of the *interpretation* . . . of [existing] agreements concerning rates of pay, rules, or working conditions. . . ." Sec. 3, First, (i). [Authors' italics.] The NRAB is made up of 34 members, of whom 17 are representative of the carriers and 17 of railway organizations. The Act requires the carriers and labor unions to pay the salaries of their own representatives.[3]

Under the Act, the NRAB is divided into four divisions. For all practical purposes the four divisions of the NRAB constitute four separate arbitration bodies with each of the four divisions having jurisdiction over a different occupational classifications of railroad employees. Powers of the NRAB are exercised in this sequence:

1. If a dispute grows out of an agreement concerning grievances, rates of pay, rules, or working conditions, such dispute is originally subject to direct negotiation and settlement between the parties.
2. Failing settlement by negotiation, the parties may petition the Board to entertain jurisdiction. Sec. 3, First, (i), provides that ". . . disputes may be referred by petition of the parties *or by either party* to the appropriate division of the Adjustment Board with a full statement of the facts and all supporting data bearing upon the disputes." [Authors' italics.]
3. Failing settlement by the NRAB because of a deadlock, which is common, Sec. 3, First, (1), provides for appointment of a neutral referee to sit with the Board to break the deadlock. If the NRAB is unable to agree upon a neutral referee, the Mediation Board may be requested to appoint one.

The NRAB has exclusive jurisdiction over matters assigned it. Congress thus has barred direct court action on disputes within the jurisdiction of the NRAB. In *Moore* v. *Illinois Central RR. Co.,*[4] an exception was preserved by the Supreme Court under which a discharged railroad employee could by-pass the NRAB and elect to bring a common-law or statutory damages suit, provided he accepted his discharge as final and claimed only money damages. However the Supreme Court overruled *Moore* some twenty years later in its recent *Andrews* v. *Louisville &*

---

[3] An amendment in 1970 to the RLA reduced the number of members of the NRAB's First Division from 10 to 8 because of a merger of four unions into the United Transportation Union.

[4] 312 U. S. 630 (1941).

Nashville RR.[5] decision, and abolished this action at law for damages as an alternative to a grievance seeking reinstatement under a collective bargaining agreement. The *Andrews* ruling has also been followed in airline cases.[6]

The Railway Labor Act, as amended in 1966, provides that National Railroad Adjustment Board awards shall be conclusive on the parties to the dispute.[7] If a carrier does not comply with an NRAB order implementing an award, a proceeding for enforcement of the award may be brought in a U. S. District Court up to two years after non-compliance with the time for compliance specified in the award. Under the 1966 amendments, the losing party may also obtain court review of an adverse order of the NRAB, but the grounds for judicial review are the narrow grounds commonly provided for review of arbitration awards. Section 3, First, (p) and (q) provide that an order may be set aside in either enforcement or review proceedings only on the following grounds:

1. failure of the board to comply with the requirements of the RLA;
2. failure of the order to conform, or confine itself, to matters within the scope of the board's jurisdiction; and
3. fraud or corruption by a member of the board.

Other Boards of Adjustment

The 1966 amendments to the Railway Labor Act provide that unions or carriers may request the establishment of special boards of adjustment (called "PL Boards" by the National Mediation board under Public Law 89–456) to resolve disputes that have been pending before the NRAB for a year or more. These boards consist of three members. The provision authorizing such special boards was added to the RLA to eliminate a large backlog of cases then pending before the NRAB and to build in a procedure for the expeditious handling of future cases. Even before the 1966 amendments the RLA, Section 3, Second, authorized the establishment of system, group or regional permanent adjustment boards by mutual consent of the parties for the local settlement of disputes otherwise referrable to the NRAB for hearing at the NRAB's headquarters in Chicago, Illinois. The awards of special, system, group or regional boards of adjustment have the same legal effect as an NRAB award.

The airlines are not subject to NRAB jurisdiction. The Railway Labor Act requires every air carrier and its employees to establish system boards of adjustment for the resolution of grievances. In *Machinists* v. *Central Airlines, Inc.,*[8] the Supreme Court ruled that awards of air carrier system boards of adjustment are enforceable by federal law in federal courts. Like NRAB procedures, the National Mediation Board aids in the designation of neutrals for service with air carrier system boards. However, the NMB does not compensate the neutrals, as is the procedure for the compensation of neutrals who serve with the NRAB. The parties are required to compensate the neutrals who serve with air carrier boards.

---

[5] 406 U. S. 320 (1972).
[6] See *West* v. *American Airlines* 352 F. Supp 1278 (N.D. Ill. 1972).
[7] The 1966 amendments eliminated an exception for money awards.
[8] 372 U. S. 682 (1963).

SECTION 19 / BARGAINING REPRESENTATION

The National Mediation Board has original jurisdiction over representation issues. The rights granted and the procedures followed closely parallel those under the National Labor Relations Act, and they are covered in detail in Chapter 5:

Sec. 2, Fourth of the Railway Labor act permits employees to ". . . bargain collectively through representatives of their own choosing" and to be free from employer interferences in their organizational efforts. The procedure for designation of representatives, elections, and certification is stated in Sec. 2, Ninth of the RLA. The rules of the Board prescribe a petition by those interested in securing bargaining agency rights, such petition to be supported by a substantial (35%) showing of interest. Following this, an election may be held, with certification accruing to the majority representative in accord with the political election principle. The RLA permits certification without the necessity of a formal election; that is, the representative may prove his majority status by means of signature lists or cards or by consent election.

It may be helpful to review a summary of the factors which the National Mediation Board considers in setting up crafts or classes. The problem presented here is quite similar to that which faces the NLRB in determining what is an "appropriate unit." The principal considerations under the RLA are these:

1. Composition of the groupings for representation and collective bargaining purposes which the employees concerned have voluntarily developed among themselves:
   a. On carriers generally of the type involved.
   b. On the carrier where the dispute under investigation exists.
2. Extent and nature of the collective bargaining arrangements developed by the employees interested in the dispute with the carriers employing them.
3. Duties, responsibilities, skill, training, and experience of the employees involved and the nature of their work.
4. Usual practices of promotion, demotion, and seniority observed or developed for the employees concerned.
5. Nature and extent of community of interest existing among the employees.
6. Previous decisions of the Board bearing upon the issues under consideration.
7. The intent and purpose of Congress in its consideration and passage of the Railway Labor Act.

In Chapter 5 a further discussion of the problems of determining bargaining representatives will be found, problems somewhat similar under the NLRA and the RLA.

A 1951 amendment to the Railway Labor Act allowed union shop agreements to be entered into, notwithstanding any law "of any state." Some nonunion employees challenged the constitutionality of this amendment in the case of *Railway Employees' Department* v. *Hanson,* 351 U.S. 225 (1956). The nonunion employees sought an injunction in a Nebraska state court, against the enforcement of a union-shop contract executed by their employer and a union. Under this agreement the nonunion employees were required to join the union in 60 days or they would be subject to discharge. They argued that this contract violated the right-to-work provision of the Nebraska Constitution. Such a provision prohibits union security arrangements which require employees to join a union as a condition of employment. The U. S. Supreme Court resolved this conflict between state and federal power by holding that Congressional power over interstate commerce prevails over state power.

SECTION 20 / INJUNCTIONS AND THE RAILWAY LABOR ACT

The employment of the injunction has previously been treated in conjunction with the enforcement of orders issued by the NMB and the NRAB. Remaining for consideration, however, is the effect of the Federal Anti-Injunction Act upon railway labor disputes. This topic is fully treated in the decisions that follow. May a carrier secure a federal court injunction against labor violence if it has failed to submit the dispute to the arbitration procedure detailed in the Railway Labor Act? Is a threatened strike enjoinable if a union fails to exert "every reasonable effort" to settle a longstanding dispute with a carrier? In the Supreme Court decisions that follow, these questions receive its consideration and decision, an injunction being disallowed in the first situation and allowable in the latter.

Brotherhood of Railroad Trainmen v. Toledo, Peoria & Western Railroad

Supreme Court of the United States, 1944. 321 U.S. 50

RUTLEDGE, J. The important question is whether the District Court properly issued an injunction which restrained respondent's employees, conductors, yardmen, enginemen, and firemen, from interfering by violence or threats of violence with its property and interstate railroad operations. The sole issues that concern us are the existence of federal jurisdiction and whether the requirements of the Norris-LaGuardia Act (29 U.S.C. Secs. 107, 108, 47 Stat. 71, 72) were satisfied.

The case arises out of a long-continued labor dispute relating to working conditions and rates of pay. Negoitations between the parties, beginning in October, 1940, failed. A long course of mediation, with the aid of the National Mediation Board, resulted likewise. Accordingly, on November 7, 1941, the mediator proposed arbitration pursuant to the Railway Labor Act's provisions. 45 U.S.C. Sec. 155, First (b), 48 Stat. 1195. Both parties refused. Thereupon, as the Act requires, the Board terminated its services. *Ibid.* This occurred November 21, 1941. . . .

With the bombing of Pearl Harbor on December 7, the Mediation Board again intervened, strongly urging both sides to settle the dispute in view of the national emergency. At the Board's request the employees had postponed the strike indefinitely. Further conference failed to bring agreement and on December 17 the Board again urged that the disputants agree to arbitration under the statute. This time the employees accepted. But respondent continued its refusal, though it also continued to urge the appointment of an emergency board. And, while the record does not show that respondent was notified formally of the employees' agreement to arbitrate until December 28, neither does it appear that respondent did not know of this this fact before that time. . . .

The strike took effect at the appointed time. Picket lines were formed. Respondent undertook to continue operations with other employees. It employed "special agents" to protect its trains and property. Clashes occurred between them and the working employees, on the one hand, and the striking employees on the other. Various incidents involving violence or threats of violence took place. Some resulted in personal attacks, others in damage to property and interruption of service. The respondent sought the aid of public authorities, including the sheriffs of counties along its right of way and police authorities in cities and towns which it served. Some assistance was offered, but in some instances the authorities replied they had forces inadequate to supply the aid respondent requested and in others no reply was given. The parties are at odds concerning the extent of the violence, the need for public protection, and the adequacy of what was supplied or available. But the findings of the District Court are that the violence was substantial and the protection supplied by the public officials was inadequate. These incidents took place through the period extending from December 29, 1941, to January 3, 1942. . . .

Three principal issues have been made in the lower courts and here. Stated in the form of petitioners' contentions, they are: (1) The District Court was without jurisdiction, since there is no claim of diversity of citizenship and, it is said, no federal question is involved; (2) the evidence was not sufficient to show that the public authorities were unwilling or unable to furnish adequate protection for respondent's property; and (3) respondent did not make every reasonable effort to settle the dispute as required by the Norris-LaGuardia Act. Without passing upon the others, we think the last contention must be sustained.

Section 8 of the Norris-LaGuardia Act (29 U.S.C. Sec. 108, 47 Stat. 72) provides:

"No restraining order or injunctive relief shall be granted to any complainant who has failed to comply with any obligation imposed by law which is involved in a labor dispute in question, or who has failed to make every reasonable effort to settle such dispute either by negotiation or with the aid of any available governmental machinery of mediation or voluntary arbitration."

The question, broadly stated, is whether respondent made "every reasonable effort" to settle the dispute, as the section requires. On the facts this narrows to whether its steadfast refusal to agree to arbitration under the Railway Labor Act's provisions made the section operative. We think it did, with the consequence that the federal courts were deprived of the power to afford injunctive relief and respondent was remitted to other forms of legal remedy which remained available.

Respondent was subject to the Railway Labor Act. Its provisions and machinery for voluntary arbitration were "available." Resort to them would have been a "reasonable effort to settle" the dispute. Clearly arbitration under the Act was a method, both reasonable and available, which respondent refused to employ, not once, but repeatedly and adamantly. If it had been used, it would have averted the strike, the violence which followed, and the need for an injunction.

Section 8 demands this method be exhausted before a complainant to whom it is available may have injunctive relief. Broadly, the section imposes two conditions. If a complainant has failed (1) to comply with any obligation imposed by law or (2) to make every reasonable effort to settle the dispute, he is forbidden relief. The latter condition is broader than the former. One must not only discharge his legal obligations. He must also go beyond them and make all reasonable effort, at the least by the methods specified if they are available, though none may involve complying with any legal duty. Any other view would make the second condition wholly redundant. It clearly is not the section's purpose, therefore, by that condition, to require only what one is compelled by law to do. Yet, as will appear, this would be the effect of accepting respondent's position.

It is wholly inconsistent with the section's language and purpose to construe it, as have respondent and the lower courts, to require reasonable effort by only one conciliatory device when others are available. The explicit terms demand "*every* reasonable effort" to settle the dispute. Three modes are specified. They were the normal ones for settlement of labor disputes by the efforts of the parties themselves and the aid of agencies adapted specially for the purpose. The Railway Labor Act provided for all of them, with the aid of governmental machinery in the stages of mediation and arbitration. Section 8 is not limited to railway labor disputes. But it includes them. And its very terms show they were used in explicit contemplation of the procedures and machinery then existing under the Railway Labor Act and with the intent of making their exhaustion conditions for securing injunctive relief, not singly or alternatively, but conjunctively or successively, when available. This purpose of Congress is put beyond question when the section's legislative history is considered in the light of the history and the basic common policy of the two statutes, the Railway Labor Act and the Norris-LaGuardia Act.

The policy of the Railway Labor Act was to encourage use of the nonjudicial processes of negotiation, mediation and arbitration for the adjustment of labor disputes. Cf. *General Committee of Adjustment* v. *Missouri-Kansas-Texas R. Co.,* 320 U.S. 323; *General Committee of Adjustment* v. *Southern Pacific Co.,* 320 U.S. 338. The overall policy of the Norris-LaGuardia Act was the same. The latter did not entirely abolish judicial power to impose previous restraint in labor controversies. But its prime purpose was to restrict the federal equity power in such matters within greatly narrower limits than it had come to occupy. It sought to make injunction a last line of defense, available not only after other legally required methods, but after all reasonable methods, as well, have been tried and found wanting. This purpose runs throughout the Act's provisions. It is dominant and explicit in Sec. 8. In short, the intent evidenced both by words and by policy was to gear the section's requirements squarely into the methods and procedures prescribed by the Railway Labor Act. . . .

. . . Respondent's failure or refusal to arbitrate has not violated any obligation imposed upon it, whether by the Railway Labor Act or by the Norris-LaGuardia Act. No one has recourse against it by any legal means on account of this failure. Respondent is free to arbitrate or not, as it chooses. But if it refuses, it loses the legal right to have an injunction issued by a federal court or, to put the matter more accurately, it fails to perfect the right to such relief. This is not compulsory arbitration. It is compulsory choice between the right to decline arbitration and the right to have the aid of equity in a federal court. . . .

The judgment is reversed and the cause is remanded for further proceedings in conformity with this opinion.

Reversed and remanded.

CASE QUESTIONS

1. Outline the failure of negotiations incident to the eventual dispute.
2. Did the employees agree to arbitration?
3. Disclose the incidents to the strike.
4. What did the District Court find as to the adequacy of police authorities?
5. What does Sec. 8 of the Norris-LaGuardia Act provide? Does it include railway labor disputes?
6. Why did the Court refuse the injunction?
7. Why did the Court believe that its action was not an unconstitutional requirement of compulsory arbitration?

Chicago and North Western Railway Company v. United Transportation Union

Supreme Court of the United States, 1971. 402 U. S. 570

HARLAN, J.: The Chicago and North Western Railway Co., petitioner in this action, brought suit in the United States District Court for the Northern District of Illinois to enjoin a threatened strike by the respondent, the United Transportation Union. The substance of the complaint was that in the negotiations between the parties over work rules, the Union had failed to perform its obligation under § 2 First of the Railway Labor Act, 45 U.S.C. § 152 First, "to exert every reasonable effort to make and maintain agreements concerning rates of pay, rules, and working conditions." Jurisdiction was said to rest on 28 U.S.C. § 1331 and 28 U.S.C. § 1337. The Union in its answer contended that §§ 4, 7, and 8 of the Norris-LaGuardia Act, 29 U.S.C. §§ 104, 107, 108, deprived the District Court of jurisdiction to issue a strike injunction and that in any event the complaint failed to state a claim upon which relief could be granted. The District Judge, having heard evidence and argument, declined to pass on whether either party had violated § 2 First. In an unreported opinion, he concluded that the question was a matter for administrative determination by the National Mediation Board and was nonjusticiable; he further ruled that §§ 4 and 7 of the Norris-LaGuardia Act deprived the court of jurisdiction to issue an injunction against the Union's threatened strike. The

Court of Appeals for the Seventh Circuit affirmed, 422 F.2d 979, construing § 2 First as a statement of the purpose and policy of the subsequent provisions of the Act, and not as a specific requirement anticipating judicial enforcement. Rather, in that court's view, the enforcement of § 2 First was solely a matter for the National Mediation Board. *Id.,* at 985–988. We granted certiorari to consider this important question under the Railway Labor Act, on which the lower courts had expressed divergent views. For reasons that follow we reverse.

For at least the past decade, the Nation's railroads and the respondent Union or its predecessors have been engaged in an off-and-on struggle over the number of brakemen to be employed on each train. We find it unnecessary to describe this history in any great detail, either generally or with particular reference to petitioner. . . . For present purposes it is sufficient to observe that the parties have exhausted the formal procedures of the Railway Labor Act: notices, conferences, unsuccessful mediation, refusal by the Union to accept the National Mediation Board's proffer of arbitration, termination of mediation, and expiration of the 30-day cooling-off period of § 5 First, 45 U.S.C. § 155 First. The Railroad's charge that the Union had violated § 2 First was based principally on its contention that the Union had consistently refused to handle the dispute on a nationwide basis while maintaining an adamant determination that no agreement should be reached with the Chicago and North Western more favorable to the carrier than agreements which the Union had already reached with other railroads. The complaint also alleged that the Union had refused to bargain on the proposals in the Railroad's counternotices.

The narrow questions presented to us are whether § 2 First imposes a legal obligation on carriers and employees or is a mere exhortation; whether the obligation is enforceable by the judiciary; and whether the Norris-LaGuardia Act strips the federal courts of jurisdiction to enforce the obligation by a strike injunction. The parties have not requested us to decide whether the allegations of the complaint or the evidence presented at the hearing was sufficient to show a violation of § 2 First, and the lower courts, by their resolution of the threshold questions, did not reach the issue. Accordingly, we intimate no view on this matter.

This Court has previously observed that "[t]he heart of the Railway Labor Act is the duty, imposed by § 2 First upon management and labor, 'to exert every reasonable effort to make and maintain agreements concerning rates of pay, rules, and working conditions, and to settle all disputes . . . in order to avoid any interruption to commerce or to the operation of any carrier growing out of any dispute between the carrier and the employees thereof.' " *Brotherhood of Railroad Trainmen* v. *Jacksonville Terminal Co.,* 394 U.S. 369, 377–378 (1969). . . .

Virginian Railway v. *System Federation No. 40,* 300 U.S. 515 (1937), furnishes an early illustration of this principle in connection with the duty to "exert every reasonable effort" under the Railway Labor Act. In that case, the railroad refused to recognize a union certified by the National Mediation Board as the duly authorized representative of its shop workers, and instead sought to coerce these employees to join a company union. The employees sought and obtained an injunction requiring the railroad to perform its duty under § 2 Ninth to "treat with" their certified representative; the injunction also compeled the railroad "to exert every reasonable effort" to make and maintain agreements with the union. This Court affirmed that decree, explicitly rejecting the argument that the duty to exert every reasonable effort was only a moral obligation. This conclusion has been repeatedly referred to without criticism in subsequent decisions.

The conclusion that § 2 First is more than merely hortatory finds support in the legislative history of the Railway Labor Act as well. As this Court has often noted, the Railway Labor Act of 1926 was, and was acknowledged to be, an agreement worked out between management and labor, and ratified by the Congress and the President. Accordingly, the statements of the spokesmen for the two parties made in the hearings on the proposed Act are entitled to great weight in the construction of the Act.

In the House hearings, Donald R. Richberg, counsel for the organized railway employees supporting the bill, was unequivocal on whether § 2 First imposed a legal obligation on the parties. He stated, "it is [the parties'] duty to exert every reasonable effort . . . to settle all disputes, whether arising out of the abrogation of agreements or otherwise, in order to avoid any interruption to commerce. In other words, the legal obligation is imposed, and as I have previously stated, and I want to emphasize it, I believe that the deliberate violation of that legal obligation could be prevented by court compulsion." Mr. Richberg went on to describe why the bill had been drafted in general language applicable equally to both parties, rather than in terms of specific requirements or prohibitions accompanied by explicit sanctions:

"[w]e believe, and this law has been written upon the theory, that in the development of the obligations in industrial relations and the law in regard thereto, there is more danger in attempting to write specific provisions and penalties into the law than there is in writing the general duties and obligations into the law and letting the enforcement of those duties and obligations develop through the courts in the way in which the common law has developed in England and America."

Accordingly, we think it plain that § 2 First was intended to be more than a mere statement of policy or exhortation to the parties; rather, it was designed to be a legal obligation, enforceable by whatever appropriate means might be developed on a case-by-case basis. . . .

Given that § 2 First imposes a legal obligation on the parties, the question remains whether it is an obligation enforceable by the judiciary. We have often been confronted with similar questions in connection with other duties under the Railway Labor Act. Our cases reveal that where the statutory language and legislative history are unclear, the propriety of judicial enforcement turns on the importance of the duty in the scheme of the Act, the capacity of the courts to enforce it effectively, and the necessity for judicial enforcement if the right of the aggrieved party is not to prove illusory.

We have already observed that the obligation under § 2 First is central to the effective working of the Railway Labor Act. The strictest compliance with the formal procedures of the Act is meaningless if one party goes through the motions with "a desire not to reach an agreement." *NLRB* v. *Reed & Prince Mfg. Co.,* 205 F.2d 131, 134 (CA1 1953). While cases in which the union is the party with this attitude are perhaps rare, they are not unknown. See *Chicago Typographical Union No. 16*, 86 NLRB 1041 (1949), enforced *sub nom. American Newspaper Publishers Assn.* v. *NLRB*, 193 F.2d 782 (CA7 1951), aff'd as to another issue, 345 U.S. 100 (1953). We think that at least to this extent the duty to exert every reasonable effort is of the essence.

The capacity of the courts to enforce this duty was considered and affirmed in the *Virginian* case. Mr. Justice Stone, speaking for the Court, noted that "whether action taken or omitted is in good faith or reasonable, are everyday subjects of inquiry by courts in framing and enforcing their decrees." 300 U.S., at 550. Section 8 of the Norris-LaGuardia Act explicitly requires district courts to determine whether plaintiffs have "failed to make every reasonable effort" to settle the dispute out of which the request for the injunction grows. We have no reason to believe that the district courts are less capable of making the inquiry in the one situation than in the other. . . .

We turn finally to the question whether § 4 of the Norris-LaGuardia Act prohibits the use of a strike injunction in all cases of violation of § 2 First. The fundamental principles in this area were epitomized in *International Association of Machinists* v. *Street*, 367 U.S. 740, 772–773 (1961):

"The Norris-LaGuardia Act, 47 Stat. 70, 29 U.S.C. §§ 101–115, expresses a basic policy against the injunction of activities of labor unions. We have held that the Act does not deprive the federal courts of jurisdiction to enjoin compliance with various mandates of the Railway Labor Act. *Virginian R. Co.* v. *System Federation*, 300 U.S. 515; *Graham* v. *Brotherhood of Locomotive Firemen & Enginemen*, 338 U.S. 232. However, the policy of the Act suggests that the courts should hesitate to fix upon the injunctive remedy for breaches of duty owing under the labor laws unless that remedy alone can effectively guard the plaintiff's right."

Similar statements may be found in many of our opinions. We consider that these statements properly accommodate the conflicting policies of our labor laws, and we adhere to them. We find it quite impossible to say that no set of circumstances could arise where a strike injunction is the only practical, effective means of enforcing the command of § 2 First. Accordingly, our prior decisions lead us to hold that the Norris-LaGuardia Act did not forbid the District Court from even considering whether this is such a case. If we have misinterpreted the congressional purpose, Congress can remedy the situation by speaking more clearly. In the meantime we have no choice but to trace out as best we may the uncertain line of appropriate accommodation of two statutes with purposes that lead in opposing directions.

We recognize, of course, that our holding that strike injunctions may issue when such a remedy is the only practical, effective means of enforcing the duty to exert every reasonable effort to make and maintain agreements falls far short of that definiteness and clarity which businessmen and labor leaders undoubtedly desire. It creates a not insignificant danger that parties will structure their negotiating positions and tactics with an eye on the courts, rather than restricting their attention to the business at hand. Moreover, the party seeking to maintain the status quo may be less willing to compromise during the determinate processes of the Railway Labor Act if he believes that there is a chance of indefinitely postponing the other party's resort to self-help after those procedures have been exhausted. See *Brotherhood of Railroad Trainmen*

v. *Jacksonville Terminal Co.,* 394 U.S. 369, 380–381 (1969); cf. Hearings, *supra* n. 8, at 17, 50, 100 (Mr. Richberg); *id.,* at 190 (Mr. Robertson). Finally, the vagueness of the obligation under § 2 First could provide a cover for freewheeling judicial interference in labor relations of the sort that called forth the Norris-LaGuardia Act in the first place.

These weighty considerations indeed counsel restraint in the issuance of strike injunctions based on violations of § 2 First. Nevertheless, the result reached today is unavoidable if we are to give effect to all our labor laws —enacted as they were by Congresses of differing political makeup and differing views on labor relations—rather than restrict our examination to those pieces of legislation which are in accord with our personal views of sound labor policy. See *Boys Markets* v. *Retail Clerks Local 770,* 398 U.S. 235, 250 (1970).

As we noted at the outset, we have not been requested to rule on whether the record shows a violation of § 2 First in circumstances justifying a strike injunction, and we do not do so. Such a question should be examined by this court, if at all only after the facts have been marshalled and the issues clarified through the decisions of lower courts.

In view of the uncertainty heretofore existing on what constituted a violation of § 2 First and what showing was necessary to make out a case for a strike injunction, we believe the appropriate course is to remand the case to the Court of Appeals with instructions to return the case to the District Court for the taking of such further evidence as the parties may deem necessary and that court may find helpful in passing on the issues which the case presents in light of our opinion today.

Reversed and remanded

CASE QUESTIONS

1. What was the substance of the Railroad's complaint against the Union?
2. What was the Union's contention about the Railroad's request for an injunction against the threatened strike?
3. Does § 2 First impose a legal obligation on management and labor to "exert every reasonable effort" to settle their disputes, or is this section a mere exhortation and a moral obligation?
4. Does § 4 of the Norris-LaGuardia Act prohibit the use of a strike injunction in all cases of violation of § 2 First?
5. What is the holding of this case on the injunction issue?

QUESTIONS ON CHAPTER 3

1. Why did Congress first regulate disputes in the railway industry?
2. How did the 1926 RLA improve the prior situation? the 1934 amendments?
3. What rights of employers are protected by the RLA?
4. Does a state right-to-work law apply to the issue of union shop agreements in the industries subject to federal statutes?
5. Does Section 4 of the Norris-LaGuardia Act prohibit the use of strike injunctions in cases arising under the RLA?

Chapter 4

The Wagner Act to the Taft-Hartley Act

SECTION 21 / HISTORICAL DEVELOPMENT

The evolution of the National Labor Relations Act as amended by the Labor-Management Relations Act (or the Taft-Hartley Act) of 1947 can be traced to the Railway Labor Act of 1926, which is analyzed in Chapter 3 of this volume. Prior to 1926, the fundamental right of workers to engage in labor organization activity without fear of employer retaliation and discrimination was unprotected. Illustrative of both employer and court resistance are the three Supreme Court pronouncements found in *Adair* v. *United States,* 208 U.S. 161, 1908, *Coppage* v. *Kansas,* 236 U.S. 1, 1915, and *Hitchman Coal Company* v. *Mitchell,* 245 U.S. 229, 1917. These three cases were authority for the proposition that an employer may legally require nonmembership in a labor union as a condition precedent to continuation of employment. In Chapter 3 it was pointed out how the yellow-dog contract was legislatively outlawed by the Railway Labor Act of 1926 and the Anti-Injunction Act of 1932, indicating legislative disapproval of the aforementioned decisions. In view of these early decisions by the Supreme Court, however, it was not without some misgiving that Congress enacted the Railway Labor Act. These legislative doubts were resolved favorably for labor in the *Texas and New Orleans Railway* case of 1930, 281 U.S. 548, wherein it was held that railway workers had the right to designate representatives of their own choosing without interference by their employers.

Three years later Congress enacted the National Industrial Recovery Act, the first in a whole series of New Deal enactments designed to lift the nation out of the depression of the thirties. In providing for codes of fair competition under the Act, it was provided that approval of any code required compliance with Section 7(a) of the Act, which read as follows:

"(1) That employees shall have the right to organize and bargain collectively through representatives of their own choosing, and shall be free from the interference, restraint, or coercion of employers of labor, or their agents, in the designation of such representatives or in self-organization or in other concerted activities for the purpose of collective bargaining or other mutual aid or protection;

"(2) That no employee and no one seeking employment shall be required as a condition of employment to join any company union or to refrain from joining, organizing or assisting a labor organization of his own choosing. . . ."

To effectuate compliance with Sec. 7(a), to adjudicate its initial interpretation, and to conduct elections to determine bargaining representatives, the President set up the National Labor Board, supplanting it, in 1934, with the National Labor Relations Board. The latter board had essentially the same powers as its predecessor, and it continued to function in labor dispute and representation cases until the National Industrial Recovery Act was declared unconstitutional by the Supreme Court in 1935, (*Schechter Corporation* v. *United States,* 295 U.S. 495) on two grounds. The Court ruled that: 1) in authorizing codes of fair competition, Congress wrongly delegated its law-making responsibility; and 2) the federal authority to regulate commerce did not extend to a wholesaler of poultry.

Undeterred by this decision, Congress enacted a comprehensive labor code on July 5, 1935, the original National Labor Relations Act, sometimes called the Wagner Act for its principal senatorial sponsor. In constructing this piece of legislation, Congress drew heavily upon experience secured under the Railway Labor Act of 1926 and Section 7(a) of NIRA, confident that, in so doing, it would avoid an adverse constitutional interpretation by the Supreme Court. The National Labor Relations Act was grounded on the power of the federal government to regulate interstate commerce, by Article 1, Sec. 8. The statement of Policy prefacing the Act (Sec. 1) recited that the purpose of the labor code was to remove obstructions to commerce and restore equality of bargaining power arising out of employers' general denial to labor of the right to bargain collectively with them from which denial resulted a number of detrimental consequences, namely, poor working conditions, depression of wage rates, and diminution of purchasing power, all of which had served to cause and aggravate business depressions.

The two most significant portions of the National Labor Relations Act are embodied in Sections 7 and 8. The substantive rights of employees are stated in Section 7 to be as follows:

> "Sec. 7. Employees shall have the right to form, join, or assist labor organizations, to bargain collectively through representatives of their own choosing, and to engage in concerted activities for the purpose of collective bargaining or other mutual aid or protection."

As can be noted, there is a close parallel between the above and Sec. 7(a) of the National Industrial Recovery Act. The rights granted by Sec. 7 were protected against employer interference by Sec. 8, which detailed and prohibited five practices deemed to be unfair to labor. These were listed in Section 8 of the Act:

1. Interference with efforts of employees to form, join, or assist labor organizations, or to engage in concerted activities for mutual aid or protection, (which made illegal antiunion threats, spying, etc.).
2. Domination of a labor organization, (which outlawed the company formed or assisted labor union, or support to one union if denied to others).
3. Discrimination in hire or tenure to influence union affiliation or to discourage group activities.
4. Discrimination for filing charges or giving testimony under the Act, (including discharge, an unfavorable employment condition, or other discipline).
5. Refusing to bargain collectively with a duly designated representative of the employees.

The labor movement secured to itself phenomenal growth and strength by reason of the broad protective cover afforded by Sections 7 and 8. The ranks of labor joined when the Supreme Court upheld the Wagner Act in a series of companion decisions beginning with *NLRB* v. *Jones and Laughlin Steel Corporation* in 1937. This case is reprinted in Section 22 of this text.

During the years that the original National Labor Relations Act was in effect, it was subjected to a continuing running battle by employer groups. They argued that legislative sponsorship of labor unions under the Wagner Act, instead of restoring equality in bargaining power, had served to tip the balance measurably in favor of labor. Criticism of the Wagner Act of 1935 and its interpretation was based on these reasons:

1. The National Labor Relations Board was said to be biased in favor of labor.
2. The constitutional free speech right of employers was severely limited by adverse interpretation of the Act.
3. The Act prescribed only employer unfair practices, leaving union unfair labor practices untouched.
4. The Act permitted all forms of union security, including the closed shop.
5. The Act left helpless the employer, caught in the midst of organizational or jurisdictional disputes, causing him damage on a matter in which he had no interest and over which he had no control.
6. Interpretation of the Act gave supervisors the right to form and assist supervisory labor organizations, along with prescribing for the employer the duty of bargaining with supervisors' unions, while holding that supervisors were management agents.

When Congress became convinced by general public pressure that many of the charges listed had support in the attitude of the public, which feared that union power would cause a serious post-war inflation, proposed legislation to restrict unions was considered in both houses of Congress. The result was the Labor-Management Relations Act of 1947 of which the revised 1935 Act became Title I.

The major changes introduced by the 1947 Act are listed at this juncture for preview summary purposes only. Detailed consideration of these changes is reserved for succeeding chapters.

1. Employees may refrain from union activity as well as engage in it. Sec. 7.
2. The closed shop was outlawed, while other union security arrangements were permitted to labor organizations. Sec. 8(a)(3) and 9(e).
3. Employers need not recognize or bargain with unions formed by supervisory personnel. Sec. 14.
4. The employer's right of free speech is broadened by Sec. 8(c).
5. Unions may not engage in unfair labor practices specified as:
   a. Coercion of workers as to their rights under Sec. 7. by Sec. 8(b)(1).
   b. Causing an employer to discriminate against his employees except where the employee, under a valid union security arrangement, fails to pay periodic dues or initiation fees by Sec. 8(b)(2).
   c. Refusing to bargain in good faith with an employer by Sec. 8(b)(3).
   d. Engaging in certain strikes and boycotts unlawful in objective as specified in Sec. 8(b)(4).
   e. Requiring payment of excessive or discriminatory initiation fees under a union security contract; Sec. 8(b)(5).

f. Engaging in "featherbed practices"; Sec. 8(b)(6).

6. Certification elections are final for the period of one year; Sec. 9(c)(3); they may be initiated by employers or by employees; Sec. 9(c)(1).
7. Labor Board determinations of unit appropriateness for bargaining purposes are modified as to professional personnel and plant guards; Sec. 9(b).
8. Employees may initiate decertification ballots under Sec. 9(e)(2).

In addition to these NLRA revisions, two new codes, Titles II and III of the 1947 Labor-Management Relations Act, included these major additions:

1. Employers and unions may both maintain suits in federal courts for damages for breach of collective agreements. Sec. 301.
2. Employers may sue unions for damages arising out of secondary boycotts and strikes for unlawful purposes; recovery is allowed only out of union assets. Sec. 303.
3. Checkoff of union dues must be authorized by employees in writing. Sec. 302(c).
4. Employee welfare funds are limited to certain uses and have joint administrative requirements. Sec. 302(c)(5).
5. Labor organizations and employers may not make contributions or expenditures in federal elections. Sec. 304. (Section 205 of the Federal Election Campaign Act of 1971 contains the present law concerning union contributions. This section expressly authorizes labor organizations to solicit contributions for political funds as long as the funds are segregated from regular union dues and assessments and the contributions are given voluntarily.)
6. National Emergency Strikes are subject to an 80-day restraining order. Secs. 206, 207 and 208.

QUESTIONS ON SECTION 21

1. Why do we trace the evolution of the National Labor Relations Act back to the Railway Labor Act of 1926 and Sec. 7(a) of the Recovery Act of 1933?
2. Is the yellow-dog contract outlawed by the Railway Labor Act?
3. Why is the *Schechter* decision famous?
4. What justification for the National Labor Relations Act is contained in the Statement of Policy (Sec. 1) of that Act?
5. State the five employer unfair labor practices under the National Labor Relations Act of 1935.
6. List five objections employers had to the Act of 1935.
7. What are union unfair labor practices under 1947 Taft-Hartley?
8. What changes have been made in the National Labor Relations Act since 1947 as to union conduct?

SECTION 22 / CONSTITUTIONALITY ISSUES

The National Labor Relations Act of 1935 followed the Court's invalidation of the National Industrial Recovery Act by only a matter of weeks. Acting under the power to regulate interstate commerce, the Congress defined the coverage of the new law so as to include not only industries in interstate and foreign commerce, but also those in which a labor dispute could be "affecting commerce."

Affecting the free flow of commerce between the states by the possible stoppage that may result, the employer's conduct would be subject to federal regulation although he might not be directly engaged in interstate activities.

Employers immediately undertook to have the new law reviewed by the Court in the effort to have it declared unconstitutional, among other things, as being in excess of federal power. The classic case on this issue is *National Labor Relations Board* v. *Jones and Laughlin;* this case also decided whether the Act violates the due process clause of the 5th Amendment. Note the Court's references to the Railway Labor Act and to its earlier decisions.

National Labor Relations Board v. Jones & Laughlin Steel Corp.

Supreme Court of the United States, 1937. 301 U.S. 1

HUGHES, C. J. In a proceeding under the National Labor Relations Act of 1935, the National Labor Relations Board found that the respondent, Jones & Laughlin Steel Corporation, had violated the Act by engaging in unfair labor practices affecting commerce. The proceeding was instituted by the Beaver Valley Lodge No. 200, affiliated with the Amalgamated Association of Iron, Steel and Tin Workers of America, a labor organization. The unfair labor practices charged were that the corporation was discriminating against members of the union with regard to hire and tenure of employment, and was coercing and intimidating its employees in order to interfere with their self-organization. The discriminatory and coercive action alleged was the discharge of certain employees.

The National Labor Relations Board, sustaining the charge, ordered the corporation to cease and desist from such discrimination and coercion, to offer reinstatement to ten of the employees named, to make good their losses in pay, and to post for thirty days notices that the corporation would not discharge or discriminate against members, or those desiring to become members, of the labor union. As the corporation failed to comply, the Board petitioned the Circuit Court of Appeals to enforce the order. The Court denied the petition, holding that the order lay beyond the range of federal power. 83 F.(2d) 998. We granted *certiorari.* . . .

Contesting the ruling of the Board, the respondent argues (1) that the Act is in reality a regulation of labor relations and not of interstate commerce; (2) that the Act can have no application to the respondent's relations with its production employees because they are not subject to regulation by the federal government; and (3) that the provisions of the Act violate Sec. 2 of Article III and the Fifth and Seventh Amendments of the Constitution of the United States.

The facts as to the nature and scope of the business of the Jones & Laughlin Steel Corporation have been found by the Labor Board and, so far as they are essential to the determination of this controversy, they are not in dispute. The Labor Board has found: The corporation is organized under the laws of Pennsylvania and has its principal office at Pittsburgh. It is engaged in the business of manufacturing iron and steel in plants situated in Pittsburgh and nearby Aliquippa, Pennsylvania. It manufactures and distributes a widely diversified line of steel and pig iron, being the fourth largest producer of steel in the United States. With its subsidiaries—nineteen in number—it is a completely integrated enterprise, owning and operating ore, coal and limestone properties, lake and river transportation facilities and terminal railroads located at its manufacturing plants. It owns or controls mines in Michigan and Minnesota. It operates four ore steamships on the Great Lakes, used in the transportation of ore to its factories. It owns coal mines in Pennsylvania. . . .

To carry on the activities of the entire steel industry, 33,000 men mine ore, 44,000 men mine coal, 4,000 men quarry limestone, 16,000 men manufacture coke, 343,000 men manufacture steel, and 83,000 men transport its product. Respondent has about 10,000 employees in its Aliquippa plant. . . .

Practically all the factual evidence in the case, except that which dealt with the nature of respondent's business, concerned its relations with the employees in the Aliquippa plant whose discharge was the subject of the complaint. These employees were active leaders in the labor union. Several were officers and others were leaders of particular groups. Two of the employees were motor inspectors; one was a tractor driver; three were crane operators; one was a washer in the coke plant; and three were laborers. Three other employees were mentioned in the complaint, but it was withdrawn as to one of them and no evidence was heard on the action taken with respect to the other two.

While respondent criticizes the evidence and the attitude of the Board, which is described as being hostile toward employers and particularly toward those who insisted upon their constitutional rights, respondent did not take advantage of its opportunity to present evidence to refute that which was offered to show discrimination and coercion. In this situation, the record presents no ground for setting aside the order of the Board so far as the facts pertaining to the circumstances and purpose of the discharge of the employees are concerned. Upon that point it is sufficient to say that the evidence supports the findings of the Board that respondent discharged these men "because of their union activity and for the purpose of discouraging membership in the union." We turn to the questions of law which respondent urges in contesting the validity and application of the Act.

First. The Scope of the Act.—The Act is challenged in its entirety as an attempt to regulate all industry, thus invading the reserved powers of the States over their local concerns. It is asserted that the references in the Act to interstate and foreign commerce are colorable at best; that the Act is not a true regulation of such commerce or of matters which directly affect it but on the contrary has the fundamental object of placing under the compulsory supervision of the federal government all industrial labor relations within the nation. The argument seeks support in the broad words of the preamble (section one) and in the sweep of the provisions of the Act, and it is further insisted that its legislative history shows an essential universal purpose in the light of which its scope cannot be limited by either construction or by the application of the separability clause.

If this conception of terms, intent and consequent inseparability were sound, the Act would necessarily fall by reason of the limitation upon the federal power which inheres in the constitutional grant, as well as because of the explicit reservation of the Tenth Amendment. . . .

There can be no question that the commerce thus contemplated by the Act (aside from that within a Territory or the District of Columbia) is interstate and foreign commerce in the constitutional sense. The Act also defines the term "affecting commerce" [Sec. 2(7)]:

"The term 'affecting commerce' means in commerce, or burdening or obstructing commerce or in the free flow of commerce, or having led or tending to lead to a labor dispute burdening or obstructing commerce or the free flow of commerce."

This definition is one of exclusion as well as inclusion. The grant of authority to the Board does not purport to extend to the relationship between all industrial employees and employers. Its terms do not impose collective bargaining upon all industry regardless of effects upon interstate or foreign commerce. It purports to reach only what may be deemed to burden or obstruct that commerce and, thus qualified, it must be construed as contemplating the exercise of control within constitutional bounds. It is a familiar principle that acts which directly burden or obstruct interstate or foreign commerce, or its free flow, are within the reach of the congressional power. Acts having that effect are not rendered immune because they grow out of labor disputes. . . . It is the effect upon commerce, not the source of the injury, which is the criterion. *Second Employers' Liability Cases,* 223 U.S. 1, 51. Whether or not particular action does affect commerce in such a close and intimate fashion as to be subject to federal control, and hence to lie within the authority conferred upon the Board, is left by the statute to be determined as individual cases arise. We are thus to inquire whether in the instant case the constitutional boundary has been passed.

Second. The unfair labor practices in question.—The unfair labor practices found by the Board are those defined in Sec. 8, subdivisions (1) and (3). These provide:

Sec. 8. It shall be an unfair labor practice for an employer—

"(1) To interfere with, restrain, or coerce employees in the exercise of the rights guaranteed in Section 7."

"(3) By discrimination in regard to hire or tenure of employment or any term or condition of employment to encourage or discourage membership in any labor organization: . . ."

Section 8, subdivision (1), refers to Sec. 7, which is as follows:

"Sec. 7. Employees shall have the right to self-organization, to form, join, or assist labor organizations, to bargain collectively through representatives of their own choosing, and to engage in concerted activities, for the purpose of collective bargaining or other mutual aid or protection."

Thus, in its present application, the statute goes no further than to safeguard the right of employees to self-organization and to select representatives of their own choosing for collective bargaining or other mutual protection without restraint or coercion by their employer. . . .

Third. The application of the Act to employees engaged in production.—

The principle involved.—Respondent says that whatever may be said of employees engaged in interstate commerce, the industrial relations and activities in the manufacturing department of respondent's enterprise are not subject to federal regulation. The argument rests upon the proposition that manufacturing in itself is not commerce. (Citing cases.) . . .

The Government distinguishes these cases. The various parts of respondent's enterprise are described as interdependent and as thus involving "a great movement of iron ore, coal and limestone along well-defined paths to the steel mills, thence through them, and thence in the form of steel products into the consuming centers of the country—a definite and well-understood course of business." It is urged that these activities constitute a "stream" or "flow" of commerce, of which the Aliquippa manufacturing plant is the focal point, and that industrial strife at that point would cripple the entire movement. . . .

Respondent contends that the instant case presents material distinctions. Respondent says that the Aliquippa plant is extensive in size and represents a large investment in buildings, machinery and equipment. The raw materials which are brought to the plant are delayed for long periods and, after being subjected to manufacturing processes, "are changed substantially as to character, utility and value." The finished products which emerge "are to a large extent manufactured without reference to pre-existing orders and contracts and are entirely different from the raw materials which enter at the other end." Hence respondent argues that "If importation and exportation in interstate commerce do not singly transfer purely local activities into the field of congressional regulation, it should follow that their combination would not alter the local situation." *Arkadelphia Milling Co.* v. *St. Louis Southwestern Ry. Co.,* 249 U.S. 134, 151; *Oliver Iron Co.* v. *Lord,* 262 U.S. 172.

We do not find it necessary to determine whether these features of defendant's business dispose of the asserted analogy to the "stream of commerce" cases. The instances in which that metaphor has been used are but particular, and not exclusive, illustrations of the protective power which the Government invokes in support of the present Act. The congressional authority to protect interstate commerce from burdens and obstructions is not limited to transactions which can be deemed to be an essential part of a "flow" of interstate or foreign commerce. Burdens and obstructions may be due to injurious action, springing from other sources. The fundamental principle is that the power to regulate commerce is the power to enact "all appropriate legislation" for "its protection and advancement" (*The Daniel Ball,* 10 Wall. 557, 564); to adopt measures "to promote its growth and insure its safety" (*Mobile County* v. *Kimball,* 102 U.S. 691, 696, 697); "to foster, protect, control and restrain." *Second Employers' Liability Cases, supra,* p. 47. See *Texas & N. O. R. Co.* v. *Railway Clerks,* 281 U.S. 548. That power is plenary and may be exerted to protect interstate commerce "no matter what the source of the dangers which threaten it." *Second Employers' Liability Cases,* p. 51; *Schechter Corp.* v. *United States,* 295 U.S. 495. Although activities may be intrastate in character when separately considered, if they have such a close and substantial relation to interstate commerce that their control is essential or appropriate to protect that commerce from burdens and obstructions, Congress cannot be denied the power to exercise that control. *Schechter Corp.* v. *United States, supra.* Undoubtedly the scope of this power must be considered in the light of our dual system of government and may not be extended so as to embrace effects upon interstate commerce so indirect and remote that to embrace them, in view of our complex society, would effectually obliterate the distinction between what is national and what is local and create a completely centralized government. *Id.* The question is necessarily one of degree. . . .

Fourth. Effects of the unfair labor practice in respondent's enterprise.
—Giving full weight to respondent's contention with respect to a break in the complete continuity of the "stream of commerce" by reason of respondent's manufacturing operations, the fact remains that the stoppage of those operations by industrial strife would have a most serious effect upon interstate commerce. In view of respondent's far-flung activities, it is idle to say that the effect would be indirect or remote. It is obvious that it would be immediate and might be catastrophic. . . . When industries organize themselves on a national scale, making their relation to interstate commerce the dominant factor in their activities, how can it be maintained that their industrial labor relations constitute a forbidden field into which Congress may not enter when it is necessary to protect interstate commerce from the paralyzing consequences of industrial war? We have often said that interstate commerce itself is a practical conception. It is equally true that interference with that commerce must be appraised by a judgment that does not ignore actual experience. . . .

The Act does not compel agreements between employers and employees. It does not compel any agreement whatever. It does not prevent the employer "from refusing to make a collective contract and hiring individuals on whatever terms" the employer "may by unilateral action determine." The Act expressly provides in Sec. 9(a) that any individual employee or a group of employees shall have the right at any time to present grievances to their employer. The theory of the Act is that free opportunity for negotiation with accredited representatives of employees is likely to promote industrial peace and may bring about the adjustments and agreements which the Act in itself does not attempt to compel. As we said in *Texas & N. O. R. Co.* v. *Railway Clerks, supra,* and repeated in *Virginian Railway Co.* v. *System Federation, No. 40, supra,* the cases of *Adair* v. *United States,* 208 U.S. 161, and *Coppage* v. *Kansas,* 236 U.S. 1, are inapplicable to legislation of this character. The Act does not interfere with the normal exercise of the right of the employer to select its employees or to discharge them. The employer may not, under cover of that right, intimidate or coerce its employees with respect to their self-organization and representation, and, on the other hand, the Board is not entitled to make its authority a pretext for interference with the right of discharge when that right is exercised for other reasons than such intimidation and coercion. The true purpose is the subject of investigation with full opportunity to show the facts. It would seem that when employers freely recognize the right of their employees to their own organizations and their unrestricted right of representation there will be much less occasion for controversy in respect to the free and appropriate exercise of the right of selection and discharge.

The Act has been criticised as one-sided in its application; that it subjects the employer to supervision and restraint and leaves untouched the abuses for which employees may be responsible; that it fails to provide a more comprehensive plan,—with better assurances of fairness to both sides and with increased chances of success in bringing about, if not compelling, equitable solutions of industrial disputes affecting interstate commerce. But we are dealing with the power of Congress, not with a particular policy or with the extent to which policy should go. . . .

The order of the Board required the reinstatement of the employees who were found to have been discharged because of their "union activity" and for the purpose of "discouraging membership in the union." That requirement was authorized by the Act. Sec. 10(c), 29 U.S.C.A. Sec. 160(c). In *Texas & N. O. R. Co.* v. *Railway & S. S. Clerks, supra,* a similar order for restoration to service was made by the court in contempt proceedings for the violation of an injunction issued by the court to restrain an interference with the right of employees as guaranteed by the Railway Labor Act of 1926. The requirement of restoration to service of employees discharged in violation of the provisions of the Act was thus a sanction imposed in the enforcement of a judicial decree. We do not doubt that Congress could impose a like sanction for the enforcement of its valid regulation. The fact that in the one case it was a judicial sanction, and in the other a legislative one, is not an essential difference in determining its propriety.

Respondent complains that the Board not only ordered reinstatement but directed the payment of wages for the time lost by the discharge, less amounts earned by the employee during that period. This part of the order was also authorized by the Act. Sec. 10(c). It is argued that the requirement is equivalent to a money judgment and hence contravenes the Seventh Amendment with respect to trial by jury. The Seventh Amendment provides that "In suits at common law, where the value in controversy shall exceed twenty dollars, the right of trial by jury shall be preserved." The Amendment thus preserves the right which existed under the common law when the Amendment was adopted. . . . Thus it has no application to cases where recovery of money damages is an incident to equitable relief even though damages might have been recovered in an action at law. . . . It does not apply where the proceeding is not in the nature of a suit at common law. . . .

The instant case is not a suit at common law or in the nature of such a suit. The proceeding is one unknown to the common law. It is a statutory proceeding. Reinstatement of the employee and payment for time lost are requirements imposed for violation of the statute and are remedies appropriate to its enforcement. The contention under the Seventh Amendment is without merit.

Our conclusion is that the order of the Board was within its competency and that the Act is valid as here applied. The judgment of the Circuit Court of Appeals is reversed and the cause is remanded for further proceedings in conformity with this opinion.

Reversed.

CASE QUESTIONS

1. What charges did the union make against the corporation?
2. What action did the Board take after investigation of the above charges?

   3. Did the Circuit Court uphold the Board? On what
   ground?
   4. Describe the "integration" aspects of the steel company's operations.
   5. Does the Supreme Court believe labor has a "fundamental" right to organize?
   6. On what basis does the company contend its activities
   are not in commerce?
   7. Does the Act compel agreements between employers
   and employees?
   8. Does the Act interfere with the employer's right to hire
   and discharge?
   9. How does the Supreme Court answer the Company's
   contention with reference to the violation of the due
   process clause and of the 7th amendment?

SECTION 23 / **ADMINISTRATION**

Administration of the amended Act is entrusted to the National Labor
Relations Board and to the General Counsel. There are five members on the
Board, appointed by the President, with the approval of the Senate, for a term
of five years. They may be removed only for neglect of duty or malfeasance, and
they may be reappointed at the expiration of five years. The General Counsel is
appointed by the President, and his term of office is four years. Generally, the
Board's function is quasi-judicial and more nearly resembles a court than a
regulatory agency. Investigative and enforcement functions are carried out by
the General Counsel.

The Board's major function is to decide all unfair labor practice cases
brought before it by the General Counsel. The Board has been granted authority
to decide cases in three-member panels in order to speed up the processing of
cases. The Board has authority over election matters, but has delegated this power
to its regional directors, retaining the right to review their decisions. The functions and powers of the Board may be summarized as follows:

1. Prevention of unfair labor practices by both employers and labor organizations. This
   power derives from Section 10 of the Act; it is judicial in character, since the General
   Counsel is vested with the authority over the investigation of unfair labor practice
   charges, the issuance of complaints, and the prosecution of those complaints before
   the Board; Sec. 3(d).
2. Conduct of representation proceedings under authority and in the manner prescribed by Section 9 of the Act, including responsibility to:
   a. Determine units appropriate for purposes of collective bargaining.
   b. Investigate petitions for certification or decertification of labor organizations.
   c. Conduct an election to determine the majority representative.
3. Securing enforcement or review of its orders by the federal courts in unfair labor
   practice cases. It is important to note that a National Labor Relations Board order
   has no final validity upon either the employer or the labor organization unless and
   until the federal courts issue an enforcing decree; Section 10(e) provides a procedure
   for judicial enforcement of Board orders, and Section 10(f) details the method
   whereunder judicial review of a Board order may be secured by an aggrieved party.

4. Conduct a poll among employees about to engage in a National Emergency Strike, the purpose of such vote being to determine whether the employees wish to accept the employer's last offer; Sec. 209.
5. Settle jurisdictional disputes between rival unions; Secs. 8(b)(4)(D), 10(1), including to petition for injunctive relief if necessary to protect the rights of an interested party.
6. Secure injunctions against all unfair labor practices of unions and employers. See Secs. 10(e), 10(f), and 10(j).
7. Secure injunctions to quell certain strikes and boycotts forbidden by Sec. 8(b)(4); an injunction secured under Sec. 10(1) applies only to unions, and is mandatory if the charge is supported by preliminary evidence.

Under Sec. 4 of the Wagner Act, the Board had authority to appoint counsel to represent it in court cases. Under the 1947 Act, the Board was divested of its powers in this regard, Section 3(d) providing for appointment by the President of a General Counsel to act for a term of four years. His powers, as first stated in House Report No. 510, 80th Congress at p. 37, are:

". . . The general counsel is to have general supervision and direction of all attorneys employed by the Board, excluding the trial examiners and the legal assistants to the individual members of the Board, and of all the officers and employees in the Board's regional offices, and is to have the final authority to act in the name of, but independently of any direction, control, or review by, the Board in respect of the investigation of charges (under Section 10) and the issuance of complaints of unfair labor practices, and in respect of the prosecution of such complaints before the Board. . . ."

The importance of the General Counsel's role should not be underestimated, especially in view of the fact that Sec. 10 provides for the prevention of unfair labor practices. Congress was wise in separating the functions of investigation and prosecution, on the one hand, from the judicial function of deciding the merits of the controversy, on the other, as the Board, under the superseded Act, had been acting in the concurrent role of investigator, prosecutor, and judge. Independence of judgment on the part of the General Counsel is preserved, in that he reports to the President and the Senate and not to the National Labor Relations Board as formerly.

There are 31 regional offices and 11 sub-regional or "field" offices located throughout the states and territories of the United States. There is a regional director in charge of every region and he is assisted by a staff of attorneys, field examiners and clerical personnel. All matters subject to the NLRA, except in unusual circumstances, must be initially filed with the regional director for the region in which the situation arose. In representation cases the action is started through the filing of a "petition" with the regional director; in unfair labor practice matters, the action is initiated by filing a "charge" with the regional director. The Board, as previously mentioned, has delegated its authority over representation matters to the regional directors. The General Counsel has delegated authority to issue complaints in unfair labor practice cases to the regional directors. Thus the Board has appellate jurisdiction over election decisions emanating from the regional offices; and the General Counsel has appellate authority over regional directors' rulings on charges of unfair labor practices.

The formal hearing on an unfair labor practice complaint issued under the authority of the General Counsel is now conducted by an administrative law judge. Until late 1972 the title used was "trial examiner." The term trial examiner is used in all reported Board cases to the date of this change, thus it continues to be important to students of Labor Law. In unfair labor practice hearings, the administrative law judge (formerly the trial examiner) functions very much like a trial court judge: he hears witnesses, rules on admissibility of evidence, makes findings of fact and draws conclusions of law. His decision may be appealed to the five member Board in Washington, D. C. by any party involved in the case. The decision is final after a twenty day appeal period expires and no exceptions to it are made. Trial examiners and now administrative law judges are free from supervision by the Board. They are appointed by the Board from a civil service roster.

QUESTIONS ON SECTION 23

1. Is the office of National Labor Relations Board member elective or appointive?
2. For what reasons may a Board member be removed?
3. Regional offices of National Labor Relations Board serve what function?
4. What is the jurisdiction of the Board?
5. List the major functions of the Board.
6. Is the office of General Counsel independent of the Board? Discuss the background of this question.
7. What are the powers of the General Counsel?

SECTION 24 / PROCEDURES AND PROCEDURAL RULES AND POLICIES

If an employee believes that an employer or a union is engaged in one or more unfair labor practices, he or she may file charges with the appropriate regional office of the National Labor Relations Board. A union or an employer also may file charges. After the charges are filed, the case is processed as follows:

1. Charges are investigated by field examiners. During this investigation, charges may be adjusted, withdrawn, dismissed, or otherwise closed without formal action.
2. A formal complaint is issued by the regional director if charges are found to be well grounded and the case is not settled by adjustment.
3. Public hearing on the complaint is held before a trial examiner.[1]
4. The trial examiner's findings and recommendations are served on the parties and sent to the Board in Washington in the form of a trial examiner's decision. At this point the case is transferred to the Board in Washington. Unless either of the parties files a statement of exceptions to the trial examiner's findings within 20 days, his recommended order takes the full effect of an order by the Board. Parties who except to the examiner's findings also may file a brief to support their exceptions and may request oral argument before the Board. Exceptions are in effect an appeal from the trial examiner's decision.

---

[1] Reference here is to "trial examiner" rather than the new title "administrative law judge" since the reported cases in this edition make reference solely to trial examiners.

5. The Board reviews the case and issues a decision and order.
6. In case a union or an employer fails to comply with a Board order, the Board may ask the appropriate U. S. court of appeals for a judgement enforcing its order. Also, any party to the case who is aggrieved by the Board's order may appeal to an appropriate U. S. court of appeals.
7. The Board or an aggrieved party may petition the Supreme Court of the United States to review the decision of the court of appeals. Failure to obey a final court judgement is punishable as either civil or criminal contempt of court, or both.

If the regional director refuses to issue a complaint, the charging party may appeal to the General Counsel in Washington, D. C., who has final authority over the issuance of complaints. Ordinarily, 10 days are allowed for making such an appeal, which should be accompanied by a full statement of the facts in the case and the reasons why it is believed that the regional director erred. If the General Counsel approves the decision not to issue the complaint, there is no further appeal. On the other hand, the General Counsel may reverse the regional director's decision and order that a complaint be issued.[2]

One of the persistent criticisms of the Wagner Act, as administered by the National Labor Relations Board, was that the NLRB disregarded rules of evidence in its conduct of hearings, admitted hearsay evidence, and made findings of fact contrary to the weight of the evidence. Administrative bodies are not usually bound to observe strict rules of law concerning the admissibility of evidence. Their proceedings may be informally conducted as distinguished from those of pure judicial bodies. Recognition of this difference was embodied in the original National Labor Relations Act which provided that "the rules of evidence prevailing in courts of law or equity shall not be controlling," and further, "the findings of the Board as to the facts, if supported by evidence, shall be conclusive."

The Act as amended in 1947 made two ostensibly important changes in the evidentiary requirements of Board proceedings. Sec. 10(b) provides "any such proceeding shall, so far as practicable, be conducted in accordance with the rules of evidence applicable in the district courts of the United States. . . ." Sec. 10 (e) stipulates that "the findings of the Board with respect to questions of fact *if supported by substantial evidence* on the record considered as a whole shall be conclusive. . . ." [Authors' italics.] Thus, by legislative mandate, the Board is required to support its findings of fact by substantial evidence to assure that the courts will sustain the orders on review, and to follow generally the rules of evidence prevailing in the federal courts. Under the Wagner Act, the courts generally refused to disturb Board findings of fact if they were supported by *some* evidence in the record. The Supreme Court had broadly construed "some evidence" to mean "more than a mere scintilla."

The changes introduced by the 1947 Act should not be misleading. They do not amount to a trial *de novo,* nor do they mean that the courts will meticulously weigh the evidence. All the courts of review are bound to do is search the record to ascertain whether there is *substantial* evidence to support the findings of fact handed down by the Board. Substantial evidence need not be the greater

---

[2] "Summary of the National Labor Relations Act," U. S. Government Printing Office, No. 3100–0094. See also Justice Douglas's dissenting opinion in the *Lockridge Case* on page 142 of this chapter.

part of the evidence; in fact, the *weight* of evidence, on the record as a whole, may be against the Board's finding and still be conclusive upon the courts of review because of substantial support. The Supreme Court said in 1962 that a reviewing court may not "displace the Board's choice between two fairly conflicting views even though the court would justifiably have made a different choice had the matter been before it *de novo.* "However, the court may set aside a Board decision "when it cannot conscientiously find that the evidence supporting that decision is substantial, when viewed in the light that the record in its entirety furnishes, including the body of evidence opposed to the Board's view." [3]

SECTION 25 / JURISDICTION: EMPLOYERS UNDER THE ACT

On the same day that the Supreme Court rendered the *Jones & Laughlin* decision, upholding the Act of 1935 on all contested constitutional grounds and placing interstate manufacturing operations within the pale of the federal commerce power, four companion cases were simultaneously handed down, all of which upheld the constitutionality and coverage of the Act. [4] Thus, in one fell stroke, manufacturing, textiles, transport, and newspapers were included in the employer coverage. Jurisdiction of the Board, however, is still based on Secs. 2(6) and 2(7) of the Act. The term *commerce* is defined in Sec. 2(6) and the term *affecting commerce* in Sec. 2(7). The broadness of the latter is herein indicated: "The term 'affecting commerce' means in commerce, or burdening or obstructing commerce or the free flow of commerce, or having led or tending to lead to a labor dispute burdening or obstructing commerce or the free flow of commerce." Purely local activities are not under the jurisdiction of the National Labor Relations Board.

The term *employer* is defined by Sec. 2(2). This section excludes from the Act's coverage the following employers:

1. Federal, state, or municipal corporations.
2. Federal Reserve Banks.
3. Charitable hospitals.
4. Railroad companies under the Railway Labor Act, airlines, and related companies.
5. Labor organizations in their representation capacity; but not in the capacity of hiring their own employees.

Although the interpretation of the jurisdictional provisions of the statute has given the Board a broad authority, it has for reasons of administrative convenience and policy exercised its authority only in situations falling within certain standards. First adopted and published in 1950, the standards have been revised from time to time.

In the 1959 amendments, Congress provided that the NLRB may continue to exercise its discretion as to jurisdiction, but set limits to that discretion by adding the following: "Provided, that the Board shall not decline to assert

---

[3] *Universal Camera Corp.* v. NLRB, 340 U.S. 474 (1951).
[4] *Associated Press* v. *NLRB*, 301 U.S. 103; *NLRB* v. *Friedman-Marks Clothing Co.,* 301 U.S. 58; *NLRB* v. *Fruehauf Trailer Co.,* 301 U.S. 49; *Washington V. & M. Coach Co.* v. *NLRB*, 301 U.S. 142.

jurisdiction over any labor dispute over which it would assert jurisdiction under the standards prevailing upon August 1, 1959." [Sec. 14(c)(1).]

In every Board proceeding, the first question investigated is the question of the Board's jurisdiction. Once the existence of general authority over the subject matter is established, the Board then determines whether or not to proceed by ascertaining whether the employer's operations satisfy the jurisdictional standards set forth below. In applying these standards, the Board considers the total operations of the employer, even though the particular labor dispute involves only a portion of those operations. The Board's jurisdictional standards are as follows:

1. *Nonretail business:* Sales of goods to consumers in other states directly, or indirectly through others (called outflow), of at least $50,000 per year, or purchases of goods from suppliers in other states directly, or indirectly through others (called inflow), of at least $50,000 per year.
2. *Office buildings:* Total annual income of at least $100,000 of which $25,000 or more is paid by other organizations which meet any of the standards except standard 1 (nonretail).
3. *Retail enterprises:* At least $500,000 total annual volume of business.
4. *Public utilities:* At least $250,000 total annual volume of business.
5. *Newspapers:* At least $200,000 total annual volume of business.
6. *Radio, telegraph, television, and telephone businesses:* At least $100,000 total annual volume of business.
7. *Hotels and motels:* At least $500,000 total annual volume of business. (In 1967 the Board extended this yardstick to include jurisdiction over permanent or residential apartment houses with annual revenues meeting this standard.)
8. *Taxicab companies:* At least $500,000 total annual volume business.
9. *Transit systems:* At least $250,000 total annual volume of business.
10. *Transportation enterprises, links, and channels of interstate commerce:* At least $50,000 total annual income from furnishing interstate transportation services or performing services valued at $50,000 or more for enterprises that meet any of the standards except the indirect outflow and indirect inflow standards established for nonretail businesses.
11. *Associations:* Regarded as a single employer in that the annual business of all members is totaled to determine whether any of the standards apply.
12. *Proprietary hospitals and nursing homes:* Operated for a profit when total annual volume of revenue is at least $250,000 in the case of hospitals and $100,000 in the case of nursing homes.
13. *Baseball:* In 1969 the Board asserted jurisdiction over organized baseball. The case is reported in this section.
14. *Nonprofit, private, educational institutions:* In 1970 the Board asserted jurisdiction over private universities and colleges having annual operating expenses of at least $1,000,000. In 1972 the Board refused to extend its jurisdiction to a private nonprofit university which was quasi-public in nature and offered low-cost higher education to state residents with the aid of state funds.

In addition, the Board exercises jurisdiction over all enterprises that affect commerce when their operations have a substantial impact on national defense. Also, all businesses in the District of Columbia come under the jurisdiction of the Board.

Ordinarily, if an enterprise does the total annual volume of business listed in the standard, it will necessarily be engaged in activities that "affect" commerce.

The Board has established the policy that where an employer whose operations "affect" commerce refuses to supply the Board with information concerning total annual business, etc., the Board may dispense with this requirement and exercise jurisdiction.

Under its jurisdictional standards the Board has applied the act to such employers as an amusement park (*Coney Island, Inc.* 140 NLRB 77); nonprofit research and educational institutions (*Woods Hole Oceanographic Institution* 140 NLRB 60); nonprofit insurance organizations (*Massachusetts Hospital Service, Inc.* 138 NLRB 1329); labor unions as employers of paid workers, and trust funds in that capacity (*Oregon Teamsters Security Plan Office* 119 NLRB 207) (*American Federation of Labor* 120 NLRB 969, 973); and over a gambling casino subject to Nevada regulation and where the industry constituted 60 percent of the state's economy (*El Dorado, Inc.* 151 NLRB 579). The definition of employer does not exclude all charitable or religious institutions, but the NLRB generally declines to assert authority over their activities. The Board has refused to assert jurisdiction over the horse racing industry.[5] Also the Board has determined that it will not take jurisdiction over the real estate brokerage business, since the services performed by brokers are essentially local in nature.[6]

Thus Congress and the courts have recognized the broadest statutory jurisdiction where the Board can establish that an employer's operations involve or affect interstate commerce, directly or otherwise; but the Board's policy excludes noncommercial public service employers and their employees.

In the *Umpires* case reported below, the American League argued that employers in the baseball industry, as a class, had an insubstantial effect on interstate commerce and thus the Board should withhold assertion of jurisdiction under § 14(c). The league argued further that umpires were supervisors within the meaning of the Act and the association of umpires was not a labor organization within the meaning of Section 2(5); and both of these arguments required the Board to decline jurisdiction. The Board's answers to these arguments are contained in the decision below.

American League and Association of Umpires

180 NLRB No. 30 (1969)

The Petitioner [Association of National Baseball League Umpires] seeks an election in a unit of umpires employed by the American League of Professional Baseball Clubs (hereinafter called the Employer or the League). The Employer, while conceding the Board's constitutional and statutory power to exercise jurisdiction herein, nevertheless urges the Board, as a matter of policy, not to assert jurisdiction pursuant to Section 14(c) of the Act.

The Employer is a nonprofit membership association consisting of 12 member clubs located in 10 states and the District of Columbia. Operating pursuant to a constitution adopted and executed by the 12 member clubs, the Employer is engaged in the business of staging baseball exhibitions and, with

---

[5] *Centennial Turf Club,* 192 NLRB No. 97 (1971).
[6] *Seattle Real Estate Board,* 130 NLRB 608 (1961).

its counterpart the National League of Professional Baseball Clubs, constitutes what is commonly known as "major league baseball." The Employer currently employs, among other persons, the 24 umpires requested herein, and one umpire-in-chief. . . .

The Board's jurisdiction under the Act is based upon the commerce clause of the Constitution, and is coextensive with the reach of that clause. In 1922 the Supreme Court in Federal Baseball Club of Baltimore v. National League of Professional Baseball Clubs, 259 U.S. 200, although characterizing baseball as a "business," ruled that it was not interstate in nature, and therefore was beyond the reach of the nation's antitrust laws. However, subsequent Supreme Court decisions appear to proceed on the assumption that baseball, like the other major professional sports, is now an industry in or affecting interstate commerce, and that baseball's current antitrust exemption has been preserved merely as a matter of judicial stare decisis. Thus, in both the Toolson and Radovich decisions the Supreme Court specifically stated that baseball's antitrust status was a matter for Congress to resolve, implying thereby that Congress has the power under the commerce clause to regulate the baseball industry. Since professional football and boxing have been held to be in interstate commerce and thus subject to the antitrust laws, it can no longer be seriously contended that the Court still considers baseball alone to be outside of interstate commerce. Congressional deliberations regarding the relationship of baseball and other professional team sports to the antitrust laws likewise reflect a Congressional assumption that such sports are subject to regulation under the commerce clause. It is, incidentally, noteworthy that these deliberations reveal Congressional concern for the rights of employees such as players to bargain collectively and engage in concerted activities. Additionally, legal scholars have agreed, and neither the parties nor those participating as amici dispute, that professional sports are in or affect interstate commerce, and as such are subject to the Board's jurisdiction. Therefore, on the basis of the above, we find that professional baseball is an industry in or affecting commerce, and as such is subject to Board jurisdiction under the Act.

Section 14(c)(1) of the National Labor Relations Act, as amended, permits the Board to decline jurisdiction over labor disputes involving any "class or category of employers, where, in the opinion of the Board, the effect of such labor dispute on commerce is not sufficiently substantial to warrant the exercise of its jurisdiction. . . ." The Employer and other employers contend that because of baseball's internal self-regulation, a labor dispute involving The American League of Professional Baseball Clubs is not likely to have any substantial effect on interstate commerce; and that application of the National Labor Relations Act to this Employer is contrary to national labor policy because Congress has sanctioned baseball's internal self-regulation. The Employer also contends that effective and uniform regulations of baseball's labor relations problems is not possible through Board processes because of the sport's international aspects.

The Petitioner and other employee representatives contend, on the other hand, that Section 14(c) precludes the Board from declining jurisdiction, as any labor dispute arising in this industry will potentially affect millions of dollars of interstate commerce and have nationwide impact. They assert that baseball's self-regulation is controlled entirely by employers, and therefore has not and will not prevent labor disputes from occurring in this industry. Additionally, it is submitted that Congressional intent does not preclude, and national labor policy requires, Board jurisdiction—for without a national forum for uniform resolution of disputes, the industry might be subject to many different labor laws depending upon the State in which any particular dispute arises.

We have carefully considered the positions of the parties, and the amicus briefs, and we find that it will best effectuate the mandates of the Act, as well as national labor policy, to assert jurisdiction over this Employer. We reach this decision for the following reasons:

Baseball's system for internal self-regulation of disputes involving umpires is made up of the Uniform Umpires Contract, the Major League Agreement, and the Major League Rules, which provide, among other things, for final resolution of disputes through arbitration by the Commissioner. The system appears to have been designed almost entirely by employers and owners, and the final arbiter of internal disputes does not appear to be a neutral third party freely chosen by both sides, but rather an individual appointed solely by the member club owners themselves. We do not believe that such a system is likely either to prevent labor disputes from arising in the future, or, having once arisen, to resolve them in a manner susceptible or conducive to voluntary compliance by all parties involved. Moreover, it is patently contrary to the letter and spirit of the Act for the Board to defer its undoubted jurisdiction to decide unfair labor practices to a disputes settlement system established unilaterally by an employer or group of employers. Finally, although the instant case involves only umpires employed by the League, professional baseball clubs employ, in addition to players, clubhouse attendants, bat boys, watchmen, scouts, ticket sellers, ushers, gatemen, trainers, janitors, office clericals, batting practice pitchers, stilemen, publicity, and advertising men, grounds keepers and maintenance men. . . . As to these other categories, there is no "self-regulation" at all. This consideration is of all the more consequence for of those employees in professional baseball whose interests are likely to call the Board's processes into play, the great majority are in the latter-named classifications.

We can find, neither in the statute nor in its legislative history, any expression of a Congressional intent that disputes between employers and employees in this industry should be removed from the scheme of the National Labor Relations Act. In 1935, 1947, and again in 1959, Congress examined the nation's labor policy as reflected in the National Labor Relations Act; and Congress has consistently affirmed the Act's basic policy, as expressed in Section 1, of encouraging collective bargaining by "protecting the exercise by workers of full freedom of association, self-organization, and designation of representatives of their own choosing." Nowhere in Congress' deliberations is there any indication that these basic rights are not to be extended to employees employed in professional baseball or any other professional sport. We do not agree that Congress, by refusing to pass legislation subjecting the sport to the antitrust laws when it considered the regulation of baseball and other sports under the antitrust statutes, sanctioned a governmentwide policy of "non-involvement" in all matters pertaining to baseball. Indeed, to the extent that Congressional deliberation on the antitrust question has reference to the issue before us, it indicates agreement that players' rights to bargain collectively and engage in concerted activities are to be protected rather than limited.

There is persuasive reason to believe that future labor disputes—should they arise in this industry—will be national in scope, radiating their impact far beyond individual State boundaries. As stated above, the Employer and its members are located and conduct business in 10 States and the District of Columbia. The stipulated commerce data establishes that millions of dollars of interstate commerce are involved in its normal business operations. The nature of the industry is such that great reliance is placed upon interstate travel. Necessarily, then, we are not here confronted with the sort of small, primarily intrastate employer over which the Board declines jurisdiction because of failure to meet its prevailing monetary standards. Moreover, it is apparent that the Employer, whose operations are so clearly national in scope, ought not have its labor relations problems subject to diverse state labor laws.

The Employer's final contention, that Board processes are unsuited to regulate effectively baseball's international aspects, clearly lacks merit, as many if not most of the industries subject to the Act have similar international features.

Accordingly, we find that the effect on interstate commerce of a labor dispute involving professional baseball is not so insubstantial as to require withholding assertion of the Board's jurisdiction, under Section 14(c) of the Act, over Employers in that industry, as a class. As the annual gross revenues of this Employer are in excess of all of our prevailing monetary standards, we find that the Employer is engaged in an industry affecting commerce, and that it will effectuate the policies of the Act to assert jurisdiction herein.

2. The Employer at the hearing denied that the Petitioner was a labor organization within the meaning of Section 2(5) of the Act. The record shows, however, that the Petitioner is an organization in which employees participate, and which exists for the purpose of dealing with employers concerning wages and other conditions of employment. Accordingly, we find that the Petitioner is a labor organization within the meaning of Section 2(5) of the Act.

3. A question affecting commerce exists concerning the representation of certain employees of the Employer within the meaning of Section 9(c)(1) and Section 2(6) and (7) of the Act.

4. The Employer contends that the petition should be dismissed on the ground that the umpires sought to be represented are supervisors as defined in Section 2(11) of the Act. It is not contended that umpires have authority to hire, fire, transfer, discharge, recall, promote, assign, or reward. We think it equally apparent that umpires do not "discipline" or "direct" the work force according to the common meaning of those terms as used in the Act.

The record indicates that an umpire's basic responsibility is to insure that each baseball game is played in conformance with the predetermined rules of the game. Thus, the umpire does not discipline except to the extent he may remove a participant from the game for violation of these rules. Testimony shows that after such a removal the umpire merely reports the incident to his superiors, and does not himself fine, suspend, or even recommend such action.

As the final arbiter on the field, the umpire necessarily makes decisions which may favor one team over another, and which may determine to some extent the movements of various players, managers, and other personnel on the ball field. The umpire does not, however, direct the work force in the same manner and for the same reasons as a foreman in an industrial setting. As every fan is aware, the umpire does not—through the use of independent judgment—tell a player how to bat, how to field, to work harder or exert more effort, nor can he tell a manager which players to play or where to play them. Thus, the umpire merely sees to it that the game is played in compliance with the rules. It is the manager and not the umpire who directs the employees in their pursuit of victory.

Accordingly, we find that the umpires are not supervisors, and thus the Employer's motion to dismiss on this ground is hereby denied. We further find that the following employees of the Employer constitute a unit appropriate for the purposes of collective bargaining within the meaning of Section 9(b) of the Act:

All persons employed as umpires in the American League of Professional Baseball Clubs, but excluding all other employees, office clerical employees, guards, professional employees and supervisors as defined in the Act.

An election by secret ballot shall be conducted among the employees in the unit found appropriate, as early as possible, but not later than 30 days from the date below. . . .

Member Jenkins dissented.

CASE QUESTIONS

1. Did the Board withhold exercising its jurisdiction over employers in the baseball industry under Section 14(c) because professional baseball does not have a substantial effect on commerce?
2. Is the association of umpires a labor organization within the meaning of Section 2(5)?
3. Are umpires supervisors as defined by Section 2(11) of the Act?

SECTION 26 / JURISDICTION: AGENTS OF EMPLOYERS

This section considers the criteria employed by the courts in distinguishing between the three legal relations of principal, agent, and independent contractor, in reviewing NLRB orders. An employer who acts in his own capacity and right does so as a *principal* and entails the full legal responsibility of a principal. When an employer acts through others who are given express or implied authority to act for him, he remains responsible as a principal because he has created an *agency* relation. This rule of imputed liability applies so long as the agent acts within the scope of his express or implied authority. Acts of an agent beyond this authority are not imputable to the employer unless they are subsequently ratified by him and thus made his own.

The legal relation of *independent contractor* is that of a principal. He contracts and performs independent acts himself or through his agents. For those acts he is liable as long as their performance is free from the control or intervention of another person or agency.

The National Labor Relations Act introduces the above legalisms in three sections:

Sec. 2(2) provides: "the term 'employer' includes any person acting as an agent of an employer, directly or indirectly. . . ."

Sec. 2(13) states: "In determining whether any person is acting as an 'agent' of another person so as to make such other person responsible for his acts, the question of whether the specific acts performed were actually authorized or subsequently ratified shall not be controlling."

Sec. 2(3) excludes independent contractors from the term "employee."

A supervisor generally acts for and commits the employer. In the *International Association of Machinists* decision presented in this section, the Supreme Court gives expression to the rules of principal and agent briefly summarized above. The former is a leading case in labor law on the question of an authority grant, by implication and acquiescence, to nonsupervisory or working leaders. The decision introduces the concept of independent contractor versus agent and joint employer. An employer can generally relieve himself of liability if the unfair labor practices committed are those of an independent contractor rather than an agent or a joint employer. The employer remains jointly liable, however, if he procures the commission of an unfair labor practice by third persons over whom he retains express or covert power of control.

Related questions of agency are found in the situation of any association of employers operating as a single entity. In a *Checker Cab* case where cab owner and operators were members of a nonprofit corporation, the Board found the corporation and the individual members to be joint employers in a common enterprise since the members had authorized the corporation to exercise substantial control over the drivers.[7] Also an attorney may or may not be acting as an agent of the client, depending on whether his conduct "exceeded the bounds of mere advocacy" and whether his acts are distinguishable from those of the employer.[8]

International Association of Machinists v. National Labor Relations Board

Supreme Court of the United States, 1940. 311 U. S. 72

DOUGLAS, J. . . . The Board found, in proceedings duly had under Sec. 10 of the Act, that the employer, Serrick Corporation, had engaged in unfair labor practices within the meaning of the Act. It ordered the employer to cease and desist from those practices and to take certain affirmative action. More specifically, it directed the employer to cease giving effect to a closed-shop

---

[7] *Checker Cab Co. and Its Members,* 141 NLRB 64.
[8] *Valley Golden Dairies, Inc., John Price, Attorney,* 152 NLRB 153.

contract with petitioner [International Association of Machinists] covering the toolroom employees; to deal with U.A.W., an industrial unit, as the exclusive bargaining agent of its employees, including the toolroom men; to desist from various discriminatory practices in favor of petitioner and against U.A.W.; and to reinstate and make whole certain employees who had been improperly discharged. The employer has complied with the Board's order. But petitioner, an intervener in the proceedings before the Board, filed a petition in the court below to review and set aside those portions of the order which direct the employer to cease and desist from giving effect to its closed-shop contract with petitioner and to bargain exclusively with U.A.W. The court below affirmed the order of the Board. . . .

. . . It is clear that the employer had an open and avowed hostility to U.A.W. It is plain that the employer exerted great effort, though unsuccessfully, to sustain its old company union, the Acme Welfare Association, as a bulwark against U.A.W. And it is evident that the employer, while evincing great hostility to U.A.W. in a contest to enlist its production force, acquiesced without protest in the organization by petitioner of the toolroom employees. The main contested issue here is narrowly confined. It is whether or not the employer "assisted" the petitioner in enrolling its majority.

Fouts, Shock, Dininger, Bolander, Byroad and Baker were all employees of the toolroom. Four of these—Fouts, Shock, Byroad and Bolander—were old and trusted employees. Fouts was "more or less an assistant foreman," having certain employees under him. Shock was in charge of the toolroom during the absence of the foreman. Dininger and Bolander were in charge of the second and third shifts respectively, working at night. Prior to mid-July, 1937, they had been actively engaged on behalf of the company union. When it became apparent at that time that the efforts to build up that union were not successful, Fouts, Shock, Byroad and Bolander suddenly shifted their support from the company union to petitioner and moved into the forefront in enlisting the support of the employees for petitioner. The general manager told Shock that he would close the plant rather than deal with U.A.W. The superintendent and Shock reported to toolroom employees that the employer would not recognize the C.I.O. The superintendent let it be known that the employer would deal with an A. F. of L. union. At the same time the superintendent also stated to one of the employees that some of the "foremen don't like the C.I.O." and added, with prophetic vision, that there was "going to be quite a layoff around here and these fellows that don't like the C.I.O. are going to lay those fellows off first." . . . Not less than a week before August 13, the personnel director advised two employees to join the A. F. of L. Byroad spent considerable time during working hours soliciting employees, threatening loss of employment to those who did not sign up with petitioner and representing that he was acting in line with the desires of the toolroom foreman, McCoy. This active solicitation for petitioner was on company time and was made openly in the shop. Much of it was made in the presence of the toolroom foreman, McCoy, who clearly knew what was being done. Yet the freedom allowed solicitors for petitioner was apparently denied solicitors for U.A.W. The plant manager warned some of the latter to check out their time for a conference with him on U.A.W. and questioned their right to discuss

U.A.W. matters on company property. The inference is justified that U.A.W. solicitors were closely watched, while those acting for petitioner were allowed more leeway.

Five U.A.W. officials had been discharged in June, 1937, because of their union activities. The known antagonism of the employer to U.A.W. before petitioner's drive for membership started made it patent that the employees were not free to choose U.A.W. as their bargaining representative. Petitioner started its drive for membership late in July, 1937, and its closed-shop contract was signed August 11, 1937. On August 10, 1937, the U.A.W., having a clear majority of all the employees, presented to the employer a proposed written contract for collective bargaining. This was refused. On August 13, 1937, all toolroom employees who refused membership in petitioner, some 20 in number, were discharged. On August 15, 1937, the management circulated among the employees a statement which, as found by the Board, was a thinly veiled attack on the U.A.W. and a firm declaration that the employer would not enter into any agreement with it.

Petitioner insists that the employer's hostility to U.A.W. cannot be translated into assistance to the petitioner *and that none of the acts of the employees above mentioned, who were soliciting for petitioner, can be attributed to the employer.* [Authors' italics.]

We disagree with that view. We agree with the court below that the toolroom episode was but an integral part of a long plant controversy. What happened during the relatively brief period from late July to August 11, 1937, cannot properly be divorced from the events immediately preceding and following. The active opposition of the employer to U.A.W. throughout the whole controversy has a direct bearing on the events during that intermediate period. Known hostility to one union and clear discrimination against it may indeed make seemingly trivial intimations of preference for another union powerful assistance for it. Slight suggestions as to the employer's choice between unions may have telling effect among men who know the consequences of incurring that employer's strong displeasure. The freedom of activity permitted one group and the close surveillance given another may be more powerful support for the former than campaign utterances.

To be sure, it does not appear that the employer instigated the introduction of petitioner into the plant. But the Board was wholly justified in finding that the employer "assisted" it in its organizational drive. Silent approval of or acquiescence in that drive for membership and close surveillance of the competitor; the intimations of the employer's choice made by superiors; the fact that the employee-solicitors had been closely identified with the company union until their quick shift to petitioner; the rank and position of those employee-solicitors; the ready acceptance of petitioner's contract and the contemporaneous rejection of the contract tendered by U.A.W.; the employer's known prejudice against the U.A.W. were all proper elements for it to take into consideration in weighing the evidence and drawing its inferences. To say that the Board must disregard what preceded and what followed the membership drive would be to require it to shut its eyes to potent imponderables permeating this entire record. The detection and appraisal of such imponderables are indeed one of the essential functions of an expert administrative agency.

Petitioner asserts that it had obtained its majority of toolroom employees by July 28, 1938, and that there was no finding by the Board that that majority was maintained between then and the date of execution of the closed-shop contract by unfair labor practices. In this case, however, that is an irrelevant refinement. The existence of unfair labor practices throughout this whole period permits the inference that the employees did not have that freedom of choice which is the essence of collective bargaining. And the finding of the Board that petitioner did not represent an uncoerced majority of toolroom employees when the closed-shop contract was executed is adequate to support the conclusion that the maintenance as well as the acquisition of the alleged majority was contaminated by the employer's aid.

Petitioner attacks the Board's conclusion that its membership drive was headed by "supervisory" employees—Fouts, Shock, Dininger and Bolander. According to petitioner these men were not foremen, let alone supervisors entrusted with executive or directorial functions, but merely "lead men" who, by reason of long experience, were skilled in handling new jobs and hence directed the set-up of the work. Petitioner's argument is that since these men were not supervisory their acts of solicitation were not coercive and not attributable to the employer.

The employer, however, may be held to have assisted the formation of a union even though the acts of the so-called agents were not expressly authorized or might not be attributable to him on strict application of the rules of *respondeat superior*. We are dealing here not with private rights (*Amalgamated Utility Workers* v. *Consolidated Edison Co.,* 309 U.S. 261) nor with technical concepts pertinent to an employer's legal responsibility to third persons for acts of his servants, but with a clear legislative policy to free the collective bargaining process from all taint of an employer's compulsion, domination, or influence. The existence of that interference must be determined by careful scrutiny of all the factors, often subtle, which restrain the employees' choice and for which the employer may fairly be said to be responsible. Thus, where the employees would have just cause to believe that solicitors professedly for a labor organization were acting for and on behalf of the management, the Board would be justified in concluding that they did not have the complete and unhampered freedom of choice which the Act contemplates. Here there was ample evidence to support that inference. As we have said, Fouts, Shock, Dininger and Bolander all had men working under them. To be sure, they were not high in the factory hierarchy and apparently did not have the power to hire or to fire. But they did exercise general authority over the employees and were in a strategic position to translate to their subordinates the policies and desires of the management. It is clear that they did exactly that. Moreover, three of them—Fouts, Shock and Bolander—had been actively engaged during the preceding weeks in promoting the company union. During the membership drive for petitioner they stressed the fact that the employer would prefer those who joined petitioner to those who joined U.A.W. They spread the idea that the purpose in establishing petitioner was "to beat the C.I.O." and that the employees might withdraw from the petitioner once this objective was reached. And in doing these things they were emulating the example set by the management. The conclusion then is justified that this is not a case where solicitors for one union merely engaged in a zealous membership drive which just happened to coincide with the management's desires. Hence the fact that they were bona fide members of petitioner did not require the Board to disregard the other circumstances we have noted. . . .

. . . The presence of such practices in this case justified the Board's conclusion that petitioner did not represent an uncoerced majority of the toolroom employees.

Affirmed.

CASE
QUESTIONS

1. Who is the petitioner in this case?
2. Why does petitioner make this appeal?
3. As between petitioner and the U.A.W., whom did the Serrick Corp. favor? Did it show favoritism by its acts?
4. What positions were held by the "trusted" employees who solicited for the I.A.M. union?
5. Does the court hold that the employees in Question No. 4 were agents of Serrick?
6. Does the act of an agent require express authorization to bind the employer?

SECTION 27 / JURISDICTION: EMPLOYEES UNDER THE ACT

Since one of the major policy objectives of the National Labor Relations Act is the protection of those employee organizational rights guaranteed by Section 7, the statutory exclusiveness of the term "employee," embodied in Sec. 2(3), becomes of prime importance.

In addition to indicating what employees are not protected against unfair labor practices, Sec. 2(3) becomes equally significant in connection with the remedial aspects of the Act. For example, should a worker lose his status as an employee protected by the Act, by virtue of his participation in unlawful strike or boycott activity, he may not be entitled to reinstatement to his position, to back pay, or to participate in representation elections. Once employee status is lost, the employer may not have to bargain with the union representing such workers and may be free to discriminate against those workers who have lost their protected status. On the other hand, the Act in the same section protects the employee in his conditional right to reinstatement with back pay if participating in pressure that is lawful in object and means.

The details of these remedial aspects are left for subsequent consideration. We shall at this point merely consider the exclusionary aspects of the term "employee" as outlined in Section 2(3). The following are not protected by the Act:

1. Workers under the Railway Labor Act.
2. Employees of employers not covered by the Act.

3. Independent contractors.
4. Domestic servants in the home.
5. Persons employed by parents or spouses.
6. Agricultural workers.
7. Supervisors.

The exclusion of workers under the Railway Labor Act follows the jurisdictional aspects of that Act as defined in Chapter 3 of this volume. The exclusion of employees of employers not covered by the law is necessitated by logical consequence of the employer noncoverage.

This leaves five excluded categories to be explained in the forthcoming materials. The relation of independent contractor was introduced in Section 26 above, under "Jurisdiction: Agents of Employers." It is further developed in this section, directly under the purview of Sec. 2(3), the test being the right to control the results of and the method of performing the work to be done; the worker is an employee if he performs services for one who retains this control and is therefore entitled to the protection against employer unfair labor practices and to inclusion in a bargaining unit. If the individual has this control over his work, he is an independent contractor. On this test the Board has found taxicab driver-owners to be employees of the "employer" under whose franchise, rules, and direction as to assignments they were working. Similarly, driver-distributors for a bottling company are held to be employees when their work is so controlled even though they own the trucks purchased from the employer, pay for all truck maintenance, and are self-employed for tax purposes and social security.[9]

In another situation, the facts caused the Board to find truck drivers who own more than one tractor, leasing them to a firm and hiring others for extra drivers, to be supervisory employees rather than independent contractors.

The application of this "right-to-control" test is explained fully in the *Phoenix Mutual* decision, reported in this section.

Union organizing activity among farmworkers has been accompanied by considerable strife, in part because there is no uniform statutory framework for the conduct of collective bargaining in the farm sector. Section 2(3) specifically excludes agricultural laborers from the Federal labor relations law. Thus, the regulation of labor relations in the farm sector is left to the individual states. Agricultural laborers do not have comparable protection and rights under State law, except in Hawaii, Wisconsin and to a limited extent Massachusetts. A recent example of state farm sector legislation is the Arizona Agriculture Employment Relations Act of 1972. Among its controversial features are a ban on certain boycott activities; a restriction on use of consumer boycotts; and a restriction on harvest-time strikes by authorizing issuance of a 10-day injunction against a strike, with the condition, however, that the dispute be submitted to binding arbitration.

The *North Whittier* case discusses the baffling problem of when agricultural labor may, nonetheless, come under the NLRA's provisions, and reveals why the courts prefer to decide each case on its own facts and merits rather than straight-jacket themselves within the confines of unyielding rules of law. Although agricultural laborers are clearly excluded from the Section 2(3) definition of

---

[9] *Coca-Cola Bottling Company of New York, Inc.,* 133 NLRB 762.

"employee," the Act does not define the term "agricultural laborer." The Board and courts had significant difficulty interpreting the meaning of this exclusion until 1947, when Congress applied the Fair Labor Standards Act definition of "agriculture" to Board proceedings. In each of its monetary appropriations for Board operations since 1947, Congress specifies that no funds are to be used for proceedings relating to agricultural workers as defined in the FLSA. *North Whittier* deals with the question of coverage of agricultural packinghouse employees under the Act.

The last point in this section covers the supervisor exemption of Sec. 2(3). The test to be applied in determining whether an employee is a supervisor is specified in Sec. 2(11), which says, "The term 'supervisor' means any individual having authority, in the interest of the employer, to hire, transfer, suspend, lay off, recall, promote, discharge, assign, reward, or discipline other employees, or responsibly to direct them, or to adjust their grievances, *or effectively to recommend such action,* if in connection with the foregoing the exercise of such authority is not of a merely routine or clerical nature, but requires the use of independent judgment." [Authors' italics.] The italicized phrase should be observed in that its effect will be to broaden the base of those falling into supervisory categories.

Sec. 14 of the Act must also be referred to in securing the complete implication of the Sec. 2(3) exemption. Sec. 14 states "Nothing herein shall prohibit any individual employed as a supervisor from becoming or remaining a member of a labor organization, *but no employer subject to this Act shall be compelled to deem individuals defined herein as supervisors as employees for the purpose of any law, either national or local, relating to collective bargaining.* [Authors' italics.] As can be seen, the italicized phrase relieves the employer from the legal obligation of collectively bargaining in good faith with supervisors or from abstaining from other unfair labor practices in their direction.[10] While supervisors can form and join unions, conduct strikes, and exert legal combined pressure on the employer, the employer is not compelled by law to recognize or bargain with supervisors, for they are no longer considered to be employees. Congressional thinking in the supervisor sections of the amended Act hinges on the idea that supervisors are management representatives and, as such, should not be encouraged to divide their loyalties.

National Labor Relations Board v. Phoenix Mutual Life Insurance Co.

Circuit Court of Appeals, Seventh Circuit, 1948. 167 F.(2d) 983

DUFFY, D. J. The National Labor Relations Board petitions this Court pursuant to Section 10(e) of the National Labor Relations Act (49 Stat. 450. Sec. 1, *et seq.;* 29 U.S.C., Sec. 151, *et seq.*) for enforcement of its order of June

---

[10] An employer may not discriminate against supervisors if his action causes nonsupervisory workers to fear retaliation for exercising their rights of self-organization. In such event, the Board has directed that the discharged supervisor be reinstated to his job with reimbursement of lost wages. *Better Monkey Grip Company,* 115 NLRB 1170.

6, 1947, based upon findings that the respondent, in discharging employees Davis and Johnson, engaged in unfair labor practices affecting commerce in violation of Section 8(1) of the Act. The Board found that respondent had interfered with, restrained, and coerced its employees in their rights guaranteed under Section 7 because they had engaged in concerted activity for their mutual aid or protection. The Board ordered respondent to cease and desist from the unfair labor practice so found and to reinstate Messrs. Davis and Johnson with back pay and to post appropriate notices of compliance.

Section 8(1) of the Act provides:

"It shall be an unfair labor practice for an employer—

"(1) To interfere with, restrain, or coerce employees in the exercise of the rights guaranteed in Section 7. . . ."

Section 7 provides:

"Employees shall have the right to self-organization, to form, join, or assist labor organizations, to bargain collectively through representatives of their own choosing, and to engage in concerted activities, for the purpose of collective bargaining or other mutual aid or protection."

The issues to be here decided are: (1) Is the National Labor Relations Act applicable to respondent's operations? (2) Were salesmen Davis and Johnson employees of respondent or independent contractors? (3) Is the Board's finding that Davis and Johnson were discharged by respondent because they engaged in concerted activities for their mutual aid or protection supported by substantial evidence, and if so did respondent's actions amount to an unfair labor practice under the Act? and (4) Was the Board's order valid and proper?

Respondent, a Connecticut corporation, is a mutual life insurance company whose business is selling and issuing life insurance policies and annuities. On the basis of total insurance in force it ranks 24th among all insurance companies in the United States. It conducts business in 33 states and in the District of Columbia. Of its two branch offices in Chicago, the one known as the Chicago-LaSalle Office is involved in this proceeding. On December 31, 1945, respondent had in force insurance amounting to the total of $814,-789,831, and its total assets amounted to $386,044,844.

There can be no doubt as to the Act's application to the business of respondent. *Polish National Alliance* v. *National Labor Relations Board,* 322 U. S. 643. . . .

Respondent strongly urges that its salesmen are not employees within the meaning of the Act and argues that Davis and Johnson were independent contractors to whom the protection of the Act may not properly be extended.

The Act does not contain a precise definition of the term "employee." As amended in 1947 by the Taft-Hartley Law (Public Law No. 101, 80th Cong., 1st Sess., Chap. 120), the Act provides that the term "employee" shall not include "any individual having the status of an independent contractor." Therefore, it was incumbent upon the Board in the first instance to determine whether the insurance salesmen involved were employees or independent contractors, and this Court likewise must determine that issue on the Board's petition for enforcement of its order.

A similar question was considered by this Court in *Williams* v. *United States,* 126 F.(2d) 129, 132, cert. den., 317 U.S. 655, where the rule was stated that each case must depend upon its own facts, and that the test most *usually* employed for determining the distinction between an independent contractor and an employee is found in the nature and the amount of control reserved by the person for whom the work is done. This Court there pointed out that the employer-employee relationship exists when the person for whom the work is done has the right to control and direct the work, not only as to the result accomplished by the work, but also as to the details and means by which that result is accomplished, and that it is the right and not the exercise of control which is the determining element. A number of tests were pointed out, such as the right to hire and discharge persons doing the work, the method and determination of the amount of the payment to the workmen, whether the person doing the work is engaged in an independent business or enterprise, whether he stands to make a profit on the work of those working under him, the question of which party furnishes the tools or materials with which the work is done, and who has control of the premises where the work is done. In addition to the tests there mentioned, consideration must be given to other factors, such as whether the relationship is of a permanent character, the skill required in the particular occupation, and who designates the place where the work is to be performed.

In the case at bar the respondent provides headquarters for its salesmen and furnishes each of them with office space, a desk, a telephone, stenographic service, stationery, postage, filing cabinets, sales supplies, and business cards. It also pays for the indemnity bonds and license fees which the State of Illinois requires of each insurance agent. Each salesman is required to devote his full time to respondent's business and may not assign his contract, nor employ anyone to work under him. Respondent requires each salesman to produce a specified minimum of new business each year, and if he fails to do so he is subject to discharge. The salesmen are engaged in soliciting life and endowment insurance within an assigned territory and usually collect the first premium. Respondent selects its agents from among those persons who make written applications for these positions, and after having a personal interview. To be selected as an insurance salesman, it is not necessary for the applicants to have previous experience at selling insurance. After an applicant is selected and after signing an agency contract, each is given an intensive training by respondent's supervisory staff. He spends the first two weeks of his employment in respondent's offices receiving instructions from the office manager and other supervisory personnel, and is taught the use of the company's various forms and records, and initiated in the sales approach. After completing this training period the salesmen are permitted to take field trips. During their first interviews they usually are accompanied by respondent's office manager or other supervisor, but as they gain experience they are subjected to less field supervision. During the first two years of their service they are known as junior salesmen and as such may operate under a financing contract rather than a regular commission contract. Under such a contract the salesmen may borrow $100.00 up to as much as $300.00 a month. These loans are in the nature of advances on commissions which the salesman is expected to earn. After they become senior salesmen they no longer are entitled to borrow under a financing contract but receive other benefits or inducements which encourage them to remain permanently with the respondent.

The evidence before the Board discloses that respondent keeps a close check on the details of its salesmen's work and exercises a large measure of control over them. Each salesman must furnish management regularly with an accurate daily record of interviews and sales, must show for each day of the week the number of hours worked in the field, the number of interviews had, the number of new prospects interviewed and many other similar details. Respondent furnishes each salesman with certain sales services, such as circularizing by mail, without cost to the salesman, and supplying the salesman with advertising specialties and miscellaneous material.

It is also persuasive evidence of the salesmen's status as employees that respondent maintains a plan for the retirement and pensioning of its salesmen. This retirement and pension plan is noncontributory, although they do have the privilege of increasing their retirement income through voluntary participation. Respondent has also made available for its salesmen special pensions providing income for total and permanent disability.

Respondent regarded its salesmen as being in a somewhat different class than ordinary insurance salesmen. In its pamphlet, "Selecting Salesmen," it said:

". . . It (respondent) then decided to take the most forward steps known to Life Insurance. These involved the cancellation of all part-time contracts and the employment thereafter of only representatives who would devote their full business time to the Phoenix . . . the Phoenix is still the only company on the American continent which employs a small, compact, and exclusively full-time sales representation."

In another pamphlet it referred to the fact that the hiring of salesmen had been put upon a scientific basis.

It is thus apparent from the undisputed facts before the Board that respondent's salesmen, by all applicable recognized standards, fall into the class of employees rather than independent contractors, and we so hold. . . .

CASE QUESTIONS

1. What legal relation does the Phoenix Company contend is applicable to Davis and Johnson?
2. What test does the *Williams* case lay down in distinguishing between independent contractors and employees?
3. Indicate the elements in the case which show that the insurance salesmen were employees.
4. Distinguish contractors as employer agents from using contractors for employees.

North Whittier Heights Citrus Ass'n. v. National Labor Relations Board

Circuit Court of Appeals, Ninth Circuit, 1940. 109 F.2d 76

STEPHENS, C. J. Charges by the Citrus Packing House Workers Union Local No. 21,091, were laid before the National Labor Relations Board, that North Whittier Heights Citrus Association was guilty of unfair practices by interfering with, restraining and coercing twenty-eight employees in the exercise of the rights guaranteed under Section 7 of the National Labor Relations Act. . . . At the opening of the hearing the Association filed its motion to dismiss the proceedings upon the ground that its employees were agricultural laborers and therefore exempt from the Board's jurisdiction, and that its operations do not directly burden or affect interstate or foreign commerce. . . .

There is competent and substantial evidence to support the following factual account of the proceeding. Petitioner is a corporate body . . . engaged in the business of receiving, handling, washing, grading, assembling, packing and shipping the citrus fruit of its members and others for marketing under a marketing contract with the Semi-Tropic Fruit Exchange, which has a marketing agreement with the California Fruit Growers Exchange. . . .

We shall proceed to consider whether or not those employed in petitioner's packing house are "agricultural laborers" and as such exempt under the Act from the Board's jurisdiction.

The pursuit of definitions of "agricultural laborers" through the cases leads to confusion because generally the case definitions have grown out of special statutory phraseology or out of judicial effort to conform to legislative intent. While it is quite impossible to phrase an all inclusive yet accurate definition of the term "agricultural laborer" as it is used in the Wagner Act, the intent of Congress is not at all obscure. . . .

In Section 2, subdivision (3), of the Act it is provided that unless the Act explicitly states otherwise, the term "employee" shall include "any individual whose work has ceased as a consequence of, or in connection with, any current labor dispute or because of any unfair labor practice, . . . but shall not include any individual employed as an agricultural laborer, or in the domestic service of any family or person at his home, or any individual employed by his parent or spouse."

The purpose of the Act is clear and we find the Act specifically excepting three kinds of employees from its provisions. It would seem profitable to consider whether or not there is a "common denominator" in these three exemptions. We think there is. Why is "any individual employed by his parent or spouse" exempted? Because (not excluding other reasons) in this classification there never would be a great number suffering under the difficulty of negotiating with the actual employer and there would be no need for collective bargaining and conditions leading to strikes would not obtain. The same holds good as to "domestic service," and the same holds good as to "agricultural laborer" if the term be not enlarged beyond the usual idea that the term suggests. Enlarge the meaning of any of these terms beyond their common usage and confusion results. When every detail of farming from plowing to delivering the produce to the consumer was done by the farmer and his "hired man," this common denominator was present. But when in the transition of citrus fruit growing from this independent action to the great industry of the present in which the fruit is passed from the individual grower through contract to a corporation for treatment in a packing house owned and run by such corporation, to be delivered by this corporation to an allied corporation for transportation and market, we think the common denominator has ceased to exist. The fact that these corporations are allied through their membership of growers does not, in our opinion, affect the situation under consideration. See *Pinnacle Packing Company et al* v. *State Unemployment Commission,* decided February 19, 1937, by the Circuit Court of Jackson County, Oregon.

Petitioner in his brief points to these important changes and concludes, "It therefore becomes important to devise some test or touchstone to determine whether certain practices are agricultural or industrial." It can hardly be contended that agriculture and industry are opposites generically speaking. Agriculture is a great industry. So, of course, petitioner has used these terms in their more limited meanings, and has perhaps unwittingly discovered his sought after "touchstone."

Industrial activity commonly means the treatment or processing of raw products in factories. When the product of the soil leaves the farmer, as such, and enters a factory for processing and marketing it has entered upon the status of "industry." . . . There would seem to be as much need for the remedial provisions of the Wagner Act, upon principle, as for any other industrial activity.

Petitioner maintains that the nature of the work is the true test. Perhaps it would more nearly conform to the true test to say that the nature of the work modified by the custom of doing it determines whether the worker is or is not an agricultural laborer.

Petitioner argues that if each member of the non-profit cooperative corporation that runs the packing house were to personally hire and direct those doing his own packing and sorting, the work would be agricultural and his employees would be agricultural laborers; that it follows, therefore, that in the case of the same members acting under a single organization to accomplish the same result there can be no change in the nature of the work nor in the status of the persons doing it. The conclusion does not follow. The factual change in the manner of accomplishing the same work is exactly what does change the status of those doing it. The premise laid down by petitioner in this phase of its argument is not, however, the exact situation facing us. The packing house activity is much more than the mere treatment of the fruit. When it reaches the packing house it is then in the practical control of a great selling organization which accounts to the individual farmer under the terms of the statute law and its own by-laws. . . .

. . . The facts show that the work done by the packing house is in every sense specialized factory work applied to fruit that has left the orchard. The major part of the fruit is moved directly by the packing house workers, through the agency of two allied corporations, into the rail cars for prompt movement in interstate trade. Most certainly any considerable interference in such work would affect the free flow of interstate commerce. . . .

Petitioner is denied relief, and the order of the Board is ordered enforced.

CASE QUESTIONS

1. State the business activities carried on by petitioner.
2. What defenses does it interpose?
3. What is the "common denominator" to which the court refers?

4. When do products of the soil enter upon the status of industry?

SECTION 28 / JURISDICTION: COVERAGE OF UNIONS AND LABOR DISPUTES

The definition of a labor organization under the National Labor Relations Act covers informal as well as definitive employee representation plans. Provided that they exist "in whole or in part, for the purpose of dealing with employers concerning grievances, labor disputes, wages, rates of pay, hours of employment or conditions of work," [11] collective efforts of employees are covered by the unfair labor practice provisions.

The Labor-Management Reporting and Disclosure Act of 1959 defines labor organizations more broadly by also including "any conference, general committee, joint or system board or joint council so engaged which is subordinate to a national or international labor organization, other than a State or local central body." [Sec. 3(i).]

In one NLRB decision, some employee committees whose function was to discuss with management matters of mutual interest, including grievances, seniority, and working conditions, were found to be labor organizations although expressly precluded from negotiating bilateral agreements. The employer's denial that these committees came within the definition or the coverage of the Act was rejected by the Board and, on appeal, by the Supreme Court. The court held that the phrase "dealing with" in the definition of labor organization is a broader term than "collective bargaining," and that committees which deal with management on employees' grievances or working conditions are covered even though not attempting "to negotiate any formal bargaining contract" with the company.[12]

In another situation, however, where the NLRB certified one individual as bargaining representative and this later stopped a union from gaining recognition, a court on appeal reversed the Board on the ground that an individual was not covered by the definition of "labor organization" . . . "in any literal sense." [13]

The concept of labor dispute is fully discussed in Chapter 2 in relation to the injunction. The statutory definition of the term is similar as defined in the Norris-LaGuardia Anti-Injunction Act, the National Labor Relations Act and in the 1959 Disclosure and Reporting Act. It should be kept in mind that this definition would cover most situations involving stoppages, but it is much broader and comprehends a great deal more than a simple strike or stoppage. Conversely, in the absence of an unfair labor practice, a work stoppage or a union refusal to provide a labor force is not necessarily covered by the National Labor Relations Act.

Courts have held that the existence of a labor dispute between an employer and employees or between labor organizations must be present in order to establish jurisdiction of the Board under certain provisions of the Act. As one example, the Board was reversed by the Fourth Circuit after reviewing an order that a

---

[11] See Sec. 2(5) of National Labor Relations Act.
[12] *NLRB* v. *Cabot Carbon Company,* 360 U.S. 203 (1959).
[13] *Bonnaz* v. *NLRB* 230 F.2d 47 (1956).

union cease and desist from refusing to work ships engaged in Cuban trade which the Board held to be a violation of Section 8(b)(4) prohibiting secondary boycotts. The Court found that political activity in the absence of a primary labor dispute was not subject to the Act. A dispute over representation rights or over terms of employment was essential to Board jurisdiction according to the Court although the NLRB disagreed.[14]

SECTION 29 / JURISDICTION: PREEMPTION

In the United States, we are subject to laws emanating from two distinct governments, state and federal. The division of power between the state and federal governments arises out of the nature of our federal system: the federal government has only those powers which are expressly or implicitly delegated to it by the Constitution of the United States; all other powers and rights are reserved to the respective states or to the people. The dualism in American government greatly complicates our legal system. Instead of having a single system, we have fifty-one separate systems, each with its own administrative agencies, court system, rules of procedure and substantive laws.

Article VI, Section 2, of the United States Constitution states that "This Constitution, and the Laws of the United States which shall be made in Pursuance thereof . . . shall be the supreme Law of the Land; and the Judges in every State shall be bound thereby, anything in the Constitution or Laws of any State to the Contrary notwithstanding." Thus, statutes passed under the authority of the United States Constitution are the supreme law of the land and take precedence over any state law. If a state law is in conflict with a federal law, the state law is invalid under the supremacy clause. We do have federal labor legislation in the form of the amended National Labor Relations Act with the National Labor Relations Board having primary jurisdiction to decide issues involved in labor disputes. Does this mean that all state laws and remedies in the area of labor relations affecting interstate commerce are preempted away from the states under the supremacy clause? The answer is no. In *Garner* v. *Teamsters Local 776*,[15] the U. S. Supreme Court held "[t]he National Labor Relations Act . . . leaves much to the states, though Congress has refrained from telling us how much. We must spell out from conflicting indications of Congressional will the area in which state action is still permissible."

The first inquiry in any case in which a claim of federal preemption is raised must be whether the conduct called into question may reasonably be asserted to be subject to National Labor Relations Board authority. The United States Supreme Court held in *San Diego Building Trade Council* v. *Garmon*,[16] a landmark decision in the area of preemption, that in the absence of an overriding state interest such as that involved in the maintenance of domestic peace, state courts must defer to the exclusive competence of the National Labor Relations Board in cases in which the activity that is subject matter of the litigation is arguably

---

[14] *NLRB* v. *I.L.A. and Local 1355,* 332 F.2d 992 (1964).
[15] 346 U.S. 485 (1953).
[16] 359 U.S. 236 (1959).

subject to the protections of § 7 or the prohibitions of § 8 of the National Labor Relations Act. This relinquishment of state jurisdiction, the *Garmon* court stated, is essential "if the danger of state interference with national policy is to be averted."

In *Garmon,* the Court certified an exception to its "arguably subject" rule by recognizing that state jurisdiction will prevail in situations marked by violence or threats to public order "because the compelling state interest in the scheme of our federalism, in the maintenance of domestic peace is not overridden in the absence of clearly expressed congressional direction."

In *Linn* v. *United Plant Guards Workers, Local 114,*[17] the Supreme Court sustained the jurisdiction of a state court to award damages in a civil action for libel instituted under state law by an official of an employer subject to the National Labor Relations Act. In allowing the state court action the Court said the state jurisdiction was a "merely peripheral concern of the Labor Management Relations Act." It also recognized that "an overriding state interest" was involved in protecting the state's residents from malicious libels. However, in *Letter Carriers* v. *Austin,*[18] the Supreme Court held that the state libel remedies for publication of a statement calling nonunion letter carriers "scabs" in a union newsletter during a continuing organizational drive by the Letter Carriers Union are preempted because the publication is protected under federal labor laws, the publication not being a reckless or knowing falsehood. The *Austin* decision clarified *Linn* pointing out that in *Linn* the Court found it appropriate to adopt by analogy the standards of *New York Times Co.* v. *Sullivan.*[19] Accordingly, the Court held that libel actions under state law were preempted by the federal labor laws to the extent that the State sought to make actionable defamatory statements in labor disputes which were published without knowledge of their falsity or reckless disregard for the truth.

In *Vaca* v. *Sipes,*[20] the Supreme Court carved out a further exception to the *Garmon* preemption doctrine for cases involving breach of union's duty of fair representation. In *Vaca,* a union member's recovery of damages in a state court for the union's refusal to take his grievance to arbitration was sustained by the Court. This case is analyzed in the *Lockridge* decision which follows.

In *Retail Clerks* v. *Schermerhorn,*[21] the Supreme Court upheld the right of a state to enforce its "right-to-work" law, prohibiting the union or agency shop, under section 14(b) of the NLRA. The Court said: "Since it is plain that Congress left the States free to legislate in that field, we can only assume that it intended to leave unaffected the power to enforce those laws."

In the *Lockridge* decision reported in this section, the Supreme Court set out a full explanation of labor relations preemption principles, and denotes the boundaries for the utilization of the Section 301 exception to the preemption doctrine. The *Machinist* v. *Gonzales*[22] case is a further exception to the preemption doctrine. It is extensively analyzed in *Lockridge.*

---

[17] 383 U.S. 53 (1966).
[18] 86 LRRM 2740 (1974).
[19] 376 U.S. 254 (1964).
[20] 386 U.S. 171 (1967).
[21] 375 U.S. 96 (1963).
[22] 356 U.S. 236 (1958).

Motor Coach Employees v. Lockridge

Supreme Court of the United States, 1971. 403 U. S. 274

HARLAN, J.: *San Diego Building Trades Council* v. *Garmon,* 359 U.S. 236 (1959), established the general principle that the National Labor Relations Act preempts state and federal court jurisdiction to remedy conduct that is arguably protected or prohibited by the Act. That decision represents the watershed in this Court's continuing effort to mark the extent to which the maintenance of a general federal law of labor relations combined with a centralized administrative agency to implement its provisions necessarily supplants the operation of the more traditional legal processes in this field. We granted certiorari in this case, 397 U.S. 1006 (1970), because the divided decision of the Idaho Supreme Court demonstrated the need for this Court to provide a fuller explication of the premises upon which *Garmon* rests and to consider the extent to which that decision must be taken to have modified or superseded this Court's earlier efforts to treat with the knotty preemption problem.

Respondent, Wilson P. Lockridge, has obtained in the Idaho courts a judgment for $32,678.56 against petitioners, Northwest Division 1055 of the Amalgamated Association of Street, Electric Railway and Motor Coach Employees of America and its parent international association, on the grounds that, in procuring Lockridge's discharge from employment, pursuant to a valid union security clause in the applicable collective bargaining agreement, the Union breached a contractual obligation embodied in the Union's constitution and bylaws. . . .

. . . No charges were filed before the National Labor Relations Board. Instead, Lockridge filed suit in September 1960 in the Idaho State District Court against the Union and Greyhound, which was later dropped as a party. That court, on the Union's motion, dismissed the complaint in April 1961 on the grounds that it charged the Union with the commission of an unfair labor practice and consequently fell within the exclusive jurisdiction of the NLRB. A year later, the Idaho Supreme Court reversed, holding that the state courts had jurisdiction under this Court's decision in *Association of Machinists* v. *Gonzales,* 356 U.S. 617 (1958), and remanded for trial on the merits. *Lockridge* v. *Amalgamated Assn. of St. El. Ry. & M. C. Emp.,* 84 Idaho 201, 369 P.2d 1006 (1962).

In 1965 Lockridge filed a second amended complaint which has since served as the basis for this lawsuit. Its first count alleged that

"in suspending plaintiff from membership in the [Union] which resulted in plaintiff's loss of employment, the [Union] . . . acted wantonly, wilfully and wrongfully and without just cause, and . . . deprived plaintiff of his . . . employment with Greyhound Corporation that accrued to him and would accrue to him by reason of his employment, seniority and experience, and plaintiff has been harassed and subject to mental anguish. . . ." App., 46–47.

Count Two, sounding squarely in contract, alleged that

"in wrongfully suspending plaintiff from membership in the [Union], which resulted in plaintiff's discharge from employment with the Greyhound Corporation, the [Union] . . . acted wrongfully, wantonly, wilfully and maliciously and without just cause and violated the constitution and general laws of the [Union] which constituted a contract between the plaintiff as a member thereof and the [Union], and as a result of said breach of contract plaintiff has been deprived of his . . . employment with . . . Greyhound Corporation . . . and plaintiff has been embarrassed and subjected to mental anguish . . ." App., 48.

The complaint sought damages in the amount of $212,000 "and such other and further relief as to the court may appear meet and equitable in the premises." *Ibid.*

After trial, the Idaho District Court found the facts as stated above and held that they did, indeed, amount to a breach of contract. The court felt itself bound by the prior determination of the Idaho Supreme Court to consider that it might properly exercise jurisdiction over the controversy and to "decide [the] case on the theories of" *Machinists* v. *Gonzales, supra.* Consequently, the trial judge concluded that Lockridge was entitled to a decree restoring him to membership in the Union, "although plaintiff has never sought such a remedy." Lockridge was also awarded $32,678.56 as compensation for wages actually lost due to his dismissal from Greyhound's employ, but his requests for future damages arising from continued loss of employment, compensation for loss of seniority or fringe benefits, and punitive damages were all denied. On appeal the Idaho Supreme Court affirmed, over one dissenting vote, except that it also ordered restoration of respondent's seniority rights. 93 Idaho 294, 460 P.2d 719 (1969). Having granted certiorari for the reasons stated at the outset of this opinion, we now reverse.

On the surface, this might appear to be a routine and simple case. Section 8(b)(2) of the National Labor Relations Act makes it an unfair labor practice for a union

"to cause or attempt to cause an employer to discriminate against an employee in violation of subsection (a)(3) . . . or to discriminate against an employee with respect to whom membership in such organization has been denied or terminated on some ground other than his failure to tender the periodic dues and the initiation fees uniformly required as a condition of acquiring or retaining membership."

Section 8(b)(1)(A) makes it an unfair labor practice for a union "to restrain or coerce . . . employees in the exercise of the right guaranteed in section 7," which includes the right not only "to form, join or assist labor organizations" but also "the right to refrain from any or all of such activities except to the extent that such right may be affected by an agreement requiring membership in a labor organization as a condition of employment as authorized in section 8(a)(3)." Section 8(a)(3) makes it an unfair labor practice for an employer

"by discrimination in regard to hire or tenure of employment . . . to encourage or discourage membership in any labor organization: *Provided,* That nothing in this Act . . . shall preclude an employer from making an agreement with a labor organization . . . to require as a condition of employment membership therein on or after the thirtieth day following the beginning of such employment or the effective date of such agreement, whichever is the later. . . : *Provided* further, That no employer shall justify any discrimination against an employee for nonmembership in a labor organization . . . if he has reasonable grounds for believing that membership was denied or terminated for reasons other than the failure of the employee to tender the periodic dues and the initiation fees uniformly required as a condition of acquiring or retaining membership. . . ."

Further, in *San Diego Building Trades Council* v. *Garmon,* 359 U.S. 236, 245 (1959), we held that the National Labor Relations Act preempts the jurisdiction of state and federal courts to regulate conduct "arguably subject to § 7 or § 8 of the Act." On their face, the above-quoted provisions of the Act at least arguably either permit or forbid the union conduct dealt with by the judgment below. For the evident thrust of this aspect of the federal statutory scheme is to permit the enforcement of union security clauses, by dismissal from employment, only for failure to pay dues. Whatever other sanctions may be employed to exact compliance with those internal union rules unrelated to dues payment, the Act seems generally to exclude dismissal from employment. See *Radio Officers' Union* v. *National Labor Relations Bd.,* 347 U.S. 17 (1954). Indeed, in the course of rejecting petitioner's preemption argument, the Idaho Supreme Court stated that, in its opinion, the Union "did most certainly violate 8(b)(1)(A), did most certainly violate 8(b)(2) . . . and probably caused the employer to violate 8(a)(3)." 93 Idaho, at __, 460 P.2d at 724. Thus, given the broad preemption principle enunciated in *Garmon,* the want of state court power to resolve Lockridge's complaint might well seem to follow as a matter of course. . . .

The constitutional principles of preemption, in whatever particular field of law they operate, are designed with a common end in view: to avoid conflicting regulation of conduct by various official bodies which might have some authority over the subject matter. A full understanding of the particular preemption rule set forth in *Garmon* especially requires, we think, appreciation of the precise nature and extent of the potential for injurious conflict that would inhere in a system unaffected by such a doctrine, and also the setting in which the general problem of accommodating conflicting claims of competence to resolve disputes touching upon labor relations has been presented to this Court.

The course of events that eventuated in the enactment of a comprehensive national labor law, entrusted for its administration and development to a centralized, expert agency, as well as the very fact of that enactment itself, reveals that a primary factor in this development was the perceived incapacity of common-law courts and state legislatures, acting alone, to provide an informed and coherent basis for stabilizing labor relations conflict and for equitably and delicately structuring the balance of power among competing forces so as to further the common good. The principle of preemption that informs our general national labor law was born of this Court's efforts, without the aid of explicit congressional guidance, to delimit state and federal judicial authority over labor disputes in order to preclude, so far as reasonably possible, conflict between the exertion of judicial and administrative power in the attainment of the multifaceted policies underlying the federal scheme.

As it appears to us, nothing could serve more fully to defeat the congressional goals underlying the Act than to subject, without limitation, the relationships it seeks to create to the concurrent jurisdiction of state and federal courts free to apply the general local law. Nor would an approach suffice that sought merely to avoid disparity in the content of proscriptive behavioral rules. As the Court observed in *Garner* v. *Teamsters Local Union,* 346 U.S. 485, 490–491 (1953), Congress in establishing overriding federal supervision of labor law

> "did not merely lay down a substantive rule of law to be enforced by any tribunal competent to apply law generally to the parties. It went on to confide primary interpretation and application of its rules to a specific and specially constituted tribunal and prescribed a particular procedure for investigation, complaint and notice, and hearing and decision. . . . Congress evidently determined that centralized administration of specially designed procedures was necessary to obtain uniform application of its substantive rules and to avoid these diversities and conflicts likely to result from a variety of local procedures and attitudes toward labor controversies. . . . A multiplicity of tribunals and a diversity of procedures are quite as apt to produce incompatible or conflicting adjudications as are different rules of substantive law."

Conflict in technique can be fully as disruptive to the system Congress erected as conflict in overt policy. As the passage from *Garner* indicates, in matters of dispute concerning labor relations a simple recitation of the formally prescribed rights and duties of the parties constitutes an inadequate description of the actual process for settlement Congress has provided. The technique of administration and the range and nature of those remedies that are and are not available is a fundamental part and parcel of the operative legal system established by the National Labor Relations Act. "Administration is more than a means of regulation; administration is regulation. We have been concerned with conflict in its broadest sense; conflict with a complex and interrelated federal scheme of law, remedy, and administration." *Garmon,* 359 U.S., at 243.

The rationale for preemption, then, rests in large measure upon our determination that when it set down a federal labor policy Congress plainly meant to do more than simply to alter the then prevailing substantive law. It sought as well to restructure fundamentally the processes for effectuating that policy, deliberately placing the responsibility for applying and developing this comprehensive legal system in the hands of an expert administrative body rather than the federalized judicial system. Thus, that a local court, while adjudicating a labor dispute also within the jurisdiction of the NLRB, may purport to apply legal rules identical to those prescribed in the federal Act or may eschew the authority to define or apply principles specifically developed to regulate labor relations does not mean that all relevant potential for debilitating conflict is absent.

A second factor that has played an important role in our shaping of the preemption doctrine has been the necessity to act without specific congressional direction. The precise extent to which state law must be displaced to achieve those unifying ends sought by the national legislature has never been determined by the Congress. This has, quite frankly, left the Court with few available options. We cannot declare preempted all local regulation that touches or concerns in any way the complex interrelationships between employees, employers, and unions; obviously, much of this is left to the States. Nor can we proceed on a case-by-case basis to determine whether each particular final judicial pronouncement does, or might reasonably be thought to, conflict in some relevant manner with federal labor policy. This Court is ill-equipped to play such a role and the federal system dictates that this problem be solved with a rule capable of relatively easy application, so that lower courts may largely police themselves in this regard. Equally important, such a principle would fail to take account of the fact, as discussed above, that simple congruity of legal rules does not, in this area, prove the absence of untenable conflict. Further, it is surely not possible for this Court to treat the National Labor Relations Act section by section, committing enforcement of some of its provisions wholly to the NLRB and others to the concurrent domain of local law. Nothing in the language or underlying purposes of the Act suggests any basis for such distinctions. Finally, treating differently judicial power to deal with conduct protected by the Act from that prohibited by it would likewise be unsatisfactory. Both areas equally involve conduct whose legality is governed by federal law, the application of which Congress committed to the Board, not courts. . . .

The failure of alternative analyses and the interplay of the foregoing policy considerations, then, led this Court to hold in *Garmon,* 359 U.S., at 244:

> "When it is clear or may fairly be assumed that the activities which a State purports to regulate are protected by § 7 of the National Labor Relations Act, or constitute an unfair labor practice under § 8, due regard for the federal enactment requires that state jurisdiction must yield. To leave the States free to regulate conduct so plainly within the central aim of federal regulation involves too great a danger of conflict between power asserted by Congress and requirements imposed by state law."

Upon these premises, we think that *Garmon* rather clearly dictates reversal of the judgment below. None of the propositions asserted to support that judgment can withstand an application, in light of those factors that compelled its promulgation, of the *Garmon* rule.

Assuredly the proposition that Lockridge's complaint was not subject to the exclusive jurisdiction of the NLRB because it charged a breach of contract rather than an unfair labor practice is not tenable. Preemption, as shown above, is designed to shield the system from conflicting regulation of conduct. It is the conduct being regulated, not the formal description of governing legal standards, that is the proper focus of concern. Indeed, the notion that a relevant distinction exists for such purposes between particularized and generalized labor law was explicitly rejected in *Garmon* itself. 359 U.S., at 244.

The second argument, closely related to the first, is that the state courts, in resolving this controversy, did deal with different conduct, *i.e.,* interpretation of contractual terms, than would the NLRB which would be required to decide whether the Union discriminated against Lockridge. At bottom, of course, the Union's action in procuring Lockridge's dismissal from employment is the conduct which Idaho courts have sought to regulate. Thus, this second point demonstrates at best that Idaho defines differently what sorts of such union conduct may permissibly be proscribed. This is to say either that the regulatory schemes, state and federal, conflict (in which case preemption is clearly called for) or that Idaho is dealing with conduct to which the federal

Act does not speak. If the latter assertion was intended, it is not accurate. As pointed out, . . . the relevant portions of the Act operate to prohibit a union from causing or attempting to cause an employer to discriminate against an employee because his membership in the union has been terminated "on some ground other than" his failure to pay those dues requisite to membership. This has led the Board routinely and frequently to inquire into the proper construction of union regulations in order to ascertain whether the union properly found an employee to have been derelict in his dues-paying responsibilities, where his discharge was procured on the asserted grounds of nonmembership in the union. . . . That a union may in good faith have misconstrued its own rules has not been treated by the Board as a defense to a claimed violation of § 8(b)(2). In the Board's view, it is the fact of misapplication by a union of its rules, not the motivation for that discrimination, that constitutes an unfair labor practice. . . .

From the foregoing, then, it would seem that this case indeed represents one of the clearest instances where the *Garmon* principle, properly understood, should operate to oust state court jurisdiction. There being no doubt that the conduct here involved was arguably protected by § 7 or prohibited by § 8 of the Act, the full range of very substantial interests the preemption doctrine seeks to protect are directly implicated here.

However, a final strand of analysis underlies the opinion of the Idaho Supreme Court, and the position of respondent, in this case. Our decision in *Association of Machinists* v. *Gonzales,* 356 U.S. 617 (1958), it is argued, fully survived the subsequent reorientation of preemption doctrine effected by the *Garmon* decision, providing, in effect, an express exception for the exercise of judicial jurisdiction in cases such as this.

The fact situation in *Gonzales* does resemble in some relevant regards that of the instant case. There the California courts had entertained a complaint by an individual union member claiming he had been expelled from his union in violation of rights conferred upon him by the union's constitution and bylaws, which allegedly constituted a contract between him and his union. Gonzales prevailed on his breach of contract theory and was awarded damages for wages lost due to the revocation of membership as well as a decree providing for his reinstatement in the union. This Court confirmed the California courts' power to award the monetary damages, the only aspect of the action below challenged in this Court. The primary rationale for the result reached was that California should be competent to "fill out," 356 U.S., at 620, the reinstatement remedy by utilizing "the comprehensive relief of equity," *id.,* at 621, which the Board did not fully possess. Secondarily, it was said that the lawsuit "did not purport to remedy or regulate union conduct on the ground that it was designed to bring about employer discrimination against an employee, the evil the Board is concerned to strike at as an unfair labor practice under § 8(b)(2)." *Id.,* at 622.

Although it was decided only one Term subsequent to *Gonzales, Garmon* clearly did not fully embrace the technique of the prior case. It was precisely the realization that disparities in remedies and administration could produce substantial conflict, in the practical sense of the term, between the relevant state and federal regulatory schemes and that this Court could not effectively and responsibly superintend on a case-by-case basis the exertion of state power over matters arguably governed by the National Labor Relations Act that impelled the somewhat broader formulation of the preemption doctrine in *Garmon.* It seems evident that the full-blown rationale of *Gonzales* could not survive the rule of *Garmon.* Nevertheless, *Garmon* did not cast doubt upon the result reached in *Gonzales,* but cited it approvingly as an example of the fact that state court jurisdiction is not preempted "where the activity regulated was a merely peripheral concern of the . . . Act." 359 U.S. at 243.

Against this background, we attempted to define more precisely the reach of *Gonzales* within the more comprehensive framework *Garmon* provided in the companion cases of *Plumbers Union* v. *Borden,* 373 U.S. 690 (1963), and *Iron Workers* v. *Perko,* 373 U.S. 701 (1963). . . .

In sum, what distinguished *Gonzales* from *Borden* and *Perko* was that the former lawsuit "was focused on purely internal union matters," *Borden, supra,* at 697, a subject the National Labor Relations Act leaves principally to other processes of law. The possibility that, in defining the scope of the union's duty to Gonzales, the state courts would directly and consciously implicate principles of federal law was at best tangential and remote. In the instant case, however, this possibility was real and immediate. To assess the legality of his union's conduct toward Gonzales the California courts needed only to focus upon the union's constitution and by-laws. Here, however, Lorkridge's entire case turned upon the construction of the applicable union security clause, a matter as to which, as shown above, federal concern is pervasive and its regulation complex. The reasons for Gonzales' deprivation of union membership had nothing to do with matters of employment, while Lockridge's cause of action and claim for damages was based solely upon the procurement of his discharge from employment. It cannot plausibly be argued, in any meaningful sense, that Lockridge's lawsuit "was focused upon purely internal matters." Although nothing said in *Garmon* necessarily suggests that States cannot relate the general conditions which unions may impose on their membership, it surely makes crystal clear that *Gonzales* does not stand for the proposition that resolution of any union-member conflict is within state competence so long as one of the remedies provided is restoration of union membership. This much was settled by *Borden* and *Perko,* and it is only upon such an unwarrantably broad interpretation of *Gonzales* that the judgment below could be sustained.

The preemption doctrine we apply today is, like any other purposefully administered legal principle, not without exception. Those same considerations that underlie *Garmon* have led this Court to permit the exercise of judicial power over conduct arguably protected or prohibited by the Act where Congress has affirmatively indicated that such power should exist, *Smith* v. *Evening News,* 371 U.S. 195 (1962); *Teamsters* v. *Morton,* 377 U.S. 252 (1964), where this Court cannot, in spite of the force of the policies *Garmon* seeks to promote, conscientiously presume that Congress meant to intrude so deeply into areas traditionally left to local law, *e. g., Linn* v. *Plant Guard Workers,* 383 U.S. 53 (1966); *Automobile Workers* v. *Russell,* 356 U.S. 634 (1958), and where the particular rule of law sought to be invoked before another tribunal is so structured and administered that, in virtually all instances, it is safe to presume that judicial supervision will not disserve the interests promoted by the federal labor statutes, *Vaca* v. *Sipes,* 386 U.S. 171 (1967).

In his brief before this Court, respondent has argued for the first time since this lawsuit was started that two of these exceptions to the *Garmon* principle independently justify the Idaho courts' exercise of jurisdiction over this controversy. First, Lockridge contends that his action, properly viewed, is one to enforce a collective-bargaining agreement. Alternatively, he asserts the suit, in essence, was one to redress petitioner's breach of its duty of fair representation. As will be seen, these contentions are somewhat intertwined.

In § 301 of the Taft-Hartley Act, Congress authorized federal courts to exercise jurisdiction over suits brought to enforce collective bargaining agreements. We have held that such actions are judicially cognizable, even where the conduct alleged was arguably protected or prohibited by the National Labor Relations Act because the history of the enactment of § 301 reveals that "Congress deliberately chose to leave the enforcement of collective agreements 'to the usual processes of law.' " *Charles Dowd Box Co.* v. *Courtney,* 368 U.S. 502, 513 (1962). It is firmly established, further, that state courts retain concurrent jurisdiction to adjudicate such claims, *Charles Dowd Box Co., supra,* and that individual employees have standing to protect rights conferred upon them by such agreements, *Smith* v. *Evening News, supra; Humphrey* v. *Moore,* 375 U.S. 335 (1964).

Our cases also clearly establish that individual union members may sue their employers under § 301 for breach of a promise embedded in the collective bargaining agreement that was intended to confer a benefit upon the individual. *Smith* v. *Evening News, supra.* Plainly, however, this is not such a lawsuit. Lockridge specifically dropped Greyhound as a named party from his initial complaint and has never reasserted a right to redress from his former employer.

This Court has further held in *Humphrey* v. *Moore,* 375 U.S. 335 (1964), that § 301 will support, regardless of otherwise applicable preemption considerations, a suit in the state courts by a union member against his union that seeks to redress union interference with rights conferred on individual employees by the employer's promises in the collective-bargaining agreement, where it is proved that such interference constituted a breach of the duty of fair representation. Indeed, in *Vaca* v. *Sipes,* 386 U.S. 171 (1967), we held that an action seeking damages for injury inflicted by a breach of a union's duty of fair representation was judicially cognizable in any event, that is, even if the conduct complained of was arguably protected or prohibited by the National Labor Relations Act and whether or not the lawsuit was bottomed on a collective agreement. Perhaps Count One of Lockridge's second amended complaint could be construed to assert either or both of these theories of recovery. However, it is unnecessary to pass upon the extent to which *Garmon* would be inapplicable if it were shown that in these circumstances petitioner not only breached its contractual obligations to respondent, but did so in a manner that constituted a breach of the duty of fair representation. For such a claim to be made out, Lockridge must have proved "arbitrary or bad faith conduct on the part of the union." *Vaca* v. *Sipes, supra,* at 193. There must be "substantial evidence of fraud, deceitful action or dishonest conduct."

Humphrey v. *Moore, supra,* at 348. Whether these requisite elements have been proved is a matter of federal law. Quite obviously, they were not even asserted to be relevant in the proceedings below. As the Idaho Supreme Court stated in affirming the verdict for Lockridge, "[t]his was a misinterpretation of a contract. Whatever the underlying motive for expulsion might have been, this case has been submitted and tried on the interpretation of the contract, not on a theory of discrimination." Thus, the trial judge's conclusion of law in sustaining Lockridge's claim specifically incorporates the assumption that the Union's "acts . . . were predicated solely upon the ground that [Lockridge] had failed to tender periodic dues in conformance with the requirements of the union Constitution and employment contract as they interpreted [it]. . . ." App., 66. Further, the trial court excluded as irrelevant petitioner's proffer of evidence designed to show that the Union's interpretation of the contract was reasonably based upon its understanding of prior collective bargaining agreements negotiated with Greyhound. Transcript of Trial, at 259–260.

Nor can it be fairly argued that our resolution or respondent's final contentions entails simply attaching variegated labels to matters of equal substance. We have exempted § 301 suits from the *Garmon* principle because of the evident congressional determination that courts should be free to interpret and enforce collective bargaining agreements even where that process may involve condemning or permitting conduct arguably subject to the protection or prohibition of the National Labor Relations Act. The legislative determination that courts are fully competent to resolve labor relations disputes through focusing on the terms of a collective bargaining agreement cannot be said to sweep within it the same conclusion with regard to the terms of union-employee contracts that are said to be implied in law. That is why the principle of *Smith* v. *Evening News* is applicable only to those disputes that are governed by the terms of the collective bargaining agreement itself.

Similarly, this Court's refusal to limit judicial competence to rectify a breach of the duty of fair representation rests upon our judgment that such actions cannot, in the vast majority of situations where they occur, give rise to actual conflict with the operative realities of federal labor policy. The duty of fair representation was judicially evolved, without the participation of the NLRB, to enforce fully the important principle that no individual union member may suffer invidious, hostile treatment at the hands of the majority of his coworkers. Where such union conduct is proved it is clear, beyond doubt, that the conduct could not be otherwise regulated by the substantive federal law. And the fact that the doctrine was originally developed and applied by courts, after passage of the Act, and carries with it the need to adduce substantial evidence of discrimination that is intentional, severe and unrelated to legitimate union objectives ensures that the risk of conflict with the general congressional policy favoring expert, centralized administration, and remedial action is tolerably slight. *Vaca* v. *Sipes, supra,* at 180–181. So viewed, the duty of fair representation, properly defined, operates to limit the scope of *Garmon* where the sheer logic of the preemption principle might otherwise cause it to be extended to a point where its operation might be unjust. *Vaca* v. *Sipes. supra,* at 182–183. If, however, the congressional policies

Garmon seeks to promote are not to be swallowed up, the very distinction, embedded within the instant lawsuit itself, between honest, mistaken conduct, on the one hand, and deliberate and severally hostile and irrational treatment, on the other, needs strictly to be maintained.

Finally, we deem it appropriate to discuss briefly two other considerations underlying the conclusion we have reached in this case. First, our decision must not be taken as expressing any views on the substantive claims of the two parties to this controversy. Indeed, our judgment is quite simply, that it is not the task of federal or state courts to make such determinations. Secondly, in our explication of the reasons for the *Garmon* rule, and the various exceptions to it, we noted that, although largely of judicial making, the labor relations preemption doctrine finds its basic justification in the presumed intent of Congress. While we do not assert that the *Garmon* doctrine is without imperfection, we do think that it is founded on reasoned principle and that until it is altered by congressional action or by judicial insights that are born of further experience with it, a heavy burden rests upon those who would, at this late date, ask this Court to abandon *Garmon* and set out again in quest of a system more nearly perfect. A fair regard for considerations of *stare decisis* and the coordinate role of the Congress in defining the extent to which federal legislation preempts state law strongly support our conclusion that the basic tenets of *Garmon* should not be disturbed.

For the reasons stated above, the judgment below is

Reversed.

[Mr. Justice White filed a dissenting opinion, in which Chief Justice Burger joined. This opinion argued that there were several cases in which the preemption doctrine had been subordinated to the interest of broader policies—for example, cases involving grievances subject to an arbitration clause. The dissenting Justices also contended that Congress sought to deal comprehensively with union member relations but has preserved state remedies and that invocation of *Garmon* was inappropriate when a union member brings suit against a union for breach of the union's constitution and bylaws.

Mr. Justice Blackman also dissented for the basic reasons set forth by Justices Douglas and White.]

Mr. Justice Douglas, dissenting: I would affirm this judgment on the basis of *Machinists* v. *Gonzales,* 356 U.S. 617 rather than overrule it. I would not extend *San Diego Building Trades Council* v. *Garmon,* 359 U.S. 236, so as to make Lockridge, the employee, seek his relief in faraway Washington, D. C., from the National Labor Relations Board.

When we hold that a grievance is "arguably" within the jurisdiction of the National Labor Relations Board and remit the individual employee to the Board for remedial relief, we impose a great hardship on him, especially where he is a lone individual not financed out of a lush treasury. I would allow respondent recourse to litigation in his home town tribunal and not require him to resort to an elusive remedy in distant and remote Washington, D. C., which takes money to reach.

He has six months within which to file an unfair labor practice charge with the Regional Director and serve it upon the other party. If he does not file within six months, the claim is barred. 29 U. S. C. § 160(b). The charge must be in writing and contain either a declaration that contents are true to best of his knowledge, or else a notarization. 29 CFR § 101.2. When the charge is received, it is filed, docketed, and given a number (29 CFR § 101.4) and assigned to a member of field staff for investigation. 29 CFR § 101.4.

Following the investigation, the Regional Director makes his decision. "If investigation reveals that there has been no violation of the National Labor Relations Act or the evidence is insufficient to substantiate the charge, the Regional Director recommends withdrawal of the charge by the person who filed." 29 CFR § 101.5. If the complaining party does not withdraw the charge, the Regional Director dismisses it. 29 CFR § 101.6. Following dismissal, the complainant has 10 days to appeal the decision to the General Counsel who reviews the decision. 29 CFR § 101.6. If the General Counsel holds against the complaining party and refuses to issue an unfair labor practice complaint, the decision is apparently unreviewable. Cox & Bok, Labor Law 138 (3d ed. 1969); *General Drivers Local 866* v. *NLRB,* 179 F.2d 492.

From the viewpoint of an aggrieved employee, there is not a trace of equity in this long-drawn, expensive remedy. If he musters the resources to exhaust the administrative remedy, the chances are that he too will be exhausted. If the General Counsel issues a complaint, then he stands in line for some time waiting for the Board's decision.[23] If the General Counsel refuses to act, then the employee is absolutely without remedy. . . .

CASE QUESTIONS

1. State the rule of the *Garmon* case.
2. What is the essence of Lockridge's amended complaint?
3. What is the fundamental design of constitutional principles of preemption?
4. What is the primary rationale for the *Garmon* preemption rule?
5. How did the court answer the plaintiff's contention that

---

[23] For the backlog of the Board see 34th Annual Report, CCH 1969. Table 1 shows the following number of Unfair Labor Practice cases:

Pending July 1, 1968	7,377
Received fiscal 1969	18,651
On docket fiscal 1969	26,028
Closed fiscal 1969	18,939
Pending June 30, 1969	7,089

Table 8 shows that the 18,939 Unfair Labor Practice cases in 1969 were as follows:

Before issuance of complaint	16,135
After issuance of complaint, before opening of hearing	1,251
After hearing opened, before issuance of Trial Examiner's decision	186
After Trial Examiner's decision, before issuance of Board decision	134
After Board order adopting Trial Examiner's decision in absence of exceptions...	131
After Board decision, before circuit court decree	606
After circuit court decree, before Supreme Court action	427
After Supreme Court action	69

Of the foregoing—
31% were dismissed before complaint.
24.9% were settled.
36% were withdrawn.
In only 5.7% did the Board issue orders. *Id.,* p. 4.

the complaint was not subject to the exclusive jurisdiction of the NLRB because it charged a breach of contract rather than an unfair labor practice?

6. Is the *Gonzales* decision, which was decided one term preceding *Garmon,* still good law?

SECTION 30 / **REMEDIAL POWERS**

Under Section 9 of the NLRA, the Board has authority to issue appropriate orders to remedy a broad range of violations concerning representation matters. These situations and their appropriate remedies will be presented in the succeeding chapter.

Remedies—Temporary and Final

Under Section 10(j) of the Act, the Board has the discretionary authority to seek injunctive relief in a federal district court in unfair labor practice cases. Section 10(j) remedies are ordinarily used against alleged employer unfair labor practices to preserve the status quo while the parties are awaiting the resolution of their basic dispute by the Board.[24] Section 10(1) *requires* the Board to seek temporary injunctive relief against unions in matters such as secondary boycotts, hot cargo agreements, recognitional picketing and jurisdictional disputes. Section 10(k) frees federal district courts from the restriction of the Norris-La Guardia Anti-Injunction Act in the above situations. It is important to remember that 10(j) and 10(1) injunctions are just temporary and can be utilized only while charges are being processed by the Board.

Under Section 10(a) the Board is given the broad responsibility "to prevent any person from engaging in any unfair labor practice." The Board has the authority under 10(b) to investigate charges, issue complaints and order hearings. Under 10(c) at a Board hearing, if upon the preponderance of the testimony taken by the Board it is determined that a person has or is engaging in an unfair labor practice, then the Board will state its findings of fact and issue an order requiring such a person to "cease and desist from such unfair labor practice, and take such affirmative action, including reinstatement of employees with or without back pay, as will effectuate the policies of this Act." If a person should choose not to comply with the Board's order, then the Board may petition an appropriate U. S. court of appeals for enforcement of its order under Section 10(e). Similarly, any person aggrieved by an order of the Board may file a petition for review of the order with the court of appeals without waiting for the Board to seek enforcement.

A complete treatment of all remedy possibilities is beyond the scope of this section. Orders against employer unfair labor practices are tailored to rectify the varied and sometimes unique misconduct of individual cases. The number of possibilities is great. Additional development of the Board's remedial options is left to Chapter 6, Employer Unfair Labor Practices.

---

[24] See *McLeod* v. *General Electric Co.,* 366 F.2d 847 (1966).

Selected Board Orders

In the *Phelps Dodge* case, reported in this section, the U. S. Supreme Court held that the Board has the power under Section 10(c) of the NLRA to order an employer to make whole any employees who have suffered loss of earnings because of the employer's discrimination in violation of Section 8(a)(3) of the Act. The usual order in discrimination cases includes reinstatement of the wronged employees with back pay and a further requirement that the employer must post a notice that he will not engage in further discriminatory activity and will take the affirmative action ordered by the Board. A wronged employee does have an obligation to mitigate damages by seeking other suitable employment. In *Reserve Supply Corp.* v. *NLRB*,[25] the U. S. court of appeals sustained a Board order requiring an employer to pay six percent interest on the back pay amount owed an employee.

The *Virginia Electric Power* decision reported in this section shows the remedy for an 8(a)(2) employer-dominated union violation. The remedy for this aspect of the case was disestablishment of the employer-dominated union and reimbursement of all dues and assessments previously deducted from wages and paid over to the disestablished organization.

The usual remedy for Section 8(a)(5) refusal to bargain violations is a "cease and desist" order from failing to bargain and an affirmative order to bargain collectively about wages, hours and working conditions at the request of the appropriate union. The Board may not order a party to agree to specific contractual items, however. In the *H. K. Porter* decision reported in this section, the U. S. Supreme Court denied enforcement of an order which would have compelled the employer to agree to a checkoff of union dues.

Usually the remedy for Section 8(b)(1)(A) and (B) cases of union restraint or coercion is a cease and desist order and the posting of a notice of compliance by the union.

In the *Radio Officers* case reported in Chapter 7, the Supreme Court held that the Board may issue a back pay order against a union for causing an employer to discriminate against an employee in violation of Section 8(b)(2). Where both the union and employer are charged, the usual remedy is an order holding both employer and union liable, reinstatement with back pay and a posting of suitable notices.

Violations of 8(b)(4) are temporarily remedied by Section 10(l) mandatory injunctions as previously mentioned. Final determinations by the Board may include cease and desist orders and posting of appropriate notices.

Phelps Dodge Corp. v. National Labor Relations Board

Supreme Court of the United States, 1941. 313 U.S. 177

FRANKFURTER, J. The dominating question which this litigation brings here for the first time is whether an employer subject to the National Labor

---

[25] 317 F.2d 785 (1963).

Relations Act may refuse to hire employees solely because of their affiliations with a labor union. . . .

The source of the controversy was a strike, begun on June 10, 1935, by the International Union of Mine, Mill and Smelter Workers at Phelps Dodge's Copper Queen Mine, Bisbee, Arizona. Picketing of the mine continued until August 24, 1935, when the strike terminated. During the strike, the National Labor Relations Act came into force. . . . The basis of the Board's conclusion that the Corporation had committed unfair labor practices in violation of Sec. 8(3) of the Act was a finding, not challenged here, that a number of men had been refused employment because of their affiliations with the Union. Of these men, two, Curtis and Daugherty, had ceased to be in the Corporation's employ before the strike but sought employment after its close. The others, thirty-eight in number, were strikers. To "effectuate the policies" of the Act, Sec. 10(c), the Board ordered the Corporation to offer Curtis and Daugherty jobs and to make them whole for the loss of pay resulting from the refusal to hire them, and it ordered thirty-seven of the strikers reinstated with back pay, and the other striker made whole for loss in wages up to a time he became unemployable. Save for a modification presently to be discussed, the Circuit Court of Appeals enforced the order affecting the strikers but struck down the provisions relating to Curtis and Daugherty. . . .

It is no longer disputed that workers cannot be dismissed from employment because of their union affiliations. Is the national interest in industrial peace less affected by discrimination against union activity when men are hired? The contrary is overwhelmingly attested by the long history of industrial conflicts, the diagnosis of their causes by official investigations, the conviction of public men, industrialists and scholars. Because of the Pullman strike, Congress in the Erdman Act of 1898 prohibited inroads upon the workingman's right of association by discriminatory practices at the point of hiring. Kindred legislation has been put on the statute books of more than half the states. And during the late war the National War Labor Board concluded that discrimination against union men at the time of hiring violated its declared policy that "The right of workers to organize in trade-unions and to bargain collectively . . . shall not be denied, abridged, or interfered with by the employers in any manner whatsoever." Such a policy is an inevitable corollary of the principle of freedom of organization. Discrimination against union labor in the hiring of men is a dam to self-organization at the source of supply. The effect of such discrimination is not confined to the actual denial of employment; it inevitably operates against the whole idea of the legitimacy of organization. In a word, it undermines the principle which, as we have seen, is recognized as basic to the attainment of industrial peace.

These are commonplaces in the history of American industrial relations. But precisely for that reason they must be kept in the forefront in ascertaining the meaning of a major enactment dealing with these relations. To be sure, in outlawing unfair labor practices Congress did not leave the matter at large. The practices condemned "are strictly limited to those enumerated in Section 8," S.Rep. No. 573, 74th Cong., 1st Sess., p. 8. Section 8(3) is the foundation of the Board's determination that in refusing employment to the two men because of their union affiliations Phelps Dodge violated the Act. And so we

turn to its provisions that "It shall be an unfair labor practice for an employer
. . . by discrimination in regard to hire or tenure of employment or any term
or condition of employment to encourage or discourage membership in any
labor organization.". . .

. . . We are asked to read "hire" as meaning the wages paid to an
employee so as to make the statute merely forbid discrimination in one of the
terms of men who have secured employment. So to read the statute would do
violence to a spontaneous textual reading of Sec. 8(3) in that "hire" would
serve no function because, in the sense which is urged upon us, it is included
in the prohibition against "discrimination in regard to . . . any term or condition of employment." Contemporaneous legislative history, and, above all, the
background of industrial experience, forbid such textual mutilation.

The natural construction which the text, the legislative settings and the
function of the statute command does not impose an obligation on the employer to favor union members in hiring employees. He is as free to hire as
he is to discharge employees. The statute does not touch "the normal exercise
of the right of the employer to select its employees or to discharge them." It
is directed solely against the abuse of that right by interfering with the counter-
vailing right of self-organization. . . .

Reinstatement is the conventional correction for discriminatory discharges. Experience having demonstrated that discrimination in hiring is twin
to discrimination in firing, it would indeed be surprising if Congress gave a
remedy for the one which it denied for the other. The powers of the Board
as well as the restrictions upon it must be drawn from 10(c), which directs
the Board "to take such affirmative action, including reinstatement of employees with or without back pay, as will effectuate the policies of this Act."
It could not be seriously denied that to require discrimination in hiring or firing
to be "neutralized," *Labor Board* v. *Mackay Co.,* 304 U.S. 333, 348, by requiring the discrimination to cease not abstractly but in the concrete victimizing
instances, is an "affirmative action" which "will effectuate the policies of this
Act." Therefore, if Sec. 10(c) had empowered the Board to "take such affirmative action as will effectuate the policies of this Act," the right to restore to
a man employment which was wrongfully denied him could hardly be doubted.
Even without such a mandate from Congress this Court compelled reinstatement to enforce the legislative policy against discrimination represented by
the Railway Labor Act. *Texas & N. O. R. Co.* v. *Railway Clerks,* 281 U.S.
548. . . . To differentiate between discrimination in denying employment and
in terminating it, would be a differentiation not only without substance but
in defiance of that against which the prohibition of discrimination is directed.

As part of its remedial action against the unfair labor practices, the Board
ordered that workers who had been denied employment be made whole for
their loss of pay. In specific terms, the Board ordered payment to the men of
a sum equal to what they normally would have earned from the date of the
discrimination to the time of employment less their earnings during this
period. The court below added a further deduction of amounts which the
workers "failed without excuse to earn," and the Board here challenges this
modification.

Making the workers whole for losses suffered on account of an unfair labor practice is part of the vindication of the public policy which the Board enforces. Since only actual losses should be made good, it seems fair that deductions should be made not only for actual earnings by the worker but also for losses which he willfully incurred. To this the Board counters that to apply this abstractly just doctrine of mitigation of damages to the situations before it, often involving substantial numbers of workmen, would put on the Board details too burdensome for effective administration. Simplicity of administration is thus the justification for deducting only actual earnings and for avoiding the domain of controversy as to wages that might have been earned.

But the advantages of a simple rule must be balanced against the importance of taking fair account, in a civilized legal system, of every socially desirable factor in the final judgment. The board, we believe, overestimates administrative difficulties and underestimates its administrative resourcefulness. . . .

The Board has a wide discretion to keep the present matter within reasonable bounds through flexible procedural devices. The Board will thus have it within its power to avoid delays and difficulties incident to passing on remote and speculative claims by employers, while at the same time it may give appropriate weight to a clearly unjustifiable refusal to take desirable new employment. By leaving such an adjustment to the administrative process we have in mind not so much the minimization of damages as the healthy policy of promoting production and employment. . . .

The decree below should be modified in accordance with this opinion. *Modified.*

CASE **QUESTIONS**	1. State the dominating question involved. 2. Were Curtis and Daugherty in the employ of the company at the time of the strike? Did this fact influence the Circuit Court of Appeals? 3. Does the Act prescribe that employers favor union men in hiring? 4. What is the conventional remedy for discriminatory discharge? 5. Phrase the rule of law covering this situation. 6. What rule is to be followed by the Board to mitigate damages for the employer?

Virginia Electric & Power Co. v. NLRB

(SUPPLEMENTAL CASE DIGEST—REMEDIAL POWERS OF NATIONAL LABOR RELATIONS BOARD)
319 U.S. 533 (1943)

After the remand of this case in 314 U.S. 469, the NLRB reconsidered it upon the original record, made new findings of fact, and concluded that the Company had violated Sections 8(1), (2) and (3) of the National Labor Relations Act. A new order was entered requiring the Company to cease and desist from the unfair labor practices found and from giving effect to its contract with the

Independent Organization of Employees, a company-wide unaffiliated labor organization. The Board held that the said I.O.E. "was not the result of the employees' free choice." The order also directed the Company to withdraw recognition from and disestablish said I.O.E. as a representative of its employees, to reinstate with back pay two of three employees found to have been discriminatorily discharged, *and to reimburse its employees in the amount of dues and assessments deducted from their wages by the Company and paid to the I.O.E.* [Authors' italics.] The Company challenged only the authority of the Board to require reimbursement of the checked-off dues. *Held:* That ". . . Section 10(c) of the Act authorizes the Board to require persons found engaged or engaging in unfair labor practices 'to take such affirmative action, including reinstatement of employees with or without back pay, as will effectuate the policies of this Act.' The declared policy of the Act in Section 1 is to prevent, by encouraging and protecting collective bargaining and full freedom of association for workers, the costly dislocation and interruption of the flow of commerce caused by unnecessary industrial strife and unrest. . . . Within this limit the Board has wide discretion in ordering affirmative action; its power is not limited to the illustrative example of one type of affirmative order namely, reinstatement with or without back pay. . . . The particular means by which the effects of unfair labor practices are to be expunged are matters for the Board, not the courts, to determine. . . .

". . . The instant reimbursement order is not a redress for a private wrong. Like a back pay order, it does restore to the employees in some measure what was taken from them because of the Company's unfair labor practices. In this, both these types of monetary awards somewhat resemble compensation for private injury, but it must be constantly remembered that both are remedies created by statute—the one explicitly and the other implicitly in the concept of effectuation of the policies of the Act—which are designed to aid in achieving the elimination of industrial conflict. They vindicate public, not private, rights. . . . The Board has here determined that the employees suffered a definite loss in the amount of the dues deducted from their wages and that the effectuation of the policies of the Act requires reimbursement of those dues in full. We cannot say this considered judgment does not effectuate the statutory purpose. . . . *Affirmed.*" (MURPHY, J.)

CASE **QUESTIONS**	1. How did this case reach the Supreme Court? 2. How did the Board rule as to the status of I.O.E.? 3. What remedies were ordered? 4. What did the Court say as to these remedies? Why did it approve them?

H. K. Porter Co., Inc. v. NLRB

Supreme Court of the United States, 1970. 397 U.S. 99

BLACK, J.: After an election respondent United Steelworkers Union was, on October 5, 1961, certified by the National Labor Relations Board as the bargaining agent for the employees at the Danville, Virginia, plant of the petitioner, H. K. Porter Co. Thereafter negotiations commenced for a collective-bargaining agreement. Since that time the controversy has seesawed between the Board, the Court of Appeals for the District of Columbia Circuit, and this Court. This delay of over eight years is not because the case is exceedingly complex, but appears to have occurred chiefly because of the skill of the company's negotiators in taking advantage of every opportunity for delay in an act more noticeable for its generality than for its precise prescriptions. The entire lengthy dispute mainly revolves around the union's desire to have the company agree to "check off" the dues owed to the union by its members, that is, to deduct those dues periodically from the company's wage payments to the employees. The record shows, as the Board found, that the company's objection to a checkoff was not due to any general principle or policy against making deductions from employees' wages. The company does deduct charges for things like insurance, taxes, and contributions to charities, and at some other plants it has a checkoff arrangement for union dues. The evidence shows, and the court below found, that the company's objection was not because of inconvenience, but solely on the ground that the company was "not going to aid and comfort the union." Efforts by the union to obtain some kind of compromise on the checkoff request were all met with the same staccato response to the effect that the collection of union dues was the "union's business" and the company was not going to provide any assistance. Based on this and other evidence the Board found, and the Court of Appeals approved the finding, that the refusal of the company to bargain about the checkoff was not made in good faith, but was done solely to frustrate the making of any collective bargaining agreement. In May 1966, the Court of Appeals upheld the Board's order requiring the company to cease and desist from refusing to bargain in good faith and directing it to engage in further collective-bargaining, if requested by the union to do so, over the checkoff. *United Steelworkers* v. *NLRB,* 124 U.S. App. D.C. 143, 363 F.2d 272, *cert. denied,* 385 U.S. 851.

In the course of that opinion, the Court of Appeals intimated that the Board conceivably might have required petitioner to agree to a checkoff provision as a remedy for the prior bad-faith bargaining, although the order enforced at that time did not contain any such provision. 363 F.2d, at 275–276, and n. 16. In the ensuing negotiations the company offered to discuss alternative arrangements for collecting the union's dues, but the union insisted that the company was required to agree to the checkoff proposal without modification. Because of this disagreement over the proper interpretation of the court's opinion, the union, in February 1967, filed a motion for clarification of the 1966 opinion. The motion was denied by the court on March 22, 1967, in an order suggesting that contempt proceedings by the Board would be the proper avenue for testing the employer's compliance with the original order. A request for the institution of such proceedings was made by the union, and in June 1967, the Regional Director of the Board declined to prosecute a contempt charge, finding that the employer had "satisfactorily complied with the affirmative requirements of the Order." App., 111. The union then filed in the Court of Appeals a motion for reconsideration of the earlier motion to clarify the

1966 opinion. The court granted that motion and issued a new opinion in which it held that in certain circumstances a "checkoff may be imposed as a remedy for bad-faith bargaining." *United Steelworkers* v. *NLRB,* 128 U.S. App. D.C. 344, 347, 389 F.2d 295, 298 (1967). The case was then remanded to the Board and on July 3, 1968, the Board issued a supplemental order requiring the petitioner to "[g]rant to the Union a contract clause providing for the checkoff of union dues." 172 NLRB No. 72. The Court of Appeals affirmed this order, *H. K. Porter Co.* v. *NLRB,* 134 U.S. App. D.C. 227, 414 F. 2d 1123 (1969). We granted certiorari to consider whether the Board in these circumstances had the power to remedy the unfair labor practice by requiring the company to agree to check off the dues of the workers. 396 U.S. 817. For reasons to be stated we we hold that while the Board does have power under the National Labor Relations Act, 61 Stat. 136, as amended, to require employers and employees to negotiate, it is without power to compel a company or a union to agree to any substantive contractual provision of a collective-bargaining agreement.

Since 1935 the story of labor relations in this country has largely been a history of governmental regulation of the process of collective bargaining. In that year Congress decided that disturbances in the area of labor relations led to undesirable burdens on and obstructions of interstate commerce, and passed the National Labor Relations Act, 49 Stat. 449. That Act, building on the National Industrial Recovery Act, 48 Stat. 195 (1933), provided that employees had a federally protected right to join labor organizations and bargain collectively through their chosen representatives on issues affecting their employment. Congress also created the National Labor Relations Board to supervise the collective bargaining process. The Board was empowered to investigate disputes as to which union, if any, represented the employees, and to certify the appropriate representative as the designated collective bargaining agent. The employer was then required to bargain together with this representative and the Board was authorized to make sure that such bargaining did in fact occur. Without spelling out the details, the Act provided that it was an unfair labor practice for an employer to refuse to bargain. Thus a general process was established that would ensure that employees as a group could express their opinions and exert their combined influence over the terms and conditions of their employment. The Board would act to see that the process worked.

The object of this Act was not to allow governmental regulation of the terms and conditions of employment, but rather to ensure that employers and their employees could work together to establish mutually satisfactory conditions. The basic theme of the Act was that through collective bargaining the passions, arguments, and struggles of prior years would be channeled into constructive, open discussions leading, it was hoped, to mutual agreement. But it was recognized from the beginning that agreement might in some cases be impossible, and it was never intended that the Government would in such cases step in, become a party to the negotiations and impose its own of a desirable settlement. This fundamental limitation was made abundantly clear in the legislative reports accompanying the 1935 Act. . . .

In 1947 Congress reviewed the experience under the Act and concluded that certain amendments were in order. In the House committee report accompanying what eventually became the Labor Management Relations Act, 1947, the committee referred to the above quoted language in *Jones & Laughlin* and said:

> "Notwithstanding this language of the Court, the present Board has gone very far, in the guise of determining whether or not employers had bargained in good faith, in setting itself up as the judge of what concessions an employer must make and of the proposals and counterproposals that he may or may not make.

*   *   *

> "[U]nless Congress writes into the law guides for the Board to follow, the Board may attempt to carry this process still further and seek to control more and more the terms of collective-bargaining agreements."

Accordingly Congress amended the provisions defining unfair labor practices and said in § 8(d) that:

> "For the purposes of this section, to bargain collectively is the performance of the mutual obligation of the employer and the representative of the employees to meet at reasonable times and confer in good faith with respect to wages, hours, and other terms and conditions of employment, or the negotiation of an agreement, or any question arising thereunder, and the execution of a written contract incorporating any agreement reached if requested by either party, *but such obligation does not compel either party to agree to a proposal or require the making of a concession.*"

In discussing the effect of that amendment, this Court said it is "clear that the Board may not, either directly or indirectly, compel concessions or otherwise sit in judgment upon the substantive terms of collective bargaining agreements." *NLRB* v. *American Ins. Co.,* 343 U.S. 395, 404 (1952). Later this Court affirmed that view stating that "it remains clear that § 8(d) was an attempt by Congress to prevent the Board from controlling the settling of the terms of collective bargaining agreements. *NLRB* v. *Insurance Agents,* 361 U.S. 477, 487 (1960). The parties to the instant case are agreed that this is the first time in the 35-year history of the Act that the Board has ordered either an employer or a union to agree to a substantive term of a collective-bargaining agreement.

Recognizing the fundamental principle "that the National Labor Relations Act is grounded on the premise of freedom of contract," 389 F.2d, at 300, the Court of Appeals in this case concluded that nevertheless in the circumstances presented here the Board could properly compel the employer to agree to a proposed checkoff clause. The Board had found that the refusal was based on a desire to frustrate agreement and not on any legitimate business reason. On the basis of that finding the Court of Appeals approved the further finding that the employer had not bargained in good faith, and the validity of that finding is not now before us. Where the record thus revealed repeated refusals by the employer to bargain in good faith on this issue, the Court of Appeals concluded that ordering agreement to the checkoff clause "may be the only means of assuring the Board, and the court, that [the employer] no longer harbors an illegal intent." 389 F.2d, at 299.

In reaching this conclusion the Court of Appeals held that § 8(d) did not forbid the Board from compelling agreement. That court felt that "[s]ection 8(d) defines collective bargaining and relates to a determination of *whether* a . . . violation has occurred and not to the *scope* of the remedy which may be necessary to cure violations which have already occurred." 389 F.2d, at 299. We may agree with the Court of Appeals that as a matter of strict, literal interpretation of that section it refers only to deciding when a violation has occurred, but we do not agree that that observation justifies the conclusion that the remedial powers of the Board are not also limited by the same considerations that led Congress to enact § 8(d). It is implicit in the entire structure of the Act that the Board acts to oversee and referee the process of collective bargaining, leaving the results of the contest to the bargaining strengths of the parties. It would be anomalous indeed to hold that while § 8(d) prohibits the Board from relying on a refusal to agree as the sole evidence of bad faith bargaining, the Act permits the Board to compel agreement in that same dispute. The Board's remedial powers under § 10 of the Act are broad, but they are limited to carrying out the policies of the Act itself. One of these fundamental policies is freedom of contract. While the parties' freedom of contract is not absolute under the Act, allowing the Board to compel agreement when the parties themselves are unable to agree would violate the fundamental premise on which the Act is based—private bargaining under governmental supervision of the procedure alone, without any official compulsion over the actual terms of the contract.

In reaching its decision the Court of Appeals relied extensively on the equally important policy of the Act that workers' rights to collective bargaining are to be secured. In this case the Court apparently felt that the employer was trying effectively to destroy the union by refusing to agree to what the union may have considered its most important demand. Perhaps the court, fearing that the parties might resort to economic combat, was also trying to maintain the industrial peace that the Act is designed to further. But the Act as presently drawn does not contemplate that unions will always be secure and able to achieve agreement even when their economic position is weak, that strikes and lockouts will never result from a bargaining impasse. It cannot be said that the Act forbids an employer or a union to rely ultimately on its economic strength to try to secure what it cannot obtain through bargaining. It may well be true, as the Court of Appeals felt, that the present remedial powers of the Board are insufficiently broad to cope with important labor problems. But it is the job of Congress, not the Board or the courts, to decide when and if it is necessary to allow governmental review of proposals for collective bargaining agreements and compulsory submission to one side's demands. The present Act does not envision such a process.

The judgment is reversed and the case is remanded to the Court of Appeals for further action consistent with this opinion.

Reversed and remanded.

CASE QUESTIONS

1. Summarize the facts of the case.
2. What is a checkoff; and how important is such to a union?

3. What is the issue before the Supreme Court?
4. What was the Supreme Court's decision on this issue?

SECTION 31 / MAKE-WHOLE REMEDIAL ORDERS

In the unfair labor practice case where an employer refuses to bargain with a union selected by employees as their bargaining representative, the ordinary remedy is a cease and desist and post-notice order. By utilizing the time-consuming procedural requirements of the Board and the courts as delaying tactics while continuing to refuse to bargain, an employer can erode a union's majority position. The ultimate cease and desist and post-notice order of the Board will fail to repair the damages caused by years of refusal to bargain. A remedy that would effectively cure this problem would be a make-whole order imposing on the employer the obligation to pay his employees what he would have paid them absent his refusal to bargain.

The District of Columbia Circuit Court of Appeals in *Electrical Workers IUE* v. *NLRB* (Tiidee),[26] held that although under the *H. K. Porter* decision, reported in the previous section, the Board could not determine what the employer and union "should" have agreed on in a refusal to bargain case, it could decide what they "would" have agreed on had they bargained in good faith. The court found justification for a make-whole order in the delaying-tactic motivation of the employer. The court ruled that a remedy limited to a cease and desist order would actually reward the employer for his "brazen" refusal. The court remanded the case to the Board for a remedy.

In *Tiidee Products, Inc.*, the Board's decision in remand held that it does not have the authority to issue a make-whole order even where the employer's refusal to bargain with the newly certified union was a "clear and flagrant violation of the Law." However, the Board went on to devise a novel remedial approach aimed at rectifying such "frivolous" refusal to bargain situations. The *Tiidee* decision with its unique remedy follows.

Tiidee Products, Inc.

194 NLRB No. 198 (1972)

[The Company manufactures metal and plastic parts for mobile homes and trailers. In July of 1967 the union began to organize the Company's employees. Prior to an election sought by the union, the Board found that the Company violated section 8(a)(1) by coercive antiunion actions taken against the employees. The election was held on September 14, 1967, and the union won 19 to 6. On September 15, the Company began a series of temporary and permanent layoffs. The Board found the layoffs and certain discharges and changes in production quotas were discriminatorily motivated in violation of section 8(a)(3). Shortly after the union's victory, the company contested the results of the election, on the basis of an election morning leaflet circulated by the union and a charge that three voters were not entitled to vote. The regional director

---

[26] 426 F.2d 1243 (1970).

determined that the leaflet did not affect the validity of the election and the 19 to 6 majority mooted the voter eligibility issue. The Company challenged the certification of the regional director and refused to bargain with the union until this litigation was disposed of. The Board found this to be a violation of 8(a)(5) of the Act and ordered the employer to bargain with the union upon request. The union's requested broader make-whole remedy was not ordered.

Subsequently, the U. S. Court of Appeals for the District of Columbia enforced the Board's order. However, upon petition for review, the court remanded the matter of a remedy to the Board. The Board accepted the remand.]

From the Board's Opinion:

The Board has given full consideration to the views of the court of appeals as expressed in the instant proceeding and the parties' contentions in their respective statements of position. For the reasons more fully set forth hereinafter, the Board has concluded that it would effectuate the policies of the Act to grant some but not all of the requested additional relief.

The Union asserts that the court of appeals' conclusion that the Board has the power under the Act to issue a make-whole remedial order is the "law of the case." It contends, moreover, that under the circumstances of these cases the Board should exercise that power and either determine on the record before the Board what dollar amount, if any, is necessary to make whole each employee for all losses sustained due to Respondent's unlawful refusal to bargain or remand this proceeding to a Trial Examiner for a hearing to determine that question. The Union also seeks organizational expenses, litigation costs, reimbursement for lost initiation fees and dues, and any other remedies that would effectuate the policies of the Act.

Respondent contends that the court of appeals erred in questioning the Board's determination not to award additional relief. Respondent argues that no additional relief is warranted; it would have the Board merely reiterate its previously announced conclusion that the Act does not empower the Board to issue a make-whole order [*Ex-Cell-O Corp.* 185 NLRB No. 20 (1970)]. . . .

We have carefully considered the Union's request for a make-whole remedy in light of the record herein and have decided that it is not practicable. The Union suggests that we determine what the parties "would have agreed to" in 1967 and thereafter on the basis of a record which contains only a proposed collective-bargaining agreement submitted by the Union to Respondent on December 18, 1967; a chart comparing the wages then paid by Respondent for certain job classifications with those paid by other employers in comparable industries in the Dayton area who were then under contract with the Union; testimonial evidence of employee wage rates as of the date of the hearing herein and a list thereof as of May 25, 1970; certain testimony about the time required to negotiate first contract; and several charts and tables depicting nationwide changes in wages and benefits since 1967. We know of no way by which the Board could ascertain with even approximate accuracy from the above what the parties "would have agreed to" if they had bargained in good faith. Inevitably, the Board would have to decide from the above what the parties "should have agreed to." And this, the court stated, the Board must not do.

Alternatively, the Union suggests that the Board remand this proceeding to a Trial Examiner apparently without standards for a hearing to devise a "make-whole" formula for backpay to be awarded employees, if any. This would result in long delay while these cases wound their way through the Trial Examiner, the Board, and, ultimately, the courts. Meanwhile, Respondent, which is under order to bargain with the Union, is not likely to agree upon any new wage benefits for employees for fear that the Board would give them retroactive effect in devising a backpay formula for the past refusal to bargain. This would further delay the commencement of meaningful collective bargaining and thus not effectuate the purposes of the Act.

However, while we find that it would be counterproductive to grant the Union's request for a remand to a Trial Examiner, the Board believes that the alternative remedies provided hereinafter will undo some of the baneful effects pointed out by the court as having resulted from Respondent's "clear and flagrant violation of the law." They will, for one, aid the Union in rebuilding its strength so that it may bargain effectively with Respondent. Also, by requiring Respondent to pay some of the Board and Union litigation costs occasioned by its misconduct, similar "brazen" refusals to bargain will be discouraged. Although these remedies are not theoretically perfect, we believe that they are as far as we can go in the circumstances.

1. In the ordinary unfair labor practice case, the notice to employees which accompanies the Board's order is posted for 60 days at the employer's place of business. However, to assure that the employees involved here fully and carefully read the notice, that Respondent's new employees unfamiliar with the history of the instant proceeding understand the reasons for the delay in collective-bargaining negotiations, and that the unit members realize that the Government protects their Section 7 right to select a collective-bargaining representative, we shall require that copies of the posted notices be mailed to each of the employees in the unit at his home.

2. Given all the circumstances of the instant proceeding and those of Tiidee Products, Inc., it is clear that the Union in essence will have to "reorganize" the unit employees despite its outstanding Board certification prior to commencing collective-bargaining negotiations with Respondent. In order that the employees may have free and ready access to information from the Union concerning all aspects of unionization and the collective-bargaining negotiations which should occur in the immediate future, the Board will order that the Union be given reasonable access to Respondent's bulletin boards and other places where notices to employees are customarily posted, during the period of contract negotiations, for the posting of union notices, bulletins, and other literature.

Similarly, and especially during the period prior to the commencement of negotiations, the Board finds that it would facilitate the Union's reclaiming the allegiance of the unit employees if it were able to meet with the individuals involved in order to explain to them the circumstances of the instant proceeding and the Union's plans for the future. While several methods for achieving this objective are available, we find least burdensome on all the parties the requirement that Respondent furnish the Union with a list of names and addresses of its employees and keep said list current for a 1-year period.

Accordingly, we shall order Respondent to furnish the Union with such lists for 1 year from the date of this Supplemental Decision.

3. The Union asserts that an award to it of organizational expenses, litigation costs and expenses, and lost initiation fees and dues would meet another of the court of appeals' objections to the Board's order; viz. that our traditional remedy rewarded Respondent's delaying tactics and increased the likelihood that similar frivolous litigation would clog future Board and court calendars.

It is clear that the Union incurred no extraordinary organizational expenses because of Respondent's patently frivolous objection to the election and subsequent refusal to bargain. Despite certain already remedied preelection unlawful Respondent conduct, the Union was selected by the employees after a 2-month campaign at the first election held. We find, therefore, no nexus between Respondent's unlawful conduct here under examination and the Union's preelection organizational expenses and, accordingly, we shall not award them to the Union.

The Union asserts that because it is union policy not to collect initiation fees and dues until a contract is executed, it has received nothing from the unit employees throughout the course of this proceeding. It therefore now seeks to recover the initiation fees and dues lost due to Respondent's refusal to bargain. We view this claim as partaking of a request for a make-whole remedy, which we have declined to order, since presumably the dues and fees sought would have come from lost wages. Moreover, since it is union policy to chance the loss of initiation fees and dues in all cases until a contract is negotiated, if ever, we find no reason to have Respondent assume that risk at this point. Clearly, the Union during the instant proceeding could have elected to assess its members for dues and fees.

We find merit, however, in the Union's request that it be reimbursed for certain litigation costs and expenses. Normally, as the Board recently noted, litigation expenses are not recoverable by the charging party in Board proceedings even though the public interest is served when the charging party protects its private interests before the Board.

We agree with the court, however, that frivolous litigation such as this is clearly unwarranted and should be kept from the nation's already crowded court dockets, as well as our own. While we do not seek to foreclose access to the Board and courts for meritorious cases, we likewise do not want to encourage frivolous proceedings. The policy of the Act to insure industrial peace through collective bargaining can only be effectuated when speedy access to uncrowded Board and court dockets is available. Accordingly, in order to discourage future frivolous litigation, to effectuate the policies of the Act, and to serve the public interest we find that it would be just and proper to order Respondent to reimburse the Board and the Union for their expenses incurred in the investigation, preparation, presentation, the conduct of these cases, including the following costs and expenses incurred in both the Board and court proceedings: reasonable counsel fees, salaries, witness fees, transcript and record costs, printing costs, travel expenses and per diem, and other reasonable costs and expenses. Accordingly, we shall order Respondent to pay to the Board and the Union the above-mentioned litigation costs and expenses.

CASE QUESTIONS

1. What remedy did the Union seek in this case?
2. What method did the Union suggest the Board follow in determining what the parties "would have agreed to" in 1967 and thereafter?
3. What was the Board response to this proposal by the Union?
4. Summarize the contents of the remedial order.

QUESTIONS ON CHAPTER 4

1. What did the 1935 Act cover?
2. What did Congress add to the NLRA in 1947 (a) in Title I; (b) in Title II; (c) in Title III?
3. Compare the duties of the NLRB and of the National Mediation Board.
4. Discuss the status of foremen today under the NLRA.
5. What control over employee activities does the law permit the employer under the law?
6. Outline (a) the procedural authority and sanctions of the NLRB; (b) the NLRB power to remedy violations.

Chapter 5

Bargaining Units and Representation

SECTION 32 / MAJORITY BARGAINING RIGHTS

The legal and the procedural problems related to the designation of employees' representatives are considered in this chapter. The Railway Labor Act and the National Labor Relations Act are both directed to similar objectives—protecting interstate economic activity, minimizing labor unrest and strife by encouraging collective bargaining, and supporting democratic freedoms. Both acts provide for free association and self-determination by employees with independence from employer influence. Both acts incorporate the right to exclusive bargaining representation by choice of the majority in an appropriate unit of employees.

These policies and principles raise many difficult questions as to minority rights, freedom of speech and electioneering activity, management conduct, and union activities. Individual employees and minority groups are protected against discriminatory treatment; but after determination of the majority's choice, everyone is subject to uniform conditions and terms agreed to between the employer and the majority representatives. Conferences between an employer and a minority are permitted subject to the contract terms of a majority choice established with the employer and subject to participation of majority representatives in any grievance settlements.

The two acts are similar in many respects. Some differences in the representation procedures exist and will be explained in the following sections. The requirements of good-faith bargaining, of noninterference, and of noncoercion in organization matters are common foundations of both laws. Administrative differences exist, however, due to the language of the two statutes, the discretion exercised by the independent boards, and the dissimilar industry labor relations.

SECTION 33 / DETERMINING EMPLOYEES' CHOICE

The two Acts do not require any particular procedure for determining the employees' wishes as to bargaining representatives as long as it clearly indicates a free choice. If a representation question is raised, the National Mediation Board is authorized by law to decide it and, as needed, to conduct representation

159

balloting. Section 9 of the National Labor Relations Act, while not requiring the parties to use the formal processes, provides the administrative machinery for the certification of a majority representative in an appropriate unit.

The NLRA also empowers the NLRB to conduct decertification elections where employees or a union official challenges the majority representation status of a currently recognized organization. Provision is also made for a secret ballot to allow employees to withdraw the authority of their representatives to continue an agreement requiring union membership as an employment condition under the NLRA, but not the RLA.

These balloting procedures raise a number of important questions, some very difficult to answer where the parties are in disagreement because of conflicting interests between the employer, the employees, and their representative or representatives. Such questions arise as whether a claim is bona fide or false or frivolous, what constitutes the appropriate bargaining unit or units, the timeliness of an election request in relation to prior elections or to existing contracts, who may vote, the conduct of elections, the freedom to electioneer, and the results of the balloting, all considered in this chapter.

The primary purpose of the NLRB proceedings is the resolution of questions over whether there will be collective bargaining, by protection of employees' rights to self-determination.

The services of the NLRB or the NMB in representation disputes must be invoked by a party to the dispute. The NLRB will not proceed to a determination in a matter of certification of employee bargaining agents unless the petitioning union or employee group presents satisfactory evidence that at least thirty percent of the group involved have indicated some support of the request for an election by signatures or by other actions. Evidence of support of the request for an election is usually in the form of signed and dated "authorization cards."

After a petition for recognition has been filed with the Board, the Board, or regional directors acting on authority delegated by the Board, will decide whether (1) the Board's jurisdictional requirements have been met, (2) the required thirty percent of the employees involved have selected the organization, and (3) the bargaining unit formed by the employees involved is appropriate. If the Board finds the above requirements have been met and thus finds the petition valid, it will conduct a union certification election. If a majority of the employees in the unit involved vote to be represented by the union, the Board then recognizes the union as the bargaining agent for the employees.

If picketed by an uncertified labor organization to force recognition or bargaining, the employer may then invoke the NLRB which will direct a prompt election regardless of the usual requirements for a union showing of substantial employee interest. If the employer filed a petition, however, and upon investigation the union named therein disclaims any interest, the Board will then dismiss the petition unless the conduct of the union contradicts its disclaimer. Continued picketing for recognition, after denying any interest, will result in an election; but picketing solely to persuade customers to trade elsewhere or not to patronize, without claims of representing the employees, may mean dismissal of an employer's petition since no question of the employees' selection or of bargaining exists. This type of situation is discussed further in Chapter 7, in connection with unfair labor practices of unions.

A decertification petition may be filed only by employees' representatives who are not acting for an employer or at his instigation. A 30 percent showing of interest is also required. To promote the policy of employee independent action, a decertification petition will be dismissed if investigation indicates that the management sponsored the employees who file it. The employer may put the burden on employee representatives to prove a claimed majority status if the employer questions it in good faith.

When one union or an employer initiates a valid petition for an election, an intervening union claiming to be also the choice of employees must produce some evidence to support that claim. The Board will allow it a place on a ballot if it can show any basis for claiming intervening rights without regard to the percent of the employees supporting it.

SECTION 34 / THE APPROPRIATE BARGAINING UNIT

Each of the labor statutes authorizes its respective board to resolve disputes over claims of majority representation and to define the appropriate bargaining unit within which the majority choice is to be certified to the parties. Each board is empowered to order and to conduct a secret ballot election, to determine who is eligible to vote, what candidates or choices appear on a ballot, and what rules of procedure and conduct shall govern the election. Such matters are generally immune from court review.

The NLRA, covering a wider scope of industries than the RLA, involves more numerous and complex problems over bargaining rights, so that most of the legal precedents have evolved from NLRB decisions. The 1947 Act authorized the Board to decide an appropriate unit so as to assure the fullest freedom of collective bargaining; included, however, are many statutory mandates. Unlike the RLA, an employee's right to refrain from collective activities receives explicit NLRA assurance in Section 7, which provides for voting against any union. Professional and nonprofessional workers may not be included in the same unit unless a majority of professionals first vote to be part of an overall unit. Separate craft units may not be found inappropriate by reason of prior certifications unless the craft majority so votes. Plant protection employees may not be included with others, or represented by a union that affiliates with representatives of other types of workers than guards.

The RLA gives no such details, merely providing that the Board investigate representation disputes at the request of either party. It may use a secret ballot or any other method for determining the majority choice in "the craft or the class."

The NLRB, although subject to more statutory guides, has broad discretion in determining an appropriate bargaining unit dispute. Among the possibilities which may be argued, it must decide whether a craft, a department, a single plant, an employer-wide multi-plant unit, or an association-wide multi-employer unit is more appropriate. Common employment interests of workers is a primary consideration: their skill and training requirements, functional unity, and the history of bargaining and personnel policy.

The Board does not permit racial or other arbitrary distinctions to be given weight in unit determinations. Such arguments or claims are considered irrelevant. As will be further discussed in Chapter 12, racial discrimination or distinctions, in agreements or representation within the bargaining unit, are a basis for revoking a representative's certification and also for finding unfair labor practice violations. Such distinctions have been held irrelevant, invidious, and unfair by the courts as well as the Board.

Relevant to unit determinations are managerial and supervisory organization and functions which, along with skill and similar functional considerations, may result in separating truck drivers or maintenance or custodial workers from a plant-wide unit. On the basis of pertinent facts, the technical employees with different group interests may be excluded from a unit of production and maintenance workers. Employees in a confidential capacity in the effectuating of management-labor policies or those with supervisory responsibilities are excluded from any unit for collective bargaining.

The following guideposts have been applied to decide what employees will be grouped or whether, in the case of a multiple-plant or store operation under unitary management, separate or combined employee units should be formed:

1. Physical location of production facilities under common ownership. If the facilities are fairly close together, the Board has tended to favor a combined unit embracing workers in all plants.
2. The skill requirements of the work to be performed by employees usually leads to a separation because the routine worker and the skilled employee are subjected to differing wage and working condition benefits and otherwise have little in common. At any rate, skilled employees under the *Globe* doctrine must be given the right to vote on the question of a separate unit or a plant-wide unit.[1]
3. Degree of ownership and managerial integration is also a factor in deciding whether employees should be grouped or separated for bargaining purposes. Are the facilities in question commonly owned? Would cessation of activity in one facility adversely affect performance in the others? Are managerial policies centrally formulated and uniformly applied to all facilities? Are conditions of employment essentially uniform among the several plants? Are employees frequently transferred and interchanged? If the answer is in the affirmative, the Board has favored a homogeneous unit.
4. The collective bargaining history of an employer has often led the Board to separate or combine bargaining units based on the employer's previous experience. If a particular employer has formerly enjoyed amicable relations with his employees under separate or combined units, such forms will generally be favored for present purposes.
5. Extent of organization is the final consideration entering into the Board's resolve to separate or combine for negotiation and representation purposes. By extent of organization is meant the degree to which employees in individual plants of multiple-plant companies have presently organized. Under the Wagner Act, the Board could decide that employees in plant A were entitled to representation as a single unit if they were desirous thereof, though the employees in plants B and C had not, as yet, been sufficiently organized to call for an election. Some limitation is placed upon the Board's discretion in this regard by the 1947 Act. Sec. 9(c)(5) provides "in determining whether a unit is appropriate . . . the extent to which the employees have organized shall not be controlling." Thus, by legislative mandate, if other

---

[1] *Globe Machine and Stamping Co.* 3 NLRB 294 (1937).

factors favor a multiple-plant unit, the Board may not base a plant unit decision upon a finding that the present extent of organization militates against a multiple-plant unit. This proviso does not outlaw consideration by the Board of organizational extent; it merely limits the *weight* that the Board can accord it in deciding whether to separate or combine for appropriate unit purposes.

Multi-employer bargaining units are strictly consensual arrangements between a union and a group of employers. All employer members of the group must stipulate that they intend to be bound by group rather than individual action. The union having representative status must also assent. The board will not sanction the creation of a multi-employer unit over the objection of any party. Once the unit is formed, the multi-employer group has substantially the same bargaining responsibilities as any single employer under the Act.

The *Leedom* v. *Kyne* case presented in this section is an example of a unit question concerning a mixture of professional and non-professional employees under Section 9(b)(1).[2] The *American District Telegraph Co.* case involves a unit question concerning plant guards under Section 9(b)(3) and a determination of the "supervisory" status of an individual employee for inclusion in a non-guard bargaining unit.

Leedom v. Kyne

(SUPPLEMENTAL CASE DIGEST—PROFESSIONAL AND CRAFT EMPLOYEES)
Supreme Court of the United States, 1958. 358 U.S. 184

The United States Supreme Court in 1958 was faced with a question of NLRB authority to include professionals and nonprofessionals in the same bargaining unit without submitting to a vote the question of whether the professionals desired inclusion in a mixed unit. The professionals, who were a majority in the unit, did not favor integration and are here asking the court to set aside a certification of the mixed unit.

The Supreme Court ruled that the Board here had exceeded its statutory powers in designating a mixed unit without consulting, through a ballot, the wishes of the professionals. It therefore upheld a District Court order which had set aside the Board certification.

American District Telegraph

(SUPPLEMENTAL CASE DIGEST—PLANT GUARDS)
160 NLRB No. 82 (1966).

Employer, who is engaged in furnishing protective services by means of electric devices which it installs and maintains, employs several classifications of servicemen. Employer also operates a one-man division responsible for selling, installing and repairing background music systems.

---

[2] The Act defines its use of "professional employee" in Section 2(12).

The union seeks to represent all of the above employees, as well as all porters. Employer contends that all of the servicemen are guards, that the background music director is a supervisor, and that these employees should consequently be excluded from any bargaining unit.

Of employer's several classifications of servicemen, only the S-2 group was specifically charged with duties related to enforcing rules to protect property or the safety of persons on customers' premises. This group was armed, wore uniforms, worked irregular hours, and was primarily responsible for detaining intruders apprehended in response to alarms. . . .

The remaining classifications, S-1 and S-3, comprised servicemen whose duties principally involved installing and repairing the electric devices or monitoring signals therefrom.

Although the music director worked in a separate administrative office building and was on a separate payroll, he remained under the supervision of the District Manager who was responsible for the servicemen.

Although the union asserts that the S-2's are primarily mechanics and have only incidental duties with respect to apprehension of intruders, the stipulation of the parties states the reverse. In view of this, as well as the fact that they are uniformed and armed, the S-2's are guards within the meaning of the Act. . . .

In contrast to the situation in ADT Company, 112 NLRB 80, there is no evidence that the regular S-1's have any responsibility other than prompt restoration of service through repairs. The instant situation being more akin to American District Telegraph Co., 128 NLRB 345, the S-1's, accordingly, are not guards within the meaning of the Act.

Although the S-3's may well be an integral part of ADT's protection operation, there is nothing in the Act which requires that they be deemed guards on that basis alone. Since they have none of the characteristics of the servicemen previously determined to be guards, but merely monitor signals, they are includable in the non-guard unit.

The music director appears to have none of the statutory indicia of supervisory status, but does seem to have a community of interests with the regular S-1's and S-3's. Consequently, he shall also be included in the non-guard unit.

CASE QUESTIONS

1. Whom did the union seek to represent in one bargaining unit?
2. Discuss the differences between the various classifications of servicemen.

SECTION 35 / **CRAFT SEVERANCE**

At the heart of labor-management relations is the bargaining unit. It is all important that the bargaining unit be truly appropriate and not contain a mix of antagonistic interests or submerge the legitimate interests of a small group of employees in the interest of a larger group. The Board has the responsibility of determining which group of employees should be considered appropriate; and in the *Mallinckrodt* case reported below, the Board spelled out the policy guidelines that it would use in determining whether the severance of a bargaining unit comprised of the craftsmen in a larger unit would be appropriate. The guidelines are summarized as follows:

1. Whether or not the proposed unit consists of a distinct and homogeneous group of skilled journeymen craftsmen.
2. The history of collective bargaining of the employees sought.
3. The extent to which the employees in the proposed unit have established and maintained their separate identity during the period of inclusion in a broader unit.
4. The history and pattern of collective bargaining in the industry involved.
5. The degree of integration of the employer's production processes.
6. The qualification of the union seeking to "carve out" a separate unit.

The above Board guidelines are not only applicable to craft severance situations in organized plants, but also to the initial formation of units in unorganized plants.[3]

Mallinckrodt Chemical Works

162 NLRB No. 48 (1966)

On July 1, 1963, the Regional Director for Region 14 issued a Decision and Direction of Election in the above-entitled proceeding. In accordance with Section 102.67 of the National Labor Relations Board Rules and Regulations, the Employer filed a timely request for review of the Regional Director's Decision, which was considered together with a statement in opposition filed by the Petitioner [International Brotherhood of Electrical Workers, Local #1, AFL-CIO]. Thereafter, on September 19, 1963, the National Labor Relations Board granted review, stayed the election, and remanded the proceedings for the purpose of taking evidence on all issues, including the craft status of the requested employees, the traditional representative status of the Petitioner, and the degree of integration of the Employer's operations. Subsequently, a hearing was held before a duly designated Hearing Officer, whose rulings made at the hearing are free from prejudicial error and are hereby affirmed. After the hearing was closed, the parties timely filed briefs in support of their respective positions. . . .

Petitioner seeks a unit composed of: All instrument mechanics, their apprentices and helpers in the Employer's instrument department at the Weldon Spring, Missouri, location. Although the Petitioner has asserted at the hearing and in its brief that it seeks severance of the instrument mechanics as a "functionally distinct and homogeneous traditional departmental group" and not as a craft—a contention upon which it based its motion for reconsideration of the Board's order granting review—it has also, on the record and in its brief, asserted its willingness to "go along with any other unit that the Board may determine to be appropriate."

---

[3] *E. I. duPont,* 162 NLRB 413 (1966).

The Employer is engaged at Weldon Spring in the purification of uranium ore and the manufacture of uranium metal under a cost plus fixed fee contract with the Atomic Energy Commission. It is the single facility contracting with AEC whose production process fully embraces the step by step extraction of uranium from its adulterated ores and converting it into a finished product in the form of solid metals, ultimately to be used by AEC and the Department of Defense.

The Employer's uranium division occupies a 200 acre tract consisting of between 40 and 50 buildings, staffed by about 560 employees. Of these, fully half are guards, supervisors, professional, technical, and clerical employees. The remaining production and maintenance unit is comprised of 130 production operators and approximately 150 maintenance employees of which 12 are instrument mechanics, the classification which Petitioner seeks to sever. . . .

Petitioner, relying on its showing that the instrument mechanics are craftsmen and on its claim that it qualifies as a traditional representative of such craftsmen, contends it has met the requirements set forth in the American Potash decision for obtaining a craft severance election. On the other hand, the Employer, though not receding from its contention that the instrument mechanics are not true craftsmen and that the Petitioner is not, in any event, the traditional representative of such mechanics, argues that the American Potash decision improperly makes the question of severance turn solely on affirmative findings with respect to the above issues, ignoring many other relevant and weighty considerations. In this latter respect, the Employer places particular emphasis on the fact that the American Potash decision precludes, for all practical purposes, consideration of the duration and character of the representation which craft employees have received while being represented in a more inclusive unit, and completely rules out any consideration of the effect that integration of the functions of the craft employees involved in the proceeding with the overall production processes of the employer may have on the Board's unit determination. With respect to both points, the Employer urges that to the extent the American Potash decision forbids realistic consideration of bargaining history and integration of the craft employees' functions in the production process unless the case involves one of the so-called National Tube industries, it is plainly discriminatory in application and requires reversal.

We believe there is much force to the Employer's arguments and contentions, and we have undertaken in this and other cases a review of our present policies regarding severance elections.

At the outset, it is appropriate to set forth the nature of the issue confronting the Board in making unit determinations in severance cases. Underlying such determinations is the need to balance the interest of the employer and the total employee complement in maintaining the industrial stability and resulting benefits of an historical plant-wide bargaining unit as against the interest of a portion of such complement in having an opportunity to break away from the historical unit by a vote for separate representation. The Board does not exercise its judgment lightly in these difficult areas. Each such case involves a resolution of "what would best serve the working man in his effort to bargain collectively with his employer, and what would best serve the interest of the country as a whole." It is within the context of this declared legislative purpose that Congress has delegated to the Board the obligation to determine appropriate bargaining units. We do not believe that the Board can properly, or perhaps even lawfully, discharge its statutory duties by delegating the performance of so important a function to a segment of the affected employee body. Thus, we accept the Court's view in Pittsburgh Plate Glass that "the Board was not authorized by . . . [the Act] to surrender to anyone else its statutory duty to determine in each case the appropriate unit for collective bargaining." *(ibid.)*

The cohesiveness and special interest of a craft or departmental group seeking severance may indicate the appropriateness of a bargaining unit limited to that group. However, the interests of all employees in continuing to bargain together in order to maintain their collective strength, as well as the public interest and the interests of the employer and the plant union in maintaining overall plant stability in labor relations and uninterrupted operation of integrated industrial or commercial facilities, may favor adherence to the established patterns of bargaining.

The problem of striking a balance has been the subject of Board and Congressional concern since the early days in the administration of the Wagner Act. In the American Can decision, the Board refused to allow craft severance in the face of a bargaining history on a broader basis. This so-called American Can doctrine was not, however, rigidly applied to rule out all opportunities for craft severance. Nevertheless, when Congress amended the Wagner Act in 1947 by enactment of the Taft-Hartley Act, it added a proviso to Section 9(b), stating in pertinent part:

"The Board shall . . . not decide that any craft unit is inappropriate on the ground that a different unit has been established by a prior Board determination, unless a majority of the employees in the proposed craft unit vote against separate representation."

Though the legislative history indicates that this proviso grew out of Congressional concern that the American Can doctrine unduly restricted the rights of craft employees to seek separate representation, it is equally clear that Congress did not intend to take away the Board's discretionary authority to find craft units to be inappropriate for collective-bargaining purposes if a review of all the facts, both pro and con severance, led to such result. . . .

Shortly after the enactment of Section 9(b)(2), the Board, in the National Tube case, dismissed a craft severance petition filed on behalf of a group of bricklayer craftsmen who were employed in the basic steel industry. After an exhaustive analysis of the section and its legislative history, the Board concluded that: "(1) the only restriction imposed by Section 9(b)(2) is that a prior Board determination cannot be the basis for denying separate representation to a craft group; (2) under the language of the statute there is nothing to bar the Board from considering either a prior determination or the bargaining history of a particular employer as a factor, even if not controlling, in determining the appropriateness of a proposed craft unit; (3) there is nothing in either statute or legislative history to preclude the Board from considering or giving such weight as it deems necessary to the factors of bargaining history in an industry, the basic nature of the duties performed by the craft employees in relation to those of the production employees, the intergration of craft functions with the overall production processes of the employer, and many other circumstances upon which the Board has customarily based its determination as to the appropriateness or inappropriateness of a proposed unit." The bricklayer unit was there found to be inappropriate because of the existence of such a pattern and history of bargaining in the basic steel industry and because the functions of the craft bricklayers were intimately connected with the basic steel production process which was highly integrated in nature. In subsequent cases, the same grounds were relied upon for denying the formation of craft units in the wet milling, basic aluminum, and lumbering industries.

In the American Potash decision, the Board, in effect, reversed the National Tube decision as to both the proper construction of Section 9(b)(2) and the propriety of denying craft severance on the basis of integrated production processes in an industry where the prevailing pattern of bargaining is industrial in character.

As to the first, the Board stated:

". . . we find that the intent of Congress will best be effectuated by a finding, and we so find, that a craft group will be appropriate for severance purposes in cases where a true craft group is sought and where, in addition, the union is one which traditionally represents that craft.

". . . All that we are considering here is whether true craft groups should have an opportunity to decide the issue for themselves. We conclude that we MUST afford them that choice in order to give effect to the statute." [Emphasis supplied.]

As to the second, the Board stated:

". . . we feel that the right of separate representation should not be denied members of a craft group merely because they are employed in an industry which involves highly integrated production processes and in which the prevailing pattern of bargaining is industrial in character. We shall, therefore, not extend the practice of denying craft severance on an industry-wide basis.". . .

Rejecting, as we do, the statutory interpretation on which the American Potash decision is premised, and recognizing that American Potash itself constituted a change in the applicable criteria, we now consider whether the tests laid down in the American Potash case nevertheless permit a satisfactory resolution of the issues posed in severance cases. We find that they do not. American Potash established two basic tests: (1) the employees involved must constitute a true craft or departmental group, and (2) the union seeking to carve out a craft or departmental unit must be one which has traditionally devoted itself to the special problems of the group involved. These tests do serve to identify and define those employee groups which normally have the necessary cohesiveness and special interests to distinguish them from the generality of production and maintenance employees, and place in the scales of judgment the interests of the craft employees. However, they do not consider the interests of the other employees and thus do not permit a weighing of the craft group against the competing interests favoring continuance of the established relationship. Thus, by confining consideration solely to the interests favoring severance, the American Potash tests preclude the Board from discharging its statutory responsibility to make its unit determinations on the basis of all relevant factors, including those factors which weigh against severance. In short, application of these mechanistic tests leads always to the conclusion that the interests of craft employees always prevail. It does this, moreover, without affording a voice in the decision to the other employees, whose unity of association is broken and whose collective strength is weakened by the success of the craft or departmental group in pressing its own special interests.

Furthermore, the American Potash decision makes arbitrary distinctions between industries by forbidding the application of the National Tube doctrine to other industries whose operations are as highly integrated, and whose plantwide bargaining patterns are as well established, as is the case in the so-called "National Tube" industries. In fact, the American Potash decision is inherently inconsistent in asserting that ". . . it is not the province of this Board to dictate the course and pattern of labor organization in our vast industrial complex," while, at the same time, establishing rules which have that very effect. Thus, American Potash clearly "dictates[s] the course and pattern of labor organization" by establishing rigid qualifications for unions seeking craft units and by automatically precluding severance of all such units in National Tube industries.

It is patent, from the foregoing, that the American Potash tests do not effectuate the policies of the Act. We shall, therefore, no longer allow our inquiry to be limited by them. Rather, we shall, as the Board did prior to American Potash, broaden our inquiry to permit evaluation of all considerations relevant to an informed decision in this area. The following areas of inquiry are illustrative of those we deem relevant:

"1. Whether or not the proposed unit consists of a distinct and homogeneous group of skilled journeymen craftsmen performing the functions of their craft on a nonrepetitive basis, or of employees constituting a functionally distinct department, working in trades or occupations for which a tradition of separate representation exists.

"2. The history of collective bargaining of the employees sought and at the plant involved, and at other plants of the employer, with emphasis on whether the existing patterns of bargaining are productive of stability in labor relations, and whether such stability will be unduly disrupted by the destruction of the existing patterns of representation.

"3. The extent to which the employees in the proposed unit have established and maintained their separate identity during the period of inclusion in a broader unit, and the extent of their participation or lack of participation in the establishment and maintenance of the existing pattern of representation and the prior opportunities, if any, afforded them to obtain separate representation.

"4. The history and pattern of collective bargaining in the industry involved.

"5. The degree of integration of the employer's production processes, including the extent to which the continued normal operation of the production processes is dependent upon the performance of the assigned functions of the employees in the proposed unit.

"6. The qualifications of the union seeking to "carve out" a separate unit, including that union's experience in representing employees like those involved in the severance action."

In view of the nature of the issue posed by a petition for severance, the foregoing should not be taken as a hard and fast definition or an inclusive or exclusive listing of the various considerations involved in making unit determinations in this area. No doubt other factors worthy of consideration will appear in the course of litigation. We emphasize the foregoing to demonstrate our intention to free ourselves from the restrictive effect of rigid and inflexible rules in making our unit determinations. Our determinations will be made only after a weighing of all relevant factors on a case-by-case basis, and we will apply the same principles and standards to all industries.

Turning to the facts of this case, we conclude that it will not effectuate the policies of the Act to permit the disruption of the production and maintenance unit by permitting Petitioner to "carve out" a unit of instrument mechanics. Our conclusion is predicated on the following considerations.

The Employer is engaged in the production of uranium metal. It is the only enterprise in the country which is engaged in all phases of such production. All of its finished product is sold to the Atomic Energy Commission. Continued stability in labor relations at such facilities is vital to our national defense.

The Employer produces uranium metal by means of a highly integrated continuous flow production system which the record herein shows is beyond doubt as highly integrated as are the production processes of the basic steel, basic aluminum, wet milling, and lumbering industries. The process itself is largely dependent upon the proper functioning of a wide variety of instrument controls which channel the raw materials through the closed pipe system and regulate the speed of flow of the materials as well as the temperatures within different parts of the system. These controls are an integral part of the production system. The instrument mechanics' work on such controls is therefore intimately related to the production process itself. Indeed, in performing such work, they must do so in tandem with the operators of the controls to insure that the system continues to function while new controls are installed, and existing controls are calibrated, maintained, and repaired.

The instrument mechanics have been represented as part of a production and maintenance unit for the last 25 years. The record does not demonstrate that their interests have been neglected by their bargaining representative. In fact, the record shows that their pay rates are comparable to those received by the skilled electricians who are currently represented by the Petitioner, and that such rates are among the highest in the plant. The instrument mechanics have their own seniority system for purposes of transfer, layoff, and recall. Viewing this long lack of concern for maintaining and preserving a separate group identity for bargaining purposes, together with the fact that Petitioner has not traditionally represented the instrument mechanic craft, we find that the interests served by maintenance of stability in the existing bargaining unit of approximately 280 production and maintenance employees outweigh the interests served by affording the 12 instrument mechanics an opportunity to change their mode of representation.

We conclude that the foregoing circumstances present a compelling argument in support of the continued appropriateness of the existing production and maintenance unit for purposes of collective bargaining, and against the appropriateness of a separate unit of instrument mechanics. In reaching this conclusion, we have not overlooked the fact that the instrument mechanics do constitute an identifiable group of skilled journeymen mechanics, similar to groups the Board heretofore has found entitled to severance from an overall unit. However, it appears that the separate community of interests which these employees enjoy by reason of their skills and training has been largely submerged in the broader community of interests which they share with other employees by reason of long and uninterrupted association in the existing bargaining unit, the high degree of integration of the employer's production processes, and the intimate connection of the work of these employees with the actual uranium metal-making process itself. We find, accordingly, that the unit sought by the Petitioner is inappropriate for the purposes of collective bargaining. We shall, therefore, dismiss the petition.

Member Fanning, dissented.

CASE QUESTIONS	1. Did the Board allow a craft severance for the petitioning bricklayers in the *National Tube* case?
	2. Summarize the Board's revised policy on craft severance as put forth in the *American Potash* decision.
	3. Was the *Mallinckrodt* Board satisfied that the *American Potash* tests permitted satisfactory resolution of the issues posed in severance cases?
	4. What factors does the Board deem relevant in evaluating cases involving craft severance?

SECTION 36 / **BARRIERS TO ELECTIONS**

In Section 9(c) the Congress prohibited the NLRB from holding an election if a valid election had been held during the preceding twelve months. The Board policy accords a similar effect to elections meeting Board standards conducted by a responsible state agency. That policy does not apply, however, to a petition under 9(e) for a union shop deauthorization vote except where that kind of election had previously been held within the twelve-month period.

The NLRB policy also precludes an election when there is a valid existing contract which contains no provisions inconsistent with the Act; it binds the parties to it unless the period of agreement was unreasonable, which means not longer than two years, after which period the Board will conduct an election notwithstanding any existing agreement.

The Board will not conduct an election in situations where unresolved unfair labor practice charges are pending, and where therefore a free election could not take place. If the charging party requests, however, an exception may be made which then disallows later objections to the election results based on these charges of violations. But if the election be then lost by the union because of subsequent employer unfair labor practices or election interferences, the union may be allowed to reinstate the prior charges along with its subsequent objections as to employer conduct as the basis of showing bad faith continuously through the entire period of organizing.

An existing agreement does not bar an election where the contracting union is not willing or able to represent the employees by reason of a schism in its ranks or because it is defunct in fact. In any case, to obtain an election where an existing contract exists, the petitioner must file for certification within a period starting no more than thirty days before a reopening date and ending at the reopening or renewal date. If renewed for a subsequent term, the agreement prevents a redetermination, usually for at least another year. This policy protects the stability of relations of contracting parties.

A certification precludes another election proceeding, even in the absence of agreement, thus requiring continuing bargaining obligations regardless of any request for change or cancellation of the certified representative. After a year a new petition for certification or for decertification in the same unit will be acted upon. Even during the year after certification an election might be held in a different, larger unit, such as among all employees including production and maintenance employees notwithstanding a prior election and inactive certification for the maintenance employees alone.

The *Brooks* decision, reprinted in this section, was decided under the amended National Labor Relations Act of 1947. Employees are thus required to accept a bona fide majority choice and may not repudiate a certified union a few months after they had voted in favor of it.

Ray Brooks v. NLRB

Supreme Court of the United States, 1954. 348 U.S. 96

FRANKFURTER, J.: The National Labor Relations Board conducted a representation election in petitioner's Chrysler-Plymouth agency on April 12, 1951. District Lodge No. 727, International Association of Machinists, won by an 8–5 vote, and the Labor Board certified it as exclusive bargaining representative on April 20. A week after the election and the day before the certification, petitioner received a handwritten letter signed by 9 of the 13 employees in the bargaining unit stating:

> "We, the undersigned majority of the employees . . . are not in favor of being represented by Union Local No. 727.". . .

Relying on this letter and the decision of the Court of Appeals for the Sixth Circuit in *Labor Board* v. *Vulcan Forging Co.,* 188 F.(2d) 927, petitioner refused to bargain with the union. The Labor Board found, 98 NLRB 976, that petitioner had thereby committed an unfair labor practice in violation of Sections 8(a)(1) and 8(a)(5) of the amended National Labor Relations Act, 61 Stat. 140–141, 29 U.S.C. Sections 158(a)(1), (a)(5), and the Court of Appeals for the Ninth Circuit enforced the Board's order to bargain, 204 F.(2d) 899. In view of the conflict between the circuits, we granted certiorari, 347 U.S. 916.

The issue before us is the duty of an employer toward a duly certified bargaining agent if, shortly after the election which resulted in the certification, the union has lost, without the employer's fault, a majority of the employees from its membership.

Under the original Wagner Act, the Labor Board was given the power to certify a union as the exclusive representative of the employees in a bargaining unit when it had determined, by election or "any other suitable method," that the union commanded majority support. Section 9(c), 49 Stat. 453. In exercising this authority the Board evolved a number of working rules, of which the following are relevant to our purpose:

(a) A certification, if based on a Board-conducted election, must be honored for a "reasonable" period, ordinarily "one year," in the absence of "unusual circumstances."

(b) "Unusual circumstances" were found in at least three situations: (1) the certified union dissolved or became defunct; (2) as a result of a schism, substantially all the members and officers of the certified union transferred their affiliation to a new local or international; (3) the size of the bargaining unit fluctuated radically within a short time.

(c) Loss of majority support after the "reasonable" period could be questioned in two ways: (1) employer's refusal to bargain, or (2) petition by a rival union for a new election.

(d) If the initial election resulted in a majority for "no union," the election—unlike a certification—did not bar a second election within a year.

The Board uniformly found an unfair labor practice where, during the so-called "certification year," an employer refused to bargain on the ground that the certified union no longer possessed a majority. While the courts in the main enforced the Board's decisions, they did not commit themselves to one year as the determinate content of reasonableness. The Board and the courts proceeded along this line of reasoning:

(a) In the political and business spheres, the choice of the voters in an election binds them for a fixed time. This promotes a sense of responsibility in the electorate and needed coherence in administration. These considerations are equally relevant to healthy labor relations.

(b) Since an election is a solemn and costly occasion, conducted under safeguards to voluntary choice, revocation of authority should occur by a procedure no less solemn than that of the initial designation. A petition or a public meeting—in which those voting for and against unionism are disclosed to management, and in which the influences of mass psychology are present —is not comparable to the privacy and independence of the voting booth.

(c) A union should be given ample time for carrying out its mandate on behalf of its members, and should not be under exigent pressure to produce hothouse results or be turned out.

(d) It is scarcely conducive to bargaining in good faith for an employer to know that, if he dillydallies or subtly undermines, union strength may erode and thereby relieve him of his statutory duties at any time, while if he works conscientiously toward agreement, the rank and file may, at the last moment, repudiate their agent.

(e) In situations, not wholly rare, where unions are competing, raiding and strife will be minimized if elections are not at the hazard of informal and short-term recall.

Certain aspects of the Labor Board's representation procedures came under scrutiny in the Congress that enacted the Taft-Hartley Act in 1947, 61 Stat. 136. Congress was mindful that, once employees had chosen a union, they could not vote to revoke its authority and refrain from union activities, while if they voted against having a union in the first place, the union could begin at once to agitate for a new election. The National Labor Relations Act was amended to provide that (a) employees could petition the Board for a decertification election, at which they would have an opportunity to choose no longer to be represented by a union, 61 Stat. 144, 29 U.S.C. Sec. 159(c)(1)(A)(ii); (b) an employer, if in doubt as to the majority claimed by a union without formal election or beset by the conflicting claims of rival unions, could likewise petition the Board for an election, 61 Stat. 144, 29 U.S.C. Sec. 159(c)(1)(B); (c) after a valid certification or decertification election had been conducted, the Board could not hold a second election in the same bargaining unit until a year had elapsed, 61 Stat. 144, 29 U.S.C. Sec. 159(c)(3); (d) Board certification could only be granted as the result of an election, 61 Stat. 144, 29 U.S.C. Sec. 159(c)(1), though an employer would presumably still be under a duty to bargain with an uncertified union that had a clear majority, see *Labor Board* v. *Kobritz,* 193 F.(2d) 8 (C.A. 1st Cir.)

The Board continued to apply its "one-year certification" rule after the Taft-Hartley Act came into force, except that even "unusual circumstances" no longer left the Board free to order an election where one had taken place within the preceding 12 months. Conflicting views became manifest in the Courts of Appeals when the Board sought to enforce orders based on refusal to bargain in violation of its rule. Some Circuits sanctioned the Board's position. The Court of Appeals for the Sixth Circuit denied enforcement. The Court of Appeals for the Third Circuit held that a "reasonable" period depended on the facts of the particular case.

The issue is open here. No case touching the problem has directly presented it. In *Franks Bros. Co.* v. *Labor Board,* 321 U.S. 702, we held that where a union's majority was dissipated after an employer's unfair labor practice in refusing to bargain, the Board could appropriately find that such conduct had undermined the prestige of the union and require the employer to bargain with it for a reasonable period despite the loss of majority. And in *Labor Board* v. *Mexia Textile Mills, Inc.,* 339 U.S. 563, we held that a claim of an intervening loss of majority was no defense to a proceeding for enforcement of an order to cease and desist from certain unfair labor practices.

Petitioner contends that whenever an employer is presented with evidence that his employees have deserted their certified union, he may forthwith refuse to bargain. In effect, he seeks to vindicate the rights of his employees to select their bargaining representative. If the employees are dissatisfied with their chosen union, they may submit their own grievance to the Board. If an employer has doubts about his duty to continue bargaining, it is his responsibility to petition the Board for relief, while continuing to bargain in good faith at least until the Board has given some indication that his claim has merit. Although the Board may, if the facts warrant, revoke a certification or agree not to pursue a charge of an unfair labor practice, these are matters for the Board; they do not justify employer self-help or judicial intervention. . . .

CASE QUESTIONS	**1.** What does the decision say as to the discretion of the NLRB to decide when to order a collective bargaining election?
	2. What does the Supreme Court say is the employer's duty when presented with evidence that employees have deserted their certified union?
	3. How did the Taft-Hartley Act in 1947 change the authority of the NLRB to conduct employee ballots on matters of bargaining agency?
	4. What purpose is served by the rules barring elections for one year or during a contract period?

SECTION 37 / **REPRESENTATION ELECTIONS**

Under either the NLRA or the RLA, the agents of the boards conduct collective bargaining elections by consent of the parties or by order of the boards. Such questions as time and place, the standards and rules of conduct, eligibility to vote, use of tellers or watchers, electioneering, and handling of challenges are settled by agreement or by ruling of the Board agent if no agreement seems possible. The time, the standards of conduct, electioneering rules, and other details are designed to assure the voters the opportunity to determine the wishes of the majority by a free and unimpeded expression of individual choice.

The first question is the bargaining unit or arrangements to allow craft workers or professionals to help decide the unit by their votes. The next issue, eligibility to vote, depends upon the status of each employee on the payroll at some date prior to the date of voting and also on the election date. An employee must be on the active payroll of the eligibility period and also working for the employer at the time of the election; those on leave, temporarily laid off, or on vacation may vote if present at the polling place.

An economic striker who has been permanently replaced and thus not entitled to reinstatement is eligible to vote in any election held within 12 months of the commencement of the strike, under Section 9(c)(3) of the Act. Replacements of economic strikers are considered eligible to vote as permanent employees, provided they were employed both at the eligibility date and the election date, unless the challenger can prove the contrary. Unfair labor practice strikers are entitled to vote regardless of the 12-month statutory restriction; and replacements for these strikers are not.[4]

For certification as bargaining agent, a labor union or an individual candidate must receive a majority of the valid votes cast in the appropriate unit. The policy of only the NLRB, unlike the NMB, requires that a substantial number of those eligible must participate although less than a majority of all employees

---

[4] See Chapter 9, Sections 79 and 80 for a detailed discussion on the status of economic strikers and unfair labor practices strikers.

may have voted. This follows the principle applied to our political elections where no requirement exists that a minimum percentage of all eligible must actually vote in an election.

In collective bargaining elections the requirements of majority choice for certification may cause the necessity of a runoff election where more than two choices on a ballot results in a majority of the voters rejecting "no union" while no majority chose any one union. The amended NLRA states in Section 9(c): "In any election where none of the choices on the ballot receives a majority, a runoff shall be conducted, the ballot providing for a selection between the two choices receiving the largest and second largest number of valid votes cast in the election." This policy as previously worked out by the NLRB is the subject of the discussion in the *Standard Lime and Stone Company* case that is printed below, the court enforcing the Board's position.

The employer may challenge the result of an election certification by refusing to bargain, or the election result may be challenged by filing objections to the conduct of the balloting or to violations of rules or interference in the voting rights of participants. Such protests must be filed within a specified number of days, usually five, for a determination by the regional office or an appeal to the Board itself. If sustained, the objections may cause the invalidation of the election, the remedying of irregularities, and a new vote with the notice sometimes stating why the first election was held void.

The court in the *Standard Lime and Stone Company* decision leaves it for the Board, not the courts, "to say whether an election is fair and representative."

National Labor Relations Board v. Standard Lime and Stone Company

Circuit Court of Appeals, Fourth Circuit, 1945. 149 Fed. (2d) 435

PARKER, C. J. This is a petition to enforce an order of the National Labor Relations Board directing the Standard Lime and Stone Company to bargain collectively with an A. F. of L. union as the bargaining representative of its employees. The company resists enforcement on the ground that the union has not been chosen as bargaining representative because (1) a majority of eligible employees did not participate in the election at which the union was chosen, (2) the election was not representative of the choice of the majority, and (3) opportunity was not given, in a runoff election between two unions, to vote against representation by either.

The facts are that a United Mine Workers union petitioned the Board to make an investigation and certify a bargaining representative for the employees of the company. An A. F. of L. union intervened in this proceeding and on April 13, 1943, the Board proceeded to hold an election at which the company's employees were allowed to indicate by secret ballot their choice of the U.M.W. union, the A. F. of L. union or "neither" as bargaining representative. 439 employees were eligible to vote in this election, but only 218 votes were cast. 99 of these were cast for the A. F. of L. union, 62 for the U.M.W. union, and 57 for "neither." The company then asked that the petition be dismissed, but both unions asked that a run-off election be held and, on May 14, 1943, one was held between the two unions, with the "neither" choice eliminated. At the time of the run-off election, 409 employees were eligible and 166 voted, one of the ballots being void. 137 votes were cast for the A. F. of L. union and 28 for the U.M.W. union.

Both elections were fairly advertised and properly held and there is no evidence of coercion or interference on the part of the company or anyone else, and nothing to indicate that they were not fairly representative of the sentiment of the employees. The Board found that the vote was "substantial and representative" and certified the A. F. of L. union as the bargaining representative. The Company's refusal to bargain with the union was found by the Board to be an unfair labor practice and the usual order was entered directing the company to bargain with it.

On the first and principal question, that presented by lack of majority participation in either of the elections, we think that the conclusive answer is found in the decision of the Supreme Court in *Virginian Railway* v. *System Federation No. 40,* 300 U.S. 515, affirming the decision of this Court reported in 84 F.2d 641. In that case both this Court and the Supreme Court held that, in employees' elections under the Railway Labor Act for the selection of bargaining representatives, the political principle of majority rule should be applied, viz., that those not participating in the election must be presumed to assent to the expressed will of the majority of those voting, so that such majority determines a choice. The Supreme Court said: "Section 2, Fourth, of the Railway Labor Act provides: 'The majority of any craft or class of employees shall have the right to determine who shall be the representative of the craft or class for the purposes of this Act.' Petitioner construes this section as requiring that a representative be selected by the votes of a majority of eligible voters. It is to be noted that the words of the section confer the right of determination upon a majority of those eligible to vote, but is silent as to the manner in which that right shall be exercised. Election laws providing for approval of a proposal by a specified majority of an electorate have been generally construed as requiring only the consent of the specified majority of those participating in the election. *Carroll County* v. *Smith,* 111 U.S. 556. . . . Those who do not participate are presumed to assent to the expressed will of the majority of those voting. *Cass County* v. *Johnston,* 95 U.S. 360, 369, and see *Carroll County* v. *Smith, supra.* We see no reason for supposing that Sec. 2, Fourth, was intended to adopt a different rule."

And we see no reason to think that a different rule was intended by the National Labor Relations Act. . . .

Although there is no decision of the Supreme Court holding that a majority of the votes cast in an election is sufficient for the choice of a bargaining representative under the National Labor Relations Act, this is the holding of the Labor Board and of all of the Circuit Courts of Appeals which have had occasion to pass upon the question. . . .

The company seeks to distinguish the Virginian Railway case and certain other of the decisions above cited on the ground that a majority of the employees participated in the elections there; but nothing in the statute furnishes the basis for such distinction. . . .

There is every reason to apply the sensible political rule to elections of this sort, and no reason that we can see to the contrary. The elections are held, not for the purpose of choosing representatives for the employees in their private and personal capacities, but for the purposes of collective bargaining, i.e., for the purpose of setting up industrial democracy by choosing someone to represent the interest of the employee in determining the rate of wages, hours of work, living conditions, etc., for the plant. The establishment of such industrial democracy is the avowed purpose of the National Labor Relations Act, which declares it to be in the public interest because of its tendency to preserve industrial peace and prevent interference with interstate commerce. . . . This being true, it would be as absurd to hold that collective bargaining is defeated because a majority of employees fail to participate in an election of representatives as it would be to hold that the people of a municipality are without officers to represent them because a majority of the qualified voters do not participate in an election held to choose such officers. In the one case, as in the other, the representative is being chosen to represent a constituency because it is in the public interest that the constituency be represented; all that should be necessary is that the election be properly advertised and fairly held and that the settled principle of majority rule be applied to the result. If the employees do not wish to be represented in collective bargaining they can so declare in the election; but where, as here, only a comparatively small number so express themselves the result should be not be the same as if a majority had so voted. We pointed out in the Virginian Railway case the disadvantages and dangers which would follow from failure to apply the political rule in such elections.

The contention that the election was not representative is without merit. The Board found that the vote was substantial and representative, and there is nothing in the record to the contrary. The company's argument on the point resolves itself into a contention that an election should not be permitted to determine a choice unless there is affirmative showing that a majority either participated or was prevented in some way from participating; but there is nothing in the statute or in reason to support such a position. It is for the Board, not us, to say whether an election is fair and representative; and where the record shows that over forty percent of the company's employees participated in it and that it was fairly advertised and conducted, we cannot say that the Board's finding that it was representative is arbitrary and unreasonable or without support in the record.

And we are not impressed with the contention that the Board's certification may be ignored because "neither" was omitted from the choices submitted in the run-off election. On the first election only 57 of the votes cast registered that choice, which was less than the votes cast for either of the unions. It could not be unreasonable to drop in the run-off the choice which had received the lowest number of votes.[5] This is quite usual procedure in other elections and we can see nothing unfair in applying it here. . . . Order enforced.[6]

---

[5] Sec. 9(c)(3) or the amended Act is in accord. Only the two highest designations participate in run-off elections.

[6] It has been held that a representation finding by the board is not reviewable in fact or law. *Inland Empire* v. *Millis,* 1945, 325 U.S. 697.

**CASE
QUESTIONS**

1. What is the "political principle" of majority rule?
2. How were the votes cast in the run-off election? State the current rule applied. Was the vote substantial?
3. Why was it justifiable to eliminate the "neither" choice in the run-off election?
4. Why is the current NLRA rule expedient?
5. Does the same majority rule apply under the Railway Labor Act as under the NLRA?

SECTION 38 / ELECTION CONDUCT AND FREE SPEECH

This section is limited in scope to identifying selected pre-election rules and incidents of employer and union conduct that have a major impact on organizational campaigns and free speech.

Pre-Election Rules

The Board has developed a body of rules that impose restrictions on pre-election activities of the parties. The Board prohibits all electioneering activities at polling places.[7] The Board, in its *Peerless Plywood* decision,[8] formulated its "24-hour rule" which prohibits both unions and employers from delivering speeches to captive audiences within 24 hours of an election. The obvious rationale for such a rule is to preserve free elections and prevent any party from obtaining undue advantage. In the *Excelsior Underwear* case, reported in this section, the Board established a prospective rule requiring employers to provide names and addresses of all employees qualified to vote in a representation election.[9] The Board requires this in order to expose all employees to all arguments for and against unionization. Violation of the above rules and other rules promulgated by the Board will be grounds for setting aside an election even if the conduct does not amount to an unfair labor practice. Conduct that is an unfair labor practice under the Act is also viewed as a violation of the Board's election rules.[10]

Employer Free Speech and Section 8(c)

In its administration of the Wagner Act, the NLRB had developed rules in its interpretation of Sec. 8(1), on employer interference, which had the effect of limiting the employers' constitutional prerogative of free speech. Critics of the Act contended that its administration was one-sided, especially in permitting freedom of speech to employees while at the same time restricting the same right as to employers. Controversies on this point arose most frequently in connection with union organizing campaigns, during which the employer might himself, or through his agents, address his employees on the subject of his opinion of labor

---

[7] *Alliance Ware, Inc.,* 92 NLRB 55 (1950); Michelm Inc., 170 NLRB 46 (1968).
[8] *Peerless Plywood Co.,* 107 NLRB 427 (1953).
[9] *Excelsior Underwear Inc.,* 156 NLRB 1236 (1966): the rule was accepted by the U. S. Supreme Court in *NLRB* v. *Wyman-Gordan Co.,* 394 U.S. 759 (1969).
[10] *Dal-Tex Optical, Co.,* 137 NLRB 1782 (1962).

unionism. More frequently than not, antiunion statements were made, giving rise to charges of interference and coercion against the employer.

In deciding whether antiunion statements amounted to interference and restraint in violation of Sec. 8(1), the Board found two questions of importance:

(a) Were the statements made coercive *per se,* such as threats to dismiss everyone who joined the union or a threat to close down the plant if the union won support of the employees? Statements that were coercive in themselves were held to constitute unlawful interference. This class of statement remains unprivileged under the 1947 Act.

(b) If the statements were not coercive *per se,* or standing alone, were they raised to coercive impact because of the total antiunion history of the employer, of which the statements were but a part? If the total conduct of the employer indicated an antilabor background, statements that were innocent in themselves could be considered as being coercive and violative of Sec. 8(1) of the Act.

The Labor Relations Act of 1947 left intact rule (a) above, but did not any longer permit the Board to apply the "totality of conduct" doctrine to antiunion statements that are innocent when standing alone. A new Sec. 8(c) now prescribes that "the expressing of any views, argument, or opinion . . . shall not constitute or be evidence of an unfair labor practice . . . if such expression contains no threat of reprisal or force or promise of benefit."

The Supreme Court, in a segment of the *Gissel* case reported in this section, considered the question of whether certain specific statements made by an employer to his employees constituted an election-voiding "threat of reprisal" and thus fell outside the protection of the First Amendment and 8(c) of the Act. In this segment of *Gissel,* the court established guidelines for employer pre-election statements and predictions about the effect of unionization of his company. An employer is free to tell only what he reasonably believes will be the likely economic consequences of unionization that are outside of his control.

Just as the "free speech" proviso of Section 8(c) of the Act will not protect an employer whose statements are found to be a "threat of reprisal" and a violation of § 8(a)(1), so also a "promise of benefit" by an employer, who times his promise to influence a representation election also violates section 8(a)(1). This is known as the *Exchange Parts* rule.[11] In *Hineline's Meat Plant, Inc.,*[12] the Board set aside an election where the employer announced a new profit-sharing plan to his employees eleven days before the election. Relying on the *Exchange Parts* rule, the Board found that since the announcement could have been delayed until after the election, it was possible that the company had timed the announcement to influence the employees' vote. Consequently the Board found a violation of 8(a)(1) and set aside the election.

No Solicitation Rules

While Section 7 of the Act gives employees the statutory right to self-organization, employers have the undisputed prerogative to make rules to maintain discipline in their establishments. Generally speaking, employers may

[11] *NLRB* v. *Exchange Parts Co.,* 375 U.S. 405 (1964).
[12] *Hineline's Meat Plant, Inc.,* 193 NLRB 135 (1971).

prohibit union solicitation by employees during work periods. As to nonworking time, employers may prohibit activity and communications if legitimate efficiency and safety reasons exist, and where not manifestly intended to impede employees' exercise of their rights under the law. In the *Armstrong Tire* case, the Board stated that "[t]he burden rests upon an employer to establish that safety conditions actually require an invasion of the normal exercise by his employees of self-organizational rights during nonworking time." [13]

Nonemployee union organizers have lesser rights than employees. The Supreme Court has held that an employer may validly post his property against nonemployee distribution of union literature if reasonable efforts by the union through other available channels of communications will enable it to reach the employees with its message.[14] The *Excelsior* case, which provides names and addresses to all interested parties, now insures that nonemployee union organizers have another available channel to reach employees.

Racial Prejudice

In recent years the use of electioneering material appealing to race consciousness or racial hostility has become the basis of election objections. The policy of the Board was stated in the *Sewell Manufacturing Company* case as placing the burden on the user of racial arguments to establish that they are true and germane to election issues rather than attempts to exacerbate or exaggerate racial feelings by irrelevant inflammatory appeals. Any doubts as to when such communication falls within or beyond permissible limits will be resolved against the party using such material.[15]

Election Propaganda

The Board may set an election aside if it finds that propaganda prejudicial to a free expression of employees' wishes accompanied the balloting. The criterion then is the employees' right to select or reject representatives in an atmosphere conducive to a free choice. Whether or not attributed to one of the parties, objections based on propaganda will be considered in relation to coercive impact, fraud, special knowledge of the facts by the promulgator, opportunity of the challenger to have rebutted any false assertions, whether the employees could be expected to evaluate the propaganda as such, and the pertinent circumstances.

In the *Hollywood Ceramics* case, the Board expressed its method of resolving objections to elections in the following explanatory dicta:

"We believe that an election should be set aside only where there has been a misrepresentation or other similar campaign trickery which involves a substantial departure from the truth, at a time which prevents the other party or parties from making an effective reply, so that the misrepresentation, whether deliberate or not, may reasonably be expected to have a significant impact on the election. However, the mere fact that a message is inartistic or vaguely worded and subject to different

---

[13] *Armstrong Tire and Rubber Co.,* 119 NLRB 382 (1958).
[14] *NLRB* v. *Babcock and Wilcox Co.,* 351 U.S. 105 (1956). See *Central Hardware* v. *NLRB,* 407 U.S. 539 (1972) reported in Chapter 8.
[15] *Sewell Manufacturing Company,* 138 NLRB 66 (1962).

interpretations will not suffice to establish such misrepresentation as would lead us to set the election aside. Such ambiguities, like extravagant promises, derogatory statements about the other party, and minor distortions of some facts, frequently occur in communication between persons. But even where a misrepresentation is shown to have been substantial, the Board may still refuse to set aside the election if it finds upon consideration of all the circumstances that the statement would not be likely to have had a real impact on the election. For example, the misrepresentation might have occurred in connection with an unimportant matter so that it could have had a *de minimis* effect. Or it could have been so extreme as to put the employees on notice of its lack of truth under the particular circumstances so that they could not reasonably have relied on the assertion. Or the Board may find that the employees possessed independent knowledge with which to evaluate the statements." [16]

In *Bausch & Lomb, Inc.* v. *NLRB*,[17] the Second Circuit affirmed the NLRB's invalidation of a representation election where an employer two days before the election mailed a letter to employees informing them that the union local at another company plant had recently agreed to a contract without a Christmas bonus provision. The letter failed to mention that the union had obtained a wage increase and extended sickpay in exchange for dropping its Christmas bonus demand. The union lost the election. In rejecting the company's allegation that the Board had abused its discretion in invalidating the election, the Court noted that the *Hollywood Ceramics* tests had been satisfied. First, the misstatement was of a material fact; the employees would obviously be concerned with such a valuable right. Second, the union did not have time to reply; the letter was received just two days prior to the election. Third, the company was in a position to have "special knowledge" of the facts. And fourth, the employees lacked independent knowledge with which to evaluate the statement.

Excelsior Underwear, Inc.

156 NLRB No. 111 (1966).

. . . We are persuaded, for the reasons set out below, that higher standards of disclosure than we have heretofore imposed are necessary, and that prompt disclosure of the information here sought by the Petitioners should be required in all representation elections. Accordingly, we now establish a requirement that will be applied in all election cases. That is, within 7 days after the Regional Director has approved a consent-election agreement entered into by the parties pursuant to Section 102.62 of the National Labor Relations Board Rules and Regulations or after the Regional Director or the Board has directed an election pursuant to Section 102.67, 102.69, or Section 102.85 thereof, the employer must file with the Regional Director an election eligibility list, containing the names and addresses of all the eligible voters. The Regional Director, in turn, shall make this information available to all parties in the case. Failure to comply with this requirement shall be grounds for setting aside the election whenever proper objections are filed.

---

[16] *Hollywood Ceramics Co.,* 140 NLRB 221 (1962).
[17] *Bausch & Lomb, Inc.* v. *NLRB,* 451 F.2d 873 (1971).

The considerations that impel us to adopt the foregoing rule are these: "The control of the election proceeding, and the determination of the steps necessary to conduct that election fairly [are] matters which Congress entrusted to the Board alone." In discharging that trust, we regard it as the Board's function to conduct elections in which employees have the opportunity to cast their ballots for or against representation under circumstances that are free not only from interference, restraint, or coercion violative of the Act, but also from other elements that prevent or impede a free and reasoned choice. Among the factors that undoubtedly tend to impede such a choice is a lack of information with respect to one of the choices available. In other words, an employee who has had an effective opportunity to hear the arguments concerning representation is in a better position to make a more fully informed and reasoned choice. Accordingly, we think that it is appropriate for us to remove the impediment to communication to which our new rule is directed.

As a practical matter, an employer, through his possession of employee names and home addresses as well as his ability to communicate with employees on plant premises, is assured of the continuing opportunity to inform the entire electorate of his views with respect to union representation. On the other hand, without a list of employee names and addresses, a labor organization, whose organizers normally have no right of access to plant premises, has no method by which it can be certain of reaching all the employees with its arguments in favor of representation, and, as a result, employees are often completely unaware of that point of view. This is not, of course, to deny the existence of various means by which a party might be able to communicate with a substantial portion of the electorate even without possessing their names and addresses. It is rather to say what seems to us obvious—that the access of all employees to such communications can be insured only if all parties have the names and addresses of all the voters. In other words, by providing all parties with employees' names and addresses, we maximize the likelihood that all the voters will be exposed to the arguments for, as well as against, union representation.

Nor are employee names and addresses readily available from sources other than the employer. The names of some employees may be secured with the assistance of sympathetic fellow employees, but, in a large plant or store, where many employees are unknown to their fellows, this method may not yield the names and addresses of a major proportion of the total employee complement. Additionally, there are not infrequently employees on layoff status, sick leave, leave of absence, military leave, etc., eligible to vote, yet unknown to their fellow employees. Furthermore, employees are frequently known to their fellows only by first names or nicknames, so that there may be significant problems in obtaining the home addresses even of those employees whose names are known. Finally, all the foregoing difficulties are compounded by the more or less constant turnover in the employee complement of any employer.

In sum, not only does knowledge of employee names and addresses increase the likelihood of an informed employee choice for or against representation, but, in the absence of employer disclosure, a list of names and addresses is extremely difficult if not impossible to obtain. Accordingly, as we have stated, we shall in the future regard an employer's refusal to make a prompt disclosure of this information as tending to interfere with prospects for a fair and free election.

A requirement that all participants in an election contest have the opportunity to ascertain the names and addresses of the voters is not uncommon. Lists of registered voters in public elections are open to inspection and copying by the public. When stockholders wish to participate in election contests (or other proxy contests), management either must provide them with the names and addresses of other stockholders or mail campaign material for them. Any candidate for union office is entitled to have the union distribute his campaign literature to all members.

We see no reason why similar opportunities should not be available in a representation election. As one thoughtful commentator has stated, "Since the opportunity for both sides to reach all the employees is basic to a fair and informed election, the reasons for requiring disclosure seem just as strong as those leading to similar requirements under other provisions of the law."

While the rule we here announce is primarily predicated upon our belief that prompt disclosure of employee names and addresses is necessary to insure an informed electorate, there is yet another basis upon which we rest our decision. As noted, an employer is presently under no obligation to supply an election eligibility list until shortly before the election. The list, when made available, not infrequently contains the names of employees unknown to the union and even to its employee supporters. The reasons for this are in large part the same as those that make it difficult for a union to obtain, other than from the employer, the names of all employees, i.e., large plants with many employees unknown to their fellows, employees on layoff status, sick leave, military leave, etc. With little time (and no home addresses) with which to satisfy itself as to eligibility of the "unknowns," the union is forced either to challenge all those who appear at the polls whom it does not know or risk having ineligible employees vote. The effect of putting the union to this choice, we have found, is to increase the number of challenges, as well as the likelihood that the challenges will be determinative of the election, thus requiring investigation and resolution by the Regional Director or the Board. Prompt disclosure of employee names as well as addresses will, we are convinced, eliminate the necessity for challenges based solely on lack of knowledge as to the voter's identity. Furthermore, bona fide disputes between employer and union over voting eligibility will be more susceptible of settlement without recourse to the formal and time-consuming challenge procedures of the Board if such disputes come to light early in the election campaign rather than in the last few days before the election when the significance of a single vote is apt to loom large in the parties' calculations. Thus, the requirement of prompt disclosure of employee names and addresses will further the public interest in the speedy resolution of questions of representation.

The arguments against imposing a requirement of disclosure are of little force, especially when weighed against the benefits resulting therefrom. . . .

CASE
QUESTIONS

1. State the Board's primary rationale for requiring employers to mail names and addresses of eligible voters to the appropriate regional director who then will make these names and addresses available to all parties to the election proceeding.
2. What action will the Board take for noncompliance with this rule?
3. Will prompt disclosure of employee names and addresses eliminate the necessity of certain election challenges?

NLRB v. Gissel Packing Co., Inc.

Supreme Court of the United States, 1969. 395 U.S. 575

[The portion of this case dealing with the establishment of bargaining rights without an election is reported on page 190 of this chapter.]

No. 585. . . . The petitioner, a producer of mill rolls, wire, and related products at two plants in Holyoke, Massachusetts, was shut down for some three months in 1952 as the result of a strike over contract negotiations with the American Wire Weavers Protective Association (AWWPA), the representative of petitioner's journeymen and apprentice wire weavers from 1933 to 1952. The Company subsequently reopened without a union contract, and its employees remained unrepresented through 1964, when the Company was acquired by an Ohio corporation, with the Company's former president continuing as head of the Holyoke, Massachusetts, division. In July 1965, the International Brotherhood of Teamsters, Local Union No. 404, began an organizing campaign among petitioner's Holyoke employees and by the end of the summer had obtained authorization cards from 11 of the Company's 14 journeymen wire weavers choosing the Union as their bargaining agent. On September 20, the Union notified petitioner that it represented a majority of its wire weavers, requested that the Company bargain with it, and offered to submit the signed cards to a neutral third party for authentication. After petitioner's president declined the Union's request a week later, claiming, *inter alia,* that he had a good faith doubt of majority status because of the cards' inherent unreliability, the Union petitioned, on November 8, for an election that was ultimately set for December 9.

When petitioner's president first learned of the Union's drive in July, he talked with all of his employees in an effort to dissuade them from joining a union. He particularly emphasized the results of the long 1952 strike, which he claimed "almost put our company out of business," and expressed worry that the employees were forgetting the "lessons of the past." He emphasized, secondly, that the Company was still on "thin ice" financially, that the Union's "only weapon is to strike," and that a strike "could lead to the closing of the plant," since the parent company had ample manufacturing facilities elsewhere. He noted, thirdly, that because of their age and the limited usefulness of their skills outside their craft, the employees might not be able to find re-employment if they lost their jobs as a result of a strike. Finally, he warned those who did not believe that the plant could go out of business to "look around Holyoke and see a lot of them out of business." The president sent letters to the same effect to the employees in early November, emphasizing that the parent company had no reason to stay in Massachusetts if profits went down.

During the two or three weeks immediately prior to the election on December 9, the president sent the employees a pamphlet captioned "Do you want another 13-week strike?" stating, *inter alia,* that "We have no doubt that the Teamsters Union can again close the Wire Weaving Department and the entire plant by a strike. We have no hopes that the Teamsters Union Bosses will not call a strike. . . . The Teamsters Union is a strike happy outfit." Similar communications followed in late November, including one stressing the Teamsters' "hoodlum control." Two days before the election, the Company sent out another pamphlet that was entitled "Let's Look at the Record," and that purported to be an obituary of companies in the Holyoke-Springfield, Massachusetts, area that had allegedly gone out of business because of union demands, eliminating some 3,500 jobs; the first page carried a large cartoon showing the preparation of a grave for the Sinclair Company and other head-stones containing the names of other plants allegedly victimized by the unions. Finally, on the day before the election, the president made another personal appeal to his employees to reject the Union. He repeated that the Company's financial condition was precarious; that a possible strike would jeopardize the continued operation of the plant; and that age and lack of education would make re-employment difficult. The Union lost the election 7–6, and then filed both objections to the election and unfair labor practice charges which were consolidated for hearing before the trial examiner.

The Board agreed with the trial examiner that the president's communications with his employees, when considered as a whole, "reasonably tended to convey to the employees the belief or impression that selection of the Union in the forthcoming election could lead [the Company] to close its plant, or to the transfer of the weaving production, with the resultant loss of jobs to the wire weavers." Thus, the Board found that under the "totality of the circumstances" petitioner's activities constituted a violation of § 8(a)(1) of the Act. The Board further agreed with the trial examiner that petitioner's activities, because they "also interfered with the exercise of a free and untrammeled choice in the election," and "tended to foreclose the possibility" of holding a fair election required that the election be set aside. . . . Consequently, the Board set the election aside, entered a cease-and-desist order, and ordered the Company to bargain on request.

On appeal, the Court of Appeals for the First Circuit sustained the Board's findings and conclusions and enforced its order in full. 397 F.2d 157. . . .

We consider finally petitioner Sinclair's First Amendment challenge to the holding of the Board and the Court of Appeals for the First Circuit. At the outset we note that the question raised here most often arises in the context of a nascent union organizational drive, where employers must be careful in waging their anti-union campaign. As to conduct generally, the above noted gradations of unfair labor practices, with their varying consequences, create certain hazards for employers when they seek to estimate or resist unionization efforts. But so long as the differences involve conduct easily avoided, such as discharge, surveillance, and coercive interrogation, we do not think that employers can complain that the distinctions are unreasonably difficult to follow. Where an employer's antiunion efforts consist of speech alone, however, the difficulties raised are not so easily resolved. The Board has eliminated some of the problem areas by no longer requiring an employer to show affirmative reasons for insisting on an election and by permitting him to make reasonable inquiries. We do not decide, of course, whether these allowances are mandatory. But we do note that an employer's free speech right to communicate his views to his employees is firmly established and cannot be infringed by a union or the Board. Thus, § 8(c) (29 U. S. C. § 158(c) (1964 ed.)) merely implements the First Amendment by requiring that the expression of "any views, argument or opinion" shall not be "evidence of an unfair labor practice," so long as such expression contains "no threat of reprisal or force or promise of benefit" in violation of § 8(a)(1). Section 8(a)(1), in turn, prohibits interference, restraint or coercion of employees in the exercise of their right to self-organization.

Any assessment of the precise scope of employer expression, of course, must be made in the context of its labor relations setting. Thus, an employer's rights cannot outweigh the equal rights of the employees to associate freely, as those rights are embodied in § 7 and protected by § 8(a)(1) and the proviso to § 8(c). And any balancing of those rights must take into account the economic dependence of the employees on their employers, and the necessary tendency of the former, because of that relationship, to pick up intended implications of the latter that might be more readily dismissed by a more disinterested ear. Stating these obvious principles is but another way of recognizing that what is basically at stake is the establishment of a nonpermanent, limited relationship between the employer, his economically dependent employee and his union agent, not the election of legislators or the enactment of legislation whereby that relationship is ultimately defined and where the independent voter may be freer to listen more objectively and employers as a class freer to talk. Compare *New York Times Co.* v. *Sullivan,* 376 U.S. 254 (1964).

Within this framework, we must reject the Company's challenge to the decision below and the findings of the Board on which it was based. The standards used below for evaluating the impact of an employer's statements are not seriously questioned by petitioner and we see no need to tamper with them here. Thus, an employer is free to communicate to his employees any of his general views about unionism or any of his specific views about a particular union, so long as the communications do not contain a "threat of reprisal or force or promise of benefit." He may even make a prediction as to the precise effects he believes unionization will have on his company. In such a case, however, the prediction must be carefully phrased on the basis of objective fact to convey an employer's belief as to demonstrably probable consequences beyond his control or to convey a management decision already arrived at to close the plant in case of unionization. See *Textile Workers* v. *Darlington Mfg. Co.,* 380 U.S. 263, 274, n. 20 (1965). If there is any implication that an employer may or may not take action solely on his own initiative for reasons unrelated to economic necessities and known only to him, the statement is no longer a reasonable prediction based on available facts but a threat of retaliation based on misrepresentation and coercion, and as such without the protection of the First Amendment. We therefore agree with the court below that "conveyance of the employer's belief, even though sincere, that unionization will or may result in the closing of the plant is not a statement of fact unless, which is most improbable, the eventuality of closing is capable of proof." 397 F.2d, at 160. As stated elsewhere, an employer is free only to tell "what he reasonably believes will be the likely economic consequences of unionization that are outside his control," and not "threats of economic reprisal to be taken solely on his own volition." *NLRB* v. *River Togs, Inc.,* 382 F.2d 198, 202 (C.A. 2d Cir. 1967).

Equally valid was the finding by the court and the Board that petitioner's statements and communications were not cast as a prediction of "demonstrable economic consequences," 397 F.2d 157, 160, but rather as a threat of retaliatory action. The Board found that petitioner's speeches, pamphlets, leaflets, and letters conveyed the following message: that the company was in a precarious financial condition; that the "strike-happy" union would in all likelihood have to obtain its potentially unreasonable demands by striking, the probable result of which would be a plant shutdown, as the past history of labor relations in the area indicated; and that the employees in such a case would have great difficulty finding employment elsewhere. In carrying out its duty to focus on the question "What did the speaker intend and the listener understand," Cox, Law and the National Labor Policy 44 (1960), the Board could reasonably conclude that the intended and understood import of that message was not to predict that unionization would inevitably cause the plant to close but to threaten to throw employees out of work regardless of the economic realities. In this connection, we need go no further than to point out (1) that petitioner had no support for its basic assumption that the union, which had not yet even presented any demands, would have to strike to be heard, and that it admitted at the hearing that it had no basis for attributing other plant closings in the area to unionism; and (2) that the Board has often found that employees, who are particularly sensitive to rumors of plant closings, take such hints as coercive threats rather than honest forecasts.

Petitioner argues that the line between so-called permitted predictions and proscribed threats is too vague to stand up under traditional First Amendment analysis and that the Board's discretion to curtail free speech rights is correspondingly too uncontrolled. It is true that a reviewing court must recognize the Board's competence in the first instance to judge the impact of utterances made in the context of the employer-employee relationship, see *NLRB* v. *Virginia Electric & Power Co.,* 314 U.S. 469, 479 (1941). But an employer, who has control over that relationship and therefore knows it best, cannot be heard to complain that he is without an adequate guide for his behavior. He can easily make his views known without engaging in " 'brinkmanship' " when it becomes all too easy to "overstep and tumble over the brink," *Wausau Steel Corp.* v. *NLRB*, 377 F.2d 369, 372 (C.A. 7th Cir. 1967). At the least he can avoid coercive speech simply by avoiding conscious overstatements he has reason to believe will mislead his employees.

CASE QUESTIONS

1. State the basis of Sinclair's challenge to the Board's decision.
2. Discuss the free speech differences between a union representation election and the election of a legislator or the enactment of legislation.
3. What standards did the Supreme Court put forth for evaluating employer statements to employees during an organizational campaign?

SECTION 39 / BARGAINING RIGHTS BASED ON AUTHORIZATION CARDS

In *NLRB* v. *Gissel Packing Co.,* which is reported in this section, the Supreme Court set forth the law regarding Board bargaining orders based on authorization cards. The bargaining order remedy is utilized by the Board in the following type of situation. A union conducts an organizational campaign and obtains authorization cards from a majority of the employees in an appropriate bargaining unit. On the basis of these cards the union demands recognition, which is refused on the grounds that the cards are inherently unreliable indicators of employee desires. The employer then conducts an anti-union campaign during which he commits unfair labor practices. Following the union loss and the filing of charges with the Board, if the Board finds that the unfair labor practices had the effect of undermining the union's majority it will set aside the election. The Board will then either order a re-run election or if the employer's conduct was so pervasive as to render a fair re-run election unlikely, the Board may certify the union on the basis of its authorization card majority and order the employer to bargain with it.

In the *Restaurant Associates* case reported below the Board found a bargaining order inappropriate.

In *Gissel,* the Supreme Court left undetermined the issue of whether it would be appropriate to find a section (8)(a)(5) violation and grant a bargaining order in cases where the employer has knowledge, on the basis of cards or other circumstantial evidence, that the union has a valid majority and the employer refuses to recognize the union but refrains from committing independent unfair labor practices. In *Summer & Co. (Linden Lumber),*[18] the Board adopted the rule that absent independent unfair labor practices a bargaining order will not issue unless the employer and the union have agreed on an alternate means of resolving the issue of majority status. The policy to be served by the *Linden* rule is that of encouraging voluntarism while ensuring that the preferred route of a secret election is available to those who do not find any alternate route more acceptable.

---

[18] 190 NLRB No. 116 (1971). See *Wilder Mfg. Co.,* 198 NLRB No. 123 (1972), which reasserts the rule of *Linden Lumber.*

NLRB v. Gissel Packing Co., Inc.

Supreme Court of the United States, 1969. 395 U.S. 575

[The portion of this case dealing with Sinclair's (Case No. 585) First Amendment challenges to the holding of the Board and the Court of Appeals for the First Circuit is reported on page 185 of this chapter.]

WARREN, Ch. J.: These cases involve the extent of an employer's duty under the National Labor Relations Act to recognize a union that bases its claim to representative status solely on the possession of union authorization cards, and the steps an employer may take, particularly with regard to the scope and content of statements he may make, in legitimately resisting such card-based recognition. The specific questions facing us here are whether the duty to bargain can arise without a Board election under the Act; whether union authorization cards, if obtained from a majority of employees without misrepresentation or coercion, are reliable enough generally to provide a valid, alternate route to majority status; whether a bargaining order is an appropriate and authorized remedy where an employer rejects a card majority while at the same time committing unfair labor practices that tend to undermine the union's majority and make a fair election an unlikely possibility; and whether certain specific statements made by an employer to his employees constituted such an election-voiding unfair labor practice and thus fell outside the protection of the First Amendment and § 8(c) of the Act. For reasons given below, we answer each of these questions in the affirmative.

Of the four cases before us, three—*Gissel Packing Co., Heck's Inc.,* and *General Steel Products, Inc.*—were consolidated following separate decisions in the Court of Appeals for the Fourth Circuit and brought here by the National Labor Relations Board in No. 573. Food Store Employees Union, Local No. 347, the petitioning Union in *Gissel,* brought that case here in a separate petition in No. 691. All three cases present the same legal issues in similar, uncomplicated factual settings that can be briefly described together. The fourth case, No. 585 *(Sinclair Company),* brought here from the Court of Appeals for the First Circuit and argued separately, presents many of the same questions and will thus be disposed of in this opinion; but because the validity of some of the Board's factual findings are under attack on First Amendment grounds, detailed attention must be paid to the factual setting of that case.

Nos. 573 and 691. In each of the cases from the Fourth Circuit, the course of action followed by the Union and the employer and the Board's response were similar. In each case, the Union waged an organizational campaign, obtained authorization cards from a majority of employees in the appropriate bargaining unit, and then, on the basis of the cards, demanded recognition by the employer. All three employers refused to bargain on the ground that authorization cards were inherently unreliable indicators of employee desires; and they either embarked on, or continued, vigorous antiunion campaigns that gave rise to numerous unfair labor practice charges. In *Gissel,* where the employer's campaign began almost at the outset of the Union's organizational drive, the Union (petitioner in No. 691) did not seek an election, but instead filed three unfair labor practice charges against the employer, for refusing to bargain in violation of § 8(a)(5), for coercion and intimidation of employees in violation of § 8(a)(1), and for discharge of Union adherents in violation of § 8(a)(3).[19] In *Heck's* an election sought by the Union was never held because of nearly identical unfair labor practice charges later filed by the Union as a result of the employer's antiunion campaign, initiated after the Union's recognition demand. And in *General Steel,* an election petitioned for by the Union and won by the employer was set aside by the Board because of the unfair labor practices committed by the employer in the preelection period.

In each case, the Board's primary response was an order to bargain directed at the employers, despite the absence of an election in *Gissel* and *Heck's* and the employer's victory in *General Steel.* More specifically, the Board found in each case that (1) the Union had obtained valid authorization cards [20] from a majority of the employees in the bargaining unit and was thus entitled to represent the employees for collective bargaining purposes; and (2) that the employer's refusal to bargain with the Union in violation of § 8(a)(5) was motivated not by a "good faith" doubt of the Union's majority status, but by a desire to gain time to dissipate that status. The Board based its conclusion as to the lack of good faith doubt on the fact that the employers had committed substantial unfair labor practices during their antiunion campaign efforts to resist recognition. Thus, the Board found that all three employers had engaged in restraint and coercion of employees in violation of § 8(a)(1)—in *Gissel,* for coercively interrogating employees about Union activities, threatening them with discharge and promising them benefits; in *Heck's,* for coercively interrogating employees, threatening reprisals, creating the appearance of surveillance, and offering benefits for opposing the Union; and in *General Steel,* for coercive interrogation and threats of reprisals, including discharge. In addition, the Board found that the employers in *Gissel* and *Heck's* had wrongfully discharged employees for engaging in Union activities in violation of § 8(a)(3). And, because the employers had rejected the card-based bargaining demand in bad faith, the Board found that all three had refused to recognize the Unions in violation of § 8(a)(5).

---

[19] At the outset of the Union campaign, the Company vice president informed two employees, later discharged, that if they were caught talking to Union men, "you God-damned things will go." Subsequently, the union presented oral and written demands for recognition, claiming possession of authorization cards from 31 of the 47 employees in the appropriate unit. Rejecting the bargaining demand, the Company began to interrogate employees as to their Union activities; to promise them better benefits than the Union could offer; and to warn them that if the "union got in, [the vice president] would just take his money and let the union run the place," that the Union was not going to get in, and that it would have to "fight" the Company first. Further, when the Company learned of an impending Union meeting, it arranged, so the Board later found, to have an agent present to report the identity of the Union's adherents. On the first day following the meeting, the vice president told the two employees referred to above that he knew they had gone to the meeting and that their work hours were henceforth reduced to half a day. Three hours later, the two employees were discharged.

[20] The cards used in all four campaigns in Nos. 573 and 691 and in the one drive in No. 585 unambiguously authorized the Union to represent the signing employee for collective bargaining purposes; there was no reference to elections. Typical of the cards was the one used in the Charleston campaign in *Heck's,* and it stated in relevant part:

"Desiring to become a member of the above Union of the International Brotherhood of Teamsters, Chauffeurs, Warehousemen and Helpers of America, I hereby make application for admission to membership. I hereby authorize you, or your agents or representatives to act for me as collective bargaining agent on all matters pertaining to rates of pay, hours or any other condition of employment."

Only in *General Steel* was there any objection by an employer to the validity of the cards and the manner in which they had been solicited, and the doubt raised by the evidence was resolved in the following manner. The customary approach of the Board in dealing with allegations of misrepresentation by the Union and misunderstanding by the employees of the purpose for which the cards were being solicited has been set out in *Cumberland Shoe Corp.*, 144 NLRB 1268 (1963), and reaffirmed in *Levi Strauss & Co.*, 172 NLRB No. 57 . . . (1968). Under the *Cumberland Shoe* doctrine, if the card itself is unambiguous (*i.e.*, states on its face that the signer authorizes the Union to represent the employee for collective bargaining purposes and not to seek an election), it will be counted unless it is proved that the employee was told that the card was to be used *solely* for the purpose of obtaining an election. In *General Steel*, the trial examiner considered the allegations of misrepresentation at length and, applying the Board's customary analysis, rejected the claims with findings that were adopted by the Board. . . .[21]

Consequently, the Board ordered the companies to cease and desist from their unfair labor practices, to offer reinstatement and back pay to the employees who had been discriminatorily discharged, to bargain with the Union on request, and to post the appropriate notices.

On appeal, the Court of Appeals for the Fourth Circuit, in *per curiam* opinions in each of the three cases (398 F.2d 336, 337, 339), sustained the Board's findings as to the §§ 8(a)(1) and (3) violations, but rejected the Board's findings that the employers' refusal to bargain violated § 8(a)(5) and declined to enforce those portions of the Board's orders directing the respondent companies to bargain in good faith. The court based its § 8(a)(5) rulings on its 1967 decisions raising the same fundamental issues. . . . The court in those cases held that the 1947 Taft-Hartley amendments to the Act, which permitted the Board to resolve representation disputes by certification under § 9(c) only by secret ballot election, withdrew from the Board the authority to order an employer to bargain under § 8(a)(5) on the basis of cards, in the absence of NLRB certification, unless the employer knows independently of the cards that there is in fact no representation dispute. The court held that the cards themselves were so inherently unreliable that their use gave an employer virtually an automatic, good faith claim that such a dispute existed, for which a secret election was necessary. Thus, these rulings established that a company could not be ordered to bargain unless (1) there was no question about a Union's majority status (either because the employer agreed the cards were valid or had conducted his own poll so indicating), or (2) the employer's §§ 8(a)(1) and (3) unfair labor practices committed during the representation campaign were so extensive and pervasive that a bargaining order was the only available Board remedy irrespective of a card majority.

Thus based on the earlier decisions, the court's reasoning in these cases was brief, as indicated by the representative holding in *Heck's:*

---

[21] "Accordingly, I reject respondent's contention that if a man is told that his card will be secret, or will be shown only to the Labor Board for the purpose of obtaining election, that this is the absolute equivalent of telling him that it will be used 'only' for the purpose of obtaining an election."

"We have recently discussed the unreliability of the cards, in the usual case, in determining whether or not a union has attained a majority status and have concluded that an employer is justified in entertaining a good faith doubt of the union's claims when confronted with a demand for recognition based solely upon authorization cards. We have also noted that the National Labor Relations Act after the Taft-Hartley amendments provides for an election as the sole basis of a certification and restricts the Board to the use of secret ballots for the resolution of representation questions. This is not one of those extraordinary cases in which a bargaining order might be an appropriate remedy for pervasive violations of § 8(a)(1). It is controlled by our recent decisions and their reasoning. . . . There was not substantial evidence to support the findings of the Board that Heck's, Inc., had no good faith doubt of the unions' claims of majorities." 398 F.2d, at 338, 339. . . .

In urging us to reverse the Fourth Circuit and to affirm the First Circuit, the National Labor Relations Board contends that we should approve its interpretation and administration of the duties and obligations imposed by the Act in authorization card cases. . . .

The traditional approach utilized by the Board for many years has been known as the *Joy Silk* doctrine. *Joy Silk Mills, Inc. v. NLRB,* 85 NLRB 1263 (1949), enforced 87 U.S. App. D.C. 360, 185 F.2d 732 (C.A.D.C. Cir. 1950). Under that rule, an employer could lawfully refuse to bargain with a union claiming representative status through possession of authorization cards if he had a "good faith doubt" as to the union's majority status; instead of bargaining, he could insist that the union seek an election in order to test out his doubts. The Board, then, could find a lack of good faith doubt and enter a bargaining order in one of two ways. It could find (1) that the employer's ind pendent unfair labor practices were evidence of bad faith, showing that the employer was seeking time to dissipate the union's majority. Or the Board could find (2) that the employer had come forward with no reasons for entertaining any doubt and therefore that he must have rejected the bargaining demand in bad faith. An example of the second category was *Snow & Sons,* 134 NLRB 709 (1961), enforced 308 F.2d 687 (C.A. 9th Cir. 1962), where the employer reneged on his agreement to bargain after a third party checked the validity of the card signatures and insisted on an election because he doubted that the employees truly desired representation. The Board entered a bargaining order with very broad language to the effect that an employer could not refuse a bargaining demand and seek an election instead "without a valid ground therefor," 134 NLRB at 710–711. . . .

The leading case codifying modifications to the *Joy Silk* doctrine was *Aaron Brothers,* 158 NLRB 1077 (1966). There the Board made it clear that it had shifted the burden to the General Counsel to show bad faith and that an employer "will not be held to have violated his bargaining obligation . . . simply because he refuses to rely upon cards, rather than an election, as the method for determining the union's majority." 158 NLRB, at 1078. Two significant consequences were emphasized. The Board noted (1) that not every unfair labor practice would automatically result in a finding of bad faith and therefore a bargaining order; the Board implied that it would find bad faith only if the unfair labor practice was serious enough to have the tendency to dissipate the union's majority. The Board noted (2) that an employer no longer needed to come forward with reasons for rejecting a bargaining demand. The Board pointed out, however, that a bargaining order would issue if it could prove that an employer's "course of conduct" gave indications as to the employer's bad faith. . . .

Although the Board's brief before this Court generally followed the approach as set out in *Aaron Brothers, supra,* the Board announced at oral argument that it had virtually abandoned the *Joy Silk* doctrine altogether. Under the Board's current practice, an employer's good faith doubt is largely irrelevant, and the key to the issuance of a bargaining order is the commission of serious unfair labor practices that interfere with the election processes and tend to preclude the holding of a fair election. Thus, an employer can insist that a union go to an election, regardless of his subjective motivation, so long as he is not guilty of misconduct; he need give no affirmative reasons for rejecting a recognition request, and he can demand an election with a simple "no comment" to the union. The Board pointed out, however, (1) that an employer could not refuse to bargain if he *knew,* through a personal poll for instance, that a majority of his employees supported the union, and (2) that an employer could not refuse recognition initially because of questions as to the appropriateness of the unit and then later claim, as an afterthought, that he doubted the union's strength. . . .

Because of the employers' refusal to bargain in each of these cases was accompanied by independent unfair labor practices which tend to preclude the holding of a fair election, we need not decide whether a bargaining order is ever appropriate in cases where there is no interference with the election processes. . . .

The first issue facing us is whether a union can establish a bargaining obligation by means other than a Board election and whether the validity of alternate routes to majority status, such as cards, was affected by the 1947 Taft-Hartley amendments. The most commonly traveled route for a union to obtain recognition as the exclusive bargaining representative of an unorganized group of employees is through the Board's election and certification procedures under § 9(c) of the Act (29 U.S.C. § 159(c) (1964 ed.)); it is also, from the Board's point of view, the preferred route. A union is not limited to a Board election, however, for, in addition to § 9, the present Act provides in § 8(a)(5) (29 U. S. C. § 158(a)(5) (1964 ed.)), as did the Wagner Act in § 8(5), that "it shall be an unfair labor practice for an employer . . . to refuse to bargain collectively with the representatives of his employees, subject to the provisions of section 9(a)." Since § 9(a), in both the Wagner Act and the present Act, refers to the representative as the one "designated or selected" by a majority of the employees without specifying precisely how that representative is to be chosen, it was early recognized that an employer had a duty to bargain whenever the union representative presented "convincing evidence of majority support." Almost from the inception of the Act, then, it was recognized that a union did not have to be certified as the winner of a Board election to invoke a bargaining obligation; it could establish majority status by other means under the unfair labor practice provision of § 8(a)(5)—by showing convincing support, for instance, by a union-called strike or strike vote, or, as here, by possession of cards signed by a majority of the employees authorizing the union to represent them for collective bargaining purposes.

We have consistently accepted this interpretation of the Wagner Act and the present Act, particularly as to the use of authorization cards. . . .

In short, we hold that the 1947 amendments did not restrict an employer's duty to bargain under § 8(a)(5) solely to those unions whose representative status is certified after a Board election.

We next consider the question whether authorization cards are such inherently unreliable indicators of employee desires that whatever the validity of other alternate routes to representative status, the cards themselves may never be used to determine a union's majority and to support an order to bargain. In this context, the employers urge us to take the step the 1947 amendments and their legislative history indicate Congress did not take, namely, to rule out completely the use of cards in the bargaining arena. Even if we do not unhesitatingly accept the Fourth Circuit's view in the matter, the employers argue, at the very least we should overrule the *Cumberland Shoe* doctrine and establish stricter controls over the solicitation of the cards by union representatives.

The objections to the use of cards voiced by the employers and the Fourth Circuit boil down to two contentions: (1) that, as contrasted with the election procedure, the cards cannot accurately reflect an employee's wishes, either because an employer has not had a chance to present his views and thus a chance to insure that the employee choice was an informed one, or because the choice was the result of group pressures and not individual decision made in the privacy of a voting booth; and (2) that quite apart from the election comparison, the cards are too often obtained through misrepresentation and coercion which compound the cards' inherent inferiority to the election process. Neither contention is persuasive, and each proves too much. The Board itself has recognized, and continues to do so here, that secret elections are generally the most satisfactory—indeed the preferred—method of ascertaining whether a union has majority support. The acknowledged superiority of the election process, however, does not mean that cards are thereby rendered totally invalid, for where an employer engages in conduct disruptive of the election process, cards may be the most effective—perhaps the only—way of assuring employee choice. As for misrepresentation, in any specific case of alleged irregularity in the solicitation of the cards, the proper course is to apply the Board's customary standards (to be discussed more fully below) and rule that there was no majority if the standards were not satisfied. It does not follow that because there are some instances of irregularity, the cards can never be used; otherwise, an employer could put off his bargaining obligation indefinitely through continuing interference with elections.

That the cards, though admittedly inferior to the election process, can adequately reflect employee sentiment when that process has been impeded, needs no extended discussion, for the employers' contentions cannot withstand close examination. The employers argue that their employees cannot make an informed choice because the card drive will be over before the employer has had a chance to present his side of the unionization issues. Normally, however, the union will inform the employer of its organization drive early in order to subject the employer to the unfair labor practice provisions of the Act; the union must be able to show the employer's awareness of the drive in order to prove that his contemporaneous conduct constituted unfair labor practices on which a bargaining order can be based if the drive is ultimately successful. See, e. g., *Hunt Oil Co.,* 157 NLRB 282 (1966); *Don Swart Trucking Co.,* 154 NLRB 1345 (1965). Thus, in all of the cases here but the Charleston campaign in *Heck's* the employer, whether informed by the union or not, was aware of the union's organizing drive almost at the outset and began his antiunion campaign at that time; and even in the *Heck's Charleston* case, where the recognition demand came about a week after the solicitation began, the employer was able to deliver a speech before the union obtained a majority. Further, the employers argue that without a secret ballot an employee may, in a card drive, succumb to group pressures or sign simply to get the union "off his back" and then be unable to change his mind as he would be free to do once inside a voting booth. But the same pressures are likely to be equally present in an election, for election cases arise most often with small bargaining units where virtually every voter's sentiments can be carefully and individually canvassed. And no voter, of course, can change his mind after casting a ballot in an election even though he may think better of his choice shortly thereafter.

The employers' second complaint, that the cards are too often obtained through misrepresentation and coercion, must be rejected also in view of the Board's present rules for controlling card solicitation, which we view as adequate to the task where the cards involved state their purpose clearly and unambiguously on their face. We would be closing our eyes to obvious difficulties, of course, if we did not recognize that there have been abuses, primarily arising out of misrepresentations by union organizers as to whether the effect of signing a card was to designate the union to represent the employee for collective bargaining purposes or merely to authorize it to seek an election to determine that issue. And we would be equally blind if we did not recognize that various courts of appeals and commentators have differed significantly as to the Board's *Cumberland Shoe* doctrine to cure such abuses.

In resolving the conflict among the circuits in favor of approving the Board's *Cumberland* rule, we think it sufficient to point out that employees should be bound by the clear language of what they sign unless that language is deliberately and clearly canceled by a union adherent with words calculated to direct the signer to disregard and forget the language above his signature. There is nothing inconsistent in handing an employee a card that says the signer authorizes the union to represent him and then telling him that the card will probably be used first to get an election. Elections have been, after all, and will continue to be, held in the vast majority of cases; the union will still have to have the signatures of 30% of the employees when an employer rejects a bargaining demand and insists that the union seek an election. We cannot agree with the employers here that employees as a rule are too unsophisticated to be bound by what they sign unless expressly told that their act of signing represents something else. In addition to approving the use of cards, of course, Congress has expressly authorized reliance on employee signatures alone in other areas of labor relations, even where criminal sanctions hang in the balance, and we should not act hastily in disregarding congressional judgments that employees can be counted on to take responsibility for their acts.

We agree, however, with the Board's own warnings in *Levi Strauss & Co.,* 172 NLRB No. 57 . . . (1968), that in hearing testimony concerning a card challenge, trial examiners should not neglect their obligation to ensure employee free choice by a too easy mechanical application of the *Cumberland* rule. We also accept the observation that employees are more likely than not, many months after a card drive and in response to questions by a company counsel, to give testimony damaging to the union, particularly where company officials have previously threatened reprisals for union activity in violation of § 8(a)(1). We therefore reject any rule that requires a probe of an employee's subjective motivations as involving an endless and unreliable inquiry. We nevertheless feel that the trial examiner's findings in *General Steel . . .* represent the limits of the *Cumberland* rule's application. We emphasize that the Board should be careful to guard against an approach any more rigid than that in *General Steel.* And we reiterate that nothing we say here indicates our approval of the *Cumberland Shoe* rule when applied to ambiguous, dual-purpose cards.

The employers argue as a final reason for rejecting the use of the cards that they are faced with a Hobson's choice under current Board rules and will almost inevitably come out the loser. They contend that if they do not make an immediate, personal investigation into possible solicitation irregularities to determine whether in fact the union represents an uncoerced majority, they will have unlawfully refused to bargain for failure to have a good faith doubt of the union's majority; and if they do make such an investigation, their efforts at polling and interrogation will constitute an unfair labor practice in violation of § 8(a)(1) and they will again be ordered to bargain. As we have pointed out, however, an employer is not obligated to accept a card check as proof of majority status, under the Board's current practice, and he is not required to justify his insistence on an election by making his own investigation of employee sentiment and showing affirmative reasons for doubting the majority status. See *Aaron Brothers,* 158 NLRB 1077, 1078. If he does make an investigation, the Board's recent cases indicate that reasonable polling in this regard will not always be termed violative of § 8(a)(1) if conducted in accordance with the requirements set out in *Struksnes Construction Co.,* 165 NLRB No. 102 (1967). And even if an employer's limited interrogation is found violative of the Act, it might not be serious enough to call for a bargaining order. See *Aaron Brothers, supra; Hammond & Irving, Inc.,* 154 NLRB No. 84 (1965). As noted above, the Board has emphasized that not "any employer conduct found violative of section 8(a)(1) of the Act, regardless of its nature or gravity, will necessarily support a refusal-to-bargain finding," *Aaron Brothers, supra,* at 1079.

Remaining before us is the propriety of a bargaining order as a remedy for a § 8(a)(5) refusal to bargain where an employer has committed independent unfair labor practices which have made the holding of a fair election unlikely or which have in fact undermined a union's majority and caused an election to be set aside. We have long held that the Board is not limited to a cease-and-desist order in such cases, but has the authority to issue a bargaining order without first requiring the union to show that it has been able to maintain its majority status. . . . And we have held that the Board has the same authority even where it is clear that the union, which once had possession of cards from a majority of the employees, represents only a minority when the bargaining order is entered. *Franks Bros. Co.* v. *NLRB,* 321 U.S. 702 (1944). We see no reason now to withdraw this authority from the Board. If the Board could enter only a cease-and-desist order and direct an election or a rerun, it would in effect be rewarding the employer and allowing him "to profit from [his] own wrongful refusal to bargain," *Franks Bros., supra,* at 704, while at the same time severely curtailing the employees' right freely to determine whether they desire a representative. The employer could continue to delay or disrupt the election processes and put off indefinitely his obligation to bargain; [22] and any election held under these circumstances would not be likely to demonstrate the employees' true, undistorted desires.[23]

The employers argue that the Board has ample remedies, over and above the cease-and-desist order, to control employer misconduct. The Board can, they assert, direct the companies to mail notices to employees, to read notices to employees during plant time and to give the union access to employees during working time at the plant, or it can seek a court injunctive order under § 10(j) (29 U. S. C. § 160(j) (1964 ed.)) as a last resort. In view of the Board's power, they conclude, the bargaining order is an unnecessarily harsh remedy that needlessly prejudices employees' § 7 rights solely for the purpose of punishing or restraining an employer. Such an argument ignores that a bargaining order is designed as much to remedy past election damage as it is to deter future misconduct. If an employer has succeeded in undermining a union's strength and destroying the laboratory conditions necessary for a fair election, he may see no need to violate a cease-and-desist order by further unlawful activity. The damage will have been done, and perhaps the only fair way to effectuate employee rights is to re-establish the conditions as they existed before the employer's unlawful campaign. There is, after all, nothing permanent in a bargaining order, and if, after the effects of the employer's acts have worn off, the employees clearly desire to disavow the union, they can do so by filing a representation petition. For, as we pointed out long ago, in finding that a bargaining order involved no "injustice to employees who may wish to substitute for the particular union some other . . . arrangement," a bargaining relationship "once rightfully established must be permitted to exist and function for a reasonable period in which it can be given a fair chance to succeed," after which the "Board may, . . . upon a proper showing, take steps in recognition of changed situations which might make appropriate changed bargaining relationships." *Frank Bros., supra,* at 705–706.

The only effect of our holding here is to approve the Board's use of the bargaining order in less extraordinary cases marked by less pervasive practices which nonetheless still have the tendency to undermine majority strength and impede the election processes. The Board's authority to issue such an order

---

[22] The Board indicates here that its records show that in the period between January and June 1968, the median time between the filing of an unfair labor practice charge and a Board decision in a contested case was 388 days. But the employer can do more than just put off his bargaining obligation by seeking to slow down the Board's administrative processes. He can also affect the outcome of a rerun election by delaying tactics, for figures show that the longer the time between a tainted election and a rerun, the lesser are the union's chances of reversing the outcome of the first election. See n. 23, *infra.*

[23] A study of 20,153 elections held between 1960 and 1962 shows that in over two-thirds of the cases, the party who caused the election to be set aside won in the rerun election. See Pollitt, NLRB Re-Run Elections: A Study, 41 N. C. L. Rev. 209, 212 (1963).

on a lesser showing of employer misconduct is appropriate, we should reemphasize, where there is also a showing that at one point the union had a majority; in such a case, of course, effectuating ascertainable employee free choice becomes as important a goal as deterring employer misbehaviour. In fashioning a remedy in the exercise of its decretion, then, the Board can properly take into consideration the extensiveness of an employer's unfair practices in terms of their past effect on election conditions and the likelihood of their recurrence in the future. If the Board finds that the possibility of erasing the effects of past practices and of ensuring a fair election (or a fair rerun) by the use of traditional remedies, though present, is slight and that employee sentiment once expressed through cards would, on balance, be better protected by a bargaining order, then such an order should issue. . . .

We emphasize that under the Board's remedial power there is still a third category of minor or less extensive unfair labor practices, which, because of their minimal impact on the election machinery, will not sustain a bargaining order. There is, the Board says, no *per se* rule that the commission of any unfair practice will automatically result in a § 8(a)(5) violation and the issuance of an order to bargain. See *Aaron Brothers, supra.*

With these considerations in mind, we turn to an examination of the orders in these cases. In *Sinclair,* No. 585, the Board made a finding, left undisturbed by the First Circuit, that the employer's threats of reprisal were so coercive that, even in the absence of a § 8(a)(5) violation, a bargaining order would have been necessary to repair the unlawful effect of those threats. The Board therefore did not have to make the determination called for in the intermediate situation above that the risks that a fair rerun election might not be possible were too great to disregard the desires of the employees already expressed through the cards. . . .

In the three cases in Nos. 573 and 691 from the Fourth Circuit, on the other hand, the Board did not make a similar finding that a bargaining order would have been necessary in the absence of an unlawful refusal to bargain. Nor did it make a finding that, even though traditional remedies might be able to ensure a fair election, there was insufficient indication that an election (or a rerun in *General Steel*) would definitely be a more reliable test of the employees' desires than the card count taken before the unfair labor practices occurred. The employees argue that such findings would not be warranted, and the court below ruled in *General Steel* that available remedies short of a bargaining order could guarantee a fair election. 398 F.2d 339, 340, n. 3. We think it possible that the requisite findings were implicit in the Board's decisions below to issue bargaining orders (and to set aside the election in *General Steel*); and we think it clearly inappropriate for the court below to make any contrary finding on its own. . . .

For the foregoing reasons, we affirm the judgment of the Court of Appeals for the First Circuit in No. 585, and we reverse the judgments of the Court of Appeals for the Fourth Circuit in Nos. 573 and 691 insofar as they decline enforcement of the Board's orders to bargain and remand these cases to that Court with directions to remand to the Board for further proceedings consistent with this opinion.

It is so ordered.

Restaurant Associates

(SUPPLEMENT CASE DIGEST—CARD BARGAINING ORDERS)
194 NLRB NO. 172 (1972)

An employer, engaged in the operation of restaurants, was charged with refusing to bargain with a union in violation of Section 8(a)(5) of the Act, and with promising wage increases and threatening a refusal to bargain in the future in violation of Section 8(a)(1) of the Act.

Employees went on strike when the employer refused to bargain on the basis of union cards signed by a majority of employees. During the strike, the employer made various promises of wage increases, including wage adjustments to conform with written rates, a ten percent across-the-board increase, and individual raises. The employer also offered a job to a union ringleader and told employees that in no event would it deal with the union. The employer wanted to end the strike without having a union come in. After the strike, all but one of the promises were broken. . . .

The Board agrees that the employer unlawfully interfered with employee rights by promising wage increases and improved working conditions, by offering a job to a union ringleader, and by stating that it would in no event deal with the union. However, the unfair labor practices were not of a kind and timeliness requiring a bargaining order.

The unfair labor practices were not so likely to have an "inevitably lingering effect" as to preclude a fair election. The employer's breaking of its promises virtually eliminated any lingering effect the promises might have had. Also, the anticipatory refusal to bargain can be dispelled by usual NLRB remedies. The employer has recognized unions at other locations and has expressed an apparent willingness to be bound by election results. That willingness, emphasized by the Board's order, should convey the employer's good-faith intentions to employees. . . .

Member Fanning dissented as to the denial of an 8(a)(5) bargaining order. . . .

Mr. Fanning did not find the breaking of the promises material, since the employer had achieved what he wanted—to reopen the restaurants without having to deal with the union. He believed that the employer's conduct met the tests for a bargaining order laid down by *NLRB* v. *Gissel Packing Co.* . . .

CASE
QUESTIONS

1. Summarize the *Cumberland Shoe* doctrine.
2. What did the Supreme Court say about the Board's *Cumberland* doctrine?
3. Did the Supreme Court hold that the Taft-Hartley amendments limited an employer's duty to bargain under Section 8(a)(5) solely to those unions whose representative status is certified after a Board election?
4. Under *Gissel* when may the Board issue a "bargaining order" remedy?
5. Were the unfair labor practices in the *Restaurant Associates* case of the kind and timeliness that would require a bargaining order remedy?

**QUESTIONS
ON
CHAPTER 5**

1. What differences can be pointed out between certification procedures under the NLRA and the RLA?
2. Why is the employer allowed by the law to be a party to a representation proceeding?
3. What rules as to freedom of electioneering will the courts sustain? What is the related statutory standard?
4. Why is an intervenor allowed easy access to a place on the ballot?

Chapter **6**

Employer Unfair
Labor Practices

SECTION 40 / **THE EMPLOYER-EMPLOYEE RELATION**

Underlying the prohibited practices contained in Section 8 of the 1935 Act, substantially unchanged in Section 8(a) of the current law, was the belief that employee rights need more protection than merely affirmation such as had appeared in the NRA legislation. Because the employer's authority over the employee's job and livelihood provided opportunity for influencing worker conduct and his personal decisions, the Congress prohibited certain practices by which employers have exercised undue control over employees' labor organizational activities.

These employer unfair labor practices, defined in Sections 8(a)(1) through (5), prohibit the following:

1. Interference, restraint, and coercion of employees as to their rights under Section 7, Sec. 8(a)(1).
2. Domination of unions, including employer interference with the administration of, or the furnishing of financial assistance to, labor organizations. Sec. 8(a)(2).
3. Discrimination against employees for union activity as to their terms of hire, tenure, or working conditions. Sec. 8(a)(3).
4. Discrimination for filing charges or giving testimony under the Act. Sec. 8(a)(4).
5. Refusing to bargain collectively with an authorized representative of labor. Sec. 8(a)(5).

SECTION 41 / **FREEDOM FROM INTERFERENCE**

Under the broad and all-inclusive wording of Section 8(a)(1), employers may not interfere with, restrain, or coerce employees in any of their Section 7 rights. Whatever unfair labor practice an employer commits, it automatically means also a violation of this subsection. Moreover, aside from such indirect derivative application of this catchall clause, independent violations occur where an employer commits such acts as these:

a. *Threatening workers*

Even implying the loss of jobs, or promising benefits, or suggesting the loss of benefits related to voting for, or joining a union, or for unionizing the operation has been held to be illegal. A promise "to take care" of those voting against the union, to "get a raise next week" for an employee affirming that he was on the employer's side, or warning that the company would close and move to another location or go out of business entirely before it would deal with a union may be the basis of a finding of interference.

b. *Inquiring on union interest*

An employer's interrogation of employees as to union allegiance or activity may be coercive in itself and unlawful. Questioning job applicants or employees on union sentiment, inquiring as to fellow workers' interests in a union, or systematic interrogation regardless of threats or promises have all been held unlawful in themselves. An employer may lawfully poll employees concerning representation attitudes. Such policy will be an unfair labor practice under the rule of the *Struknes Construction Co.*[1] case unless the following safeguards are observed: (1) the purpose of the poll must be to determine the truth of a union's claim of majority, (2) this purpose must be communicated to the employees, (3) assurances against reprisal must be given, (4) the employees must be polled by secret ballot, and (5) the employer must not have engaged in unfair labor practices or otherwise created a coercive atmosphere.

c. *Prohibiting union activity*

An employer may have a rule against union activity on company working time if fairly applied and if not for discriminating purposes as between unions. Such a rule during nonworking time is illegal unless need can be shown for it to maintain order and discipline or for safe work conditions and production. In one decision the Board found unlawful interference where the employer conduct included "ordering a union business agent to leave company premises where there was no rule against salesmen's solicitations during working hours and where the agent was delivering insurance policies to employees and serving Board subpoenas. . . ."[2]

The peculiar needs of retail operations are recognized by the Board in allowing store rules to prohibit union discussion or solicitation on the selling floors at any time. Such a rule may not legally apply to the entire store premises at all times, nor may management have a rule restricting employees if at the same time it engages in antiunion communications with employees.

The right to talk with fellow workers on nonworking time regarding grievances may not be restricted by management. The Board has found such rules would obstruct the self-organization and representation rights of employees.

d. *Espionage and surveillance*

An employer violates Section 8(a)(1) if managment or its agent attempts surveillance over employee union activities or spies on union conversation or conduct, or even creates the impression of watching such activity. In the *Montgomery Ward* decision, using detectives for this purpose was found unlawful. Other decisions have found interference where supervisors kept a union meeting under surveillance by repeatedly slowly driving by the meeting hall, and where electronic devices in the plant working areas were used to overhear employees' union conversations while at work; when a company official pretended to take motion pictures of employees who were talking to handbill distributing union representatives, this was held to be illegal interference.

---

[1] 165 **NLRB** 1062 (1967).
[2] *Sachs & Sons, et al.,* 135 NLRB No. 111 (1962).

SECTION 42 / DOMINATION OF LABOR ORGANIZATIONS

Employer-formed and -dominated unions are outlawed by the Act in Sec. 8(a)(2). The Board can draw inferences as to domination in those cases where the company contributes aid financially or otherwise, or is instrumental in its formation, and has its agents or supervisory staff solicit membership therein. The Board is entitled to make its decision on domination under the totality of conduct doctrine; namely, many little acts when summed up place the conduct in the unfair labor practice category, even when they are unimportant taken individually.

The National Labor Relations Act, Sec. 10(c) provides that in deciding interference and domination charges, the Board is to treat independent, unaffiliated, and affiliated unions alike. Under the Wagner Act, the Board overlooked some employer-assistance conduct directed toward an affiliated union, but was doubly circumspect with reference to independent unions.

According to the Board, the statute forbids any employer domination of a labor organization in forming it to meet his wishes rather than to represent the free choice of employees. Thus supervisors' attendance and active participation at meetings or by other actions in the formation, subsidies by paying for time spent in organizing or controlling the formal structure and internal composition, or requiring automatic membership of all workers have all been found to be evidences of 8(a)(2) violations.

Illegal employer assistance and support may be less than domination, but still has been found illegal. A favorable action toward one union over another, such as assistance in soliciting employee signatures for membership or dues checkoff cards, recognition by a contract while a majority claim of another union was pending, or recognition of a union representing no employee majority in the bargaining unit, or allowing a supervisor to be a union officer have been held evidences of illegality. The Board and the courts find that even if management or supervisory people, excluded from the bargaining unit, are union members and vote for the union officers who negotiate and administer agreements, an illegal intrusion into union affairs occurs which constitutes illegal employer domination.

SECTION 43 / DISCRIMINATION AS TO HIRE AND TENURE

In the *Jones and Laughlin Steel* decision in Chapter 4, the Supreme Court discussed how Section 8(a)(3) of the National Labor Relations Act forbids the employer all forms of discrimination tending to encourage as well as to discourage membership in a labor union. This rule is subject to the proviso that he may lawfully discriminate in instances where the labor organization is functioning under authority of a union shop or maintenance-of-membership agreement and the union seeks the discharge of an employee because he has failed to pay his dues or initiation fees. See Section 46 in this chapter.

The National Labor Relations Board has found evidence of discrimination against active union supporters where the employer:

a. Gives inconsistent reasons for discharge.
b. Discharges on the strength of past misdeeds that were condoned.
c. Neglects to give customary warning prior to discharge.
d. Discharges for a rule generally unenforced.
e. Applies disproportionately severe punishment to union supporters.
f. Effects layoffs in violation of seniority status, with disproportionate impact on union supporters.

The Act preserves the right of the employer to maintain control over his work force in the interest of discipline, efficiency, and pleasant and safe customer relations. Employees, on the other hand, have the right to be free from coercive discrimination resulting from union activity. Also job applicants, as in the *Phelps Dodge* case reported in Chapter 4, receive the same protection from illegal discrimination.

At times these two rights collide. For example, an employee may be discharged for two reasons: (a) violation of a valid company rule and (b) union activity. The former is given by the employer as the reason for severance; the latter remains unstated on his part, causing the labor organization to file a Sec. 8(a)(3) charge against the employer. These are known as *dual-motive* cases. The general rule in this type of situation is to hold the employer guilty of an unfair labor practice and to remedy the effect of discrimination by ordering reinstatement with back pay or employment and back pay. See the *Goodyear* decision reported in this section.

The exception to the general rule in dual-motive situations is invoked where the *compelling reason* for deciding on a person was not union activity, but some other extenuating circumstance. If the employer finds it necessary to lay off workers because of business inactivity, and does so in accordance with seniority rules, it cannot be held discriminative if, by chance, those workers with the least seniority happen to be the most active in the union.

Then again, suppose that the employee being discharged is an active labor adherent, but that the reason for discharge, coexisting with labor activity, is insubordination, refusal to perform assigned duties or to work overtime, defective performance of work, dangerous or violent conduct, inefficient performance of work, participation in an unlawful strike or property seizure or intoxication. It may be successfully maintained that the compelling reason for discharge was the reason stated rather than union activity. The Board may not "require the reinstatement of any individual . . . if such individual was discharged for cause," as Section 10(c) of the Act defines NLRB powers.

Goodyear Tire & Rubber Co. v. NLRB

United States Court of Appeals, 1972. 456 F.2d 465

MORGAN, C. J.: The issue on this appeal is whether there is substantial evidence in the record to support the Board's decision which overturned the holding by the Trial Examiner and held that Goodyear Tire and Rubber Company violated Section 8(a)(3) of the Act by discharging an employee because of his union activities. Having found a substantial basis in the record to support the Board's holding, we grant the petition for enforcement.

Richard O. Dobbs was an employee of Goodyear. Under contractual arrangement with Greyhound Bus Lines, Goodyear assigned five of its employees to the Greyhound bus terminal in Atlanta, Georgia, for the purpose of changing and repairing bus tires. As one of these employees, Dobbs' principal duties were to perform various types of manual labor in connection with the tire maintenance program. Dobbs' immediate superior was Foreman James M. Porter.

In December of 1970 Goodyear changed its existing two-shift-per-day schedule and initiated a new work schedule providing for three shifts on each day. When Dobbs learned of the new work schedule on December 22nd, he and another Goodyear employee, John Jennings, approached Porter and complained about having their hours changed. In the course of the conversation Dobbs informed Porter that he was going to seek union representation because the employees needed a union in order to "have a say-so as to what hours we would work." Porter replied that if the employees selected a union they would have to punch a time clock, pay their own insurance premiums, and forfeit the right to make up days lost due to sickness.

On January 26, 1971, Porter ordered Dobbs to work the third shift. Dobbs again complained to Porter about the three-shift work schedule and repeated his view that the employees needed union representation. Dobbs then informed Porter that he would take up the matter of shift changes with Porter's superior, District Field Manager E. D. Tracy.

The next day Dobbs went to Tracy's office to complain about the schedule changes. During this conversation Dobbs stated that the employees needed a union and Tracy replied that he remembered Dobbs having had some trouble with a union on a previous job. When Tracy suggested that Dobbs resign if the working conditions were unsatisfactory, Dobbs refused saying he "was going to try to make it better for the next guy that was hired. . . ."

On January 29, 1971, Dobbs contacted a union representative and obtained several authorization cards and pamphlets. Dobbs then discussed forming a union with his fellow employees and obtained authorization card signatures from all but one of them.

On February 9, 1971, Dobbs was discharged by Goodyear. The final decision to fire Dobbs was approved by Tracy who took action after discussing the matter with Porter. In a letter authorizing Dobbs' termination Tracy stated as follows:

> "After talking to you this morning we are in agreement with your thought that Mr. Dobbs should be discharged due to his lack of cooperation with you and with Greyhound supervisors and his attitude in general as regards work, and though it will impair your servicing of buses somewhat you may discharge Mr. Dobbs."

At the hearing before the Trial Examiner, Tracy testified that Dobbs was fired because of several complaints Goodyear had received from Greyhound personnel. Tracy testified that Dobbs was not performing satisfactory work and that Goodyear's "relations with Greyhound were deteriorating from things that he (Dobbs) was doing."

Tracy's testimony was supported by Greyhound Supervisor John W. Carter, who stated that he had received several complaints that Dobbs caused work delays by talking for long periods of time with other employees. On one particular occasion it became necessary to remove a bus from the schedule because Dobbs was talking and failed to repair a tire on time. Carter complained several times to Goodyear about Dobbs' work performance.

At the close of the evidence the Trial Examiner held that Goodyear violated Section 8(a)(1) of the Act by threatening employees with reprisals if they formed a union. This holding is not challenged by Goodyear on appeal.

However, as to the Section 8(a)(3) charge, the Trial Examiner held that Dobbs' discharge was provoked not by his union activities but by complaints from Greyhound.

On review the Board affirmed the Section 8(a)(1) violation but reversed the Trial Examiner's holding that Goodyear did not violate Section 8(a)(3). Considering the evidence *in toto,* the Board found that the General Counsel made out a *prima facie* case of unlawful motivation which Goodyear failed to rebut. For the reasons that follow, we find ample evidence in the record to support the Board's holding.

On a petition for enforcement we are bound by the general principle that the Board's decision may not be overturned if supported by substantial evidence in the record as a whole. *Universal Camera Corp.* v. *NLRB,* 1951, 340 U.S. 474; *NLRB* v. *Brown,* 1965, 380 U.S. 278. In applying the substantial evidence test to cases where the Board has reversed the holding of the Trial Examiner, this court has attached much significance to credibility choices made by the Trial Examiner. . . . The reason for this rule is that the Trial Examiner obviously has the superior advantage in selecting which witness to believe. On the other hand, it is not the function of this court to deny enforcement simply because the evidence might reasonably support other conclusions or because we might have reached a different conclusion had the matter come before us *de novo.* . . . The Board's decision cannot be reversed for an alleged refusal to accept Trail Examiner credibility choices where the Board merely draws a different inference than that drawn by the Trial Examiner from established facts. . . .

Applying these standards to the case at hand, we must first resolve the question of which Goodyear supervisor actually discharged Dobbs. Although Field Manager Tracy's consent was necessary before Dobbs could be fired, it is clear from Tracy's letter, *supra,* that he relied heavily upon unspecified information from Porter in authorizing the termination. The Board apparently concluded, and we agree, that the prime mover in Dobbs' discharge was Porter. Any examination of Goodyear's motive for discharge, therefore, must necessarily concentrate on Porter's reasons for firing Dobbs.

And at this point we are confronted with the most perplexing problem in this case—Porter never testified. The reasons for his failure to testify seem even more perplexing in view of the fact that Porter was present in the room at the hearing before the Trial Examiner. In any event, we must proceed without the benefit of testimony from the one person who was in the best position to testify under oath as to the actual motive for the employee's discharge.

An examination of the record reveals valid business reasons, i. e., the complaints from Greyhound, which could have prompted Porter to fire Dobbs.

However, the record also reveals other facts from which an unlawful motive could be inferred. Porter indisputably threatened Dobbs and another employee with reprisals at the first mention of union representation. Dobbs was very active in attempting to secure a union for the Goodyear employees, and his discharge came less than two weeks after he had obtained authorization card signatures from a majority of his fellow employees. Field Manager Tracy admitted that Goodyear usually discussed Greyhound complaints with the particular employee involved in an effort to "get it straightened out," and, yet, Tracy equivocated and gave contradictory testimony when asked whether this procedure had been followed prior to the discharge of Dobbs.

Contrary to the arguments of Goodyear, we find that the Board did not overturn credibility choices made by the Trial Examiner. While Tracy did testify that to his knowledge the discharge had nothing to do with union activity, Tracy was not the one who initiated the dismissal of Dobbs. Even accepting the truth of Tracy's statements, it was Porter who actually fired Dobbs and Porter did not testify. Thus, the Board's holding could have reversed credibility choices only if Porter had taken the witness stand and said that he was not motivated by Dobbs' protected activity in initiating the dismissal.

Under these circumstances we hold that the General Counsel met his burden of proving that the discharge of Dobbs was unlawfully motivated. Considering the record as a whole, there was substantial evidence before the Board to support its holding that Goodyear violated Section 8(a)(3) of the Act. Accordingly, the petition for enforcement is hereby

Granted.

CASE QUESTIONS

1. State the facts of the case.
2. Was there substantial evidence to support the Board's decision that an employee was discharged because he was a proponent of unionization among his fellow workers?
3. May the Court of Appeals deny enforcement of a Board order because the evidence might support other conclusions?

SECTION 44 / DISCRIMINATORY LOCKOUTS

The legality of a layoff or lockout of employees during bargaining raises difficult issues concerning motive of the employer and effect on the employees' rights. If a defensive act to protect the employer's business in the face of a threatened strike or to improve his bargaining position, rather than to interfere with bargaining rights or union activity, no violation of the Act occurs. As shown by the latest decisions presented in this section, the NLRB has been inclined to conclude anything is illegal except a strictly defensive shutdown, but the courts have been willing to allow the employer more freedom temporarily to lockout, as in the *Brown* case reversing the NLRB ruling of illegality.

In another decision referred to in the *Brown* decision, known as the *Buffalo Linen* case,[3] the Board found legal a lockout for defending an association-wide bargaining unit, and the Supreme Court agreed. There one member company was struck as a whipsaw tactic against one competitor to pressure the others, and the others legally shut down to defend their position. A lockout to force a union to accept, however, multiemployer bargaining rather than to protect the existing unit, is an illegal offensive lockout according to the Board.[4]

In the *Brown* case the Board found illegal discrimination in that lockout where the employer continued operations with temporary workers. A divided Court majority rejected this distinction. The *American Shipbuilding Company* decision printed in this section extends further the legal "defensive lockout" theory. There, the Supreme Court reversed the Board's ruling of discrimination, finding no antiunion or antibargaining motives in a shutdown to improve the employer's economic position in negotiating.

Similarly an NLRB ruling of an unfair labor practice in a *Detroit News* case involving lockout of employees was reversed upon court review. The Teamsters Union had there struck another publisher for which the Newspaper Publishers Association was seeking to negotiate a new uniform agreement. The Court held the lockout by an unstruck employer was legally employed to affect the bargaining outcome rather than for discrimination or interference with the employees' rights or for employees' support of union demands.

Similarly lawful was held a New York Publishers' Association agreement that all members would suspend publication in the event of a craft union stoppage in breach of an association-wide contract.[5] A defensive measure to combat unauthorized strikes, rather than an unlawful lockout of the nonstriking employees, was the NLRB ruling.

National Labor Relations Board v. Brown, d.b.a. Brown Food Stores

Supreme Court of the United States, 1965. 580 U.S. 278

BRENNAN, J. The respondents, who are members of a multiemployer bargaining group, locked out their employees in response to a whipsaw strike against another member of the group. They and the struck employer continued operations with temporary replacements. The National Labor Relations Board found that the struck employer's use of temporary replacements was lawful under *Labor Board* v. *Mackay Radio & Telegraph Co.,* 304 U.S. 333, but that the respondents had violated §§ 8(a)(1) and (3) of the National Labor Relations Act by locking out their regular employees and using temporary replacements to carry on business. 137 NLRB 73. The Court of Appeals for the Tenth Circuit disagreed and refused to enforce the Board's order. 319 F.2d 7. We granted certiorari, 375 U.S. 962. We affirm the Court of Appeals.

Five operators of six retail food stores in Carlsbad, New Mexico, make

---

[3] *NLRB* v. *Truck Drivers Local Union 449,* 353 U.S. 87 (1956).
[4] *Great Atlantic and Pacific Tea Co.,* 145 NLRB 361 (1963).
[5] *Publishers Ass'n of New York City,* 139 NLRB 1092 (1962).

up the employer group. The stores had bargained successfully on a group basis for many years with Local 462 of the Retail Clerks International Association. Negotiations for a new collective bargaining agreement to replace the expiring one began in January, 1960. Agreement was reached by mid February on all terms except the amount and effective date of a wage increase. Bargaining continued without result, and on March 2 the Local informed the employers that a strike had been authorized. The employers responded that a strike against any member of the employer group would be regarded as a strike against all. On March 16, the union struck Food Jet, Inc., one of the group. The four respondents, operating five stores, immediately locked out all employees represented by the Local, telling them and the Local that they would be recalled to work when the strike against Food Jet ended. The stores, including Food Jet, continued to carry on business by using management personnel, relatives of such personnel, and a few temporary employees; all of the temporary replacements were expressly told that the arrangement would be discontinued when the whipsaw strike ended. Bargaining continued until April 22 when an agreement was reached. The employers immediately released the temporary replacements and restored the strikers and the locked out employees to their jobs.

The Board and the Court of Appeals agreed that the case was to be decided in light of our decision in the so-called *Buffalo Linen* case, *Labor Board* v. *Truck Drivers Union,* 353 U.S. 87. There we sustained the Board's finding that, in the absence of specific proof of unlawful motivation, the use of a lockout by members of a multiemployer bargaining unit in response to a whipsaw strike did not violate either § 8(a)(1) or § 8(a)(3). We held that, although the lockout tended to impair the effectiveness of the whipsaw strike, the right to strike "is not so absolute as to deny self-help by employers when legitimate interests of employees and employers collide. . . . The ultimate problem is the balancing of the conflicting legitimate interests." 353 U.S., at 96. We concluded that the Board correctly balanced those interests in upholding the lockout, since it found that the nonstruck employers resorted to the lockout to preserve the multiemployer bargaining unit from the disintegration threatened by the whipsaw strike. But in the present case the Board held, two members dissenting, that the respondents' continued operating with temporary replacements constituted a "critical difference" from *Buffalo Linen* —where all members of the employer group shut down operations—and that in this circumstance it was reasonable to infer that the respondents did not act to protect the multiemployer group, but "for the purpose of inhibiting a lawful strike." 137 NLRB at 76. Thus the respondents' act was both a coercive practice condemned by § 8(a)(1) and discriminatory conduct in violation of § 8(a)(3).

The Board's decision does not rest upon independent evidence that the respondents acted either out of hostility toward the Local or in reprisal for the whipsaw strike. It rests upon the Board's appraisal that the respondents' conduct carried its own indicia of unlawful intent, thereby establishing, without more, that the conduct constituted an unfair labor practice. It was disagreement with this appraisal, which we share, that led the Court of Appeals to refuse to enforce the Board's order.

It is true that the Board need not inquire into employer motivation to support a finding of an unfair labor practice where the employer conduct is demonstrably destructive of employee rights and is not justified by the service of significant or important business ends. See, *e.g., Labor Board* v. *Erie Resistor Corp.*, 373 U.S. 221; *Labor Board* v. *Burnup & Sims, Inc.*, 379 U.S. 21. We agree with the Court of Appeals that, in the setting of this whipsaw strike and Food Jet's continued operations, the respondents' lockout and their continued operations with the use of temporary replacements, viewed separately or as a single act, do not constitute such conduct.

We begin with the proposition that the Act does not constitute the Board as an "arbiter of the sort of economic weapons the parties can use in seeking to gain acceptance of their bargaining demands." *Labor Board* v. *Insurance Agents*, 361 U.S. 477, 497. In the absence of proof of unlawful motivation, there are many economic weapons which an employer may use that either interfere in some measure with concerted employee activities, or which are in some degree discriminatory and discourage union membership, and yet the use of such economic weapons does not constitute conduct that is within the prohibition of either § 8(a)(1) or § 8(a)(3). See, *e.g., Labor Board* v. *Mackay Radio & Telegraph Co., supra; Labor Board* v. *Dalton Brick & Tile Corp.*, 301 F.2d 886, 896. Even the Board concedes that an employer may legitimately blunt the effectiveness of an anticipated strike by stockpiling inventories, readjusting contract schedules, or transferring work from one plant to another, even if he thereby makes himself "virtually strikeproof." As a general matter he may completely liquidate his business without violating either § 8(a)(1) or § 8(a)(3), whatever the impact of his action on concerted employee activities. *Textile Workers* v. *Darlington Mfg. Co.*, Nos. 37 and 41, decided today. Specifically, he may in various circumstances use the lockout as a legitimate economic weapon. See, *e.g., Labor Board* v. *Truck Drivers Union, supra; Labor Board* v. *Dalton Brick & Tile Corp., supra; Leonard* v. *Labor Board*, 205 F.2d 355; *Betts Cadillac Olds, Inc.*, 96 NLRB 268; *International Shoe Co.*, 93 NLRB 907; *Pepsi-Cola Bottling Co.*, 72 NLRB 601, 602; *Duluth Bottling Assn.*, 48 NLRB 1335; *Link-Belt Co.*, 26 NLRB 227. And in *American Ship Building Co.* v. *Labor Board*, No. 255, decided today, we hold that lockout is not an unfair labor practice simply because used by an employer to bring pressure to bear in support of his bargaining position after an impasse in bargaining negotiations has been reached.

In circumstances of this case, we do not see how the continued operations of respondents and their use of temporary replacements any more imply hostile motivation, nor how they are inherently more destructive of employee rights, than is the lockout itself. Rather, the compelling inference is that this was all part and parcel of respondents' defensive measure to preserve the multiemployer group in the face of the whipsaw strike. Since Food Jet legitimately continued business operations, it is only reasonable to regard respondents' action as evincing concern that the integrity of the employer group was threatened unless they also managed to stay open for business during the lockout. For with Food Jet open for business and respondents' stores closed, the prospect that the whipsaw strike would succeed in breaking up the employer association was not at all fanciful. The retail food industry is very competitive and repetitive patronage is highly important. Faced with the prospect of a loss of patronage to Food Jet, it is logical that respondents should have been concerned that one or more of their number might bolt the group and come to terms with the Local, thus destroying the common front essential to multiemployer bargaining. The Court of Appeals correctly pictured the respondents' dilemma in saying, "If . . . the struck employer does choose to operate with replacements and the other employers cannot replace after lockout, the economic advantage passes to the struck member, the nonstruck members are deterred in exercising the defensive lockout, and the whipsaw strike . . . enjoys an almost inescapable prospect of success." 319 F.2d, at 11. Clearly respondents' continued operations with the use of temporary replacements following the lockout was wholly consistent with a legitimate business purpose.

Nor are we persuaded by the Board's argument that justification for the inference of hostile motivation appears in the respondents' use of temporary employees rather than some of the regular employees. It is not common sense, we think, to say that the regular employees were "willing to work at the employers' terms." 137 NLRB at 76. It seems probable that this "willingness" was motivated as much by their understandable desire to further the objective of the whipsaw strike—to break through the employers' united front by forcing Food Jet to accept the Local's terms—as it was by a desire to work for the employers under the existing unacceptable terms. As the Board's dissenting members put it, "These employees are willing only to receive wages while their brethren in the rest of the associationwide unit are exerting whipsaw pressure on one employer to gain benefits that will ultimately accrue to all employees in the associationwide unit, including those here locked out." 137 NLRB, at 78. Moreover, the course of action to which the Board would limit the respondents would force them into the position of aiding and abetting the success of the whipsaw strike and consequently would render "largely illusory," 137 NLRB, at 78–79, the right of lockout recognized by *Buffalo Linen;* the right would be meaningless if barred to nonstruck stores that find it necessary to operate because the struck store does so. . . .

Nor does the record show any basis for concluding that respondents violated § 8(a)(3). Under that section both discrimination and a resulting discouragement of union membership are necessary, but the added element of unlawful intent is also required. In *Buffalo Linen* itself the employers treated the locked-out employees less favorably because of their union membership, and this may have tended to discourage continued membership, but we rejected the notion that the use of the lockout violated the statute. The discriminatory act is not by itself unlawful unless intended to prejudice the employees' position because of their membership in the union; some element of antiunion animus is necessary. . . .

It is argued, finally, that the Board's decision is within the area of its expert judgment and that, in setting it aside, the Court of Appeals exceeded the authorized scope of judicial review. This proposition rests upon our statement in *Buffalo Linen* that in reconciling the conflicting interests of labor and management the Board's determination is to be subjected to "limited judicial review." 353 U.S., at 96. When we used the phrase "limited judicial review," we did not mean that the balance struck by the Board is immune from judicial examination and reversal in proper cases. Courts are expressly empowered to enforce, modify, or set aside, in whole or in part, the Board's orders, except that the findings of the Board with respect to questions of fact, if supported by substantial evidence on the record considered as a whole, shall be conclusive. 29 U.S.C. §§ 160(e), (f). Courts should be "slow to overturn an administrative decision," *Labor Board* v. *Babcock & Wilcox Co.,* 351 U.S. 105, 112, but they are not left "to 'sheer acceptance' of the Board's conclusions," *Republic Aviation Corp.* v. *Labor Board,* 324 U.S. 793, 803. Reviewing courts are not obliged to stand aside and rubber stamp their affirmance of administrative decisions that they deem inconsistent with a statutory mandate or that frustrate the congressional policy underlying a statute. Such review is always properly within the judicial province, and courts would abdicate their responsibility if they did not fully review such administrative decisions. Of course due deference is to be rendered to agency determinations of fact, so long as there is substantial evidence to be found in the record as a whole. But where, as here, the review is not of a question of fact, but of a judgment as to the proper balance to be struck between conflicting interests, "[t]he deference owed to an expert tribunal cannot be allowed to slip into a judicial inertia which results in the unauthorized assumption by an agency of major policy decisions properly made by Congress." *American Ship Building Co.* v. *Labor Board, supra.*

Courts must, of course, set aside Board decisions which rest on an "erroneous legal foundation." *Labor Board* v. *Babcock & Wilcox, supra,* at 112–113. Congress has not given the Board untrammelled authority to catalogue which economic devices shall be deemed freighted with indicia of unlawful intent. *Labor Board* v. *Insurance Agents, supra,* at 498. In determining here that the respondents' conduct carried its own badge of improper motive, the Board's decision, for the reasons stated, misapplied the criteria governing the application of §§ 8(a)(1) and (3). Since the order therefore rested on an "erroneous legal foundation," the Court of Appeals properly refused to enforce it.

Affirmed.

Mr. Justice Goldberg wrote a concurring opinion in which Chief Justice Warren joined.

Mr. Justice White dissented.

CASE QUESTIONS	1. What factual differences existed in the *Buffalo Linen* case and the *Brown* case?
	2. Why did the Court reverse the Board's thinking?
	3. What is an illegal lockout?
	4. What is meant by a "whipsaw strike"?
	5. What limits NLRB discretion in rulings in economic disputes?

American Ship Building Co. v. NLRB

Supreme Court of the United States, 1965. 380 U.S. 300

STEWART, J. The American Ship Building Company seeks review of a decision of the United States Court of Appeals for the District of Columbia

Circuit enforcing an order of the National Labor Relations Board which found that the company had committed an unfair labor practice under §§ 8(a)(1) and 8(a)(3) of the National Labor Relations Act. The question presented is that expressly reserved in *Labor Board* v. *Truck Drivers Local Union,* 353 U.S. 87, 93; namely, whether an employer commits an unfair labor practice under these sections of the Act when he temporarily lays off or "locks out" his employees during a labor dispute to bring economic pressure in support of his bargaining position. To resolve an asserted conflict among the circuits upon this important question of federal labor law we granted certiorari, 379 U.S. 814.

The American Ship Building Company operates four shipyards on the Great Lakes—at Chicago, at Buffalo, and at Toledo and Lorain, Ohio. The company is primarily engaged in the repairing of ships, a highly seasonal business concentrated in the winter months when the freezing of the Great Lakes renders shipping impossible. What limited business is obtained during the shipping season is frequently such that speed of execution is of the utmost importance to minimize immobilization of the ships.

Since 1952 the employer has engaged in collective bargaining with a group of eight unions. Prior to the negotiations here in question, the employer had contracted with the unions on five occasions, each agreement having been preceded by a strike. The particular chapter of the collective bargaining history with which we are concerned opened shortly before May 1, 1961, when the unions notified the company of their intention to seek modification of the current contract, due to expire on August 1.

At the initial bargaining meeting on June 6, 1961, the company took the position that its competitive situation would not allow increased compensation. The unions countered with demands for increased fringe and some unspecified wage increase. Several meetings were held in June and early July during which negotiations focussed upon the fringe benefit questions without any substantial progress. At the last meeting, the parties resolved to call in the Federal Mediation and Conciliation Service, which set the next meeting for July 19. At this meeting, the unions first unveiled their demand for a 20-cent-an-hour wage increase and proposed a six-month extension of the contract pending continued negotiations. The employer rejected the proposed extension because it would have led to expiration during the peak season.

Further negotiations narrowed the dispute to five or six issues, all involving substantial economic differences. On July 31, the eve of the contract's expiration, the employer made a proposal; the unions countered with another, revived their proposal for a six-month extension, and proposed in the alternative that the existing contract, with its no-strike clause, be extended indefinitely with the terms of the new contract to be made retroactive to August 1. After rejection of the proposed extensions, the employer's proposal was submitted to the unions' membership; on August 8 the unions announced that this proposal had been overwhelmingly rejected. The following day, the employer made another proposal which the unions refused to submit to their membership; the unions made no counteroffer and the parties separated without setting a date for further meetings, leaving this to the discretion of the conciliator.

Thus on August 9, after extended negotiations, the parties separated without having resolved substantial differences on the central issues dividing them and without having specific plans for further attempts to resolve them—a situation which the trial examiner found was an impasse. Throughout the negotiations, the employer displayed anxiety as to the unions' strike plans, fearing that the unions would call a strike as soon as a ship entered the Chicago yard or delay negotiations into the winter to increase strike leverage. The union negotiator consistently insisted that it was his intention to reach an agreement without calling a strike; however, he did concede incomplete control over the workers—a fact borne out by the occurrence of a wildcat strike in February, 1961. Because of the danger of an unauthorized strike and the consistent and deliberate use of strikes in prior negotiations, the employer remained apprehensive of the possibility of a work stoppage.

In light of the failure to reach an agreement and the lack of available work, the employer decided to lay off certain of his workers. On August 11 the employees received a notice which read: "Because of the labor dispute which has been unresolved since August 1, 1961, you are laid off until further notice." The Chicago yard was completely shut down, and all but two employees laid off at the Toledo yard. A large force was retained at Lorain to complete a major piece of work there, and the employees in the Buffalo yard were gradually laid off as miscellaneous tasks were completed. Negotiations were resumed shortly after these layoffs and continued for the following two months until a two-year contract was agreed upon on October 27. The employees were recalled the following day.

Upon claims filed by the unions, the General Counsel of the Board issued a complaint charging the employer with violations of §§ 8(a)(1), (a)(3), and (a)(5). The trial examiner found that although there had been no work in the Chicago yard since July 19, its closing was not due to lack of work. Despite similarly slack seasons in the past, the employer had for 17 years retained a nucleus crew to do maintenance work and remain ready to take such work as might come in. The examiner went on to find that the employer was reasonably apprehensive of a strike at some point. Although the unions had given assurances that there would be no strike, past bargaining history was thought to justify continuing apprehension that the unions would fail to make good their assurances. It was further found that the employer's primary purpose in locking out his employees was to avert peculiarly harmful economic consequences which would be imposed on him and his customers if a strike were called either while a ship was in the yard during the shipping season or later when the yard was fully occupied. The examiner concluded that the employer:

> "was economically justified and motivated in laying off its employees when it did, and the fact that its judgment was partially colored by its intention to break the impasse which existed is immaterial in the peculiar and special circumstances of this case. Respondent, by its actions, therefore, did not violate Sections 8(a)(1), (3), and (5) of the Act."

A three-to-two majority of the Board rejected the trial examiner's conclusion that the employer could reasonably anticipate a strike. Finding the unions' assurances sufficient to dispel any such apprehension, the Board was able to find only one purpose underlying the layoff: a desire to bring economic pressure to secure prompt settlement of the dispute on favorable terms. The Board did not question the examiner's finding that the layoffs had not occurred until after the bargaining impasse had been reached. Nor did the Board remotely suggest that the company's decision to lay off its employees was based either on union hostility or on a desire to avoid its bargaining obligations under the Act. The Board concluded that the employer "by curtailing its operations at the South Chicago yard with the consequent layoff of the employees, coerced employees in the exercise of their bargaining rights in violation of Section 8(a)(1) of the Act, and discriminated against its employees within the meaning of Section 8(a)(3) of the Act."

The difference between the Board and the trial examiner is thus a narrow one turning on their differing assessments of the circumstances which the employer claims gave him reason to anticipate a strike. Both the Board and the examiner assumed, within the established pattern of Board analysis, that if the employer had shut down his yard and laid off his workers solely for the purpose of bringing to bear economic pressure to break an impasse and secure more favorable contract terms, an unfair labor practice would be made out. "The Board has held that, absent special circumstances, an employer may not during bargaining negotiations either threaten to lock out or lock out his employees in aid of his bargaining position. Such conduct the Board has held presumptively infringes upon the collective-bargaining rights of employees in violation of Section 8(a)(1) and the lockout, with its consequent layoff, amounts to discrimination within the meaning of Section 8(a)(3). In addition, the Board has held that such conduct subjects the Union and the employees it represents to unwarranted and illegal pressure and creates an atmosphere in which the free opportunity for negotiations contemplated by Section 8(a)(5) does not exist." *Quaker State Oil Refining Corp.,* 121 NLRB 334, 337.

The Board has, however, exempted certain classes of lockouts from proscription. "Accordingly, it has held that lockouts are permissible to safeguard against loss where there is reasonable ground for believing that a strike was threatened or imminent." *Quaker State Oil Refining Corp.,* 121 NLRB 334, 337. Developing this distinction in its rulings, the Board has approved lockouts designed to prevent seizure of a plant by a sitdown strike, *Link-Belt Co.,* 26 NLRB 227; to forestall repetitive disruptions of an integrated operation by quickie strikes. *International Shoe Co.,* 93 NLRB 907; to avoid spoilage of materials which would result from a sudden work stoppage, *Duluth Bottling Assn.,* 48 NLRB 1335; and to avert the immobilization of automobiles brought in for repair, *Betts Cadillac-Olds Inc.,* 96 NLRB 268. In another distinct class of cases the Board has sanctioned the use of the lockout by a multiemployer bargaining unit as a response to a whipsaw strike against one of its members. *Buffalo Linen Supply Co.,* 109 NLRB 447, rev'd, 231 F.2d 110, rev'd *sub nom. Truck Drivers Union* v. *Labor Board,* 353 U.S. 87.

In analyzing the status of the bargaining lockout under §§ 8(a)(1) and 8(a)(3) of the National Labor Relations Act, it is important that the practice with which we are here concerned be distinguished from other forms of temporary separation from employment. No one would deny that an employer is free to shut down his enterprise temporarily for reasons of renovation or lack of profitable work unrelated to his collective bargaining situation. Similarly, we put to one side cases where the Board has concluded on the basis of substantial evidence that the employer has used a lockout as a means to injure a labor organization or to evade his duty to bargain collectively. *Hopwood Retinning Co.,* 4 NLRB 922; *Scott Paper Box Co.,* 81 NLRB 535. What we are here concerned with is the use of a temporary layoff of employees solely as a means to bring economic pressure to bear in support of the employer's bargaining position, after an impasse has been reached. This is the only issue before us, and all that we decide.

To establish that this practice is a violation of § 8(a)(1), it must be shown that the employer has interfered with, restrained, or coerced employees in the exercise of some right protected by § 7 of the Act. The Board's position is premised on the view that the lockout interferes with two of the rights guaranteed by § 7: the right to bargain collectively and the right to strike. In the Board's view, the use of the lockout "punishes" employees for the presentation of and adherence to demands made by their bargaining representatives and so coerces them in the exercise of their right to bargain collectively. It is important to note that there is here no allegation that the employer used the lockout in the service of designs inimical to the process of collective bargaining. There was no evidence and no finding that the employer was hostile to his employees, banding together for collective bargaining or that the lockout was designed to discipline them for doing so. It is therefore inaccurate to say that the employer's intention was to destroy or frustrate the process of collective bargaining. What can be said is that he intended to resist the demands made of him in the negotiations and to secure modification of these demands. We cannot see that this intention is in any way inconsistent with the employees' rights to bargain collectively.

Moreover, there is no indication, either as a general matter or in this specific case, that the lockout will necessarily destroy the unions' capacity for effective and responsible representation. The unions here involved have vigorously represented the employees since 1952, and there is nothing to show that their ability to do so has been impaired by the lockout. Nor is the lockout one of those acts which is demonstrably so destructive of collective bargaining that the Board need not inquire into employer motivation, as might be the case, for example, if an employer permanently discharged his unionized staff and replaced them with employees known to be possessed of a violent antiunion animus. Cf. *Labor Board* v. *Erie Resistor Corp.,* 373 U.S. 221. The lockout may well dissuade employees from adhering to the position which they initially adopted in the bargaining, but the right to bargain collectively does not entail any "right" to insist on one's position free from economic disadvantage. Proper analysis of the problem demands that the simple intention to support the employer's bargaining position as to compensation and the like be distinguished from a hostility to the process of collective bargaining which could suffice to render a lockout unlawful. See *Labor Board* v. *Brown,* 380 U.S. 278.

The Board has taken the complementary view that the lockout interferes with the right to strike protected under §§ 7 and 13 of the Act in that it allows the employer to preempt the possibility of a strike and thus leave the union with "nothing to strike against." Insofar as this means that once employees are locked out, they are deprived of their right to call a strike against the employer because he is already shut down, the argument is wholly specious, for the work stoppage which would have been the object of the strike has in fact occurred. It is true that recognition of the lockout deprives the union of exclusive control of the timing and duration of work stoppages calculated to influence the result of collective bargaining negotiations, but there is nothing in the statute which would imply that the right to strike "carries with it" the right exclusively to determine the timing and duration of all work stoppages. The right to strike as commonly understood is the right to cease work—nothing more. No doubt a union's bargaining power would be enhanced if it possessed not only the simple right to strike but also the power exclusively to determine when work stoppages should occur, but the Act's provisions are not indefinitely elastic, content-free forms to be shaped in whatever manner the Board might think best conforms to the proper balance of bargaining power.

Thus, we cannot see that the employer's use of a lockout solely in support of a legitimate bargaining position is in any way inconsistent with the right to bargain collectively or with the right to strike. Accordingly, we conclude that on the basis of the findings made by the Board in this case, there has been no violation of § 8(a)(1).

Section 8(a)(3) prohibits discrimination in regard to tenure or other conditions of employment to discourage union membership. Under the words of the statute there must be both discrimination and a resulting discouragement of union membership. It has long been established that a finding of violation under this section will normally turn on the employer's motivation. See *Labor Board* v. *Brown,* 380 U.S. 278; *Radio Officers' Union* v. *Labor Board,* 347 U.S. 17, 43; *Labor Board* v. *Jones & Laughlin Steel Corp.,* 301 U.S. 1, 46. Thus when the employer discharges a union leader who has broken shop rules, the problem posed is to determine whether the employer has acted purely in disinterested defense of shop discipline or has sought to damage employee organization. It is likely that the discharge will naturally tend to discourage union membership in both cases, because of the loss of union leadership and the employees' suspicion of the employer's true intention. But we have consistently construed the section to leave unscathed a wide range of employer actions taken to serve legitimate business interests in some significant fashion, even though the act committed may tend to discourage union membership. See, *e.g., Labor Board* v. *Mackay Radio & Telegraph Co.,* 304 U.S. 333, 347. Such a construction of § 8(a)(3) is essential if due protection is to be accorded the employer's right to manage his enterprise. See *Textile Workers* v. *Darlington Mfg. Co.*

This is not to deny that there are some practices which are inherently so prejudicial to union interests and so devoid of significant economic justification that no specific evidence of intent to discourage union membership or other antiunion animus is required. In some cases, it may be that the employer's conduct carries with it an inference of unlawful intention so compelling that it is justifiable to disbelieve the employer's protestations of innocent purpose. *Radio Officers' Union* v. *Labor Board, supra,* at 44–45; *Labor Board* v. *Erie Resistor Corp., supra.* Thus where many have broken a shop rule, but only union leaders have been discharged, the Board need not listen too long to the plea that shop discipline was simply being enforced. In other situations, we have described the process as the "far more delicate task . . . of weighing the interests of employees in concerted activity against the interest of the employer in operating his business in a particular manner. . . ." *Labor Board* v. *Erie Resistor Corp., supra,* at 229.

But this lockout does not fall into that category of cases arising under § 8(a)(3) in which the Board may truncate its inquiry into employer motivation. As this case well shows, use of the lockout does not carry with it any necessary implication that the employer acted to discourage union membership or otherwise discriminate against union members as such. The purpose and effect of the lockout were only to bring pressure upon the union to modify its demands. Similarly, it does not appear that the natural tendency of the lockout is severely to discourage union membership while serving no significant employer interest. In fact, it is difficult to understand what tendency to discourage union membership or otherwise discriminate against union members was perceived by the Board. There is no claim that the employer locked out only union members, or locked out any employee simply because he was a union member; nor is it alleged that the employer conditioned rehiring upon resignation from the union. . . .

To find a violation of § 8(a)(3), then, the Board must find that the employer acted for a proscribed purpose. Indeed, the Board itself has always recognized that certain "operative" or "economic" purposes would justify a lockout. But the Board has erred in ruling that only these purposes will remove a lockout from the ambit of § 8(a)(3), for that section requires an intention to discourage union membership or otherwise discriminate against the union. There was not the slightest evidence, and there was no finding, that the employer was actuated by a desire to discourage membership in the union as distinguished from a desire to affect the outcome of the particular negotiations in which he was involved. We recognize that the "union membership" which is not to be discouraged refers to more than the payment of dues and that measures taken to discourage participation in protected union activities may be found to come within the proscription. *Radio Officers' Union* v. *Labor Board, supra,* at 39–40. However, there is nothing in the Act which gives employees the right to insist on their contract demands, free from the sort of economic disadvantage which frequently attends bargaining disputes. Therefore, we conclude that where the intention proven is merely to bring about a settlement of labor dispute on favorable terms, no violation of § 8(a)(3) is shown. . . .

The Board has justified its ruling in this case and its general approach to the legality of lockouts on the basis of its special competence to weigh the competing interests of employers and employees and to accommodate these interests according to its expert judgment. "The Board has reasonably concluded that the availability of such a weapon would so substantially tip the scales in the employer's favor as to defeat the Congressional purpose of placing employees on a par with their adversary at the bargaining table." To buttress its decision as to the balance struck in this particular case, the Board points out that the employer has been given other weapons to counterbalance the employees' power of strike. The employer may permanently replace workers who have gone out on strike, or by stockpiling and subcontracting, maintain his commercial operations while the strikers bear the economic brunt of the work stoppage. Similarly, the employer can institute unilaterally the working conditions which he desires once his contract with the union has expired. Given these economic weapons, it is argued, the employer has been adequately equipped with tools of economic self-help.

There is of course no question that the Board is entitled to the greatest deference in recognition of its special competence in dealing with labor problems. In many areas its evaluation of the competing interests of employer and employee should unquestionably be given conclusive effect in determining the application of §§ 8(a)(1), (a)(3), and (a)(5). However, we think that the Board construes its functions too expansively when it claims general authority to define national labor policy by balancing the competing interests of labor and management.

While a primary purpose of the National Labor Relations Act was to redress the perceived imbalance of economic power between labor and management, it sought to accomplish that result by conferring certain affirmative rights on employees and by placing certain enumerated restrictions on the activities of employers. The Act prohibited acts which interfered with, restrained, or coerced employees in the exercise of their rights to organize a union, to bargain collectively, and to strike; it proscribed discrimination in regard to tenure and other conditions of employment to discourage membership in any labor organization. The central purpose of these provisions was to protect employee self-organization and the process of collective bargaining from disruptive interferences by employers. Having protected employee organization in countervailance to the employers' bargaining power, and having established a system of collective bargaining whereby the newly coequal adversaries might resolve their disputes, the Act also contemplated resort to economic weapons should more peaceful measures not avail. Sections 8(a)(1) and 8(a)(3) do not give the Board a general authority to assess the relative economic power of the adversaries in the bargaining process and to deny weapons to one party or the other because of its assessment of that party's bargaining power. *Labor Board* v. *Brown*, 380 U.S. 278. In this case the Board has, in essence, denied the use of the bargaining lockout to the employer because of its conviction that use of this device would give the employer "too much power." In so doing, the Board has stretched §§ 8(a)(1) and 8(a)(3) far beyond their functions of protecting the rights of employee organization and collective bargaining. What we have recently said in a closely related context is equally applicable here:

> "[W]hen the Board moves in this area . . . it is functioning as an arbiter of the sort of economic weapons the parties can use in seeking to gain acceptance of their bargaining demands. It has sought to introduce some standard of properly 'balanced' bargaining power, or some new distinction of justifiable and unjustifiable, proper and 'abusive' economic weapons into . . . the Act. . . . We have expressed our belief that this amounts to the Board's entrance into the substantive aspects of the bargaining process to an extent Congress has not countenanced." *Labor Board* v. *Insurance Agents' International Union*, 361 U.S. 477, 497–498.

We are unable to find that any fair construction of the provisions relied on by the Board in this case can support its finding of an unfair labor practice.

Indeed, the role assumed by the Board in this area is fundamentally inconsistent with the structure of the Act and the function of the sections relied upon. The deference owed to an expert tribunal cannot be allowed to slip into a judicial inertia which results in the unauthorized assumption by an agency of major policy decisions properly made by Congress. Accordingly, we hold that an employer violates neither § 8(a)(1) nor § 8(a)(3) when, after a bargaining impasse has been reached, he temporarily shuts down his plant and lays off his employees for the sole purpose of bringing economic pressure to bear in support of his legitimate bargaining position.

Reversed.

GOLDBERG, J., joined by WARREN, J., concurring: I concur in the Court's conclusion that the employer's lockout in this case was not a violation of either § 8(a)(1) or § 8(a)(3) of the National Labor Relations Act, 49 Stat. 452, as amended, 29 U.S.C. §§ 158(a)(1) and (3), and I therefore join in the judgment reversing the Court of Appeals. I reach this result not for the Court's reasons, but because, from the plain facts revealed by the record, it is crystal clear that the employer's lockout here was justifiable. The very facts recited by the Court in its opinion show that this employer locked out his employees in the face of a threatened strike under circumstances where, had the choice of timing been left solely to the unions, the employer and his customers would have been subject to economic injury over and beyond the loss of business normally incident to a strike upon the termination of the collective bargaining agreement. A lockout under these circumstances has been recognized by the Board itself to be justifiable and not a violation of the labor statutes. *Betts Cadillac Olds, Inc.,* 96 NLRB 268; see *Packard Bell Electronics Corp.,* 130 NLRB 1122; *International Shoe Co.,* 93 NLRB 907; *Duluth Bottling Assn.,* 48 NLRB 1335; *Quaker State Oil Refining Corp.,* 121 NLRB 334, 337. . . .

CASE QUESTIONS	1. Distinguish between a legal layoff and a lockout; a legal and an illegal lockout.
	2. What sort of lockouts appear to be permitted by the NLRA?
	3. How does the right legally to strike compare to that legally to layoff? to lockout?
	4. What does the Court say as to NLRB authority to balance labor and management interests in bargaining?
	5. Does the Congress or the Board or the Court decide permissible bargaining tactics?

SECTION 45 / PERMANENT SHUTDOWNS

As distinct from a temporary shutdown or layoff, the permanent shutdown of a unionized plant raises some other difficult questions. In the liquidation or removal of an operation, a violation of Section 8(a)(3) may be found by the NLRB if union membership or the purpose of avoiding collective bargaining is found to be the controlling motivation. This does not apply where legitimate economic considerations rather than antiunion reasons were the controlling factors.

In the *Darlington Manufacturing Company* case printed below, a recently unionized mill owned by a multi-plant parent corporation was liquidated, some economic factors contributing along with unionization to its shutting down. The employer's claim of a right to go out of business as absolute was denied by the NLRB; sustained on court review, the claim was in part sustained by the Supreme Court when it remanded the case to the NLRB for further evidence as to any coercive impact of the shutdown on employees at other plants of the parent corporation. The conclusion now is that the mill closing was an unfair labor practice under Section 8(a)(3) "if motivated by a purpose to chill unionism in any of the remaining plants . . . much the same as that found to exist in runaway shop and temporary closing cases."

Textile Workers of America v. Darlington Manufacturing Company

Supreme Court of the United States, 1965. 380 U.S. 263

HARLAN, J.: We here review a judgment of the Court of Appeals refusing to enforce an order of the National Labor Relations Board which found respondent Darlington guilty of an unfair labor practice by reason of having permanently closed its plant following petitioner union's election as the bargaining representative of Darlington's employees.

Darlington Manufacturing Company was a South Carolina corporation operating one textile mill. A majority of Darlington's stock was held by Deering Milliken, a New York "selling house" marketing textiles produced by others. Deering Milliken in turn was controlled by Roger Milliken, president of Darlington, and by other members of the Milliken family. The National Labor Relations Board found that the Milliken family, through Deering Milliken, operated 17 textile manufacturers, including Darlington, whose products, manufactured in 27 different mills, were marketed through Deering Milliken.

In March, 1956, petitioner Textile Workers Union initiated an organizational campaign at Darlington which the company resisted vigorously in various ways, including threats to close the mill if the union won a representation election. On September 6, 1956, the union won an election by a narrow margin. When Roger Milliken was advised of the union victory, he decided to call a meeting of the Darlington board of directors to consider closing the mill. Mr. Milliken testified before the Labor Board:

> "I felt that as a result of the campaign that had been conducted and the promises and statements made in these letters that had been distributed [favoring unionization], that if before we had had some hope, possible hope of achieving competitive [costs] . . . by taking advantage of new machinery that was being put in, that this hope had diminished as a result of the election because a majority of the employees had voted in favor of the union. . . ." (R. 457.)

The board of directors met on September 12 and voted to liquidate the corporation, action which was approved by the stockholders on October 17. The plant ceased operations entirely in November, and all plant machinery and equipment was sold piecemeal at auction in December.

The Union filed charges with the Labor Board claiming that Darlington had violated §§ 8(a)(1) and (a)(3) of the National Labor Relations Act by closing its plant, and § 8(a)(5) by refusing to bargain with the union after the election. The Board, by a divided vote, found that Darlington had been closed because of the antiunion animus of Roger Milliken, and held that to be a violation of § 8(a)(3). The Board also found Darlington to be part of a single integrated employer group controlled by the Milliken family through Deering Milliken; therefore Deering Milliken could be held liable for the unfair labor practices of Darlington. Alternatively, since Darlington was a part of the Deering Milliken enterprise, Deering Milliken had violated the Act by closing part of its business for a discriminatory purpose. The Board ordered back pay for all Darlington employees until they obtained substantially equivalent work or were put on preferential hiring lists at the other Deering Milliken mills. Respondent Deering Milliken was ordered to bargain with the union in regard to details of compliance with the Board order. 139 NLRB 241.

On review, the Court of Appeals sitting *en banc,* denied enforcement by a divided vote. 325 F.2d 682. The Court of Appeals held that even accepting *arguendo* the Board's determination that Deering Milliken had the status of a single employer, a company has the absolute right to close out a part or all of its business regardless of antiunion motives. The court therefore did not review the Board's finding that Deering Milliken was a single integrated employer. We granted certiorari, 377 U.S. 903, to consider the important questions involved. We hold that so far as the Labor Relations Act is concerned, an employer has the absolute right to terminate his entire business for any reason he pleases, but disagree with the Court of Appeals that such right includes the ability to close part of a business no matter what the reason. We conclude that the case must be remanded to the Board for further proceedings.

Preliminarily it should be observed that both petitioners argue that the Darlington closing violated § 8(a)(1) as well as § 8(a)(3) of the Act. We think, however, that the Board was correct in treating the closing only under § 8 (a)(3). Section 8(a)(1) provides that it is an unfair labor practice for an employer "to interfere with, restrain, or coerce employees in the exercise of" § 7 rights. Naturally, certain business decisions will, to some degree, interfere with concerted activities by employees. But it is only when interference with § 7 rights outweighs the business justification for the employer's action that § 8 (a)(1) is violated. See, *e.g., Labor Board* v. *Steelworkers,* 357 U.S. 357; *Republic Aviation Corp.* v. *Labor Board,* 324 U.S. 793. A violation of § 8(a)(1) alone therefore presupposes an act which is unlawful even absent a discriminatory motive. Whatever may be the limits of § 8(a)(1), some employer decisions are so peculiarly matters of management prerogative that they would never constitute violations of § 8(a)(1), whether or not they involved sound business judgment, unless they also violated § 8(a)(3). Thus it is not questioned in this case that an employer has the right to terminate his business, whatever the impact of such action on concerted activities, if the decision to close is motivated by other than discriminatory reasons. But such action, if indiscriminatorily motivated, is encompassed within the literal meaning of § 8(a)(3). We therefore deal with the Darlington closing under that section.

I. We consider first the argument, advanced by the petitioner union but not by the Board, and rejected by the Court of Appeals, that an employer may not go completely out of business without running afoul of the Labor Relations Act if such action is prompted by a desire to avoid unionization. Given the Board's findings on the issue of motive, acceptance of this contention would carry the day for the Board's conclusion that the closing of this plant was an unfair labor practice, even on the assumption that Darlington is to be regarded as an independent unrelated employer. A proposition that a single businessman cannot choose to go out of business if he wants to would represent such a startling innovation that it should not be entertained without the clearest manifestation of legislative intent or unequivocal judicial precedent so construing the Labor Relations Act. We find neither.

So far as legislative manifestation is concerned, it is sufficient to say that there is not the slightest indication in the history of the Wagner Act or of the Taft-Hartley Act that Congress envisaged any such result under either statute. . . .

The AFL-CIO suggests in its *amicus* brief that Darlington's action was similar to a discriminatory lockout, which is prohibited "because designed to frustrate organizational efforts, to destroy or undermine bargaining representation, or to evade the duty to bargain." One of the purposes of the Labor Relations Act is to prohibit the discriminatory use of economic weapons in an effort to obtain future benefits. The discriminatory lockout designed to destroy a union, like a "runaway shop," is a lever which has been used to discourage collective employee activities in the future. But a complete liquidation of a business yields no such future benefit for the employer, if the termination is bona fide. It may be motivated more by spite against the union than by business reasons, but it is not the type of discrimination which is prohibited by the Act. The personal satisfaction of such an employer may derive from standing on his beliefs and the mere possibility that other employers will follow this example are surely too remote to be considered dangers at which the labor statutes were aimed. . . .

We are not presented here with the case of a "runaway shop," whereby Darlington would transfer its work to another plant or open a new plant in another locality to replace its closed plant. Nor are we concerned with a shutdown where the employees, by renouncing the union, could cause the plant to reopen. Such cases would involve discriminatory employer action for the purpose of obtaining some benefit from the employees in the future. We hold here only that when an employer closes his entire business, even if the liquidation is motivated by vindictiveness toward the union, such action is not an unfair labor practice.

II. While we thus agree with the Court of Appeals that viewing Darlington as an independent employer the liquidation of its business was not an unfair labor practice, we cannot accept the lower court's view that the same conclusion necessarily follows if Darlington is regarded as an integral part of the Deering Milliken enterprise.

The closing of an entire business, even though discriminatory, ends the employer-employee relationship; the force of such a closing is entirely spent as to that business when termination of the enterprise takes place. On the other hand, a discriminatory partial closing may have repercussions on what remains of the business, affording employer leverage for discouraging the free exercise of § 7 rights among remaining employees of much the same kind as that found to exist in the "runaway shop" and "temporary closing" cases. See *supra.* Moreover, a possible remedy open to the Board in such a case, like the remedies available in the "runaway shop" and "temporary closing" cases, is to order reinstatement of the discharged employees in the other parts of the business. No such remedy is available when an entire business has been terminated. By analogy to those cases involving a continuing enterprise we are constrained to hold, in disagreement with the Court of Appeals, that a partial closing is an unfair labor practice under § 8(a)(3) if motivated by a purpose to chill unionism in any of the remaining plants of the single employer and if the employer may reasonably have foreseen that such closing would likely have that effect.

While we have spoken in terms of a "partial closing" in the context of the Board's finding that Darlington was part of a larger single enterprise controlled by the Milliken family, we do not mean to suggest that an organizational integration of plants or corporations is a necessary prerequisite to the establishment of such a violation of § 8(a)(3). If the persons exercising control over a plant that is being closed for antiunion reasons (1) have an interest in another business, whether or not affiliated with or engaged in the same line of commercial activity as the closed plant, of sufficient substantiality to give promise of their reaping a benefit from the discouragement of unionization in that business; (2) act to close their plant with the purpose of producing such a result; and (3) occupy a relationship to the other business which makes it realistically foreseeable that its employees will fear that such business will also be closed down if they persist in organizational activities, we think that an unfair labor practice has been made out.

Although the Board's single employer finding necessarily embraced findings as to Roger Milliken and the Milliken family which, if sustained by the Court of Appeals, would satisfy the elements of "interest" and "relationship" with respect to other parts of the Deering Milliken enterprise, that and the other Board findings fall short of establishing the factors of "purpose" and "effect" which are vital requisites of the general principles that govern a case of this kind.

Thus, the Board's findings as to the purpose and foreseeable effect of the Darlington closing pertained *only* to its impact on the Darlington employees. No findings were made as to the purpose and effect of the closing with respect to the employees in the other plants comprising the Deering-Milliken group. It does not suffice to establish the unfair labor practice charged here to argue that the Darlington closing necessarily had an adverse impact upon unionization in such other plants. We have heretofore observed that employer action which has a foreseeable consequence of discouraging concerted activities generally does not amount to a violation of § 8(a)(3) in the absence of a showing of motivation which is aimed at achieving the prohibited effect. See *Teamsters*

Local v. *Labor Board,* 365 U.S. 667, and the concurring opinion therein, at 677. In an area which trenches so closely upon otherwise legitimate employer prerogatives, we consider the absence of Board findings on this score a fatal defect in its decision. The Court of Appeals for its part did not deal with the question of purpose and effect at all, since it concluded that an employer's right to close down his entire business because of distaste for unionism also embraced a partial closing so motivated. . . .

In these circumstances, we think the proper disposition of this case is to require that it be remanded to the Board so as to afford the Board the opportunity to make further findings on the issue of purpose and effect. See, *e.g., Labor Board* v. *Virginia Elec. & Power Co.,* 314 U.S. 469, 479–480. This is particularly appropriate here since the case involves issues of first impression. If such findings are made, the case will then be in a posture for further review by the Court of Appeals on all issues. Accordingly, without initimating any view as to how any of these matters should eventuate, we vacate the judgment of the Court of Appeals and remand the case to that court with instructions to remand it to the Board for further proceedings consistent with this opinion.

It is so ordered.

CASE QUESTIONS

1. State the facts of the case.
2. May an employer close down his business for any reason he pleases?
3. What remedy did the Board order?
4. Summarize the rule promulgated by the Supreme Court.

SECTION 46 / UNION SECURITY CONTRACT DISCRIMINATION

Under Section 8(3) of the 1935 Act, any union security contract that an employer agreed to with legal representatives of the employees was a valid defense against charges of discrimination for observing the agreement's closed-shop requirements.

After the 1947 amendments the employer could legally agree to union membership only if the agreement allowed nondiscriminatory hiring without a pre-hire union membership requirement. Membership can be now required not sooner than thirty days after hiring, provided the employee is given equal opportunity for union membership. Only when the employee is unwilling to meet the initiation fees and dues always required of all, can discharge under the agreement be defended as not an unfair labor practice. The NLRB has found violations of Section 8(a)(3) where closed-shop or preferential hiring conditions were in effect, or where the union was permitted by contract to decide if probationary employees could become permanent, or even if union dues deductions were wrongly obtained under an agreement.

The Board has placed upon the employer the obligation to investigate union requests for discharge of employees, such as determining if the employee or the union failed to meet the statutory requirements as to membership conditions.

Some Board orders have been reversed on review by the courts, however, on the ground that the employer had a right to assume the validity of a union demand for discharge under the contract.

The 1947 amendments also prohibited a union from charging excessive or discriminatory membership fees or dues if union membership is required by agreement (Section 8(b)(5)); and dues deductions are conditioned upon individual employee signed authorizations that must be revocable after one year (Section 302(c)). The paying or receiving by a union of checkoff deductions is a crime if these conditions are not met, regardless of any agreement in effect.

The application of these union security provisions of the law is mostly a matter of union practices, fully covered in Chapters 7 and 11 under the subjects of union unfair labor practices, and union duties and responsibilities. These rules may be applied to both the employer and the union in the same situation, however, as the cases in those chapters indicate.

These rules of federal law apply to all employers whose operations affect interstate commerce, but Congress explicitly excluded employers in a state or territory where membership in a labor organization may not be legally enforced by contract. These so-called "right-to-work laws" are permitted by Section 14(b) of the NLRA. The Supreme Court in 1956 conceded their constitutionality in relation to federal statutes, in *Railway Employees' Department* v. *Hanson.*[6] The state courts have jurisdiction to construe and enforce a right-to-work law if not involving NLRA violations, as decided in the *Schermerhorn* case.[7] Twenty states have enacted such laws.

SECTION 47 / DISCRIMINATION FOR NLRB ACTION

Under Section 8(a)(4) an employer may not "discharge or otherwise discriminate against an employee because he has filed charges or given testimony under this act." This provision protects employees from discharge, layoff, or other working conditions discrimination for testifying or making out a charge or an affidavit in any NLRA proceeding. It applies to laid-off employees or applicants for open jobs if refused employment due to appearing at an NLRB hearing. Discharging an employee or discriminating against an employee or applicant for testifying, filing a charge, or refusing to withdraw charges has been found to be cause for finding an 8(a)(4) violation. The Board decision said the following on 8(a)(4) violation:

Beiser Aviation Corporation

135 NLRB 399 (1962)

From the Trial Examiner's Opinion:
There is no doubt in my mind that the above-described conduct of the Respondent towards Byrd was violative of the Act. The vital issue here is not

---

[6] 351 U.S. 225 (1956).
[7] *Retail Clerks Local 1625* v. *Schermerhorn,* 375 U.S. 96 (1963).

whether the Respondent was entitled to know the details of the incidents about which Byrd had testified at the Board hearing. Had the Respondent or its attorney sought the information from Byrd subsequent to his having testified in the proper manner to prepare its defense or to avoid a repetition of the incidents no violation could be found. But where, as here, the Respondent took measures against Byrd which he and the other employees considered as a reprisal for the manner in which he had testified at the hearing, a different situation is presented. In the first place, the Respondent made no explanation why it was necessary to seat Byrd in the middle of the jet engine room to make the report. Obviously this step was taken to put Byrd on display as an object lesson to the other employees that giving testimony against the Respondent would result in similar treatment. Secondly, the removal of Byrd from his regular job of keeping records and his being put to work as an ordinary mechanic after a period of isolation at a table placed in the middle of the jet engine shop could not fail to bring home to the other employees that giving testimony against the Respondent at a Board hearing was a risky thing to do. I have no difficulty in finding that this conduct of the Respondent was calculated to intimidate and coerce other employees not to give damaging testimony against the Respondent at a Board hearing. This conduct was clearly violative of Section 8(a)(1) of the Act and I so find. There is no question also that the change in Byrd's work conditions was motivated by the testimony he gave against the Respondent when he testified on May 5, 1960. This constituted a violation of Section 8(a)(4) of the Act but the General Counsel saw fit to allege it as a violation of Section 8(a)(3) instead. I do not deem it necessary to here decide whether every discrimination which is violative of Section 8(a)(4) of the Act is also a violation of Section 8(a)(3) of the same Act. I do not decide here whether the Respondent's conduct towards Byrd after he testified was violative of Section 8(a)(3) as well as of Section 8(a)(1) inasmuch as the remedy necessary to effectuate the policies of the Act would be identical in either case. The Respondent's conduct was not only a flagrant violation of the employees' rights under the Act but also a serious interference with the orderly processes of the Board, and it should be condemned.

From the Board's Opinion:

. . . We agree with the Trial Examiner that the Respondent, commencing May 6, 1960, relieved employee David Byrd of his normal work, seated Byrd in the center of its jet engine room and demoted him to the job of ordinary mechanic as a reprisal for testifying as a witness for the General Counsel in the instant proceeding and that such conduct on the part of the Respondent violated Section 8(a)(1) of the Act because it clearly indicated to employees, generally, that they also would be subjected to reprisals for similarly testifying.

We find, however, that the Trial Examiner erred in not permitting the General Counsel to amend the complaint to allege that this conduct of the Respondent also violated Section 8(a)(4) of the Act. We do not believe that the General Counsel's request, which came before the close of this phase of the case, was untimely made; the request to amend is hereby granted. And as the facts were fully litigated, we therefore find that, by engaging in the foregoing conduct, the Respondent violated Section 8(a)(4) of the Act. Moreover, we believe it imperative, in order to protect the integrity of Board processes, that such specific finding be made, as Respondent's conduct constitutes a flagrant interference not only with employees' rights but also with the orderly processes of this Act.

CASE   1. State the facts of the case.
QUESTIONS   2. Was the employer conduct in question found to be an 8(a)(4) violation as well as an 8(a)(1) violation?

SECTION 48 / DISCRIMINATION FOR CONCERTED ACTIVITIES

Different types of strikes and pressure tactics will be discussed in Chapter 9 with explanations of the extent of legal protection for the participants. During an economic strike an employer may legally replace such strikers permanently. However, *economic strikers* who unconditionally apply for reinstatement and make known their continued availability are entitled to reinstatement by the employer as long as a vacancy exists for which they are qualified; and if the strikers have been permanently replaced, they are entitled to reinstatement when permanent replacements leave their jobs. Strikers violating the labor unfair labor practices of Section 8(b) or a no-strike contract provision, or engaging in other serious misconduct, may be lawfully discharged on a nondiscriminatory basis. Employer *unfair labor practice strikers* receive full reinstatement protection regardless of replacements, with back pay ordered from the date of a refusal to reemploy upon request up to the date of reemployment in the vast majority of cases.

When strikers' job rights exist, it is illegal for the employer to deprive them of seniority rights by giving superior or superseniority to replacements or to those strikers returning to work first. In *NLRB* v. *Erie Resistor Corp.*[8] a strike was called when bargaining on a new contract reached an impasse. The company, under intense competitive pressures, decided to continue production operations and after a period of weeks, it notified the union that it would begin hiring replacements. Several weeks later, the company informed the union that it had decided to award 20 years additional seniority, for credit against future layoffs, to replacements and strikers who returned by a certain date. The union charged that this granting of superseniority during a strike was an unfair labor practice. The Supreme Court held that such action unavoidably discouraged protected collective activities and must have been so intended. A weighing process was used to consider the conflict between employer interests in operating his business in a particular way and the employees' interest in concerted economic action. Answering the problem, the Court said the employer's asserted business purpose did not balance the violation of the strikers' rights in the light of the federal law's deference to the strike weapon.

---

[8] 373 U.S. 221 (1963).

The *Great Dane Trailers* case reported in this section deals with another type of employer action affecting economic strikers. In this case the employer paid accrued vacation benefits to nonstrikers and announced the extinction of these benefits to strikers. The Supreme Court considered the factor of employer motivation in the context of an 8(a)(3) violation and set forth the controlling principles on the matter.

NLRB v. Great Dane Trailer, Inc.

Supreme Court of the United States, 1967. 388 U.S. 26

WARREN, Ch. J.: The issue here is whether, in the absence of proof of an antiunion motivation, an employer may be held to have violated §§ 8(a) (3) and (1) of the National Labor Relations Act when it refused to pay striking employees vacation benefits accrued under a terminated collective bargaining agreement while it announced an intention to pay such benefits to striker replacements, returning strikers, and nonstrikers who had been at work on a certain date during the strike.

The respondent company and the union entered into a collective bargaining agreement which was effective by its terms until March 31, 1963. The agreement contained a commitment by the company to pay vacation benefits to employees who met certain enumerated qualifications. In essence, the company agreed to pay specified vacation benefits to employees who, during the preceding year, had worked at least 1,525 hours. It was also provided that, in the case of a "lay-off, termination or quitting," employees who had served more than 60 days during the year would be entitled to pro rata shares of their vacation benefits. Benefits were to be paid on the Friday nearest July 1 of each year.

The agreement was temporarily extended beyond its termination date, but on April 30, 1963, the union gave the required 15 days' notice of intention to strike over issues which remained unsettled at the bargaining table. Accordingly, on May 16, 1963, approximately 350 of the company's 400 employees commenced a strike which lasted until December 26, 1963. The company continued to operate during the strike, using nonstrikers, persons hired as replacements for strikers, and some original strikers who had later abandoned the strike and returned to work. On July 12, 1963, a number of the strikers demanded their accrued vacation pay from the company. The company rejected this demand, basing its response on the assertion that all contractual obligations had been terminated by the strike and, therefore, none of the company's employees had a right to vacation pay. Shortly thereafter, however, the company announced that it would grant vacation pay—in the amounts and subject to the conditions set out in the expired agreement—to all employees who had reported for work on July 1, 1963. The company denied that these payments were founded on the agreement and stated that they merely reflected a new "policy" which had been unilaterally adopted.

The refusal to pay vacation benefits to strikers, coupled with the payments to nonstrikers, formed the bases of an unfair labor practice complaint filed with the Board while the strike was still in progress. Violations of §§ 8(a)(3) and (1) were charged. A hearing was held before a trial examiner who found that the company's action in regard to vacation pay constituted a discrimination in terms and conditions of employment which would discourage union membership, as well as an unlawful interference with protected activity. He held that the company had violated §§ 8(a)(3) and (1) and recommended that it be ordered to cease and desist from its unfair labor practice and to pay the accrued vacation benefits to strikers. The Board, after reviewing the record, adopted the Trail Examiner's conclusions and remedy.

A petition for enforcement of the order was filed in the Court of Appeals for the Fifth Circuit. That court first dealt with the company's contention that the Board had lacked jurisdiction and that the union should have been relegated either to the bargaining table or to a lawsuit under § 301 of the Act, since the basic question was one of contract interpretation and application. It noted that the company's announced policy relating to vacation pay clearly concerned a "term or condition of employment"; since it was alleged that the company had discriminated between striking and nonstriking employees in regard to that term or condition of employment, the complaint stated "an unfair labor practice charge in simplest terms" and the Board had properly exercised its jurisdiction. Reviewing the substantive aspects of the Board's decision next, the Court of Appeals held that, although discrimination between striking and nonstriking employees had been proved, the Board's conclusion that the company had committed an unfair labor practice was not well-founded inasmuch as there had been no affirmative showing of an unlawful motivation to discourage union membership or to interfere with the exercise of protected rights. Despite the fact that the company itself had not introduced evidence of a legitimate business purpose underlying its discriminatory action, the Court of Appeals speculated that it might have been motivated by a desire "(1) to reduce expenses; (2) to encourage longer tenure among present employees; or (3) to discourage early leaves immediately before vacation periods." Believing that the possibility of the existence of such motives was sufficient to overcome the inference of an improper motive which flowed from the conduct itself, the court denied enforcement of the order. 363 F. 2d 130 (1966). We granted certiorari to determine whether the treatment of the motivation issue by the Court of Appeals was consistent with recent decisions of this Court. 385 U.S. 1000 (1967).

The unfair labor practice charged here is grounded primarily in § 8(a) (3) which requires specifically that the Board find a discrimination and a resulting discouragement of union membership. *American Ship Building Co.* v. *Labor Board,* 380 U.S. 300, 311 (1965). There is little question but that the result of the company's refusal to pay vacation benefits to strikers was discrimination in its simplest form. Compare *Republic Aviation Corp.* v. *Labor Board,* 324 U.S. 793 (1945), with *Teamsters Union* v. *Labor Board,* 365 U.S. 667 (1961). Some employees who met the conditions specified in the expired collective bargaining agreement were paid accrued vacation benefits in the amounts set forth in that agreement, while other employees who also met the conditions but who had engaged in protected concerted activity were denied such benefits. Similarly, there can be no doubt but that the discrimination was capable of discouraging membership in a labor organization within the meaning of the statute. Discouraging membership in a labor organization "includes discouraging participation in concerted activities . . . such as a legitimate strike." *Labor Board* v. *Erie Resistor Corp.,* 373 U.S. 221, 233 (1963). The act of paying accrued benefits to one group of employees while announcing the extinction of the same benefits for another group of employees who are distinguishable only by their participation in protected concerted activity surely may have a discouraging effect on either present or future concerted activity.

But inquiry under § 8(a)(3) does not usually stop at this point. The statutory language "discrimination . . . to . . . discourage" means that the finding of a violation normally turns on whether the discriminatory conduct was motivated by an antiunion purpose. *American Ship Building Co.* v. *Labor Board,* 380 U.S. 300 (1965). It was upon the motivation element that the Court of Appeals based its decision not to grant enforcement, and it is to that element which we now turn. In three recent opinions we considered employer motivation in the context of asserted § 8(a)(3) violations. *American Ship Building Co.* v. *Labor Board, supra; Labor Board* v. *Brown,* 380 U.S. 278 (1965); and *Labor Board* v. *Erie Resistor Corp., supra.* We noted in *Erie Resistor, supra,* at 227, that proof of an antiunion motivation may make unlawful certain employer conduct which would in other circumstances be lawful. Some conduct, however, is so "inherently destructive of employee interests" that it may be deemed proscribed without need for proof of an underlying improper motive. *Labor Board* v. *Brown, supra,* at 287; *American Ship Building Co.* v. *Labor Board, supra,* at 311. That is, some conduct carries with it "unavoidable consequences which the employer not only foresaw but which he must have intended" and thus bears "its own indicia of intent." *Labor Board* v. *Erie Resistor Corp., supra,* at 228, 231. If the conduct in question falls within this "inherently destructive" category, the employer has the burden of explaining away, justifying or characterizing "his actions as something different than they appear on their face," and if he fails, "an unfair labor practice charge is made out." *Id.,* at 228. And even if the employer does come forward with counter explanations for his conduct in this situation, the Board may nevertheless draw an inference of improper motive from the conduct itself and exercise its duty to strike the proper balance between the asserted business justifications and the invasion of employee rights in light of the Act and its policy. *Id.,* at 229. On the other hand, when "the resulting harm to employee rights is . . . comparatively slight, and a substantial and legitimate business end is served, the employers' conduct is prima facie lawful," and an affirmative showing of improper motivation must be made. *Labor Board* v. *Brown, supra,* at 289; *American Ship Building Co.* v. *Labor Board, supra,* at 311–313.

From this review of our recent decisions, several principles of controlling importance here can be distilled. First, if it can reasonably be concluded that the employer's discriminatory conduct was "inherently destructive" of important employee rights, no proof of an antiunion motivation is needed and the Board can find an unfair labor practice even if the employer introduces evidence that the conduct was motivated by business considerations. Second, if the adverse effect of the discriminatory conduct on employee rights is "comparatively slight," an antiunion motivation must be proved to sustain the charge *if* the employer has come forward with evidence of legitimate and substantial business justifications for the conduct. Thus, in either situation, once it has been proved that the employer engaged in discriminatory conduct which could have adversely affected employee rights to *some* extent, the burden is upon the employer to establish that he was motivated by legitimate objectives since proof of motivation is most accessible to him.

Applying the principles to this case then, it is not necessary for us to decide the degree to which the challenged conduct might have affected employee rights. As the Court of Appeals correctly noted, the company came forward with no evidence of legitimate motives for its discriminatory conduct. 363 F.2d at 134. The company simply did not meet the burden of proof, and the Court of Appeals misconstrued the function of judicial review when it proceeded nonetheless to speculate upon what *might have* motivated the company. Since discriminatory conduct carrying a potential for adverse effect upon employee rights was proved and no evidence of a proper motivation appeared in the record, the Board's conclusions were supported by substantial evidence, *Universal Camera Corp.* v. *Labor Board,* 340 U.S. 474 (1951), and should have been sustained.

The judgment of the Court of Appeals is reversed and the case is remanded with directions to enforce the Board's order.

It is so ordered.

HARLAN, J., joined by STEWART, J., dissented.

CASE QUESTIONS

1. What is the issue that the Supreme Court is called upon to resolve?
2. What are the controlling principles set forth by the Supreme Court concerning the significance of employer motivation in the context of an alleged Section 8(a) (3) violation?
3. What was the holding of the case?

SECTION 49 / REFUSAL OF EMPLOYER TO BARGAIN

Section 1 of the National Labor Relations Act declares the policy of the United States to protect commerce "by encouraging the practice and procedure of collective bargaining and by protecting the exercise by workers of full freedom of association, self-organization, and designation of representatives of their own choosing, for the purpose of negotiating the terms and conditions of their employment. . . ." To effectuate this policy, § 8(a)(5) provides that it is an unfair labor practice for an employer "to refuse to bargain collectively with the representatives of his employees subject to the provisions of Section 9(a)." Section 8(d) defines "to bargain collectively" as "the performance of the mutual obligation of the employer and the representative of the employees to meet at reasonable times and confer in good faith with respect to wages, hours, and other terms and conditions of employment. . . ." Section 9(a) declares: "Representatives designated or selected for the purposes of collective bargaining by the majority of the employees in a unit appropriate for such purposes, shall be the exclusive representatives of all the employees in such unit for the purposes of collective bargaining in respect to rates of pay, wages, hours of employment, or other conditions of employment. . . ."

Together, these provisions establish the obligation of the employer to bargain collectively, "with respect to wages, hours, and other terms and conditions of employment," with "the representatives of his employees" designated or selected by the majority "in a unit appropriate for such purposes."

The procedural requirements are partly defined by Section 8(d), including the following duties: (a) to meet at reasonable times and confer in good faith; (b) to execute a written contract if agreement is reached, but without legal compulsion on either party to agree or to make any concessions; (c) for termination or modification of an existing contract, to give a sixty-day notice to the other party with an offer to confer for negotiating proposals and a thirty-day notice to federal and state mediation services of a pending dispute over the new agreement; (d) no strikes or lockouts during the sixty-day notice period, subject to loss of employee status for so striking.

In *NLRB* v. *Wooster Division of the Borg-Warner Corp.,*[9] the Supreme Court approved a distinction between *mandatory* and *permissive* subjects of bargaining. Concerning the mandatory category, the Court held that the statutory duty to bargain is limited to the subjects of "wages, hours and other terms and conditions of employment." All parties must bargain in good faith on these items. They need not agree and may bargain to an impasse without committing an unfair labor practice. However, under *Borg-Warner,* a party commits an unfair labor practice by insisting to impasse upon incorporation of permissive subject matter in the collective bargaining contract, that is, subject matter outside the scope of "wages, hours and other terms and conditions of employment." The decision on what items fall within the classification of "wages, hours and other terms and conditions of employment" is made by the Board and the courts. For example in *Allied Chemical Workers Local 1* v. *Pittsburg Plate Glass Co.,*[10] the Supreme Court held that benefits of already retired employees were not mandatory subjects of bargaining and that an employer's unilateral modification of a contract term did not breach his duty to bargain, if that modification related to a permissive rather than mandatory subject of bargaining.

The scope of bargaining subjects which are mandatory under the Board and court decisions covers any matter affecting conditions of employment, work opportunity, or benefits. Insurance, pension, and stock purchase programs are included. In the *Fibreboard* decision printed in this section, the Supreme Court ruled that an employer must also bargain about a decision to subcontract work formerly performed by his own employees. The NLRB for a period of time held that *Fibreboard* stood for the broad principle that termination of employment, including such matters as closing or moving part of a business, were included within the scope of "conditions of employment" which are mandatory bargaining subjects. However in the *Summit Tooling* case, the Board reversed its previous

---

[9] 356 U.S. 342 (1958).
[10] 404 U.S. 157 (1971).

position, holding that an employer did not unlawfully refuse to bargain with a union over its decision to shutdown its manufacturing operations. While the Board did not require the employer to bargain about the initial decision, the employer does have a duty to bargain about the effects of the decision.

The question of good faith bargaining arises in many ways, one aspect being employer unilateral action on mandatory bargaining subjects without good faith negotiations with employee representatives. It also may involve an employer communicating directly with employees as to its bargaining position. The Board held in the *General Electric* [11] case that presenting an insurance proposal to union negotiators and other proposals as rigid "fair-and-firm" offers or on a take-it-or-leave-it basis is illegal, as is attempting to bypass national negotiators by direct dealing with local unions. General Electric's collective bargaining policy, called "Boulwareism" for the company vice president who formulated the bargaining concept of a fair-and-firm offer which would be subject to change only if new information showed the company wrong, was thus held to be an unfair labor practice. The Board found this technique "calculated to disparage the union and to impose, without substantial alteration, respondent's fair and firm proposal, rather than to satisfy the true standards and good faith collective bargaining required by the statute."

As a general rule bypassing a union and dealing directly with employees so as to undermine a certified bargaining agent is unlawful. In the *C & C Plywood* [12] decision, the Supreme Court upheld a Board determination that an employer's inauguration of a premium pay plan during the term of a collective bargaining agreement, without prior consultation with the union, violated section 8(a)(5) of the Act.

A further significant requirement imposed by collective bargaining arises from rulings that any relevant information for intelligent consideration of the employer's position under a union's representation responsibility must be provided upon request. [13] Included have been such matters as job description information; job classification wage data (within the unit or outside if comparable); time study data, and the right to make independent check studies; financial data as to employer inability to meet union demands; and competitive wage data to support claimed noncompetitive rates. An unwillingness to cooperate in these areas may result in a finding of refusal to bargain and a cease-and-desist order.

The *H. K. Porter* [14] decision held that while the Board does have the power under the Act to require employers and employees to negotiate, the Board is without power to compel a company or union to agree to any specific substantive contractual provision of a collective bargaining agreement. In the *Burns International Security Services* [15] case, the Supreme Court held that in view of the Act's premise that the parties to collective bargaining cannot be compelled to make agreements (the *H. K. Porter* rationale) successor employers obligated to bargain with a union certified to represent employees of the prior employer are under no obligation to honor the substantive terms of collective bargaining

---

[11] *General Electric Co.,* 150 NLRB 192 (1965); enforced 418 F.2d 736 (1969).
[12] *NLRB* v. *C & C Plywood,* 385 U.S. 421 (1967).
[13] See *NLRB* v. *Truit Mfg. Co.,* 351 U.S. 149 (1956).
[14] *H. K. Porter, Inc.* v. *NLRB,* 397 U.S. 99 (1970).
[15] *NLRB* v. *Burns International Security Services,* 406 U.S. 272 (1972).

agreements negotiated by their predecessors but not agreed to or assumed by the successors.

Howard Johnson Co. v. *Detroit Joint Board* [16] involved a franchiser (Howard Johnson Co.) that purchased assets of a restaurant and motor lodge and hired only a small fraction of the sellers' employees and none of their supervisors. The Supreme Court held that, based on *Burns,* Howard Johnson Co. erroneously was ordered to arbitrate the extent of its obligations under the sellers' collective bargaining contract to the sellers' employees who were not hired. The Court held that there was no obligation to arbitrate since there plainly was no substantial continuity of the work force hired by the franchiser with that of the sellers and no express or implied assumption by the franchiser of an agreement to arbitrate.

Fibreboard Paper Products Corp. v. NLRB

Supreme Court of the United States, 1964. 379 U.S. 203

WARREN, Ch. J. This case involves the obligation of an employer and the representative of his employees under §§ 8(a)(5), 8(d) and 9(a) of the National Labor Relations Act to "confer in good faith with respect to wages, hours, and other terms and conditions of employment." The primary issue is whether the "contracting out" of work being performed by employees in the bargaining unit is a statutory subject of collective bargaining under those sections.

Petitioner, Fibreboard Paper Products Corporation (the Company), has a manufacturing plant in Emeryville, California. Since 1937 the East Bay Union Machinists, Local 1304, United Steelworkers of America, AFL-CIO (the Union) has been the exclusive bargaining representative for a unit of the Company's maintenance employees. In September, 1958, the Union and the Company entered the latest of a series of collective bargaining agreements which was to expire on July 31, 1959. The agreement provided for automatic renewal for another year unless one of the contracting parties gave 60 days' notice of a desire to modify or terminate the contract. On May 26, 1959, the Union gave timely notice of its desire to modify the contract and sought to arrange a bargaining session with Company representatives. On June 2, the Company acknowledged receipt of the Union's notice and stated:

"We will contact you at a later date regarding a meeting for this purpose."

As required by the contract, the Union sent a list of proposed modifications on June 15. Efforts by the Union to schedule a bargaining session met with no success until July 27, four days before the expiration of the contract, when the Company notified the Union of its desire to meet.

The Company, concerned with the high cost of its maintenance operation, had undertaken a study of the possibility of effecting cost savings by engaging an independent contractor to do the maintenance work. At the July 27 meeting, the Company informed the Union that it had determined that substantial savings could be effected by contracting out the work upon expiration of its

[16] 86 LRRM 2449 (1974).

collective bargaining agreements with the various labor organizations representing its maintenance employees. The Company delivered to the Union representatives a letter which stated in pertinent part:

"For some time we have been seriously considering the question of letting out our Emeryville maintenance work to an independent contractor, and have now reached a definite decision to do so effective August 1, 1959.

"In these circumstances, we are sure you will realize that negotiation of a new contract would be pointless. However, if you have any questions, we will be glad to discuss them with you."

After some discussion of the Company's right to enter a contract with a third party to do the work then being performed by employees in the bargaining unit, the meeting concluded with the understanding that the parties would meet again on July 30.

By July 30, the Company had selected Fluor Maintenance, Inc., to do the maintenance work. Fluor had assured the Company that maintenance costs could be curtailed by reducing the work force, decreasing fringe benefits and overtime payments, and by preplanning and scheduling the services to be performed. The contract provided that Fluor would:

"furnish all labor, supervision and office help required for the performance of maintenance work . . . at the Emeryville plant of Owner as Owner shall from time to time assign to Contractor during the period of this contract; and shall also furnish such tools, supplies and equipment in connection therewith as Owner shall order from Contractor, it being understood however that Owner shall ordinarily do its own purchasing of tools, supplies and equipment."

The contract further provided that the Company would pay Fluor the costs of the operation plus a fixed fee of $2,250 per month.

At the July 30 meeting, the Company's representative, in explaining the decision to contract out the maintenance work, remarked that during bargaining negotiations in previous years the Company had endeavored to point out through the use of charts and statistical information "just how expensive and costly our maintenance work was and how it was creating quite a terrific burden upon the Emeryville plant." He further stated that unions representing other Company employees "had joined hands with management in an effort to bring about an economical and efficient operation," but "we had not been able to attain that in our discussions with this particular Local." The Company also distributed a letter stating that "since we will have no employees in the bargaining unit covered by our present Agreement, negotiation of a new or renewed Agreement would appear to us to be pointless." On July 31, the employment of the maintenance employees represented by the Union was terminated and Fluor employees took over. That evening the Union established a picket line at the Company's plant.

The Union filed unfair labor practice charges against the Company, alleging violations of §§ 8(a)(1), 8(a)(3), and 8(a)(5). After hearings were held upon a complaint issued by the National Labor Relations Board's Regional Director, the Trial Examiner filed an Intermediate Report recommending dismissal of the complaint. The Board accepted the recommendation and dismissed the complaint. 130 NLRB 1558.

Petitions for reconsideration, filed by the General Counsel and the Union, were granted. Upon reconsideration, the Board adhered to the Trial Examiner's finding that the Company's motive in contracting out its maintenance work was economic rather than antiunion but found nonetheless that the Company's "failure to negotiate with . . . [the Union] concerning its decision to subcontract its maintenance work constituted a violation of Section 8(a) (5) of the Act." This ruling was based upon the doctrine established in *Town & Country Mfg. Co.,* 136 NLRB 1022, 1027 *enforcement granted,* 316 F.2d 846 (C.A. 5th Cir. 1963), that contracting out work, "albeit for economic reasons, is a matter within the statutory phrase 'other terms and conditions of employment' and is a mandatory subject of collective bargaining within the meaning of Section 8(a)(5) of the Act."

The Board ordered the Company to reinstitute the maintenance operation previously performed by the employees represented by the Union, to reinstate the employees to their former or substantially equivalent positions with back pay computed from the date of the Board's supplemental decision, and to fulfill its statutory obligation to bargain.

On appeal, the Court of Appeals for the District of Columbia Circuit granted the Board's petition for enforcement 322 F.2d 411. Because of the importance of the issues and because of an alleged conflict among the courts of appeals, we granted certiorari limited to a consideration of the following questions:

> 1. Was Petitioner required by the National Labor Relations Act to bargain with a union representing some of its employees about whether to let to an independent contractor for legitimate business reasons the performance of certain operations in which those employees had been engaged?
> 2. Was the Board, in a case involving only a refusal to bargain, empowered to order the resumption of operations which had been discontinued for legitimate business reasons and reinstatement with back pay of the individuals formerly employed therein?

We agree with the Court of Appeals that, on the facts of this case, the "contracting out" of the work previously performed by members of an existing bargaining unit is a subject about which the National Labor Relations Act requires employers and the representatives of their employees to bargain collectively. We also agree with the Court of Appeals that the Board did not exceed its remedial powers in directing the Company to resume its maintenance operations, reinstate the employees with back pay, and bargain with the Union.

I. Section 8(a)(5) of the National Labor Relations Act provides that it shall be an unfair labor practice for an employer "to refuse to bargain collectively with the representatives of his employees." Collective bargaining is defined in § 8(d) as

> the performance of the mutual obligation of the employer and the representative of the employees to meet at reasonable times and confer in good faith with respect to wages, hours, and other terms and conditions of employment.

"Read together, these provisions establish the obligation of the employer and the representative of its employees to bargain with each other in good faith with respect to 'wages, hours, and other terms and conditions of employment. . . .' The duty is limited to those subjects, and within that area neither party is legally obligated to yield. *Labor Board* v. *American Ins. Co.,* 343 U.S. 395. As to other matters, however, each party is free to bargain or not to bargain. . . ." *Labor Board* v. *Wooster Div. of Borg-Warner Corp.,* 356 U.S. 342, 349. Because of the limited grant of certiorari, we are concerned here only with whether the subject upon which the employer allegedly refused to bargain—contracting out of plant maintenance work previously performed by employees in the bargaining unit, which the employees were capable of continuing to perform—is covered by the phrase "terms and conditions of employment" within the meaning of § 8(d).

The subject matter of the present dispute is well within the literal meaning of the phrase "terms and conditions of employment." See *Order of Railroad Telegraphers* v. *Chicago & N. W. R. Co.,* 362 U.S. 330. A stipulation with respect to the contracting out of work performed by members of the bargaining unit might appropriately be called a "condition of employment." The words even more plainly cover termination of employment which, as the facts of this case indicate, necessarily results from the contracting out of work performed by members of the established bargaining unit.

The inclusion of "contracting out" within the statutory scope of collective bargaining also seems well designed to effectuate the purposes of the National Labor Relations Act. One of the primary purposes of the Act is to promote the peaceful settlement of industrial disputes by subjecting labor-management controversies to the mediatory influence of negotiation. The Act was framed with an awareness that refusals to confer and negotiate had been one of the most prolific causes of industrial strife. *Labor Board* v. *Jones & Laughlin Steel Corp.,* 301 U.S. 1, 42–43. To hold, as the Board has done, that contracting out is a mandatory subject of collective bargaining would promote the fundamental purpose of the Act by bringing a problem of vital concern to labor and management within the framework established by Congress as most conducive to industrial peace.

The conclusion that "contracting out" is a statutory subject of collective bargaining is further reinforced by industrial practices in this country. While not determinative, it is appropriate to look to industrial bargaining practices in appraising the propriety of including a particular subject within the scope of mandatory bargaining. *Labor Board* v. *American Nat'l Ins. Co.,* 343 U.S. 395, 408. Industrial experience is not only reflective of the interests of labor and management in the subject matter but is also indicative of the amenability of such subjects to the collective bargaining process. Experience illustrates that contracting out in one form or another has been brought, widely and successfully, within the collective bargaining framework. Provisions relating to contracting out exist in numerous collective bargaining agreements, and "contracting out work is the basis of many grievances; and that type of claim is grist in the mills of the arbitrators." *United Steelworkers* v. *Warrior & Gulf Nav. Co.,* 363 U.S. 574, 584.

The situation here is not unlike that presented in *Local 24, Teamsters Union* v. *Oliver,* 358 U.S. 283, where we held that conditions imposed upon contracting out work to prevent possible curtailment of jobs and the undermining of conditions of employment for members of the bargaining unit constituted a statutory subject of collective bargaining. The issue in that case was whether state antitrust laws could be applied to a provision of a collective bargaining agreement which fixed the minimum rental to be paid by the employer motor carrier who leased vehicles to be driven by their owners rather than the carrier's employees. We held that the agreement was upon a subject matter as to which federal law directed the parties to bargain and hence that state antitrust laws could not be applied to prevent the effectuation of the agreement. We pointed out that the agreement was a

> "direct frontal attack upon a problem thought to threaten the maintenance of the basic wage structure established by the collective bargaining contract. The inadequacy of a rental which means that the owner makes up his excess costs from his driver's wages not only clearly bears a close relation to labor's efforts to improve working conditions but is a fact of vital concern to the carrier's employed drivers; an inadequate rental might mean the progressive curtailment of jobs through withdrawal of more and more carrier-owned vehicles from service. [*Id.*, at 294.]"

Thus, we concluded that such a matter is a subject of mandatory bargaining under § 8(d). *Id.*, at 294–295. The only difference between that case and the one at hand is that the work of the employees in the bargaining unit was let out piecemeal in *Oliver,* whereas here the work of the entire unit has been contracted out. In reaching the conclusion that the subject matter in *Oliver* was a mandatory subject of collective bargaining, we cited with approval *Timken Roller Bearing Co.,* 70 NLRB 500, 518, *enforcement denied on other grounds,* 161 F.2d 949 (C.A. 6th Cir. 1947), where the Board in a situation factually similar to the present case held that §§ 8(a)(5) and 9(a) required the employer to bargain about contracting out work then being performed by members of the bargaining unit.

The facts of the present case illustrate the propriety of submitting the dispute to collective negotiation. The Company's decision to contract out the maintenance work did not alter the Company's basic operation. The maintenance work still had to be performed in the plant. No capital investment was contemplated; the Company merely replaced existing employees with those of an independent contractor to do the same work under similar conditions of employment. Therefore, to require the employer to bargain about the matter would not significantly abridge his freedom to manage the business.

The Company was concerned with the high cost of its maintenance operation. It was induced to contract out the work by assurances from independent contractors that economies could be derived by reducing the work force, decreasing fringe benefits, and eliminating overtime payments. These have long been regarded as matters peculiarly suitable for resolution within the collective bargaining framework, and industrial experience demonstrates that collective negotiation has been highly successful in achieving peaceful accommodation of the conflicting interests. Yet, it is contended that when an employer can effect cost savings in these respects by contracting the work out, there is no need to attempt to achieve similar economies through negotiation with existing employees or to provide them with an opportunity to negotiate a mutually acceptable alternative. The short answer is that, although it is not possible to say whether a satisfactory solution could be reached, national labor policy is founded upon the congressional determination that the chances are good enough to warrant subjecting such issues to the process of collective negotiation.

The appropriateness of the collective bargaining process for resolving such issues was apparently recognized by the Company. In explaining its decision to contract out the maintenance work, the Company pointed out that in the same plant other unions "had joined hands with management in an effort to bring about an economical and efficient operation," but "we had not been able to attain that in our discussions with this particular Local." Accordingly, based on past bargaining experience with this union, the Company unilaterally contracted out the work. While "the Act does not encourage a party to engage in fruitless marathon discussions at the expense of frank statement and support of his position," *Labor Board* v. *American Nat'l Ins. Co.,* 343 U.S. 395, 404, it at least demands that the issue be submitted to the mediatory influence of collective negotiations. As the Court of Appeals pointed out,

"it is not necessary that it be likely or probable that the union will yield or supply a feasible solution but rather that the union be afforded an opportunity to meet management's legitimate complaints that its maintenance was unduly costly."

We are thus not expanding the scope of mandatory bargaining to hold, as we do now, that the type of "contracting out" involved in this case—the replacement of employees in the existing bargaining unit with those of an independent contractor to do the same work under similar conditions of employment—is a statutory subject of collective bargaining under § 8(d). Our decision need not and does not encompass other forms of "contracting out" or "subcontracting" which arise daily in our complex economy.

II. The only question remaining is whether, upon a finding that the Company had refused to bargain about a matter which is a statutory subject of collective bargaining, the Board was empowered to order the resumption of maintenance operations and reinstatement with back pay. We believe that it was so empowered.

Section 10(c) provides that the Board, upon a finding that an unfair labor practice has been committed,

"shall issue . . . an order requiring such person to cease and desist from such unfair labor practice, and to take such affirmative action including reinstatement of employees with or without back pay, as will effectuate the policies of this subchapter. . . ."

That section "charges the Board with the task of devising remedies to effectuate the policies of the Act." *Labor Board* v. *Seven-Up Bottling Co.,* 344 U.S. 344, 346. The Board's power is a broad discretionary one, subject to limited judicial review. *Ibid.* "[T]he relation of remedy to policy is peculiarly a matter for administrative competence. . . ." *Phelps Dodge Corp.* v. *Labor Board,* 313 U.S. 177, 194. "In fashioning remedies to undo the effects of violations of the Act, the Board must draw on enlightenment gained from experience." *Labor Board* v. *Seven-Up Bottling Co.,* 344 U.S. 344, 346. The Board's order will not be disturbed "unless it can be shown that the order is a patent attempt to achieve ends other than those which can fairly be said to effectuate the policies of the Act." *Virginia Elec. & Power Co.* v. *Labor Board,* 319 U.S. 533, 540. Such a showing has not been made in this case.

There has been no showing that the Board's order restoring the *status quo ante* to insure meaningful bargaining is not well designed to promote the policies of the Act. Nor is there evidence which would justify disturbing the Board's conclusion that the order would not impose an undue or unfair burden on the Company.

It is argued, nonetheless, that the award exceeds the Board's powers under § 10(c) in that it infringes the provision that "no order of the Board shall require the reinstatement of any individual as an employee who has been suspended or discharged, or the payment to him of any back pay, if such individual was suspended or discharged for cause. . . ." The legislative history of that provision indicates that it was designed to preclude the Board from reinstating an individual who had been discharged because of misconduct. There is no indication, however, that it was designed to curtail the Board's power in fashioning remedies when the loss of employment stems directly from an unfair labor practice as in the case at hand.

The judgment of the Court of Appeals is affirmed.

Mr. Justice GOLDBERG took no part in the consideration or decision of this case.

CASE	1. What Company action caused this complaint?
QUESTIONS	2. What did the Board conclude as to legality?
	3. What remedy did it order?
	4. Did the Court believe the order imposed an undue burden on this company?
	5. What does this case add to an understanding of "terms and conditions of employment"?

Summit Tooling Co.

(SUPPLEMENTAL CASE DIGEST—REFUSAL OF EMPLOYER TO BARGAIN)
195 NLRB No. 91 (1972)

The Board adopts the findings, conclusions and recommendations of the Trial Examiner to the extent consistent with the following.

The Board agrees with the Trial Examiner that the denial of information regarding contributions to the pension plan was violative of Section 8(a)(5) of the Act, since the memorandum agreement specifically provided that the union trustee receive a monthly report of the amount paid to the insurance underwriter in order to effectively administer the contract.

The Board also agrees with the finding that the employer's refusal to sign the collective bargaining agreement demonstrated bad-faith dealing and was violative of Section 8(a)(5) of the Act. . . .

Contrary to the Trial Examiner, the Board finds that the employer did not violate Section 8(a)(5) of the Act by closing its manufacturing operation without giving the union a chance to bargain concerning the decision to close. While the closing may be characterized as a partial closing, as the non-manufacturing end of the employer's business remained in operation, staffed in part by former production employees, the effect of the cessation of manufacturing was to remove the employer from the business of manufacturing tools.

Therefore, to require the employer to bargain about its decision to close its manufacturing operation would significantly abridge its freedom to manage its own affairs. Accordingly, it is found that the employer did not violate Section 8(a)(5) of the Act by its unilateral decision to close its manufacturing operation.

The Trial Examiner's suggested remedy of ordering the employer to reopen its operations has no precedent and is not adopted. . . .

CASE QUESTIONS

1. Did the Board find that the employer violated Section 8(a)(5) of the Act by closing its manufacturing operation without giving the union a chance to bargain concerning its decision to close?
2. What was the Board's rationale for its decision?
3. Distinguish *Summit Tooling* from the *Darlington* decision.

QUESTIONS ON CHAPTER 6

1. What theory of labor relations underlies Section 8(a) of the Act?
2. What does the law prohibit as regards employer conduct?
3. Explain the restrictions on assisting a "company union," an "independent union," and an "affiliated union."
4. What does the law require as to nondiscrimination against (a) job seekers; (b) workers; (c) striking employees?
5. List the elements required for good faith bargaining by employers.
6. What general rules apply to (a) furnishing of information; (b) the scope of mandatory bargaining subjects?

Chapter 7

Union Unfair
Labor Practices

SECTION 50 / FROM COMMON LAW TO 8(b)

Except for the common law, unions were unrestricted in their expansion of the 1930's. Far-reaching changes were introduced into the National Labor Relations Act of 1947 by adding Sec. 8(b), which prohibits union unfair labor practices. The Wagner Act had provided for employer unfair labor practices but left untouched the practices of labor organizations. The statement of policy in Sec. 1 of the Act outlines the reasoning behind the new restrictions imposed upon labor, as follows:

> "Experience has further demonstrated that certain practices by some labor organizations . . . have the intent or the necessary effect of burdening or obstructing commerce by preventing the free flow of goods in such commerce through strikes and other forms of industrial unrest or through concerted activities which impair the interest of the public in the free flow of such commerce. The elimination of such practices is a necessary condition to the assurance of the rights herein guaranteed."

The protection of "the right to refrain" from union activities was included in Section 7 by the 1947 revision. The employee right to reject unionization was affirmed further in the amended Act by providing "deauthorizing" procedures. In 1959 the Landrum-Griffin Bill, officially entitled the Labor-Management Reporting and Disclosure Act of 1959, further tightened the restrictions of Sections 8(b)(4) and added 8(b)(7), 8(e) and 8(f) to the NLRA. In its remedial aspects, the reader will recall that all unfair labor practices are subject to injunctive restraint by the NLRB without regard to the limitation by the Federal Anti-Injunction Act. Further than this, certain strikes and secondary boycotts, detailed in Sec. 8(b)(4), may be made the subject of damage suits against the unions' assets by the injured party. (See Sec. 303 of the Act, as well as Chapter 11 of this volume, covering the suability of labor unions.)

Under the statutory prohibition of Sec. 8(b) a labor organization becomes amenable to an unfair labor practice charge if it:

(1) Coerces or restrains employees in their freedom to engage in or to refrain from union activities, or employers in choosing spokesmen.
(2) Coerces an employer to discriminate against employees under a union security agreement, except where the employee fails to pay reasonable dues and initiation fees to the union.

(3) Refuses to engage in good faith bargaining with the employer or his representative.
(4) Engages in conduct, including picketing, that influences nonperformance of work by employees in order to:
   (A) force an employer or one who is self-employed to join a labor organization or an employer organization; or to force him to refuse to deal with or handle products of another company; or
   (B) force another employer to recognize an uncertified union; or
   (C) force any employer to bargain where any other union has been certified as representative; or
   (D) force the assigning of work to one craft or group instead of another unless in accordance with an NLRB order.
(5) Levies excessive or discriminatory dues and initiation fees if it enjoys a union shop contract.
(6) Engages in featherbed practices exactions.
(7) Engages in picketing to coerce unionization without seeking any election.

The statutory prohibitions against labor organizations use of certain types of strikes, picketing and boycotts including some that fall into the "secondary" category will be covered in the two succeeding chapters.

SECTION 51 / COERCION BY LABOR UNIONS

The first union unfair labor practice is predicated upon the Sec. 7 right of employees to refrain from union activities as well as to participate in them. Sec. 8(b)(1) provides as follows:

"It shall be an unfair labor practice for a labor organization or its agents to restrain or coerce (A) employees in the exercise of the rights guaranteed in Sec. 7; provided that this paragraph shall not impair the right of a labor organization to prescribe its own rules with respect to the acquisition or retention of membership therein; or, (B) an employer in the selection of his representatives for the purposes of collective bargaining or the adjustment of grievances."

Congressional reasoning in including Sec. 8(b)(1) can clearly be determined from an extract of Senate Report 105, 80th Congress:

". . . The committee heard many instances of union coercion of employees such as that brought about by threats of reprisal against employees and their families in the course of organizing campaigns; also direct interference by mass picketing and other violence. Some of these acts are made illegal by state law, but we see no reason why they should not also constitute unfair labor practices to be investigated by the National Labor Relations Board, and at least deprive the violators of any protection furnished by the Wagner Act. We believe that the freedom of the individual workman should be protected from duress by the union as well as from duress by the employer."

The legislative history of this provision indicates that Congress had no intention to proscribe the normal exercise by unions of the right to appeal to employees or members by persuasive speech or conduct which carried no threat of force or reprisal. If they pass these allowable bounds, however, by violence to the employee's person or to his rights or property, or by threats, a violation of 8(b)(1) will have resulted. Massed picketing may also have an unlawful restraining effect upon workers under Sec. 8(b)(1)(A).

The prohibition of union restraint on employees' rights contains the proviso that the law allows unions to prescribe their own membership rules. Section 8(b)

(1)(A) has been applied, however, to prevent union coercion to force upon employees membership or even representation by a union, or to enforce strike activity or picket line respect. Threatening harm by pickets or strikers in the presence of union officials who do not repudiate them, blocking plant entrances and exits, threats of job loss for antiunion actions or attitudes constitute violations of Section 8(b)(1)(A).

Under Section 8(b)(1)(B) union coercion of an employer's rights to select his bargaining representatives is forbidden. This restriction applies to a union strike threat for insistence on bargaining with the company owners or executives rather than with an attorney engaged to negotiate for the management. It has been applied to unions striking to compel members of an employer association to sign individual agreements in conflict with a multiemployer-established single unit. It has also been applied to picketing activity to require a nonmember to accept the association as his representative or to require participation in association activity against his wishes. In other words the employers are protected against union coercion in their right to representation, to engage in joint activities, or to refrain from such activities in the absence of an established pattern.

The United States Supreme Court decision below in the *I.L.G.W.* and *Bernhard Altmann* situation found an 8(b)(1)(A) violation along with employer violations where the employer recognized the union as exclusive representative at a time when it had only the minority's authorization. The Board makes this application of 8(b)(1)(A) where it finds that the union executes and enforces a contract for exclusive rights when it has no majority authorization or has had some assistance by the employer in gaining the majority of the employees as supporters or members. It is often difficult to distinguish between employer interference and union coercion of employees in these cases. In the following situations the facts outlined and the party against which charges were filed determined the union responsibility for the unfair labor practices against the employees.

In the decision finding that Local 404 of the Teamsters' Union coerced employees, the charges came from the Machinists' Union. Both organizations represented some of the Company's workers and both sought to represent employees at a new plant by reason of their respective agreements. Included in the pressure exerted by the Teamsters was a work stoppage resulting in signing up the employees "under protest."

In this case and in the one involving Teamsters Local 886, which also involved coercion of employees, the Board order to reimburse the workers for the Union fees and dues was sustained by the court.

NLRB v. General Drivers, Local No. 886

Circuit Court of Appeals, Tenth Circuit, 1959. 225 F.2d 205

MURRAH, C. J.: This is a proceeding under Section 10(e) of the Labor Management Relations Act, 61 Stat. 136, 147; 29 U.S.C. 160(e), to enforce an order of the National Labor Relations Board, based upon a finding that the respondent violated Section 8(b)(1)(A); 29 U.S.C. 158 (b)(1)(A) of the Act, by coercively withholding contractual benefits from certain of the complainant's employees until about 80 percent of them signed union membership applications and dues checkoff authorizations. The order required the respondent to reimburse the employees for the dues checked off during the critical period involved here.

The ultimate findings are derived from these facts. In February, 1956, the respondent Union became the exclusive bargaining representative for the complaining company's production and maintenance employees. After a series of bargaining conferences between the Union representative and management, the parties tentatively agreed upon a contract providing for a 7¢ per hour increase. The contract thus agreed upon was drafted by the company and submitted to the Union representative on June 7, 1956, and the company thereafter stood ready to sign the same "any time." On the same date, about 40 of the company's employees met to consider the contract. There is a sharp conflict concerning the attitude of the Union representative, but the Board found from conflicting evidence that the Union representative told the assembled employees that the 7¢ increase would not become effective until the contract was signed, and that the contract would not be signed until about 80 percent of the employees signed union membership applications and checkoff dues authorizations; that the employees then voted to accept the Company's proposal "on condition that it was satisfactory to the Contract Committee and to the Union." On July 20, about 62 of the 83 employees had joined the Union and signed dues checkoff authorization.

From this the Board concluded that the employees' action in joining the Union and executing the dues checkoff authorizations was not voluntary, but the direct result of respondent's coercive conduct; and that it was reasonably calculated to restrain and coerce the employees in the exercise of their right under Section 7 of the Act to refrain from joining or assisting the respondent Union.

The respondent insists that the Union representative's condemned remarks at the employees' meeting were made as agent of the Employees Contract Committee, and not of the Union, and furthermore, having voted for the Union as its bargaining representative, it is "inconceivable" that the employees would have to be coerced to join it and sign checkoff cards; and that in any event, since the contract had not been executed when the remarks were made, they could not be construed as a threat to deprive the employees of any benefits thereunder, i.e., there could be no contractual benefits from a nonexisting contract.

. . . But the Board took a different view of the effects of and the remedy for the unfair labor practice. Having concluded that the execution of the checkoff authorizations was the "direct result of respondent's coercive conduct," the Board thought the appropriate remedy was reimbursement of the dues. It did not believe subjective evidence necessary to warrant the order.

"The relation of remedy to policy is peculiarly a matter of administrative competence." *Phelps Dodge Corp.* v. *NLRB,* 313 U.S. 177, 194; *NLRB* v. *Seven-Up,* 344 U.S. 344. It is the primary responsibility of the Board to fashion an appropriate remedy for an unfair labor practice in order to effectuate the purposes of the Act, and we should not interfere with the designed remedy unless we can say from the whole record that it is "oppressive and therefore not calculated to effect a policy of the Act." *NLRB* v. *Seven-Up, supra; Virginia Electric Co.* v. *NLRB*, 319 U.S. 533.

The reimbursement of initiation fees and dues as an appropriate remedy cannot be doubted. *NLRB* v. *Local 404, etc.,* 205 F.(2d) 104. And, this is so even though the employees who were coerced to pay the dues may have received some value therefor in the form of Union services. . . .

CASE
QUESTIONS

1. What coercive action did the Union take in this case?
2. What remedy did the Board order which the Court approved?

Chauffeurs, Teamsters and Helpers v. Newell and El Dorado Dairy

(SUPPLEMENTAL CASE DIGEST—COERCION OF EMPLOYEES BY LABOR UNIONS)
Supreme Court of the United States, 1958. 356 U.S. 341

In a labor dispute with attendant picketing, a union official ostensibly photographed nonstrikers crossing the picket line. The employer secured an injunction in a state court, Kansas, which restrained all future picketing adjacent the premises of the Dairy Co. The union pursued this appeal on the theory that the restraining order of the lower court restrained even peaceful picketing and therefore violated the free speech guaranty of the Constitution.

The U. S. Supreme Court peremptorily reversed the trial court, citing *Thornhill* v. *Alabama*, evidently agreeing with the labor union's position. It should be noted there was an absence of *past* violence in the instant case.

National Labor Relations Board v. Bernhard Altmann Texas Corp.
International Ladies' Garment Workers Union v. NLRB

Supreme Court of the United States, 1961. 366 U.S. 731

BURTON, J.: These cases present the question whether it was an unfair labor practice, under §§ 8(a)(1) and (2) and 8(b)(1)(A) of the National Labor Relations Act, as amended in 1947, for an employer and a union to enter into a collective-bargaining agreement recognizing the union as the exclusive bargaining representative of all of the employees in the proposed bargaining unit, although the union had not been authorized to act as their collective-bargaining representative by a majority of the employees. For the reasons hereafter stated, we are of the opinion that such an agreement unlawfully restrained nonparticipating employees from their free exercise of the rights of self-organization guaranteed to them by § 7 of the Act and also gave unlawful support to the participating union. We therefore agree with the National Labor Relations Board's decision that such conduct in the cases before us was an unfair labor practice which the Board properly ordered discontinued.

The General Counsel for the National Labor Relations Board filed a complaint against the Bernhard-Altmann Texas Corporation, an employer, manufacturing knit-wear for interstate commerce at San Antonio, Texas. The complaint charged the employer with entering into an exclusive recognition agreement with the International Ladies' Garment Workers' Union, AFL-CIO, at a time when the union did not represent a majority of the corporation's employees in any appropriate bargaining unit. It also charged the employer with thus contributing to the support of the union in violation § 8(a)(2), and with interfering with the free exercise of rights, guaranteed to the employees by § 7 of such Act, in violation of § 8(a)(1). In a separate complaint the General Counsel also charged that the union had violated § 8(b)(1)(A) by entering into the above-mentioned agreement with the employer and thus restraining and coercing some of the latter's employees in the free exercise of rights guaranteed to them by § 7. After a hearing in which the cases were consolidated, the trial examiner issued an intermediate report recommending that each complaint be dismissed in its entirety. However, the Board, on exceptions filed by the General Counsel, disagreed with the trial examiner's conclusions. The Board found that the employer and the union had respectively engaged in the alleged unfair labor practices. It accordingly ordered each of them to cease and desist from such practices and to hold a representative election. One member concurred in part and dissented in part. 122 NLRB 1289, 1297. The union now asks this Court to set aside the Board's order, whereas the Board asks that its order be enforced. Except for filing its answer, the employer had not participated in these proceedings.

The facts found by the Board are supported by substantial evidence on the record considered as a whole and are conclusive here. 61 Stat. 148, 29 U.S.C. § 160(e). Our jurisdiction is not questioned.

Beginning in 1956, the union engaged in a campaign to organize the employer's plant. It obtained a substantial number of authorization cards signed by employees designating the union as their bargaining representative. In July, 1957, a number of the employees struck in protest against a wage reduction, and the union, on behalf of some of the strikers, endeavored to settle the controversy. On August 30, 1957, during these negotiations, a "memorandum of understanding" was signed by the employer and the union. In that memorandum the employer expressly recognized the union as the exclusive bargaining agent for its production and shipping employees, and the union stated that it had been designated by a majority of such production and shipping employees to act as the exclusive bargaining representative of all of such employees. There was testimony that the union maintained a running check of the number of authorization cards it held against a list of the employees believed by it to be working in the bargaining unit. When the union's Regional Director became convinced that the union had obtained cards from a majority of the workers in the unit, he so stated to the employer. The latter made no independent check of the cards and took no other steps to investigate the assertion. Likewise, there is no evidence that at the time of concluding the agreement the union attempted to obtain a definitive list of the employees within the proposed bargaining unit.

In October, 1957, the memorandum was followed by a formal collective-bargaining agreement. This covered many subjects appropriate for such a contract and recited that a majority of the employees in the bargaining unit had designated the union as their exclusive bargaining representative. The Board found that, on the critical date of August 30, the union had not been designated as a bargaining agent, either by the votes or by the signed cards of a majority of the employees in an appropriate bargaining unit. The union disputes the Board's finding of lack of majority status on August 30. While there were questions raised as to the status of some employees, the Board was justified in the finding that the union did not represent a majority of the employees in the designated unit on the critical date.

The intent of the National Labor Relations Act, as amended, and especially § 7, is that the decision whether or not to be represented by a bargaining representative and also the choice of that representative shall be the uncoerced decision of a majority of the employees in an appropriate unit. Obstruction of that freedom of choice, by either the employer or the union, deprives some of the employees of this guaranteed right and is an unfair labor practice under § 8. It is difficult to conceive of a clearer restraint on the employees' right of self-organization than for their employer to enter into a collective-bargaining agreement with a minority of the employees. If upheld, that action would foreclose any other choice of a bargaining representative by a majority of the workers in the unit. It would not only impose the minority's bargaining agent upon the nonparticipating majority, it would also practically preclude the majority, during the term of the contract, from casting off the union as bargaining representative. Even if the employees might surmount the difficulties inherent in challenging the established order by presenting a petition for decertification under § 9(c), it is quite likely, under the Board's decisions, that the "contract-bar" rule would prevent the majority from asserting the union's lack of majority status during the two-year term of the contract. It has been held repeatedly by the Board that in a decertification proceeding, where the contract bar has been asserted, the petitioners are not permitted to show the lack of majority status of the union at the time the contract was made.

It has been repeatedly found an unfair labor practice under § 8(a)(1) and (2) for an employer to conclude a collective-bargaining agreement with a minority union. In most of these cases there were aggravating factors such as the presence of a rival union or the imposition of a union security provision, but those cases do not appear to turn on the presence of these aggravating factors, nor are these factors always present. We see no material distinction from the viewpoint of the employees' § 7 organizational rights between the rival union situation, where there is interference in the choice between bargaining agents, and the instant cases, where the interference affects the choice whether to bargain through a collective representative or individually.

As early as *NLRB* v. *Jones & Laughlin Steel Corp.*, 301 U.S. 1, 44–45, it has been recognized that implicit in the duty of the employer to recognize the majority's representative of his employees as the exclusive bargaining representative is the correlative duty to deal with no agent other than that chosen by the majority. Also implicit is the obligation on the part of the employer to make sure that the representative does in fact represent a majority of the employees. Conversely, it is the duty of those who seek to establish themselves as exclusive bargaining agents to make sure that they have the mandate of those in whose name they speak.

Section 8(b)(1)(A), as enacted in 1947, prohibits unions from invading the rights of employees under § 7 in a fashion comparable to the activities of employers prohibited under § 8(a)(1). That the provisions were intended to be parallel is indicated by the similarity of the language employed, and is confirmed by the legislative history of the provisions.

Section 8(a)(1), as it appeared in the original Wagner Act as § 8(1), applied only to employer conduct. The major purpose which the sponsors of the 1947 amendments sought to achieve, was to impose on unions the same restrictions as those imposed by § 8(1) on employers respecting intrusion on protected employee activity. The omission of the word "interference" from subsection (b) (1) may not be devoid of significance when considering whether labor organizations are permitted wider latitude in peacefully persuading employees to organize than is permitted employers in opposing collective bargaining. But where union activities go beyond the level of persuasion and amount to a foreclosure of the exercise of § 7 rights by the employees, we find no basis for holding that the provisions should have a different meaning when applied to a labor organization than when applied to an employer.

The practices involved here, unlike recognitional and organizational picketing, are not specifically limited in the other unfair labor practice provisions of § 8.

An employer need not bargain with an uncertified representative if he has grounds in good faith for doubting the union's majority status, but he is under a duty to bargain if he has adequate grounds for believing that the union does represent a majority. It is difficult to establish ground for believing or disbelieving the existence of a majority status for a union in the face of a failure to take any steps to determine that status.

The central consideration here is not merely whether the employer or the union entertained a bona fide belief that the union had majority support, but whether that belief was arrived at through an adequate effort to determine the true facts of the situation.

Questions may arise as to the membership of particular employees in the bargaining unit or the validity of the union authorizations. In most of these situations clear and convincing proof of the employees' status will be readily available to the parties in the form of personnel records and other direct proof of employment status. If informal methods are not available, or they do not prove dispositive, § 9(c) provides a formal method for an authoritative Board determination of majority representative status.

Organizational efforts will not generally turn on such thin majorities as to require a complex computation of majority status. In such a case, simple procedures are available to demonstrate majority status. It is only when the question is close that more is required. If the parties' determination of majority status is questionable, the burden is on the General Counsel to establish the alleged unfair practice and lack of majority status.

The net effect of the Board's policy is to require that labor organizations and employers refrain from recognizing by agreement a sole bargaining representative until such time as they have adequately established that such agent represents a majority of the employees in the bargaining unit. Allowing the union or the employer to do otherwise would permit them, by agreement, to undermine the employees' rights under § 7.

Accordingly, the union's petition to set aside the order is denied and the Board's order shall be enforced in full.

CASE QUESTIONS	1. Which violations of the Act involved "interference"— the Union's or the Company's? which "coercion"?
	2. What should the employer's course of conduct be in such situations?
	3. Does the Act place a burden of proof as to majority authorization on the Union? on the Company? or on the NLRB counsel?
	4. Do the rights of employees or of the Union or of the Company receive the Court's primary concern? Why?

SECTION 52 / CAUSING EMPLOYER TO DISCRIMINATE

Sec. 8(b)(2) makes it an unfair labor practice for a union "to cause or attempt to cause an employer to discriminate against an employee in violation of subsection 8(a)(3) or to discriminate against an employee with respect to whom membership in such organization has been denied or terminated on some ground other than his failure to tender the periodic dues and the initiation fees uniformly required as a condition of acquiring or retaining membership."

Under Sec. 8(3) of the Wagner Act of 1935, as explained in Chapter 4, all forms of union security were permitted, including the closed shop, union shop, maintenance-of-membership, preferential hiring, and the checkoff of union dues. By virtue of the Labor Management Relations Act of 1947, Sec. 8(a)(3) allows only union shop and maintenance-of-membership agreements to be entered into with employers, by a union representing the majority of employees as provided in Sec. 9(a). The checkoff of union dues is still allowed, provided the employee consents to the deduction in writing, under Sec. 302(c).

The significance of this present Sec. 8(b)(2) limitation upon union power is apparent from the fact that under the Wagner Act a closed shop or union security agreement with the employer often legally compelled him to discharge employees who had been refused admittance to, or who had been expelled from, the union for any reason whatsoever. Under the Act as amended in 1947, an employer is obligated to discharge an employee, at the behest of the union, only if the following circumstances prevail:

a. A valid union shop or maintenance-of-membership agreement is in force.

b. The employee has been denied membership in the labor association for failure to

pay a reasonable initiation fee, or is expelled from membership because he has failed to pay dues which are reasonable under Sec. 8(b)(5).
c. The contractual requirement of union membership is not effective before the thirtieth day after the date of employment or after the start of the contract period, whichever comes later.

It is illegal under the 1947 provision to discharge for a refusal by an employee to pay any retroactive financial obligations for the time before this thirty-day grace period, irrespective of the contract language. If the employee is discharged for refusing to pay such "back dues," or "reinstatement fees" after lapse of membership on a prior job, discrimination will be found under Sec. 8(b)(2); and possibly also under 8(a)(3). The order of reinstatement with reimbursement of lost earnings may be issued against the employer or the union or both; payment is imposed on only the union if the employer is innocent of illegal intent or of knowledge of illegal union purpose.[1]

The 1959 amendments changed the building and construction industry requirement to permit legal agreements: (a) before any hiring commences, and (b) allowing notice to unions of any vacancies to be filled, and (c) requiring union membership after the seventh day of employment on the job. Such an agreement would not be a legal defense against a charge of discrimination in any other industry.

If a union demands illegal payment of dues or fees under conditions not permitted by the law, such as under an illegal agreement, and the employee pays rather than suffer discharge for not paying, the union will be liable for repaying such monies for a period that may go back to a date six months prior to the date that charges are filed with the National Labor Relations Board.[2]

This remedy has subsequently been sustained but qualified by a Supreme Court ruling in 1961 that irrespective of "closed shop preferential hiring conditions there must be evidence that employees were coerced by unfair labor practices into membership and into paying dues and fees." The Court distinguished between the *Radio Officers* case given below and the later case by pointing to the lack of evidence of coercion in the latter. It supported the NLRB authority to remedy the victims of unfair labor practices but not to make punitive orders requiring a union to refund payments made "by a lot of old-time union men" where the evidence did not show that "their membership was induced, obtained or retained in violation of the Act."[3]

Where a union illegally causes an employer to discriminate against applicants for employment through refusing to allow nonmember applicants to be given work, the union also will be held liable for losses of earnings. Discriminatory referral practices of a union hiring hall resulted in an order for the union to reimburse nonunion men who were denied work assignments for all consequent losses in earnings.[4] In another case a union was held liable along with the employer for lost earnings of applicants where the union urged its members not to work with newly hired nonmembers, causing an illegal discrimination.[5] The union

---

[1] See *Radio Officers Union* v. *NLRB* on page 254 of this chapter.
[2] *Plumbers and Pipefitters Local 231* v. *Brown and Olds*, 115 NLRB 594 (1956).
[3] *Local 60, United Brotherhood of Carpenters & Joiners* v. *NLRB*, 365 U.S. 651 (1961).
[4] *Pacific Coast Marine Firemen, Oilers, Water Tenders and Wipers Assn.*, 107 NLRB, 593 (1953).
[5] *NLRB* v. *Newspaper and Mail Deliverers' Union of N. Y. and Vicinity and Hearst Consolidated Publications*, 192 F.2d 654 (1951).

alone is held liable where the employer is not charged with any violation, or is not shown to have any knowledge of the illegal union actions or motives.

Examples of union actions in violation of Section 8(b)(2) included forcing agreements on employers requiring that only those "satisfactory" to the union be hired; or union-caused discharges because an employee opposed the method of selecting shop stewards; or because the employee was a "troublemaker," a "bad actor," or otherwise disliked by the union members. Although the right of a union to determine its own rules for membership is protected explicitly by 8(b), employees' jobs or the job conditions fall outside lawful union discrimination.

The Board also has found violations of 8(b)(1), (2) in union discrimination for racial reasons. Where only white employees are eligible for membership and the union refused to process a grievance of a black employed in the unit, its unequal treatment is a violation of Section 8(b)(1), (2).[6]

Union discrimination toward employees or members for unfair, arbitrary, or irrelevant conditions, or its failure to act for bargaining unit members due to such unfair reasons, has been held unlawful at common law for many years, as well as grounds for loss of NLRB or NMB certification of a bargaining representative. The Civil Rights Act of 1964 also forbids sex, racial, religious, and national origin discrimination by unions or employers by Title VII of that Act, as discussed in Chapter 12.

The NLRB has recently been extending its authority further in reviewing union discrimination against bargaining unit members for racial reasons. Violations of Sec. 8(b)(1), (2), (3) were found where a white segregated local of the Int'l. Longshoremen's Association enforced segregated work assignment rules by its agreement with an employer association for limiting its segregated black members to 25 percent of the work.[7] A later decision printed below,[8] ruled the United Rubber Workers Local in Gadsden, Alabama, to have caused discriminatory conditions and to have failed to bargain in good faith for black members. Note that the order of the NLRB required unusual union action to correct the violations of the law; also note the Board's discussion of concurrent NLRA authority and Title VII Civil Rights Act authority in such matters.

In the *Radio Officers Union* decision the Board was upheld by the Court in finding that only the union violated Sec. 8(b)(2), without finding an employer violation of Sec. 8(a)(3).

Radio Officers Union, A.F.L. v. NLRB

Supreme Court of the United States, 1954. 347 U.S. 17

PER CURIAM. . . . Section 8(b)(2) was added to the National Labor Relations Act by the Taft-Hartley amendments in 1947. It provides that "it shall be an unfair labor practice for a labor organization or its agents . . . to

---

[6] *Independent Metal Workers Union, Local 1* (Hughes Tool Co.), 147 NLRB No. 166 (1964).
[7] *Local 1367 International Longshoremen's Assn.* (Galveston Maritime Assn.), 148 NLRB 8978 (1964).
[8] *Local Union No. 12, United Rubber Workers (Business League of Gadsden)*, 150 NLRB 312 (1964).

cause or attempt to cause an employer to discriminate against an employee in violation of subsection (a)(3) or to discriminate against an employee with respect to whom membership in such organization has been denied or terminated on some ground other than his failure to tender the periodic dues and initiation fees uniformly required as a condition of acquiring or retaining membership." Petitioner in *Radio Officers* contends that it was fatal error for the Board to proceed against it, a union, without joining the employer, and that absent a finding of violation of Sec. 8(a)(3) by and a reinstatement order against such employer, the Board could not order the union to pay back pay under Sec. 8(b)(2).

We find no support for these arguments in the Act. No such limitation is contained in the language of Sec. 8(b)(2). That section makes it clear that there are circumstances under which charges against a union for violating the section must be brought without joining a charge against the employer under Sec. 8(a)(3) for attempts to cause employers to discriminate are proscribed. Thus a literal reading of the section requires only a showing that the union caused or attempted to cause the employer to engage in conduct which, if committed, would violate Sec. 8(a)(3). No charge was filed against the company by Fowler when he filed his charge against the union. The General Counsel is entrusted with "final authority, on behalf of the Board, in respect of the investigation of charges and issuance of complaints," but without a charge he has no authority to issue a complaint. Even when a charge is filed, many factors must influence exercise by the General Counsel of this discretion relative to prosecution of unfair labor practices. Abuse of discretion has not been shown, and, when a complaint is prosecuted, the Board is empowered by Sec. 10(a) "to prevent any person from engaging in any unfair labor practice. . . ." It, therefore, had the power to find that the union had violated Sec. 8(b)(2).

Nor does the absence of joinder of the employer preclude entry of a back pay order against the union. The union cites in support of its position the language of Sec. 10(c) which empowers the Board to issue orders requiring "such affirmative action including reinstatement of employees with or without back pay, as will effectuate the policies of this Act: *Provided,* That where an order directs reinstatement of an employee, back pay may be required of the employer or labor organization as the case may be, responsible for the discrimination suffered by him: . . . ." In *Phelps Dodge Corp.* v. *Labor Board,* 313 U.S. 177, 189, we interpreted the phrase giving the Board power to order "reinstatement of employees with or without back pay" not to limit, but merely to illustrate the general grant of power to award affirmative relief. Thus we held that the Board could order back pay without ordering reinstatement. The proviso in Sec. 10(c) was added by the 1947 amendments. The purpose of Congress in enacting this provision was not to limit the power of the Board to order back pay without ordering reinstatement but to give the Board power to remedy union unfair labor practices comparable to the power it possessed to remedy unfair labor practices by employers. Petitioner argues, however, that it will not "effectuate the policies of this Act" to require it to reimburse back pay if the employer is not made to share this burden, but, on the contrary, will frustrate the Act's purposes. We do not agree. It does not follow that because one form of remedy is not available or appropriate in a case, as here, that no remedy should be granted. . . . discriminated against.

CASE
QUESTIONS

1. How does the General Counsel enter into this case?
2. What does Section 8(b)(2) of the NLRA provide?
3. May a back pay order issue against a union?
4. When is the employer held liable?

Business League of Gadsden (United Rubber Workers)

150 NLRB No. 18 (1964)

. . . Briefly, since 1943 the Respondent Union has been the bargaining representative of the employees of Goodyear Tire and Rubber Company at the latter's plant at East Gadsden, Alabama. The collective labor agreement which was in effect at all material times, and, insofar as appears, all earlier agreements did not contain provisions discriminating racially against Negroes in the bargaining unit. In practice, however, the Respondent and the Company construed the contracts as permitting racial job discrimination and racial seniority rosters, so that, to quote the Trial Examiner, "Certain jobs were allocated to white employees and other jobs to Negro employees" and "as to promotions, transfers, layoffs, and recalls Negro employees with greater plant seniority had no rights over white employees with less seniority, and vice versa." In addition, as the Trial Examiner found, racially segregated dining and toilet facilities are maintained in the plant, although there has been no contractual provision with respect to the subjects, and the evidence "indicated" that use of the plant's golf course is limited to white employees.

David Buckner is one of eight Negro complainants in this case. During or before October, 1961, Buckner bid on a job that was then posted, but his bid was rejected by management because the job was a "white job." Buckner was laid off. He protested to both the Company and the Respondent that a white employee of less seniority was being retained. Other complainants also had been laid off. Thereafter, as detailed in the Trial Examiner's Decision, Buckner and the other complainants filed grievances with the Respondent by which they undertook to obtain (1) elimination of racially discriminatory practices by the Respondent and the Company, and (2) back pay for the periods of their layoffs. The Respondent refused to process the grievances. . . .

We turn to a consideration of the remaining exceptions. These relate to the Respondent's refusal, within the 10(b) period, to process grievances seeking (1) back pay for layoffs and (2) desegregation of the plant facilities.

"Discrimination in representation because of race is prohibited by the" Act (*Conley* v. *Gibson,* 355 U.S. 41, 46), and we held in *Independent Metal Workers Union, Local No. 1* (Hughes Tool Co.), 147 NLRB No. 166, that a statutory bargaining representative violates Section 8(b)(1)(A), (2), and (3) when it refuses, on racial grounds, to process the grievance of a member of the bargaining unit. See also *Local 1367, International Longshoremen's As-*

sociation (Galveston Maritime Association), 148 NLRB No. 44, in which we analyzed a statutory representative's duty to bargain collectively as including the duty to represent employees fairly and without invidious discrimination. The right of employees to be represented fairly by their statutory representative is analogous to their right to require their employer to bargain collectively, and their representative cannot bargain for the denial of equal employment and promotion opportunities to a part of the unit upon grounds of race, *Steele* v. *L & N Railroad,* 323 U.S. 192, 207 (1944); *Graham* v. *Brotherhood of Locomotive Firemen and Enginemen,* 338 U.S. 232, 238–239 (1949). Moreover, the duty of fair representation may be breached not only by action, but by inaction as well, such as the refusal to process a grievance. "Discrimination in refusing to represent" an employee has been held to constitute such a breach, *Conley* v. *Gibson,* 355 U.S. at 47; "So long as a labor union assumes to act as the statutory representative of a [unit], it cannot rightly refuse to perform the duty, which is inseparable from the power of representation conferred upon it, to represent the entire membership of the [unit]," *Steele,* 323 U.S. at 204. The duty of fair representation which the Act imposes upon a statutory representative "stands on no different footing" than the duty to bargain collectively which the Act imposes upon an employer. *Steele,* 323 U.S. at 207. In the absence of legislative history to establish that the Act contemplates resort to different forums when the analogous duties are breached, i.e., judicial remedies against a statutory representative and administrative remedies against an employer, the effective administration of the Act requires that administrative remedies be available in the instance of either breach. *Cf. Steele* 323 U.S. at 204–207. . . .

. . . We hold that the Respondent's statutory duty was to process the grievances through arbitration, and that the Respondent demonstrated manifest bad faith and invidious motivation in refusing because of the past invalid interpretations of its collective labor agreements. Upon the basis of the *Hughes Tool* and *Galveston Maritime* cases, *supra,* and for the additional reasons recited herein, we find violations of Section 8(b)(1)(A), 8(b)(2), and 8(b)(3) in the Respondent's refusal within the 10(b) period to process the grievances concerning back pay. We are not to be understood as holding that the Respondent or any other labor organization must process to arbitration any grievance other than the precise ones discussed herein. We hold only that where the record demonstrates that a grievance would have been processed to arbitration but for racially discriminatory reasons, the failure so to process it violates the Act because the statutory agent's duty is to represent without regard to race. To paraphrase a portion of the Intermediate Report of Trial Examiner Reel in *Hughes Tool, supra,* whatever may be the bases on which a statutory representative may properly decline to process grievances, the bases must bear a reasonable relation to the union's role as bargaining representative or to its functioning as a labor organization; manifestly racial discrimination bears no such relationship. . . .

We are not unmindful that in Title VII of the Civil Rights Act of 1964 the Congress has legislated concerning racial discrimination by labor organizations. But the reach of Title VII goes far beyond such discrimination, proscribing as it does discrimination on the basis of race, color, religion, sex, or national origin by employers, employment agencies, and joint labor-management committees, as well as labor organizations. Moreover, the Board's powers and duties are in no way limited by Title VII. On June 12, 1964, before the passage of the Civil Rights Act of 1964, the Senate rejected by a vote of 59 to 29 an amendment to Title VII which had been proposed by Senator Tower (R, Texas) and which perhaps would have had the effect of limiting the Board's powers. See the *Congressional Record* (daily copy) 88th Congress, 2nd Session, pp. 13171–73. The proposed amendment read:

"Sec. 717. Beginning on the effective date of Sections 703, 704, 706, and 707 of this title, as provided in Section 716, the provisions of this title shall constitute the exclusive means whereby any department, agency, or instrumentality in the executive branch of the Government, or any independent agency of the United States, may grant or seek relief from, or pursue any remedy with respect to, any employment practice of any employer, employment agency, labor organization, or joint labor-management committee covered by this title, if such employment practice may be the subject of a charge or complaint filed under this title."

The Respondent, by refusing to process the grievances relating to (1) back pay for some or all of the complainants and (2) desegregation of plant facilities restrained and coerced employees in the exercise of their Section 7 right to be represented without invidious discrimination, caused and attempted to cause the Company to discriminate against employees in violation of Section 8(a)(3), and refused to bargain in their behalf, thereby engaging in unfair labor practices affecting commerce within the meaning of Section 8(b)(1)(A), (2), and (3) and Section 2(6) and (7) of the Act.

Having found that the Respondent has engaged in unfair labor practices, we shall order it to cease and desist therefrom and to take affirmative action designated to effectuate the purposes of the Act. Specifically, we shall order the Respondent to comply with its duty of fair representation by processing the grievances concerning back pay and desegregation of plant facilities. The processing shall include arbitration because the record establishes that that step is essential to assure the complainants an impartial resolution of the merit of their grievances. Finally, we note anew that the Respondent, when purportedly ending its invalid interpretations of contracts in 1962, agreed orally with the Company that future interpretations will not result in racial discrimination. We shall order the Respondent to implement that oral agreement by proposing to the Company specific contractual provisions to prohibit racial discrimination in terms and conditions of employment, and to bargain in good faith to obtain such provisions in a written contract. We are convinced that such an order is necessary in view of (1) the long history of the Respondent's invalid interpretations of contracts, (2) the failure of the Respondent to do more in 1962 than reach an oral agreement with the Company, and (3) the Respondent's continuing resistance to its duty of fair representation as reflected by other facts recited herein. The oral agreement of 1962 must be reduced to writing in particularized form if the Respondent's unfair labor practices are to be rectified and if there is to be a fulfillment of its statutory duty of fair representation. Our order in this respect does not differ materially from those in scores of cases in which we ordered employers to reduce to writing, and sign, oral agreements which they had reached with their employees' representatives. See, e.g., the early case, *H. J. Heinz Co.* v. *NLRB*,

311 U.S. 514, 524 (1941), in which the Court said that a written agreement is essential "to provide an authentic record of its terms which [can] be exhibited to employees. . . ."

CASE QUESTIONS	1. What was the discriminatory representation complained of here?
	2. What consideration does the Board give to the Civil Rights Act's effects on its jurisdiction?
	3. What remedy is ordered and against whom? Why?
	4. Why is union racial discrimination less amenable to the NLRA than to the Civil Rights Act, Title VII?

SECTION 53 / REFUSAL BY UNION TO BARGAIN

The original National Labor Relations Act imposed no explicit duty upon a labor organization to engage in good faith bargaining, presumably under the theory that such a provision would be superfluous since the basic purpose of a labor association is to represent employees for purposes of collective bargaining. The amended Act, in Sec. 8(b)(3), imposes an affirmative duty upon unions. This union requirement, like that for employers, as discussed in Chapter 6, includes the duties stated in Section 8(d) of the law to give 60 days' notice of proposed changes in agreements, with the *status quo* to be maintained during the notice period.[9] Failure to notify the government agencies as required by 8(d)(3) connotes a union's refusal of good faith bargaining, with the result that striking employees thereafter are unprotected as to job rights. Failure to give proper notice to a state mediation service also is held by the NLRB to be a violation of 8(b)(3). In one case it was held that the union's failure to notify the Federal Mediation and Conciliation Service as well as the State agency made a subsequent strike an

---

[9] The pertinent language of 8(d) states the following:

(d) For the purposes of this section, to bargain collectively is the performance of the mutual obligation of the employer and the representative of the employees to meet at reasonable times and confer in good faith with respect to wages, hours, and other terms and conditions of employment, or the negotiation of an agreement, or any question arising thereunder, and the execution of a written contract incorporating any agreement reached if requested by either party, but such obligation does not compel either party to agree to a proposal or require the making of a concession: *Provided,* That where there is in effect a collective-bargaining contract covering employees in an industry affecting commerce, the duty to bargain collectively shall also mean that no party to such contract shall terminate or modify such contract, unless the party desiring such termination or modification—

(1) serves a written notice upon the other party to the contract of the proposed termination or modification sixty days prior to the expiration date thereof, or in the event such contract contains no expiration date, sixty days prior to the time it it is proposed to make such termination or modification;

(2) offers to meet and confer with the other party for the purpose of negotiating a new contract or a contract containing the proposed modifications;

(3) notifies the Federal Mediation and Conciliation Service within thirty days after such notice of the existence of a dispute, and simultaneously therewith notifies any State or Territorial agency established to mediate and conciliate disputes within the State or Territory where the dispute occurred, provided no agreement has been reached by that time; and

(4) continues in full force and effect, without resorting to strike or lockout, all the terms and conditions of the existing contract for a period of sixty days after such notice is given or until the expiration date of such contract, whichever occurs later. . . .

unprotected union unfair labor practice stoppage. Replacing the strikers and refusing to deal further with the union, this employer's conduct was held to be lawful under the Act, with the complaint dismissed as to 8(a)(1), (2), (3), and (5) violations.[10]

The union duty to bargain in good faith also includes the same procedural requirements that the employer must meet, including a willingness to consider in good faith the position of the other party. Insisting on illegal clauses which fall outside the scope of mandatory bargaining subjects constitutes a union violation of 8(b)(3), as the reciprocal of 8(a)(5). The use of economic power to coerce agreement to such proscribed contract demands compounds the evidence of a violation. The NLRB has no authority to find mere use of economic power or harsh bargaining methods to be evidence of a violation of the duty to bargain where demands are lawful and the union remains willing to negotiate in good faith at bargaining conferences. But illegal demands as a condition to further bargaining are evidence of 8(b)(3) violations.

A union refusal to bargain may be caused also by insistence on contract provisions for a discriminatory hiring hall, for other illegal union preferences, for any illegal clause against "hot cargo" or struck work requirements. The latter prohibition of Section 8(e) of the Act is discussed below under that heading, along with some of the demands that may violate this restriction on union demands.

A violation of 8(b)(3) may also be caused by the failure to sign a contract by the authorized union representatives after agreement is reached with the employer because national union officials insist on further provisions before execution is permitted; or where improved bargaining power at another plant of the employer is sought through delaying of signed provisions such as no-strike clauses. These rulings are consistent with the Board holding that an employer refusal to sign a written contract violates 8(a)(5).

It was pointed out in the previous section of the chapter that a union violates the Act by not giving fair, nondiscriminatory representation to bargaining unit members regardless of race, color, religion, national origin, or sex in contract negotiations and administration or in grievance handling. For such bad faith representation the NLRB may order affirmative action to correct the illegal practices, may cancel certification as bargaining agent, or order other corrective steps as in the *United Rubber Workers* decision already presented in Section 52. But in the *Insurance Agents* decision, the Supreme Court upholds the labor position by restricting the discretionary powers of the NLRB.

NLRB v. Insurance Agents' International Union

Supreme Court of the United States, 1960. 361 U.S. 477

BRENNAN, J.: This case presents an important issue of the scope of the National Labor Relations Board's authority under Sec. 8(b)(3) of the National

---

[10] *Fort Smith Chair Company,* 143 NLRB No. 2 (1963).

Labor Relations Act, which provides that "It shall be an unfair labor practice for a labor organization or its agents . . . to refuse to bargain collectively with an employer, provided it is the representative of his employees. . . ." The precise question is whether the Board may find that a union, which confers with an employer with the desire of reaching agreement on contract terms, has nevertheless refused to bargain collectively, thus violating that provision, solely and simply because during the negotiations it seeks to put economic pressure on the employer to yield to its bargaining demands by sponsoring on-the-job conduct designed to interfere with the carrying on of the employer's business.

Since 1949 the respondent Insurance Agents' International Union and the Prudential Insurance Company of America have negotiated collective bargaining agreements covering district agents employed by Prudential in 35 States and the District of Columbia. The principal duties of a Prudential district agent are to collect premiums and to solicit new business in an assigned locality known in the trade as his "debit." He has no fixed or regular working hours except that he must report at his district office two mornings a week and remain for two or three hours to deposit his collections, prepare and submit reports, and attend meetings to receive sales and other instructions. He is paid commissions on collections made and on new policies written.

However, in April, 1956, Prudential filed a Sec. 8(b)(3) charge of refusal to bargain collectively against the union. The charge was based upon actions of the union and its members outside the conference room, occurring after the old contract expired in March. The union had announced in February that if agreement on the terms of the new contract was not reached when the old contract expired, the union members would then participate in a "Work-Without-Contract" program—which meant that they would engage in certain planned, concerted on-the-job activities designed to harass the company.

A complaint of violation of Sec. 8(b)(3) issued on the charge and hearings began before the bargaining was concluded. It was developed in the evidence that the union's harassing tactics involved activities by the member agents such as these: refusal for a time to solicit new business, and refusal (after the writing of new business was resumed) to comply with the company's reporting procedures; refusal to participate in the company's "May Policyholders' Month Campaign"; reporting late at district offices the days the agents were scheduled to attend them, and refusing to perform customary duties at the offices, instead engaging there in "sit-in-mornings," "doing what comes naturally" and leaving at noon as a group; absenting themselves from special business conferences arranged by the company; picketing and distributing leaflets outside the various offices of the company on specified days and hours as directed by the union; distributing leaflets each day to policyholders and others and soliciting policyholders' signatures on petitions directed to the company; and presenting the signed policyholders' petitions to the company at its home office while simultaneously engaging in mass demonstrations there. . . .

. . . The hearing examiner found that there was nothing in the record, apart from the mentioned activities of the union during the negotiations, that could be relied upon to support an inference that the union had not fulfilled its statutory duty; in fact nothing else was relied upon by the Board's General Counsel in prosecuting the complaint. The hearing examiner's analysis of the congressional design in enacting the statutory duty to bargain led him to conclude that the Board was not authorized to find that such economically harassing activities constituted a Sec. 8(b)(3) violation. The Board's opinion answers flatly "We do not agree" and proceeds to say

". . . the Respondent's reliance upon harassing tactics during the course of negotiations for the avowed purpose of compelling the Company to capitulate to its terms is the antithesis of reasoned discussion it was duty-bound to follow. Indeed, it clearly revealed an unwillingness to submit its demands to the consideration of the bargaining table where argument, persuasion, and the free interchange of views could take place. In such circumstances, the fact that the Respondent continued to confer with the Company and was desirous of concluding an agreement does not alone establish that it fulfilled its obligation to bargain in good faith. . . ." 119 NLRB, at 769, 770–771.

Thus the Board's view is that irrespective of the union's good faith in conferring with the employer at the bargaining table for the purpose and with the desire of reaching agreement on contract terms, its tactics during the course of the negotiations constituted *per se* violation of Sec. 8(b)(3). Accordingly, as is said in the Board's brief,

"The issue here . . . comes down to whether the Board is authorized under the Act to hold that such tactics, which the Act does not specifically forbid but Section 7 does not protect, support a finding of a failure to bargain in good faith as required by Section 8(b)(3)."

. . . Obviously there is tension between the principle that the parties need not contract on any specific terms and a practical enforcement of the principle that they are bound to deal with each other in a serious attempt to resolve differences and reach a common ground. And in fact criticism of the Board's application of the "good-faith" test arose from the belief that it was forcing employers to yield to union demands if they were to avoid a successful charge of unfair labor practice. Thus, in 1947 in Congress the fear was expressed that the Board had "gone very far, in the guise of determining whether or not employers had bargained in good faith, in setting itself up as the judge of what concessions an employer must make and of the proposals and counter proposals that he may or may not make." H. R. Rep. No. 245, 80th Cong., 1st Sess., p. 19. Since the Board was not viewed by Congress as an agency which should exercise its powers to arbitrate the parties' substantive solutions of the issues in their bargaining, a check on this apprehended trend was provided by writing the good-faith test of bargaining into Sec. 8(d) of the Taft-Hartley Act. That section defines collective bargaining as follows:

"For the purposes of this section, to bargain collectively is the performance of the mutual obligation of the employer and the representative of the employees to meet at reasonable times and confer in good faith with respect to wages, hours, and other terms and conditions of employment, or the negotiation of an agreement, or any question arising thereunder, and the execution of a written contract incorporating any agreement reached if requested by either party, but such obligation does not compel either party to agree to a proposal or require the making of a concession. . . ."

But it remains clear that Sec. 8(d) was an attempt by Congress to prevent the Board from controlling the settling of the terms of collective bargaining agreements. *Labor Board* v. *American National Ins. Co.,* 343 U.S. 395.

At the same time as it was statutorily defining the duty to bargain collectively, Congress, by adding Sec. 8(b)(3) of the Act through the Taft-Hartley amendments, imposed that duty on labor organizations. Unions obviously are formed for the very purpose of bargaining collectively; but the legislative history makes it plain that Congress was wary of the position of some unions, and wanted to ensure that they would approach the bargaining table with the same attitude of willingness to reach an agreement as had been enjoined on management earlier. It intended to prevent employee representatives from putting forth the same "take it or leave it" attitude that had been condemned in management.

It is apparent from the legislative history of the whole Act that the policy of Congress is to impose a mutual duty upon the parties to confer in good faith with a desire to reach agreement, in the belief that such an approach from both sides of the table promotes the overall design of achieving industrial peace. See *Labor Board* v. *Jones & Laughlin Steel Corp.,* 301 U.S. 1. Discussion conducted under that standard of good faith may narrow the issues, making the real demands of the parties clearer to each other, and perhaps to themselves, and may encourage an attitude of settlement through give and take. The mainstream of cases before the Board and in the courts reviewing its orders, under the provisions fixing the duty to bargain collectively, is concerned with insuring that the parties approach the bargaining table with this attitude. But apart from this essential standard of conduct, Congress intended that the parties should have wide latitude in their negotiations, unrestricted by any governmental power to regulate the substantive solution of their differences.

We believe that the Board's approach in this case—unless it can be defended, in terms of Sec. 8(b)(3), as resting on some unique character of the union tactics involved here—must be taken as proceeding from an erroneous view of collective bargaining. It must be realized that collective bargaining, under a system where the Government does not attempt to control the results of negotiations, cannot be equated with an academic collective search for truth—or even with what might be thought to be the ideal of one. The parties —even granting the modification of views that may come from a realization of economic interdependence—still proceed from contrary, and to an extent antagonistic viewpoints and concepts of self-interest. The system has not reached the ideal of the philosophic notion that perfect understanding among people would lead to perfect agreement among them on values. The presence of economic weapons in reserve, and their actual exercise on occasion by the parties, is part and parcel of the system that the Wagner and Taft-Hartley Acts have recognized. Abstract logical analysis might find inconsistency between the command of the statute to negotiate toward an agreement in good faith and the legitimacy of the use of economic weapons, frequently having the most serious effect upon individual workers and productive enterprises, to induce one party to come to the terms desired by the other. But the truth of the matter is that at the present statutory stage of our national labor relations policy, the two factors—necessity for good-faith bargaining between parties, and the availability of economic pressure devices to each to make the other party incline to agree on one's terms—exist side by side. . . .

For similar reasons, we think the Board's approach involves an intrusion into the substantive aspects of the bargaining process—again, unless there is some specific warrant for its condemnation of the precise tactics involved here. The scope of Sec. 8(b)(3) and the limitations on Board power which were the design of Sec. 8(d) are exceeded, we hold, by inferring a lack of good faith not from any deficiencies of the union's performance at the bargaining table by reason of its attempted use of economic pressure, but solely and simply because tactics designed to exert economic pressure were employed during the course of the good faith negotiations. Thus the Board in the guise of determining good or bad faith in negotiations could regulate what economic weapons a party might summon to its aid. And if the Board could regulate the choice of economic weapons that may be used as part of collective bargaining, it would be in a position to exercise considerable influence upon the substantive terms on which the parties contract. As the parties' own devices became more limited, the Government might have to enter even more directly into the negotiation of collective agreements. Our labor policy is not presently erected on a foundation of government control of the results of negotiations. See S. Rep. No. 105, 80th Cong., 1st Sess., p. 2. Nor does it contain a charter for the National Labor Relations Board to act at large in equalizing disparities of bargaining power between employer and union. . . .

. . . It is suggested here that the time has come for a reevaluation of the basic content of collective bargaining as contemplated by the federal legislation. But that is for Congress. Congress has demonstrated its capacity to adjust the Nation's labor legislation to what, in its legislative judgment, constitutes the statutory pattern appropriate to the developing state of labor relations in the country. Major revisions of the basic statute were enacted in 1947 and 1959. To be sure, then, Congress might be of opinion that greater stress should be put on the role of "pure" negotiation in settling labor disputes, to the extent of eliminating more and more economic weapons from the parties' grasp, and perhaps it might start with the ones involved here; or in consideration of the alternatives, it might shrink from such an undertaking. But Congress' policy has not yet moved to this point, and with only Sec. 8(b)(3) to lean on, we do not see how the Board can do so on its own. *Affirmed.*

CASE QUESTIONS

1. What was done by the Union to harass the employer?
2. Under what Section did the employer file charges?
3. What position did the Board take in deciding the matter?
4. Did the Supreme Court uphold the Board? Why did the Court take its position?

SECTION 54 / ORGANIZATIONAL OR RECOGNITION PICKETING

The Reporting and Disclosure Act of 1959 provided a very important amendment to the National Labor Relations Act when it added Section 8(b)(7) to the list of union unfair labor practices. Peaceful picketing is ordinarily accorded constitutional protection, but may be curbed under certain circumstances, as when it is untruthful, massed, or enmeshed in inseparable violent conduct. Section 8(b)(7) adds a statutory prohibition against organizational and recognition picketing on the part of an *uncertified* union even though such picketing is peaceful and truthful.

Congress enacted Section 8(b)(7) in an effort to provide statutory protection of employers who, though innocent of any misconduct or illegality on their part, might be subjected to long, extended, and harrassing picketing, the effect of which, in some cases, would be to compel the employer to illegally grant recognition to an uncertified union that did not, in fact, command a sufficiency of employee interest to win an election under the provisions of Section 9 of the NLRA.

Normal procedure providing for orderly representation and elections is treated in this volume in Chapter 5. At this juncture we are concerned with the type of picketing for recognition that has been now designated a union unfair labor practice. The summary language of Section 8(b)(7) reads as follows: "(b) It shall be an unfair labor practice for a labor organization or its agents (7) to picket or cause to be picketed, or threaten to picket . . . any employer . . . to force him to recognize or bargain with a labor organization . . . unless such labor organization is currently certified as the representative of such employees:

(A) where the employer has lawfully recognized . . . any other labor organization and a question concerning representation may not appropriately be raised under Section 9(c) of this Act.
(B) where within the preceding twelve months a valid election under Section 9(c) of this Act has been conducted, or
(C) where such picketing has been conducted without a petition under Section 9(c) being filed [to secure NLRB resolution of representation rights] [11] within a reasonable period of time *not to exceed thirty days* from the commencement of such picketing."

To illustrate the manner in which the above three provisions will operate, let us take an assumed set of facts and proceed with the action, with initial focus upon subsections (A) and (B) above. An uncertified union is peacefully picketing an employer for recognition even though said employer is already legally bargaining under the circumstances detailed in (A) and (B) above. The employer may then file an unfair union labor practice charge under Section 8(b)(7) with the NLRB. If the Board finds that the employer's statement truly represents the facts of the case, upon hearing, etc., it will find the union guilty of the commission of an unfair labor practice and take appropriate steps for its cessation.

Let us now examine subsection (C) above, altering the facts in one particular, namely, that there is a valid question of representation involved, or where there

---

[11] Brackets and italics ours.

is, at present, no union representative and the uncertified union peacefully pickets to secure recognition by the employer. If, within thirty days of the beginning of picketing, no party files a petition for an election under Section 9(c), the picketing becomes violative of Section 8(b)(7) and subject to injunctive relief. The party filing a Section 9(c) election petition can be an employer, employee, a rival union, or the union doing the primary picketing.

Suppose, however, that one of the parties involved in the organizational picketing does file such petition within the prescribed thirty days and accompanies or precedes the petition with a Section 8(b)(7) charge, "the Board shall *forthwith*,[12] without regard to the provisions of Section 9(c)(1) or the absence of a showing of substantial interest on the part of the labor organization, direct an election . . . and shall certify the results thereof."

One final portion of Section 8(b)(7)(C) is important and the statute is quoted directly. "That nothing in this subparagraph (C) shall be construed to prohibit any picketing or other publicity for the purpose of truthfully advising the *public (including consumers)*[13] that an employer does not employ members of . . . a labor organization, unless an effect of such picketing is to induce any individual employed by any other person in the course of his employment, not to pick up, deliver, or transport any goods or not to perform any services."

The purport of this proviso is to specifically legalize publicity or informational picketing as heretofore, but to interdict even primary peaceful picketing if it produces unlawful secondary results as when the effect of the picket is to cause, say, a teamster to refuse to make deliveries or pickups. As a caution to the layman, it should be realized that a Section 8(b)(7) charge by an employer will not be sustained by the General Counsel of the NLRB if a Section 8(a)(2) domination or interference charge is pending before the Board.

QUESTIONS ON SECTION 54

1. Does Section 8(b)(7) apply to all labor organizations involved in recognition picketing disputes?
2. Why did Congress enact Section 8(b)(7)?
3. What are the principal provisions of Section 8(b)(7)?
4. Under what circumstances does an "expedited" election take place?

SECTION 55 / **JURISDICTIONAL DISPUTES**

In Section 8(b)(4)(D) some additional economic pressures by unions are prohibited. Where the purpose of a strike or boycott is to compel work assignment to members of a trade, craft, class, or organization in the absence of a Board certification or ruling concerning that particular work, a violation of the sanction occurs.

This particular violation receives a different accelerated treatment since the Act gives the parties ten days after notice of charges filed for attempting to adjust the dispute. If satisfactory evidence of adjustment or of an agreed upon method

---

[12] Authors' italics. This means that an election is held on an expedited schedule.
[13] Authors' italics.

for adjustment is submitted within ten days, the proceeding ends; otherwise, under Section 10(k), or if later renewed, the dispute may be heard and determined. A complaint may issue if violation continues. In addition to the usual cease-and-desist orders, the Board may also obtain from a court a temporary restraining order against jurisdictional or work assignment unfair activity prior to issuing its complaint. Thus a neutral employer and the public should receive prompt relief from a jurisdictional struggle between unions.

Such strife may be continuing over long periods, however, where two unions are contesting each other's right. For example, in one case the respondent union contended that the case was a moot one since the work had been completed before any restraining order issued. The court found grounds, however, to believe that the dispute would be renewed on future jobs. Although the parties had agreed on voluntary methods of adjustment, the Court of Appeals upheld the Board authority to decide the matter by a cease-and-desist order.[14]

Interesting questions arise as to the purpose of union activity where both such unlawful and also protected objectives are said to be present. The picketing respondent union may claim its sole aim to be consumer or public information, while the Board may believe work reassignment to have been the objective. If any basis exists for the latter conclusion, even though multiple objectives are present, the Board will proceed under the 8(b)(4)(D) provision, and the courts agree to this.

In making work assignment determination, the criteria used include past practice and customs, existing contracts, efficiency and economy of operations, previous certification of bargaining units, or other significant considerations. Usually several significant considerations may be in conflict, the problem then being to decide which will have the controlling weight. The courts do not upset the NLRB judgments in such matters.

After a charge is filed under Section 8(b)(4)(D), Section 10(k) then requires the Board to hold a hearing to resolve the jurisdictional dispute unless "the parties to such dispute" adjust or agree upon a method for the voluntary adjustment of the dispute. Ever since 10(k) was enacted, the Board has consistently interpreted the term "parties to such dispute" to include the employer as well as the disputing unions and has refused to dismiss the 10(k) proceedings when the unions, but not the employer, have agreed to settle. In the *Plasterers' Local 79* decision, reported below, the Supreme Court upheld the Board's interpretation and reversed the District of Columbia Circuit Court's decision that an employer had no right to insist upon participation in a 10(k) proceeding.

NLRB v. Plasterers' Local 79

Supreme Court of the United States, 1971. 404 U.S. 116

WHITE, J.: When a charge is filed under § 8(b)(4)(D), the provision of the Labor Management Relations Act banning so-called jurisdictional disputes, the Board must under § 10(k) "hear and determine the dispute out of

---

[14] *Douds* v. *Local Union No. 46, Wood, Wire, and Metal Lathers Int'l Assn.*, 245 F.2d 223 (1957).

which [the] unfair labor practice shall have arisen unless . . . the parties to such dispute" adjust or agree upon a method for the voluntary adjustment of the dispute. The issue here is whether an employer, picketed to force reassignment of work, is a "party" to the "dispute" for purposes of § 10(k). When the two unions involved, but not the employer, have agreed upon a method of settlement, must the Board dismiss the § 10(k) proceedings or must it proceed to determine the dispute with the employer afforded a chance to participate?

I. Texas State Tile & Terrazzo Company (Texas State) and Martini Tile & Terrazzo Company (Martini) are contractors in Houston, Texas, engaged in the business of installing tile and terrazzo. Both have collective bargaining agreements with Tile, Terrazzo and Marble Setters Local Union No. 20 (Tile Setters) and have characteristically used members of the Tile Setters union for laying tile and also for work described in the collective bargaining contract as applying "a coat or coats of mortar, prepared to proper tolerance to receive tile on floors, walls and ceilings regardless of whether the mortar coat is wet or dry at the time the tile is applied to it."

These cases arose when Plasterers' Local Union No. 9, Operative Plasterers' and Cement Masons' International Association of Houston, Texas (Plasterers), picketed the job sites of Texas State and Martini claiming that the work of applying the mortar to receive tile was the work of the Plasters' union and not of the Tile Setters. Neither Texas State nor Martini had a collective bargaining contract with the Plasterers or regularly employed workers represented by that union.

Before the Texas State picketing began, the Plasterers submitted their claim to the disputed work to the National Joint Board for Settlement of Jurisdictional Disputes (Joint Board), a body established by the Building Trades Department, AFL-CIO, and by certain employer groups. Both the Plasterers' and the Tile Setters' locals were bound by Joint Board decisions because their international unions were members of the AFL-CIO's Building Trades Department. Neither Texas State nor Martini had agreed to be bound by Joint Board procedures and decisions, however. The Joint Board found the work in dispute to be covered by an agreement of August 1917, between the two international unions, and awarded the work to the Plasterers. When Texas State and the Tile Setters refused to acquiesce in the Joint Board decision and change the work assignment, the Plasterers began the picketing of Texas State which formed the basis for the § 8(b)(4)(D) charges. The Plasterers also picketed a job site where Martini employees, members of the Tile Setters, were installing tile, although this dispute had not been submitted to the Joint Board.

Martini and Southwestern Construction Company, the general contractor which had hired Texas State, filed § 8(b)(4)(D) unfair labor practice charges against the Plasterers, and the NLRB's regional director noticed a consolidated § 10(k) hearing to determine the dispute. Southwestern, Texas State, Martini, and the two unions participated in the hearing. A panel of the Board noted that the Tile Setters admitted being bound by Joint Board procedures, but deemed the Joint Board decision to lack controlling weight and "after taking into account and balancing all relevant factors" awarded the work to the Tile Setters. When the Plasterers refused to indicate that they would abide by the Board's award, an § 8(b)(4)(D) complaint was issued against them, and they were found to have committed an unfair labor practice by picketing to force Texas State and Martini to assign the disputed work to them. In making both the § 10(k) and § 8(b)(4)(D) decisions, the Board rejected the Plasterers' contention that even though the employer had not agreed to be bound by the Joint Board decision, the provisions of § 10(k) precluded a subsequent Board decision because the competing unions had agreed upon a voluntary method of adjustment.

On petition to review by the Plasterers and cross petition to enforce by the Board, a divided panel of the Court of Appeals set aside the order of the Board. It held that "It is not the employer but the rival unions (or other employee groups) who are parties to the jurisdictional dispute contesting which employees are entitled to seek the work in question." It concluded that the Board may not make a § 10(k) determination of a jurisdictional dispute where the opposing unions have agreed to settle their differences through binding arbitration. Both the Board and the employers petitioned for certiorari, and we granted the petitions.

II. Section 8(b)(4)(D) makes it an unfair labor practice for a labor organization to strike or threaten or coerce an employer or other person in order to force or require an employer to assign particular work to one group of employees rather than to another, unless the employer is refusing to honor a representation order of the Board. On its face, the section would appear to cover any union challenge to an employer work assignment where the prohibited means are employed. *Labor Board* v. *Radio and Television Broadcast Engineers Union, Local 1212 (CBS)*, 364 U.S. 573, 576 (1960). As the charging or intervening party, the employer would normally be a party to any proceedings under that section. Section 8(b)(4)(D), however, must be read in light of § 10(k) with which it is interlocked. *Labor Board* v. *Radio and Television Broadcast Engineers, supra,* at 576. When an § 8(b)(4)(D) charge is filed and there is reasonable cause to believe that an unfair labor practice has been committed, issuance of the complaint is withheld until the provisions of § 10(k) have been satisfied. That section directs the Board to "hear and determine" the dispute out of which the alleged unfair labor practice arose; the Board is required to decide which union or group of employees is entitled to the disputed work in accordance with acceptable, Board-developed standards, unless the parties to the underlying dispute settle the case or agree upon a method for settlement. Whether the § 8(b)(4)(D) charge will be sustained or dismissed is thus dependent on the outcome of the § 10(k) proceeding. The Board allows an employer to fully participate in a § 10(k) proceeding as a party. If the employer prefers the employees to whom he has assigned the work, his right to later relief against the other union's picketing is conditioned upon his ability to convince the Board in the § 10(k) proceeding that his original assignment is valid under the criteria employed by the Board.

The alleged unfair labor practice in this case was the picketing of the job sites by the Plasterers, and the dispute giving rise to this picketing was the disagreement over whether Plasterers or Tile Setters were to lay the final plaster coat. This dispute was a three-cornered one. The Plasterers made demands on both Texas State and the Tile Setters and on both Martini and the Tile Setters. In both cases, the employer's refusal to accede to the Plasterers' demands inevitably and inextricably involved him with the Tile Setters against the Plasterers. It was this triangular dispute which the § 10(k) proceeding was intended to resolve.

It may be that in some cases employers have no stake in how a jurisdictional dispute is settled and are interested only in prompt settlement. Other employers, as shown by this case, are not neutral and have substantial economic interests in the outcome of the § 10(k) proceeding. A change in work assignment may result in different terms or conditions of employment, a new union to bargain with, higher wages or costs, and lower efficiency or quality of work. In the construction industry, in particular, where employers frequently calculate bids on very narrow margins, small cost differences are likely to be extremely important. In the present case, both employers had collective bargaining contracts with the Tile Setters specifically covering the work at issue; neither had contracts with the Plasterers nor employed Plasterers regularly. Both employers determined it to be in their best interests to participate vigorously in the Board's § 10(k) proceeding. The employers contended it was more efficient and less costly to use the same craft for applying the last coat of plaster, putting on the bonding coat, and laying the tile and that it was more consistent with industry practice to use the Tile Setters as they did. Both companies claimed that their costs would be substantially increased if the award went to the Plasterers, and that without collective bargaining contracts with the Plasterers, they would lose 30%–40% of their work to plastering contractors. It is obvious, therefore, that both Texas State and Martini had substantial stakes in the outcome of the § 10(k) proceeding.

The phrase "parties to the dispute" giving rise to the picketing must be given its common-sense meaning corresponding to the actual interests involved here. *Cf. International Union, United Automobile, Aerospace & Agricultural Implement Workers of America, AFL-CIO, Local 283* v. *Scofield,* 382 U.S. 205, 220 (1965). Section 10(k) does not expressly or impliedly deny party status to an employer, and since the section's adoption in 1947, the Board has regularly accorded party status to the employer and has refused to dismiss the proceeding when the unions, but not the employer, have agreed to settle.

The Court of Appeals rejected this construction of § 10(k). Its reasoning, which we find unpersuasive, was that because the employer is not bound by the § 10(k) decision, he should have no right to insist upon participation. But the § 10(k) decision standing alone, binds no one. No cease-and-desist order against either union or employer results from such a proceeding; the impact of the § 10(k) decision is felt in the § 8(b)(4)(D) hearing because for all practical purposes the Board's award determines who will prevail in the unfair labor practice proceeding. If the picketing union persists in its conduct despite a § 10(k) decision against it, an § 8(b)(4)(D) complaint issues and the union will likely be found guilty of an unfair labor practice and be ordered to cease and desist. On the other hand, if that union wins the § 10(k) decision and the employer does not comply, the employer's § 8(b)(4)(D) case evaporates and the charges he filed against the picketing union will be dismissed. Neither the employer nor the employees to whom he has assigned the work are legally bound to observe the § 10(k) decision, but both will lose their § 8(b)(4)(D) protection against the picketing which may, as it did here, shut down the job. The employer will be under intense pressure, practically, to conform to the Board's decision. This is the design of the Act; Congress provided no other way to implement the Board's § 10(k) decision.

We do not find that the legislative history of § 8(b)(4)(D) and § 10(k) requires a different conclusion. The Court of Appeals and the Plasterers rely upon various statements in the legislative history of the two sections, particularly the remarks of Senator Morse, referring to jurisdictional disputes as controversies between two labor unions, and a passage in the House Conference Report referring to § 10(k) as directing the Board to "hear and determine disputes between unions giving rise to unfair labor practices under § 8(b)(4)(D)." Nothing in these remarks or in the other relevant legislative documents indicates an affirmative intent to exclude an interested employer from participating in a § 10(k) proceeding. The usual focus of the legislative debates was on ways of protecting the employer from the economic havoc of jurisdictional strikes. But it does not follow from statements condemning the economically deleterious effects of inter-union strife that Congress intended an employer to have no say in a decision that may, practically, affect his business in a radical way. Congress did not expressly focus on the non-neutral employer, but there is nothing in the legislative history that negatives employer standing; and in referring to the "parties to the dispute," Congress used terminology that would ordinarily include the employer in cases such as these.

The Court has frequently cautioned that "[i]t is at best treacherous to find in congressional silence alone the adoption of a controlling rule of law." *Girouard* v. *U.S.,* 328 U.S. 61, 69 (1946). *Boys Markets Inc.* v. *Retail Clerks Union, Local 770,* 398 U.S. 235, 241 (1970). It is clear that Congress intended to protect employers and the public from the detrimental economic impact of "indefensible" jurisdictional strikes. It would therefore be myopic to transform a procedure which was meant to protect employer interests into a device which could injure them. In the absence of an "unmistakable directive," the Court has refused to construe legislation aimed to protect a certain class in a fashion that will run counter to the goals Congress clearly intended to effectuate. *F. T. C.* v. *Fred Meyer Inc.,* 390 U.S. 341, 349 (1968). We conclude, therefore, that these sections were enacted to protect employers who are partisan in a jurisdictional dispute as well as those who are neutral.

Nothing in *Labor Board* v. *Radio and Television Broadcast Engineers (CBS), supra,* mandates a different conclusion. . . . But the issue before us is whether the employer is also a party to that dispute and to the proceeding which decides that question. The Court in *CBS* did not have before it a case in which the employer was particularly interested in which union did the work, since it had collective bargaining contracts with both unions and since both unions were able to do the disputed work with equal skill, expense, and efficiency. The Court recognized that there, *"as in most instances"* the quarrel was of "so little interest to the employer that he seems perfectly willing to assign work to either [union] if the other will just let him." 364 U.S., at 579 (emphasis added). We have no doubt, therefore, that the Court had no intention of deciding the case now before us.

If employers must be considered parties to the dispute that the Board must decide under § 10(k), absent private agreement, they must also be deemed parties to the adjustment or agreement to settle that will abort the § 10(k) proceedings. It is insisted that so holding will encourage employers to avoid private arbitrations, whereas holding union agreement alone sufficient to foreclose Board action will pressure employers to become part of private settlement mechanisms productive of sound result and much swifter decision.

The difficulties with this argument are several. First of all, if union agreements to arbitrate are sufficient to terminate § 10(k) proceedings, there is no assurance that these private procedures will always be open to employer participation, that an employer will be afforded a meaningful chance to participate, or that all relevant factors will be properly considered.

Second, the argument for regarding the employer as a dispensable neutral is reminiscent of the position taken by the Board and rejected by the Court in the *CBS* case. There, the Board sought to justify a narrow view of its function and its failure to make affirmative awards as generating pressure to settle or arbitrate privately. As § 10(k) passed the Senate, it directed the Board to decide the dispute *or* to order arbitration, but the arbitration alternative was deleted in Conference, and the amended bill was passed by the Senate over the strenuous objections of Senator Morse and others. By this amendment, the Court in *CBS* held that Congress had expressed a clear preference for Board decision as compared with compelled arbitration, and that this policy preference must be respected. 364 U.S., at 581–582. Although this Court has frequently approved an expansive role for private arbitration in the settlement of labor disputes, this enforcement of arbitration agreements and settlements has been predicated on the view that the parties have voluntarily bound themselves to such a mechanism at the bargaining table. In both *Carey* v. *Westinghouse Electric Corp.,* 375 U.S. 261, 262 (1964) and *Boys Markets, Inc.* v. *Retail Clerks, Local 770,* 398 U.S. 235, 238 (1970), the employers had acceded to binding arbitration as the terminal step of the grievance procedure. This concession is not present in the instant case; the employers here did not even have a collective bargaining contract with the Plasterers. Section 10(k) contemplates only a voluntary agreement as a bar to a Board decision. As in *CBS,* we decline to narrow the Board's powers under § 10(k) so that employers are coerced to accept compulsory private arbitration when Congress has declined to adopt such a policy. . . .

Reversed.

CASE	1. State the facts of the case.
QUESTIONS	2. If the unions involved in a jurisdictional dispute, but not the employers, have agreed to arbitrate the dispute, must the Board defer to the arbitrators' findings and dismiss the 10(k) proceedings?
	3. What interest, if any, did the employers have in which union performed the work?

SECTION 56 / EXCESSIVE INITIATION FEES AND DUES

Labor organizations that operate under permitted forms of union security may not charge excessive or discriminatory dues or initiation fees by virtue of Sec. 8(b)(5). The General Counsel of the NLRB has issued a statement that shows a disposition to handle each charge on this issue as it arises, with the determination of unfair labor practice resting on a study of custom in the trade, the earnings made by the constituents, and the extent of protection offered to them. Thus what might be considered excessive in one case may be entirely reasonable in another. Rate discrimination within a specific class because of race, color, or creed is, on the other hand, uniformly outlawed. See the *Eclipse* case, which follows, for an example of a violation. The Board also held discriminatory against part-time and temporary employees an increase in initiation fee from $50 to $500 in a 1962 decision.[15]

NLRB v. Eclipse Lumber Co.

Circuit Court of Appeals, Ninth Circuit, 1952. 199 F.2d 684

DENMAN, C. J. This is a petition by the National Labor Relations Board to enforce certain orders of the Board against respondent company and respondent union.

A. *The Board's Order Against the Company.*

This order is based on a claimed violation of Section 8(a)(3)(B) of the Labor Management Act, hereafter called the Act, which provides "That no employer shall justify any discrimination against an employee for nonmembership in a labor organization. . . . (B) if he has reasonable grounds for believing that membership was denied or terminated for reasons other than the failure of the employee to tender the periodic dues and the initiation fees uniformly required as a condition of acquiring or retaining membership."

That is to say, that when a union-shop agreement is entered into under Section 8(a)(3) of the Act, the Company could not discharge a member of the Union on the Union's demand if it had reasonable grounds for believing that the Union's demand for his discharge was on grounds other than for nonpayment of periodic dues and required initiation fees. The Company does not question that the "periodic dues" are those due the Union, subsequent to the making of the union-shop contract. *NLRB* v. *International Union,* 194 F.(2d) 698, 701. *Colonial Fibre Co.* v. *NLRB,* 163 F.(2d) 65.

The facts, in brief, are: In 1944, one Marl, then working for the Company, refused to pay a Union political assessment and thereupon left the Union and paid no more dues. Under the Union rules he remained a member until he was "dropped" by some affirmative act of the Union, which was not taken. He remained a "suspended" member of the Union.

---

[15] *Television and Radio Broadcasting Studio Employees Local 804 and Radio and Television Division of Triangle Publications,* 135 NLRB No. 64 (1962).

In 1948, he returned to work with the Company and was working there when on April 25, 1950, the Union entered into a union-shop contract providing that:

> "All employees shall be required, as a necessary condition of continued employment, to become members of the Union in good standing not later than thirty (30) days from the effective date of this agreement or the beginning date of their first employment, whichever occurs later, and to maintain such membership in good standing thereafter.
>
> "The Union shall notify the Employer in writing of any employee who fails to become or remain a member of the Union in good standing, and the Employer shall, immediately upon receipt of such notification dismiss any such employee from employment."

The Union had a constitutional provision to the effect that a delinquent member could be reinstated upon payment of the regular new member initiation fee of $10 and six months' back dues of $2.50 a month, and one month's dues at the increased rate of $2.75, totaling $27.75. On inquiry of the Union, Marl was told the amount he had to pay was the sum of $85.25, consisting of $70.50 past dues, $10 initiation fee, one month's advanced dues of $2.75, and a $2 fine for non-picketing in a prior strike.

When Marl protested, he was told by the Union treasurer that if he did not pay ". . . at the end of 30 days you know what happens." After thirty days had expired the Union notified the Company to dismiss Marl, which the Company did. . . .

We agree with the finding of both the Board and trial examiner, that Carpenter, a company executive, knew that the Union's demand for Marl's discharge was for Union obligations other than current dues or initiation fees.

We are of the opinion that the evidence supports the Board's finding that Carpenter, who told Marl, *"We* will have to let you go," was a supervisory employee of a rank to charge the Company with knowledge that Marl's discharge was in violation of Section 8(a)(3)(B) of the Act. Carpenter's title was General Sales Manager, but "with reference to the company's *operations* he was the next responsible person" to General Manager Stuchell. . . .

We order enforced the Board's orders against the Company. . . .

B. *The Board's order against the Union for its wrong to Marl.*

It is obvious from the above evidence that the Union violated Section 8(b)(2) of the Act providing that:

> "(b) It shall be an unfair labor practice for a labor organization or its agents—
>
> "(2) to cause or attempt to cause an employer to discriminate against an employee in violation of subsection (a)(3) of this section or to discriminate against an employee with respect to whom membership in such organization has been denied or terminated on some ground other than his failure to tender the periodic dues and the initiation fees uniformly required as a condition of acquiring or retaining membership; . . ."

The Board's order respecting the Union is ordered enforced.

C. *The Board's Order Against the Union Because of Coercive Statements to Union Members Requiring Them to Pay Excessive Amounts to Remain in Proper Standing for Employment under the Union Shop Agreement.*

The evidence amply supports the findings of the Board that such coercion by the Union caused some fourteen members of the Union to pay it sums in excess of the $12.75 required to be in good standing under the union-shop agreement.

The Board's order respecting the fourteen Union members is ordered enforced.

CASE	**1.** What are the facts surrounding Marl's claim?
QUESTIONS	**2.** What did the union's constitution provide?
	3. What type of union security is here under scrutiny?
	4. How did the court hold with respect to the employer and to the union?

SECTION 57 / FEATHERBED PRACTICES

Featherbedding in common parlance is the receiving of compensation for work that is not required by the employer or tendered or performed by the employee recipients of the indicated compensation. The work or services in question may not, in the employer's opinion, be at all necessary but, through industry usage, have become customary as was the situation in the *American Newspaper Publishers Association* decision presented on page 278.

In a second type of situation the services may be required by an employer, but in spite of the fact that he pays for services, he receives neither a tender nor performance of such services on the worker's part. A union steward who ostensibly is being paid for operating a lathe on company time may actually spend his time in assisting co-workers for the benefit of the union from which he may also draw compensatory rewards. If an agreement permits this, it is legal.

In the third nonwork category, we find that type of featherbedding where the services are not required, are not tendered for performance, and are of course not performed. See the decision in *United States* v. *Jack Green* on the Hobbs Act concerning conduct that borders upon the area of criminal extortion.

The Supreme Court held in *U.S.* v. *Enmons* [16] that union members could not be prosecuted under the Hobbs Act on a charge of conspiracy to extort higher wages from a company by the use of wrongful force, even though strikers fired rifles at three company transformers and blew up a substation. The Court ruled that "wrongful force" under the Hobbs Act means force with a wrongful objective; and in this case the objective of higher wages through collective bargaining was legitimate. The Court pointed out that strike violence is properly prosecuted under state criminal laws.

Specifically, Section 8(b)(6) of the NLRA makes unlawful those attempts to cause an employer to "pay for services which are not performed or not to be

---

[16] *U.S.* v. *Enmons,* 93 Sup. Ct. 284 (1973).

performed." Its phrasing permits certain make-work forms of featherbedding, which would include those situations where two men do the work which, conceivably or reasonably, one man could do. Section 8(b)(6) is inapplicable, then, where unnecessary work is performed. The test is *performance* and not *necessity of performance* as stated by the Supreme Court of the United States in the decision in the 1953 *American Newspaper Publishers Assn.* case.

The Lea Act, which outlawed featherbedding in the broadcasting industry, attaches criminal penalties for violation, as does the Anti-Racketeering Act. Under the National Labor Relations Act of 1947, the remedy provided is an NLRB cease and desist order, followed by an injunction secured by the Board if necessary. This provision has been ineffective.

Complex interrelations of featherbedding, management rights, and the duty to bargain collectively are analyzed by the U. S. Supreme Court in the *Order of Telegraphers* v. *Chicago and Northwestern Railway* case arising under the Railway Labor Act. The bargaining duties of that law being similar to those of the NLRA, the decision is relevant to the negotiation of any change that may abolish jobs. There the Court stated:

"We cannot agree with the Court of Appeals that the union's efforts to negotiate about the job security of its members represents an attempt to usurp legitimate managerial prerogative in the exercise of business judgment with respect to the most economical and efficient conduct of its operations. . . . It goes without saying, therefore, that added railroad expenditures for employees cannot always be classified as wasteful. . . ." [17]

United States v. Jack Green

Supreme Court of the United States, 1956. 350 U.S. 415

REED, J.: An indictment was found in the Southern District of Illinois against appellees Green and a local union. The jury adjudged them guilty under counts one and two thereof. The court sustained their separate motions in arrest of judgment, setting out in its order that its action was "solely" on the following grounds:

"2. This Court is without jurisdiction of the offense. . . . .
"(b) The facts alleged in the Indictment failed to set forth an offense against the United States such as to give this Court jurisdiction.
"(c) A proper construction of the statute in question clearly indicates that it does not cover the type of activity charged. . . ."

Appeal was taken by the United States directly to this Court.

The two counts in question were based upon alleged violations of 18 U.S.C. Sec. 1951, popularly known as the Hobbs Act. The pertinent statutory provisions are subsections (a) and (b)(2) thereof, reading as follows:

"(a) Whoever in any way or degree obstructs, delays, or affects commerce or the movement of any article or commodity in commerce, by robbery or extortion or attempts or conspires so to do, or commits or threatens physical violence to any

---

[17] 362 U.S. 330 (1960).

person or property in furtherance of a plan or purpose to do anything in violation of this section shall be fined not more than $10,000 or imprisoned not more than twenty years, or both.

"(2) The term 'extortion' means the obtaining of property from another, with his consent, induced by wrongful use of actual or threatened force, violence, or fear, or under color of official right."

Each of the two counts charged appellees with acts of extortion under Sec. 1951 directed against a different employer. The extortions alleged consisted of attempts to obtain from the particular employer

"his money, in the form of wages to be paid for imposed, unwanted, superfluous and fictitious services of laborers commonly known as swampers, in connection with the operation of machinery and equipment then being used and operated by said (employer) in the execution of his said contract for maintenance work on said levee, the attempted obtaining of said property from said [employer] as aforesaid being then intended to be accomplished and accomplished with the consent of said [employer], induced and obtained by the wrongful use, to wit, the use for the purposes aforesaid, of actual and threatened force, violence and fear made to said [employer], and his employees and agents then and there being; in violation of Section 1951 of Title 18, United States Code. . . . ."

We do not agree with that interpretation of the section. The Hobbs Act was passed after this Court had construed Section 2 of the federal Anti-Racketeering Act of 1934, 48 Stat. 979, in *United States* v. *Local 807*, 315 U.S. 521. Subsection (a) of Section 2 barred, with respect to interstate commerce, exaction of valuable considerations by force, violence or coercion, "not including, however, the payment of wages by a bona fide employer to a bona fide employee." We held in *Local 807* that this exception covered members of a city truck drivers' union offering superfluous services to drive arriving trucks to their city destination with intent, if the truck owners refused their offer, to exact the wages by violence. In the Hobbs Act, 60 Stat. 420, carried forward as 18 U.S.C. Section 1951, which amended the Anti-Racketeering Act, the exclusion clause involved in the *Local 807* decision was dropped. The legislative history makes clear that the new Act was meant to eliminate any grounds for future judicial conclusions that Congress did not intend to cover the employer-employee relationship. The words were defined to avoid any misunderstanding.

Title II of the Hobbs Act provides that the provisions of the Act shall not affect the Clayton Act, Sections 6 and 20, 38 Stat. 731, . . . ; the Norris-LaGuardia Act, 47 Stat. 70; the Railway Labor Act, 44 Stat. 577; or the National Labor Relations Act. There is nothing in any of those Acts, however, that indicates any protection for unions or their officials in attempts to get personal property through threats of force or violence. Those are not legitimate means for improving labor conditions. If the trial court intended by its references to the Norris-LaGuardia and Wagner Acts to indicate any such labor exception, which we doubt, it was in error. . . .

On this appeal the record does not contain the evidence upon which the court acted. The indictment charges interference with commerce by extortion in the words of the Act's definition of that crime. We rule only on the allegations of the indictment and hold that the acts charged against appellees fall within the terms of the Act. The order in arrest of judgment is reversed and the cause remanded to the District Court. *It is so ordered.*

CASE	**1.** What was the offense with which Green was charged?
QUESTIONS	**2.** How did the lower court dispose of the case?
	3. Why does the U. S. Supreme Court reverse and remand?

American Newspaper Publishers Assn. v. NLRB

Supreme Court of the United States, 1953. 345 U.S. 100

BURTON, J. . . . . The question here is whether a labor organization engages in an unfair labor practice, within the meaning of Sec. 8(b)(6) of the National Labor Relations Act, as amended by the Labor Management Relations Act, 1947, when it insists that newspaper publishers pay printers for reproducing advertising matter for which the publishers ordinarily have no use. For the reasons hereafter stated, we hold that it does not.

Petitioner, American Newspaper Publishers Association, is a New York corporation the membership of which includes more than 800 newspaper publishers. They represent over 90 percent of the circulation of the daily and Sunday newspapers in the United States and carry over 90 percent of the advertising published in such papers.

In November, 1947, petitioner filed with the National Labor Relations Board charges that the International Typographical Union, here called ITU, and its officers were engaging in unfair labor practices within the meaning of Sec. 8(b)(1), (2) and (6) of the National Labor Relations Act, as amended by the Labor Management Relations Act, 1947, here called the Taft-Hartley Act. . . .

Printers in newspaper composing rooms have long sought to retain the opportunity to set up in type as much as possible of whatever is printed by their respective publishers. In 1872, when printers were paid on a piecework basis, each diversion of composition was at once reflected by a loss in their income. Accordingly, ITU, which had been formed in 1852 from local typo graphical societies, began its long battle to retain as much typesetting work for printers as possible.

With the introduction of the linotype machine in 1890, the problem took on a new aspect. When a newspaper advertisement was set up in type, it was impressed on a cardboard matrix, or "mat." These mats were used by their makers and also were reproduced and distributed, at little or no cost, to other publishers who used them as molds for metal casting from which to print the same advertisement. This procedure bypassed all compositors except those who made up the original form. Facing this loss of work, ITU secured the agreement of newspaper to permit their respective compositors, at convenient times, to set up duplicate forms for all local advertisements in precisely the same manner as though the mat had not been used. For this reproduction work the printers received their regular pay. The doing of this "made work" came to be known in the trade as "setting bogus." It was a wasteful procedure. Nevertheless, it has become a recognized idiosyncrasy of the trade and a customary feature of the wage structure and work schedule of newspaper printers. . . .

On rare occasions the reproduced compositions are used to print the advertisement when rerun, but, ordinarily, they are promptly consigned to the "hell box" and melted down. . . .

However desirable the elimination of all industrial featherbedding practices may have appeared to Congress, the legislative history of the Taft-Hartley Act, 29 U.S.C.A. Sec. 141 et seq., demonstrates that when the legislation was put in final form Congress decided to limit the practice but little by law.

A restraining influence throughout this congressional consideration of featherbedding was the fact that the constitutionality of the Lea Act penalizing featherbedding in the broadcasting industry was in litigation. That Act, known also as the Petrillo Act, had been adopted April 16, 1946, as an amendment to the Communications Act of 1934, 47 U.S.C.A. Sec. 151 et seq. . . . On December 2, 1946, the United States District Court for the Northern District of Illinois held that it violated the First, Fifth, and Thirteenth Amendments to the Constitution of the United States. *United States* v. *Petrillo,* D.C., 68 F. Supp. 845. The case was pending here on appeal throughout the debate on the Taft-Hartley bill. Not until June 23, 1947, on the day of the passage of the Taft-Hartley bill over the President's veto, was the constitutionality of the Lea Act upheld. *United States* v. *Petrillo,* 332 U.S. 1, 67 S. Ct. 1538, 91 L. Ed. 1877.

The purpose of the sponsors of the Taft-Hartley bill to avoid the controversial features of the Lea Act is made clear in the written statement which Senator Taft, cosponsor of the bill and Chairman of the Senate Committee on Labor and Public Welfare, caused to be incorporated in the proceedings of the Senate, June, 1947. . . .

The Act now limits its condemnation to instances where a labor organization or its agents exact pay from an employer in return for services not performed or not to be performed. Thus, where work is done by an employee, with the employer's consent, a labor organization's demand that the employee be compensated for time spent in doing the disputed work does not become an unfair labor practice. The transaction simply does not fall within the kind of featherbedding defined in the statute. In the absence of proof to the contrary, the employee's compensation reflects his entire relationship with his employer. . . .

Accordingly, the judgment of the Court of Appeals sustaining dismissal of the complaint, insofar as it was based upon Sec. 8(b)(6), is affirmed.

Affirmed.

CASE QUESTIONS

1. What do you believe is meant by the term "featherbedding"?
2. How may featherbedding be related to racketeering or to machine displacement?

3. What was the alleged violation by the Typographical Union?
4. What is a "hell box"?
5. What was the decision of the court and why?

QUESTIONS ON CHAPTER 7

1. What purpose did including "labor unfair practices" seek to accomplish when added in 1947?
2. What major issues are raised that have to be answered by the NLRB under each section of 8(b)(4)?
3. Does 8(b)(3) impose any more duties than 8(a)(5)? Explain.
4. Compare the sanctions and restraints on labor with those on management under Taft-Hartley's provisions.
5. Does 8(b) restrict unions in terms of means or aims or both?

Chapter 8

Picket and Boycott Activity

SECTION 58 / ECONOMIC PRESSURE TACTICS LEGALITY

In addition to strike activity, which will be discussed in the succeeding chapter, two other forms of economic pressure may be applied in labor disputes. They are picketing and boycott activities. The use of picketing and the boycott and the protection of property may cause a conflict of rights. The Constitution and the labor laws do not establish any absolute right to picket or boycott regardless of purpose or effect, according to the views of the courts. The intent, the circumstances, and the result usually receive consideration.

SECTION 59 / TYPES OF PICKETING

Picketing of an establishment may take a number of forms, may be engaged in for a variety of reasons or purposes, and may or may not coexist with a strike. Though picket activity usually accompanies a strike, the converse is not necessarily true. If a union believes that the economic compulsion inherent in the publication of a labor dispute through picket activity is sufficient to enforce compliance with demands, a picket line may be established without the existence of a strike against the employer in question.

Where workers, fearful of employer retaliation for engaging in union activity therefore refrain from joining a union, that union may set up a picket line to exert pressure on the employer to induce his workers to join it. A strike will not exist under these conditions. When third parties, not in the relation of employer and employee, picket an employer, it is known as *outsider* or *stranger* picketing.

In addition to outsider picketing, we may distinguish two other major forms, *primary* and *secondary* picketing. The *primary* picket results when workers in a given establishment patrol around it with placards, usually to inform workers and the public that the employer is unfair to union labor. A strike may or may not have been called. The gist of the primary picket is a dispute with the employer whose establishment is being patrolled. The *secondary* picket, which is a species of secondary boycott, involves the stationing of pickets around the place of business of a customer or supplier of the primary employer with whom the union has a dispute, to cause him to refrain from dealing with the primary employer.

SECTION 60 / PICKETING AND THE FIRST AMENDMENT

The Supreme Court decision in the *American Steel Foundries* case (pages 31–32), which drastically limited the right to engage in picket activity, spurred on many states to enact antipicketing statutes. These statutes incorporated provisions such as the prohibition of outsider, violent, massed, fraudulent, and secondary picketing. The *Thornhill* case in this section involves the constitutionality of an Alabama statute that prohibited *all* picketing as a misdemeanor. *Thornhill* is a landmark case in labor law because it held that the dissemination of information about the facts of a labor dispute must be regarded as within that area of free discussion that is guaranteed by the First and Fourteenth Amendments of the U. S. Constitution. A reading of the *Logan Valley* decision as restricted by the *Central Hardware* decision, both of which are reported in the next section of this chapter, shows that peaceful picketing carried out on public property or on private property which has assumed to some significant degree the functional attributes of public property devoted to public use is still protected by the First Amendment. The *Logan Valley* decision pointed out that peaceful picketing could be limited because it involves elements of both speech and conduct, i.e., patroling, and thus it can be subjected to controls that would not be constitutionally permissible in the case of pure speech.

The Supreme Court will not generally find a statute unconstitutional on its face unless it is clearly so. It usually does seek to determine whether the statute was *applied* and *construed* by the lower court to give full expression to constitutional guarantees. Thus, the same enactment may be constitutional in one case, where properly applied, and unconstitutional where improperly applied. It was impossible for the Court to uphold the Alabama statute in *Thornhill,* since it was incapable of anything but an unconstitutional construction.

Thornhill v. State of Alabama

Supreme Court of the United States, 1940. 310 U.S. 88

MURPHY, J. Petitioner, Byron Thornhill, was convicted in the Circuit Court of Tuscaloosa County, Alabama, of the violation of Section 3448 of the State Code of 1923. The Code Section reads as follows: "Sec. 3448. Loitering or picketing forbidden.—Any person or persons, who, without a just cause or legal excuse therefor, go near to or loiter about the premises or place of business of any other person, firm, corporation, or association of people, engaged in a lawful business, for the purpose, or with intent of influencing, or inducing other persons not to trade with, buy from, sell to, have business dealings with, or be employed by such persons, firm, corporation, or association of persons, for the purpose of hindering, delaying, or interfering with or injuring any lawful business or enterprise of another, shall be guilty of a misdemeanor; but nothing herein shall prevent any person from soliciting trade or business for a competitive business."

At the close of the case for the State, petitioner moved to exclude all the testimony taken at the trial on the ground that Section 3448 was violative of the Constitution of the United States. The Circuit Court overruled the motion, found petitioner "guilty of Loitering and Picketing as charged in the complaint," and entered judgment accordingly. The judgment was affirmed by the Court of Appeals, which considered the constitutional question and sustained the section on the authority of two previous decisions in the Alabama courts.

The proofs consist of the testimony of two witnesses for the prosecution. It appears that petitioner on the morning of his arrest was seen "in company with six or eight other men" "on the picket line" at the plant of the Brown Wood Preserving Company. Some weeks previously a strike order had been issued by a Union, apparently affiliated with the American Federation of Labor, which had as members all but four of the approximately one hundred employees of the plant. Since that time a picket line with two picket posts of six to eight men each had been maintained around the plant twenty-four hours a day. The picket posts appear to have been on Company property, "on a private entrance for employees, and not on any public road." One witness explained that practically all of the employees live on Company property. No demand was ever made upon the men not to come on the property. There is not testimony indicating the nature of the dispute between the Union and the Preserving Company, or the course of events which led to the issuance of the strike order, or the nature of the efforts for conciliation.

The Company scheduled a day for the plant to resume operations. One of the witnesses, Clarence Simpson, who was not a member of the Union, on reporting to the plant on the day indicated, was approached by petitioner who told him that "they were on strike and did not want anybody to go up there to work." None of the other employees said anything to Simpson, who testified: "Neither Mr. Thornhill nor any other employee threatened me on the occasion testified to. Mr. Thornhill approached me in a peaceful manner, and did not put me in fear; he did not appear to be mad." "I then turned and went back to the house, and did not go to work." The other witness, J. M. Walden, testified: "At the time Mr. Thornhill and Clarence Simpson were talking to each other, there was no one else present, and I heard no harsh words and saw nothing threatening in the manner of either man." For engaging in some or all of these activities, petitioner was arrested, charged, and convicted as described.

First. The freedom of speech and of the press, which are secured by the First Amendment against abridgment by the United States, are among the fundamental personal rights and liberties which are secured to all persons by the Fourteenth Amendment against abridgment by a state.

The safeguarding of these rights to the ends that men may speak as they think on matters vital to them and that falsehoods may be exposed through the processes of education and discussion is essential to free government. Those who won our independence had confidence in the power of free and fearless reasoning and communication of ideas to discover and spread political and economic truth. Noxious doctrines in those fields may be refuted and their evil averted by the courageous exercise of the right of free discussion. Abridgment of freedom of speech and of the press, however, impairs those opportunities for public education that are essential to effective exercise of the power of correcting error through the processes of popular government. Compare *United States* v. *Carolene Products,* 304 U.S. 144, 152, 153n, 58 S. Ct. 778, 783, 784, 82 L. Ed. 1234. Mere legislative preference for one rather than another means for combating substantive evils, therefore, may well prove an inadequate foundation on which to rest regulations which are aimed at or in their operation diminish the effective exercise of rights so necessary to the maintenance of democratic institutions. It is imperative that, when the effective exercise of these rights is claimed to be abridged, the courts should "weigh the circumstances" and "appraise the substantiality of the reasons advanced" in support of the challenged regulations. *Schneider* v. *State,* 309 U.S. 147, 161, 162, 60 S. Ct. 146, 150, 151, 84 L. Ed. 155.

Second. The section in question must be judged upon its face. The finding against petitioner was a general one. It did not specify the testimony upon which it rested. The charges were framed in the words of the statute and so must be given a like construction. The courts below expressed no intention of narrowing the construction put upon the statute by prior State decisions. In these circumstances, there is no occasion to go behind the fact of the statute or of the complaint for the purpose of determining whether the evidence, together with the permissible inferences to be drawn from it, could ever support a conviction founded upon different and more precise charges. "Conviction upon a charge not made would be sheer denial of due process." *De Jonge* v. *Oregon,* 299 U.S. 353, 362, 57 S. Ct. 255, 259, 81 L. Ed. 278; *Stromberg* v. *California,* 283 U.S. 359, 367, 368, 51 S. Ct. 532, 535, 75 L. Ed. 1117, 73 A.L.R. 1484. The State urges that petitioner may not complain of the deprivation of any rights but his own. It would not follow that on this record petitioner could not complain of the sweeping regulations here challenged.

Third. Section 3448 has been applied by the State courts so as to prohibit a single individual from walking slowly and peacefully back and forth on the public sidewalk in front of the premises of an employer, without speaking to anyone, carrying a sign or placard on a staff above his head stating only the fact that the employer did not employ union men affiliated with the American Federation of Labor; the purpose of the described activity was concededly to advise customers and prospective customers of the relationship existing between the employer and its employees and thereby to induce such customers not to patronize the employer. *O'Rourke* v. *City of Birmingham,* 27 Ala. App. 133, 168 So. 206, certiorari denied 232 Ala. 355, 168 So. 209. The statute as thus authoritatively construed and applied leaves room for no exceptions based upon either the number of persons engaged in the proscribed activity, the peaceful character of their demeanor, the nature of their dispute with an employer, or the restrained character and the accurateness of the terminology used in notifying the public of the facts of the dispute.

The numerous forms of conduct proscribed by Section 3448 are subsumed under two offenses: the first embraces the activities of all who "without a just cause or legal excuse" "go near to or loiter about the premises" of any person engaged in a lawful business for the purpose of influencing or inducing others to adopt any of certain enumerated courses of action; the second, all who "picket" the place of business of any such person "for the purpose of hindering, delaying, or interfering with or injuring any lawful business or enterprise of another." It is apparent that one or the other of the offenses comprehends every practicable method whereby the facts of a labor dispute may be publicized in the vicinity of the place of business of an employer. The phrase "without a just cause or legal excuse" does not in any effective manner restrict the breadth of the regulation; the words themselves have no ascertainable meaning either inherent or historical.

Fourth. We think that Section 3448 is invalid on its face.

The freedom of speech and of the press guaranteed by the Constitution embraces at least the liberty to discuss publicly and truthfully all matters of public concern without previous restraint or fear of subsequent punishment.

In the circumstances of our times the dissemination of information concerning the facts of a labor dispute must be regarded as within that area of free discussion that is guaranteed by the Constitution. *Hague* v. *C.I.O.,* 307 U.S. 496, 59 S. Ct. 954, 83 L. Ed. 1423; *Schneider* v. *State,* 308 U.S. 147, 155, 162, 163, 60 S. Ct. 146, 151, 84 L. Ed. 155. See *Senn* v. *Tile Layers Union,* 301 U.S. 468, 478, 57 S. Ct. 857, 862, 81 L. Ed. 1229. It is recognized now that satisfactory hours and wages and working conditions in industry and a bargaining position which makes these possible have an importance which is not less than the interests of those in the business or industry directly concerned. The health of the present generation and of those as yet unborn may depend on these matters, and the practices in a single factory may have economic repercussions upon a whole region and affect widespread systems of marketing. The merest glance at State and Federal legislation on the subject demonstrates the force of the argument that labor relations are not matters of mere local or private concern. Free discussion concerning the conditions in industry and the causes of labor disputes appears to us indispensable to the effective and intelligent use of the processes of popular government to shape the destiny of modern industrial society. The issues raised by regulations, such as are challenged here, infringing upon the right of employees effectively to inform the public of the facts of a labor dispute are part of this larger problem. We concur in the observation of Mr. Justice Brandeis, speaking for the Court in *Senn's* case (301 U.S. at page 478, 57 S. Ct. at page 862, 81 L. Ed. 1229): "Members of a union might, without special statutory authorization by a state, make known the facts of a labor dispute, for freedom of speech is guaranteed by the Federal Constitution."

It is true that the rights of employers and employees to conduct their economic affairs and to compete with others for a share in the products of industry are subject to modification or qualification in the interests of the society in which they exist. This is but an instance of the power of the State to set the limits of permissible contest open to industrial combatants. See Mr. Justice Brandeis in *Duplex Printing Press Co.* v. *Deering,* 254 U.S. 443, at page 488, 41 S. Ct. 172, 184, 65 L. Ed. 349, 16 A.L.R. 196. It does not follow that the State in dealing with the evils arising from industrial disputes may impair the effective exercise of the right to discuss freely industrial relations which are matters of public concern. A contrary conclusion could be used to support abridgment of freedom of speech and of the press concerning almost every matter of importance to society.

The range of activities proscribed by Section 3448, whether characterized as picketing or loitering or otherwise, embraces nearly every practicable, effective means whereby those interested—including the employees directly affected—may enlighten the public on the nature and causes of a labor dispute. The safeguarding of these means is essential to the securing of an informed and educated public opinion with respect to a matter which is of public concern.

The State urges that the purpose of the challenged statute is the protection of the community from the violence and breaches of the peace, which, it asserts, are the concomitants of picketing. The power and the duty of the State to take adequate steps to preserve the peace and to protect the privacy, the lives, and the property of its residents cannot be doubted. But no clear and present danger of destruction of life or property, or invasion of the right of privacy, or breach of the peace can be thought to be inherent in the activities of every person who approaches the premises of an employer and publicizes the facts of a labor dispute involving the latter. We are not now concerned with picketing en masse or otherwise conducted which might occasion such imminent and aggravated dangers to these interests as to justify a statute narrowly drawn to cover the precise situation giving rise to the danger. Compare *American Steel Foundries* v. *Tri-City Council,* 257 U.S. 184, 205, 42 S. Ct. 72, 77, 66 L. Ed. 189, 27 A.L.R. 360. Section 3448 in question here does not aim specifically at serious encroachments on these interests and does not evidence any such care in balancing these interests against the interest of the community and that of the individual in freedom of discussion on matters of public concern.

It is not enough to say that Section 3448 is limited or restricted in its application to such activity as takes place at the scene of the labor dispute. "The streets are natural and proper places for the dissemination of information and opinion; and one is not to have the exercise of his liberty of expression in appropriate places abridged on the plea that it may be exercised in some other place." *Schneider* v. *State,* 308 U.S. 147, 161, 60 S. Ct. 146, 150, 84 L. Ed. 155; *Hague* v. *C.I.O.,* 307 U.S. 496, 515, 516, 59 S. Ct. 954, 963, 964, 83 L. Ed. 1423. The danger of breach of the peace or serious invasion of rights of property or privacy at the scene of a labor dispute is not sufficiently imminent in all cases to warrant the legislature in determining that such place is not appropriate for the range of activities outlawed by Section 3448.

Reversed.

CASE **QUESTIONS**	1. State the gist of Sec. 3448 of the Alabama Code. 2. What facts gave rise to the Thornhill indictment? 3. Was the picketing on company property? Was it peaceful? Was it fraudulent?

4. Under what amendment to the Constitution does Thornhill defend?

5. Did the Supreme Court hold Sec. 3448 invalid on its face?

6. What defense of the statute was made by the State? How was the defense disposed of?

SECTION 61 / UNION ACTIVITY ON PRIVATE PROPERTY

The *Central Hardware* case, with its landmark *Babcock and Wilcox* precedent, and the *Logan Valley* case, both of which are presented in this section, give the law relating to peaceful nonemployee union activity on private property. An interesting decision decided before *Central* by the Seventh Circuit Court of Appeals, denied enforcement of a Board order based on *Logan*.[1] The case involved union solicitation in the parking lot of a tenant in an industrial park complex. The court held that the Board's findings that the park was "quasi-public" in nature was not supported by the evidence.

Central Hardware Company v. NLRB

Supreme Court of the United States, 1972. 407 U.S. 539

Mr. Justice Powell delivered the opinion of the Court: Petitioner, Central Hardware Company (Central), owns and operates two retail hardware stores in Indianapolis, Indiana. Each store is housed in a large building, containing 70,000 square feet of floor space, and housing no other retail establishments. The stores are surrounded on three sides by ample parking facilities, accommodating approximately 350 automobiles. The parking lots are owned by Central, and are maintained solely for the use of Central's customers and employees. While there are other retail establishments in the vicinity of Central's stores, these establishments are not a part of a shopping center complex, and they maintain their own separate parking lots.

Approximately a week before Central opened its stores, the Retail Clerks Union, Local 725, Retail Clerks International Association, AFL-CIO (the Union), began an organization campaign at both stores. The campaign consisted primarily of solicitation by nonemployee Union organizers on Central's parking lots. The nonemployee organizers confronted Central's employees in the parking lots and sought to persuade them to sign cards authorizing the Union to represent them in an appropriate bargaining unit. As a part of the organization campaign, an "undercover agent for the Union" was infiltrated into the employ of Central, receiving full-time salary from both the Union and the company. This agent solicited employees to join the Union, and obtained

---

[1] *NLRB* v. *Solo Cup Co.,* 422 F.2d 1149 (1970).

a list of the employees of the two stores which was about 80% complete.

Central had a no-solicitation rule which it enforced against all solicitational activities in its stores and on its parking lots. A number of employees complained to Central's local management that they were being harassed by the organizers, and these complaints were forwarded to Central's corporate headquarters in St. Louis, Missouri. The St. Louis officials directed the Indianapolis management to enforce the nonemployee no-solicitation rule and keep all Union organizers off the company premises, including the parking lots. Although most of the nonemployee Union organizers had either left Indianapolis or ceased work on the Central organization campaign, the Indianapolis management had occasion to assert the nonemployee no-solicitation rule on several occasions.

One arrest was made when a field organizer for the Union was confronted by the manager of one of the stores on its parking lot, and refused to leave after being requested to do so. The field organizer asserted that he was a "customer" and insisted upon entering the store. The police were called, and when the organizer persisted in his refusal to leave, he was arrested.

Shortly after Central received complaints from its employees as to harassment by the organizers, Central filed unfair labor practice charges against the Union. The Union subsequently filed unfair labor practice charges against Central. After an investigation, the General Counsel of the National Labor Relations Board (the Board) dismissed Central's charges against the Union, and issued a complaint against Central on the Union's charges.

The Board held that Central's nonemployee no-solicitation rule was overly broad, and that its enforcement violated § 8(a)(1) of the National Labor Relations Act. The Board reasoned that the character and use of Central's parking lots distinguished the case from *NLRB* v. *Babcock & Wilcox Co.,* 351 U.S. 105 (1956), and brought it within the principle of *Amalgamated Food Employees Union Local 590* v. *Logan Valley Plaza, Inc.,* 391 U.S. 308 (1968). 181 NLRB 491 (1970). A divided Court of Appeals for the Eighth Circuit agreed, and ordered enforcement of the Board's order enjoining Central from enforcing any rule prohibiting nonemployee Union organizers from using its parking lots to solicit employees on behalf of the Union. 439 F.2d 1321 (CA 8 1971). We granted certiorari to consider whether the principle of *Logan Valley* is applicable to this case. 404 U.S. 1014 (1972). We conclude that it is not.

I. Section 7 of the National Labor Relations Act, 29 U.S.C. § 157, guarantees to employees the right "to self-organization, to form, join, or assist labor organizations." This guarantee includes both the right of union officials to discuss organization with employees, and the right of employees to discuss organization among themselves.[2] Section 8(a)(1) of the Act, 29 U.S.C. § 158 (a)(1), makes it an unfair labor practice for an employer "to interfere with, restrain, or coerce employees in the exercise of the rights guaranteed" in § 7. But organization rights are not viable in a vacuum; their effectiveness depends in some measure on the ability of employees to learn the advantages and disadvantages of organization from others. Early in the history of the adminis-

---

[2] See *Thomas* v. *Collins,* 323 U.S. 516, 533–534 (1945).

tration of the Act the Board recognized the importance of freedom of communication to the free exercise of organization rights. See *Peyton Packing Co.,* 49 NLRB 828 (1943), enforced, 142 F.2d 1009 (CA 5), cert. denied, 323 U.S. 730 (1944).

In seeking to provide information essential to the free exercise of organization rights, union organizers have often engaged in conduct inconsistent with traditional notions of private property rights. The Board and the courts have the duty to resolve conflicts between organization rights and property rights, and to seek a proper accommodation between the two. This Court addressed the conflict which often arises between organization rights and property rights in *NLRB* v. *Babcock & Wilcox Co.,* 351 U.S. 105 (1956). The Babcock & Wilcox Company operated a manufacturing plant on a 100-acre tract about one mile from a community of 21,000 people. The plant buildings were enclosed within a fence, employee access being through several gates. Approximately 90% of the employees drove to work in private cars, and the company maintained a parking lot for the employees. Only employees and deliverymen normally used the parking lot. The company had a rule forbidding the distribution of literature on company property. The Board found that the company's parking lot and the walkway leading from it to the plant entrance were the only "safe and practicable" places in the vicinity of the plant for distribution of union literature, and held the company guilty of an unfair labor practice for enforcing the no-distribution rule and thereby denying union organizers limited access to company property. The Board ordered the company to rescind its no-distribution rule insofar as it related to nonemployee union representatives seeking to distribute union literature on the parking lot and walkway area.

The Court of Appeals for the Fifth Circuit refused enforcement of the Board's order on the ground that the Act did not authorize the Board to impose a servitude on an employer's property where no employee was involved. This Court affirmed on the ground that the availability of alternative channels of communication made the intrusion on the employer's property rights ordered by the Board unwarranted. The Court in *Babcock* stated the guiding principle for adjusting conflicts between § 7 rights and property rights:

> "Organization rights are granted to workers by the same authority, the National Government, that preserves property rights. Accommodation between the two must be obtained with as little destruction of one as is consistent with the maintenance of the other. The employer may not affirmatively interfere with organization; the union may not always insist that the employer aid organization. But when the inaccessibility of employees makes ineffective the reasonable attempts by nonemployees to communicate with them through the usual channels, the right to exclude from property has been required to yield to the extent needed to permit communication of information on the right to organize." 351 U.S., at 112.

The principle of *Babcock* is limited to this accommodation between organization rights and property rights. This principle requires a "yielding" of property rights only in the context of an organization campaign. Moreover, the allowed intrusion on property rights is limited to that necessary to facilitate the exercise of employees' § 7 rights. After the requisite need for access to the employer's property has been shown, the access is limited to (i) union organizers; (ii) prescribed nonworking areas of the employer's premises; and (iii) the duration of organization activity. In short, the principle of accommodation announced in *Babcock* is limited to labor organization campaigns, and the "yielding" of property rights it may require is both temporary and minimal.

II. The principle applied in *Amalgamated Food Employees Union Local 590* v. *Logan Valley Plaza, Inc.,* 391 U.S. 308 (1968), is quite different. While it is true that *Logan Valley* involved labor picketing, the decision rests on constitutional grounds; it is not a § 7 case.

Logan Valley had its genesis in *Marsh* v. *Alabama,* 326 U.S. 501 (1946). *Marsh* involved a "company town," an economic anachronism rarely encountered today. The town was wholly owned by the Gulf Shipbuilding Corporation, yet it had all of the characteristics of any other American town. Gulf Shipbuilding held title to all the land in the town, including that covered by streets and sidewalks. Gulf Shipbuilding also provided municipal services, such as sewerage service and police protection, to the residents of the town. A Jehovah's Witness undertook to distribute religious literature on a sidewalk near the post office in the "business block" of the town, and was arrested on a trespassing charge. She was subsequently convicted of the crime of trespassing, and the Alabama courts upheld the conviction on appeal. This Court reversed, holding that Alabama could not permit a corporation to assume the functions of a municipal government and at the same time deny First Amendment rights through the application of the State's criminal trespass law.

In *Logan Valley,* over a strong dissent by Mr. Justice Black, the author of *Marsh,* the Court applied the reasoning of *Marsh* to a modern economic phenomenon, the shopping center complex. The Logan Valley Mall was a complex of retail establishments, which the Court regarded under the factual circumstances as the functional equivalent of the "community business block" of the company town in *Marsh.* The corporate owner of Logan Valley Mall obtained a state court injunction against peaceful picketing on the shopping center property, and the Pennsylvania Supreme Court affirmed the issuance of the injunction on the ground that the picketing constituted a trespass on private property. This Court reversed, holding that Pennsylvania could not "delegate the power, through the use of its trespass laws, wholly to exclude those members of the public wishing to exercise their First Amendment rights on the premises in a manner and for a purpose generally consonant with the use to which the property is actually put." 391 U.S., at 319–320.

III. The Board and the Court of Appeals held that *Logan Valley* rather than *Babcock* controlled this case. The Board asserts that the distinguishing feature between these two cases is that in *Logan Valley* the owner had "diluted his property interest by opening his property to the general public for his own economic advantage." The emphasis, both in the argument on behalf of the Board and in the opinion below, is on the opening of the property "to the general public."

This analysis misconceives the rationale of *Logan Valley. Logan Valley* involved a large commercial shopping center which the Court found has displaced, in certain relevant respects, the functions of the normal municipal "business block." First and Fourteenth Amendment free-speech rights were deemed infringed under the facts of that case when the property owner invoked the trespass laws of the State against the pickets.

Before an owner of private property can be subjected to the commands of the First and Fourteenth Amendments the privately owned property must assume to some significant degree the functional attributes of public property devoted to public use. The First and Fourteenth Amendments are limitations on state action, not on action by the owner of private property used only for private purposes. The only fact relied upon for the argument that Central's parking lots have acquired the characteristics of a public municipal facility is that they are "open to the public." Such an argument could be made with respect to almost every retail and service establishment in the country, regardless of size or location. To accept it would cut *Logan Valley* entirely away from its roots in *Marsh.* It would also constitute an unwarranted infringement of long-settled rights of private property protected by the Fifth and Fourteenth Amendments. We hold that the Board and the Court of Appeals erred in applying *Logan Valley* to this case.

The Trial Examiner concluded that no reasonable means of communication with employees were available to the nonemployee Union organizers other than solicitation in Central's parking lots. The Board adopted this conclusion. Central vigorously contends that this conclusion is not supported by substantial evidence in the record as a whole. The Court of Appeals did not consider this contention, because it viewed *Logan Valley* as controlling rather than *Babcock & Wilcox.* The determination whether on the record as a whole there is substantial evidence to support agency findings is a matter entrusted primarily to the Courts of Appeals. *Universal Camera Corp.* v. *NLRB,* 340 U.S. 474 (1951). Since the Court of Appeals has not yet considered this question in light of the principles of *NLRB* v. *Babcock & Wilcox,* 351 U.S. 105 (1956), the judgment is vacated, and the case will be remanded to that court for such consideration.

It is so ordered.

MR. JUSTICE MARSHALL, with whom MR. JUSTICE DOUGLAS and MR. JUSTICE BRENNAN join, dissenting.

I agree with the Court that this case should have been considered under *NLRB* v. *Babcock & Wilcox Co.,* 351 U.S. 105 (1956). That case is, as the opinion of the Court suggests, narrower than *Amalgamated Food Employees Union* v. *Logan Valley Plaza, Inc.,* 391 U.S. 308 (1968). It does not purport to interpret the National Labor Relations Act (NLRA) so as to give union members the same comprehensive rights to free expression on the private property of an employer that the First Amendment gives to all citizens on private property that is the functional equivalent of a public business district. But, *Babcock & Wilcox* is, in another sense, even broader than *Logan Valley.* It holds that where a union has no other means at its disposal to communicate with employees other than to use the employer's property or where the union is denied the access to employees that the employer gives antiunion forces, the union may communicate with employees on the property of the employer.

Congress gave unions this right in Section 7 of the NLRA, 61 Stat. 140, 29 U.S.C. § 157. The First Amendment gives no such broad right to use private property to ordinary citizens.

The National Labor Relations Board found that petitioner permitted antiunion solicitation on its premises at the same time that it barred union solicitation. 181 NLRB 491 (1970). It made no explicit finding as to whether access to the employees was reasonably available to the union outside of the petitioner's property, but suggested that it was not. Rather than deciding the case under *Babcock & Wilcox, supra,* which would appear to control and to provide that the union activity in the case is protected by the NLRA, the Board appears to have decided the case under *Logan Valley, supra.* The United States Court of Appeals for the Eighth Circuit affirmed on the basis of *Logan Valley* and found it unnecessary to review the Board's finding of discrimination by the employer against the union in the use of its property or to remand the case for a determination of whether it was necessary for the union to use petitioner's property to communicate with the employees. 439 F.2d 1321 (1971).

It is obvious, then, that neither the Board nor the Court of Appeals has fully considered whether the employer's conduct was proscribed by *Babcock & Wilcox* even though the indications in the Board's opinion are that it was. In reaching out to decide this case under *Logan Valley,* the agency and the lower court decided a difficult constitutional issue that might well have been avoided by deciding the case under the NLRA. This was error. The principle is well established that decisions on constitutional questions should not be reached unnecessarily. See, *e.g., Dandridge* v. *Williams,* 397 U.S. 471, 476 (1970); *Rosenberg* v. *Fleuti,* 374 U.S. 449 (1963).

Since both the agency and the Court of Appeals should have first decided whether or not *Babcock & Wilcox* controlled the instant case before proceeding to decide it under *Logan Valley,* before this Court decides whether or not the decision below was correct under the Constitution, we should remand the case to the Board, rather than to the Court of Appeals, for a square holding as to the applicability of *Babcock & Wilcox* to the facts of this case. MR. JUSTICE WHITE has recently re-emphasized the point that when an agency decides a case under an incorrect legal approach, courts should not seek to predict whether the agency would have decided the case the same way under the correct approach, but should instead remand the case to the agency for further proceedings. *Federal Trade Commission* v. *Sperry & Hutchinson Co.,* 405 U.S. 233 (1972). See also *Burlington Truck Lines* v. *United States,* 371 U.S. 156, 168 (1962).

Accordingly, I would remand this case to the Board for further proceedings without deciding the constitutional question.

CASE QUESTIONS

1. What is the issue before the Supreme Court?
2. Under the *Babcock* rule, when do property rights yield to organizational rights?
3. As a result of *Central Hardware,* when does an owner of private property become subject to the First and Fourteenth Amendments of the Constitution?

Food Employees Local 590 v. Logan Valley Plaza

(SUPPLEMENTAL CASE DIGEST—UNION ACTIVITY ON PRIVATE PROPERTY)
Supreme Court of the United States, 1968. 391 U.S. 308

MARSHALL, J.: This case presents the question whether peaceful picketing of a business enterprise located within a shopping center can be enjoined on the ground that it constitutes an unconsented invasion of the property rights of the owners of the land on which the center is situated. . . .

Logan Valley Plaza, Inc. (Logan), one of the two respondents herein, owns a large, newly developed shopping center complex, known as the Logan Valley Mall, located near the City of Altoona, Pennsylvania. . . .

At the time of the events in this case, Logan Valley Mall was occupied by two businesses, Weis Markets, Inc. (Weis), the other respondent herein, and Sears, Roebuck and Co. (Sears), although other enterprises were then expected and have since moved into the center.

On December 8, 1965, Weis opened for business, employing a wholly nonunion staff of employees. A few days after it opened for business, Weis posted a sign on the exterior of its building prohibiting trespassing or soliciting by anyone other than its employees on its porch or parking lot. On December 17, 1965, members of Amalgamated Food Employees Union, Local 590 began picketing Weis. They carried signs stating that the Weis market was nonunion and that its employees were not "receiving union wages or other benefits." The pickets did not include any employees of Weis, but rather were all employees of competitors of Weis. The picketing continued until December 27, during which time the number of picketers varied between four and 13 and averaged around six. The picketing was carried out almost entirely in the parcel pickup area and that portion of the parking lot immediately adjacent thereto. Although some congestion of the parcel pickup area occurred, such congestion was sporadic and infrequent. The picketing was peaceful at all times and unaccompanied by either threats or violence.

On December 27, Weis and Logan instituted an action in equity in the Court of Common Pleas of Blair County, and that court immediately issued an *ex parte* order enjoining petitioners from, *inter alia,* "picketing and trespassing upon . . . the [Weis] storeroom, porch and parcel pick-up area . . . [and] the [Logan] parking area and entrances and exits leading to said parking area." The effect of this order was to require that all picketing be carried on along the berms beside the public roads outside the shopping center. . . . The Court of Common Pleas continued indefinitely its original *ex parte* injunction without modification.

That court explicitly rejected petitioners' claim under the First Amendment that they were entitled to picket within the confines of the shopping center, and their contention that the suit was within the primary jurisdiction of the NLRB. The trial judge held that the injunction was justified both in order to protect respondents' property rights and because the picketing was unlawfully aimed at coercing Weis to compel its employees to join a union. On appeal the Pennsylvania Supreme Court, with three Justices dissenting, affirmed the issuance of the injunction on the sole ground that petitioners' conduct constituted a trespass on respondents' property.

We start from the premise that peaceful picketing carried on in a location open generally to the public is, absent other factors involving the purpose or manner of the picketing, protected by the First Amendment. *Thornhill* v. *Alabama,* 310 U.S. 88 (1940); *AFL* v. *Swing,* 312 U.S. 321 (1941); . . . To be sure, this Court has noted that picketing involves elements of both speech and conduct, *i.e.,* patrolling, and has indicated that because of this intermingling of protected and unprotected elements, picketing can be subjected to controls that would not be constitutionally permissible in the case of pure speech. . . .

This Court has also held, in *Marsh* v. *Alabama,* 326 U.S. 501 (1946), that under some circumstances property that is privately owned may, at least for First Amendment purposes, be treated as though it were publicly held. . . .

. . . All we decide here is that because the shopping center serves as the community business block "and is freely accessible and open to the people in the area and those passing through," *Marsh* v. *Alabama,* 346 U.S., at 508, the State may not delegate the power, through the use of its trespass laws, wholly to exclude those members of the public wishing to exercise their First Amendment rights on the premises in a manner and for a purpose generally consonant with the use to which the property is actually put. . . .

The sole justification offered for the substantial interference with the effectiveness of petitioners' exercise of their First Amendment rights to promulgate their views through handbilling and picketing is respondents' claimed absolute right under state law to prohibit any use of their property by others without their consent. However, unlike a situation involving a person's home, no meaningful claim to protection of a right of privacy can be advanced by respondents here. Nor on the facts of the case can any significant claim to protection of the normal business operation of the property be raised. Naked title is essentially all that is at issue.

The economic development of the United States in the last 20 years reinforces our opinion of the correctness of the approach taken in *Marsh.* The large-scale movement of this country's population from the cities to the suburbs has been accompanied by the advent of the suburban shopping center, typically a cluster of individual retail units on a single large privately owned tract. It has been estimated that by the end of 1966 there were between 10,000 and 11,000 shopping centers in the United States and Canada, accounting for approximately 37% of the total retail sales in those two countries.

These figures illustrate the substantial consequences for workers seeking to challenge substandard working conditions, consumers protesting shoddy or overpriced merchandise, and minority groups seeking nondiscriminatory hiring policies that a contrary decision here would have. Business enterprises located in downtown areas would be subject to on-the-spot public criticism for their practices, but businesses situated in the suburbs could largely immunize themselves from similar criticism by creating a *cordon sanitaire* of parking lots around their stores. Neither precedent nor policy compels a result so at variance with the goal of free expression and communication that is the heart of the First Amendment.

Therefore, as to the sufficiency of respondents' ownership of the Logan Valley Mall premises as the sole support of the injunction issued against petitioners, we simply repeat what was said in *Marsh* v. *Alabama*, 326 U.S., at 506, "Ownership does not always mean absolute dominion. The more an owner, for his advantage, opens up his property for use by the public in general, the more do his rights become circumscribed by the statutory and constitutional rights of those who use it." Logan Valley Mall is the functional equivalent of a "business block" and for First Amendment purposes must be treated in substantially the same manner.

The judgment of the Supreme Court of Pennsylvania is reversed and the case is remanded for further proceedings not inconsistent with this opinion.

It is so ordered.

CASE QUESTIONS

1. Compare the essential facts of *Logan Valley* and *Central Hardware*.
2. What was the sole justification offered by the respondents for the legality of the prohibition of picketing and handbilling in front of the Weis market?
3. If the injunction was allowed to stand, what consequences did the Supreme Court foresee?

SECTION 62 / **VIOLENT PICKETING**

Violent and intimidatory picketing is unlawful in all jurisdictions. This, however, is not what causes difficulty. What is violence and intimidation? When is intimidation of sufficient intensity to cast it in the proscribed category? While the general rule is uniformly applicable, the problem is largely one of permissible degree, and it is in this particular that the several jurisdictions vary in their application of the general rule.

The *Meadowmoor* decision in this section leaves not much doubt as to the original illegal conduct of the union men and to the fact that the injunction was properly issued. The court finds no problem on this score, but has no little difficulty in reconciling its decision here with that in *Thornhill* v. *Alabama* (page 282) decision, wherein it was held that peaceful picketing was constitutionally protected as a right of free speech. The issue in the *Meadowmoor* case is whether currently peaceful picketing, enmeshed in contemporaneously violent conduct, is properly enjoinable. The union contends that the picketing injunction should be dissolved, as the picketing is presently peaceful.

Milk Wagon Drivers' Union of Chicago v. Meadowmoor Dairies, Inc.

Supreme Court of the United States, 1941. 312 U.S. 287

FRANKFURTER, J. The Supreme Court of Illinois sustained an injunction against the Milk Wagon Drivers' Union over the latter's claim that it involved an infringement of the freedom of speech guaranteed by the Fourteenth

Amendment. Since this ruling raised a question intrinsically important, as well as affecting the scope of *Thornhill* v. *Alabama,* 310 U.S. 88, and *Carlson* v. *California,* 310 U.S. 106, we brought the case here. 310 U.S. 655.

The "vendor system" for distributing milk in Chicago gave rise to the dispute. Under that system, which was fully analyzed in *Milk Wagon Drivers' Union* v. *Lake Valley Farm Products,* 311 U.S. 91, milk is sold by the dairy companies to vendors operating their own trucks who resell to retailers. These vendors departed from the working standards theretofore achieved by the Union for its members as dairy employees. The Union, in order to compel observance of the established standards, took action against dairies using the vendor system. The present respondent, Meadowmoor Dairies, Inc., brought suit against the Union and its officials to stop interference with the distribution of its products. A preliminary injunction restraining all union conduct, violent and peaceful, was promptly issued, and the case was referred to a master for report. Besides peaceful picketing of the stores handling Meadowmoor's products, the master found that there had been violence on a considerable scale. Witnesses testified to more than fifty instances of window-smashing; explosive bombs caused substantial injury to the plants of Meadowmoor and another dairy using the vendor system and to five stores; stench bombs were dropped in five stores; three trucks of vendors were wrecked, seriously injuring one driver, and another was driven into a river; a store was set on fire and in large measure ruined; two trucks of vendors were burned; a storekeeper and a truck driver were severely beaten; workers at a dairy which, like Meadowmoor, used the vendor system, were held up with guns and severely beaten about the head while being told "to join the union"; carloads of men followed vendors' trucks, threatened the drivers, and in one instance shot at the truck and driver. In more than a dozen of these occurrences, involving window-smashing, bombings, burnings, the wrecking of trucks, shootings, and beatings, there was testimony to identify the wrongdoers as union men. In the light of his findings, the master recommended that all picketing, and not merely violent acts, should be enjoined. The trial court, however, accepted the recommendations only as to acts of violence and permitted peaceful picketing. The reversal of this ruling by the Supreme Court, 371 Ill. 377, 21 N.E. 2d 308, directing a permanent injunction as recommended by the master, is now before us.

The question which thus emerges is whether a state can choose to authorize its courts to enjoin acts of picketing in themselves peaceful when they are enmeshed with contemporaneously violent conduct which is concededly outlawed. The Constitution is invoked to deny Illinois the power to authorize its courts to prevent the continuance and recurrence of flagrant violence, found after an extended litigation to have occurred under specific circumstances, by the terms of a decree familiar in such cases. Such a decree, arising out of a particular controversy and adjusted to it, raises totally different constitutional problems from those that would be presented by an abstract statute with an overhanging and undefined threat to free utterance. To assimilate the two is to deny to the states their historic freedom to deal with controversies through the concreteness of individual litigation rather than through the abstractness of a general law.

The starting point is Thornhill's case. That case invoked the constitutional protection of free speech on behalf of a relatively modern means for "publicizing, without annoyance or threat of any kind, the facts of a labor dispute." 310 U.S. 100. The whole series of cases defining the scope of free speech under the Fourteenth Amendment are facets of the same principle in that they all safeguard modes appropriate for assuring the right to utterance in different situations. Peaceful picketing is the workingman's means of communication.

It must never be forgotten, however, that the Bill of Rights was the child of the Enlightenment. Back of the guarantee of free speech lay faith in the power of an appeal to reason by all the peaceful means for gaining access to the mind. It was in order to avert force and explosions due to restrictions upon rational modes of communication that the guarantee of free speech was given a generous scope. But utterance in a context of violence can lose its significance as an appeal to reason and become part of an instrument of force. Such utterance was not meant to be sheltered by the Constitution.

Still it is of prime importance that no constitutional freedom, least of all the guarantees of the Bill of Rights, be defeated by insubstantial findings of fact screening reality. That is why this Court has the ultimate power to search the records in the state courts where a claim of constitutionality is effectively made. And so the right of free speech cannot be denied by drawing from a trivial rough incident, or a moment of animal exuberance, the conclusion that otherwise peaceful picketing has the taint of force. . . .

These acts of violence are neither episodic nor isolated. Judges need not be so innocent of the actualities of such an industrial conflict as this record discloses as to find in the Constitution a denial of the right of Illinois to conclude that the use of force on such a scale was not the conduct of a few irresponsible outsiders. The Fourteenth Amendment still leaves the state ample discretion in dealing with manifestations of force in the settlement of industrial conflicts. And in exercising its power a state is not to be treated as though the technicalities of the laws of agency were written into the Constitution. Certainly a state is not confined by the Constitution to narrower limits in fashioning remedies for dealing with industrial disputes than the scope of discretion open to the National Labor Relations Board. It is true of a union as of an employer that it may be responsible for acts which it has not expressly authorized or which might not be attributable to it on strict application of the rules of respondeat superior. *International Association of Machinists* v. *Labor Board,* 311 U.S. 72, 80; *Heinz Co.* v. *Labor Board,* 311 U.S. 514. To deny to a state the right to a judgment which the National Labor Relations Board has been allowed to make in cognate situations, would indeed be distorting the Fourteenth Amendment with restrictions upon state power which it is not our business to impose. A state may withdraw the injunction from labor controversies, but no less certainly the Fourteenth Amendment does not make unconstitutional the use of the injunction as a means of restricting violence. We find nothing in the Fourteenth Amendment that prevents a state if it so chooses from placing confidence in a chancellor's decree and compels it to rely exclusively on a policeman's club.

We have already adverted to the generous scope that must be given to the guarantee of free speech. Especially is this attitude to be observed where, as in labor controversies, the feelings of even the most detached minds may become engaged and a show of violence may make still further demands on calm judgment. It is therefore relevant to remind that the power to deny what otherwise would be lawful picketing derives from the power of the states to prevent future coercion. Right to free speech in the future cannot be forfeited because of disassociated acts of past violence. Nor may a state enjoin peaceful picketing merely because it may provoke violence in others. *Near* v. *Minnesota,* 283 U.S. 697, 721–22; *Cantwell* v. *Connecticut,* 310 U.S. 296. In as much as the injunction was based on findings made in 1937, this decision is no bar to resort to the state court for modification of the terms of the injunction should that court find that the passage of time has deprived the picketing of its coercive influence. In the exceptional cases warranting restraint upon normally free conduct, the restraint ought to be defined by clear and guarded language. According to the best practice, a judge himself should draw the specific terms of such restraint and not rely on drafts submitted by the parties. But we do not have revisory power over state practice, provided such practice is not used to evade constitutional guarantees. See *Fox River Co.* v. *Railroad Comm'n,* 274 U.S. 651, 655; *Long Sault Development Co.* v. *Call,* 242 U.S. 272, 277. We are here concerned with power and not with the wisdom of its exercise. We merely hold that in the circumstances of the record before us the injunction authorized by the Supreme Court of Illinois does not transgress its constitutional power. That other states have chosen a different path in such a situation indicates differences of social view in a domain in which states are free to shape their local policy. Compare *Busch Jewelry Co.* v. *United Retail Employees' Union,* 281 N.Y. 150; 22 N.E. 2d 320, and *Baillis* v. *Fuchs,* 283 N.Y. 133, 27 N.E. 2d 812.

To maintain the balance of our federal system, in so far as it is committed to our care, demands at once zealous regard for the guarantees of the Bill of Rights and due recognition of the powers belonging to the state. Such an adjustment requires austere judgment, and a precise summary of the result may help to avoid misconstruction.

We do not qualify the *Thornhill* and *Carlson* decisions. We reaffirm them. They involved statutes baldly forbidding all picketing near an employer's place of business. Entanglement with violence was expressly out of those cases. The statutes had to be dealt with on their face, and therefore we struck them down. Such an unlimited ban on free communication declared as the law of a state by a state court enjoys no greater protection here. *Cantwell* v. *Connecticut,* 310 U.S. 296; *American Federation of Labor* v. *Swing,* 312 U.S. 321. But just as a state through its legislature may deal with specific circumstances menacing the peace by appropriately drawn act, *Thornhill* v. *Alabama, supra,* so the law of a state may be fitted to a concrete situation through the authority given by the state to its courts. This is precisely the kind of situation which the *Thornhill* opinion excluded from its scope. "We are not now concerned with picketing en masse or otherwise conducted which might occasion such imminent and aggravated danger . . . as to justify a statute narrowly drawn to cover the precise situation giving rise to the danger." 310 U.S. 105. We would not strike down a statute which authorized the courts of Illinois to prohibit picketing when they should find that violence had given to the picketing a coercive effect whereby it would operate destructively as force and intimidation. Such a situation is presented by this record. It distorts the meaning of things to generalize the terms of an injunction derived from and directed towards violent misconduct as though it were an abstract prohibition of all picketing wholly unrelated to the violence involved.

The exercise of the state's power which we are sustaining is the very antithesis of a ban on all discussion in Chicago of a matter of public importance. Of course we would not sustain such a ban. The injunction is confined to conduct near stores dealing in respondent's milk, and it deals with this narrow area precisely because the coercive conduct affected it. An injunction so adjusted to a particular situation is in accord with the settled practice of equity, sanctioned by such guardians of civil liberty as Mr. Justice Cardozo. Compare *Nann* v. *Raimist,* 255 N.Y. 307, 174 N.E. 690. Such an injunction must be read in the context of its circumstances. Nor ought state action be held unconstitutional by interpreting the law of the state as though, to use a phrase of Mr. Justice Holmes, one were fired with a zeal to pervert. If an appropriate injunction were put to abnormal uses in its enforcement, so that encroachments were made on free discussion outside the limits of violence, as for instance discussion through newspaper or on the radio, the doors of this Court are always open.

The injunction which we sustain is "permanent" only for the temporary period for which it may last. It is justified only by the violence that induced it and only so long as it counteracts a continuing intimidation. Familiar equity procedure assures opportunity for modifying or vacating an injunction when its continuance is no longer warranted. Here again, the state courts have not the last say. They must act in subordination to the duty of this Court to enforce constitutional liberties even when denied through spurious findings of fact in a state court. Compare *Chambers* v. *Florida,* 309 U.S. 227. Since the union did not urge that the coercive effect had disappeared either before us or, apparently, before the state court, that question is not now here.

A final word. Freedom of speech and freedom of the press cannot be too often invoked as basic to our scheme of society. But these liberties will not be advanced or even maintained by denying to the states with all their resources, including the instrumentality of their courts, the power to deal with coercion due to extensive violence. If the people of Illinois desire to withdraw the use of the injunction in labor controversies, the democratic process for legislative reform is at their disposal. On the other hand, if they choose to leave their courts with the power which they have historically exercised, within the circumscribed limits which this opinion defines, and we deny them that instrument of government, that power has been taken from them permanently. Just because these industrial conflicts raise anxious difficulties, it is most important for us not to intrude into the realm of policy-making by reading our own motions into the Constitution.

Affirmed.

CASE QUESTIONS

1. Describe the "vendor system" of milk distribution.
2. Had the union resorted to previous violence?
3. What question does the United States Supreme Court say is before it?

4. May the right to free speech in the future be "forfeited because of disassociated acts of past violence"?
5. Did the court qualify the *Thornhill* decision?
6. Is the scope of the injunction confined to a particular physical area?
7. When may the union petition for dissolution of the injunction?
8. In view of the Norris-LaGuardia Act, how was the Meadowmoor Dairy able to secure an injunction?
9. State the rule of law developed by this case.
10. Do you believe the case is soundly reasoned?

SECTION 63 / FRAUDULENT PICKETING

If the conduct incident to even peaceful picketing activity can be established as involving serious misrepresentation of fact, fraud, and the usage of opprobious and profane language, then such picketing ceases to be clothed with constitutional immunity from injunction.

Most jurisdictions permit some degree of misrepresentation, as in the case of a salesman who becomes unduly expansive about the merits of his product, but variance is found both in the matter of permissible degree and in the punishment invoked. For illustration, some courts permanently enjoin the picketing if fraud is found; others require the injunction to remain in effect only as long as the misrepresentation continues. The court decisions included in this section are principally concerned with the degree to which misrepresentation of fact is allowable before it is subject to restraint.

Busch Jewelry Co., Inc. v. United Retail Employees' Union, Local 830

Supreme Court of New York County, 1938. 168 Misc. 224, 5 N.Y.S.(2d) 575

CORTILLO, J. In this action, brought by three plaintiffs against the defendant Union Local and its officers, approximately one hundred specific instances (some repetitious) of illegal, unwarranted and socially improper conduct are claimed to have been established upon the trial as the basis for the permanent injunction demanded. The plaintiff Busch Credit Jewelry Co., Inc., operates five stores in the Boroughs of Manhattan and Bronx. . . .

The defendant Local is, as its name implies, an organization of employees of retail merchants, the individual defendants being officers of said Local. . . .

The strike . . . was called on May 17th, and the picketing complained of here began shortly thereafter. The sole question presented by this action is whether the numerous acts shown by the evidence to have accompanied the strike and picketing are legal or illegal. The grant or refusal of the permanent injunction sought by plaintiffs depends upon the answer to that question. The right to strike and the right to picket have been repeatedly upheld by the courts, and in this day and age require no discussion. Neither the right to strike or picket, however, justifies or excuses acts which are illegal per se. . . .

Numerous acts of misconduct were established by the proof, some of which are violative of law and order and distinctly conducive to a breakdown of the public peace. They may be classified as (1) acts of physical and forcible obstruction to the proper and orderly conduct of plaintiffs' business; (2) threats, intimidation and coercion inducing a breach of the public peace and tending to constitute a violation of constitutional rights of others; (3) promulgation of false, deceitful and misleading statements calculated to deceive the public as to the true state of affairs, for which purpose the facilities of the post office were used along with other means; and (4) false propaganda and appeals to class hatreds circulated to build up an esprit de corps among the strikers and their sympathizers, based upon unsound social economics tending to cheapen the intelligence of the workers and foment organized opposition to orderly processes and the administration of the law.

In view of the great number of acts complained of and which are established by the proofs, it will suffice for the purposes of this opinion and to keep it within proper bounds to generalize such acts and their effect and influence upon plaintiffs, their employees and customers and the public. Illustrative of the first class of acts above mentioned is the case of a customer who was stopped by two pickets as she was about to enter one of plaintiffs' stores and threatened with physical violence if she went in. The threat had its intended effect and the customer left without entering. A day or two later a prospective customer was stopped by another picket as he was about to enter another store of one of the plaintiffs. The picket referred the intending buyer to a store belonging to the picket's father and furnished him with a card bearing that store's address. At least two members of the defendant Local admitted that during the strike they called at homes of plaintiffs' customers to prevent payment by the latter of installments due to plaintiffs, one of defendant's members actually collecting an installment from one customer and pocketing the money. Another member of the Local accompanied by two other men not identified, entered the home of a female relative of one of plaintiffs' employees and threatened to picket her home and that of the employee if the relative did not compel the employee to leave his job and join the strikers. Many other similar instances were established by satisfactory proof.

While strikers may use any and all peaceful and lawful efforts to induce workers to join their ranks, the evidence shows many instances of threats, intimidation and coercion exceeding legal bounds. A female employee was followed by several members of the Local from the store where she was employed to the restaurant where she lunched and there denounced by them as a scab and a strikebreaker and otherwise vilified. Their manner and language was such as to cause her to fear for her physical safety. Another young lady was seized by a negro picket as she was about to enter plaintiffs' store where she was employed. Aided by a co-employee, she gained the safety of the store, but was subjected to a torrent of abusive language from the picket, who applied to her the vilest term known to our language. On another occasion a different member of the defendant Local accosted this same employee in vulgar terms and threatened to spit in her face. Other employees were warned by members of the Local that they would "get" them.

The third class of acts above specified, namely, false and misleading statements concerning plaintiffs and the controversy, directly involves the public, for it was to the public that such statements were issued. This is the first case that has come to my attention wherein the United States mails were used to disseminate false propaganda relating to labor controversies. On May 27th of this year a tenant in the apartment house 306 Union Avenue, Brooklyn, wherein one of the plaintiffs' employees, Rose Esposito, lived, found in his letter box a circular signed "The Busch Strikers, Members Retail Employees Union, Local 830—U.R. & W.E.A.—C.I.O., United Optical Workers Union—Local 208 C.I.O." and which among other things contained the statement: "Your neighbor Rose Esposito, 306 Union Street, is a scab at Busch's!" Similarly the home of Dr. Benjamin Meyerowitz at Long Beach was picketed by members of the defendant Local with placards bearing the statement "Your neighbor Dr. Benjamin Meyerowitz is a scab at Busch's." Dr. Meyerowitz is an employee of one of the plaintiffs.

Other statements, both oral and printed, circulated in the immediate neighborhood of various of plaintiffs' stores, were: "We are locked out. Help us get our jobs back." "Anybody but a louse would not enter this store while the strike is on." "While the strike is on you don't have to make any payments. After the strike is settled even then you don't have to pay them if you are smart." "If you buy a radio you will have to bring it back tomorrow because this is not a reputable company." "Busch's are making prostitutes of their women." "They cheated us, they will cheat you too." "Don't make any payments. They will give you phoney receipts." "They sell cracked diamonds." "You won't get credit for the money you pay." "Don't make any payments. They can't do anything to you." "Busch's doesn't hire colored people."

Not only were these false statements exhibited on signs by defendants, but they were uttered in a loud, boisterous tone in singsong fashion by such defendants while encircling the fronts of plaintiffs' stores. The monotonous repetitions and the encircling process were definite disturbances of the peace, interfering unreasonably with the orderly process of business, and exceeded legal and orderly picketing as usually conducted and as permitted under the laws and decisions of this jurisdiction. . . .

The law is well settled that where, as in the instant case, defendant unions have repeatedly and constantly engaged in unlawful picketing accompanied by disorder, intimidation, loud and boisterous language, the issuance of false and misleading statements, congregation in great numbers in front of plaintiffs' places of business, thereby causing crowds to collect and to block ingress and egress to plaintiffs' stores, and by disorderly, offensive, abusive and insulting remarks to plaintiffs' employees, customers and prospective customers and that where it appears upon the facts of the case, as it does in this case, that there is danger of the continuance of such unlawful acts with consequent injury to plaintiffs if any picketing whatsoever is permitted, courts of equity will and have enjoined all picketing.

An early expression of this doctrine appeared in *Exchange Bakery & Restaurant, Inc.* v. *Rifkin,* 1927, 245 N.Y. 260, 157 N.E. 130, when the Court of Appeals stated at page 269, 157 N.E. at page 135:

"Where unlawful picketing has been continued, where violence and intimidation have been used, and where misstatements as to the employers' business have been distributed, a broad injunction prohibiting all picketing may be granted. The course of conduct of the strikers has been such as to indicate the danger of injury to property if any picketing whatever is allowed."

In *Nann* v. *Raimist*, 1931, 255 N.Y. 307, 174 N.E. 690, 73 A.L.R. 669, Justice Cardozo said at page 315, 174 N.E. at page 693:

"Whether the trial court, in view of this record of defiance, would give the defendant still another chance to picket peacefully and in order, was something to be determined in the exercise of a wise discretion. This court may not interfere except for manifest abuse. . . . The injunction is sustained upon the theory that the defendant, having been permitted to picket subject to conditions, violated those conditions, and in contempt of the existing mandate picketed with violence and with falsehood, spreading terror with a strong hand and a multitude of people. In the judgment of the trial court, 'the (defendant's) course of conduct . . . has been such as to indicate the danger of injury to property if any picketing whatever is allowed.' *Exchange Bakery & Restaurant, Inc.* v. *Rifkin, supra.* We cannot say that a basis for that belief is lacking altogether."

An abuse of picketing was sufficient to enjoin all picketing in *Stillwell Theatre, Inc.* v. *Kaplan,* 1932, 259 N.Y. 405, 182 N.E. 63, 84 A.L.R. 6. Pound, C. J., cited with approval the *Exchange Bakery Case, Nann* v. *Raimist* and *Steinkritz Amusement Corporation* v. *Kaplan,* 257 N.Y. 294, 178 N.E. 11, pointing out, at page 411, 182 N.E. page 66, that the holding in the latter case had been as follows: "By abuse of picketing, it was held that the union had forfeited the right to picket.". . .

On all the facts established, the court is constrained to permanently enjoin the picketing complained of and the defendants, individually and severally, are so enjoined. Injunction granted. Findings passed on. Judgment signed.

Denver Local Union No. 13 v. Perry Truck Lines

(SUPPLEMENTAL CASE DIGEST—FRAUDULENT PICKETING)
Supreme Court of Colorado, 1940. 101 P.2d 436

"The trial court found that the placards carried by the pickets, declaring, 'This Firm Unfair to Teamsters Union No. 13,' were highly misleading and false. We cannot agree with that conclusion. This involves only a battle over words. We do not doubt that the employer considered the slogan false. He had the right to entertain that opinion. Under the facts, defendants also had the right to their opinions. The statement on the placards was not fraudulent." (Otto Bock, J.) In accord on the proposition that an "unfair" statement is privileged is the case of *Taxi Cab Drivers* v. *Yellow Cab Operating Co.,* Circuit Court of Appeals, Tenth Circuit, 1941, 123 Fed. (2d) 262. For a case involving enjoinable misrepresentation of labor dispute facts by picketers, see *Sachs Quality Furniture Co.* v. *Hensley,* New York Supreme Court, 1945, 269 App. Div. 264, 55 N.Y.S. (2d) 450.

NLRB v. Local Union 1229, I.B.E.W.

(SUPPLEMENTAL CASE DIGEST—FRAUDULENT PICKETING)
Supreme Court of the United States, 1953. 346 U.S. 464

As a concomitant of contract negotiations, the union resorted to pressurized picketing by publicly distributing thousands of handbills which stated that the television station by which they were employed as telecast technicians televised inferior programs. The employer retaliated by discharging the malcontent pickets for their ridicule and disparagement of his broadcasts.

The Supreme Court ruled that the picket activity in question was not legitimate and privileged, but rather was representative of such "disloyalty" as to legalize discharge under the NLRA notwithstanding its protective provisions.

CASE QUESTIONS

1. List the classes of improper acts by the Union in *Busch.*
2. In *Busch,* what means did the union employ to publicize the labor dispute?
3. State the rule quoted from the *Exchange Bakery* case.
4. Distinguish the fraudulent statements found in the parent case and the *Denver* case digest.

SECTION 64 / MASSED PICKETING

Another form of peaceful picketing which may be illegal is that in which the pickets are so massed as to contain elements of implicit coercion growing out of the force of numbers. Some courts have been disposed to limit substantially the number of pickets on station or patrol and the manner of their position. Others have been more liberal as long as the picketing retained its essentially peaceful character.

The Supreme Court decision of 1921 in *Truax* v. *Corrigan* lent early weight to the proposition that numbers and mass may alone cast peaceful picketing into an unlawful category. The modern representative view on this question is found in the *Carnegie-Illinois* decision, presented in this section, precluding any such activity as coercive.

Carnegie-Illinois Steel Corporation v. United Steelworkers of America

Supreme Court of Pennsylvania, 1946. 353 Pa. 420

MAXEY, C. J. The plaintiff filed a bill in equity against the defendants, making certain allegations as to the commission of acts of force and violence against employees of the plaintiff and interfering with the ingress of such employees to the plaintiff's property, an extensive steel works situated at

Homestead. These employees who were allegedly barred from plaintiff's plant were not engaged in the work of producing steel and were in no sense of the term "strikebreakers." None of the manufacturing and productive facilities at the Homestead Steel Works have been in operation at any time during the strike. These barred-out employees were assigned to the work of maintaining the powerhouses, the boilers, the pumps, the steam lines and the sprinkler system, and to guard against the constant hazard of fire and to prevent the freezing of water lines essential to water cooling systems in the plant. The steam lines and water lines in the plant total several hundred miles in length. The work of these maintenance men was essential to the keeping of the steel plant in condition to resume the production of steel as soon as the steel strike should come to an end. . . .

On January 25, 1946, a large group of pickets, estimated to be from one hundred to two hundred in number, standing three deep, extended across the gate and blocked the entrance to plaintiff's Homestead plant and thus denied access to the plant to individuals below the rank of superintendent. . . .

There were other similar injunction affidavits filed all purporting to show that supervisory officials were denied access to plaintiff's plant and that the defendant labor union and its officials and agents had arrogated to itself and themselves the authority to determine what employees of the plaintiff corporation should and should not, respectively, enter the corporation's plant, and that the Union enforced its assumed authority by massing approximately 200 pickets at the gate leading into the plant.

The court below in response to the above bill of complaint, supported by the above injunction affidavits and others, granted the injunction prayed for. . . .

The court in its opinion made the following apt statement: "Picketing which results in the intimidation and coercion of officers and employees of the plaintiff and denies workmen from legitimate business access to plaintiff's plant is not legal picketing. Picketing which results in the kidnaping of individuals and placing them under restraint and depriving them of their personal liberty is not legal picketing. Picketing which consists of at least one hundred or more pickets massed and grouped together at the main entrance of a plant for the purpose of denying the right of access is not legal picketing." . . .

Forcibly to deny an owner of property or his agents and employees access to that property for the purpose of protecting and maintaining it and its equipment or for any other legitimate purpose is in practical and legal effect a seizure or holding of that property. Such a lawless seizure of property no government worthy of the name will tolerate or condone. The employment of hostile force against persons and property is exclusively a governmental function, and exercisable even by the government only by due process of law. When any individual or organization under whatsover name attempts to use force to gain his or its ends they are attempting to usurp governmental functions. . . .

Nowhere in the defendants' voluminous brief or in their hour's oral argument before the Supreme Court, was it asserted that the affidavits in response to which this injunction was issued were *untrue*. The defense was that on the state of the record (no hearing having been had) the court had no power to issue the injunction. This contention we overrule. When property needs protection from the acts of lawless groups, it needs it *at once.* Delays are dangerous. It is self-evident that such a vast and complex structure as plaintiff's plant, representing an investment of over $200,000,000, could be irreparably injured by failure of proper maintenance and protection against fire and other hazards, for even a day or a lesser period. . . .

When this case reached this court and the record was before us, it then became our duty to decide whether or not the facts showed that what the defendants were doing constituted a "holding" or "seizure" of the plant or any part of it. The holding or seizure of even one gateway to the plant entitled the plaintiff to the protection of a court of equity just as fully as would the seizure of the entire plant. When a "picket line" becomes a picket *fence* it is time for government to act. Collective coercion is not a legitimate child of collective bargaining. The forcible seizure of an employer's property is the very essence of communism.

Injunctions are not issued against picketing when the latter's only purposes are to advertise the fact that there is a strike in a certain plant and to persuade workers to join in that strike and to urge the public not to patronize the employer. For these purposes, a limited number of pickets is all that is necessary. But when hundreds of pickets are massed, as at least two hundred were here at a single gate, it is obvious that this force was not mustered for a peaceful purpose. . . .

We dismiss this appeal. . . .

<table>
<tr><td>CASE
QUESTIONS</td><td>1. What workers did the pickets exclude from the plant?
2. Suppose regular production workers were the only ones excluded. Would this have made a difference in the decision of the court?
3. How many pickets were at the main entrance?
4. How did the court characterize the picket line in its analogy?
5. State the rule of law of this case.</td></tr>
</table>

SECTION 65 / OUTSIDER PICKETING

The term *outsider-stranger picketing* is self-explanatory, describing the picketing of an employer by persons who are not in the employ of the employer. It is also characterized by the fact that there is usually no overt dispute between the employer and his workers, the economic pressure being exerted to force the employer to meet certain demands of those picketing. Some state courts have been prone to denounce this type of picketing as unjustified under proper circumstances.

The *Swing* case in this section is the Supreme Court's leading pronouncement on the legality of outsider pressure. Outsider pressure, it should be recalled, is protected both by the Federal Anti-Injunction Act and the National Labor

Relations Act, which broadly define a labor dispute as not requiring the existence of the proximate relation of employer and employee.

American Federation of Labor v. Swing

Supreme Court of the United States, 1941. 312 U.S. 321

FRANKFURTER, J. In *Milk Wagon Drivers Union* v. *Meadowmoor Dairies, Inc.,* 312 U.S. 287, 61 S. Ct. 552, 85 L. Ed.—, decided this day, we held that acts of picketing when blended with violence may have a significance which neutralizes the constitutional immunity which such acts would have in isolation. When we took this case, 310 U.S. 620, 60 S. Ct. 1081, 84 L. Ed. 1393, it seemed to present a similar problem. More thorough study of the record and full argument have reduced the issue to this: is the constitutional guarantee of freedom of discussion infringed by the common law policy of a state forbidding resort to peaceful persuasion through picketing merely because there is no immediate employer-employee dispute?

A union of those engaged in what the record describes as beauty work unsuccessfully tried to unionize Swing's beauty parlor. Picketing of the shop followed. To enjoin this interference with his business and with the freedom of his workers not to join a union, Swing and his employees began the present suit. In addition, they charged the use of false placards in picketing and forcible behavior towards Swing's customers. A preliminary injunction was granted. . . . The union sought review of this decree in the Supreme Court by writ of error. Swing and his employees moved to dismiss the writ because in seeking to obtain it the union had conceded that "all issues of the case have been settled on prior appeal and that the decree entered by the appellate court is in conformity with the mandate issued" to the appellate court. The writ was dismissed.

Such is the case as we extract it from a none too clear record. It thus appears that in passing upon the temporary injunction the Supreme Court of Illinois sustained it in part because of allegations of violence and libel. But our concern is with the final decree of the appellate court. On its face the permanent injunction in that decree rested on the explicit avowal that "peaceful persuasion" was forbidden in this case because those who were enjoined were not in Swing's employ. . . .

Since the case clearly presents a substantial claim of the right to free discussion and since, as we have frequently indicated, that right is to be guarded with a jealous eye, *Herndon* v. *Lowry,* 301 U.S. 242, 258, 57 S. Ct. 732, 739, 81 L. Ed. 1066; *Schneider* v. *State,* 308 U.S. 147, 161, 60 S. Ct. 146, 150, 84 L. Ed. 155; *United States* v. *Carolene Products Co.,* 304 U.S. 144, 152 note, 58 S. Ct. 778, 783 note, 82 L. Ed. 1234, it would be improper to dispose of the case otherwise than on the face of the decree, which is the judgment now under review. We are therefore not called upon to consider the applicability of *Milk Wagon Drivers Union* v. *Meadowmoor Dairies, Inc., supra,* the circumstances of which obviously present quite a different situation from the controlling allegations of violence and libel made in the present bill.

All that we have before us, then, is an instance of "peaceful persuasion" disentangled from violence and free from "picketing en masse or otherwise conducted" so as to occasion "imminent and aggravated danger." *Thornhill* v. *Alabama,* 310 U.S. 88, 105, 60 S. Ct. 736, 746, 84 L. Ed. 1093. We are asked to sustain a decree which for purposes of this case asserts as the common law of a state that there can be no "peaceful picketing or peaceful persuasion" in relation to any dispute between an employer and a trade union unless the employer's own employees are in controversy with him.

Such a ban of free communication is inconsistent with the guarantee of freedom of speech. That a state has ample power to regulate the local problems thrown up by modern industry and to preserve the peace is axiomatic. But not even these essential powers are unfettered by the requirements of the Bill of Rights. The scope of the Fourteenth Amendment is not confined by the notion of a particular state regarding the wise limits of an injunction in an industrial dispute, whether those limits be defined by statute or by the judicial organ of the state. A state cannot exclude workingmen from peacefully exercising the right of free communication by drawing the circle of economic competition between employers and workers so small as to contain only an employer and those directly employed by him. The interdependence of economic interest of all engaged in the same industry has become a commonplace. *American Steel Foundries* v. *Tri-City Council,* 257 U.S. 184, 209, 42 S. Ct. 72, 78, 66 L. Ed. 189, 27 A.L.R. 360. The right of free communication cannot therefore be mutilated by denying it to workers, in a dispute with an employer, even though they are not in his employ. Communication by such employees of the facts of a dispute, deemed by them to be relevant to their interests, can no more be barred because of concern for the economic interests against which they are seeking to enlist public opinion than could the utterance protected in Thornhill's case. "Members of a union might, without special statutory authorization by a state, make known the facts of a labor dispute, for freedom of speech is guaranteed by the Federal Constitution." *Senn* v. *Tile Layers Union,* 301 U.S. 468, 478, 57 S. Ct. 857, 862, 81 L. Ed. 1229.

Reversed.

CASE QUESTIONS

1. State the issue of this case in the words of the Supreme Court.
2. Outline the facts leading to the lower court injunction.

SECTION 66 / INFORMATIONAL PICKETING

Communication of ideas is constitutionally protected, but peaceful persuasion may be qualified when in conflict with other important considerations. Thus the National Labor Relations Act, as amended, both protects and limits boycotting and picketing. Restrictions on striking written into the union unfair practices of Section 8(b) of the law sometimes also constitute barriers to picketing or boycotting even in the absence of a stoppage.

Such prohibitive terms as: "to restrain or coerce"; "to attempt to cause"; "to induce or encourage . . . to engage in"; "to threaten, coerce or restrain . . . where an object thereof" clearly apply also to picketing and boycotting activities regardless of actual stoppages, if a prohibited purpose of any result prohibited by law is found to exist in whole or in part.

The Act explicitly prohibits not only picketing but even "to threaten to picket" in order to force illegal recognition of or membership in an uncertified labor organization under conditions spelled out in Section 8(b)(7). However, these restrictions on picketing and on boycotting are not to be construed to prohibit "picketing or other publicity for the purpose of truthfully advising the public (including customers) that an employer does not employ members of or have a contract with a labor organization" if no interruption of service or work is induced.

An interpretation of the statutory language of 8(b)(7)(C), which regulates informational picketing, was set out by the Board and enforced by the Ninth Circuit Court of Appeals in the *Barker Brothers*[3] case. The court held that informing the public by handbills and pickets that a furniture store did not have a labor agreement with the Retail Clerks Union and asking customers not to patronize it, was legal notwithstanding some minor interruptions of deliveries. The Board found a meaning for 8(b)(7)(C) that accomplished, as nearly as possible, two results, namely, permitting "informational" picketing, as the second proviso to subparagraph (C) was designed to do, while at the same time outlawing picketing if it had the "signal" effect of stopping deliveries and services, at which the "unless" clause in 8(b)(7)(C) is aimed.

SECTION 67 / ORGANIZING AND JURISDICTIONAL PICKETING

Jurisdictional disputes prior to the National Labor Relations Act of 1947 were a thorn in the side of many an employer who was caught in the middle of a dispute in which he had no interest and over which he could exercise no control. The amended Act remedied this situation in the following particulars:

1. Sec. 8(b)(4)(C) makes it an unfair labor practice for a union to force or require any "employer to recognize or bargain with a particular labor organization . . . if another . . . has been certified . . . under the provisions of Sec. 9."
2. Sec. 8(b)(4)(D) makes it an unfair labor practice for a union to engage in a work jurisdictional dispute. The Board must decide these disputes under Sec. 10(k), and, if necessary, secure an injunction under Sec. 10(l) to preserve the *status quo* while it is deciding to whom certain work shall be assigned.

Since the 1959 amendments of the federal law, a qualifying proviso to these limitations on jurisdictional picketing explicitly permits "publicity other than picketing." Also section 8(b)(7) makes it an unfair labor practice to picket or even threaten such tactics to force recognition or bargaining rights when another union

---

[3] 328 F.2d 431 (1964).

is lawfully recognized and an election would be untimely, as where a valid election was conducted in the preceding twelve months. As discussed in the previous section, "informational" picketing is permitted for the purpose of truthfully advising the public that an employer does not have a labor agreement in effect, while "signal" picketing, the purpose of which is to enlist other unions not to make deliveries and perform services, is illegal.

SECTION 68 / SECONDARY BOYCOTTS: INTRODUCTION

The thrust of Section 8(b)(4)(ii)(B), the principal secondary boycott section of the Act, is to protect neutral employers from the effects of labor disputes between other employers and their employees. This protection has been limited by rulings that have recognized the right of striking employees, under certain circumstances, to picket "allies" of their employer, to picket "common situs" locations where neutral as well as primary employer activity is present, and, again under certain circumstances, to conduct secondary consumer boycotts. Section 8(e) outlaws "hot cargo" agreements where an employer contracts with a union not to handle specified "unfair" goods; however, rulings permit agreements containing job protecting "work preservation" clauses. The law concerning the above matters is covered in the following sections.

The student is cautioned that this area of labor law presents problems of great complexity. It is recommended that the student may better understand the law of secondary boycotts by examining the cases in the following sections with great care and studying the relevant statutory language that applies to each case.

SECTION 69 / SECONDARY BOYCOTTS: THE ALLY DOCTRINE

The *Douds* decision presented below discusses in detail the "ally" doctrine. In *NLRB* v. *Denver Building & Construction Trades Council*[4] the Supreme Court stated that § 8(b)(4) reflects "the dual congressional objectives of preserving the right of labor organizations to bring pressure to bear on offending employers in primary labor disputes and of shielding unoffending employers and others from pressures and controversies not their own." This policy then protects unoffending or innocent third parties from labor disputes which are not their affair. An employer who performs the "struck work" of a primary employer is no such innocent party and is not protected under § 8(b)(4). Additionally the "ally" doctrine is applied to those employers who because of common ownership, control and integration of operations, become so identified with the primary employer that the businesses are considered as a single enterprise.

---

[4] 341 U.S. 675 (1951).

Douds v. Metropolitan Federation

United States District Court, Southern District of New York, 1948. 75 Fed. Supp. 672

RIFKIND, D. J. This is a petition brought by Charles T. Douds, Regional Director of the Second Region of the National Labor Relations Board to enjoin the respondent, Metropolitan Federation of Architects, Engineers, Chemists and Technicians, Local 231, United Office & Professional Workers of America, C.I.O., from engaging in certain activities alleged to be in violation of Section 8(b)(4)(A) of the Labor Management Relations Act of 1947, Public Law 101, 80th Congress, popularly known as the Taft-Hartley Act. Project Engineering Company, a partnership, is the "charging party," and has asked for and received permission to intervene.

The relevant portions of the Act are set out in the margin.[5]

The testimony offered by the petitioner, the respondent, and the charging party at the hearings established the following facts:

Ebasco Services, Inc., is a corporation engaged, since 1905, in the business of supplying engineering services, such as planning and designing and drafting plans for industrial and public utility installations. During the year ending September 1, 1947, the respondent union was the bargaining agent for Ebasco's employees. On that day the agreement between Ebasco and the union expired. A new agreement was not reached and a strike against Ebasco was commenced on September 5, 1947.

James P. O'Donnell and Guy M. Barbolini in 1946 organized a partnership, styled Project Engineering Company, herein called "Project." Its business is identical with Ebasco's—planning and designing and drafting plans for industrial installations, although they seem to have specialized in chemical and petroleum plants. The partnership had an inception completely independent of Ebasco or its influence. There is no common ownership of any kind. It was through Project's solicitations that Ebasco first employed the partnership. An open contract dated December 19, 1946, marked the beginning of their business relations.

Prior to August, 1946, Ebasco never subcontracted any of its work. Subsequent to that date it subcontracted some of its work. At the time the strike was called, part of Ebasco's work had been let out to Project. An appreciable percentage of Project's business for some months antedating the strike consisted of work secured from Ebasco. After the strike had begun, an even greater percentage—about 75%—of its work was Ebasco's. Some work, which had been begun by Ebasco's workers, was transferred, after the commencement of the strike, in an unfinished condition, to Project for completion. . . .

---

[5] "Sec. 8(b). It shall be an unfair labor practice for a labor organization or its agents—

"(4) To engage in, or to induce or encourage the employees of any employer to engage in, a strike or a concerted refusal in the course of their employment to use, manufacture, process, transport, or otherwise handle or work on any goods, articles, materials, or commodities or to perform any services, where an object thereof is: (A) forcing or requiring any employer or self-employed person to join any labor or employer organization or any employer or other person to cease using, selling, handling, transporting, or otherwise dealing in the products of any other producer, processor, or manufacturer, or to cease doing business with any other person; . . ."

Ebasco supervisory personnel made regular visits to Project to oversee the work on the subcontracts. After the strike was called and the work subcontracted increased, these visits increased in frequency and number of personnel involved. Ebasco supervisory personnel, whose subordinates were on strike, continued to supervise their "jobs," at Project's plant, where such work had been transferred. The working hours of Project employees were increased after the commencement of the Ebasco strike.

Delegations representing the respondent union approached the charging party on more than one occasion and asked, among other things, that it refuse to accept work which had come "off the boards" of Ebasco.

On October 28, 1947, respondent union ordered Project picketed and such picketing has continued since that day. The pickets carry signs which denominate Project a scab shop for Ebasco. A number of resignations at Project are attributable to the picketing.

The number of pickets has usually been reasonable and the picketing was ordinarily unaccompanied by violence. However, on a number of occasions, to-wit, October 28, November 6 and November 25, there was picketing by thirty-five men or more. Such occasions were marked by pushing, kicking and blocking the entrance way to the buildings. Epithets such as "scab," "louse," "rat" and others were hurled at Project employees by the pickets. On those occasions the assistance of the police was requested by Project employees and order was promptly restored. Project continues to do engineering work for Ebasco—the kind of work which Ebasco employees themselves would be doing if they were not striking.

The Taft-Hartley Act has thus far had but little judicial attention. . . . Even cursory examination of the stated facts and the quoted portions of the Act reveals that the case bristles with questions of constitutional law, statutory construction and practical application. It is necessary in this instance to find the answers to but a few of these.

One of the prohibitions of Section 8(b)(4)(A) of the Act is:

"It shall be an unfair labor practice for a labor organization . . . to encourage the employees of any employer to engage in a strike . . . where an object thereof is . . . requiring . . . any . . . person . . . to cease doing business with any other person."

Is Project "doing business" with Ebasco within the meaning of the Act? The term is not defined in the Act itself. Section 2 contains thirteen definitions, but none of doing business. The term itself has, of course, received a vast amount of judicial construction but always in a context so different that it is pointless to explore that field for help in construing the term in the present context. Nor is it possible to attach legal consequences to all the relationships which the dictionary meaning of the term embraces. So to do would destroy the Act by driving it to absurdity. To give such broad scope to the term would, for instance, reach out to and include the business relation between an employee of the primary employer (Ebasco, in this case) and the primary employer, or the business relationship between a primary employer and a professional supplier of strikebreakers. Certainly it is *an* object of very many strikes and picket lines to induce a reduction in the struck employer's business by an appeal to customers—"any person"—to cease dealing with the employer. This is one of the most conspicuous weapons employed in many labor disputes. The effect of a strike would be vastly attenuated if its appeals were limited to the employer's conscience. I shall proceed on the assumption, warranted by the history of the Act, that it was not the intent of Congress to ban such activity, although the words of the statute, given their broadest meaning, may seem to reach it. Moreover, such broad construction would probably run afoul of Section 13 of the Act which reads:

"Sec. 13. Nothing in this Act, except as specifically provided for herein, shall be construed so as either to interfere with or impede or diminish in any way the right to strike, or to affect the limitations or qualifications on that right."

To find the limitations to which "doing business" must be confined recourse may be had to the legislative history to discover the mischief which Congress intended to remedy. In describing the "necessity for legislation" the House Committee on Education and Labor reported, Report No. 245, pp. 4–5:

"The employers' plight has likewise not been happy. . . .

"His business on occasions has been virtually brought to a standstill by disputes to which he himself was not a party and in which he himself had no interest."

The Senate Committee on Labor and Public Welfare reported the bill which it in part described thus, Report No. 105, p. 3:

"The major changes which the bill would make in the National Labor Relations Act may be summarized as follows. . . .

"3. It gives employers and individual employees rights to invoke the processes of the Board against unions which engaged in certain enumerated unfair labor practices, including secondary boycotts and jurisdiction strikes, which may result in the Board itself applying for restraining orders in certain cases."

Page 22 of the report goes on to say:

"Under paragraph (A) strikes or boycotts, or attempts to induce or encourage such action, are made violations of the Act if the purpose is to force an employer or other person to cease using, selling, handling, transporting, or otherwise dealing in the products of another, or to cease doing business with any other person. Thus, it would not be lawful for a union to engage in a strike against employer A for the purpose of forcing that employer to cease doing business with employer B; nor would it be lawful for a union to boycott employer A because employer A uses or otherwise deals in the goods of or does business with employer B (with whom the union has a dispute)."

During the Congressional debates on the Bill, Senator Pepper objected to the provision relating to the secondary boycott and stated an illustration in which he thought it would be unjust to apply them. Senator Taft, in reply, said:

"I do not quite understand the case which the Senator has put. This provision makes it unlawful to resort to a secondary boycott to injure the business of a third person who is wholly unconcerned in the disagreement between an employer and his employees." (April 29, 1947, p. 4323 of the Congressional Record, Vol. 93.)

Examination of these expositions of Congressional purpose indicates that the provision was understood to outlaw what was theretofore known as secondary boycott. It is to the history of the secondary boycott, therefore, that attention should be directed and it is in the light of that history that the term "doing business" should be evaluated. See Hellerstein, *Secondary Boycotts in Labor Disputes,* 1938, 47 Yale Law J. 341; Gramfine, *Labor's Use of Secondary Boycotts,* 1947, 15 Geo. Washington Law Rev. 327.

When the term is read with the aid of the glossary provided by the law of secondary boycott it becomes quite clear that Project cannot claim to be a victim of that weapon in labor's arsenal. To suggest that Project had no interest in the dispute between Ebasco and its employees is to look at the form and remain blind to substance. In every meaningful sense it had made itself party to the contest. . . . It was firmly allied to Ebasco and it was its conduct as ally of Ebasco which directly provoked the union's action.

Significant is the unique character of the contract between Ebasco and Project. Ebasco did not buy any articles of commerce from Project. Ebasco did not retain the professional services of Project. Ebasco "bought" from Project, in the words of the basic contract, "services of your designers and draftsmen . . . to work under the direction and supervision of the Purchaser." The purchase price consisted of the actual wages paid by Project plus a factor for overhead and profit. In practice the terms and implications of the agreement were fully spelled out. Ebasco supplied both direction and supervision of a detailed and pervasive character. It established the maximum wage rates for which it would be charged. Invoices were in terms of man-hours, employee by employee. Daily tally was taken of the number of men at work on Ebasco assignments and communicated to Ebasco. The final product, the plans and drawings, were placed upon forms supplied by Ebasco, bearing its name, and were thus delivered to Ebasco's clients as Ebasco's work. In advertising its services to the industries which it served Ebasco held itself out as "having available" a number of designers and draftsmen which included those employed by Project.

True enough, the contract prescribes that "all employees furnished by the seller shall at all times be and remain employees of the seller." I do not, however, draw therefrom the inference advocated by the petitioner and the charging party. The very need for such a provision emphasizes the realization of the parties that they were doing business on terms which cast a shadow of doubt upon the identity of the employer. Without question, Ebasco and Project were free to contract who, as between themselves, should be subject to the burden and possessed of the privileges that attach to the employer of those on Project's payroll. But the law is not foreclosed by such agreements to examine the reality relevant to the purposes of a particular statute. Cf. *Rutherford Food Corp.* v. *McComb,* 1947, 331 U.S. 722; *NLRB* v. *Hearst Publications, Inc.,* 1944, 322 U.S. 111. I am unable to hold that corporate ownership or insulation of legal interests between two businesses can be conclusive as to neutrality or disinterestedness in a labor dispute.

The evidence is abundant that Project's employees did work, which, but for the strike of Ebasco's employees, would have been done by Ebasco. The economic effect upon Ebasco's employees was precisely that which would flow from Ebasco's hiring strikebreakers to work on its own premises. The conduct of the union in inducing Project's employees to strike is not different in kind from its conduct in inducing Ebasco's employees to strike. If the latter is not amenable to judicial restraint, neither is the former. In encouraging a strike at Project the union was not extending its activity to a front remote from the immediate dispute but to one intimately and indeed inextricably united to it. See *Bakery Drivers Local* v. *Wohl,* 1942, 315 U.S. 769. Cf. *Carpenters Union* v. *Ritter's Cafe,* 1942, 315 U.S. 722.

The nexus between the labor dispute and the firm picketed in the instant case is immeasurably closer than in the *Ritter* case where the injunction against picketing was upheld, or in the *Wohl* case where it was condemned. It must be apparent that a construction of the Act which outlaws the kind of union activity here involved would almost certainly cast grave doubts upon its constitutionality. It is preferable to interpret the disputed section so as to restrain only that kind of union activity which does not enjoy constitutional immunity.

The case at bar is not an instance of a secondary boycott.

For these reasons it is clear that there has been no violation of Section 8(b)(4)(A) and the court is therefore without power to grant the requested relief.

Petitioner's evidence has tended to prove that the nature of the business relation between Project and Ebasco is common in this type of business—that it is not an unusual practice for one firm to purchase the services of another firm's employees, nor for the former to supply active supervision of the latter's employees so engaged. These facts do not affect my conclusion. All it can mean is that the practices in a particular industry may be such that the normal contractor-subcontractor relationship carries with it the label of "ally" in a labor dispute context. The decision in this case is not dispositive of subcontracting in other industries, nor do I indicate any opinion as to the application of the Act if the normal volume of subcontracting work in this case had not been increased by reason of the primary contractor's strike. For the same reasons the existence of a contract between Project and Ebasco antedating the strike is without legal significance. . . .

Petition denied.

CASE QUESTIONS

1. State in detail the relationship prevailing between Ebasco and the Project Engineering Co.
2. Who is being picketed? By whom?
3. Who is the "charging party?"
4. What does Section 10(l) of the National Labor Relations Act provide? What section of the Act must be violated before an injunction may be requested by the officer of the Board?
5. Why does the court search the legislative history of the Act? What conclusion does it draw as to the applicability of Sec. 8(b)(4)(A)?
6. Did the court find unity of interest present?
7. State the rule of the case.

SECTION 70 / SECONDARY BOYCOTTS: NEUTRAL EMPLOYERS

In the *Miami Pressmen's Local 46* v. *NLRB*[6] decision it was held that common ownership of two newspapers, one in Florida and the other in Michigan, with the potentiality of common control did not justify picketing of one paper in support of a strike against the other. They were not considered "allies" because they had separate and largely unrelated operations despite their common ownership.

In the *AFTRA* decision reported in this section, the Court of Appeals for the District of Columbia considered whether or not a television station and a newspaper located six miles from each other, both being unincorporated divisions of the same parent corporation, were different "persons" within the meaning of the Act.

AFTRA, Washington-Baltimore Local v. NLRB

United States Court of Appeals, District of Columbia, 1972. 462 F.2d 887

ROBB, C. J.: The question in this case is whether the record supports the finding and conclusion of the National Labor Relations Board that two unincorporated divisions of The Hearst Corporation must be treated as separate "persons" in applying the secondary boycott provisions of the National Labor Relations Act. § 8(b)(4)(i)—(ii)(B), 29 U.S.C. § 158(b)(4)(i)—(ii)(B) (1970). We think the board's decision is supported by the record as a whole.

WBAL Television, The Hearst Corporation, (WBAL) maintains and operates radio and television stations in Baltimore, Maryland. Baltimore News American Newspaper Division, The Hearst Corporation, (News American) publishes and distributes a daily and Sunday newspaper in Baltimore. WBAL and the News American are divisions of The Hearst Corporation, a Delaware corporation, whose principal offices are in New York City. American Federation of Television and Radio Artists, Washington-Baltimore Local, AFL-CIO, (AFTRA) is a union that for many years represented WBAL's staff announcers and employees appearing before cameras and microphones.

The collective bargaining agreement between AFTRA and WBAL expired on September 1, 1968. On September 21, after negotiations for a new contract were broken off, AFTRA struck and picketed WBAL in support of its demands. Two days later, in furtherance of its dispute with WBAL, the Union picketed the News American premises in Baltimore, six miles from WBAL. Although the News American employees were not members of AFTRA, some of them refused to cross the picket line, forcing the newspaper to curtail publication, distribution and circulation.

In response to a petition by the Regional Director of the Board, the United States District Court for the District of Maryland enjoined the picketing of the News American. The court held that this picketing violated the

---

[6] 332 F.2d 405 (CA DC 1963).

secondary boycott provisions of the National Labor Relations Act. *Penello* v. *American Federation of Television and Radio Artists Washington-Baltimore Local, AFL-CIO,* 291 F. Supp. 409 (D. C. Md. 1968). Also, upon a charge filed by the News American, the Regional Director issued a complaint alleging that AFTRA had engaged in prohibited secondary boycott activities. More specifically, the complaint alleged that, in furtherance of its labor dispute with WBAL, AFTRA picketed the premises of the News American, a secondary or neutral employer, with the objects of (a) inducing employees of the News American to strike or withhold their services, and (b) forcing or requiring the News American to cease doing business with WBAL and customers and suppliers of the News American.

After a hearing, at which the evidence was substantially undisputed, the trial examiner found that the charges were sustained, and he recommended that AFTRA be ordered to cease and desist from its unfair labor practices. The Board, with one member dissenting, adopted the examiner's decision. The Union now petitions for review and the Board applies for enforcement of its order. . . .

. . . Section 2(1) of the Act, 29 U. S. C. § 152(1), provides:

> The term "person" includes one or more individuals, labor organizations, partnerships, associations, corporations, legal representatives, trustees, trustees in bankruptcy, or receivers.

The Union argues, as it has from the beginning of this litigation, that WBAL and the News American are not separate "persons" within the meaning of the Act, and that the News American therefore cannot be a neutral "person" entitled to the protection of the secondary boycott provisions.

At the outset the Union contends that the "plain language of the statute" demonstrates that the News American cannot be a separate "person." The argument is that the definition of a "person" in section 2(1) of the Act does not include or refer to an unincorporated division of a corporation, that "according to Section 2(1) of the Act, the only 'person' for the purposes of Sections 8(b)(4)(i) and (ii)(B) is *The Hearst Corporation itself,* and the separate operating divisions of The Hearst Corporation are merely *parts of one 'person'.*" (Emphasis in original) We do not find the argument persuasive.

Section 2(1) of the Act states that the "term 'person' *incudes* one or more individuals, labor organizations, partnerships, associations, corporations * * * or receivers." (Emphasis added) We think that as used in this context the word "includes" is a term of enlargement, not of limitation, and that the reference to certain entities or categories is not intended to exclude all others. *See Federal Land Bank* v. *Bismarck Lumber Co.,* 314 U.S. 95, 99–100 (1941). . . . The statute must be construed in light of the congressional purpose, which is "to confine labor conflicts to the employer in whose labor relations the conflict had arisen, and to wall off the pressures generated by that conflict from unallied employers." *Mami Newspaper Pressmen's Local No. 46* v. *NLRB,* 322 F.2d 405, 410 (1963). The Act has "the dual congressional objectives of preserving the right of labor organizations to bring pressure to bear on offending employers in primary labor disputes and of shielding unoffending employers and others from pressures in controversies not their own." *NLRB* v. *Denver*

Building & Construction Trades Council, 341 U.S. 675, 692 (1951). The question therefore is not whether legally the News American is a separate corporation but whether it is in fact an autonomous and unoffending employer. If it is autonomous and unoffending, the News American does not forfeit the protection of the Act because of its technical corporate status; the potential for harmful consequences that the Act seeks to avoid is the same whether WBAL and the News American are separate corporations or separate and autonomous "divisions" of one corporation.

The trial examiner and the Board concluded from the evidence that WBAL and the News American were operated as separate autonomous entities and that the News American was therefore a "person" under section 8(b)(4) of the Act, entitled to protection against secondary pressures. In our opinion the record as a whole supports this conclusion.

The record discloses that The Hearst Corporation, with headquarters in New York City, comprises more than twenty separate divisions. These divisions publish newspapers in Seattle, San Francisco, Los Angeles, San Antonio, Boston, Albany, New York, and Baltimore. Television and radio stations are maintained by divisions in Pittsburgh, Milwaukee, Puerto Rico, and Baltimore. Other divisions operate or maintain motion picture studios, cattle ranches, real estate enterprises and timberlands.

Hearst's three executives in New York are its president, executive vice-president and treasurer. As chief executive, the president appoints division heads, including publishers of newspapers and general managers of television and radio stations. Brent Gunts is general manager of WBAL-TV, Alfred Burk is general manager of WBAL-Radio, and Mark Collins is publisher of the News American. Each has the corporate title "Vice-President"; for example, Gunts is designated "Vice-President and General Manager, WBAL Division, The Hearst Corporation" (the television and radio stations together compose one division, known as WBAL). None of the vice-presidents sits on Hearst's board of directors, but each is responsible to Hearst's president and executive vice-president. Hearst President Richard A. Berlin testified that he has instructed his division heads to "run it [the division] as if they owned it.". . .

We think this summary of the evidence amply supports the Board's conclusion that at the time of the labor dispute WBAL and the News American were so independent of Hearst and so unrelated to each other that the News American was an unoffending employer within the meaning of the statute. True, the ultimate power to control each division belonged to Hearst, since each division manager was answerable to Hearst. As the Board correctly held, however, the test is not whether an unexercised power to control exists. "There must be in addition such actual or active common control, as distinguished from merely a potential, as to denote an appreicable integration of operations and management policies." *Drivers, Chauffeurs and Helpers Local No. 639 (Poole's Warehousing, Inc.),* 158 NLRB 1281, 1286 (1966). Here the record establishes that The Hearst Corporation's ultimate power to control has not been exercised. With respect to all matters except capital expenditures exceeding $10,000, Gunts, Burk and Collins have exercised final and independent control over their divisions. They have had complete discretion in the areas of management policy, labor relations, production, purchasing, and all other aspects of planning and operation which might touch on labor's interests in this dispute. Their responsibility to Hearst for their divisions' financial performance does not detract from their independence.

In their operations WBAL and the News American are competitors, dealing with each other at arms length. Neither division has confided in the other or sought the other's counsel with respect to labor relations matters. Labor policies have been independently formulated and labor contracts independently negotiated and concluded. We find it difficult to imagine two more independent divisions, whether they be unincorporated or incorporated separately.

Finding ample support for the Board's conclusions that common active control of the two divisions does not exist and that the News American is therefore an unoffending employer, not concerned in WBAL's labor dispute, we dismiss the petition for review and enforce the Board's order.

**CASE
QUESTIONS**

1. What was the Union's position as to the "neutrality" of the newspaper?
2. What did the Court of Appeals consider to be the fundamental issue of the case?
3. Is the ultimate power of a corporate owner to control each corporate division sufficient to make a television station and newspaper "allies" and thus not entitled to the protection of the secondary boycott provision?

SECTION 71 / **SECONDARY BOYCOTTS: COMMON SITUS PICKETING**

The line between legitimate primary and unlawful secondary activity is relatively easy to draw where the primary and secondary employers have separate work sites. A more difficult problem is presented in the common situs cases where both the struck or primary employer and the secondary or neutral employer are carrying on business activities at the same location. In the *Moore Dry Dock Co.*[7] case, where a union which had a dispute with a shipowner was refused permission to enter a shipyard to picket alongside the ship and thus set up a picket line at the entrance to the secondary employer's shipyard, the Board set forth standards outlining the types of picketing permissible in common situs situations. The Board ruled that picketing is primary and beyond the scope of 8(b)(4) if:

a. the picketing is strictly limited to times when the common situs of the dispute is located on the secondary employer's premises;
b. at the time of the picketing the primary employer is engaged in its normal business at the situs;
c. the picketing is limited to places reasonably close to the location of the situs; and
d. the picketing discloses clearly that the dispute is with the primary employer.

In *Auburndale Freezer Corp.* v. *NLRB*,[8] a common situs issue arose when striking employees of Cypress Garden Citrus Products picketed a warehouse

---

[7] *Sailors Union of the Pacific (Moore Dry Dock Co.)*, 92 NLRB 547 (1950).
[8] 434 F.2d. 1219 (5th Cir. 1970).

owned by Auburndale and used by Cypress and nineteen other processors for storage purposes. The Board, with two members dissenting, found that the picketing was within the common situs guidelines of *Moore Dry Dock* and therefore was not prohibited by § 8(b)(4)(ii)(B). The majority of the Board concluded that use of the warehouse was an integrated step in the primary employer's production process. The Court of Appeals for the Fifth Circuit overruled the Board's decision. The Court stressed the fact that Cypress was limited by contract to occupy no more than ten percent of the warehouse. The Court was concerned that the operations of the nineteen other neutral employers would be interrupted. Indeed this decision demonstrates that while *Moore Dry Dock* continues to be good law, its criteria will be applied flexibly on a case to case basis so as to balance the interest of the employees' right to strike with the congressional intent to protect neutral employers.

In the *Carrier* decision presented in this section, the Supreme Court relied on the precedent of *General Electric*[9] in clarifying its "reserved gate" doctrine. A reserved gate is an entrance to an employer's premises which is used only by employees of neutral employers. The object of any picketing activity at such a gate would clearly be to pressure neutral employees to join in the union action against the primary employer. Such conduct falls within the literal language of § 8(b)(4)(ii)(B) and would thus appear to be unlawful. However, under *General Electric* and *Carrier*, picketing of neutral contractors at the site of the primary employer's plant is permissible when the neutral employer's work is related to the normal operations of the struck employer's plant.

United Steelworkers of America v. NLRB & Carrier Corp.

Supreme Court of the United States, 1964. 376 U.S. 492

WHITE, J.: The question presented by this case is whether a union violates § 8(b)(4) of the National Labor Relations Act by picketing an entrance, used exclusively by railroad personnel, to a railroad spur track located on a right-of-way owned by the railroad and adjacent to the struck employer's premises.

On March 2, 1960, after the petitioning union and the respondent company, Carrier Corporation, failed to agree upon a collective bargaining contract the union, which was the certified bargaining agent, called a strike in support of its demands. During the course of the strike the union picketed the several entrances to the plant. Along the south boundary of Carrier's property was a 35-foot railroad right-of-way used by the railroad for deliveries to Carrier and to three other companies in the area, General Electric, Western Electric, and Brace-Mueller-Huntley. The railroad spur ran across Thompson Road, a public thoroughfare which bounded Carrier's property on the west, and through a gate in a continuous chain-link fence which enclosed both the property of Carrier Corporation and the railroad right-of-way. The gate was locked when the spur was not in use and was accessible only to rail-

---

[9] *Electrical Workers* v. *NLRB (General Electric)*, 366 U.S. 667 (1961).

road employees. The picketing with which we are concerned occurred at this gate.

Between March 2 and March 10, railroad personnel made several trips through the gate for the purpose of switching out cars for General Electric, Western Electric, and Brace-Mueller-Huntley, and also to supply coal to Carrier and General Electric. On March 11 a switch engine manned by a regular switching crew made one trip serving the three nonstruck corporations. It then returned, this time manned by supervisory personnel, with 14 empty boxcars. The pickets, being aware that these cars were destined for use by Carrier, milled around the engine from the time it reached the western side of Thompson Road, attempting to impede its progress. By inching its way across the road, however, the locomotive succeeded in reaching and entering the gate. After uncoupling the empties just inside the railroad right-of-way, for future use by Carrier, the engine picked up 16 more cars which Carrier wanted shipped out and made its way back toward the gate. This time resistance from the picketing strikers was more intense. Some of the men stood on the footboard of the engine, others prostrated themselves across the rails and one union official parked his car on the track. Invective and threats were directed toward the operators of the train, and only after the pickets were dispersed by deputies from the Onandaga County sheriff's office was it able to pass. . . .

The activities of the union in this case clearly fall within clauses (i) and (ii) of § 8(b)(4); likewise the objective, to induce the railroad to cease providing freight service to Carrier for the duration of the strike, is covered by the language of subsection (B), exclusive of the proviso. The question we have is whether the activities of the union, although literally within the definition of secondary activities contained in clauses (i) and (ii) of § 8(b)(4), are nevertheless within the protected area of primary picketing carved out by Congress in the proviso to subsection (B).

The dividing line between forbidden secondary activity and protected primary activity has been the subject of intense litigation both before and after the 1959 amendments to § 8(b)(4), which broadened the coverage of the section but also added the express exceptions for the primary strike and primary picketing. We need not detail the course of this sometimes confusing litigation; for in the *General Electric* case, 366 U.S. 667, the Court undertook to survey the cases dealing with picketing at both primary and secondary sites and the result reached in that case largely governs this one. In the *General Electric* case, because the union's object was to enmesh "employees of the neutral employers in its dispute" with the primary employer, the Board ordered the union to cease picketing a separate gate used exclusively by employees of certain independent contractors who had been doing work on the primary premises on a regular and continuous basis for a considerable period of time. 123 NLRB 1547. In this Court, the Board conceded that when the struck premises are occupied by the primary employer alone, the right of the union to engage in primary activity at or in connection with the primary premises may be given unlimited effect—"all union attempts, by picketing and allied means to cut off deliveries, pickups, and employment at the primary employer's plant will be regarded as primary and outside the purview of § 8(b)

(4)(A)." But, the Board insisted that the facts presented a common situs problem since the regular work of the contractors was continuously done on the primary premises and hence the rules of the *Moore Dry Dock* case should be applied. The union, on the other hand, argued that no picketing at the primary premises should be considered as secondary activity.

The Court accepted the approach neither of the Board nor of the Union. The location of the picketing, though important, was not deemed of decisive significance; picketing was not to be protected simply because it occurred at the site of the primary employer's plant. Neither, however, was all picketing forbidden where occurring at gates not used by primary employees. The legality of separate gate picketing depended upon the type of work being done by the employees who used that gate; if the duties of those employees were connected with the normal operations of the employer, picketing directed at them was protected primary activity, but if their work was unrelated to the day-to-day operation of the employer's plant, the picketing was an unfair labor practice. The order of the NLRB was vacated to permit determination of the case in accordance with the proper test.

It seems clear that the rejection of the Board's position in *General Electric* leaves no room for the even narrower approach of the Court of Appeals in this case, which is that the picketing at the site of a strike could be directed at secondary employees only where incidental to appeals to primary employees. Under this test, no picketing at gates used only by employees of delivery men would be permitted, a result expressly disapproved by the Court in *General Electric:* "On the other hand, if a separate gate were devised for regular plant deliveries, the barring of picketing at that location would make a clear invasion on traditional primary activity of appealing to neutral employees whose tasks aid the employer's everyday operations." 366 U.S. at 680–681.

Although the picketing in the *General Electric* case occurred prior to the 1959 amendments to § 8(b)(4), the decision was rendered in 1961 and the Court bottomed its decision upon the amended law and its legislative history. We think *General Electric's* construction of the proviso to § 8(b)(4)(B) is sound and we will not disturb it. The primary strike, which is protected by the proviso, is aimed at applying economic pressure by halting the day-to-day operations of the struck employer. But Congress not only preserved the right to strike; it also saved "primary picketing" from the secondary ban. Picketing has traditionally been a major weapon to implement the goals of a strike and has characteristically been aimed at all those approaching the situs whose mission is selling, delivering or otherwise contributing to the operations which the strike is endeavoring to halt. In light of this traditional goal of primary pressures we think Congress intended to preserve the right to picket during a strike a gate reserved for employees of neutral deliverymen furnishing day-to-day service essential to the plant's regular operations.

Nor may the *General Electric* case be put aside for the reason that the picketed gate in the present case was located on property owned by New York Central Railroad and not upon property owned by the primary employer. The location of the picketing is an important but not decisive factor. . . . The railroad gate adjoined company property and was in fact the railroad entrance gate to the Carrier plant. For the purposes of § 8(b)(4) picketing at a situs so proximate and related to the employer's day-to-day operations is no more illegal than if it has occurred at a gate owned by Carrier. . . .

Reversed.

Mr. Justice DOUGLAS concurs in the result.

Mr. Justice GOLDBERG took no part in the consideration or decision of this case.

CASE   1. What are the significant facts?
QUESTIONS   2. What statutory wording applies?

SECTION 72 / SECONDARY BOYCOTTS: PRODUCT PICKETING

The "publicity proviso" to 8(b)(4) states that:

". . . nothing contained in such paragraph shall be construed to prohibit publicity, other than picketing, for the purpose of truthfully advising the public, including consumers and members of a labor organization, that a product or products are produced by an employer with whom the labor organization has a primary dispute and are distributed by another employer, as long as such publicity does not have an effect of inducing any individual employed by any person other than the primary employer in the course of his employment to refuse to pick up, deliver, or transport any goods, or not to perform any services, at the establishment of the employer engaged in such distribution . . ."

A union thus has the right to publicize a dispute with a primary employer at retail establishments that sell the goods of the primary employer. Truthful handbilling, billboards, newspaper advertisements and radio and television messages are all clearly protected. Despite the "other than picketing" language of the "publicity proviso," the Supreme Court held in the *Tree Fruits* decision that consumer picketing limited to asking customers not to purchase the struck product at the neutral employer's store is legal. If the purpose of the picketing is to cut off all trade with the neutral employer, it is then an 8(b)(4)(ii)(B) violation. The *Tree Fruits* decision is presented in this section.

In the *Honolulu Typographical Union* case, the union, for support of its strike against a newspaper, picketed at a shopping center with signs requesting shoppers not to buy products advertised in the struck newspaper. Single picket signs named each of four restaurants that regularly advertised in the newspaper. The Court of Appeals held that such picketing was an unlawful secondary boycott and outside the protection of the *Tree Fruits* limited product boycott. The court found that the "products," advertising, had become an integral part of the restaurant owners' entire offerings, so that the product boycott will of necessity encompass the entire business of the secondary employers which is contrary to *Tree Fruits*.

In *NLRB* v. *Servette, Inc.,*[10] union representatives contacted managers of supermarkets, advised them that they were engaged in a strike against Servette, and requested that they discontinue handling merchandise supplied by Servette. The union representatives also warned that handbills asking the public not to buy Servette products would be passed out in front of those stores that refused to cooperate. The Supreme Court held that such conduct was lawful. The court found that warnings which threatened distribution of handbills were not "threats" within the meaning of 8(b)(4)(ii), reasoning that the statutory protection for the distribution of handbills would be undermined if a threat to engage in protected conduct were not itself protected.

National Labor Relations Board v. Fruit and Vegetable Packers and Warehousemen, Local 760 (Tree Fruits Inc.)

Supreme Court of the United States, 1964. 377 U.S. 58

BRENNAN, J. Under § 8(b)(4)(ii)(B) of the National Labor Relations Act, as amended, it is an unfair labor practice for a union "to threaten, coerce, or restrain any person," with the object of "forcing or requiring any person to cease using, selling, handling, transporting, or otherwise dealing in the products of any other producer . . . or to cease doing business with any other person . . . ." A proviso excepts, however, "publicity, *other than picketing,* for the purpose of truthfully advising the public . . . that a product or products are produced by an employer with whom the labor organization has a primary dispute and are distributed by another employer, as long as such publicity does not have an effect of inducing any individual employed by any person other than the primary employer in the course of his employment to refuse to pick up, deliver, or transport any goods, or not to perform any services, at the establishment of the employer engaged in such distribution." (Italics supplied.) The question in this case is whether the respondent unions violated this section when they limited their secondary picketing of retail stores to an appeal to the customers of the stores not to buy the products of certain firms against which one of the respondents was on strike.

Respondent Local 760 called a strike against fruit packers and warehousemen doing business in Yakima, Washington. The struck firms sold Washington State apples to the Safeway chain of retail stores in and about Seattle, Washington. Local 760, aided by respondent Joint Council, instituted a consumer boycott against the apples in support of the strike. They placed pickets who walked back and forth before the customers' entrances of 46 Safeway stores in Seattle. The pickets—two at each of 45 stores and three at the 46th store—wore placards and distributed handbills which appealed to Safeway customers, and to the public generally, to refrain from buying Washington

---

[10] 377 U.S. 46 (1964).

State apples, which were only one of numerous food products sold in the stores. Before the pickets appeared at any store, a letter was delivered to the store manager informing him that the picketing was only an appeal to his customers not to buy Washington State apples, and that the pickets were being expressly instructed "to patrol peacefully in front of the customer entrances of the store, to stay away from the delivery entrances and not to interfere with the work of your employees, or with deliveries to or pickups from your store." A copy of written instructions to the pickets—which included the explicit statement that "you are also forbidden to request that the customers not patronize the store"—was enclosed with the letter. Since it was desired to assure Safeway employees that they were not to cease work, and to avoid any interference with pickups or deliveries, the pickets appeared after the stores opened for business and departed before the stores closed. At all times during the picketing, the store employees continued to work, and no deliveries or pickups were obstructed. Washington State apples were handled in normal course by both Safeway employees and the employees of other employers involved. Ingress and egress by customers and others was not interfered with in any manner.

A complaint issued on charges that this conduct violated § 8(b)(4) as amended. The case was submitted directly to the National Labor Relations Board on a stipulation of facts and the waiver of a hearing and proceedings before a Trial Examiner. The Board held, following its construction of the statute in *Upholsterers Frame & Bedding Workers Twin City Local No. 61,* 132 NLRB 40, that "by literal wording of the proviso [to § 8(b)(4)] as well as through the interpretative gloss placed thereon by its drafters, consumer picketing in front of a secondary establishment is prohibited." 132 NLRB 1172, 1176. Upon respondents' petition for review and the Board's cross-petition for enforcement, the Court of Appeals for the District of Columbia Circuit set aside the Board's order and remanded. The court rejected the Board's construction and held that the statutory requirement of a showing that respondents' conduct would "threaten, coerce, or restrain" Safeway could only be satisfied by affirmative proof that a substantial economic impact on Safeway had occurred, or was likely to occur as a result of the conduct. Under the remand the Board was left "free to reopen the record to receive evidence upon the issue whether Safeway was in fact threatened, coerced, or restrained." 113 U.S. App. D. C. 356, 357, 308 F.2d 311, 318. We granted certiorari, 374 U.S. 804.

The Board's reading of the statute—that the legislative history and the phrase "other than picketing" in the proviso reveal a congressional purpose to outlaw all picketing directed at customers at a secondary site—necessarily rested on the finding that Congress determined that such picketing always threatens, coerces, or restrains the secondary employer. We therefore have a special responsibility to examine the legislative history for confirmation that Congress made that determination. Throughout the history of federal regulation of labor relations, Congress has consistently refused to prohibit peaceful picketing except where it is used as a means to achieve specific ends which experience has shown are undesirable. "In the sensitive area of peaceful picketing Congress has dealt explicitly with isolated evils which experience has established flow from such picketing." *Labor Board* v. *Drivers Local Union,* 362 U.S. 274, 284. We have recognized this congressional practice and have not ascribed to Congress a purpose to outlaw peaceful picketing unless "there is the clearest indication in the legislative history," *ibid.,* that Congress intended to do so as regards the particular ends of the picketing under review. Both the congressional policy and our adherence to this principle of interpretation reflect concern that a broad ban against peaceful picketing might collide with the guarantees of the First Amendment.

We have examined the legislative history of the amendments to § 8(b)(4), and conclude that it does not reflect with the requisite clarity a congressional plan to proscribe all peaceful consumer picketing at secondary sites, and, particularly, any concern with peaceful picketing when it is limited, as here, to persuading Safeway customers not to buy Washington State apples when they traded in the Safeway stores. All that the legislative history shows in the way of an "isolated evil" believed to require proscription of peaceful consumer picketing at secondary sites, was its use to persuade the customers of the secondary employer to cease trading with him in order to force him to cease dealing with, or to put pressure upon, the primary employer. This narrow focus reflects the difference between such conduct and peaceful picketing at the secondary site directed only at the struck product. In the latter case, the union's appeal to the public is confined to its dispute with the primary employer, since the public is not asked to withhold its patronage from the secondary employer, but only to boycott the primary employer's goods. On the other hand, a union appeal to the public at the secondary site not to trade at all with the secondary employer goes beyond the goods of the primary employer, and seeks the public's assistance in forcing the secondary employer to cooperate with the union in its primary dispute. This is not to say that this distinction was expressly alluded to in the debates. It is to say, however, that the consumer picketing carried on in this case is not attended by the abuses at which the statute was directed.

The story of the 1959 amendments, which we have detailed at greater length in our opinion filed today in *Labor Board* v. *Servette, Inc.,* begins with the original § 8(b)(4) of the National Labor Relations Act. Its prohibition, in pertinent part, was confined to the inducing or encouraging of "the employees of any employer to engage in a strike or a concerted refusal . . . to . . . handle . . . any goods . . ." of a primary employer. This proved to be inept language. Three major loopholes were revealed. Since only inducement of "employees" was proscribed, direct inducement of a supervisor or the secondary employer by threats of labor trouble was not prohibited. Since only a "strike or a concerted refusal" was prohibited, pressure upon a single employee was not forbidden. Finally, railroads, airlines, and municipalities were not "employers" under the Act and therefore inducement or encouragement of their employees was not unlawful. . . .

Senator Kennedy presided over the Conference Committee. He and Congressman Thompson prepared a joint analysis of the Senate and House bills. This analysis pointed up the First Amendment implications of the broad language in the House revisions of § 8(b)(4) stating,

"This prohibition [of the House bill] reaches not only picketing but leaflets, radio broadcasts and newspaper advertisements, thereby interfering with freedom of speech.

". . . one of the apparent purposes of the amendment is to prevent unions from appealing to the general public as consumers for assistance in a labor dispute. This is a basic infringement upon freedom of expression."

This analysis was the first step in the development of the publicity proviso, but nothing in the legislative history of the proviso alters our conclusion that Congress did not clearly express an intention that amended § 8(b)(4) should prohibit all consumer picketing. Because of the sweeping language of the House bill, and its implications for freedom of speech, the Senate conferees refused to accede to the House proposal without safeguards for the right of unions to appeal to the public, even by some conduct which might be "coercive." The result was the addition of the proviso. But it does not follow from the fact that same coercive conduct was protected by the proviso, that the exception "other than picketing" indicates that Congress had determined that all consumer picketing was coercive.

No Conference Report was before the Senate when it passed the compromise bill, and it had the benefit only of Senator Kennedy's statement of the purpose of the proviso. He said the proviso preserved "the right to appeal to consumers by methods other than picketing asking them to refrain from buying goods made by nonunion labor *and* to refrain from trading with a retailer who sells such goods. . . . We were not able to persuade the House conferees to permit picketing in front of that secondary shop, but were able to persuade them to agree that the union shall be free to conduct informational activity short of picketing. In other words, the union can hand out handbills at the shop . . . and can carry on all publicity short of having ambulatory picketing. . . ." (Italics supplied.) This explanation does not compel the conclusion that the Conference Agreement contemplated prohibiting any consumer picketing at a secondary site beyond that which urges the public, in Senator Kennedy's words, to "refrain from trading with a retailer who sells such goods." To read into the Conference Agreement, on the basis of a single statement, an intention to prohibit all consumer picketing at a secondary site would depart from our practice of respecting the congressional policy not to prohibit peaceful picketing except to curb "isolated evils" spelled out by the Congress itself.

Peaceful consumer picketing to shut off all trade with the secondary employer unless he aids the union in its dispute with the primary employer, is poles apart from such picketing which only persuades his customers not to buy the struck product. The proviso indicates no more than the Senate conferees' constitutional doubts led Congress to authorize publicity other than picketing which persuades the customers of a secondary employer to stop all trading with him, but not such publicity which has the effect of cutting off his deliveries or inducing his employees to cease work. On the other hand, picketing which persuades the customers of a secondary employer to stop all trading with him was also to be barred.

In sum, the legislative history does not support the Board's finding that Congress meant to prohibit all consumer picketing at a secondary site, having determined that such picketing necessarily threatened, coerced, or restrained the secondary employer. Rather, the history shows that Congress was following its usual practice of legislating against peaceful picketing only to curb "isolated evils."

This distinction is opposed as "unrealistic" because, it is urged, all picketing automatically provokes the public to stay away from the picketed establishment. The public will, it is said, neither read the signs and handbills, nor note the explicit injunction that "This is not a strike against any store or market." Be that as it may, our holding today simply takes note of the fact that a broad condemnation of peaceful picketing, such as that urged upon us by petitioners, has never been adopted by Congress, and an intention to do so is not revealed with that "clearest indication in the legislative history," which we require. *Labor Board* v. *Drivers Local Union, supra.*

We come then to the question whether the picketing in this case, confined as it was to persuading customers to cease buying the product of the primary employer, falls within the area of secondary consumer picketing which Congress did clearly indicate its intention to prohibit under § 8(b)(4)(ii). We hold that it did not fall within that area, and therefore did not "threaten, coerce, or restrain" Safeway. While any diminution in Safeway's purchases of apples due to a drop in consumer demand might be said to be a result which causes respondents' picketing to fall literally within the statutory prohibition, "it is a familiar rule, that a thing may be within the letter of the statute and yet not within the statute, because not within its spirit, nor within the intention of its makers." *Holy Trinity Church* v. *United States,* 143 U.S. 457, 459. See *United States* v. *American Trucking Assn.,* 310 U.S. 534, 543–544. When consumer picketing is employed only to persuade customers not to buy the struck product, the union's appeal is closely confined to the primary dispute. The site of the appeal is expanded to include the premises of the secondary employer, but if the appeal succeeds, the secondary employers' purchases from the struck firm are decreased only because the public has diminished its purchases of the struck product. On the other hand, when consumer picketing is employed to persuade customers not to trade at all with the secondary employer, the latter stops buying the struck product, not because of a falling demand, but in response to pressure designed to inflict injury on his business generally. In such case, the union does more than merely follow the struck product; it creates a separate dispute with the secondary employer.

We disagree therefore with the Court of Appeals that the test of "to threaten, coerce, or restrain" for the purposes of this case is whether Safeway suffered or was likely to suffer economic loss. A violation of § 8(b)(4)(ii)(B) would not be established, merely because respondents' picketing was effective to reduce Safeway's sales of Washington State apples, even if this led or might lead Safeway to drop the item as a poor seller.

The judgment of the Court of Appeals is vacated and the case is remanded with direction to enter judgment setting aside the Board's order.

It is so ordered.

1. What was the union conduct complained of by Safeway Stores?
2. On what grounds did the NLRB prohibit the picketing?
3. How does the Supreme Court view the legality of this boycott?
4. Is its reversal based on law or on judgment of facts?
5. What is the legal attitude today toward secondary activity from the Court's judgment?

SECTION 73 / SECONDARY BOYCOTTS: "CEASING TO DO BUSINESS" OBJECTIVE

In *NLRB* v. *Local 825, Operating Engineers (Burns and Roe)*, which is reported below, the Supreme Court considered the question of whether union pressure upon neutral employers, with the object of forcing a change in a work assignment by the primary employer, amounted to coercion to "cease doing business" with the primary employer under Section 8(b)(4)(B).

NLRB v. Local 825, Operating Engineers (Burns and Roe)

Supreme Court of the United States, 1971. 400 U.S. 297

MARSHALL, J.: In this case we are asked to determine whether strikes by Operating Engineers at the site of the construction of a nuclear power generator plant at Oyster Creek, New Jersey, violated § 8(b)(4)(B) of the National Labor Relations Act. Although the National Labor Relations Board found the strikes to be in violation of this section, the Court of Appeals refused to enforce the Board's order. We believe the Court of Appeals construed the Act too narrowly. Accordingly, we reverse and remand the case for consideration of the propriety of the Board's order.

The general contractor for the project, Burns and Roe, Inc., subcontracted all of the construction work to three companies—White Construction Company, Chicago Bridge and Iron Company, and Poirier and McClane Corporation. All three employed operating engineers who were members of Local 825, International Union of Operating Engineers. But White, unlike Chicago Bridge and Poirier, did not have a collective-bargaining agreement with Local 825.

In the latter part of September 1965, White installed an electric welding machine and assigned the job of pushing the buttons that operated the machine to members of the Ironworkers Union, who were to perform the actual welding. Upon learning of this work assignment, Local 825's job steward and its lead engineer threatened White with a strike if operating engineers were not given the work. White, however, refused to meet the demand. On September 29, 1965, the job steward and lead engineer met with the construction manager for Burns, the general contractor. They informed him that the members of

Local 825 working at the jobsite had voted to strike unless Burns signed a contract, which would be binding on all three subcontractors as well as Burns, giving Local 825 jurisdiction over all power equipment, including electric welding machines, operated on the jobsite. On October 1, after White and Burns refused to accede to the demands, the operating engineers employed by Chicago Bridge and Poirier as well as those employed by White walked off the job. They stayed out from 8:00 a.m. to 1:00 p.m., returning to work when negotiations over their demands started.

On October 6, Burns submitted the work assignment dispute to the National Joint Board for the Settlement of Jurisdictional Disputes for the Construction Industry. The same day, Local 825 threatened Burns and all the subcontractors with another work stoppage unless the contracts were signed and the work transferred to the operating engineers. The employers again refused, and the operating engineers walked off the project. This strike lasted from October 7 to October 11.

On October 20, the Joint Board notified the parties that there was no reason to change the assignment of the disputed work. Local 825 did not accept this resolution; and when the welding machine was started on November 4, the operating engineers surrounded the machine and physically prevented its operation. On November 8, the NLRB Regional Director obtained from the United States District Court a temporary injunction under § 10(1) of the Act restraining the union from coercing a cessation of business on the project or to compel White to change the work assignment.

An unfair labor practice proceeding against Local 825 subsequently ensued. The Board found that the union had violated § 8(b)(4)(D) of the Act by inducing employees of White, Chicago Bridge, and Poirier to strike to force White to take the disputed work away from the Ironworkers and assign it to the Operating Engineers. The Court of Appeals' approval of this finding is not questioned here. But the Board's finding that Local 825's encouragement of the Chicago Bridge and Poirier employees to strike and the union's coercion of Burns violated § 8(b)(4)(B) of the Act was not approved by the Court of Appeals and is in issue here.

I. Congressional concern over the involvement of third parties in labor disputes not their own prompted § 8(b)(4)(B). This concern was focused on "secondary boycotts," which was conceived of as pressure brought to bear not "upon the employer who is a party [to a dispute] but upon some third party who has no concern in it" with the objective of forcing the third party to bring pressure on the employer to agree to the union's demands.

Section 8(b)(4)(B) is, however, the product of legislative compromise and also reflects a concern with protecting labor organizations' right to exert legitimate pressure aimed at the employer with whom there is a primary dispute. This primary activity is protected even though it may seriously affect neutral third parties. *Steelworkers (Carrier Corp.)* v. *NLRB* 376 U.S. 492, 502 (1964); *Electrical Workers (General Electric)* v. *NLRB,* 366 U.S. 667, 673 (1961).

Thus there are two threads to § 8(b)(4)(B) that require disputed conduct to be classified as either "primary" or "secondary." And the tapestry that has been woven in classifying such conduct is among the labor law's most intricate.

See *Brotherhood of Railroad Trainmen* v. *Jacksonville Terminal Co.,* 394 U.S. 369 (1969). But here the normally difficult task of classifying union conduct is easy. As the Court of Appeals said, the "record amply justifies the conclusion that [Burns and the neutral subcontractors] were subjected to coercion in the form of threats or walkouts, or both." 410 F.2d, at 9. And as the Board said, it is clear that this coercion was designed "to achieve the assignment of [the] disputed work" to operating engineers. 162 NLRB, at 1621.

Local 825's coercive activity was aimed directly at Burns and the subcontractors that were not involved in the dispute. The union engaged in a strike against these neutral employers for the specific, overt purpose of forcing them to put pressure on White to assign the job of operating the welding machine to operating engineers. Local 825 was not attempting to apply the full force of primary action by directing its efforts at all phases of Burns' normal operation as was the case in *Steelworkers (Carrier)* v. *NLRB,* 376 U.S. 492 (1964), and *Electrical Workers (General Electric)* v. *NLRB,* 366 U.S. 677 (1961). It was instead using a sort of pressure that was unmistakably and flagrantly secondary. *Labor Board* v. *Denver Building & Construction Trade Council,* 341 U.S. 675 (1951).

The more difficult task is to determine whether one of Local 825's objectives was to force Burns and the other neutrals to "cease doing business" with White as § 8(b)(4)(B) requires. The Court of Appeals concluded that the union's objective was to force Burns "to use its influence with the subcontractor to change the subcontractor's conduct, not to terminate their relationship" and that this was not enough. That court read the statute as requiring that the union demand nothing short of a complete termination of the business relationship between the neutral and the primary employer. Such a reading is too narrow.

Some disruption of business relationships is the necessary consequence of the purest form of primary activity. These foreseeable disruptions are, however, clearly protected. *Steelworkers (Carrier),* 376 U.S., at 492; *Electrical Workers (General Electric),* 366 U.S., at 682. Likewise, secondary activity could have such a limited goal and the foreseeable result of the conduct could be, while disruptive, so slight that the "cease doing business" requirement is not met.

Local 825's goal was not so limited nor were the foreseeable consequences of its secondary pressure slight. The operating engineers sought to force Burns to bind all the subcontractors on the project to a particular form of job assignments. The clear implication of the demands was that Burns would be required either to force a change in White's policy or to terminate White's contract. The strikes shut down the whole project. If Burns was unable to obtain White's consent, Local 825 was apparently willing to continue disruptive conduct that would bring all the employers to their knees.

Certainly, the union would have preferred to have the employers capitulate to its demands; it wanted to take the job of operating the welding machines away from the Ironworkers. It was willing, however, to try to obtain this capitulation by forcing neutrals to compel White to meet union demands. To hold that this flagrant secondary conduct with these most serious disruptive effects was not prohibited by § 8(b)(4)(B) would be largely to ignore the original congressional concern. *NLRB* v. *Carpenters Dist. Council,* 407 F.2d 804, 806 (CA5 1969).

II. In addition to its argument that § 8(b)(4)(B) does not cover its conduct, Local 825 argues that § 8(b)(4)(D) provides the exclusive remedy. Clearly, § 8(b)(4)(D) is, as the Board and Court of Appeals held, applicable. But that section is aimed at protecting "the employer trapped between the . . . claims" of rival unions. *National Woodwork Mfgrs. Assn.,* 386 U.S., at 625. Although § 8(b)(4)(D) also applies to neutrals, the basic purpose is different from that of § 8(b)(4)(B). The practices here were unfair under both sections and there is no indication that Congress intended either section to have exclusive application.

III. Since the Court of Appeals did not believe that § 8(b)(4)(B) was applicable, it did not consider the propriety of the portion of Board's order relating to that section. But the order was not narrowly confined to the conduct involved here; so we must remand this case for the Court of Appeals to consider whether the order is necessary to further the goals of the Act. See *Communications Workers* v. *NLRB,* 362 U.S. 479 (1960); *NLRB* v. *Express Publishing Co.,* 312 U.S. 426 (1941).

Reversed and remanded.

MR. JUSTICE DOUGLAS, with whom MR. JUSTICE STEWART concurs, dissented.

CASE	1. Explain the secondary nature of Local 825's conduct.
QUESTIONS	2. Who were the "neutral" employers in this case?
	3. Must a union make an overt demand on a neutral employer that a subcontractor be terminated in order to find a "cessation of business" objective?
	4. Does § 8(b)(4)(D) provide the exclusive remedy for disputes involving strikes to force assignment of work?

SECTION 74 / **HOT CARGO AGREEMENTS**

After Section 8(b)(4) was enacted to make illegal secondary economic activity for the purpose of compelling one employer to cease doing any business with another person, the problem of contracts providing for such results remained. In 1959 Section 8(e), the so-called "hot cargo" section of the Act, was added. This section prohibits collective bargaining agreements whereby members of the contracting bargaining unit need not handle nonunion or struck goods of other employers.

Explicit exceptions to the prohibitions of § 8(e) were made for two industries, garment manufacturing and building construction, where subcontracting commonly is practiced under the contractual requirements that only unionized shops will be used.

The construction industry proviso to § 8(e) has been interpreted to allow unions in this industry to use economic pressures to secure "hot cargo" subcontracting clauses limited to work to be done at the site of the construction. The

Board and the courts however have held that it is not legal for unions to use any economic pressure to enforce such clauses.[11] The union's only recourse is to bring a § 301 lawsuit. A union may use economic pressure however to enforce a "work preservation" clause as will be seen in the *National Woodwork* decision presented below.

Garment industry unions were treated more favorably by Congress than construction industry unions and may use economic pressure to obtain and enforce hot cargo clauses in their collective bargaining agreements.

National Woodwork Manufacturers Association v. NLRB

Supreme Court of the United States, 1967. 386 U.S. 612

BRENNAN, J.: Under the Landrum-Griffin Act amendments enacted in 1959, § 8(b)(4)(A) of the National Labor Relations Act became § 8(b)(4)(B) and § 8(e) was added. The questions here are whether, in the circumstances of this case, the Metropolitan District Council of Philadelphia and Vicinity of the United Brotherhood of Carpenters and Joiners of America, AFL-CIO (hereafter the Union), committed the unfair labor practices prohibited by §§ 8(e) and 8(b)(4)(B).

Frouge Corporation, a Bridgeport, Connecticut, concern, was the general contractor on a housing project in Philadelphia. Frouge had a collective bargaining agreement with the Carpenters' International Union under which Frouge agreed to be bound by the rules and regulations agreed upon by local unions with contractors in areas in which Frouge had jobs. Frouge was therefore subject to the provisions of a collective bargaining agreement between the Union and an organization of Philadelphia contractors, the General Building Contractors Association, Inc. A sentence in a provision of that agreement entitled Rule 17 provides that ". . . No member of this District Council will handle . . . any doors . . . which have been fitted prior to being furnished on the job . . . ." Frouge's Philadelphia project called for 3,600 doors. Customarily, before the doors could be hung on such projects, "blank" or "blind" doors would be mortised for the knob, routed for the hinges, and beveled to make them fit between jambs. These are tasks traditionally performed in the Philadelphia area by the carpenters employed on the jobsite. However, precut and prefitted doors ready to hang may be purchased from door manufacturers. Although Frouge's contract and job specifications did not call for premachined doors, and "blank" or "blind" doors could have been ordered, Frouge contracted for the purchase of premachined doors from a Pennsylvania door manufacturer which is a member of the National Woodwork Manufacturers Association, petitioner in No. 110 and respondent in No. 111. The Union ordered its carpenter members not to hang the doors when they arrived at the jobsite. Frouge thereupon withdrew the prefabricated doors and substituted "blank" doors which were fitted and cut by its carpenters on the jobsite.

The National Woodwork Manufacturers Association and another filed

---

[11] See *NLRB* v. *IBEW, Local 769,* 405 F.2d 159 (CA 9, 1968).

charges with the National Labor Relations Board against the Union alleging that by including the "will not handle" sentence of Rule 17 in the collective bargaining agreement the Union committed the unfair labor practice under § 8(e) of entering into an "agreement . . . whereby the employer . . . agrees to cease or refrain from handling . . . any of the products of any other employer . . . ," and alleging further that in enforcing the sentence against Frouge, the Union committed the unfair labor practice under § 8(b)(4)(B) of "forcing or requiring any person to cease using . . . the products of any other . . . manufacturer. . . ." The National Labor Relations Board dismissed the charges, 149 NLRB 646. The Board adopted the findings of the Trial Examiner that the "will not handle" sentence in Rule 17 was language used by the parties to protect and preserve cutting out and fitting as unit work to be performed by the jobsite carpenters. The Board also adopted the holding of the Trial Examiner that both the sentence of Rule 17 itself and its maintenance against Frouge were therefore "primary" activity outside the prohibitions of §§ 8(c) and 8(b)(4)(B). The following statement of the Trial Examiner was adopted by the Board:

> "I am convinced and find that the tasks of cutting out and fitting millwork, including doors, has, at least customarily, been performed by the carpenters employed on the jobsite. Certainly, this provision of Rule 17 is not concerned with the nature of the employer with whom the contractor does business nor with the employment conditions of other employers or employees, nor does it attempt to control such other employers or employees. The provision guards against encroachments on the cutting out and fitting work of the contract unit employees who have performed that work in the past. Its purpose is plainly to regulate the relations between the general contractor and his own employees and to protect a legitimate economic interest of the employees by preserving their unit work. Merely because it incidentally also affects other parties is no basis for invalidating this provision.
>
> "I find that . . . (the provision) is a lawful work-protection or work-preservation provision and that Respondents have not violated Section 8(e) of the Act by entering into agreements containing this provision and by thereafter maintaining and enforcing this provision." 149 NLRB, at 657.

The Court of Appeals for the Seventh Circuit reversed the Board in this respect. . . . The court held that the "will not handle" agreement violated § 8(e) without regard to any "primary" or "secondary" objective, and remanded to the Board with instructions to enter an order accordingly. In the court's view, the sentence was designed to effect a product boycott like the one condemned in *Allen Bradley Co.* v. *Local Union No. 3,* 325 U.S. 797, and Congress meant, in enacting § 8(c) and § 8(b)(4)(B), to prohibit such agreements and conduct forcing employers to enter into them.

The Court of Appeals sustained, however, the dismissal of the § 8(b)(4)(B) charge. The court agreed with the Board that the Union's conduct as to Frouge involved only a primary dispute with it and held that the conduct was therefore not prohibited by that section but expressly protected by the proviso "[t]hat nothing contained in this clause (B) shall be construed to make unlawful, where not otherwise unlawful, any primary strike or primary picketing . . . ." *Id.,* at 597.

I. Even on the doubtful premise that the words of § 8(e) unambiguously embrace the sentence of Rule 17, this does not end inquiry into Congress' purpose in enacting the section. It is a "familiar rule, that a thing may be within the letter of the statute and yet not within the statute, because not within its spirit, nor within the intention of its makers." *Holy Trinity Church v. United States,* 143 U.S. 457, 459. That principle has particular application in the construction of labor legislation which is "to a marked degree, the result of conflict and compromise between strong contending forces and deeply held views on the role of organized labor in the free economic life of the Nation and the appropriate balance to be struck between the uncontrolled power of management and labor to further their respective interests." *Carpenters* v. *Labor Board (Sand Door),* 357 U.S. 93, 99–100. . . .

Strongly held opposing views have invariably marked controversy over labor's use of the boycott to further its aims by involving an employer in disputes not his own. But congressional action to deal with such conduct has stopped short of proscribing identical activity having the object of pressuring the employer for agreements regulating relations between him and his own employees. That Congress meant §§ 8(e) and 8(b)(4)(B) to prohibit only "secondary" objectives clearly appears from an examination of the history of congressional action on the subject. . . .

Despite . . . virtually overwhelming support for the limited reading of § 8(b)(4)(A), the Woodwork Manufacturers Association relies on *Allen Bradley Co.* v. *Local 3, Electrical Workers,* 325 U.S. 797, as requiring that the successor section, § 8(b)(4)(B), be read as proscribing the District Council's conduct in enforcing the "will not handle" sentence of Rule 17 against Frouge. The Association points to the references to *Allen Bradley* in the legislative debates leading to the enactment of the predecessor § 8(b)(4)(A). We think that this is an erroneous reading of the legislative history. *Allen Bradley* held violative of the antitrust laws a combination between Local 3 of the International Brotherhood of Electrical Workers and both electrical contractors and manufacturers of electrical fixtures in New York City to restrain the bringing in of such equipment from outside the city. The contractors obligated themselves to confine their purchases to local manufacturers, who in turn obligated themselve to confine their New York City sales to contractors employing members of the local, this scheme supported by threat of boycott by the contractors' employees. While recognizing that the union might have had an immunity for its contribution to the trade boycott had it acted alone, citing *Hutcheson,* 321 U.S. 219, the Court held immunity was not intended by the Clayton or Norris-LaGuardia Acts in cases in which the union's activity was part of a larger conspiracy to abet contractors and manufacturers to create a monopoly. . . .

. . . [E]ven on the premise that Congress meant to prohibit boycotts such as that in *Allen Bradley* without regard to whether they were carried on to affect labor conditions elsewhere, the fact is that the boycott in *Allen Bradley* was carried on not as a shield to preserve the jobs of Local 3 members, traditionally a primary labor activity, but as a sword, to reach out and monopolize all the manufacturing job tasks for Local 3 members. It is arguable that Congress may have viewed the use of the boycott as a sword as different from labor's traditional concerns with wages, hours, and working conditions.

But the boycott in the present case was not used as a sword; it was a shield carried solely to preserve the members' jobs. We therefore have no occasion today to decide the questions which might arise where the workers carry on a boycott to reach out to monopolize jobs or acquire new job tasks when their own jobs are not threatened by the boycotted product. . . .

In effect Congress, in enacting § 8(b)(4)(A) of the Act, returned to the regime of *Duplex Printing Press Co.* and *Bedford Cut Stone Co.* . . . and barred as a secondary boycott union activity directed against a neutral employer, including the immediate employer when in fact the activity directed against him was carried on for its effect elsewhere.

Indeed, Congress in rewriting § 8(b)(4)(A) as § 8(b)(4)(B) took pains to confirm the limited application of the section to such "secondary" conduct. The word "concerted" in former § 8(b)(4) was deleted to reach secondary conduct directed to only one individual. This was in response to the Court's holding in *Labor Board* v. *International Rice Milling Co.,* 341 U.S. 665, that "concerted" required proof of inducement of two or more employees. But to make clear that the deletion was not to be read as supporting a construction of the statute as prohibiting the incidental effects of traditional primary activity, Congress added the proviso that nothing in the amended section "shall be construed to make unlawful, where not otherwise unlawful, any primary strike or primary picketing." Many statements and examples proffered in the 1959 debates confirm this congressional acceptance of the distinction between primary and secondary activity.

II. The Landrum-Griffin Act amendments in 1959 were adopted only to close various loopholes in the application of § 8(b)(4)(A) which had been exposed in Board and court decisions. We discussed some of these loopholes, and the particular amendments adopted to close them, in *Labor Board* v. *Servette, Inc.,* 377 U.S. 46, 51–54. We need not repeat that discussion here, except to emphasize, as we there said, that "these changes did not expand the type of conduct which § 8(b)(4)(A) condemned, that is, union pressures calculated to induce the employees of a secondary employer to withhold their services in order to force their employer to cease dealing with the primary employer." *Id.,* at 52–53.

Section 8(e) simply closed still another loophole. In *Carpenters* v. *Labor Board (Sand Door),* 357 U.S. 93, the Court held that it was no defense to an unfair labor practice charge under § 8(b)(4)(A) that the struck employer had agreed, in a contract with the union, not to handle nonunion material. However, the Court emphasized that the mere execution of such a contract provision (known as a "hot cargo" clause because of its prevalence in Teamsters Union contracts), or its voluntary observance by the employer, was not unlawful under § 8(b)(4)(A). Section 8(e) was designed to plug this gap in the legislation by making the "hot cargo" clause itself unlawful. The *Sand Door* decision was believed by Congress not only to create the possibility of damage actions against employers for breaches of "hot cargo" clauses, but also to create a situation in which such clauses might be employed to exert subtle pressures upon employers to engage in "voluntary" boycotts. Hearings in late 1958 before the Senate Select Committee explored seven cases of "hot cargo" clauses in Teamster Union contracts, the use of which the Committee found conscripted neutral employers in Teamsters organizational campaigns.

This loophole closing measure likewise did not expand the type of conduct which § 8(b)(4)(A) condemned. Although the language of § 8(e) is sweeping, it closely tracks that of § 8(b)(4)(A), and just as the latter and its successor § 8(b)(4)(B) did not reach employees' activity to pressure their employer to preserve for themselves work traditionally done by them, § 8(e) does not prohibit agreements made and maintained for that purpose. . . .

However, provisos were added to § 8(e) to preserve the *status quo* in the construction industry, and exempt the garment industry from the prohibitions of §§ 8(e) and 8(b)(4)(B). This action of the Congress is strong confirmation that Congress meant that both §§ 8(e) and 8(b)(4)(B) reach only secondary pressures. If the body of § 8(e) applies only to secondary activity, the garment industry proviso is a justifiable exception which allows what the legislative history shows it was designed to allow, secondary pressures to counteract the effects of sweatshop conditions in an industry with a highly integrated process of production between jobbers, manufacturers, contractors and subcontractors. First, this motivation for the proviso sheds light on the central theme of the body of § 8(e), from which the proviso is an exception. Second, if the body of that provision and § 8(b)(4)(B) were construed to prohibit primary agreements and their maintenance, such as those concerning work preservation, the proviso would have the highly unlikely effect, unjustified in any of the statute's history, of permitting garment workers, but garment workers only, to preserve their jobs against subcontracting or prefabrication by such agreements and by strikes and boycotts to enforce them. Similarly, the construction industry proviso, which permits "hot cargo" agreements only for jobsite work, would have the curious and unsupported result of allowing the construction worker to make agreements preserving his traditional tasks against jobsite prefabrication and subcontracting, but not against nonjobsite prefabrication and subcontracting. On the other hand, if the heart of § 8(e) is construed to be directed only to secondary activites, the construction proviso becomes, as it was intended to be, a measure designed to allow agreements pertaining to certain secondary activities on the construction site because of the close community of interests there, but to ban secondary-objective agreements concerning nonjob-site work, in which respect the construction industry is no different from any other. The provisos are therefore substantial probative support that primary work preservation agreements were not to be within the ban of § 8(e). . . .

In addition to all else, "the silence of the sponsors of (the) Amendments is pregnant with significance. . . ." *Labor Board* v. *Fruit & Vegetable Packers,* 377 U.S. 58, at 66. Before we may say that Congress meant to strike from workers' hands the economic weapons traditionally used against their employers' efforts to abolish their jobs, that meaning should plainly appear. "(I)n this era of automation and onrushing technological change, no problems in the domestic economy are of greater concern than those involving job security and employment stability. Because of the potentially cruel impact upon the lives and fortunes of the working men and women of the Nation, these problems have understandably engaged the solicitous attention of government, of responsible, private business, and particularly of organized labor." *Fibreboard Paper Prods. Corp.* v. *Labor Board,* 379 U.S. 203, 225 (concurring opinion of STEWART, J.). We would expect that legislation curtailing the ability of management and labor voluntarily to negotiate for solutions to these significant and difficult problems would be preceded by extensive congressional study and debate, and consideration of voluminous economic, scientific, and statistical data. . . . We cannot lightly impute to Congress an intent in § 8(e) to preclude labor-management agreements to ease these effects through collective bargaining on this most vital problem created by advanced technology.

Moreover, our decision in *Fibreboard Paper Prods. Corp., supra,* implicitly recognizes the legitimacy of work preservation clauses like that involved here. Indeed, in the circumstances presented in *Fibreboard,* we held that bargaining on the subject was made mandatory by § 8(a)(5) of the Act, concerning as it does "terms and conditions of employment," § 8(d). . . . It would therefore be incongruous to interpret § 8(e) to invalidate clauses over which the parties may be mandated to bargain and which have been successfully incorporated through collective bargaining in many of this Nation's major labor agreements. . . .

The Woodwork Manufacturers Association and *amici* who support its position advance several reasons, grounded in economic and technological factors, why "will not handle" clauses should be invalid in all circumstances. Those arguments are addressed to the wrong branch of government. It may be "that the time has come for a reevaluation of the basic content of collective bargaining as contemplated by the federal legislation. But that is for Congress. . . .

III. The determination whether the "will not handle" sentence of Rule 17 and its enforcement violated § 8(e) and § 8(b)(4)(B) cannot be made without an inquiry into whether, under all the surrounding circumstances, the Union's objective was preservation of work for Frouge's employees, or whether the agreements and boycott were tactically calculated to satisfy union objectives elsewhere. Were the latter the case, Frouge, the boycotting employer, would be a neutral bystander, and the agreement or boycott would, within the intent of Congress, become secondary. There need not be an actual dispute with the boycotted employer, here the door manufacturer, for the activity to fall within this category, so long as the tactical object of the agreement and its maintenance is that employer, or benefits to other than the boycotting employees or other employees of the primary employer thus making the agreement or boycott secondary in its aim. The touchstone is whether the agreement or its maintenance is addressed to the labor relations of the contracting employer *vis-à-vis* his own employees. This will not always be a simple test to apply. But "[h]owever difficult the task of drawing of lines more nice than obvious, the statute compels the task." *Local 761, Electrical Workers* v. *Labor Board,* 366 U.S. 667, 674.

That the "will not handle" provision was not an unfair labor practice in this case is clear. The finding of the Trial Examiner, adopted by the Board, was that the objective of the sentence was preservation of work traditionally performed by the jobsite carpenters. This finding is supported by substantial evidence, and therefore the Union's making of the "will not handle" agreement was not a violation of § 8(e).

Similarly, the Union's maintenance of the provision was not a violation of § 8(b)(4)(B). The Union refused to hang prefabricated doors whether or not they bore a union label, and even refused to install prefabricated doors manufactured off the jobsite by members of the Union. This and other substantial evidence supported the finding that the conduct of the Union on the Frouge jobsite related solely to preservation of the traditional tasks of the jobsite carpenters.

The judgment is affirmed in No. 110, and reversed in No. 111.

It is so ordered.

Justice Harlan wrote a concurring opinion.

STEWART, J., joined by BLACK, J., DOUGLAS, J., and CLARK, J., dissenting: The Union's boycott of the prefitted doors clearly falls within the express terms of the Federal labor law, which makes such conduct unlawful when "an object thereof" is "forcing or requiring any person to cease using . . . the products of any other . . . manufacturer. . . . ." And the collective bargaining provision that authorizes such a boycott likewise stands condemned by the law's prohibition of any agreement whereby an employer "agrees to cease or refrain from handling . . . any of the products of any other employer . . . ." The Court undertakes a protracted review of legislative and decisional history in an effort to show that the clear words of the statute should be disregarded in these cases. But the fact is that the relevant history fully confirms that Congress meant what it said, and I therefore dissent. . . .

CASE QUESTIONS	1. Define the term "hot cargo" clause.
	2. Distinguish the *Allen Bradley* case from *National Woodwork*.
	3. Why was Section 8(e) of the Landrum-Griffin Act made law?
	4. What test did the Supreme Court set out for determining whether the "will not handle" clause and its enforcement was in violation of Section 8(e) and Section 8(b)(4)(B)?
	5. State the findings of the Supreme Court concerning the objective of the union's "will not handle" clause.

SECTION 75 / DAMAGES FROM BOYCOTTS AND PICKETING

In addition to unfair labor practice and injunction procedures providing redress against illegal boycotts and for picketing activities, the Labor-Management Relations Act of 1947 provides for damage suits in the federal courts. Section 303 makes it unlawful for any labor organization to engage in conduct prohibited by Section 8(b)(4) of the National Labor Relations Act, which includes all the boycott and picketing activities previously discussed in this chapter.

Suits for damages, with judgments and costs enforceable against the union's assets, but not against individual members, are specifically permitted by Section 303, similar to suits against labor organizations for violating union agreements. The right to sue is discussed in detail in Chapter 11 of this volume.

1. Distinguish between the strike and the boycott; between the boycott and the picketing weapons in labor disputes.
2. Can secondary activity be found at a single building site? On a primary employer's own property?
3. What is the authority of state courts in boycott situations? Of federal courts?
4. To what extent may consumer boycotts be carried on legally?

Legality of Strikes

SECTION 76 / BARGAINING POWER AND LAW

We have in prior chapters reviewed the law that was applied to the use of power and collective effort in the labor market. Government possesses the authority to establish and protect constitutional rights of workers and of property owners, and to limit the extent that one group may interfere in the rights of the other in promoting economic self-interest. The application of government authority to regulate the exercise of economic power by striking or other nonperformance tactics, by pickets, boycotts, blacklists, and by lockouts has been traced through the doctrines of conspiracy, restraint of trade, ends and means, contract protection, and other judicial reasons.

Labor law developed to a large extent from court actions in disputes arising out of conflicts of interest in which one party used direct or indirect pressures on the other. Up to the early part of the twentieth century, labor law had been primarily the creation of judges. Not until 1926 when the Railway Labor Act was passed and in 1932 when the Anti-Injunction Act became law did Congressional authority prevail. Since then federal courts have held that labor policy is a legislative responsibility, subject only to due process court review.

This chapter brings up to date the legal status of economic tactics employed by labor and by management and the doctrinal changes that were developed since modern statutory enactments. As construed by the administrative and judicial rulings, not only were radical changes effectuated by labor law but the extent and the scope of this government influence has in fact become a major positive factor in labor-management relations instead of only a negative force. Applied too frequently in denying labor its freedom to organize, from 1930 on the pendulum swung to emphasize the protection of labor's right to organize, to use collective power tactics, and to withhold its services.

SECTION 77 / TYPES OF STOPPAGES

The strike is perhaps the most potent weapon possessed by labor to force its demands upon an employer. Its usual concomitant is the establishment of a picket line. Sometimes the boycott is simultaneously employed against an especially resistant employer.

The strike may generally be defined as a temporary and concerted withdrawal of workers from an employer's service to enforce their demands, the workers retaining a contingent interest in their jobs. The degree to which workers retain a vested or contingent interest in the positions they leave will depend largely upon the purpose of the strike, the means employed to effectuate the strike, and the success of the employer in securing effective replacements. Interpretations under the National Labor Relations Act have clarified, to some extent *ab initio,* the status of workers engaging in the various forms of strikes. The determination of a striker's status becomes important with respect to deciding questions of reinstatement of workers, awarding of back pay, and granting of permission to the men to participate in representation elections.

While the general definition has been given, it is important to distinguish the several forms of strike activity. The *primary strike* involves a withdrawal of a single employer's workers who seek a direct and immediate benefit to themselves. The *secondary strike* involves a withdrawal of another employer's workers who thereby exert pressure on their own employer in the expectation that he will, in turn, bring pressure upon an employer with whom the union has a dispute. Thus the unionized workers of X Company withdraw to force X to bring pressure upon the Y Company, with whom the union has an unsettled dispute. The secondary strike has sympathetic elements, but is distinguishable from a *sympathetic strike* in that to fall in the secondary rather than the sympathetic category, the strike in question must be conducted for the direct benefit of the union involved. If the strike is for the direct benefit of some other union, and if the strikers secure only an incidental benefit therefrom, then we have a sympathetic or sympathy strike.

The *general strike* involves work cessation by most, if not all, workers in a particular industry, such as coal or steel; or most, if not all, workers in a particular city. In its widest and most serious application, the workers of an entire nation are involved. European countries have seen more rashes of national general strikes, which may be traced to the broad economic and political character of this strike form. Strongly unified labor employs the general strike for the assertion of strength to protest against adverse industry-wide conditions of employment or antilabor legislation. The general strike was restricted by the inclusion in the amended Labor Relations Act of 1947 of Sections 206–210 on National Emergency Strikes; thus usage of the general strike weapon is now subject to executive action and injunction.

The *sitdown strike* covers a cessation of work by laborers without withdrawal from the plant, employees remaining at their work stations but machines and tools remaining idle. The *slowdown* is a variant of the sitdown, there being no withdrawal from the work station with cessation of work being only partial. The slowdown is an aggravated form of soldiering and brings pressure by embarrassing production schedules. In a *partial strike* only part of the workers leave their work stations, a technique that has been employed successfully in large-scale firms when a union selects a vulnerable department or departments and strikes only in those areas. No merchandise can enter and none can leave, especially if outside unions give sympathetic aid by respecting picket lines established at the receiving and shipping docks. The bulk of union members continue working and draw their pay, that is, if the employer does not lock them out. The union strike fund is often used for assisting partial strikers.

The *wildcat strike* is one for which the parent union disclaims responsibility. Presumably, or in fact, it is unauthorized and generally is in breach of a collective agreement. Forces lying dormant may spontaneously flare into flame in retaliation against dilatory action by management with respect to the handling of unredressed employee grievances, or for other reasons. The union, for example, may not effectively represent the desires of the workmen, in which case they fully or partially strike on their own volition.

A *jurisdictional strike* involves a dispute between two or more unions. In order to compel the employer to take sides, one or both unions instigate a strike. New materials and new production methods, especially in the building trades, often precipitate controversy between two or more unions, where each seeks to obtain work assignments for its own members.

A *whipsaw strike* is a strike against one strategically situated employer in order to weaken the opposition of other employers or force them to capitulate, one company being played off against other companies. The *Brown Food Stores* case, in Chapter 6, is an example.

The National Labor Relations Board lumps all the above strike variants into three broad groupings. The first may be termed the economic strike; the second, the employer unfair labor practice strike; and the third, the union unfair labor practice strike. The *economic strike* is one concerned with material or nonmaterial demands concerning improvements as to hours of work, wages, and working conditions. The *employer unfair labor practice strike* involves retaliation against unfair employer practices, more fully developed in Chapter 6. These unfair practices include the denial to workers of the right to bargain collectively, discrimination against union members, and other proscribed interferences with legitimate collective activity.

The third type of strike under the National Labor Relations Act is designated an unprotected activity strike, or a union unfair practice strike. Activities made unfair by the amendments of 1947 and 1959, or in violation of no-strike agreements, and other strikes which remove the strikers from the protection of the law will be discussed below so as to show how the rights of strikers differ in each type of situation.

Two questions arise in connection with each strike or lockout activity, questions which can be traced to earlier legal doctrines: Is the purpose or objective illegal; and, if so, are the means or tactics applied in a lawful way? In the past five decades the answers to these questions have no longer been left solely to the discretion and value judgments of courts since in such legislation as the Railway Labor Act, the Anti-Injunction Act and the Labor-Management Relations Act, the Congress has established policies as to what are legitimate ends and means for labor-management relations. The courts are no longer free to use only personal standards of morality or equity in ruling on permissible conduct in strikes and lockouts or to apply judicial favoritism to support owners or workers in labor disputes.

As a tactic available to labor for placing economic pressure upon another group or individual, usually but not necessarily an employer, the right to cease work individually or collectively has been recognized at common law for over a hundred years. In the case of *Commonwealth* v. *Hunt* referred to previously, the Massachusetts jurist, Chief Justice Shaw, stated in 1842: "The case supposes that these persons are not bound by contract but are free to work for whom they please, or not to work, if they so prefer. In this state of things, we cannot perceive that it is criminal for men to agree together to exercise their own acknowledged rights, in such a manner as best to subserve their own interests . . . associations may be entered into, the object of which is to adapt measures that may have a tendency to impoverish another, that is, to diminish his gains and profits, and yet so far from being criminal or unlawful, the object may be highly meritorious and public-spirited."

In the absence of a statutory limitation on striking under specified circumstances, or an agreement limiting the right to cease work, the strike is a legal exercise of economic pressure. The National Labor Relations Act of 1935 in Section 13 provided: "Nothing in this Act shall be construed so as either to interfere with or impede or diminish in any way the right to strike. . . ."[1]

The right to strike can be limited by action of the legislative branch of government, under appropriate constitutional authority. Thus, since 1947 Congress has required that certain steps be followed by the parties when seeking to negotiate any changes of contractual provisions which postpone the legal exercise of the right to strike; it also provided for further delays in situations that might imperil the national health or welfare.

With these specific provisions affecting the right to strike, the Labor-Management Relations Act has expanded the language of Sec. 13 to read: "Nothing in this Act, *except as specifically provided for herein,* shall be construed so as either to interfere with or impede or diminish in any way the right to strike, or to affect the limitations or qualifications of that right."

Although stoppages can and do occur irrespective of the formal existence of unions, it might be expected that the growth of union resources under organizational leadership would increase the number and intensity of work stoppages. On the other hand, the practice of collective bargaining should diminish the need for work stoppages by more readily providing alternatives in the form of negotiating committees, grievance machinery, mediation, and arbitration. The causes of stoppages have also changed since 1935; prior to the NLRA enactment, those stoppages involving questions of union organization, such as issues of recognition and union shop and union jurisdiction, constituted the major category, while in the later period these causes fell to about 10 percent of the total. Thus with the clarification and acceptance of the law through administrative and judicial decisions and legislative additions, the organizational issue was no longer a major cause of stoppages, and about 90 percent of the disputes reported were being caused by differences over wages or working conditions.

The cases presented in the following sections on strikes could all be classed as labor disputes, a term defined similarly in the Anti-Injunction Act and the National Labor Relations Act in broad terms that would cover most situations

---

[1] Sec. 501(2) of Amended National Labor Relations Act states that "the term 'strike' includes any strike or other concerted stoppage of work by employees (including a stoppage by reason of the expiration of a collective-bargaining agreement) and any concerted slowdown or other concerted interruption of operations by employees."

involving strikes, lockouts, and other forms of work stoppage. Of course, not all labor disputes are accompanied by stoppages initiated by employees or their representatives. The essence of the stoppage appears in the concerted refusal to perform work as expected or a refusal to provide services until some concession or a change in position is indicated by the opposing party to the dispute.

QUESTIONS ON SECTION 77

1. Define a strike.
2. Why does it become important to determine a striker's status?
3. Distinguish the various types of strikes.
4. What is the principal usage of the general strike?
5. Why are partial strikes disconcerting to employers?
6. What three strike categories are recognized by the National Labor Relations Board?
7. What has been the impact of growing union strength upon law as to work stoppages?

SECTION 78 / UNION UNFAIR LABOR OBJECTIVES

The National Labor Relations Act outlaws strikes for purposes defined as union unfair labor objectives. Section 8(b)(4) prohibits to labor organizations the employment of certain types of strikes, pickets, and boycotts if they fall into the "secondary" or "jurisdictional" category. As amended in 1959, subsections A, B, and C were supplemented by Sections 8(b)(7) and 8(e) to prohibit any primary or secondary strike, picketing, or boycott where the object is:

a. To force an employer to join an employer organization.
b. To force a self-employed person to join a labor union.
c. To force one employer to cease dealing with another person.
d. To require recognition after another union has obtained bargaining rights by certification under the Act where redetermination of such rights is barred.

SECTION 79 / EMPLOYER UNFAIR LABOR PRACTICE STRIKES

A strike by lawful nonviolent methods in protest of an unfair labor practice committed by the struck employer protects the strikers from discharge or from the loss of employment by replacements. Replacements may be hired to fill the strikers' jobs, but only for the period until the strikers seek to return to work.

The *Mastro Plastics* case established the right of employees striking against employer violations of the NLRA to reinstatement with reimbursement of earnings lost through the employer's discrimination before reinstatement. This remedy was sustained notwithstanding an agreement prohibiting strikes and also the failure of the employees to observe obligations that would otherwise have been in effect except for the employer's unfair labor practices.

In the *Kohler* case, the company was ordered to reinstate the strikers where the NLRB found that what started as an economic strike became an unfair labor practice by employer conduct after the employees stopped work. The courts rejected the company contentions as to striker misconduct which the employer claimed to justify the refusal to reemploy, except where serious criminal convictions were previously established by the courts.

Mastro Plastics Corp. v. NLRB

Supreme Court of the United States, 1956. 350 U.S. 270

BURTON, J. This case presents two principal questions: (1) whether, in the collective-bargaining contract before us, the union's undertaking "to refrain from engaging in any strike or work stoppage during the term of this agreement" waives not only the employees' right to strike for economic benefits but also their right to strike solely against unfair labor practices of their employers, and (2) whether Par. 8(d) of the National Labor Relations Act, as amended, deprives individuals of their status as employees if, within the waiting period prescribed by Par. 8(d)(4), they engage in a strike solely against unfair labor practices of their employers. For the reasons hereafter stated, we answer each in the negative.

Mastro Plastics Corp. and French-American Reeds Manufacturing Co., Inc., petitioners herein, are New York corporations which, in 1949 and 1950, were engaged in interstate commerce, manufacturing, selling and distributing plastic articles, including reeds and other accessories for musical instruments. They operated in the City of New York within the same plant, under the same management and with the same employees. For collective bargaining, their employees were represented by Local 22045, American Federation of Labor, or by Local 3127, United Brotherhood of Carpenters and Joiners of America, AFL. These locals occupied the same office and used the services of the same representatives. During the period in question, the right of representation of petitioners' employees was transferred back and forth between them for reasons not material here. Accordingly, they are referred to in this opinion as the "Carpenters."

In August 1950, Local 65 of the Wholesale and Warehouse Workers Union began a campaign among petitioners' employees in an effort to become their collective-bargaining representatives. Petitioners bitterly opposed the movement, believing Local 65 to be communist-controlled. Feeling that the Carpenters were too weak to cope successfully with Local 65, petitioners asked the Carpenters to transfer their bargaining rights to Local 318, International Brotherhood of Pulp, Sulphite and Paper Mill Workers, AFL. When the Carpenters declined to do so, petitioners selected a committee of employees to visit 318, obtain membership cards and seek members for that union. The cards were distributed during working hours and petitioners paid their employees for time spent in the campaign, including attendance at a meeting of 318. Petitioners' officers and supervisors instructed employees to sign these cards and indicated that those refusing to do so would be "out."

September 28, Local 65 filed with the National Labor Relations Board its petition for certification as bargaining representative. October 24, Local 318 intervened in the representation proceedings and asked that it be certified. However, many employees revoked their applications for membership in 318 and reaffirmed their adherence to the Carpenters. This was followed on October 31 by the Carpenters' refusal to consent to an election on the ground that petitioners had unlawfully assisted 318 in the campaign.

November 10, 1950, a crisis developed when the president of petitioners summarily discharged Frank Ciccone, an employee of over four years' standing, because of the latter's activity in support of the Carpenters and his opposition to 318. We accept the finding of the National Labor Relations Board that petitioners "discriminatorily discharged, and thereafter refused to reinstate, Frank Ciccone because of his organizational activities in support of the . . . [Carpenters]." This discharge at once precipitated the strike which is before us and which the Board found "was clearly caused and prolonged by the cumulative effects of the [petitioners'] unfair labor practices culminating in the discriminatory discharge of Ciccone." There was no disorder, but the plant was virtually shut down until December 11; and it was March 9, 1951, before the Carpenters, on behalf of petitioners' employees, made an unconditional request to return to work. Petitioners ignored that request and neither Ciccone nor any of the other 76 striking employees has been reinstated.

While the strike against petitioners' unfair labor practices continued, the collective-bargaining contract between petitioners and the Carpenters approached its expiration date of November 30, 1950, and, apart from the above-described organizational controversy, the Carpenters had taken timely steps to secure modification of their agreement. October 10, they had delivered to petitioners a notice (dated September 29, 1950) "requesting modification" of the contract. They thus had started the statutory negotiating period running as prescribed by the above-mentioned § 8(d). The Carpenters met several times with petitioners and pressed their demands for changes in the contract, but the expiration date passed without any agreement being reached.

In January 1951, the Carpenters initiated the present proceedings before the National Labor Relations Board by charging petitioners with unfair labor practices. Acting on those charges, the Board's general counsel filed a complaint alleging petitioners' support of Local 318 and discharge of numerous employees, including Ciccone, as violations of § 8(a)(1), (2) and (3) of the Act.

Petitioners admitted that they had discharged the employees in question and had not rehired them. They denied, however, that in so doing they had committed any unfair labor practices. Their first affirmative defense was that the waiver of the right to strike, expressed by their employees in their collective-bargaining contract, applied to strikes not only for economic benefits but to any and all strikes by such employees, including strikes directed solely against unfair labor practices of the employer.

Petitioners' other principal defense was that the existing strike began during the statutory waiting period initiated by the employees' request for modifications of the contract and that, by virtue of § 8(d) of the Act, the strikers had lost their status as employees. That defense turned upon petitioners' interpretation of § 8(d), applying it not only to strikes for economic benefits but to any and all strikes occurring during the waiting period, including strikes solely against unfair labor practices of the employer.

The trial examiner made findings of fact sustaining the complaint and recommended that petitioners be ordered to cease and desist from the interference complained of and be required to offer to Ciccone and the 76 other discharged employees full reinstatement, together with back pay for Ciccone from November 10, 1950, and for the other employees from March 9, 1951. See 103 NLRB 511, 526–563. With minor modifications, the Board adopted the examiner's findings and conclusions and issued the recommended order. 103 NLRB 511. The chairman and one member dissented in part.

The Court of Appeals, with one judge dissenting in part, accepted the Board's findings of fact and conclusions of law and enforced the Board's order. 214 F.2d 462. Since then, the Court of Appeals for the Seventh Circuit has reached a similar conclusion. *Labor Board* v. *Wagner Iron Works,* 220 F.2d 126. Because of the importance of the issues in industrial relations and in the interpretation of the National Labor Relations Act, as amended, we granted certiorari. 348 U.S. 910.

Apart from the issues raised by petitioners' affirmative defenses, the proceedings reflect a flagrant example of interference by the employers with the expressly protected right of their employees to select their own bargaining representative. The findings disclose vigorous efforts by the employers to influence and even to coerce their employees to abandon the Carpenters as their bargaining representatives and to substitute Local 318. Accordingly, unless petitioners sustain at least one of their affirmative defenses, they must suffer the consequences of their unfair labor practices violating § 8(a)(1), (2) or (3) of the Act, as amended.

In the absence of some contractual or statutory provision to the contrary, petitioners' unfair labor practices provide adequate ground for the orderly strike that occurred here. Under those circumstances, the striking employees do not lose their status and are entitled to reinstatement with back pay, even if replacement for them have been made. Failure of the Board to enjoin petitioners' illegal conduct or failure of the Board to sustain the right to strike against that conduct would seriously undermine the primary objectives of the Labor Act. See *Labor Board* v. *Rice Milling Co.,* 341 U.S. 665, 673. While we assume that the employees, by explicit contractual provision, could have waived their right to strike against such unfair labor practices and that Congress, by explicit statutory provision, could have deprived strikers, under the circumstances of this case, of their status as employees, the questions before us are whether or not such a waiver was made by the Carpenters in their 1949–1950 contract and whether or not such a deprivation of status was enacted by Congress in § 8(d) of the Act, as amended in 1947. . . .

As neither the collective-bargaining contract nor § 8(d) of the National Labor Relations Act, as amended, stands in the way, the judgment of the Court of Appeals is *Affirmed.*

CASE QUESTIONS

1. What unfair labor practices did the employer commit?
2. Was the agreement a strike deterrent? Why?
3. What did the Board state as its reason for absolving the Union?

4. How did the Court find as to the legality of the Union conduct?

Kohler Co. v. Local 833, United Automobile Workers

U. S. Court of Appeals, D. C., 1962. 300 F.2d 699

[Board supplemental order enforced April 20, 1965, in full after remand and finding that 57 unfair labor practice strikers should be reinstated.]

BAZELON, C. J. These are petitions for review and enforcement of an order of the National Labor Relations Board concerning a strike by Local 833, UAW-AFL-CIO, against the Kohler Company. The strike began on April 5, 1954, and was still unsettled when the Board issued its order on August 26, 1960. The dispute has a long and bitter history—more typical of "a bygone era"—which is set forth in detail in the Board's decision. *Kohler Co.,* 128 NLRB 1062. In this opinion we relate only those facts required to understand the issues we consider.

The Board found that a disagreement over contract terms and not Kohler's alleged refusal to bargain caused the strike, but that it was prolonged by such refusals on and after June 1, 1954. On that date Kohler granted a three-cent wage increase to nonstriking employees working under the conditions specified in an expired contract, but failed to make a similar offer to the Union. The Board also found that Kohler subsequently refused to bargain in good faith in the following respects, among others: by unilaterally putting into effect a second wage increase; by discharging striking employees and transferring nonstriking employees without notification to or consultation with the Union; and by refusing to furnish wage information pertinent to the negotiations. The Board also determined that Kohler violated §§ 8(a)(3) and (1) of the Act by discriminatorily treating some employees and unlawfully discharging others because of their participation in strike activities. In addition, the Board found that after June 1, 1954, Kohler interfered with, restrained, and coerced its employees in the exercise of their right to join labor unions and bargain collectively by engaging in surveillance and antiunion espionage, evicting certain strikers from Company-owned dwellings, and other conduct violating § 8(a)(1) of the Act. . . .

Having concluded that Kohler's unfair labor practices on and after June 1, 1954, converted what the Board thought had been an economic strike into an unfair labor practice strike, the Board issued a remedial order directing the Company, *inter alia,* to reinstate strikers replaced after the June 1 unilateral wage increase, excepting, however, employees discharged on March 1, 1955, for misconduct in connection with the strike.

In No. 16182 Kohler seeks review of the Board's adverse determinations. We think they are amply supported by the record considered as a whole and that Kohler's attack must fail. Since we fully adopt the Board's analysis of the evidence on these matters, further discussion would serve no useful purpose.

<table>
<tr><td>CASE
QUESTIONS</td><td>1. In an economic strike can the employer discharge strikers? Refuse to reinstate them?
2. When may an economic strike become an unfair labor practice?
3. How can the employer change conditions of employment during a strike?
4. Is all strike conduct a ground for refusing to reinstate employees who wish to return?</td></tr>
</table>

SECTION 80 / **ECONOMIC STRIKES**

Reinstatement rights of strikers vary depending on the cause of the strike. As established in the previous section, employees engaging in an *unfair labor practice strike* have an unlimited right to reinstatement. The NLRB has the authority to order the reinstatement of these employees, as well as ordering back pay awards. An employer must rehire these strikers even though their reinstatement results in the discharge of workers hired to replace them. In contrast, employees who engage in an *economic strike* have lesser reinstatement rights. In the 1938 case of *NLRB* v. *MacKay Radio & Telegraph,* the Supreme Court ruled that an employer could hire permanent replacements for economic strikers.[2] The effect was that where economic strikers had been permanently replaced, the NLRB had no authority to direct their reinstatement. However, in 1968 in the *Laidlaw* case, the NLRB developed a new rule regarding reinstatement of economic strikers. This new rule is based on the 1967 decision of the U. S. Supreme Court, *NLRB* v. *Fleetwood Trailer Company.* The rule requires that economic strikers not rehired at the termination of a strike because of low levels of production must be rehired when jobs become available. The *Fleetwood* case and the *Laidlaw* rule are reported in this section.

In *NLRB* v. *International Van Lines,* where three employees engaged in an economic strike were discharged before their replacements were actually hired, the Supreme Court held the discharges constituted an unfair labor practice so that the employer was obligated to reinstate the strikers.[3] The Court recertified that an employer may refuse to reinstate economic strikers (subject to the *Laidlaw* rule) if in the interim he has taken on permanent replacements.

National Labor Relations Board v. Fleetwood Trailer Company, Inc.

Supreme Court of the United States, 1967. 389 U.S. 375

FORTAS, J.: Respondent is a manufacturer of mobile homes. On August 5, 1964, it employed about 110 persons. On August 6, 1964, as a result of a

---

[2] 304 U.S. 333 (1938).
[3] 409 U.S. 48 (1972).

breakdown in collective bargaining negotiations between respondent and the Union, about half of the employees struck. Respondent cut back its production schedule from the prestrike figure of 20 units to 10 units per week, and curtailed its orders for raw materials correspondingly. On August 18, the Union accepted the respondent's last contract offer, terminated the strike, and requested reinstatement of the strikers.

Respondent explained that it could not reinstate the strikers "right at that moment" because of the curtailment of production caused by the strike. The evidence is undisputed that it was the company's intention "at all times" to increase production to the full prestrike volume "as soon as possible."

The six strikers involved in this case applied for reinstatement on August 20 and on a number of occasions thereafter. On that date, no jobs were available, and their applications were rejected. However, between October 8 and 16, the company hired six new employees, who had not previously worked for it, for jobs which the striker-applicants were qualified to fill. Later, in the period from November 2 through December 14, the six strikers were reinstated.

An NLRB complaint was issued upon charges filed by the six employees. As amended, the complaint charged respondent with unfair labor practices within the meaning of §§ 8(a)(1) and (3) of the National Labor Relations Act (29 U.S.C. §§ 158(a)(1) and (3)) because of the hirings of new employees instead of the six strikers. After hearing, the Trial Examiner concluded that respondent had discriminated against the strikers by failing to accord them their rights to reinstatement as employees in October when respondent hired others to fill the available jobs. Accordingly, the Examiner recommended that respondent should make each of the six whole for loss of earnings due to its failure to return them to employment at the time of the October hirings and until they were reemployed. A three-member panel of the Board adopted the findings, conclusions and recommendations of the Trial Examiner.

The Board filed a petition for enforcement of the order, The Court of Appeals for the Ninth Circuit, one judge dissenting, denied enforcement. 366 F.2d 126 (1966). It held that the right of the strikers to jobs must be judged as of the date when they apply for reinstatement. Since the six strikers applied for reinstatement on August 20, and since there were no jobs available on that date, the court concluded that the respondent had not committed an unfair labor practice by failing to employ them. We granted certiorari on petition of the Board. 386 U.S. 990 (1967). We reverse.

Section 2(3) of the Act (29 U.S.C. § 152(3)) provides that an individual whose work has ceased as a consequence of a labor dispute continues to be an employee if he has not obtained regular and substantially equivalent employment. If, after conclusion of the strike, the employer refuses to reinstate striking employees, the effect is to discourage employees from exercising their rights to organize and to strike guaranteed by §§ 7 and 13 of the Act (29 U.S.C. §§ 157 and 163). Under §§ 8(a)(1) and (3) it is an unfair labor practice to interfere with the exercise of these rights. Accordingly, unless the employer who refuses to reinstate strikers can show that his action was due to "legitimate and substantial business justifications," he is guilty of an unfair labor practice. *NLRB* v. *Great Dane Trailers*, 388 U.S. 26, 34 (1967). The burden of proving justification is on the employer. *Ibid.* It is the primary responsibility of the Board and not of the courts "to strike the proper balance between the asserted business justifications and the invasion of employee rights in light of the Act and its policy." *Id.*, at 33–34. . . .

In two types of situations, "legitimate and substantial business justifications" for refusing to reinstate striking employees have been recognized. The first is when the jobs which the strikers claim are occupied by workers hired as permanent replacements during the strike in order to continue operations. *NLRB* v. *Mackay Radio & Telegraph Co.*, 304 U.S. 333, 345–346 (1938); *NLRB* v. *Plastilite Corp.*, 375 F. 2d 343 (C.A. 8th Cir. 1967) *Brown & Root*, 132 NLRB 486 (1961). In the present case, respondent hired 21 replacements during the strike compared with about 55 strikers; but it is clear that the jobs of the six strikers were available after the strike. Indeed, they were filled by new employees.

A second basis for justification is suggested by the Board—when the striker's job has been eliminated for substantial and bona fide reasons other than considerations relating to labor relations: for example, "the need to adapt to changes in business conditions or to improve efficiency." We need not consider this claimed justification because in the present case no changes in methods of production or operation were shown to have been instituted which might have resulted in eliminating the strikers' jobs.

The Court of Appeals emphasized in the present case the absence of any antiunion motivation for the failure to reinstate the six strikers. But in *NLRB* v. *Great Dane Trailers, supra,* which was decided after the Court of Appeals' opinion in the present case, we held that proof of antiunion motivation is unnecessary when the employer's conduct "could have adversely affected employee rights to *some* extent" and when the employer does not meet his burden of establishing "that he was motivated by legitimate objectives." *Id.*, at 34. *Great Dane Trailers* determined that payment of vacation benefits to nonstrikers and denial of those payments to strikers carried "a potential for adverse effect upon employee rights." Because "no evidence of a proper motivation appeared in the record," we agreed with the Board that the employer had committed an unfair labor practice. *Id.*, at 35. A refusal to reinstate striking employees, which is involved in this case, is clearly no less destructive of important employee rights than a refusal to make vacation payments. And because the employer here has not shown "legitimate and substantial business justifications," the conduct constitutes an unfair labor practice without reference to intent.

The Court of Appeals, however, held that the respondent did not discriminate against the striking employees because on the date when they applied for work, two days after the end of the strike, respondent had no need for their services. But it is undisputed that the employees continued to make known their availability and desire for reinstatement, and that "at all times" respondent intended to resume full production to reactivate the jobs and to fill them.

It was clearly error to hold that the right of the strikers to reinstatement expired on August 20, when they first applied. This basic right to jobs cannot depend upon job availability as of the moment when the applications are filed. The right to reinstatement does not depend upon technicalities relating to application. On the contrary, the status of the striker as an employee continues until he has obtained "other regular and substantially equivalent employment." (29 U.S.C. § 152(3).) Frequently a strike affects the level of production and the number of jobs. It is entirely normal for striking employees to apply for reinstatement immediately after the end of the strike and before full production is resumed. If and when a job for which the striker is qualified becomes available, he is entitled to an offer of reinstatement. The right can be defeated only if the employer can show "legitimate and substantial business justifications." *NLRB* v. *Great Dane Trailers, supra.*

Accordingly, the judgment of the Court of Appeals is vacated and the cause is remanded for further proceedings consistent with this opinion.

Laidlaw Corporation

(SUPPLEMENTAL CASE DIGEST—ECONOMIC STRIKERS)
171 NLRB 175 (1968), 414 F.2d 94 (7 cir. 1969), cert denied 397 U.S. 920 (1970)

We hold, therefore, that economic strikers who unconditionally apply for reinstatement at a time when their positions are filled by permanent replacements: (1) remain employees; (2) are entitled to full reinstatement upon departure of replacements unless they have in the meantime acquired regular and substantially equivalent employment, or the employer can sustain his burden of proof that the failure to offer full reinstatement was for legitimate and substantial business reasons. . . .

CASE QUESTIONS

1. What reason did the Company give for not reinstating all the economic strikers?
2. Did the Company hire "new" employees before reinstating the six strikers.
3. What did the Trial Examiner conclude regarding the unfair labor practice charges filed against the Company?
4. State the rule of law developed by this case.
5. State the rule of law developed in the *Laidlaw* case.

SECTION 81 / **NO-STRIKE AGREEMENTS**

Since the purpose of collective bargaining is to promote industrial stability, it is common for the parties to negotiate a no-strike clause into their collective bargaining contracts. In the *Kellogg* case, reported in this section, the court points out that the right to strike may be relinquished by appropriate provisions in the collective bargaining agreements provided the relinquishment is expressed in clear and unmistakable language. In *Kellogg,* however, the court found that there was not an explicit contractual waiver of the employees' right to strike under the narrow circumstance of the case.

In the 1970 *Boys Markets* case, reported in Chapter 2, the Supreme Court held that employers may obtain an injunction from the federal courts to stop a strike that is in actual violation of a no-strike clause.

Kellogg Company v. National Labor Relations Board

United States Court of Appeals, Sixth Circuit, 1972. 457 F.2d 519

KENT, C. J.: This is a petition for review of an order of the National Labor Relations Board and a cross petition for enforcement of such order.

The Board ordered reinstatement of two employees of the petitioner with back pay. The Board reversed its Trial Examiner in reaching the conclusion that the employees were entitled to reinstatement. There is little dispute about the facts.

Petitioner's plant in Battle Creek, Michigan, employs approximately 3,500 people. The majority of the hourly rated employees are members of Local No. 3, American Federation of Grain Millers, AFL-CIO (herein referred to as the Millers). The remainder of the employees (approximately 150) are represented by Printing Specialty and Paper Products Union Local No. 480, International Printing Pressman and Assistants' Union of North America AFL-CIO (herein referred to as the Pressmen).

During the month of April, 1969, the contracts which the petitioner had with each of the Unions expired. The contract of the Millers expired on April 15, but the parties agreed to an extension to May 2 while negotiations continued. A new agreement was reached on April 26, 1969, which was made retroactive to April 15. The agreement between the petitioner and the Millers Local No. 3 was termed a supplemental agreement and included all of the provisions of a master agreement between the Millers International Union and the Company, negotiated in February, 1969, and designed to cover four of the Company's plants. The Pressmen were not as successful as the Millers with their negotiations with the Petitioner and went on strike on April 25, 1969. The strike was not settled until July 22, 1969. The two employees who were the subject to these proceedings refused to cross the Pressmen's picket line and after hearing, in accordance with the Millers' contract, were discharged (for nonattendance). They were not discharged for violation of the no strike clause.

Robert Sutfin, one of the employees, was the son, and Elaine Putnam was a wife, of striking members of the Pressmen. Each employee had been previously warned in regard to excess absenteeism on more than one occasion.

While the basic issues involved relate to the interpretation of the contract between the Petitioner and the Millers, there are also presented questions as to whether the employees' refusal to cross the picket line was because they were honoring the picket line or because of personal reasons, and also as to whether or not each of the employees had made an unconditional demand for reinstatement.

The Master Agreement, incorporated into the supplemental Agreement negotiated by Local No. 3 of the Millers, contained the following provisions relating to strikes and lockouts:

NO STRIKES—NO LOCKOUTS
Section 1101
(a) During the life of this Supplemental Agreement no strike or work stoppages in connection with disputes arising hereunder shall be caused or sanctioned by the Union, or by any member thereof, and no lockout shall be ordered by the Company in connection with such disputes.

(b) It is agreed that any authorized legal strike that may be called by the Union, or any lockout by the Company on or after the expiration of the Master Agreement in an effort to secure a new Master Agreement shall not be deemed a breach of the provisions of this Supplemental Agreement prohibiting strikes or work stoppages and lockouts during the life of this Supplemental Agreement.

(c) It is agreed that any authorized legal strike that may be called, or any lockout by the Company, on or after the expiration of this Supplemental Agreement in an effort to secure changes in or a new agreement, shall not be deemed a breach of the provisions of the Master Agreement.

NO SYMPATHY STRIKE
Section 1102
During the life of this Supplemental Agreement, no sympathy strike shall be caused or sanctioned by the Union because of differences between the AFL-CIO or any of its affiliated Unions and any other local or national employers, except for differences between the AFL-CIO or any of its affiliated Unions involving other plants of the Company.

STRIKE AUTHORIZATION
Section 1103
It is agreed that before a strike may be called the Company will be given a copy of the written authorization which is provided to the local Union by the President of the AMERICAN FEDERATION OF GRAIN MILLERS authorizing such action to be taken in accordance with its Constitution and Bylaws.

The petitioner has at all times taken the position that the terms of the contract, quoted above, made it a violation of the contract for the members of the Millers to honor a picket line of another Union at the Battle Creek plant.

At the outset of the Pressmen's strike many of the members of the Millers refused to cross the Pressmens' picket line. All, except the two here involved, returned to work after the Company warned them that they were violating the Collective Bargaining Agreement by refusing to cross the picket line, and after Representatives of the Local and International of the Millers informed the members of that Union that a sympathy strike was not permitted under the newly negotiated contract. The position taken by Union officials in their interpretation of the contract was communicated to the members through statements given to the local newspapers, to the local radio stations, and by means of notices posted on Company bulletin boards asking workers to report to work and honor their contract.

The Trial Examiner took evidence relating to the advice given by Local and International officers of the Millers and based his conclusion in part upon such evidence. The Board in reversing the Trial Examiner took a different view of this evidence, extraneous to the contract, and reached a different conclusion, as pointed out above.

The Court of Appeals for the District of Columbia in *News Union of Baltimore* v. *NLRB*, 393 F.2d 673 (D.C. Cir., 1968), concluded that the position taken by Union officials that the no strike provisions of the contract covered sympathy strikes was strong evidence that the clause was intended to bar such strikes; and in *NLRB* v. *Rockaway News Co.*, 345 U.S. 71 (1953), the United States Supreme Court approved the consideration of extrinsic evidence as an aid in determining the coverage intended by a broad no strike agreement. However, this Circuit in weighing the effect of the attitude of Union officers in regard to refusal to cross another Union's picket line stated in *NLRB* v. *Difco Laboratories, Inc.*, 427 F.2d 170, 172 (6th Cir., 1970):

> "Finally, whether the UAW did or did not want the two discharged employees to strike obviously has no bearing on their right to do so if they considered such action to be in their own best interest."

Thus, we conclude that if the Millers contract did not prohibit the sympathetic honoring of another Union's picket line then Putnam and Sutfin were engaging in protected concerted activity (as will be pointed out hereafter), and if the contract did prohibit such activity then they were properly discharged. We, therefore, conclude that after removing the factual issues we are faced with one fundamental problem: The interpretation of the Millers contract no strike clauses.

The right to strike is guaranteed by the National Labor Relations Act, 29 U.S.C. § 151 et seq., as interpreted in numerous cases. The United States Supreme Court in *NLRB* v. *Erie Resistor Corp.*, 373 U.S. 221 (1963), stated at page 233:

> "Section 7 guarantees, and § 8(a)(1) protects from employer interference the rights of employees to engage in concerted activities, which, as Congress has indicated, H. R. Rep. No. 245, 80th Cong., 1st Sess. 26, include the right to strike. . . ."

We reiterate that the right to strike is protected by law, whether it be for economic reasons, for the purpose of improving working conditions, or for mutual aid or protection of employees who are members of another Union. This right may be surrendered or waived by appropriate provisions in the collective bargaining agreement. *Mastro Plastics Corporation* v. *NLRB*, 350 U.S. 270, 280 (1956):

> "On the premise of fair representation, collective-bargaining contracts frequently have included certain waivers of the employees' right to strike and of the employers' right to lockout to enforce their respective economic demands during the terms of those contracts. *Provided the selection of the bargaining representative remains free,* such waivers contribute to the normal flow of commerce and to the maintenance of regular production schedules. Individuals violating such clauses appropriately lose their status as employees."

and the right to engage in a sympathy strike or the right to refuse to cross a picket line may be waived in the same manner. *NLRB* v. *Rockaway News Co.*, 345 U.S. 71, 80 (1953).

"In the section by which the Labor Management Relations Act prescribes certain practices of labor organizations which shall be deemed unfair, there is a proviso that nothing therein "shall be construed to make unlawful a refusal by any person to enter upon the premises of any employer (other than his own employer), if the employees of such employer are engaged in a strike ratified or approved by a representative of such employees whom such employer is required to recognize under this Act. . . ." This clearly enables contracting parties to embody in their contract a provision against requiring an employee to cross a picket line if they so agree. And nothing in the Act prevents their agreeing upon contrary provisions if they consider them appropriate to the particular kind of business involved. An employee's breach of such an agreement may be made grounds for his discharge without violating § 7 of the Act. *Labor Board* v. *Sands Co.,* 306 U.S. 332, 334. . . ."

This Court has held that the relinquishment of a right to strike must be expressed in "clear and unmistakable language." In *Timken Roller Bearing Co.* v. *NLRB,* 325 F.2d 746 (6th Cir., 1963), this Court said at page 751:

"Even so, we recognize that the Union could have relinquished this right under the provisions of the bargaining agreement if it, as a part of the bargaining process, elected to do so. But such a relinquishment must be in "clear and unmistakable" language. *Tide Water Associated Oil Company,* 85 NLRB 1096. . . . Silence in the bargaining agreement on such an issue does not meet this test. This Court said in *NLRB* v. *J. H. Allison & Co.,* 165 F.2d 766, 768, . . . "Nor do we see logical justification in the view that in entering into a collective bargaining agreement for a new year, *even though the contract was silent* upon a controverted matter, the union should be held to have waived *any rights secured under the Act,* including its right to have a say-so as to so-called merit increases." (Emphasis added.) We are of the opinion that the execution of the 1960 bargaining agreement, which was silent on this controversial question did not constitute a relinquishment of the Union's statutory right to the wage information which it now seeks. . . ."

In this contract Section 1101, *supra,* prohibits strikes or work stoppages because of disputes arising under the contract, and prohibits any strike "caused or sanctioned by the Union, or by any member thereof . . . ." Section 1102 provides:

"NO SYMPATHY STRIKE
Section 1102
    During the life of this Supplemental Agreement, no sympathy strike shall be caused or sanctioned by the Union because of differences between the AFL-CIO or any of its affiliated Unions and any other local or national employers, except for differences between the AFL-CIO or any of its affiliated Unions involving other plants of the Company."

By its terms the contract prohibits any member of the Union from striking because of a dispute under the contract. The sympathy strike clause relates only to sympathy strikes caused or sanctioned by the Union and makes no reference to the right of the members to refrain from crossing a picket line.

We find nothing in the language of this contract which prohibits a member of the Millers Union at the Battle Creek Plant from honoring the picket line of another Union at the same plant. If only the broad no strike clause of Section 1101 were considered perhaps the extrinsic evidence offered would be sufficient to justify the conclusion reached by the Trial Examiner, but in the light of the decision of this Court in *Timken Roller Bearing* v. *NLRB,* 325 F.2d 746 (6th Cir., 1963), we find no need for extrinsic evidence. We, therefore, conclude that the employees in question were engaged in protected concerted activity within the meaning of Section 7 and Section 8(a)(1) of the Act.

The claims of the petitioner that the employees in question refused to cross the picket line for personal reasons and that they failed to make an unconditional demand for reinstatement are clearly issues of fact which were resolved against the petitioner by the Board. These conclusions are supported by substantial evidence on the record as a whole and may not, therefore, be reviewed by this Court. 29 U. S. C. § 160(e). *NLRB* v. *Southern Greyhound Lines,* 426 F.2d 1299 (5th Cir., 1970);

Finally, there is a claim by the Petitioner that Putnam and Sutfin had been replaced. Clearly an employer who has replaced striking workers in order to keep his plant functioning is not required to discharge the workers he employed as replacements once the strike is over. *NLRB* v. *Mackay Co.,* 304 U.S. 333, 345–346 (1938):

> "Nor was it an unfair labor practice to replace the striking employees with others in an effort to carry on the business. Although § 13 provides, "Nothing in this Act shall be construed so as to interfere with or impede or diminish in any way the right to strike," it does not follow that an employer, guilty of no act denounced by the statute, has lost the right to protect and continue his business by supplying places left vacant by strikers. And he is not bound to discharge those hired to fill the places of strikers upon the election of the latter to resume their employment, in order to create places for them. The assurance by respondent to those who accepted employment during the strike that if they so desired their places might be permanent was not an unfair labor practice nor was it such to reinstate only so many of the strikers as there were vacant places to be filled."

However, the record is clear that no one was employed to replace either Putnam or Sutfin. As we read the record no one was ever assigned or hired to fill the position of Putnam. Sutfin's position was filled by another employee who was simply moved into Sutfin's position. There is no evidence in this record that anyone was hired to fill the position of the individual who was promoted to Sutfin's work. The Petitioner relies upon *NLRB* v. *Union Carbide Corporation,* 440 F.2d 54 (4th Cir., 1971). But in *Union Carbide* the Court held that workers who had honored the picket line of another union were entitled to the same status as economic strikers including the right to reinstatement if replacement had not been hired. This record reflects no new hiring and, therefore, the reason for the rule *i.e.* to protect the workers hired to replace the strikers does not exist because there is no one to protect.

The orders of the Board will be enforced.

CASE QUESTIONS

1. Should extrinsic evidence of the Union's interpretation of the contract language be used to determine the coverage intended by the no-strike agreement?
2. What is the one fundamental problem to be resolved by the Court?
3. May the right to strike be surrendered or waived by

appropriate provisions in the collective bargaining contract?

4. What effect did the "No Sympathy Strike" section of the collective bargaining agreement have on the individual members of the Millers Union?
5. Does an employer have a right to replace striking workers in order to keep his plant functioning?
6. Had the two employees in the case actually been replaced?

SECTION 82 / **NATIONAL EMERGENCY STRIKE**

As was previously pointed out, notwithstanding the limitations imposed on the use of the federal court injunction by the Anti-Injunction Act of 1932, these restrictions do not apply to suits initiated by the government to protect the public interest from actual or threatened national emergency strikes.[4]

Several strikes in 1946, particularly in the bituminous coal industry, were stimulants for inclusion of Sections 206 to 210 in the Labor-Management Relations Act of 1947. These are in purpose parallel to Section 10 of the Railway Labor Act. After the courts sustained employment of the injunction in mines seized under the War Labor Disputes Act, Congress included in the 1947 legislation authority for the President to invoke this power after required preliminary steps had been taken, for intervention in major disputes.

Under these provisions of the Act, as in the emergency strike provisions of the Railway Labor Act, the President is authorized to appoint a Board of Investigation which submits a report to him concerning the issues in dispute. Unlike the Railway Labor Act, the Taft-Hartley Act specifies that the Presidential Board's report "shall not contain any recommendations"; no such limitations as to Board recommendations is found in the Railway Labor Act. Under the latter Act, moreover, the parties are precluded from changing the "status quo" for a period of thirty days after a Board report is submitted to the President, or for a maximum of sixty days, after which the right to strike may legally be exercised by Railway Act workers. The Labor-Management Relations Act of 1947 under Sections 206–210 enables the government to secure what amounts to an 80-day injunctive forestalling of strikes or lockouts affecting all or a substantial part of an industry in interstate commerce, if such dispute were to imperil the national health or safety. During the interim, the government mediation service is to be invoked, but recommendations for settlement are not mandatory on the disputants. If an accord is not reached, the NLRB must poll the workers as to whether they wish to accept the employer's last offer in settlement. If the last offer is not acceptable, the injunction is dissolved and the President refers the case to Congress for such "appropriate action" as they deem advisable.

The reader should note that the LMRA does not provide for a compulsory method of dispute settlement, but leaves ultimate disposition of an unresolved national emergency case in the hands of the federal Congress upon referral by

---

[4] See *United States* v. *United Mine Workers,* 1947, 330 U.S. 258, 67 Sup. Ct. 677.

the President. The Act of 1947, Sections 206–210, expresses Congressional intention to leave open all legitimate methods of labor union self-help, subject to dilatory action by Presidential injunctive intervention and by providing facilities for mediation and conciliation in the hope that the parties will reach a settlement and avoid a crippling strike.

In *United Steelworkers of America* v. *U. S.*, 1959, 361 U.S. 39, the Supreme Court upheld the authority of the government to secure an injunction under Sections 206–210 in a case where a steel strike impeded production of vital weapons needed for defense. The court found that the facts adduced in the lower courts revealed . . ."the judgment below is amply supported on the ground that the strike imperils the national safety . . . the statute does recognize certain rights in the public to have unimpeded for a time production in industries vital to the national health or safety. . . . We are of opinion that the provision (of the statute) in question as applied here is not violative of the constitutional limitation prohibiting courts from exercising power of a legislative or executive nature. . . ."

At the other end of the spectrum, however, the U.S. Supreme Court in *Youngstown Sheet and Tube* v. *Sawyer,* 1952, 343 U.S. 579, denied that the existence of emergency alone, in the absence of prior Congressional authority, gave the President constitutional power to effect a seizure of major American steel mills which he attempted to accomplish by Executive Order in a steel strike stalemate in 1951. This case is included in this text at Chapter 10.

QUESTIONS ON SECTION 82

1. Briefly outline the pertinent national emergency strike provisions of the LMRA.
2. What question was involved in the *Steelworker* case?
3. Does national emergency vest in the President the power to seize American industry?

QUESTIONS ON CHAPTER 9

1. What constitutional basis supports the right to strike as written into labor legislation?
2. What types of strike activity are unprotected by law?
3. Distinguish between economic and unprotected and unfair labor practice strikes.
4. What are the reinstatement rights of economic strikers as opposed to unfair labor practice strikers?
5. When may strikers be discharged legally for strike activity?

Chapter 10

Dispute Settlement Law

SECTION 83 / PRIVATE AND PUBLIC INTEREST

This chapter will discuss the legal aspects of the procedures which aid the collective bargaining process, or occasionally act as substitutes, when the result is a stalemate rather than a settlement of differences between labor and management. These supplementary procedures to bargaining are mediation, arbitration, fact-finding, and similar third-party methods for settlement.

In Chapter 3 the procedures of the Railway Labor Act were discussed as applicable to the rail and air transportation industries covered by that statute. The more extensive coverage of Title II of the 1947 Labor-Management Relations Act has led to some other important legal decisions. Also the provisions for contract enforcement and damage suits in Title III of the Act have caused significant changes in the legal aspects of the bargaining process and in the relative authority of arbitration, the administrative bodies, and courts.

The labor relations laws treat collective bargaining as a private instrument, but at the same time as a public institution. The public interest grows out of the need to control conflict and to protect the economy from strikes as two inherent elements of labor relations.

The laws state their aims as reducing one source of industrial strife, resistance to good faith bargaining, and as encouraging "practices fundamental to the friendly adjustment of industrial disputes." [1] Private negotiation was to be relied upon as far as possible. Government direct action concerned primarily enforcing the duties of the negotiators toward one another with employee self-determination a prime consideration.

Both the Railway Labor Act and the Taft-Hartley Act do more than sponsor private bargaining over conflicts of interest. To protect the community and in order to avoid "jeopardy" to the "public health, safety, or interest," the laws include statutory limitations on labor in its organizing, striking, and bargaining activities. Conflicts over diverse interests of the bargaining parties are made subject to machinery established by Congress in the Taft-Hartley Act, as in the Railway Labor Act, including mediation and conciliation, fact-finding boards of inquiry, and injunctive restraints for disputes "imperiling the national health and safety."

---

[1] Policy of NLRA and RLA.

Although the law in a market-regulated economy is poorly suited to resolve union-management differences over economic questions and conflicts of economic power, or security, or status, it can be used to aid the parties to such disputes in resolving these bitterly disputed issues. Especially for situations of a public emergency nature, the government now has rules and procedures by enactment of Congress to guide the parties and to direct the executive and judicial branches.

SECTION 84 / DEFINITIONS AND TERMS

In order to understand the effects of this legislation and of the judicial opinions on the use of economic power in collective bargaining, it is important to understand the terms that are applied to labor dispute settlement. Six major supplements to collective bargaining are detailed below.

1. *Negotiation* is the act of settling the issues of a labor dispute directly between the immediate parties thereto, namely, between the representatives of each through the medium of collective bargaining. It is the first phase of dispute settlement. If it fails, it may be followed by the conciliatory devices of mediation and/or arbitration, on the one hand, as against self-help in the form of strike or picket pressure on the other.
2. *Mediation* is the act of a third-party intermediary, directed toward inducing the parties to a labor dispute to agree to a collective contract. It is synonymous with the term conciliation. It is directed to forestall resort to self-help pressure tactics or to stop their exercise if they have already begun. Pure mediation does not concern itself with the direct settlement of the issues at stake; the mediator makes no decision for the parties. He usually acts in the role of a neutral expert to aid the parties to the dispute to resume or continue their bargaining efforts. In some cases, the mediator may be called upon to make findings of fact looking to a solution, but his recommendations do not bind the parties.
3. *Voluntary Arbitration* is the act of resolving a labor dispute between the immediate parties through the medium of a neutral third party whom they empower to decide the issue(s) causing the dispute. His decision is binding upon the disputants and is enforceable in the courts. Most collective bargaining agreements today incorporate a provision requiring the submission of certain or all disputes to the arbitration process.
4. *Compulsory Arbitration* may be defined as arbitration compelled by a state or a federal statute, rather than obligatory by agreement of the parties.
5. *Fact-finding* covers a report on the issues and contentions, with or without recommendations for settling differences.
6. *Plant Seizure* is a final supplement which is explored in the *Youngstown* decision and which means that government "takes over" operations for protection of the public.

SECTION 85 / ASSISTING NEGOTIATIONS

Mandatory bargaining laws date back to 1926. Both the Railway Labor Act and the National Labor Relations Act impose a mandatory duty on management and the union representatives to negotiate in a bona fide effort to reach an agreement, covering conditions of employment and other related matters affecting management or union authority or employee welfare. This duty to negotiate in good faith continues throughout the period of an agreement. If controversies arise or grievances develop over the application of the contract, the interpretation of its language, or other appropriate matters, a legal duty to negotiate continues.

Negotiations may fail to resolve differences notwithstanding good faith efforts of the participants. Sometimes the economic, political, or personality differences preclude a mutually acceptable adjustment between a union and management. A strike threat or an actual strike may add to the difficulties because the interests and the viewpoints of union and management representatives may then become more inflexible.

Labor disputes differ from negotiations between commercial interests where disagreement can result in the termination of efforts at further dealing, and where disputes over language of an existing agreement can be decided by a court. A buyer may simply look for another seller and a seller for a different buyer. In labor negotiations, however, no alternative exists because employers and unions are not free agents. In the absence of an accord, a stoppage of operations will usually occur when no acceptable substitute or supplement can be found; court action is not a possibility to settle nonlegal disputes. Neutral third-party intervention is the usual course, by way of mediation and conciliation or by arbitration if the parties will agree to that course.

The Labor-Management Relations Act of 1947 established the Federal Mediation and Conciliation Service by Title II, with the function of aiding the parties to labor difficulties "to settle such disputes through conciliation and mediation." The Service is an independent agency reporting directly to the office of the President. Its duties may be summarized as follows, as given in Section 203 of the Labor-Management Relations Act of 1947:

1. "The Service may proffer its services in any labor dispute . . . whenever in its judgment such dispute threatens to cause a substantial interruption of commerce."
2. "If the Director (of the Service) is not able to bring the parties to agreement by conciliation . . . he shall seek to induce the parties voluntarily to seek other means of settling the dispute without resort to strike, lockout, or other coercion."
3. ". . . The Service is directed to make (itself) available in the settlement of grievance disputes only as a last resort and in exceptional cases."
4. Although parties to disputes are encouraged to use the Service, "the failure or refusal of either party to agree to any procedure suggested by the Director shall not be deemed a violation of any duty or obligation imposed by this Act."

The Federal Mediation and Conciliation Service concerns itself primarily with disputes arising from new agreement negotiations or from disagreements as to what shall be the changes in the renegotiation of an old agreement. Most of the states also have provided for the mediation of labor disputes by *ad hoc* or permanent mediators or boards of conciliation, and local facilities exist in a few cities. Dispute settlements that are worked out by such agencies may be enforced under the federal law procedures available for enforcing performance of collective agreements.

SECTION 86 / **VOLUNTARY ARBITRATION**

As a substitute for strikes or other direct action self-help weapons in disputes between labor and management, the parties may agree to have an outsider or a board determine their differences, agreeing in advance to accept this decision as final and binding. Such a tool exists in the form of arbitration, which may be used in many types of disagreements.

Voluntary arbitration of labor disagreements is a process having a widespread use in American labor-management relations. It rests entirely on the consent of the parties to collective bargaining. In practice arbitration operates usually without any implementation by legislation or any government sanction as a mutually adopted instrument for the maintenance of industrial operations by avoiding strikes and lockouts. Evidence of this acceptance is the Bureau of Labor Statistics' estimate that over 90 per cent of approximately 100,000 labor agreements in the nation contain a provision for the arbitration of unresolved grievances.

If the parties cannot resolve a dispute over the meaning or the application of the agreement, they have agreed in advance to accept the decisions of a neutral arbitrator who is acceptable to both the union and management. The authority of the arbitrator is defined by the stipulation of the parties. If the difference arises under the provisions of the existing collective bargaining agreement, that document may restrict the discretion of the arbitrator by its terms. A definition of the dispute or the issue to be resolved by the arbitrator is submitted to the arbitrator before a hearing gets started, often limiting his discretion to a greater degree than the collective bargaining contract.

By agreeing to arbitrate there exists an alternative to economic action for the disputing bargainers. Contractual arbitration has legal support as an alternative to formal judicial or administrative proceedings through courts of law and government agencies and also as an alternative to strikes or lockouts arising from grievances or other bargaining stalemates. Use of arbitration may be obligatory under a previously executed agreement or it may be accepted upon a mediator's recommendation to avoid the threat of any stoppage or other economic pressure, or perhaps to terminate such tactics which may have already been initiated.

In comparison to the almost universal use of grievance arbitration as the terminal step for disputes over contract interpretations and applications, voluntary third party arbitration of disputes over new or reopened agreements are much less frequently used. Under a standing agreement for such determination of a dispute, the acceptance of arbitration is obligatory upon the other party if requested by either party when direct negotiation or mediation has failed to bring about an agreement. However invoking such a step can cause a complicated argument over the arbitrability of the issues or over the applicability of arbitration to the situation involved in the dispute.

Unlike grievance arbitration which serves a quasi-judicial function and as a *quid pro quo* for waiving the right to direct action by either party, the arbitration of terms for a new or revised set of conditions can be distinquished as a quasi-legislative or rule-making function. Thus it is sometimes less acceptable, although as legally valid; it is also administratively supported by such agencies as the

Federal Mediation and Conciliation Service, the American Arbitration Association or the state mediation services.

In practice an arbitration agreement may be implemented by using an individual or by establishing a three-man tribunal composed of neutral members or of a neutral chairman with two partisan nominees. If difficulty develops in the selection of an acceptable neutral board member or if the parties are unable to agree on an acceptable single arbitrator, then by agreement a request for a panel of qualified professional labor arbitrators is sent to the American Arbitration Association (a nonprofit, nongovernment voluntary association) or to the Federal Mediation and Conciliation Service or to a state conciliation service. The Federal Service maintains a list of experienced arbitrators acceptable to both management and labor representatives, under the authority of its legislation. Title II of the Labor Management Relations Act includes in its policy statement "making available full and adequate government facilities for conciliation, mediation and voluntary arbitration." If there exists some difficulty between the parties in agreeing on a neutral so that even a list of names is of no value, the services will select and appoint an individual from its list. In some agreements where considerable use of an arbitrator is anticipated, such as in multi-plant or multi-employer agreements, the "permanent arbitrator" or umpire for a tri-partite arbitration arrangement may be named in the contract, although in practice his services will be continued only as long as both parties find him acceptable to the constituents of the contracting organizations. This method of appointment has the advantage over temporary or *ad hoc* appointments in that it saves the time and sometimes the difficulty involved in determining mutually on arbitrators to hear each dispute as it arises. To assist those who use arbitrators infrequently on an *ad hoc* basis the service agencies furnish pertinent biographical data when names are requested; sometimes an individual selected from such a list performs subsequently as the regular chairman for the parties without being so designated in any formal agreement. Whether he acts as permanent arbitrator under a contract designating him as such or as an *ad hoc* appointee, the usual practice assigns to each party to the dispute the duty to meet one half of the costs of the proceedings, including the per diem fee for each day of hearing, studying and opinion writing by the arbitrator and any other expenses.

Prior to or at the outset of a hearing the parties stipulate whatever precise issue or issues are to be decided by the individual arbitrator or board. If there is disagreement on this it may be left to the impartial arbitrator to define the issues after hearing preliminary opening statements from each side. Occasionally one party fails to appear at the duly noticed hearing or may only appear to object to its conduct, in which situation the arbitrator must decide whether to proceed on an extensive hearing, possibly subject to a court challenge as to propriety of the hearing.

SECTION 87 / NLRB DEFERRAL TO ARBITRATION

As stated in a previous section of this chapter, in arbitration of the grievances, the arbitrator or board of arbitrators are appointed by the parties pursuant to an arbitration clause in a collective bargaining agreement. The powers and duties of an arbitrator are limited by the terms of the agreement and he is generally confined to questions of whether or not a particular action was valid under the collective bargaining agreement. The arbitrator is concerned then with private rights under a private agreement between private parties. In contrast the NLRB has the statutory obligation to resolve unfair labor practice charges under the amended National Labor Relations Act. The Board's powers are statutory and it is concerned with public rights rather than private rights. What is the law when a particular action affects *both* a private contractual right and at the same time a public right guaranteed by statute? The answer to this question is developed below.

As a general rule the NLRB has the statutory powers to resolve unfair labor practice charges in matters relating to contract interpretation and is not ousted from jurisdiction by the existence of contract grievance-arbitration machinery. However, under the Board's *Spielberg* standards, the Board will defer to an existing arbitration award when (1) the arbitration proceedings were fair and regular, (2) all parties had agreed to be bound by the award, and (3) the results were not "clearly repugnant to the purposes and policies of the Act." [2] Thus, if a party was not allowed to be present at an arbitration proceeding, or to present witnesses or to cross-examine witnesses or to have a reasonable time to prepare its case, the Board would not defer to the award and would consider the unfair labor practice charge on its merits. In cases where a party had not agreed to be bound by the award, the Board will not defer. The final *Spielberg* standard that the award "not be repugnant to the purpose and policies of the Act" means that the award must be so contrary to the statutory policies contained in the Act as to *compel* a different conclusion. It does not mean that an arbitrator has to reach the same conclusions that the Board would reach if it were to decide the case on its merits.

In the *Collyer Insulated Wire* decision reported in this section, the Board announced that it will defer, at least contingently, to available contract arbitration procedures where alleged wrongful conduct may violate both the contract and the NLRA. The Board then will dismiss charges where grievance-arbitration machinery is available to the parties to resolve disputes even though an award has not yet been rendered or arbitration proceedings have not been instituted. The Board will retain jurisdiction for the limited purpose of ensuring compliance with its *Spielberg* standards once the arbitration award is rendered.

The *Collyer* case involved alleged violations of section 8(a)(5) of the Act. The Board has extended its *Collyer* deferral rule to cases involving discharges alleged to be violations of Section 8(a)(3) of the Act. In *National Radio Co.* where a union official was discharged for failing to notify his supervisor that he was going to another part of the plant on a grievance matter, the Board deferred pursuant to the *Collyer* rule even though no arbitration decision had yet been issued, but where arbitration machinery was available to resolve the dispute.[3] The Board stated in *National Radio* that the crucial determinant of deferral was the reasonableness of the assumption that the contractual arbitration procedure

---

[2] *Spielberg Mfg. Co.,* 112 NLRB 1080 (1955).
[3] 198 NLRB 1 (1972).

would resolve the dispute in a manner consistent with the *Spielberg* criteria.

The General Counsel of the NLRB has issued a memorandum on guidelines for the application of *Collyer.*[4] He has indicated that a *prima facie* warrant for the deferral of a dispute is established by the existence of a contract between the parties which makes binding arbitration available to the charging party, provided the dispute does not concern a special subject matter inappropriate for deferral. Some subject matters not appropriate for deferral include disputes over requests for information relevant to contract negotiations, disputes over the processing of grievances and disputes over union recognition.

Collyer Insulated Wire Co.

192 NLRB No. 150 (1971)

The employer, engaged in the manufacture and sale of insulated wire cable, was charged with violating Section 8(a)(5) of the Act by making assertedly unilateral changes in certain wages and working conditions.

The employer contended that its authority to make the changes was sanctioned by the collective-bargaining contract between the parties and by their course of dealing under the contract. The employer further contended that any of its actions in excess of contractual authorization should properly have been remedied by grievances and arbitration proceeding, as provided in the contract.

The union has represented the employer's production and maintenance employees under successive contracts since 1937. The contract provided for a job evaluation plan and for the adjustment of rates, subject to the grievance procedure, during the term of the contract. Throughout the bargaining relationship, the employer has routinely made adjustments in incentive rates to accommodate new or changed production methods.

Since early 1968, the employer's wage rates for skilled tradesmen have not been sufficiently high to attract and retain the numbers of skilled maintenance mechanics and electricians required for the efficient operation of the plant.

During negotiations, the employer several times proposed wage raises for maintenance employees over and above those being negotiated for the production and maintenance unit generally. The union rejected those proposals and the contract did not include any provision for such raises.

Following conclusion of the contract negotiations, the employer and the union continued to discuss the employer's desire to raise the rates for maintenance employees. Finally, the employer instituted an upward adjustment of 20 cents per hour. . . .

The contract between the parties made provision for adjustment by the employer in the wages of its employees during the contract term. The arbitra-

---

[4] Peter G. Nash, Memorandum: Arbitration Deferral Policy Under *Collyer*-Revised Guidelines (May 10, 1973).

tion provision made clear that the parties intended to make the grievance and arbitration machinery the exclusive forum for resolving contract disputes.

Trial Examiner's Decision:

It was found that the subject of the skill factor increase for maintenance tradesmen was discussed at meetings and that the employer's decision to grant such an increase was announced on November 12. It was found that despite these discussions, the union did not accede to the proposed change.

The Trial Examiner further found that the contract did not authorize the employer to act unilaterally in the matter and that by so acting the employer had sought to escape from the basic wage framework established in the contract. It was concluded that this was in violation of Section 8(a)(5) of the Act.

In considering the reassignment of duties related to the worm gear removal, the Trial Examiner found that the employer's actions were not sanctioned by the contract and had not been made the subject of bargaining between the union and the employer. Accordingly, he found that Section 8(a)(5) of the Act had been violated.

Concerning changes in the computation of incentive rates of extruder operators, it was found that the matter had been discussed at two of the three meetings. It was concluded that the contract and practice under it sanctioned the employer's action.

From the Board's Opinion:

We find merit in Respondent's exceptions that because this dispute in its entirety arises from the contract between the parties, and from the parties' relationship under the contract, it ought to be resolved in the manner which that contract prescribes. We conclude that the Board is vested with authority to withhold its processes in this case, and that the contract here made available a quick and fair means for the resolution of this dispute including, if appropriate, a fully effective remedy for any breach of contract which occurred. We conclude, in sum, that our obligation to advance the purposes of the Act is best discharged by the dismissal of this complaint.

In our view, disputes such as these can better be resolved by arbitrators with special skill and experience in deciding matters arising under established bargaining relationships than by the application by this Board of a particular provision of our statute. The necessity for such special skill and expertise is apparent upon examination of the issues arising from Respondent's actions with respect to the operators' rates, the skill factor increase, and the reassignment of duties relating to the worm gear removal. Those issues include, specifically: (a) the extent to which these actions were intended to be reserved to the management, subject to later adjustment by grievance and arbitration; (b) the extent to which the skill factor increase should properly be construed, under article IX of the agreement, as a "change in the general scale of pay" or, conversely, as "adjustments in individual rates . . . to remove inequalities or for other proper reason"; (c) the extent, if any, to which the procedures of article XIII governing new or changed jobs and job rates should have been made applicable to the skill factor increase here; and (d) the extent to which any of these issues may be affected by the long course of dealing between the parties. The determination of these issues, we think, is best left to discussions in the grievance procedure by the parties who negotiated the applicable provisions or, if such discussions do not resolve them, then to an arbitrator chosen under the agreement and authorized by it to resolve such issues.

The Board's authority, in its discretion, to defer to the arbitration process has never been questioned by the courts of appeals, or by the Supreme Court. Although Section 10(a) of the Act clearly vests the Board with jurisdiction over conduct which constitutes a violation of the provisions of Section 8, notwithstanding the existence of methods of "adjustment or prevention that might be established by agreement," nothing in the Act intimates that the Board must exercise jurisdiction where such methods exist. On the contrary in *Carey* v. *Westinghouse Electric Corporation,* 375 U.S. 261, 271 (1964), the Court indicated that it favors our deference to such agreed methods. . . .

In an earlier case, *Smith* v. *Evening News Assn.* the Supreme Court had likewise observed that, "the Board has, on prior occasions, declined to exercise its jurisdiction to deal with unfair labor practices in circumstances where, in its judgment, federal labor policy would best be served by leaving the parties to other processes of law." As in *Carey* v. *Westinghouse,* the decision carries a clear implication that the Court approved the informed use of such discretion.

The policy favoring voluntary settlement of labor disputes through arbitral processes finds specific expression in Section 203(d) of the LMRA, in which Congress declared:

> Final adjustment by a method agreed upon by the parties is hereby declared to be the desirable method for settlement of grievance disputes arising over the application or interpretation of an existing collective-bargaining agreement. And, of course, disputes under Section 301 of the LMRA called forth from the Supreme Court the celebrated affirmation of that national policy in the Steelworkers trilogy. . . .

The question whether the Board should withhold its process arises, of course, only when a set of facts may present not only an alleged violation of the Act but also an alleged breach of the collective-bargaining agreement subject to arbitration. Thus, this case like each such case compels an accommodation between, on the one hand, the statutory policy favoring the fullest use of collective bargaining and the arbitral process and, on the other, the statutory policy reflected by Congress' grant to the Board of exclusive jurisdiction to prevent unfair labor practices.

We address the accommodation required here with the benefit of the Board's full history of such accommodations in similar cases. From the start the Board has, case by case, both asserted jurisdiction and declined, as the balance was struck on particular facts and at various stages in the long ascent of collective bargaining to its present state of wide acceptance. Those cases reveal that the Board has honored the distinction between two broad but distinct classes of cases, those in which there has been an arbitral award, and those in which there has not.

In the former class of cases the Board has long given hospitable acceptance to the arbitral process. In *Timken Roller Bearing Company,* 70 NLRB 500, the Board refrained from exercising jurisdiction, in deference to an arbitrator's decision, despite the fact that the Board would otherwise have found that an unfair labor practice had been committed. The Board explained "[I]t would not comport with the sound exercise of our administrative discretion to permit the Union to seek redress under the Act after having initiated arbitration proceedings which, at the Union's request, resulted in a determination upon the merits." Id. at 501. The Board's policy was refined in *Spielberg Manufacturing Company,* where the Board established the now settled rule that it would limit its inquiry, in the presence of an arbitrator's award, to whether the procedures were fair and the results not repugnant to the Act.

In those cases in which no award had issued, the Board's guidelines have been less clear. At times the Board has dealt with the unfair labor practice, and at other times it has left the parties to their contract remedies. . . .

Jos. Schlitz Brewing Company,[5] is the most significant recent case in which the Board has exercised its discretion to defer. The underlying dispute in *Schlitz* was strikingly similar to the one now before us. In *Schlitz* the respondent employer decided to halt its production line during employee breaks. That decision was a departure from an established practice of maintaining extra employees, relief men, to fill in for regular employees during breaktime. The change resulted in, among other things, elimination of the relief man job classification. The change elicited a union protest leading to an unfair labor practice proceeding in which the Board ruled that the case should be "left for resolution within the framework of the agreed upon settlement procedures." The majority there explained its decision in these words:

> Thus, we believe that where, as here, the contract clearly provides for grievance and arbitration machinery, where the unilateral action taken is not designed to undermine the Union and is not patently erroneous but rather is based on a substantial claim of contractual privilege, and it appears that the arbitral interpretation of the contract will resolve both the unfair labor practice issue and the contract interpretation issue in a manner compatible with the purposes of the Act, then the Board should defer to the arbitration clause conceived by the parties. This particular case is indeed an appropriate one for just such deferral. The parties have an unusually long established and successful bargaining relationship; they have a dispute involving substantive contract interpretation almost classical in its form, each party asserting a reasonable claim in good faith in a situation wholly devoid of unlawful conduct or aggravated circumstances of any kind; they have a clearly defined grievance-arbitration procedure which Respondent has urged the Union to use for resolving their dispute; and, significantly, the Respondent, the party which in fact desires to abide by the terms of its contract, is the same party which, although it firmly believed in good faith in its right under the contract to take the action it did take, offered to discuss the entire matter with the Union prior to taking such action. Accordingly, under the principles above stated, and the persuasive facts in this case, we believe that the policy of promoting industrial peace and stability through collective bargaining obliges us to defer the parties to the grievance-arbitration procedures they themselves have voluntarily established. [175 NLRB No. 23, sl. op. at 5–6. Footnotes omitted.]

The circumstances of this case, no less than those in *Schlitz,* weigh heavily in favor of deferral. Here, as in *Schlitz,* this dispute arises within the confines of a long and productive collective-bargaining relationship. The parties before

---

[5] 175 NLRB No. 23 (1969).

us have, for 35 years, mutually and voluntarily resolved the conflicts which inhere in collective bargaining. Here, as there, no claim is made of enmity by Respondent to employees' exercise of protected rights. Respondent here has credibly asserted its willingness to resort to arbitration under a clause providing for arbitration in a very broad range of disputes and unquestionably broad enough to embrace this dispute.

Finally, here, as in *Schlitz,* the dispute is one eminently well suited to resolution by arbitration. The contract and its meaning in present circumstances lie at the center of this dispute. In contrast, the Act and its policies become involved only if it is determined that the agreement between the parties, examined in the light of its negotiating history and the practices of the parties thereunder, did not sanction Respondent's right to make the disputed changes, subject to review if sought by the Union, under the contractually prescribed procedure. That threshold determination is clearly within the expertise of a mutually agreed-upon arbitrator. In this regard we note especially that here, as in *Schlitz,* the dispute between these parties is the very stuff of labor contract arbitration. The competence of a mutually selected arbitrator to decide the issue and fashion an appropriate remedy, if needed, can no longer be gainsaid.

We find no basis for the assertion of our dissenting colleagues that our decision here modifies the standards established in *Spielberg* for judging the acceptability of an arbitrator's award. *Spielberg, supra* at 1082, established that such awards would not be contravened by this Board where:

> [T]he proceedings appear to have been fair and regular, all parties had agreed to be bound, and the decision of the arbitration panel is not clearly repugnant to the purposes and policies of the Act.

As already noted, the contract between Respondent and the Union unquestionably obligates each party to submit to arbitration any dispute arising under the contract and binds both parties to the result thereof. It is true, manifestly, that we cannot judge the regularity or statutory acceptability of the result in an arbitration proceeding which has not occurred. However, we are unwilling to adopt the presumption that such a proceeding will be invalid under *Spielberg* and to exercise our decisional authority at this juncture on the basis of a mere possibility that such a proceeding might be unacceptable under *Spielberg* standards. That risk is far better accommodated, we believe, by the result reached here of retaining jurisdiction against an event which years of experience with labor arbitration have now made clear is a remote hazard.

Member Fanning's dissenting opinion incorrectly characterizes this decision as instituting "compulsory arbitration" and as creating an opportunity for employers and unions to "strip parties of statutory rights."

We are not compelling any party to agree to arbitrate disputes arising during a contract term, but are merely giving full effect to their own voluntary agreements to submit all such disputes to arbitration, rather than permitting such agreements to be sidestepped and permitting the substitution of our processes, a forum not contemplated by their own agreement.

Nor are we "stripping" any party of "statutory rights." The courts have long recognized that an industrial relations dispute may involve conduct which, at least arguably, may contravene both the collective agreement and our statute. When the parties have contractually committed themselves to mutually agreeable procedures for resolving their disputes during the period of the contract, we are of the view that those procedures should be afforded full opportunity to function. The long and successful functioning of grievance and arbitration procedures suggests to us that in the overwhelming majority of cases, the utilization of such means will resolve the underlying dispute and make it unnecessary for either party to follow the more formal, and sometimes lengthy, combination of administrative and judicial litigation provided for under our statute. At the same time, by our reservation of jurisdiction, *infra,* we guarantee that there will be no sacrifice of statutory rights if the parties' own processes fail to function in a manner consistent with the dictates of our law. This approach, we believe, effectuates the salutary policy announced in *Spielberg,* which the dissenting opinion correctly summarizes as one of not requiring the "serious machinery of the Board where the record indicates that the parties are in the process of resolving their dispute in a manner sufficient to effectuate the policies of the Act."

We are especially mindful, finally, that the policy of this Nation to avoid industrial strife through voluntary resolution of industrial disputes is not static, but is dynamic. The years since enactment of Section 203(d) have been vital ones, and the policy then expressed has helped to shape an industrial system in which the institution of contract arbitration has grown not only pervasive but, literally, indispensable. The Board has both witnessed and participated in the growth, a complex interaction where the growth of arbitration in response to Congress' will has called forth and nurtured gradually broader conceptions of the basic policy. The Supreme Court which in *Lincoln Mills,* first upheld the enforceability of agreements to arbitrate disputes has recently, in *Boys Markets, Inc.* v. *Retail Clerks,* suggested that arbitration has become "the central institution in the administration of collective bargaining contracts." After *Boys Market* it may truly be said that where a contract provides for arbitration, either party has at hand legal and effective means to ensure that the arbitration will occur. We believe it to be consistent with the fundamental objectives of Federal law to require the parties here to honor their contractual obligations rather than, by casting this dispute in statutory terms, to ignore their agreed-upon procedures.

Without prejudice to any party and without deciding the merits of the controversy, we shall order that the complaint herein be dismissed, but we shall retain jurisdiction for a limited purpose. Our decision represents a developmental step in the Board's treatment of these problems and the controversy here arose at a time when the Board decisions may have led the parties to conclude that the Board approved dual litigation of this controversy before the Board and before an arbitrator. We are also aware that the parties herein have not resolved their dispute by the contractual grievance and arbitration procedure and that, therefore, we cannot now inquire whether resolution of the dispute will comport with the standards set forth in *Spielberg, supra.* In order to eliminate the risk of prejudice to any party we shall retain jurisdiction over this dispute solely for the purpose of entertaining an appropriate and timely motion for further consideration upon a proper showing that either (a) the dispute has not, with reasonable promptness after the issuance of this decision, either been resolved by amicable settlement in the grievance procedure or submitted promptly to arbitration, or (b) the grievance or arbitration procedures have not been fair and regular or have reached a result which is repugnant to the Act.

Member Brown wrote a concurring opinion.

Members Fanning and Jenkins wrote separate dissenting opinions. Their principal concern was that the Board was permitting statutory rights to be determined by private arbitrators and this they felt was an abdication of the authority vested in the Board under the Statute.

CASE QUESTIONS	1. What question was the Board called upon to decide?
	2. What action did the Board take on the complaint against the employer alleging 8(a)(5) unfair labor practices?
	3. What rationale did the Board give for its action on the complaint?
	4. Did the Board modify the *Spielberg* standards in this decision?

SECTION 88 / THE COURTS AND THE ARBITRATION PROCESS

In *Atkinson* v. *Sinclair Refining Co.,* the Supreme Court held that it is the responsibility of a court to determine whether a union and employer have agreed to arbitration.[6] Additionally, the Court held in *Sinclair* that the scope of the arbitration clause remains a matter for judicial decision. But once a court finds that the parties are subject to an agreement to arbitrate, and that agreement extends to "any difference" between them, then a claim that a particular grievance is barred by an equitable defense is itself an arbitrable issue under the agreement.[7] In *John Wiley & Sons* v. *Livingston,* where an employer refused to arbitrate on the ground that the union had failed to follow grievance procedures required by the collective bargaining agreement, the Supreme Court ordered arbitration, holding that "once it is determined . . . that the parties are obligated to submit the subject matter of a dispute to arbitration, 'procedural' questions which grow out of the dispute and bear on its final disposition should be left to the arbitrator."[8]

In *Textile Workers Union* v. *Lincoln Mills,* reported in this section, the Supreme Court held that under Section 301 of the LMRA, the courts could compel performance of an arbitration provision. In the famous *Steelworkers* Trilogy,[9] the Supreme Court further expanded the use of Section 301 suits to compel not only performance of grievance arbitration agreements but also to enforce arbitration awards. These cases established that the function of the courts

---

[6] 370 U.S. 238, 241 (1962).
[7] *Operating Engineers, Local 150* v. *Flair Builders, Inc.* 80 LRRM 2441 (1972).
[8] 376 U.S. 543 (1964).
[9] *United Steelworkers* v. *American Mfg. Co.* 363 U.S. 561 (1960); *United Steelworkers* v. *Warrior & Gulf Navigation Co.* 363 U.S. 574 (1960); *United Steelworkers* v. *Enterprise Wheel & Car Corp.* 363 U.S. 593 (1960).

is limited "to ascertaining whether the party seeking arbitration is making a claim which on its face is governed by the contract." [10] As pointed out in the *Capital Airways* decision printed in this section, the *Steelworkers* precedents also hold that the courts have no authority to substitute their interpretations of contractual provisions for interpretations rendered by arbitrators, where the authority to interpret has been granted to arbitrators.[11] Finally, the *Steelworkers* Trilogy sets out the rule that doubts concerning the coverage of the arbitration clause should be resolved in favor of coverage.[12]

The Supreme Court, which in *Lincoln Mills* first upheld the enforceability of agreements to arbitrate disputes, has submitted in its *Boys Markets, Inc.* v. *Retail Clerks* decision reported in Chapter 2, that arbitration has become "the central institution in the administration of collective bargaining contracts." Because of the *Boys Markets* decision, each party to a collective bargaining agreement which provides for arbitration now has a legal and effective means to guarantee that the arbitration will occur.

Textile Workers v. Lincoln Mills

Supreme Court of the United States, 1957. 353 U.S. 448

DOUGLAS, J.: Petitioner-union entered into a collective bargaining agreement in 1953 with respondent-employer, the agreement to run one year and from year to year thereafter, unless terminated on specified notices. The agreement provided that there would be no strikes or work stoppages and that grievances would be handled pursuant to a specified procedure. The last step in the grievance procedure—a step that could be taken by either party—was arbitration.

This controversy involves several grievances that concern work loads and work assignments. The grievances were processed through the various steps in the grievance procedure and were finally denied by the employer. The union requested arbitration, and the employer refused. Thereupon the union brought this suit in the District Court to compel arbitration.

The District Court concluded that it had jurisdiction and ordered the employer to comply with the grievance arbitration provisions of the collective bargaining agreement. The Court of Appeals reversed by a divided vote, 230 F.(2d) 81. It held that, although the District Court has jurisdiction to entertain the suit, the court had not authority founded either in federal or state law to grant the relief. The case is here on a petition for a writ of certiorari which we granted because of the importance of the problem and the contrariety of views in the courts. 352 U.S. 821.

The starting point of our inquiry is § 301 of the Labor Management Relations Act of 1947, which provides:

(a) Suits for violation of contracts between an employer and a labor organization representing employees in an industry affecting commerce as defined in this

---

[10] *United Steelworkers* v. *American Mfg. Co.* 363 U.S. 561, 568 (1960).
[11] *United Steelworkers* v. *Enterprise Wheel & Car Corp.* 363 U.S. 593 (1960).
[12] *United Steelworkers* v. *Warrior & Gulf Navigation Co.,* 363 U.S. 574 (1960).

chapter, or between any such labor organizations, may be brought in any district court of the United States having jurisdiction of the parties, without respect to the amount in controversy or without regard to the citizenship of the parties.

(b) Any labor organization which represents employees in an industry affecting commerce as defined in this chapter and any employer whose activities affect commerce as defined in this chapter shall be bound by the acts of its agents. Any such labor organization may sue or be sued as an entity and in behalf of the employees whom it represents in the courts of the United States. Any money judgment against a labor organization in a district court of the United States shall be enforceable only against the organization as an entity and against its assets, and shall not be enforceable against any individual member or his assets.

There has been considerable litigation involving § 301 and courts have construed it differently. There is one view that § 301(a) merely gives federal district courts jurisdiction in controversies that involve labor organizations in industries affecting commerce, without regard to diversity of citizenship or the amount in controversy. Under that view § 301(a) would not be the source of substantive law; it would neither supply federal law to resolve these controversies nor turn the federal judges to state law for answers to the questions. Other courts—the overwhelming number of them—hold that § 301(a) is more than jurisdictional—that it authorizes federal courts to fashion a body of federal law for the enforcement of these collective bargaining agreements and includes within that federal law specific performance of promises to arbitrate grievances under collective bargaining agreements. Perhaps the leading decision representing that point of view is the one rendered by Judge Wyzanski in *Textile Workers Union* v. *American Thread Co.,* 113 F. Supp. 137. That is our construction of § 301(a), which means that the agreement to arbitrate grievance disputes, contained in this collective bargaining agreement, should be specifically enforced.

From the face of the Act it is apparent that § 301(a) and § 301(b) supplement one another. Section 301(b) makes it possible for a labor organization, representing employees in an industry affecting commerce, to sue and be sued as an entity in the federal courts. Section 301(b) in other words provides the procedural remedy lacking at common law. Section 301(a) certainly does something more than that. Plainly, it supplies the basis upon which the federal district courts may take jurisdiction and apply the procedural rule of § 301(b). The question is whether § 301(a) is more than jurisdictional.

The legislative history of § 301 is somewhat cloudy and confusing. But there are a few shafts of light that illuminate our problem. . . .

. . . Both the Senate and the House took pains to provide for "the usual processes of the law" by provisions. which were the substantial equivalent of § 301(a) in its present form. Both the Senate Report and the House Report indicate a primary concern that unions as well as employees should be bound to collective bargaining contracts. But there was also a broader concern—a concern with a procedure for making such agreements enforceable in the courts by either party. At one point the Senate Report, *supra,* p. 15, states, "We feel that the aggrieved party should also have a right of action in the Federal courts. Such policy is completely in accord with the purpose of the Wagner Act which the Supreme Court declared was 'to compel employers to bargain collectively with their employees to the end that an employment contract, binding on both parties, should be made. . . .' "

Congress was also interested in promoting collective bargaining that ended with agreements not to strike. The Senate Report, *supra,* p. 16, states:

> If unions can break agreements with relative impunity, then such agreements do not tend to stabilize industrial relations. The execution of an agreement does not by itself promote industrial peace. The chief advantage which an employer can reasonably expect from a collective labor agreement is assurance of uninterrupted operation during the term of the agreement. Without some effective method of assuring freedom from economic warfare for the term of the agreement, there is little reason why an employer would desire to sign such a contract.
>
> Consequently, to encourage the making of agreements and to promote industrial peace through faithful performance by the parties, collective agreements affecting interstate commerce should be enforceable in the Federal courts. Our amendment would provide for suits by unions as legal entities and against unions as legal entities in the Federal courts in disputes affecting commerce.

Thus collective bargaining contracts were made "equally binding and enforceable on both parties."

Plainly the agreement to arbitrate grievance disputes is the *quid pro quo* for an agreement not to strike. Viewed in this light, the legislation does more than confer jurisdiction in the federal courts over labor organizations. It expresses a federal policy that federal courts should enforce these agreements on behalf of or against labor organizations and that industrial peace can be best obtained only in that way.

The question then is, what is the substantive law to be applied in suits under § 301(a)? We conclude that the substantive law to apply in suits under § 301(a) is federal law which the courts must fashion from the policy of our national labor laws. See Mendelsohn, Enforceability of Arbitration Agreements Under Taft-Hartley Section 301, 66 Yale L. J. 167. The Labor Management Relations Act expressly furnishes some substantive law. It points out what the parties may or may not do in certain situations. Other problems will lie in the penumbra of express statutory mandates. Some will lack express statutory sanction but will be solved by looking at the policy of the legislation and fashioning a remedy that will effectuate that policy. The range of judicial inventiveness will be determined by the nature of the problem. See *Board of Commissioners* v. *United States,* 308 U.S. 343, 351. Federal interpretation of the federal law will govern, not state law. Cf. *Jerome* v. *United States,* 318 U.S. 101, 104. But state law, if compatible with the purpose of § 301, may be resorted to in order to find the rule that will best effectuate the federal policy. See *Board of Commissioners* v. *United States, supra,* 351–352. Any state law applied, however, will be absorbed as federal law and will not be an independent source of private rights.

The question remains whether jurisdiction to compel arbitration of grievance disputes is withdrawn by the Norris-LaGuardia Act, 47 Stat. 70, 29 U.S.C. § 101. Section 7 of that Act prescribes stiff procedural requirements for issuing an injunction in a labor dispute. The kinds of acts which had given rise to abuse of the power to enjoin are listed in § 4. The failure to arbitrate was not a part and parcel of the abuses against which the Act was aimed.

Section 8 of the Norris-LaGuardia Act does, indeed, indicate a congressional policy toward settlement of labor disputes by arbitration, for it denies injunctive relief to any person who has failed to make "every reasonable effort" to settle the dispute by negotiation, mediation, or "voluntary arbitration." Though a literal reading might bring the dispute within the terms of the Act (see Cox, Grievance Arbitration in the Federal Courts, 67 Harv. L. Rev. 591, 602–604), we see no justification in policy for restricting § 301(a) to damage suits, leaving specific performance of a contract to arbitrate grievance disputes to the inapposite procedural requirements of that Act. Moreover, we held in *Virginian R. Co.* v. *System Federation,* 300 U.S. 515, and in *Graham* v. *Brotherhood Firemen,* 338 U.S. 232, 237, that the Norris-LaGuardia Act does not deprive federal courts of jurisdiction to compel compliance with the mandates of the Railway Labor Act. The mandates there involved concerned racial discrimination. Yet those decisions were not based on any peculiarities of the Railway Labor Act. We followed the same course in *Syres* v. *Oil Workers International Union,* 350 U.S. 892 which was governed by the National Labor Relations Act. There an injunction was sought against racial discrimination in application of a collective bargaining agreement; and we allowed the injunction to issue. The congressional policy in favor of the enforcement of agreements to arbitrate grievance disputes being clear, there is no reason to submit them to the requirements of § 7 of the Norris-LaGuardia Act. . . .

CASE QUESTIONS	1. Under what theory does the Court hold that Section 301(a) can be used to enforce arbitration agreements?
	2. What is said to be the relation of a no-strike clause to the arbitration of grievances?
	3. Does this decision make clear the applicability of any other labor law besides Taft-Hartley? How does this question affect the result?
	4. What was the Circuit Court decision?
	5. Does this decision reject the prior rule under common law as to enforcement of agreements to arbitrate?
	6. What does the Court say as to the applicability of state law along with Section 301?

Air Line Pilots Association v. Capitol International Airways, Inc.

United States Court of Appeals, Sixth, 1972. 458 F.2d 1344

Before PECK, MILLER and KENT, Circuit Judges.

PER CURIAM: This is an appeal by Capitol International Airways, Inc. (Capitol) from a decision of the District Court granting a summary judgment to enforce a decision of the arbitrator under a collective bargaining agreement. The facts are not complicated.

Paul J. Spivack was an employee of the defendant from 1966 until his discharge in 1969. Pursuant to the collective bargaining agreement he applied, and was accepted for training as a co-pilot on the company's DC-8 airplanes (a large jet airliner). For various reasons he was not permitted to complete this training while other employees of the defendant with less seniority did complete the training. On December 23, 1968 Spivack filed a grievance through the Air Line Pilots Association International (Association) pursuant to a collective bargaining agreement between Capitol and the Association. At the time he filed the grievance Spivack was on "furlough" because of the regular winter decline in the business of Capitol, a supplemental carrier. The grievance related to Capitol's use of personnel junior to Spivack in seniority, contrary to the collective bargaining agreement. After the filing of the grievance, and on January 2, 1969, Spivack's furlough was cancelled and he was ordered to report to Frankfort, Germany. He refused to report and his employment was terminated on February 13, 1969.

Spivack filed a second grievance protesting the discharge. The grievances were submitted to the System Board of Adjustment, pursuant to the collective bargaining agreement, which Board was unable to resolve the disputes. Thereafter, in accordance with the collective bargaining agreement the dispute was submitted to arbitration. The arbitrator found in favor of Spivack and ordered him reinstated with full seniority. Capitol refused to reinstate Spivack and this action was instituted in the District Court for specific performance of the arbitration award.

The arbitrator found that there was a conflict between the provisions of Sections 24(c) and 24(e) of the Collective Bargaining Agreement, which provide as follows:

> "(c) The right of preference to reemployment shall expire at the end of three (3) years from the date of last furlough.
>
> "(e) A furloughed pilot shall not be entitled to recall and reinstatement preference if he does not return to the service of the Company within two (2) weeks after notice to do so has been sent by registered mail or telegram to the last address filed with the Company."

The trial court, while stating a disagreement with the arbitrator's interpretation of the contract, recognized that under Provision (e) of the Supplemental Agreement between the parties:

> "(e) The Board shall have jurisdiction over disputes between any employee covered by the Pilots' Agreement and the Company, growing out of grievances or out of interpretation or application of any of the terms of the Pilots' Agreement. . . ."

the interpretation of the agreement was for the arbitrator and that the arbitrator's decision was binding upon the parties as provided in Provision (1) of the Supplemental Agreement:

> "Decisions of the Board in all cases properly referrable to it shall be final and binding upon the parties thereto."

Since the Steelworkers trilogy, *United Steelworkers* v. *American Mfg. Co.,* 363 U.S. 565 (1959); *United Steelworkers* v. *Warrior & Gulf Co.,* 363 U.S. 574 (1959); *United Steelworkers* v. *Enterprise Corp.,* 363 U.S. 593 (1959), the Courts of the United States have recognized that in labor arbitration cases there is no authority to substitute their interpretations of contractual provisions for interpretations rendered by arbitrators, where the authority to interpret has been granted to arbitrators. See *Machinists* v. *Central Airlines,* 372 U.S. 682 (1962). As stated in the *Enterprise* decision at 363 U.S. 599:

> "It is the arbitrator's construction that was bargained for; and so far as the arbitrator's decision concerns construction of the contract, the courts have no business overruling him because their interpretation of the contract is different from his."

We cannot say that the arbitrator's decision is so contrary to the agreement that it does not "draw its essence from the . . . agreement," nor can we say that there is a complete lack of ambiguity between Sections 24(c) and 24(e) of the Collective Bargaining Agreement.

For the reasons herein stated and for the reasons stated by District Judge L. Clure MORTON the judgment of the District Court is affirmed.

CASE QUESTIONS	1. Does a court have authority to substitute its interpretations of contractual provisions for that of an arbitrator? 2. What leading precedent did the court of appeals rely on for its decision?

SECTION 89 / **COMPULSORY ARBITRATION**

Compulsory arbitration means, under statutory requirements, that a public arbitration board or a single arbitrator shall decide disputes under specified circumstances. Laws requiring compulsory arbitration exist in Australia and in New Zealand, negating the right to strike.

Experience with compulsory arbitration of labor disputes in the United States dates back to 1888 in the form of the Federal Arbitration Act which applied to railway labor disputes. Though on the statute books for ten years, it was never resorted to and was replaced by the Erdman Act in 1898 which provided for voluntary arbitration of railway labor-management tensions.

Mandatory arbitration has since been resorted to at the federal level. Under conditions of war, for example, the National War Labor Board exercised arbitration authority under a War Labor Disputes Act of 1943. Predating this statute was the Adamson Act of 1916 which provided for compulsory arbitration of railway labor disputes. Both laws were repealed when hostilities ceased.

Presently the Supreme Court has precluded the states from forcing arbitration, unless by agreement, in industries subject to federal authority under the doctrine of preemption.[13] However, Congress has the authority to require arbitration of public interest emergency disputes. The *Brotherhood of Locomotive Firemen* decision shows that this power has been upheld by the courts, but that power is denied the executive branch of government if it is not exercised in accordance with a congressional prior authorization, an effective way of maintaining a system of checks and balances.[14]

The limited present use of compulsory arbitration in the area of public employee bargaining is discussed in Chapter 13.

SECTION 90 / **SEIZURE OF VITAL INDUSTRY**

Sections 206–210 of the LMRA set out procedures for the resolution of national emergency strikes. Provision is made for Presidential Boards of Inquiry, the injunctive process to forestall such strikes for 80 days, interim mediation and conciliation to restore bargaining, strike ballots, and ultimate reporting by the President to Congress for legislative action, all other efforts having failed.

The procedures are both complex and dilatory; it must be emphasized that it does not require compulsory arbitration since ultimately the right of the union to call a strike is preserved. Since passage of the Act of 1947, no President has, as of this writing, secured special enabling legislation of the Congress. The *United Mine Workers* decision of 1947 involved federal seizure of soft coal mines and subsequently required civil and criminal contempt proceedings instituted by the federal government to terminate a nationwide strike of coal miners which had been called in ostensible violation of an outstanding injunction. The Supreme Court of the United States upheld the Executive Order for seizure and found that the Norris-LaGuardia Act was inapplicable where the federal government was properly exercising a "sovereign function" under Congressional authority found in the War Labor Disputes Act. This Act was, however, permitted to lapse in June of 1947.

This brings us to the crippling steel strike of 1952 in which the President, instead of resorting to the dilatory procedures of the LMRA, seized the steel industry by Executive Order as being a proper exercise of presidential power in time of national emergency. The United States Supreme Court scrutinizes the Presidential seizure power in the *Youngstown* case next following. Compulsion as a means of settling labor-management conflicts of interest involves constitutional problems of freedom of contract, of person, and of property rights. The Supreme Court also makes clear that legislation is necessary to enable the seizure of plants by the President, emphasizing the separation of legislative and executive powers in our government. Notwithstanding the reluctance of government to coerce in the sphere of economic action, it must be remembered that man-made law is not immutable and that future exigencies may change the direction of public policy as it has in other democratic countries.

---

[13] *Amalgamated Association* v. *Wisconsin Employment Relations Board,* 340 U.S. 383 (1951).
[14] *Brotherhood of Locomotive Firemen and Engineermen* v. *Chicago, Burlington and Quincy R.R. Co.,* 225 F. Supp. 11 (1964).

Youngstown Sheet and Tube Co. v. Sawyer

Supreme Court of the United States, 1952. 343 U.S. 579

BLACK, J.: We are asked to decide whether the President was acting within his constitutional power when he issued an order directing the Secretary of Commerce to take possession of and operate most of the Nation's steel mills. The mill owners argue that the President's order amounts to law-making, a legislative function which the Constitution has expressly confided to the Congress and not to the President. The Government's position is that the order was made on findings of the President that his action was necessary to avert a national catastrophe which would inevitably result from a stoppage of steel production, and that in meeting this grave emergency the President was acting within the aggregate of his constitutional powers as the Nation's Chief Executive and the Commander in Chief of the Armed Forces. . . .

In the latter part of 1951, a dispute arose between the steel companies and their employees over terms and conditions that should be included in new collective bargaining agreements. Long-continued conferences failed to resolve the dispute. On December 18, 1951, the employees' representative, United Steelworkers of America, CIO, gave notice of an intention to strike when the existing bargaining agreements expired on December 31. Thereupon the Federal Mediation and Conciliation Service intervened in an effort to get labor and management to agree. This failing, the President on December 22, 1951, referred the dispute to the Federal Wage Stabilization Board to investigate and make recommendations for fair and equitable terms of settlement. This Board's report resulted in no settlement. On April 4, 1952, the union gave notice of a nation-wide strike called to begin at 12:01 a.m. April 9. The indispensability of steel as a component of substantially all weapons and other war materials led the President to believe that the proposed work stoppage would immediately jeopardize our national defense and that governmental seizure of the steel mills was necessary in order to assure the continued availability of steel. Reciting these considerations for his action, the President, a few hours before the strike was to begin, issued Executive Order 10340. . . . The order directed the Secretary of Commerce to take possession of and operate most of the steel mills throughout the country. . . .

Obeying the Secretary's orders under protest, the companies brought proceedings against him in the District Court. Their complaints charged that the seizure was not authorized by an act of Congress or by any constitutional provisions. The District Court was asked to declare the orders of the President and the Secretary invalid and to issue preliminary and permanent injunctions restraining their enforcement. Opposing the motion for preliminary injunction, the United States asserted that a strike disrupting steel production for even a brief period would so endanger the well-being and safety of the nation that the President has "inherent power" to do what he had done—power "supported by the Constitution, by historical precedent, and by court decisions.". . . Deeming it best that the issues raised be promptly decided by this Court, we granted certiorari on May 3. . . .

The President's power to issue the order must stem either from an act of Congress or from the Constitution itself. There is no statute that expressly authorizes the President to take possession of property as he did here. Nor is there any act of Congress to which our attention has been directed from which such a power can fairly be implied. Indeed, we do not understand the Government to rely on statutory authorization for this seizure. There are two statutes which do authorize the President to take both personal and real property under certain conditions. However, the Government admits that these conditions were not met and that the President's order was not rooted in either of them. The Government refers to the seizure provisions of one of these statutes [Sec. 201(b) of the Defense Production Act] as "much too cumbersome, involved, and time-consuming for the crisis which was at hand."

Moreover, the use of the seizure technique to solve labor disputes in order to prevent work stoppages was not only unauthorized by any congressional enactment; prior to this controversy, Congress had refused to adopt that method of settling labor disputes. When the Taft-Hartley Act was under consideration in 1947, Congress rejected an amendment which would have authorized such governmental seizures in cases of emergency. Apparently it was thought that the technique of seizure, like that of compulsory arbitration, would interfere with the process of collective bargaining. Consequently, the plan Congress adopted in that Act did not provide for seizure under any circumstances. Instead, the plan sought to bring about settlements by use of the customary devices of mediation, conciliation, investigation by boards of inquiry, and public reports. In some instances temporary injunctions were authorized to provide cooling-off periods. All this failing, the unions were left free to strike after a secret vote by employees as to whether they wished to accept their employer's final settlement offer.". . .

The order cannot properly be sustained as an exercise of the President's military power as Commander in Chief of the Armed Forces. The Government attempts to do so by citing a number of cases upholding broad powers in military commanders engaged in day-to-day fighting in a theater of war. Such cases need not concern us here. Even though "theater of war" be an expanding concept, we cannot with faithfulness to our constitutional system hold that the Commander in Chief of the Armed Forces has the ultimate power as such to take possession of private property in order to keep labor disputes from stopping production. This is a job for the Nation's lawmakers, not for its military authorities.

Nor can the seizure order be sustained because of the several constitutional provisions that grant executive power to the President. In the framework of our Constitution, the President's power to see that the laws are faithfully executed refutes the idea that he is to be a lawmaker. The Constitution limits his functions in the law-making process to the recommending of laws he thinks wise and the vetoing of laws he thinks bad. And the Constitution is neither silent nor equivocal about who shall make laws which the President is to execute. . . .

It is said that other Presidents without congressional authority have taken possession of private business enterprises in order to settle labor disputes. But even if this be true, Congress has not thereby lost its exclusive constitutional authority to make laws necessary and proper to carry out the powers vested by the Constitution "in the Government of the United States, or any Department or Officer thereof."

The Founders of this Nation entrusted the lawmaking power to the Congress alone in both good and bad times. It would do no good to recall the historical events, the fears of power and the hopes for freedom that lay behind their choice. Such a review would but confirm our holding that this seizure order cannot stand.

The judgment of the District Court is *Affirmed.*

CASE QUESTIONS

1. Did the President in the *Youngstown* decision follow procedures outlined in the LMRA?
2. Who initiated this court action?
3. From where does the President derive his powers?
4. Discuss the view of the Supreme Court regarding the President's power as chief of the military.

QUESTIONS ON CHAPTER 10

1. Was conciliation and mediation effected by the 1947 Act? How?
2. Does the Supreme Court approve of the seizure of plants in vital industries?
3. Is compulsory arbitration constitutional?
4. Is a voluntary arbitration decision enforceable? How?

Chapter 11

Regulating Internal Union Conduct

SECTION 91 / INTRODUCTION

We have seen how labor organizations are legally permitted to engage in conduct that is prohibited to other groups by such statutes as the antitrust laws. Labor has been restricted, however, from engaging in some activities permitted to other voluntary associations, as was made clear in Chapters 7, 8, and 9.

The unique legal status of organized labor reflects the legislative and judicial thinking concerning the power and authority of unions *vis-a-vis* employers, employees, and the entire community. That power developed after the National Labor Relations Act assured employees the right to join a labor organization without employer interference, and permitted agreements requiring all of the employees to join the majority's choice of labor organization as a condition of employment.

In 1947 union responsibilities toward employees and toward employers were added to the law. Employees were now protected as to the right to refrain from union activities while union membership could no longer be demanded as the condition of hiring under closed-shop agreements. The 1947 amendments also prohibited unions from coercing employees or from forcing employers to discriminate, and other responsibilities were imposed by the provisions making it unfair for a union to charge a discriminatory or excessive initiation fee or to have dues deducted by the employer unless individually authorized by each member of the bargaining unit. Chapter 7 covered these practices.

The duties of the union officers and the union's responsibility to its members were further defined in 1947. To protect employees from irregularities of union officials and from representation for subversive political ends, detailed reports were to be sent to the Secretary of Labor, with copies furnished all members; and Union campaign contributions for federal elections were prohibited if derived from members' dues or assessments as unfair to the individual member who voted differently.

Continued dissatisfaction with the conduct of some unions and companies toward employees and with abuse of power by union officers resulted in investigation by Congress that brought about the Labor-Management Reporting and Disclosure Act of 1959. That law imposed further duties and responsibilities on

384

labor unions and their officials for the protection of the members, and required also employer disclosure of his part in irresponsible dealings.

Chapter 7 covered union unfair practices in organizing and bargaining resulting from the 1947 and 1959 legislation. In this chapter the duties imposed on unions in relation to workers and to union members will be discussed and explained under existing law up through the Federal Election Campaign Act of 1971.

Most unions are unincorporated voluntary associations at common law. The limits of proper authority over the members, the liability of the union officials to the members, the financial responsibilities of unions and their members' liability have not been clearly or uniformly defined at common law. The federal statutes concerned with these questions, the common law rules and statutory provisions as to the internal responsibilities and liabilities of labor organizations, of their officials, and of the members are all included in this chapter as matters of internal union practices.

The present chapter is concerned with the laws as applied by courts and agencies that have authority to rule on internal union practices affecting individual or group rights. Matters of discrimination by unions on grounds of race, color, national origin or sex are covered in Chapter 12. This present chapter covers the procedures and the standards that have been established by law for protecting the union members, either the individual or a minority, from abuse by leaders or arbitrary application of union bylaws and constitutions. The statutory restraints and remedies are included.

Although the union organization and its officials are generally not opponents of the employees who make up the membership, conflict issues arise between individuals and minority groups over rights or interests. Disputes arise also between the majority and their representatives, including conflicts over the application of the fair representation principle underlying the collective bargaining statutes. As in other political activities and institutions based on majority rule, the individual's freedom will often be sacrificed to protect the benefits or the bargaining power of the group or to enhance the long run bargaining position of the organization. A labor organization's constitution and bylaws usually provide internal avenues for legal protection with remedies against unfair or arbitrary action by union officials.

In the cases that follow, the Supreme Court affirms the right of a union majority to make and to enforce its own rules and procedures.

SECTION 92 / SELECTED RESPONSIBILITIES AND DUTIES

Union officials have a duty to provide fair and nondiscriminating representation for all persons in a bargaining unit. The employees have a duty to accept the conditions negotiated on their behalf. Within the membership group or between the members and their union officials there exists the duty to fulfill obligations established under the union constitution and bylaws as well as the obligations created in collective bargaining agreements.

The duties of the officials and the members may be thought of as mutual and reciprocal. The officials must serve the interests of the members in good faith while the members have the duty to accept the conditions negotiated and agreed to by properly selected officials and to comply with internal union rules and policies if properly adopted by constitutional procedures.

In the event that a member believes that the Union or its officials have violated his rights through malicious or arbitrary action, he has the legal redress to sue for damages, in addition to any relief that may be available through any agency of government established to enforce specific statutory rights.

In *Vaca* v. *Sipes*,[1] the Supreme Court set out the requirements imposed upon a union in processing an employee's grievance under a collective bargaining contract. In *Vaca*, an employee who suffered from high blood pressure took an extended sick leave. He was later certified by his family physician as fit to resume his work. The employer's doctor examined him and refused him reinstatement. The employee received a second authorization from another outside doctor but ultimately was permanently discharged for poor health. The union processed a grievance on behalf of the employee through the pre-arbitration steps of the collective bargaining agreement; but, based on a negative medical opinion which the union itself had required and paid for, the union refused to take the case to arbitration. The employee brought suit against the union under Section 301 of the LMRA for damages for failure to represent him fairly in processing his grievance with the employer. The Missouri Supreme Court sustained a jury award of damages in favor of the employee. The Supreme Court of the United States, on appeal, held that the union has the discretion to make decisions "in good faith and in a nonarbitrary manner" as to the merits of any particular grievance. Citing the case of *Ford Motor Company* v. *Huffman*,[2] the majority opinion stated that while a union "may not arbitrarily ignore a meritorious grievance or process it in perfunctory fashion we do not agree that the individual employee has an absolute right to have his grievance taken to arbitration regardless of the provisions of the applicable agreement." In the absence of evidence of personal hostility to the member or of any bad faith, the Court said that a union could not be found to have breached its duty of fair representation to the member when it decided not to arbitrate his grievance as not meritorious. In a dissent, Justice Black said the majority imposed too much of a burden on the employee by requiring that he prove that the union had acted in bad faith or arbitrarily.

In the *Boilermakers* case presented in this section, an expelled member had filed suit under Section 102 of the LMRDA alleging violation of his rights, as protected under Section 101 which requires specific charges, time to prepare a defense and a full and fair hearing before being disciplined or expelled. He won his suit in the trial court, receiving a damages award from a jury of $152,150 which was affirmed by the Court of Appeals. The Supreme Court reversed, however, on the ground that the lower courts had not followed the usual rule of judicial nonintervention in internal union affairs. The due process requirements

---

[1] 386 U.S. 171 (1967). The significant jurisdictional aspects of this case were discussed in Chapter 4, Section 29, "Jurisdiction: Preemption."
[2] 345 U.S. 330 (1953).

had been observed within the union; therefore it said, a court should not inject itself into internal union matters or substitute its judgment for that of the union.

Boilermakers v. Hardeman

Supreme Court of the United States, 1971. 401 U.S. 233

BRENNAN, J.: Section 102 of the Labor-Management Reporting and Disclosure Act (hereafter LMRDA) provides that a union member who charges that his union violated his rights under Title I of the Act may bring a civil action against the union in a district court of the United States for appropriate relief.[3] Respondent was expelled from membership in petitioner union and brought this action under § 102 in the District Court for the Southern District of Alabama. He alleged that in expelling him the petitioner violated § 101(a)(5) of the Act, 73 Stat. 519, 29 U.S.C. § 411(a)(5) which provides: "No member of any labor organization may be fined, suspended, expelled, or otherwise disciplined except for nonpayment of dues by such organization or by any officer thereof unless such member has been (A) served with written specific charges; (B) given a reasonable time to prepare his defense; (C) afforded a full and fair hearing." A jury awarded respondent damages of $152,150. The Court of Appeals for the Fifth Circuit affirmed. 420 F.2d 485 (1969). We granted certiorari limited to the questions whether the subject matter of the suit was preempted because exclusively within the competence of the National Labor Relations Board and, if not preempted, whether the courts below had applied the proper standard of review to the union proceedings, 398 U.S. 926 (1970). We reverse.

The case arises out of events in the early part of October 1960. Respondent, George Hardeman, is a boilermaker. He was then a member of petitioner's Local Lodge 112. On October 3, he went to the union hiring hall to see Herman Wise, business manager of the Local Lodge and the official responsible for referring workmen for jobs. Hardeman had talked to a friend of his, an employer who had promised to ask for him by name for a job in the vicinity. He sought assurance from Wise that he would be referred for the job. When Wise refused to make a definite commitment, Hardeman threatened violence if no work was forthcoming in the next few days.

On October 4, Hardeman returned to the hiring hall and waited for a referral. None was forthcoming. The next day, in his words, he "went to the hall . . . and waited from the time the hall opened until we had the trouble. I tried to make up my mind what to do, whether to sue the local or Wise or beat hell out of Wise, and then I made up my mind." When Wise came out of his office to go to a local jobsite, as required by his duties as business

---

[3] Section 102 of the Act, 73 Stat. 519, 29 U.S.C. § 412, provides:

"Any person whose rights secured by the provisions of this title have been infringed by any violation of this title may bring a civil action in the district court of the United States for such relief (including injunctions) as may be appropriate. Any such action against a labor organization shall be brought in the district court of the United States for the district where the alleged violation occurred, or where the principal office of such labor organization is located."

manager, Hardeman handed him a copy of a telegram asking for Hardeman by name. As Wise was reading the telegram, Hardeman began punching him in the face.

Hardeman was tried for this conduct on charges of creating dissension and working against the interest and harmony of the Local Lodge,[4] and of threatening and using force to restrain an officer of the Local Lodge from properly discharging the duties of his office.[5] The trial committee found him "guilty as charged," and the Local Lodge sustained the finding and voted his expulsion for an indefinite period. Internal union review of this action, instituted by Hardeman, modified neither the verdict nor the penalty. Five years later, Hardeman brought this suit alleging that petitioner violated § 101(a)(5) by denying him a full and fair hearing in the union disciplinary proceedings.

We consider first the union's claim that the subject matter of this lawsuit is, in the first instance, within the exclusive competence of the National Labor Relations Board. The union argues that the gravamen of Hardeman's complaint—which did not seek reinstatement, but only damages for wrongful expulsion, consisting of loss of income, loss of pension and insurance rights, mental anguish and punitive damages—is discrimination against him in job referrals; that any such conduct on the part of the union is at the very least arguably an unfair labor practice under §§ 8(b)(1)(A) and 8(b)(2) of the National Labor Relations Act, 29 U.S.C. §§ 158(b)(1)(A), 158(b)(2); and that in such circumstances, "the federal courts must defer to the exclusive competence of the National Labor Relations Board if the danger of . . . interference with national policy is to be averted." *San Diego Building Trades Council* v. *Garmon*, 359 U.S. 236, 245 (1959); see *Local 100, Journeymen* v. *Borden*, 373 U.S. 690 (1963).

We think the union's argument is misdirected. Hardeman's complaint alleged that his expulsion was unlawful under § 101(a)(5), and sought compensation for the consequences of the claimed wrongful expulsion. The critical issue presented by Hardeman's complaint was whether the union disciplinary proceedings had denied him a full and fair hearing within the meaning of § 101(a)(5)(C).[6] Unless he could establish this claim, Hardeman would be out of court. We hold that this claim was not within the exclusive competence of the National Labor Relations Board.

---

[4] Article 13, § 1, of the Subordinate Lodge Constitution then in force provided:
"Any member who endeavors to create dissension among the members; or who works against the interest and harmony of the International Brotherhood or of any District or Subordinate Lodge; who advocates or encourages a division of the funds, or the dissolution of any District or Subordinate Lodge, or the separation of any District or Subordinate Lodge from the International Brotherhood; who supports or becomes a member of any dual or subversive organization which shall be hostile to the International Brotherhood or to any of its Subordinate Lodges, or which is antagonistic to the principles and purposes of the International Brotherhood, shall upon conviction thereof be punished by expulsion from the International Brotherhood."
[5] Article 12, § 1, of the Subordinate Lodge By-Laws then in force provided that "It shall be a violation of these By-Laws for any member through the use of force or violence or the threat of the use of force or violence to restrain, coerce, or intimidate, or attempt to restrain, coerce, or intimidate any official of this International Brotherhood or Subordinate Lodge to prevent or attempt to prevent him from properly discharging the duties of his office." Violators of Article 12 are to "be punished as warranted by the offense."
[6] Hardeman's complaint did not claim that the charges were insufficiently specific, or that he did not have adequate time to prepare his defense in the union proceedings.

" 'The doctrine of primary jurisdiction . . . applies where a claim is originally cognizable in the courts, and comes into play whenever enforcement of the claim requires the resolution of issues which, under a regulatory scheme, have been placed within the special competence of an administrative body; in such a case the judicial process is suspended pending referral of such issues to the administrative body for its views.' *United States* v. *Western Pac. R. Co.,* 352 U.S. 59, 63–64. The doctrine is based on the principle 'that in cases raising issues of fact not within the conventional experience of judges or cases requiring the exercise of administrative discretion, agencies created by Congress for regulating the subject matter should not be passed over,' *Far East Conference* v. *United States,* 342 U.S. 570, 574, and 'requires judicial abstention in cases where protection of the integrity of a regulatory scheme dictates preliminary resort to the agency which administers the scheme,' *United States* v. *Philadelphia Nat. Bank,* 374 U.S. 321, 353." *Local 189, Amalgamated Meat Cutters* v. *Jewel Tea Co.,* 381 U.S. 676, 684–685 (1965) (opinion of WHITE, J., announcing judgment).

Those factors suggesting that resort must be had to the administrative process are absent from the present case. The fairness of an internal union disciplinary proceeding is hardly a question beyond "the conventional experience of judges," nor can it be said to raise issues "within the special competence" of the NLRB. See *NLRB* v. *Allis-Chalmers Mfg. Co.,* 388 U.S. 175, 181, 193–194 (1967). As we noted in that case, the Eighty-Sixth Congress which enacted § 101(a)(5) was "plainly of the view" that the protections embodied therein were new material in the body of federal labor law. 388 U.S. at 194. And that same Congress explicitly referred claims under § 101(a)(5) not to the NLRB, but to the federal district courts. This is made explicit in the opening sentence of § 102: "Any person whose rights secured by the provisions of this title have been infringed by any violation of this title may bring a civil action in a district court of the United States for such relief (including injunctions) as may be appropriate." Of course, "[t]he purpose of Congress is the ultimate touchstone." *Retail Clerks Local 1625* v. *Schermerhorn,* 375 U.S. 96, 103 (1963). And in § 102 Congress has clearly indicated a purpose to refer claims regarding violation of § 101(a)(5) to the district courts.

The union argues that Hardeman's suit should nevertheless have been dismissed because he did not seek an injunction restoring him to membership, and because he did seek damages for loss of employment said to be the consequence of his expulsion from the union. Taken together, these factors are said to shift the primary focus of the action from a review of Hardeman's expulsion to a review of alleged union discrimination against him in job referrals. Since this is a matter normally within the exclusive competence of the NLRB, see *Local 100, Journeymen* v. *Borden* 373 U.S., at 695–696, the union argues that Hardeman's suit was beyond the competence of the district court.

The argument has no merit. To begin with, the language of § 102 does not appear to make the availability of damages turn upon whether an injunction is requested as well. If anything, § 102 contemplates that damages will be the usual, and injunctions the extraordinary form of relief. Requiring that injunctive relief be sought as a precondition to damages would have little effect other than to force plaintiffs, as a matter of course, to add a few words to their complaint seeking an undesired injunction. We see no reason to import into § 102 so trivial a requirement.

Nor are our prior cases authority for such a result. We have repeatedly held, of course, that state law may not regulate conduct either protected or prohibited by the National Labor Relations Act. *Local 100, Journeymen* v. *Borden, supra; San Diego Building Trades Council* v. *Garmon,* 359 U.S., at 244; *Weber* v. *Anheuser-Busch, Inc.,* 348 U.S. 468, 480–481 (1955); *Garner* v. *Teamsters Union,* 346 U.S. 485, 490–491 (1953). Where it has not been clear whether particular conduct is protected, prohibited, or left to state regulation by that Act, we have likewise required courts to stay their hand, for "courts are not primary tribunals to adjudicate such issues. It is essential to the administration of the Act that these determinations be left in the first instance to the National Labor Relations Board." *Building Trades Council* v. *Garmon, supra,* at 244–245. Nor may courts intervene in such matters even to apply the National Labor Relations Act, except by the normal mechanism of review of actions of the NLRB. For recognizing that "[a] multiplicity of tribunals and a diversity of procedures are quite as apt to produce incompatible or conflicting adjudications as are different rules of substantive law," *Garner* v. *Teamsters Union, supra,* Congress confided to the NLRB the primary power of interpretation and application of the Act. See *Guss* v. *Utah Labor Relations Board,* 353 U.S. 1 (1957).

The present case, however, implicates none of the principles discussed above. There is no attempt, in this lawsuit, to apply state law to matters preempted by federal authority. Nor is there an attempt to apply federal law of general application, which is limited in the particular circumstances by the National Labor Relations Act. Nor is there an attempt to have the district court enforce the provisions of the National Labor Relations Act itself, without guidance from the NLRB. As we have said, the critical question in this action is whether Hardeman was afforded the rights guaranteed him by § 101 (a)(5) of the LMRDA. If he was denied them, Congress has said that he is entitled to damages for the consequences of that denial. Since these questions are irrelevant to the legality of conduct under the National Labor Relations Act, there is no danger of conflicting interpretation of its provisions. And since the law applied is federal law explicitly made applicable to such circumstances by Congress, there is no danger that state law may come in through the back door to regulate conduct that has been removed by Congress from state control. Accordingly, this action was within the competence of the district court.

Two charges were brought against Hardeman in the union disciplinary proceedings. He was charged with violation of Article 13, § 1, of the Subordinate Lodge Constitution, which forbids attempting to create dissension or working against the interest and harmony of the union, and carries a penalty of expulsion. He was also charged with violation of Article 12, § 1, of the Subordinate Lodge By-Laws, which forbids the threat or use of force against any officer of the union in order to prevent him from properly discharging the duties of his office; violation may be punished "as warranted by the offense." Hardeman's conviction on both charges was upheld in internal union procedures for review.

The trial judge instructed the jury that "whether or not he [respondent] was rightfully or wrongfully discharged or expelled is a pure question of law for me to determine." He assumed, but did not decide, that the transcript of the union disciplinary hearing contained evidence adequate to support conviction of violating Article 12. He held, however, that there was no evidence at all in the transcript of the union disciplinary proceedings to support the charge of violating Article 13. This holding appears to have been based on the Fifth Circuit's decision in *Boilermakers* v. *Braswell*, 388 F.2d 193 (CA-5 1968). There the Court of Appeals for the Fifth Circuit had reasoned that "penal provisions in union constitutions must be strictly construed" and that as so construed Article 13 was directed only to "threats to the union as an organization and to the effective carrying out of the union's aims," not to merely personal altercations. 388 F.2d at 199. Since the union tribunals had returned only a general verdict, and since one of the charges was thought to be supported by no evidence whatsoever, the trial judge held that Hardeman had been deprived of the full and fair hearing guaranteed by § 101(a)(5). The Court of Appeals affirmed, simply citing *Braswell.* 420 F.2d 485 (CA-5 1970).

We find nothing in either the language or the legislative history of § 101 (a)(5) that could justify such a substitution of judicial for union authority to interpret the union's regulations in order to determine the scope of offenses warranting discipline of union members. . . .

Of course, § 101(a)(5)(A) requires that a member subject to discipline be "served with written specific charges." These charges must be, in Senator McClellan's words, "specific enough to inform the accused member of the offense that he has allegedly committed." Where, as here, the union's charges make reference to specific written provisions, § 101(a)(5)(A) obviously empowers the federal courts to examine those provisions and determine whether the union member had been misled or otherwise prejudiced in the presentation of his defense. But it gives courts no warrant to scrutinize the union regulations in order to determine whether particular conduct may be punished at all.

Respondent does not suggest, and we cannot discern, any possibility of prejudice in the present case. Although the notice of charges with which he was served does not appear as such in the record, the transcript of the union hearing indicates that the notice did not confine itself to a mere statement or citation of the written regulations that Hardeman was said to have violated: the notice appears to have contained a detailed statement of the facts relating to the fight which formed the basis for the disciplinary action. Section 101 (a)(5) requires no more. . . .

Applying this standard to the present case, we think there is no question that the charges were adequately supported. Respondent was charged with having attacked Wise without warning, and with continuing to beat him for some time. Wise so testified at the disciplinary hearing, and his testimony was fully corroborated by one other witness to the altercation. Even Hardeman, although he claimed he was thereafter held and beaten, admitted having struck the first blow. On such a record there is no question but that the charges were supported by "some evidence."

Reversed.

CASE QUESTIONS	1. What factual situation led to Hardeman's suit?
	2. What defense did the Union make?
	3. Under what provisions of the LMRDA did the Trial Court review Hardeman's case?

4. What did the District Court find?
5. What did the Supreme Court rule?

SECTION 93 / UNION DISCIPLINE: SECTION 8(b) (1)(A)

Section 8(b)(1)(A) protects employees' rights in their relations with labor organizations. The main clause of the section makes it an unfair labor practice for a union to "restrain or coerce employees in the exercise of the rights guaranteed in Section 7. A proviso reduces the sweep of the section: "*Provided,* that this paragraph shall not impair the right of a labor organization to prescribe its own rules with respect to the acquisition or retention of membership therein." The problem inherent in Section 8(b)(1)(A), then, is the seeming conflict between the main clause, which offers employees protection of their Section 7 rights, and the proviso, which protects from Board action certain union disciplinary rules that may abridge those rights.

In *NLRB* v. *Allis-Chalmers Mfg. Co.,*[7] the Supreme Court sustained an NLRB decision finding that union discipline in the form of fines for crossing a picket line involved internal union matters that were not subject to the employees' right to refrain from concerted activities under Section 7. The Court expressly left open the question of whether employees holding less than "full membership" in the labor organization could, consistent with 8(b)(1)(A), be subjected to union disciplinary measures. By less than full membership is meant those individuals who make payment of periodic dues and initiation fees to a union in compliance with a union security clause, but elect not to otherwise participate in the labor organization.

In *NLRB* v. *Marine & Shipbuilding Workers,*[8] the Supreme Court held that a union's enforcement of a rule requiring its members to exhaust internal union remedies before filing an unfair labor practice charge with the NLRB was an 8(b)(1)(A) violation. The Court found that the union's "exhaustion of internal remedies" rule would frustrate the overriding statutory policy of allowing unimpeded access to the Board.

In *Scofield* v. *NLRB,*[9] reported in this section, the Supreme Court held that union fines imposed on members who exceeded a union piecework rule were lawful. In *Scofield* the Supreme Court set out the standards for lawful imposition of union fines: "§ 8(b)(1)(A) leaves a union free to enforce a properly adopted rule which reflects a legitimate union interest, impairs no policy Congress has imbedded in the labor laws, and is reasonably enforced against union members who are free to leave the union and escape the rule." The third *Scofield* standard, of reasonable enforcement against union members, has been modified by the Supreme Court in *NLRB* v. *Boeing Company.*[10] In *Boeing* the Court held that when union disciplinary fines against members do not interfere with the employer-employee relationship or otherwise violate a policy of the NLRA, the Board does not have authority to determine the reasonableness of the fines in making a ruling on whether or not the fines are an unfair labor practice. If the

---

[7] 388 U.S. 175 (1967).
[8] 391 U.S. 418 (1968).
[9] 394 U.S. 423 (1969).
[10] 83 LRRM 2183 (1973).

Board investigated a fine's reasonableness, the Court held it would be delving into internal union affairs in a manner which Congress did not intend. The Court recognizes that state courts will continue to have jurisdiction to determine reasonableness, in a fine enforcement context. The dissenting opinions in Boeing argued that it is no answer to say that the reasonableness of a fine may be tested in a state court suit since individual employees are often indigent and such a suit is likely to be no contest. Under Board procedures, the General Counsel represents the employee without cost to the employee if the employee's charge has merit. Further, the dissenting justices argued, state judges have no expertise in labor-management relations; and national standards to be set by the Board are needed in the matter of union disciplinary fines.

In *NLRB* v. *Textile Workers (Granite State Joint Board)*,[11] the Supreme Court found that the union's imposition of court-collectible fines against former members, who had resigned during a lengthy strike which they had previously voted for, constituted illegal interference with employees' freedom to refrain from collective activities. Since nothing in the union's constitution or in any contract limited this right to resign or to work thereafter, the fines interfered with rights guaranteed in Section 7 in violation of Section 8(b)(1)(A). In *Machinists, Lodge 405* v. *NLRB*,[12] reported below, the Supreme Court held that a union committed an 8(b)(1)(A) unfair labor practice in seeking court enforcement of fines imposed for strikebreaking activities by employees who had resigned from the union, even though the union constitution expressly prohibited members from strikebreaking. The United States Supreme Court, in *Florida Power and Light Co.* v. *IBEW*,[13] considered the issue of whether a union committed an unfair labor practice under Section 8(b)(1)(B) when it disciplined its supervisor-members for crossing picket lines and performing rank and file struck work during a lawful economic strike against an employer. The Court held that the NLRB erred in finding that the union violated Section 8(b)(1)(B). The Court pointed out that a union's discipline of supervisor-members can violate Section 8(b)(1)(B) only when it adversely may affect their conduct in performing duties of, and acting in capacity of grievance adjusters or collective bargainers on behalf of an employer, but supervisor-members in the present case were not engaged in such conduct when they crossed the picket lines. The Court found that Congress addressed the problem of supervisors' loyalty to the employer not through Section 8(b)(1)(B), but instead through Sections 2(3), 2(11), and 14(a), which permit an employer to refuse to hire union members as supervisors because of union activities or membership, and refuse to engage in collective bargaining with them.

Scofield v. NLRB

Supreme Court of the United States, 1969. 393 U.S. 995

WHITE, J.: Half the production employees of the Wisconsin Motor Corporation are paid on a piecework or incentive basis. They and the other employees are represented by respondent union, which has had contractual

---

[11] 409 U.S. 213 (1972).
[12] 83 LRRM 2189 (1973).
[13] 86 LRRM 2689 (1974).

relations with the company since 1937.[14] In 1938 the union initiated a ceiling on the production for which its members would accept immediate piecework pay. This was done at first by gentlemen's agreement among the members, but since 1944 by union rule enforceable by fines and expulsion. As the rule functions now, members may produce as much as they like each day, but may only draw pay up to the ceiling rate. The additional production is "banked" by the company; that is, wages due for it are retained by the company and paid out to the employee for days on which the production ceiling has not been reached because of machine breakdown or for some other reason. If the member demands to be paid in full each pay period over the ceiling rate the company will comply, but the union assesses a fine of $1 for each violation, and in cases of repeated violation may fine the member up to $100 for "conduct unbecoming a union member." Failure to pay the fine may lead to expulsion. As the trial examiner found, the company's complaint is not and cannot be that "the employee, for the pay he receives, has not given the requisite *quid pro quo* in production." Rather, the question is the extent to which the group will forgo for pay the rest periods it has bargained for, and the discipline which the union may invoke to achieve unity toward this end which, the trial examiner found, was "manifestly a matter affecting the interest of the group and in which its collective bargaining strength hinges upon the cooperation of its individual components."

The collective bargaining contract between employer and union defines a "machine rate" of hourly pay guaranteed to the employees. The piecework rate, as defined by the contract, is set at a level such that "the average competent operator working at a reasonable pace [as determined by a time study] shall earn not less than the machine rate at his assigned task." [15] Allowances are made in the time study for setting up machinery, cleaning tools, fatigue, and personal needs. By ignoring these allowances or by speed and efficiency it is possible for an industrious employee to produce faster than the machine rate. If he does so, he is entitled to additional pay. Union members, however, are subject to the banking procedures imposed by the union rule.

The margin between the "machine" rate set by the contract and the ceiling rate set by the union was 10¢ per hour in 1944. As a result of collective bargaining between company and union over both the machine and ceiling rates, the margin has been increased to between 45 and 50¢, depending on the skill level of the job. The company has regularly urged the union to abandon the ceiling and has never agreed to refuse employees immediate pay for work done over the ceiling. However, the parties have bargained over the ceiling rate and the company has extracted from the union promises to increase the ceiling rate. The company opens its work records to the union to permit them to check compliance with the ceiling; pays union stewards for time spent in this checking activity as legitimate union business; and banks money for union

---

[14] There is a union security clause in the current contract, giving each employee, after a 30-day waiting period, the option of becoming and remaining a member in good standing of the union, or of declining membership but paying the union a "service fee."

[15] There is also a "day rate," lower than the machine rate, which applies to periods in which the incentive worker has not been producing, or has produced scrap, through no fault of the company's. That rate is of no concern here.

members complying with the rule. The ceiling rate is also used in computing piece rate increases and in settling grievances.

This case arose in 1961 when a random card check by the union showed that petitioners, among other union members, had exceeded the ceiling. The union membership imposed fines of $50 to $100, and a year's suspension from the union. Petitioners refused to pay the fines, and the union brought suit in state court to collect the fines as a matter of local contract law.[16] Petitioners then initiated charges before the National Labor Relations Board, arguing that union enforcement of its rule through the collection of fines was an unfair labor practice. Petitioners asserted that their right to refrain from "concerted activities," National Labor Relations Act, § 7, 49 Stat. 452, as amended, 29 U.S.C. § 157, was impaired by the union's effort to "restrain or coerce" them, in violation of NLRA, § 8(b)(1)(A). The trial examiner, after extensive findings, concluded that there was no violation of the Act, and his findings and recommendations were adopted by the Board, whose order was enforced by the Court of Appeals for the Seventh Circuit, 393 F.2d 49 (1968). We affirm. . . .

Section 8(b)(1) makes it an unfair labor practice to "restrain or coerce (A) employees in the exercise of the rights guaranteed in [§ 7]: Provided, that this paragraph shall not impair the right of a labor organization to prescribe its own rules with respect to the acquisition or retention of membership therein. . . ."

Based on the legislative history of the section, including its proviso, the Court in *NLRB* v. *Allis-Chalmers Mfg. Co.,* 388 U.S. 175, 195 (1967), distinguished between internal and external enforcement of union rules and held that "Congress did not propose any limitations with respect to the internal affairs of unions, aside from barring enforcement of a union's internal regulations to affect a member's employment status." A union rule, duly adopted and not the arbitrary fiat of a union officer, forbidding the crossing of a picket line during a strike was therefore enforceable against voluntary union members by expulsion or a reasonable fine. The Court thus essentially accepted the position of the National Labor Relations Board dating from *Minneapolis Star and Tribune Co.,* 109 NLRB 727 (1954) where the Board also distinguished internal from external enforcement [17] in holding that a union could fine a member for violating a rule against working during a strike but that the same rule could not be enforced by causing the employer to exclude him from the work force or by affecting his seniority without triggering violations of §§ 8(b)(1), 8(b)(2), 8(a)(1), 8(a)(2), and 8(a)(3). These sections form a web, of which § 8(b)(1)(A) is only a strand, preventing the union from inducing the employer to use the emoluments of the job to enforce the union's rules.

This interpretation of § 8(b)(1), as the Court explained in *Allis-Chalmers,*

---

[16] Unless the rule or its enforcement impinge[s] on some policy of the federal labor law, the regulation of the relationship between union and employee is a contractual matter governed by local law. As the trial examiner put it in this case, the Board "never intended . . . to suggest that the disciplinary action in enforcement of [union] rules . . . were affirmatively protected under the Act, as opposed to merely being not violations thereof." It is thus a "federally unentered enclave" open to state law.

[17] The Board has long held that § 8(b)(1)(A)'s legislative history requires a narrow construction which nevertheless proscribes unacceptable methods of union coercion, such as physical violence to induce employees to join the union or to join in a strike. *In re Maritime Union,* 78 NLRB 971, enforced 175 F.2d 686 (C.A. 2d Cir. 1949).

388 U.S., at 193–195, was reinforced by the Landrum-Griffin Act of 1959 which, although it dealt with the internal affairs of unions, including the procedures for imposing fines or expulsion, did not purport to overturn or modify the Board's interpretation of § 8(b)(1). And it was this interpretation which the Board followed in *Allis-Chalmers* and in the case now before us.

Although the Board's construction of the section emphasizes the sanction imposed, rather than the rule itself, and does not involve the Board in judging the fairness or wisdom of particular union rules, it has become clear that if the rule invades or frustrates an overriding policy of the labor laws the rule may not be enforced, even by fine or expulsion, without violating § 8 (b)(1). . . .

Under this dual approach, § 8(b)(1) leaves a union free to enforce a properly adopted rule which reflects a legitimate union interest, impairs no policy Congress has imbedded in the labor laws, and is reasonably enforced against union members who are free to leave the union and escape the rule. This view of the statute must be applied here.

In the case at hand, there is no showing in the record that the fines were unreasonable or the mere fiat of a union leader, or that the membership of petitioners in the union was involuntary. Moreover, the enforcement of the rule was not carried out through means unacceptable in themselves, such as violence or employer discrimination. It was enforced solely through the internal technique of union fines, collected by threat of expulsion or judicial action. The inquiry must therefore focus on the legitimacy of the union interests vindicated by the rule and the extent to which any policy of the Act may be violated by the union-imposed production ceiling.

As both the trial examiner and the Court of Appeals noted, union opposition to unlimited piecework pay systems is historic. Union apprehension, not without foundation, is that such systems will drive up employee productivity and in turn create pressures to lower the piecework rate so that at the new, higher level of output employees are earning little more than they did before. The fear is that the competitive pressure generated will endanger workers' health, foment jealousies, and reduce the work force. In addition, the findings of the trial examiner were that the ceiling served as a yardstick for the statement of job allowance grievances, that it has played an important role in negotiating the minimum hourly rate and that it is the standard for "factoring" the hourly rate raises into the piecework rate. The view of the trial examiner was that "[i]n terms of a union's traditional function of trying to serve the economic interests of the group as a whole, the union has a very real, immediate, and direct interest in it." 145 NLRB, at 1135.

It is doubtless true that the union rule in question here affects the interests of all three participants in the labor-management relation: employer, employee, and union. Although the enforcement of the rule is handled as an internal union matter, the rule has and was intended to have an impact beyond the confines of the union organization. But as *Allis-Chalmers* and *Marine Workers* made clear, it does not follow from this that the enforcement of the rule violates § 8(b)(1)(A), unless some impairment of the statutory labor policy can be shown.

Petitioner purports to characterize the union rule as featherbedding, but it is hard to square this with his collective agreement that an average efficient employee produces at a "machine" rate substantially below the ceiling. Beyond that, however, Congress has addressed itself specifically to the problem of featherbedding in § 8(b)(6), making it an unfair labor practice "to cause or attempt to cause an employer to pay or deliver or agree to pay or deliver any money or other thing of value, in the nature of an exaction, for services which are not performed or not to be performed. . . .' 61 Stat. 142, 29 U.S.C. § 158(b)(6). This narrow prohibition was enacted partly because the Congress found it difficult to define with more particularity just where the area between shiftlessness and over-work should lie. Since Congress has addressed itself to the problem specifically and left a broad area for private negotiation, there is no present occasion for the courts to interfere with private decision. Indeed, there is no claim before us that the rule violates § 8(b)(6). If the company wants to require more work of its employees, let it strike a better bargain. The labor laws as presently drawn will not do so for it.

This leaves the possible argument that because the union has not successfully bargained for a contractual ceiling, it may not impose one on its own members, for doing so will discriminate between members and those others who are free to earn as much as the contract permits. All members of the bargaining unit, however, have the same contractual rights. In dealing with the employer as bargaining agent, the union has accorded all employees uniform treatment. If members are prevented from taking advantage of their contractual rights bargained for all employees it is because they have chosen to become and remain union members. In *Allis-Chalmers,* the union members were subject to the discipline of an internal rule which strengthened the union's hand in bargaining and in this respect benefited both the members who obeyed the rule and the nonmembers who did not. The same is true here, and the price of obeying the rule is not as high as in *Allis-Chalmers.* There the member could be replaced for his refusal to report to work during a strike; here he needs simply limit his production and suffer whatever consequences that conduct may entail. If a member chooses not to engage in this concerted activity and is unable to prevail on the other members to change the rule, then he may leave the union and obtain whatever benefits in job advancement and extra pay may result from extra work, at the same time enjoying the protection from competition, the high piece rate, and the job security which compliance with the union rule by union members tends to promote.

That the choice to remain a member results in differences between union members and other employees raises no serious issue under § 8(b)(2) and § 8(a)(3) of the Act, because the union has not induced the employer to discriminate against the member but has merely forbidden the member to take advantage of benefits which the employer stands willing to confer. Those sections are not aimed at completely internal union discipline of union members, even though the discipline may result in the member's refusal to accept work offered by the employer. *Allis-Chalmers* makes this quite clear.

The union rule here left the collective bargaining process unimpaired, breached no collective contract, required no pay for unperformed services, induced no discrimination by the employer against any class of employees, and represents no dereliction by the union of its duty of fair representation. In light of this, and the acceptable manner in which the rule was enforced, vindicating a legitimate union interest, it is impossible to say that it contravened any policy of the Act.

We affirm, holding that the union rule is valid and that its enforcement by reasonable fines does not constitute the restraint or coercion proscribed by § 8(b)(1)(A).

Affirmed.

CASE QUESTIONS

1. What is the legal question in this case?
2. Does the decision of the NLRB mean a union can exclude the member from the job or reduce his seniority standing as a penalty for violating the rule?
3. What does the court say as to legal relief the employee may invoke to avoid such a fine?
4. What does the court say as to the legality of the production ceiling rule?

Machinists, Lodge 405 v. NLRB (Boeing Co.)

Supreme Court of the United States, 1973. 83 LRRM 2189

PER CURIAM:—In this companion case to *National Labor Relations Board* v. *The Boeing Company, . . .* — U.S. —, 83 LRRM 2183, we must decide whether our decision in *National Labor Relations Board* v. *Granite State Joint Board,* 409 U.S. 213, 81 LRRM 2853 authorizes the Board to find that a union commits an unfair labor practice in seeking court enforcement of fines imposed for strikebreaking activities by employees who have resigned from the union, even though the union constitution expressly prohibits members from strikebreaking. We hold that it does.

On September 16, 1965, the day after the expiration of the collective bargaining agreement between Booster Lodge No. 405, International Association of Machinists and Aerospace Workers, AFL-CIO (the Union), and the Boeing Company (the Company), the Union called a lawful strike and picketed the Company's Michoud, Louisiana, plant to further its demands for a new contract. The strike continued for 18 days, during which time 143 of the 1,900 production and maintenance employees represented by the Union crossed the picket line to work. All of these employees had been members of the Union before the strike, but 61 resigned their membership prior to returning to work and another 58 resigned after they returned to work. These resignations were tendered in registered or certified letters to the Union. Neither its constitution nor its by-laws contained any provision expressly permitting or forbidding such resignations.

The strike ended on October 4, 1965, after ratification of a new collective bargaining agreement by the Union membership. During late October and early November the Union notified all employees who had crossed the picket line to work during the strike that charges had been preferred against them under the Union constitution for "Improper Conduct of a Member" because of their having "accept[ed] employment . . . in an establishment where a strike or lockout exist[ed]." They were advised of the dates of their union trials, which were to be held even in their absence, and of their right to be represented by any counsel who was a member of the International Union. Fines were imposed on all employees who had worked during the strike without regard to whether or not such employees had resigned or had remained members. None of the disciplined employees processed intra-union appeals. To the extent that fines were not paid, the Union sent written notices to the offending employees stating that the matter had been referred to an attorney for collection. Suits were initiated in state court against nine employees for the purpose of collecting the fines plus attorneys' fees and interest. None of these suits has been resolved.

The Company filed an unfair labor practice charge with the National Labor Relations Board alleging that the Union had violated § 8(b)(1)(A) of the National Labor Relations Act, 29 U.S.C. § 158(b)(1)(A). The General Counsel issued a complaint, and the Board held that the Union violated § 8(b)(1)(A), *supra,* by fining those employees who had resigned from the Union before returning to work during the strike, and by fining those who had resigned after returning to work to the extent that such fines were based on post-resignation work. No violation was found in the Union's fining members for crossing the picket line to work during the strike or in its fining those employees who resigned after they returned to work for work performed prior to resignation. The Board ordered the Union to cease and desist from fining employees who had resigned from the Union for their post-resignation work during the strike and from seeking court enforcement of such fines. It further order reimbursement to employees who had already paid fines for any amount imposed because of post-resignation work The Court of Appeals sustained these holdings, — U.S. App. D.C. —, 459 F.2d 1143 79 LRRM 2443 (1972), and on the Union's petition for review, we granted certiorari. 409 U.S. 1074.

In *National Labor Relations Board* v. *Granite State Joint Board, supra,* 409 U.S., at 217, 81 LRRM, at 2854, we held that "[w]here a member lawfully resigns from a union and thereafter engages in conduct which the union rule proscribes, the union commits an unfair labor practice when it seeks enforcement of fines for that conduct." Since [in] that case there was no provision in the union's constitution or bylaws limiting the circumstances in which a member could resign, we conclude that the members were free to resign at will and that § 7 of the Act, 29 U.S.C. § 157, protected their right to return to work during a strike which had been commenced while they were union members. The union's imposition of court-collectible fines against the former members for such work was therefore held to violate § 8(b)(1)(A), *supra.*

Here, as in Granite State, the Union's constitution and by-laws are silent on the subject of voluntary resignation from the Union. And here as there we leave open the question of the extent to which contractual restriction on a member's right to resign may be limited by the Act. Since there is no evidence that the employees here either knew of or had consented to any limitation on their right to resign, we need "only to apply the law which normally is reflected in our free institutions—the right of the individual to join or to resign from associations, as he sees fit "subject of course to any financial obligations due and owing' the group with which he was associated." *Granite State, supra,* at 216, 81 LRRM, at 2854.

The Union contends, however, that a result different from Granite State is warranted in this case because, even though its constitution does not expressly restrict the right to resign during a strike, it does impose on members an obligation to refrain from strikebreaking. The Union asserts that this provision has been consistently interpreted to bind a member, notwithstanding his resignation, to abstain from strikebreaking for the duration of an existing strike. It urges that this provision may be enforced as a matter of contract law against one whose membership has ceased, because it was an obligation he undertook while a member.

The provision in the Union's constitution which proscribes strikebreaking by its terms purports only to define "misconduct of a member." Nothing in the record indicates that Union members were informed, prior to the bringing of the charges that were the basis of this action, that the provision was interpreted as imposing any obligation on a resignee. Thus, in order to sustain the Union's position, we would first have to find, contrary to the determination of the Board and of the Court of Appeals, that the Union constitution by implication extended its sanctions to nonmembers, and then further conclude that such sanctions were consistent with the Act. But we are no more disposed to find an implied post-resignation commitment from the strikebreaking proscription in the Union's constitution here than we were to find it from the employees' participation in the strike vote and ratification of penalties in Granite State. Accordingly, the judgment of the Court of Appeals sustaining the Board's finding of an unfair labor practice on the part of petitioner Union is

Affirmed.

Mr. Justice BLACKMUN, concurring in the judgment.

In *NLRB* v. *Textile Workers,* 409 U.S. 213, 81 LRRM 2853 (1972), the strikebreaking employees, while they were members of the union, had all voted to strike. On the day following the inception of the strike, these employees also voted in favor of a union resolution that anyone aiding or abetting the company during the strike would be subject to a fine. And all had participated in the strike prior to resigning from the union.

I was in solitary dissent in *Textile Workers,* 409 U.S., at 218, 81 LRRM, at 2855. I emphasized there that "it seems likely that the three factors of a member's strike vote, his ratification of strikebreaking penalties, and his actual participation in the strike, would be far more reliable indicia of his obligation to the union and its members than the presence of boiler-plate provisions in a union's constitution," *id.,* at 220, 81 LRRM, at 2856, that the Court's opinion seemed to me "to exalt the formality of resignation over the substance of the various interests and national labor policies that [were] at stake," *id.,* at 221, 81 LRRM, at 2856, that § 7 of the National Labor Relations Act "does not necessarily give him [the employee] the right to abandon these [union] activities in midcourse once he has undertaken them voluntarily," *id.,* at 222,

81 LRRM, at 2857, quoting from 446 F.2d 369, 373, 77 LRRM 2711, 2714, and that the policy of § 7 would not be frustrated by a holding that an employee, in the circumstances of that case, could "knowingly waive his § 7 right to resign from the union and to return to work without sanction." *Id.,* at 222–223, 81 LRRM, at 2857.

The present case, however, is a very different situation. None of the Boeing employees who resigned from the Union had been given notice of a strikebreaking penalty before the strike vote or before their participation in the strike. The imposition of a penalty was never ratified formally by the union membership. The members were not notified that post-resignation strikebreaking was proscribed and would subject them to union discipline. And the provision in the Union's constitution, referred to by the Court, *ante,* as to a member's general obligation to refrain from strikebreaking, surely does not make up for this lack of notice, and it would not do so even if it were clearly applicable, which it is not, to strikebreaking after resignation from the Union.

Without effective notice of obligations that are supposed to be assumed, there can be no waiver of a member's § 7 right to refrain from participation in a legal strike. In the absence of such notice, § 8(b)(1)(A) bars the union from subjecting a member to a choice between the substantial obligation of weathering the strike and that of being subjected to court-collectible fines for failure to do so.

I, therefore, join in the Court's judgment.

CASE
QUESTIONS

1. State the issue of the case.
2. Who filed the unfair labor practice charges in this case?
3. Distinguish the *Granite State* precedent from the present case.
4. What is the gist of the concurring Justice's opinion?

SECTION 94 / RIGHTS OF MEMBERS

Certain of the rights of members in relation to their union are established by the constitution and bylaws, which the courts have held to be in the nature of a contract between a union and its members. A number of statutory rights, applicable irrespective of union documents or rules, are also incorporated into the Reporting and Disclosure Act of 1959 in Title I, the "Bill of Rights" provisions. In addition to the provisions that were discussed in the prior section as protecting the membership from improper or arbitrary discipline, the basic rights of equal treatment with regard to nominations and voting, of assembly, free expression and appeal to the courts or to other government agencies are included.

The legislative rights have precedence over inconsistent provisions of a union constitution or bylaws. The law further provides, however, that it is not to be applied as to impair "reasonable rules" concerning a member's responsibility to the organization and to the performance of its obligations.

Freedom of participation in all membership affairs, such as elections, referendums, meetings, and discussions, are specifically provided for with the qualifying condition that the matter is "properly before the meeting, subject to the organization's established and reasonable rules pertaining to the conduct of meetings." In *Hall* v. *Cole* [18] the respondent John Cole, at a regular meeting of the membership of petitioner Seafarers Union, introduced a set of resolutions alleging various instances of undemocratic actions and shortsighted policies on the part of the union officers. The resolutions were defeated and Cole was expelled from the union on the ground that his presentation of the resolutions violated a union rule proscribing "deliberate and malicious vilification with regard to the execution or the duties of any office." After exhausting his intra-union remedies, respondent filed suit under § 102 of the LMRDA, claiming that his expulsion violated his right of free speech as secured by § 101(a)(2) of the Act. He regained his union membership and was awarded $5,500 in legal fees by the trial court. The Supreme Court, considering only the issue of the propriety of awarding the legal fees, held that a trial judge has the inherent equitable power to award legal fees whenever overriding considerations indicate the need for such recovery: the Court found such considerations since Cole's vindiction of free speech rights worked to the benefit of all members of the union.

An increase of dues or assessments and changes in initiations fees can only be made by a majority of members voting in a secret ballot or in a convention. The Disclosure Act of 1959 specifies different requirements for national unions and for local unions.

Members may not be restricted in their right to initiate a suit or proceeding in a court of law or equity, or to testify or communicate. The right to sue is subject to any reasonable internal procedures provided by the union, if extending not beyond four months' duration.

Collective agreements must be available for all employees affected, whether members or not and whether negotiated by the local or by a parent organization. Members must be given the facts as to the law and their rights under it. They may bring civil actions to gain relief in a federal court. They have the right for just cause to examine union records and accounts and to have copies of all documents and information which the union must submit to the Secretary of Labor.

Title IV of the law establishes democratic standards for all elections including the following:

1. Secret ballots in local union elections.
2. Opportunity for members to nominate candidates.
3. Advance notice of elections.
4. Freedom of choice among all the candidates.
5. Observers at polling and at ballot counting stations for all candidates.
6. Publication of results and preservation of records for one year.
7. Prohibition of any income from dues or assessments being used to support candidates for union office.
8. The frequency of elections for officers and advance opportunity of each candidate to inspect the membership name and address lists are provided for, along with other detailed procedural requirements for balloting.

---

[18] 83 LRRM 1390 (1973).

Members of local unions that are under the trusteeship of a parent body are also protected by limitations on the purposes and the duration of a valid trusteeship, and by protection of their right to vote for representatives. The property and finances of trusteed locals also are subjected to certain control rules in the interest of the membership.

Violations or negligence as to the provisions may be the basis of a member's law suit in the federal court. A member may also file a complaint with the Secretary of Labor charging that trusteeship standards have been violated, or that union agreements are not available.

When a violation of the election requirements is charged, any internal union procedures in the bylaws and constitution must be pursued for a three-month period. If not adjusted then, a complaint to the Secretary of Labor can bring about action in the court at the Secretary's initiation. The Secretary, upon application of a local union member, may also conduct an investigation and determine the adequacy of procedures for removal of local officers "guilty of serious misconduct." If no adequate procedures are available, the Secretary may provide an alternate procedure for removal of any officer found guilty of malfeasance. In the two cases on member rights printed below, the Courts applied Section 101 broadly.

Johnson v. Local 58, International Electrical Workers

(SUPPLEMENTAL CASE DIGEST—RIGHTS OF MEMBERS)
U. S. District Court, Eastern District, Michigan, 1960.

An injunction was issued on petition of members where threats were made by local union agents concerning job rights of members who had been holding meetings to discuss petitioning for a new local charter. The court decided that it was doubtful that the acts complained of were offenses under the union constitution, and the members' right to assemble freely was interfered with in violation of Section 101(a)(2) of the Bill of Rights of Members in Title I of the Reporting and Disclosure Act of 1959.

Wirtz v. Local 125, Laborers

Supreme Court of the United States, 1968. 389 U.S. 477

BRENNAN, J.: Petitioner, the Secretary of Labor, filed the action in the District Court for the Northern District of Ohio, Eastern Division, under § 402(b) of the Labor-Management Reporting and Disclosure Act of 1959, 29 U.S.C. § 482(b). His complaint challenged the validity of a general election of union officers conducted by the respondent Local Union on June 8, 1963, and the validity of a runoff election for the single office of Business Representative made necessary by a tie vote for that office at the June 8 election. The complaint alleged, in part, violations of § 401(e), 29 U.S.C. § 481 (e), in permitting members not "in good standing" to vote and to run for office on both occasions. However, the only allegation that internal union remedies had been exhausted, as is required by § 402(a), was in regard to the runoff election of July 13; the complaint stated that the loser in the runoff election, one Dial, protested and appealed to the General Executive Board of the International Union concerning the conduct of that election and having received a final denial of his protest by the General Executive Board filed a timely complaint with the Secretary. The District Court held that the omission in the complaint of an allegation that a member complained internally about the conduct of the June 8 general election was fatal to the Secretary's action addressed to that election and dismissed that part of the complaint. 231 F. Supp. 590. The Secretary appealed to the Court of Appeals for the Sixth Circuit. During pendency of the appeal, respondent Local conducted its next regular triennial election of officers. The Court of Appeals thereupon vacated the judgment of dismissal and remanded to the District Court with instructions that the portion of the Secretary's complaint dealing with the June 8 election be dismissed as moot. 375 F.2d 921. We granted certiorari. 387 U.S. 904. In light of our decision today in *Wirtz* v. *Local 153,* 389 U.S. 463, the action of the Court of Appeals must be reversed; we there held that ". . . the fact that the union has already conducted another unsupervised election does not deprive the Secretary of his right to a court order declaring the challenged election void and directing that a new election be conducted under his supervision."

In the circumstances we might remand to the Court of Appeals to decide the merits of the Secretary's appeal. The issue on the merits is whether the District Court erred in holding that the Secretary in his suit may not challenge the alleged violations affecting the general election of June 8 because Dial specifically challenged only the runoff election of July 13 with respect to the office of Business Representative. The merits of this question have been fully briefed and argued in this Court and the underlying issue of statutory construction has already been the subject of several and conflicting rulings by various federal courts. The interests of judicial economy are therefore best served if we proceed to resolve this important question now.

Respondent Local is governed by the Constitution and the Uniform Local Union Constitution of the Laborers' International Union of North America. Under the Uniform Local Union Constitution as it existed during the period relevant here, a member's good standing was lost by failure to pay membership dues within a specified grace period, and the member was automatically suspended without notice and with loss of all membership rights except the right to readmission (but as a new member) upon payment of a fee. The eligibility of voters and candidates in both elections in this case was determined by reference to a report to the International Union of the names of members for whom a per capita tax had been paid. This report included some 50 to 75 members who were delinquent in the payment of their Local dues and had therefore actually lost good standing under the provisions of the Uniform Local Union Constitution. The cause of this patent disregard of the Local's own constitution was the practice of its Secretary-Treasurer of paying from Local funds the per capita tax of delinquent members selected by him, thus making it appear on the per capita tax report that those members had met their dues obligations when in fact they had not.[19] The Secretary's investigation disclosed that approximately 50 of the members voting in the June 8 general election and approximately 60 voting in the July 13 runoff election were ineligible to vote; and that 16 of the 27 candidates for office in the general election, including Dial's opponent who ultimately won the runoff, were ineligible for the same reason.

The question is one of statutory construction and must be answered by inference since there is lacking an explicit provision regarding the permissible scope of the Secretary's complaint. On the facts of this case we think the Secretary is entitled to maintain his action challenging the June 8 general election because respondent union had fair notice from the violation charged by Dial in his protest of the runoff election that the same unlawful conduct probably occurred at the earlier election as well. We therefore need not consider and intimate no view on the merits of the Secretary's argument that a member's protest triggers at § 402 enforcement action in which the Secretary would be permitted to file suit challenging any violation of § 401 discovered in his investigation of the member's complaint.

We reject the narrow construction adopted by the District Court and supported by respondent limiting the Secretary's complaint solely to the allegations made in the union member's initial complaint. Such a severe restriction upon the Secretary's powers should not be read into the statute without a clear indication of congressional intent to that effect. Neither the language of the statute nor its legislative history provides such an indication; indeed, the indications are quite clearly to the contrary.

First, it is most improbable that Congress deliberately settled exclusive enforcement jurisdiction on the Secretary and granted him broad investigative powers to discharge his responsibilities,[20] yet intended the shape of the enforcement action to be immutably fixed by the artfulness of a layman's complaint which often must be based on incomplete information. The expertise and resources of the Labor Department were surely meant to have a broader play.[21] Second, so to constrict the Secretary would be inconsistent with his vital role, which we emphasize today in *Wirtz* v. *Local 153, supra,* in protecting the public interest bound up in Title IV. The Act was not designed merely to protect the right of a union member to run for a particular union office in a particular election. Title IV's special function in furthering the general goals of the LMRDA is to insure free and democratic union elections, the regulations of the union electoral process enacted in the Title having been regarded

---

[19] The International Constitution required respondent Local to remit to the International a per capita tax payment of $1 per member per month. These payments were to be made only for members who had in fact made current payment of their dues to the Local.

[20] The Secretary's authority under § 601, 29 U.S.C. § 521, both supplements his investigative mandate under § 402(b) and authorizes inquiry without regard to the filing of a complaint by a union member. But when the Secretary investigates pursuant to § 601 without a member's complaint, his remedy is limited to disclosure of violations discovered. Whether violations of § 401 uncovered by a § 601 investigation may be the predicate of a member's protest to the union and an enforcement proceeding under § 402 if the union denies relief is a question we need not and do not reach in this case.

[21] Senator Kennedy's reference to the Secretary as the complaining "union member's lawyer." 104 Cong. Rec. 10947, Leg. Hist. 1093 (Dept. Labor 1964), does not support the District Court's conclusion. The lawyer's function is to use his skills to give shape and substance to his client's often incompletely expressed complaint.

as necessary protections of the public interest as well as of the rights and interests of union members.

We can only conclude, therefore, that it would be anomalous to limit the reach of the Secretary's cause of action by the specifics of the union member's complaint. In an analogous context we rejected such a limiting construction of the National Labor Relations Board's authority to fashion unfair labor practice complaints. *NLRB* v. *Fant Milling Co.,* 360 U.S. 301, 306–309; *National Licorice Co.* v. *NLRB,* 309 U.S. 350, 369.

Respondent argues, however, that the spirit and letter of the statutory requirement that the member first exhaust his internal union remedies before the Secretary may intervene compels the suggested limitation. It contends that even to allow the Secretary to challenge the earlier election for the same violation established as having occurred in the runoff election would be inconsistent with Congress' intention to allow unions first opportunity to redress violations of § 401. This argument is not persuasive.

It is true that the exhaustion requirement was regarded by Congress as critical to the statute's objective of fostering union self-government. By channeling members through the internal appellate processes, Congress hoped to accustom members to utilizing the remedies made available within their own organization; at the same time, however, unions were expected to provide responsible and responsive procedures for investigating and redressing members' election grievances. These intertwined objectives are not disserved but furthered by permitting the Secretary to include in his complaint at least any § 401 violation he has discovered which the union had a fair opportunity to consider and redress in connection with a member's initial complaint.

Here the Secretary sought to challenge the June 8 general election, alleging that the same unlawful conduct occurring in the runoff affected the general election held only five weeks before. Dial's complaint had disclosed the fraudulent practice with respect to the runoff, and he was apparently able to prove at the hearing before the General Executive Board that that practice enabled nine ineligible members to vote in the runoff election; but his protest was denied because he had lost by 19 votes. The Secretary's investigation, however, discovered that a much larger number of ineligible members had been permitted to vote in that runoff election and that the Secretary-Treasurer responsible for the falsification prepared the per capita tax reports used to determine the eligiblity of voters and candidates at both elections. Yet in the face of Dial's evidence raising the almost overwhelming probability that the misconduct affecting the runoff election had also occurred at the June 8 election, the union insists that it was under no duty to expand its inquiry beyond the specific challenge to the runoff election made by Dial. Surely this is not the responsible union self-government contemplated by Congress in allowing the unions great latitude in resolving their own internal controversies. In default of respondent's action on a violation which it had a fair opportunity to consider and resolve in connection with Dial's protest, the Secretary was entitled to seek relief from the court with respect to the June 8 election. Again, Congress having given the Secretary a broad investigative power cannot have intended that his right to relief be defined by a complaining member's ignorance of the law or the facts or by the artlessness of the member's protest.

Because the complaint as to the June 8 election was dismissed for deficiency in pleading, the factual allegations have not been tried. We therefore reverse the judgment of the Court of Appeals and remand to that court with direction to enter a judgment reversing the District Court's judgment of dismissal and directing further proceedings by that court consistent with this opinion.

It is so ordered.

CASE QUESTIONS

1. What was Dial's complaint against the Union as filed with the Secretary of Labor?
2. What does the court state to be the purpose of Title IV of LMRDA?
3. How does the court want this law applied?
4. How was ignorance of the law at issue?

SECTION 95 / **DUTIES OF OFFICERS**

The obvious duties of a union officer are to abide by the constitution and bylaws of the organization, to represent his constitutents fairly, and to handle the union's funds honestly. These duties are fully developed in the cases given below.

The duty to represent all those employees for whom a union has been certified as bargaining agent, without discrimination or favoritism, was discussed in Chapters 3 and 5, referring to the Railway Labor Act and the National Labor Relations Act requirements respectively.

The Labor-Management Reporting and Disclosure Act of 1959 placed additional duties on union officers in relations to their members. Title I contains a "Bill of Rights of Members of Labor Organizations" with specific restrictions on discipline (covering fines, suspension, or expulsion) and requiring that certain procedural standards be met. Excepting discipline for nonpayment of dues, the member is entitled to be:

1. Served with written specific charges,
2. Given a reasonable time to prepare his defense, and
3. Afforded a full and fair hearing.

The law states that these procedural requirements stand ahead of any union constitutions or bylaw provisions that may be inconsistent. In addition, union officers have the duty of complying with the requirements of the Reporting and Disclosure Act of 1959 as to the filing of detailed financial reports with the Secretary of Labor as outlined in Section 96 and complying with the voting and election standards of the 1959 law covered in Section 94 of this volume.

The 1959 Reporting and Disclosure Act also defines the financial duties imposed upon officers to safeguard the funds of the organization. These duties include the requirement that officers and key personnel must manage, invest, and disburse funds and property of the union strictly in accordance with the authorization requirements of the constitution and bylaws, *holding the funds solely for the benefit of the organization and its members.* They must refrain from financial or personal interests that conflict with the interests of the union and give an accounting of any profits that are received in the transaction of union affairs.

All officers, agents, stewards, and other representatives or employees handling union funds must be bonded if the annual income plus all property of the union amounts to $5,000 or more. This requirement also applies to all union representatives serving as trustees for the members' welfare funds.

Persons who have been members of the Communist Party, or anyone who was convicted of a heinous crime, or of violating the reporting or trustee requirements of the statute, may not serve as an officer, steward, agent, or staff employee of the union for five years following either termination of party membership or an imprisonment or conviction. It is a crime to violate these rules, or even knowingly to permit a prohibited person to hold a union position. Further, any union officials who are convicted of violations of the 1959 Reporting and Disclosure Act may not receive help from funds of the union or of an employer for payment of fines. It appears, however, that expenses, other than fines, may be forthcoming to union officials who are subjected to any legislative or judicial investigation, and incur expenses of any kind, other than fines.

In the case presented in this section Ferrara and other union officials were found to have violated Section 302 of the 1947 LMRA as revised by the 1959 LMRDA by agreeing with the Walgreen Company, whose employees they represented, to drop a contractual benefit in return for "commissions" the union officials would receive on coffee bought by Walgreen from another employer whose workers also were represented by the same union.

U.S. v. Ferrara

United States Court of Appeals, Second Circuit, 1972. 458 F.2d 868

TIMBERS, C. J.: These appeals graphically depict how corrupt labor union officials can use their positions to promote their own selfish interests at the expense of the interests of those they ostensibly represent.

Appellants Fred Ferrara, Arthur Russell, Elmer Hauck and George Papalexis were convicted after a three-day non-jury trial in the District Court for the Southern District of New York, Milton Pollack, *District Judge,* of conspiring to violate and of violating §§ 302(a)(1), (a)(4) and (b)(1) of the Taft-Hartley Act, 29 U.S.C. §§ 186(a)(1), (a)(4) and (b)(1) (1970), by demanding and receiving money and a thing of value from employers of employees whom they represented. The trial judge fined each appellant $4,500, and Ferrara, Russell and Hauck received prison terms of one year, two months and one month, respectively. On appeal, appellants claim that the evidence was insufficient to support the trial judge's findings; that the government failed to show that the Taft-Hartley Act applied to the payments in question; that the application of the Taft-Hartley Act, as amended in 1959, to their activities violated the *ex post facto* clause of the Constitution; and that they were denied their right to a speedy trial. Finding no error, we affirm.

The evidence presented at trial established that from 1954 through 1965, the period covered by the indictment, appellants and co-defendant James Gleason were officers of Local 11, Chain Service Restaurant, Luncheonette and Soda Fountain Employees and Bartenders Union (AFL-CIO) (hereafter "Local 11"). During this same period, Local 11 represented employees of the Walgreen Company.

During the course of contract negotiations between Walgreen and Local 11 in 1954, management's representative, co-conspirator Casey LaFramenta, complained that the provision in the contract which allowed fountain employees to eat free of charge was costing the company a great deal and that its employees were the only ones in New York with such a "free food" provision. Gleason, the union's business agent for Walgreen's employees, and Ferrara, then president of Local 11, told LaFramenta that the "free food" provision could not be eliminated.

Thereafter appellant Ferrara approached Gleason privately about the prospect of convincing Walgreen employees to give up the free food benefit. Ferrara explained that if the employees would accept a modification of this benefit and if Ferrara could persuade Walgreen to purchase its coffee from Abraham Wechsler, chairman of the board of Wechsler Coffee Company, then Ferrara, Gleason, Russell, Hauck and Papalexis could arrange a lucrative deal which would earn them several thousand dollars. Gleason agreed to help Ferrara implement this proposal.

At about this time, Ferrara asked Walgreen's negotiator, LaFramenta, whether Walgreen would purchase its coffee from Wechsler. LaFramenta relayed this suggestion to Donald Haas, who was then head of the Walgreen purchasing division. Thereafter, Local 11 dropped its demand that the free food provision be included in the contract.

Gleason then used his position as union business agent for the Walgreen employees to convince them to accept a modification of the food benefit provision. The Walgreen employees eventually agreed to give up free food in exchange for a $3 weekly increase in salary and a 50% discount on food purchases.

In exchange for Local 11's promoting this modification of the food benefit provision, Walgreen agreed to purchase its coffee from Wechsler. Ferrara then arranged with Edward Wechsler, brother of Abraham Wechsler, to have Wechsler Coffee make an annual payment to a person designated by Ferrara, Hauck or Russell of four cents a pound on all sales of Wechsler coffee to Walgreen.

Thus, from 1954 to 1965, Walgreen purchased its coffee requirements in the New York City area from Wechsler Coffee, despite the absence of any business justification for doing so. Prior to 1954, Walgreen had been using coffee roasted and gound in its own plant in Chicago, and Walgreen's representatives could give no plausible explanation for changing its source of supply. Moreover, while Walgreen was purchasing its coffee from Wechsler, James

Plummer, the food and fountain supervisor for Walgreen's New York stores, received numerous consumer complaints about the coffee, and informed his superiors that the coffee was overpriced and of poor quality. Plummer was told by co-conspirator LaFramenta to "keep [his] hands off the coffee." Plummer was later told that Wechsler coffee would be purchased because Local 11 had "something to do with it."

Furthermore, each year from 1954 through 1965 Wechsler Coffee made the agreed-upon payments to nominees of Ferrara, Hauck and Russell. In 1954, 1955 and 1956, Ferrara paid Gleason $800, $700 and $650–700 in cash, respectively, as Gleason's share on the Wechsler deal. In 1957 and 1958, Ferrara gave Gleason checks drawn on the account of Wechsler Coffee, payable to Gleason. Gleason then cashed the checks and divided the proceeds equally with Ferrara, Russell, Hauck and Papalexis. In 1959 the check was made payable to Riese Enterprises, owned by Irving Riese, Ferrara's brother-in-law. In 1961, 1962, 1963 and 1964, the Wechsler checks were made payable to Rudolph Wetter, Gleason's cousin. After each check was cashed, Wetter received 10% of the proceeds, and appellants reimbursed Wetter for whatever income tax liability he incurred. In 1965, the check also was made payable to Wetter, who again received 10% of the proceeds. However, this year, rather than dividing the proceeds equally between the five defendants as had been done in each previous year, Gleason kept half of the proceeds and gave the other half to Ferrara.

To uphold their end of this tripartite arrangement, appellants, who as previously noted were officers of Local 11, did not again demand that the free food provision be included in the collective bargaining agreements negotiated by appellants on behalf of Local 11 in each of the years 1959, 1962 and 1965.

Shortly after appellants received their 1965 payment from Wechsler, Walgreen discontinued the use of Wechsler coffee. . . .

. . . [A]ppellants contend that even if Gleason's testimony were sufficient to show that Wechsler Coffee Company made annual payments to appellants, the government failed to establish that these payments were outlawed by § 302 of the Taft-Hartley Act, 29 U.S.C. § 186. The resolution of this issue requires a brief summary of the theories upon which the government relied to prove violations of the various provisions of this statute.

The government relied on three theories to show that appellants had conspired to violate 29 U.S.C. § 186: (1) by receiving annual payments from an employer (Rikers Restaurants and Restaurant Associates) of members of their union, in violation of §§ 186(a)(1) and (b)(1); (2) by receiving a "thing of value" (an agreement to purchase Wechsler coffee) from another employer (Walgreen) of members of their union, in violation of §§ 186(a)(1) and (b)(1); and (3) by receiving annual payments from employers (Abraham Wechsler, James Slater and Irwin Chapman) with intent to be influenced as union officials, in violation of §§ 186(a)(4) and (b)(1). A review of the record reveals that the government presented sufficient evidence to support each one of these three theories.

With respect to the first theory, appellants' claim that the government failed to show that Wechsler and his subordinates were employers of employees represented by appellants is without merit. It is true that Wechsler

Coffee did not employ anyone represented by Local 11. The evidence presented at trial showed, however, that during the period covered by the indictment, Local 11 organized the employees of many of the restaurants operated by Restaurant Associates, Inc., a corporation which operates a wide variety of food service establishments ranging from luxury restaurants to coffee shops and cafeterias, all of which are in the New York Metropolitan area. The evidence also indicated that Rikers Restaurants, Inc., a chain of fourteen restaurants, had been organized by Local 11 prior to 1954. The government then showed that Abraham Wechsler and his immediate family ran Rikers Restaurants and Restaurant Associates during the period covered by the indictment. Abraham Wechsler testified that in 1954 he was sole stockholder of both companies. In 1956 Wechsler began giving away his shares to his family, including his son-in-law, co-conspirator James Slater. During the entire period covered by the indictment, Wechsler and his family continued to control Restaurant Associates and Rikers Restaurants. Even after a public offering of Restaurant Associates stock in 1961, the Wechsler family was to retain 62% of its common stock. Although Wechsler was no longer a director of Restaurant Associates in 1961, he continued to control the business. James Slater, who was secretary-treasurer and later president of Wechsler Coffee, was a director of Restaurant Associates from 1961 on. Wechsler's personal control over Restaurant Associates was demonstrated by his ability to have his other son-in-law, Jerome Brody, removed from the presidency of Restaurant Associates in 1963, after Brody and Wechsler's daughter were separated. Furthermore, in 1963, Wechsler arranged for co-conspirator Irwin Chapman, then secretary-treasurer of Wechsler Coffee, to be named a director of Restaurant Associates, although Chapman was, at most, a nominal shareholder in that company. In view of these facts, there was sufficient evidence to support Judge Pollack's finding that Abraham Wechsler, James Slater and Irwin Chapman, by virtue of their control over and involvement with Restaurant Associates and Rikers Restaurants, were employers or persons acting in the interest of employers, within the meaning of 29 U.S.C. § 186(a).

Appellants' claim that the evidence was insufficient to show that Walgreen promised to buy its coffee from Wechsler also is refuted by the record. The existence of this promise is shown by Walgreen's purchasing its coffee requirements from Wechsler from 1954 through 1965 despite Walgreen's dissatisfaction with the price and quality of Wechsler coffee. Moreover, when Plummer, a Walgreen employee, made complaints about the coffee, he was informed that coffee would continue to be purchased from Wechsler because Local 11 was involved. Furthermore, in view of the fact that Walgreen had its own roasting plant which had supplied its coffee in New York prior to 1955, Local 11's involvement with Wechsler provides the only plausible explanation for Walgreen's purchasing coffee from Wechsler. Moreover, Walgreen's agreement with appellants to switch coffee suppliers was a "thing of value" within the meaning of 29 U.S.C. § 186(a)(1), since the agreement enabled defendants to exact a "commission" on every pound of coffee sold to Walgreen thereafter.

There also was ample evidence to show that appellants had conspired to violate 29 U.S.C. §§ 186(a)(4) and (b)(1), since the money was requested by them and received by appellants with the intent of being influenced as union officials. As previously noted, the evidence showed the existence of an arrangement, pursuant to which Walgreen would buy its coffee requirements from Wechsler Coffee, Wechsler Coffee would pay appellants a commission on the coffee sold to Walgreen, and the union would relinquish its demand for retention of the "free meal" provision in its contract with Walgreen. The fact that relinquishing the "free food" provision was unacceptable to Gleason and Ferrara, until it appeared that they could use their position to make a profit out of relinquishing the free food provision, indicates that appellants received the money with the intent of being influenced in their actions as officers of Local 11. Moreover, the fact that this arrangement was adhered to despite the demands of some members that the free food provision be reinstated indicates that appellants continued to receive the money with the intent of being influenced.

Relying on the theory that their conduct could not have been criminal prior to the 1959 amendments to the Taft-Hartley Act, appellants maintain that the introduction of evidence concerning their activities prior to September of 1959 was reversible error and that the application of the amended statute to them constituted a violation of the *ex post facto* clause of the Constitution. These claims are without merit.

Even assuming appellants' activities were not criminal prior to the 1959 amendments to the Taft-Hartley Act, the application of amended 29 U.S.C. § 186 to the conspiracy did not violate the *ex post facto* clause. Although the evidence established that the initial agreements among appellants Walgreen and Wechsler Coffee were consummated in 1954, there was clear proof that the conspiracy was reaffirmed and adhered to long after September of 1959. Merely because appellants' actions prior to 1959 did not violate § 186 does not mean that acts committed after that date, done in violation thereof, are in any way excused or that the conspiracy had ended. Here, a number of overt acts, the most obvious of which were the annual payments to appellants, occurred after the effective date of the amendments to the Taft-Hartley Act. Accordingly, the *ex post facto* clause was not violated, as the conspiracy, and overt acts in furtherance thereof, continued long after the 1959 amendment to the statute.

Furthermore, the trial judge did not commit reversible error in admitting evidence relating to the period before the statute was amended. Such evidence was admissible to show the existence and purpose of the conspiracy, as well as to prove the intent and purpose of the conspirators' later acts. In view of the fact that the conspiracy continued long after 1959, evidence of prior acts was both admissible and necessary to enable the trial judge to appreciate fully the reasons for the payments made after 1959. . . .

CASE QUESTIONS

1. What statutory charge was used in this indictment of criminal conduct?
2. What are the material facts?
3. What theory did the prosecution use?
4. How did this decision protect members from their union?

SECTION 96 / UNION AND MANAGEMENT REPORTING REQUIREMENTS

The Labor-Management Relations Act of 1947 contained provisions for reports and affidavits, but unions were not required to comply unless they wanted to obtain the services of the National Labor Relations Board. Some organizations preferred to forego access to the Board rather than meet these filing conditions.

The Labor-Management Reporting and Disclosure Act rescinded this 1947 provision and replaced it with a mandatory reporting requirement. Every labor union *must* now file with the Secretary of Labor a complete report containing the following:

1. The name and title of each officer,
2. The initiation fees and work permit fees required of members or others, and regular dues or other fees required of members;
3. Provisions as to membership qualifications or restrictions, assessments, benefit plan participation, authorization for fund disbursements, and audits; calling of meetings for selection of officers or representatives and for their discipline or removal; discipline of members; authorization of bargaining demands and of strikes; ratification of contracts; and issuing work permits.

Any changes in union constitutions, bylaws, or rules must be reported, along with an annual report containing the following information:

1. Assets and liabilities at the beginning and end of the fiscal year;
2. Receipts and the sources thereof;
3. Salary and allowances and other disbursements to anyone receiving more than $10,000 total from the union and from any affiliated organization;
4. Any loan aggregating over $250 with full details;
5. Any other disbursements.

All the information reported to the Secretary of Labor must be made available to the members. The reports must be signed by the union officials, who, in addition, must each file a signed report each year with the following information:

1. Any security holdings or other financial interest in or benefit received from any employer whose employees the union represents or seeks to represent, including transactions in the name of a spouse or child.
2. Anything of value received from an employer or consultant (except the allowable union dues or welfare fund payments), including any valuable benefit received from a business dealing in any way connected with the union.

Employers must also file annual reports containing information as to any expenditures or transactions with union representatives, and as to the following additional transactions:

1. Payments to employees for influencing others as to organizational or bargaining activities.
2. Expenditures to influence such activities or to obtain information concerning any activities in connection with a labor dispute.
3. Arrangements with labor relations consultants or other agencies for the same purpose and payments pursuant to such arrangements, with full details.

Any other persons party to arrangements such as those referred to in the above three paragraphs must file a report within thirty days, giving all details. All reports to the Secretary of Labor are public information available to anyone. These reporting requirements can be enforced by criminal or civil prosecution in federal courts.

SECTION 97 / WELFARE AND PENSION PLANS

The Labor Management Relations Act prohibits by its Section 302 any employer from paying and any employee representative from receiving "any money or other thing of value," with specified exceptions, under penalty of fine or imprisonment. The exceptions include such lawful transactions as paying checkoff dues deductions to the union where the employee has signed a written authorization for such wage deduction and assignments. Another exception allows the employer to make payments into a trust fund for the sole benefit of employees and their dependents.

Such trust funds may only be for medical or hospital care, disability or death benefits, and retirement pensions, as are specified in an agreement between an employer and the union. The agreement must provide that both parties be equally represented in the administration of any fund and that there be neutral determination of any deadlocked item. An annual audit with the results available to any interested person has to be provided, and under the statute payments for pension funds must be made to a separate fund limited to that purpose.

In 1958 a Welfare and Pension Plans Disclosure Act further required that details of all such funds must be filed with the Secretary of Labor and made available to each beneficiary. The only compliance provided for enforcing the requirements was a private lawsuit undertaken by an interested individual. In March of 1962, however, the 1958 Act was strengthened by Congress by adding to the Secretary of Labor's power. He is authorized now to disclose pertinent details of any fund covered by the Act, defined as those having 100 or more covered employees; to investigate alleged violations; and to enforce the law through undertaking injunctive actions. Criminal penalties for false reports or for dishonest conduct are also included.[22]

SECTION 98 / SUABILITY AND LIABILITY

In Chapter 2 we saw that the Supreme Court in a suit for damages under the Sherman Act affirmed a lower court's finding that the members of the union were jointly liable with the officers for damages which the United Hatters of North America had caused the employer (*Lawlor* v. *Loewe*). It was noted there also that Section 301 of the Labor Management Relations Act later made a money judgment enforceable only against the union as an entity, but not against any members as individuals.

This section is directed to the suability character of labor organizations; to

---

[22] Welfare and Pension Plans Disclosure Act, Public Law 85–836 72 Stat. 997.

the responsibility of officers, members, and agents; and the liability of the union for unlawful conduct. While today members are immune from financial liability as individuals in union damage suits, a union's treasury and assets are liable under the 1947 Act in both federal and state court actions. Formerly, as an unincorporated association, a union at common law could be a plaintiff only in the name of all its members and a defendant only if personal service of summons was had against its constituents. The money judgment against the association could then be satisfied only out of the assets of those members who had been served a summons. These common law rules made it very difficult to sue or to be sued.

A related question arises as to what is the responsibility of the union for acts of individuals, e.g. who is a union agent. We saw in Chapter 2 of this volume that the Norris-LaGuardia Anti-Injunction Act laid down the strict rule that, in a labor dispute, actual participation or authorization or ratification after knowledge was necessary to affix responsibility so as to hold officers liable for the unlawful acts of others. Under the Labor Management Relations Act of 1947, however, damages may be awarded under the authority of Section 301(e) for acts of others irrespective of whether the specific acts were actually authorized or ratified subsequently. In other words, the union as an entity and its assets may now be held liable for actions of agents with authorization or ratification not being the controlling consideration.

State courts and federal courts have jurisdiction to award damages against a local union for striking. Where the contract required arbitration, even in the absence of an explicit no-strike clause, the United States Supreme Court agreed with the courts of the State of Washington that such a damages award to the employer was permitted under Section 302 of the federal LMRA.[23]

Unions may be sued also under the 1959 LMRDA, Section 102, as seen in the *Boilermakers* decision printed in a previous section. In *Yablonski* v. *United Mine Workers,* the Court of Appeals sustained a murdered member's estate in continuing a LMRDA suit against then UMW President Boyle and the Mineworkers Union for actual and punitive money damages resulting from union reprisals made because of his seeking office as union president against incumbent President Boyle.

Estate of Yablonski v. United Mine Workers

United States Court of Appeals, District of Columbia Circuit, 1972. 459 F.2d 1201

PER CURIAM: Joseph A. Yablonski filed suit June 27, 1969, against appellees, the United Mine Workers of America (UMWA), W. A. ("Tony") Boyle, its International President, George J. Titler, its International Vice President, and John Owens, its International Secretary-Treasurer. Plaintiff was a long-standing member of the UMWA, a labor organization subject in the conduct of its affairs to provisions of the Labor-Management Reporting and Disclosure Act of 1959 (LMRDA). Plaintiff had announced his candidacy

---

[23] *Local 174 Teamsters* v. *Lucas Flour Company,* 365 U.S. 809 (1962).

for President of the UMWA, in opposition to the candidacy for re-election of incumbent defendant Boyle. The election was to be held December 9, 1969. The complaint, which invoked provisions of the LMRDA, particularly Sections 609 (29 U.S.C. § 529) and 102 (29 U.S.C. § 412), may for our purposes be further described as having two basic thrusts. One was to obtain a declaratory ruling that the defendants' purported removal of Yablonski as Acting Director of Labor's Non-Partisan League was illegal, and a preliminary injunction compelling effective reinstatement to that position and preventing further reprisals by defendants against plaintiff for exercising rights conferred upon him by various cited provisions of the LMRDA. In the second place, the complaint prayed for an award to plaintiff as against all defendants of actual damages in the sum of $20,000, reasonable attorneys fees and expenses, and, as against defendant Boyle, for an award of such punitive damages as the court should deem sufficient to deter incumbent officials seeking office from actions such as those alleged in the complaint.

Proceedings in the District Court, which followed shortly upon the filing of the complaint, led the court to issue a preliminary injunction for reinstatement of plaintiff as Acting Director of the League and for related relief. According to further pleadings filed by plaintiff, however, defendants never effectively complied with the order of the District Court.

On December 9, 1969, with the litigation initiated by the complaint still pending, the election for President of the Union was held, after which defendant Boyle announced his own re-election. Plaintiff filed charges with the UMWA to set aside the election. On January 5, 1970, plaintiff and his wife and daughter were found slain in their home.

Two days after the discovery of the bodies of plaintiff and his wife and daughter, defendants filed a suggestion of plaintiff's death, and on January 21, 1970, filed a motion to dismiss the complaint on the grounds that the death of plaintiff had "either rendered moot or deprived the court of jurisdiction" of all issues in the case except those arising under Sections 501(a) and (b) of the LMRDA (29 U.S.C. §§ 501(a), (b)), and that as to those matters the complaint fails to state a claim. On April 6, 1970, appellants Kenneth J. Yablonski and Joseph A. Yablonski, as administrators of the estate of their father, the original plaintiff, sought in the District Court substitution for the deceased and continuation of the suit. Their motion in that regard was not acted upon by the District Court. They have been substituted as appellants by *sua sponte* order of this court.

The District Court, on June 22, 1970, entered its Order that, "the motion of the defendants to dismiss . . . C. A. 1799–69 . . . as moot is granted. . . ." On the same day the court filed an "Opinion and Order" in which the court referred to C. A. 1799–69—the "reinstatement case"—as having been orally dismissed after argument because "mooted by reason of the fact that the election is over and no further relief is available in this court." Mention was made in the Opinion and Order of Sections 501(a) and (b), but no mention was made in either the Opinion and Order or in the Order of the claims for damages advanced in the complaint.

Neither the holding of the election, nor the death of the original plaintiff, rendered moot the claims for actual and punitive damages, or the question of appellants' right to continue the suit in respect of those claims. For this reason, without intimating any view as to the merits of those issues, and without intimating any view as to right of survivorship, we reverse the Order dismissing the complaint as moot insofar as the complaint seeks damages and a right in appellants to continue the suit in that respect, and we remand for further proceedings not inconsistent with this opinion.

It is so ordered.

CASE QUESTIONS

1. What was the issue before the Court?
2. What had the Union done?
3. What did the District Court award?
4. What was the Circuit Court opinion?

SECTION 99 / POLITICAL CONTRIBUTIONS AND EXPENDITURES

The Labor-Management Relations Act of 1947 contains a provision concerning union political expenditures. Its Section 304 presents the amended Section 313 of the Federal Corrupt Practices Act. As amended, the section now includes unions, as well as previously covered corporations, under the bans imposed on expending or contributing funds in federal election activities. The section provides as follows:

> SEC. 313. It is unlawful for any national bank, or any corporation organized by authority of any law of Congress, to make a contribution or expenditure in connection with any election to any political office, or in connection with any primary election or political convention or caucus held to select candidates for any political office, or for any corporation whatever, or any labor organization to make a contribution or expenditure in connection with any election at which Presidential and Vice Presidential electors or a Senator or Representative in, or a Delegate or Resident Commissioner to Congress are to be voted for, or in connection with any primary election or political convention or caucus held to elect candidates for any of the foregoing offices, or for any candidate, political committee, or other person to accept or receive any contribution prohibited by this section. Every corporation or labor organization which makes any contribution or expenditure in violation of this section shall be fined not more than $5,000; and every officer or director of any corporation, or officer of any labor organization, who consents to any contribution or expenditure by the corporation or labor organization, as the case may be, in violation of this section shall be fined not more than $1,000 or imprisoned for not more than one year, or both. For the purposes of this section 'labor organization' means any organization of any kind, or any agency or employee representation committee or plan, in which employees participate and which exists for the purpose, in whole or in part, of dealing with employers concerning grievances, labor disputes, wages, rates of pay, hours of employment, or conditions of work.

It should be noted that the prohibition and penalties of Section 304, as it incorporates Section 313 of the F.C.P. Act, extends to both the *maker* and the *receiver* of the forbidden expenditure and applies to corporations as well as labor organizations.

In 1972 another pertinent law affecting political activity of labor organizations became effective when President Nixon signed the Federal Election Campaign Act of 1971 which revised the provisions of the Corrupt Practices Act and the parallel Section 304 of the 1947 Labor Management Relations Act.[24] In *Pipefitters Local 562* v. *U.S.*, which is presented below, the Supreme Court found that union political funds are legal if they are segregated from regular dues and assessments, are earmarked for political activity purposes with the members so informed, and there is no actual or threat of reprisal by job or membership discrimination in connection with the collection of the members' contributions. The Court considered the 1947 and the 1971 enactments as the accrued thinking of Congress, including an explicit codification of prior court rulings as to what could and could not be done under Section 304 of the Labor Management Relations Act.

In *U.S.* v. *Boyle* in which the President of the Mineworkers Union was found to have violated the 1947 law by making contributions to candidates for political offices, the union officials were found guilty of the crime even though the union itself was not indicted or convicted. The District Court of the District of Columbia held that indirect or direct transmission of funds from general union dues for electioneering purposes was illegal, finding that use of such funds for the purpose prohibited by the statute was unfair to union members opposing those candidates for whom union leaders made contributions or expenditures.[25]

Pipefitters Local No. 562 v. United States

Supreme Court of the United States, 1972. 407 U.S. 385

MR. JUSTICE BRENNAN delivered the opinion of the Court: Petitioners— Pipefitters Local Union No. 562 and three individual officers of the Union— were convicted by a jury in the United States District Court for the Eastern District of Missouri of conspiracy under 18 U.S.C. § 371 to violate 18 U.S.C. § 610. At the time of trial § 610 provided in relevant part:

> "It is unlawful . . . for any corporation whatever, or any labor organization to make a contribution or expenditure in connection with any election at which Presidential and Vice Presidential electors or a Senator or Representative in . . . Congress are to be voted for, or in connection with any primary election or political convention or caucus held to select candidates for any of the foregoing offices. . . .
>
> "Every corporation or labor organization which makes any contribution or expenditure in violation of this section shall be fined not more than $5,000; and every officer or director of any corporation, or officer of any labor organization, who consents to any contribution or expenditure by the corporation or labor organization, as the case may be, . . . in violation of this section, shall be fined not more than $1,000 or imprisoned not more than one year, or both; and if the violation was willful, shall be fined not more than $10,000 or imprisoned not more than two years, or both.
>
> "For the purposes of this section 'labor organization' means any organization of any kind, or any agency or employee representation committee or plan, in which employees participate and which exist [*sic*] for the purpose, in whole or in part, of

---

[24] Federal Election Campaign Act of 1971, 18 U.S.C. 610 (1972).
[25] *United States* v. *Boyle,* 338 F. Supp 1028 (1972).

dealing with employers concerning grievances, labor disputes, wages, rates of pay, hours of employment, or conditions of work."

The indictment charged, in essence, that petitioners had conspired from 1963 to May 9, 1968, to establish and maintain a fund that (1) would receive regular and systematic payments from Local 562 members and members of other locals working under the Union's jurisdiction; (2) would have the appearance, but not the reality of being an entity separate from the Union; and (3) would conceal contributions and expenditures by the Union in connection with federal elections. . . .

The evidence tended to show, in addition to disbursements of about $150,000 by the fund to candidates in federal elections, an identity between the fund and the Union and a collection of well over $1 million in contributions to the fund by a method similar to that employed in the collection of dues or assessments. In particular, it was established that from 1949 through 1962 the Union maintained a political fund to which Union members and others working under the Union's jurisdiction were in fact required to contribute and that that fund was then succeeded in 1963 by the present fund, which was, in form, set up as a separate "voluntary" organization. Yet a principal Union officer assumed the role of director of the present fund with full and unlimited control over its disbursements. The Union's business manager, petitioner Lawler, became the first director of the fund and was later succeeded by petitioner Callanan, whom one Local 562 member described as "the Union" in explaining his influence within the local. Moreover, no significant change was made in the regular and systematic method of collection of contributions at a prescribed rate based on hours worked, and Union agents continued to collect donations at jobsites on Union time. In addition, changes in the rate of contributions were tied to changes in the rate of members' assessments. In 1966, for example, when assessments were increased from 2½% to 3¾% of gross wages, the contribution rate was decreased from $1 to 50¢ per day worked with the result that the change did not cause, in the words of the Union's executive board, "one extra penny cost to members of Local Union 562." At the same time, the contribution rate for nonmembers, who were not required to pay the prescribed travel card fee for working under Local 562's jurisdiction, remained the same at $2 per day worked, approximately matching the total assessment and contribution of members. Finally, in addition to political contributions, the fund used its monies for nonpolitical purposes, such as aid to financially distressed members on strike, and for a period of a few months, upon the vote of its members, even suspended collections in favor of contributions to a separate gift fund for petitioner Callanan. Not surprisingly, various witnesses testified that during the indictment period contributions to the fund were often still referred to as—and actually understood by some to be—assessments, or that they paid their contributions "voluntarily" in the same sense that they paid their dues or other financial obligations.

On the other hand, the evidence also indicated that the political contributions by the fund were made from accounts strictly segregated from Union dues and assessments and that donations to the fund were not, in fact, necessary for employment or Union membership. The fund generally required contributors to sign authorization cards, which contained a statement that their donations were "voluntary . . . [and] no part of the dues or financial obligations of Local Union No. 562 . . . ," and the testimony was overwhelming from both those who contributed and those who did not, as well as from the collectors of contributions, that no specific pressure was exerted, and no reprisals were taken, to obtain donations. Significantly, the Union's attorney who had advised in the organization of the fund testified on cross-examination that his advice had been that payments to the fund could not be made a condition of employment or Local 562 membership, but it was immaterial whether contributions appeared compulsory to those solicited. . . .

The jury instructions embody an interpretation of § 610 that is plainly erroneous. The trial court refused requests by petitioners for instructions that the jury should acquit if it found that contributions to the Pipefitters fund were made voluntarily. Adopting a contrary view, the court instructed the jury, over petitioners' objections, that it should return verdicts of guilty if the fund "was in fact a union fund, . . . the money therein was union money, and . . . the real contributor to the candidates was the union." "In determining whether the Pipefitters Voluntary Fund was a bona fide fund, separate and distinct from the union or a mere artifice or device," the jury was further instructed to "take into consideration all the facts and circumstances in evidence, and in such consideration . . . [to] consider" 19 factors, several of which related to the regularity, rate, method of collection, and segregation from Union monies of payments to the fund. Others concerned the kinds of expenditures the fund made and the Union's control over them. Still others involved whether the payments to the fund were made voluntarily. In the latter regard the court charged (emphasis added):

> "A great deal of evidence has been introduced on the question of whether the payments into the Pipefitters Voluntary . . . Fund by members of Local 562 and others working under its jurisdiction were voluntary or involuntary. This evidence is relevant for your consideration, along with all other facts and circumstances in evidence, in determining whether the fund is a union fund. *However, the mere fact that the payments into the fund may have been made voluntarily by some or even all of the contributors thereto does not, of itself, mean that the money so paid into the fund was not union money."*

On appeal the Court of Appeals did not address the validity of these instructions other than to agree with the trial judge that "the issue of whether the payments to the fund were voluntary is relevant and material [but not determinative] on the issue of whether the fund is the property of Local 562."

The instructions, as the Court of Appeals confirmed, clearly permitted the jury to convict without finding that donations to the Pipefitters fund had been actual or effective dues or assessments. This was plain error.

The judgment of the Court of Appeals as to petitioners Callanan and Lawler is vacated, and the case is remanded to the District Court with directions to dismiss the indictment against them. The judgment of the Court of Appeals as to petitioners Local 562 and Seaton is reversed, and the case is remanded to the District Court for proceedings as to them not inconsistent with this opinion.

It is so ordered.

MR. JUSTICE BLACKMUN took no part in the consideration or decision of this case.

MR. JUSTICE POWELL, with whom THE CHIEF JUSTICE joins, dissenting: The decision of the Court today will have a profound effect upon the role of labor unions and corporations in the political life of this country. The holding, reversing a trend since 1907, opens the way for major participation in politics by the largest aggregations of economic power, the great unions and corporations. This occurs at a time, paradoxically, when public and legislative interest has focused on limiting—rather than enlarging—the influence upon the elective process of concentrations of wealth and power.

The majority opinion holds that *unions* lawfully may make political contributions so long as they come from funds voluntarily given to the union for such purpose. The Court seeks to buttress this holding by a long and scholarly presentation of the legislative history of § 610 of the Labor Management Relations Act. But some of that history invites conflicting inferences, and the background of § 205 of the Federal Election Campaign Act of 1971, to which the majority also devotes extensive attention, is of dubious value in interpreting an earlier statute which on its face is clear and unambiguous.

In its preoccupation with the legislative history, the Court has overlooked the central point involved in this case: that the conviction of petitioners accords with the plain language of the controlling statute. Nor does the majority demonstrate an ambiguity in that statutory language that makes relevant its long journey into the legislative history. . . .

The consequences of today's decision could be far-reaching indeed. The opinion of the Court provides a blueprint for compliance with § 610, as now construed, which will be welcomed by every corporation and union which wishes to take advantage of a heretofore unrecognized opportunity to influence elections in this country.

It may be that the unions, by virtue of a system of collecting "political contributions" simultaneously with the collection of dues and regularizing such collections to the point where they are indistinguishable from dues, will be the primary beneficiaries. But the corporations are more numerous than the unions. They have millions of stockholders and hundreds of thousands of nonunion employees. Both unions and corporations have large financial resources. Today's interpretation of § 610 will enable a more direct and extensive political employment of these resources by both union and corporation.

By refusing to affirm the judgment below, the majority renders the ultimate fate of this litigation uncertain. If, on remand, the techniques of Local 562 should be sanctioned, other unions and corporations could easily follow Local 562 and obtain from members, employees and shareholders a consent form attesting that the contribution (or withholding) is "voluntary." The trappings of voluntariness might be achieved while the substance of coercion remained. Union members and corporate employees might find themselves the objects of regular and systematized solicitation by the very agent which exercised direct control over their jobs and livelihood.

The only remaining requirement to meet the new standards is that the fund be separate from other union or corporate funds, although under the majority's interpretation of § 205 it may be established, administered and the contributions to it solicited by the union or corporation with their own funds. Again, if Local 562 were to provide the standards, the separateness of such a fund need be nothing more than separate ledger and bank account.

In sum, the opinion of the Court today, adopting an interpretation of § 610 at variance with its language and purpose, goes a long way toward returning unions and corporations to an unregulated status with respect to political contributions. This opening of the door to extensive corporate and union influence of the elective and legislative processes must be viewed with genuine concern. This seems to me to be a regressive step as contrasted with the numerous legislative and judicial actions in recent years designed to assure that elections are indeed free and representative.

I would affirm the judgment below.

CASE QUESTIONS	1. What was the basis of violation by the union in the district court action?
	2. What does the Supreme Court find to be a fatal error in the lower court proceeding?
	3. Why does the dissenting opinion object to the majority decision?
QUESTIONS ON CHAPTER 11	1. How are union members given protection by the law from unfair or arbitrary treatment by union officers or a union majority?
	2. What reporting requirements are contained in the federal laws regulating unions?
	3. What financial responsibility does a union have at law? Where does this liability rest?
	4. To what extent are labor unions or similar organizations representing workers restricted in expenditures of their funds?

Chapter 12

Fair Employment Practices

SECTION 100 / INTRODUCTION

There are three major federal laws which regulate equal rights in employment. The *Civil Rights Act of 1964 Title VII* as amended by the *Equal Employment Opportunities Act of 1972* forbids employer and union discrimination based on race, color, religion, sex or national origin. The *Equal Pay Act of 1963* requires equal pay for men and women doing equal work. The *Age Discrimination in Employment Act of 1967* forbids discriminatory hiring practices against job applicants between the ages of 40 and 65. Additionally, *Executive Order 11246,* which has the force and effect of a statute enacted by Congress, regulates contractors and subcontractors doing business with the federal government. This order forbids discrimination against minorities and in certain situations requires "affirmative action" to be taken to better employment opportunities for minorities. This chapter covers the law of fair employment practices which includes the above statutes and executive order, the U. S. Constitution, and the court decisions construing them.

SECTION 101 / TITLE VII AS AMENDED

The general purpose of Title VII of the Civil Rights Act of 1964 is the elimination of employer and union practices which discriminate against employees and job applicants on the basis of race, color, religion, sex, or national origin.

Prohibited Practices

Title VII forbids discrimination in hiring, terms or conditions of employment, union membership and representation, and in the referral of applicants by employment agencies. Title VII specifically forbids any employer from failing or refusing to hire, or to discharge or otherwise to discriminate against any individual with respect to his compensation, terms, conditions, or privileges of employment; or to limit, segregate, or classify his employees in any way which

423

would deprive or tend to deprive any individual of employment opportunity or otherwise adversely affect his status as an employee due to race, color, religion, sex, or national origin.

A union is forbidden to exclude or expel from its membership or otherwise discriminate against any individual, or to limit, segregate, or classify its membership; or to classify or fail or refuse to refer for employment any individual in any way which would deprive or tend to deprive the individual of employment opportunities or limit such employment opportunities or otherwise adversely affect his status as an employee or as an applicant for employment because of race, color, religion, national origin or sex. It is further unlawful for any employer or union to discriminate against an individual in any program established to provide apprenticeship or other training.[1]

The Equal Employment Opportunity Commission

Compliance with Title VII is achieved through the Equal Employment Opportunity Commission (EEOC). The Civil Rights Act of 1964, which created the EEOC, granted it the authority to investigate and conciliate grievances alleging racial, religious, national origin, or sex discrimination. Where there is a state or local agency with the power to act on allegations of discriminatory practices, a grievant must first file his or her complaint with that agency. He or she must then wait sixty days or until the termination of the state proceedings, whichever occurs first, before filing a charge with the EEOC. The Commission then conducts an investigation to determine whether reasonable cause exists to believe that the charge is true. If such cause is found to exist, the EEOC attempts to remedy the unlawful practice through conciliation. Under the 1964 Act, if the Commission was unable to satisfactorily resolve the dispute through conciliation and persuasion, it notified the grievant of his or her right to sue the respondent in federal court, with the court having the right to waive costs and to grant attorneys fees. Also under the 1964 Act, the Attorney General of the United States was authorized to initiate court action in the limited circumstances of an allegation of a "pattern or practice" of discrimination. The Equal Employment Opportunities Act of 1972, which amends Title VII in several important areas to be enumerated below, authorizes the EEOC itself to litigate court actions on behalf of an individual grievant when conciliation fails. The EEOC also was given authority under the 1972 amendments to bring class action suits and, as of March 24, 1974, it will have exclusive authority to initiate and litigate "pattern and practice" actions.

The 1972 Act created the Office of General Counsel to the Commission in order to provide the legal resources for its new litigation powers. The General Counsel is appointed by the President with the advice and consent of the Senate. He or she is responsible for the conduct of litigation and the supervision of EEOC regional offices.

The new amendments to Title VII significantly enlarge the class of persons under the Act. State and local governments and their political subdivisions are now included in the Act's definition of "persons" which makes them employers

---

[1] See Section 703 of the Civil Rights Act, printed in the Appendix of this volume.

subject to the Act.[2] The elimination of an exemption for educational institutions with respect to individuals whose work involves educational activities brings teachers and professional and non-professional staff members within the Act's coverage. The amendments also lower from twenty-five to fifteen the number of employees required to bring their employer under the coverage of Title VII.[3] Labor unions with at least 15 members are now subject to the law.[4] The inclusion within the coverage of the Act continues for all unions operating hiring halls and all employment agencies regardless of size.[5]

The statute of limitations for filing charges with the EEOC is now 180 days after the occurrence of the discriminatory act.[6] Limitations for filing charges is 300 days after the occurrence of the discriminatory act when the grievant is required to first file with a state or local agency.[7]

The remedial powers of federal courts deciding Title VII actions may include an injunction against the unlawful practice and the issuance of affirmative orders which may include reinstatement or the hiring of employees with or without back pay. However the 1972 amendments limit back pay orders to a period of two years prior to the filing of the charge.[8]

The Bona Fide Occupational Qualification Exception

Section 703(e) provides an exception to the broad prohibitions of Title VII against discrimination based on race, color, religion, sex or national origin. This section stipulates that it shall not be an unlawful employment practice for an employer to hire employees on the basis of his or her religion, sex, or national origin in those certain instances where religion, sex, or national origin is a bona fide occupational qualification (BFOQ) reasonably necessary to the normal operation of a particular enterprise. The so-called "BFOQ" clause is contrued narrowly by the courts and the burden of proving the business necessity for any such restrictive occupational qualifications is on the employer.[9] The *Diaz* decision reported in this section is a good example of the narrow application of this statutory exception. It is important to note that there is no BFOQ exception for either race or color.

Testing and Educational Requirements

The Supreme Court held in *Griggs* v. *Duke Power Company* that employment testing and educational requirements must be "job related"; that is, the employer must prove that the tests and educational requirements bear a demonstrable relationship to job performance. The court ruled that despite absence of any intent on the part of the employer to discriminate against blacks, the lack of intention to discriminate was irrelevant when the effect was to discriminate.

---

[2] 42 U.S.C. § 701(a).
[3] 42 U.S.C. § 701(b).
[4] 42 U.S.C. § 701(e).
[5] 42 U.S.C. § 701(e).
[6] 42 U.S.C. § 706(e).
[7] 42 U.S.C. § 706(e).
[8] 42 U.S.C. § 706(g).
[9] See *Phillips* v. *Martin Marietta Corp.*, 400 U.S. 542 (1971). See *McDonnell-Douglas Corp.* v. *Green*, 411 U.S. 792 (1973), for procedures regarding proof of discrimination.

Indeed, it is not enough for an employer to demonstrate a legitimate business *purpose* for adhering to its challenged practices, for the test devised in the *Griggs* decision is a business *necessity* test. The *Griggs* decision is reported in this section.

Arrest and Convicton Inquiries

In *Gregory* v. *Litton Systems Inc.,*[10] the Ninth Circuit Court of Appeals upheld a district court's order for damages and attorneys fees awarded pursuant to Title VII of the Civil Rights Act. It was stipulated that Litton's decision not to hire Gregory as a sheet-metal worker was predicated upon his statement in Litton's employment questionnaire that he had been arrested fourteen times and not upon any consideration of convictions. The trial court held, and it was approved on appeal, that Litton's employment questionnaire, which required each applicant to reveal his or her arrest record, was discriminatory against black job-seekers. It was held that Litton had not demonstrated that it had any reasonable business purpose for asking prospective employees about their arrest records.

The EEOC has taken the position that review of arrest records is irrelevant. The EEOC has also maintained that convictions cannot always be regarded as relevant to the ability of an individual to perform a job. The burden of proof is on the employer to justify inquiries into an applicant's arrest-conviction record. The EEOC has ruled that an employee's false answer to an inquiry regarding his arrest-conviction record did not justify discharge.[11] The EEOC relied on the Federal Bureau of Investigation statistics showing that "Negroes as a class are arrested and convicted substantially more frequently than Caucasians" and found that

> the foreseeable impact of respondent's arrest-conviction inquiry is that a substantially disproportionate percentage of those persons rejected or discharged because of the inquiry either because they answered in the affirmative, not at all, or falsely, will be Negro. In these circumstances the arrest-conviction policy is unlawful, absent a showing of business necessity.

The EEOC in this particular decision found that "business necessity" was not involved since the charging party had performed satisfactorily during an 18-month period of employment prior to the discovery of the false statement in the job application.[12]

Religion

Title VII of the Civil Rights Act of 1964 prohibits employment discrimination because of religion. The 1972 amendments provide a new definition of "religion" to include all aspects of religious observance, practice and belief, so as to require employers to make reasonable accommodations for employees whose "religion" may include observances, practices and beliefs, such as Friday

---

[10] 472 F.2d 631 (9th Cir. 1972).

[11] Decision of EEOC No. 72–1460, 1972 CCH Employment Practice Guide 6341.

[12] In the case of *Peters* v. *Kiff,* 407 U.S. 493 (1972), the Supreme Court indicated that a legal right which can be claimed by a minority group member can be claimed by someone who does not fall into that category.

evening and Saturday religious observances which differ from the employer's or potential employer's requirements regarding schedules or other business-related employment conditions. Failure to make accommodations is unlawful unless an employer can demonstrate that he or she cannot reasonably accommodate such beliefs, practices, or observances without undue hardship on the conduct of his or her business.[13] As an example of accommodation, the U. S. Department of Labor excused members of the Amish religion from regulations requiring the wearing of hard hats on construction sites, because the Amish religion requires the wearing of a black felt hat even when working and it is considered a breach of Amish religious principles to wear a hard hat.[14]

Griggs v. Duke Power Company

Supreme Court of the United States, 1971. 401 U.S. 424

BURGER, Ch. J.: We granted the writ in this case to resolve the question whether an employer is prohibited by the Civil Rights Act of 1964, Title VII, from requiring a high school education or passing of a standardized general intelligence test as a condition of employment in or transfer to jobs when (a) neither standard is shown to be significantly related to successful job performance, (b) both requirements operate to disqualify Negroes at a substantially higher rate than white applicants, and (c) the jobs in question formerly had been filled only by white employees as part of a longstanding practice of giving preference to whites.[15]

Congress provided, in Title VII of the Civil Rights Act of 1964, for class actions for enforcement of provisions of the Act and this proceeding was brought by a group of incumbent Negro employees against Duke Power Company. All the petitioners are employed at the Company's Dan River Steam Station, a power generating facility located at Draper, North Carolina. At the time this action was instituted, the Company had 95 employees at the Dan River Station, 14 of whom were Negroes; 13 of these are petitioners here.

The District Court found that prior to July 2, 1965, the effective date of the Civil Rights Act of 1964, the Company openly discriminated on the basis of race in the hiring and assigning of employees at its Dan River plant. The plant was organized into five operating departments: (1) Labor, (2) Coal Handling, (3) Operations, (4) Maintenance, and (5) Laboratory and Test.

---

[13] 42 U.S.C. § 701(j).

[14] 1972 CCH Employment Practices Guide, No. 5077.

[15] The Act provides:

"Sec. 703. (a) It shall be an unlawful employment practice for an employer—

"(2) to limit, segregate, or classify his employees in any way which would deprive or tend to deprive any individual of employment opportunities or otherwise adversely affect his status as an employee, because of such individual's race, color, religion, sex, or national origin.

"(h) Notwithstanding any other provision of this title, it shall not be an unlawful employment practice for an employer . . . to give and to act upon the results of any professionally developed ability test provided that such test, its administration or action upon the results is not designed, intended or used to discriminate because of race, color, religion, sex or national origin. . . ." 78 Stat. 255, 42 U.S.C. § 2000e–2.

Negroes were employed only in the Labor Department where the highest paying jobs paid less than the lowest paying jobs in the other four "operating" departments in which only whites were employed. Promotions were normally made within each department on the basis of job seniority. Transferees into a department usually began in the lowest position.

In 1955 the Company instituted a policy of requiring a high school education for initial assignment to any department except Labor, and for transfer from the Coal Handling to any "inside" department (Operations, Maintenance, or Laboratory). When the Company abandoned its policy of restricting Negroes to the Labor Department in 1965, completion of high school also was made a prerequisite to transfer from Labor to any other department. From the time the high school requirement was instituted to the time of trial, however, white employees hired before the time of the high school education requirement continued to perform satisfactorily and achieve promotions in the "operating" departments. Findings on this score are not challenged.

The Company added a further requirement for new employees on July 2, 1965, the date on which Title VII became effective. To qualify for placement in any but the Labor Department it became necessary to register satisfactory scores on two professionally prepared aptitude tests, as well as to have a high school education. Completion of high school alone continued to render employees eligible for transfer to the four desirable departments from which Negroes had been excluded if the incumbent had been employed prior to the time of the new requirement. In September 1965 the Company began to permit incumbent employees who lacked a high school education to qualify for transfer from Labor or Coal Handling to an "inside" job by passing two tests—the Wonderlic Personnel Test, which purports to measure general intelligence, and the Bennett Mechanical Comprehension Test. Neither was directed or intended to measure the ability to learn to perform a particular job or category of jobs. The requisite scores used for both initial hiring and transfer approximated the national median for high school graduates.[16]

The District Court had found that while the Company previously followed a policy of overt racial discrimination in a period prior to the Act, such conduct had ceased. The District Court also concluded that Title VII was intended to be prospective only and, consequently, the impact of prior inequities was beyond the reach of corrective action authorized by the Act.

The Court of Appeals was confronted with a question of first impression, as are we, concerning the meaning of Title VII. After careful analysis a majority of that court concluded that a subjective test of the employer's intent should govern, particularly in a close case, and that in this case there was no showing of a discriminatory purpose in the adoption of a diploma and test requirements. On this basis, the Court of Appeals concluded there was no violation of the Act.

The Court of Appeals reversed the District Court in part, rejecting the holding that residual discrimination arising from prior employment practices

---

[16] The test standards are thus more stringent than the high school requirement, since they would screen out approximately half of all high school graduates.

was insulated from remedial action. The Court of Appeals noted, however, that the District Court was correct in its conclusion that there was no finding of a racial purpose or invidious intent in the adoption of the high school diploma requirement or general intelligence test and that these standards had been applied fairly to whites and Negroes alike. It held that, in the absence of a discriminatory purpose, use of such requirements was permitted by the Act. In so doing, the Court of Appeals rejected the claim that because these two requirements operated to render ineligible a markedly disproportionate number of Negroes, they were unlawful under Title VII unless shown to be job-related. We granted the writ on these claims. 399 U.S. 926.

The objective of Congress in the enactment of Title VII is plain from the language of the statute. It was to achieve equality of employment opportunities and remove barriers that have operated in the past to favor an identifiable group of white employees over other employees. Under the Act, practices, procedures, or tests neutral on their face, and even neutral in terms of intent, cannot be maintained if they operate to "freeze" the status quo of prior discriminatory employment practices.

The Court of Appeals' opinion, and the partial dissent, agreed that, on the record in the present case, "whites register far better on the Company's alternative requirements" than Negroes.[17] 400 F.2d 1225, 1239 N. 6 This consequence would appear to be directly traceable to race. Basic intelligence must have the means of articulation to manifest itself fairly in a testing process. Because they are Negroes, petitioners have long received inferior education in segregated schools and this Court expressly recognizes these differences in *Gaston County* v. *United States,* 395 U.S. 285 (1969). There, because of the inferior education received by Negroes in North Carolina, this Court barred the institution of a literacy test for voter registration on the ground that the test would abridge the right to vote indirectly on account of race. Congress did not intend by Title VII, however, to guarantee a job to every person regardless of qualifications. In short, the Act does not command that any person be hired simply because he was formerly the subject of discrimination, or because he is a member of a minority group. Discriminatory preference for any group, minority or majority, is precisely and only what Congress has proscribed. What is required by Congress is the removal of artificial, arbitrary, and unnecessary barriers to employment when the barriers operate invidiously to discriminate on the basis of racial or other impermissible classification.

Congress has now provided that tests or criteria for employment or promotion may not provide equality of opportunity merely in the sense of the fabled offer of milk to the stork and the fox. On the contrary, Congress has now required that the posture and condition of the job-seeker be taken into account. It has—to resort again to the fable—provided that the vessel in which the milk is proffered be one all seekers can use. The Act proscribes not only

---

[17] In North Carolina, 1960 census statistics show that, while 34% of white males had completed high school, only 12% of Negro males had done so. U. S. Bureau of the Census, U. S. Census of Population: 1960, Vol. 1, Characteristics of the Population, Part 35, Table 47.

Similarly, with respect to standardized tests, the EEOC in one case found that use of a battery of tests, including the Wonderlic and Bennett tests used by the Company in the instant case, resulted in 58% of whites passing the tests, as compared with only 6% of the blacks.

overt discrimination but also practices that are fair in form, but discriminatory in operation. The touchstone is business necessity. If an employment practice which operates to exclude Negroes cannot be shown to be related to job performance, the practice is prohibited.

On the record before us, neither the high school completion requirement nor the general intelligence test is shown to bear a demonstrable relationship to successful performance of the jobs for which it was used. Both were adopted, as the Court of Appeals noted, without meaningful study of their relationship to job-performance ability. Rather, a vice president of the Company testified, the requirements were instituted on the Company's judgment that they generally would improve the overall quality of the work force.

The evidence, however, shows that employees who have not completed high school or taken the tests have continued to perform satisfactorily and make progress in departments for which the high school and test criteria are now used. The promotion record of present employees who would not be able to meet the new criteria thus suggests the possibility that the requirements may not be needed even for the limited purpose of preserving the avowed policy of advancement within the Company. In the context of this case, it is unnecessary to reach the question whether testing requirements that take into account capability for the next succeeding position or related future promotion might be utilized upon a showing that such long-range requirements fulfill a genuine business need. In the present case the Company has made no such showing.

The Court of Appeals held that the Company had adopted the diploma and test requirements without any "intention to discriminate against Negro employees." 420 F.2d, at 1232. We do not suggest that either the District Court or the Court of Appeals erred in examining the employer's intent; but good intent or absence of discriminatory intent does not redeem employment procedures or testing mechanisms that operate as "built-in headwinds" for minority groups and are unrelated to measuring job capability.

The Company's lack of discriminatory intent is suggested by special efforts to help the undereducated employees through Company financing of two-thirds the cost of tuition for high school training. But Congress directed the thrust of the Act to the *consequences* of employment practices, not simply the motivation. More than that, Congress has placed on the employer the burden of showing that any given requirement must have a manifest relationship to the employment in question.

The facts of this case demonstrate the inadequacy of broad and general testing devices as well as the infirmity of using diplomas or degrees as fixed measures of capability. History is filled with examples of men and women who rendered highly effective performance without the conventional badges of accomplishment in terms of certificates, diplomas, or degrees. Diplomas and tests are useful servants, but Congress has mandated the commonsense proposition that they are not to become masters of reality.

The Company contends that its general intelligence tests are specifically permitted by § 703(h) of the Act. That section authorizes the use of "any professionally developed ability test" that is not "designed, intended *or used* to discriminate because of race . . ." (Emphasis added.)

The Equal Employment Opportunity Commission, having enforcement responsibility, has issued guidelines interpreting § 703(h) to permit only the use of job-related tests. The administrative interpretation of the Act by the enforcing agency is entitled to great deference. See, *e.g., United States* v. *City of Chicago,* 400 U.S. 8 (1970); *Udall* v. *Tallman,* 380 U.S. 1 (1965); *Power Reactor Co.* v. *Electricians,* 367 U.S. 396 (1961). Since the Act and its legislative history support the Commission's construction, this affords good reason to treat the guidelines as expressing the will of Congress.

Section 703(h) was not contained in the House version of the Civil Rights Act but was added in the Senate during extended debate. For a period, debate revolved around claims that the bill as proposed would prohibit all testing and force employers to hire unqualified persons simply because they were part of a group formerly subject to job discrimination. Proponents of Title VII sought throughout the debate to assure the critics that the Act would have no effect on job-related tests. Senators Case of New Jersey and Clark of Pennsylvania, comanagers of the bill on the Senate floor, issued a memorandum explaining that the proposed Title VII "expressly protects the employer's right to insist that any prospective applicant, Negro or white, *must meet the applicable job qualifications.* Indeed, the very purpose of Title VII is to promote hiring on the basis of job qualifications, rather than on the basis of race or color." 110 Cong. Rec. 7247. (Emphasis added.) Despite these assurances, Senator Tower of Texas introduced an amendment authorizing "professionally developed ability tests." Proponents of Title VII opposed the amendment because, as written, it would permit an employer to give any test, "whether it was a good test or not, so long as it was professionally designed. Discrimination could actually exist under the guise of compliance with the statute." 110 Cong. Rec. 13504 (remarks of Sen. Case).

The amendment was defeated and two days later Senator Tower offered a substitute amendment which was adopted verbatim and is now the testing provision of § 703(h). Speaking for the supporters of Title VII, Senator Humphrey, who had vigorously opposed the first amendment, endorsed the substitute amendment, stating: "Senators on both sides of the aisle who were deeply interested in Title VII have examined the text of this amendment and have found it to be in accord with the intent and purpose of that title." 110 Cong. Rec. 13724. The amendment was then adopted. From the sum of the legislative history relevant in this case, the conclusion is inescapable that the EEOC's construction of § 703(h) to require that employment tests be job-related comports with congressional intent.

Nothing in the Act precludes the use of testing or measuring procedures; obviously they are useful. What Congress has forbidden is giving these devices and mechanisms controlling force unless they are demonstrably a reasonable measure of job performance. Congress has not commanded that the less qualified be preferred over the better qualified simply because of minority origins. Far from disparaging job qualifications as such, Congress has made such qualifications the controlling factor, so that race, religion, nationality, and sex become irrelevant. What Congress has commanded is that any tests used must measure the person for the job and not the person in the abstract.

The judgment of the Court of Appeals is, as to that portion of the judgment appealed from, reversed.

1. What is the question before the Supreme Court?
2. What was the objective of Congress in the enactment of Title VII?
3. Would the Court order the case against the employer to be dismissed if it found that the employer had adopted the diploma and test requirements without any intention to discriminate against minority employees?
4. As a result of the *Griggs* decision, may employers insist that both minority and white job applicants meet the applicable job qualifications by the use of testing or measuring procedures?

Diaz v. Pan American World Airways, Inc.

United States Court of Appeals, Fifth Circuit, 1971. 442 F.2d 385

TUTTLE, C. J.: This appeal presents the important question of whether Pan American Airlines' refusal to hire appellant and his class of males solely on the basis of their sex violates § 703(a)(1) of Title VII of the 1964 Civil Rights Act. Because we feel that being a female is not a "bona fide occupational qualification" for the job of flight cabin attendant, appellee's refusal to hire appellant's class solely because of their sex, does constitute a violation of the Act.

The facts in this case are not in dispute. Celio Diaz applied for a job as flight cabin attendant with Pan American Airlines in 1967. He was rejected because Pan Am had a policy of restricting its hiring for that position to females. He then filed charges with the Equal Employment Opportunity Commission (EEOC) alleging that Pan Am had unlawfully discriminated against him on the grounds of sex. The Commission found probable cause to believe his charge, but was unable to resolve the matter through conciliation with Pan Am. Diaz next filed a class action in the United States District Court for the Southern District of Florida on behalf of himself and others similarly situated, alleging that Pan Am had violated Section 703 of the 1964 Civil Rights Act by refusing to employ him on the basis of his sex; he sought an injunction and damages.

Pan Am admitted that it had a policy of restricting its hiring for the cabin attendant position to females. Thus, both parties stipulated that the primary issue for the District Court was whether, for the job of flight cabin attendant, being a female is a "bona fide occupational qualification (hereafter BFOQ) reasonably necessary to the normal operation" of Pan American's business.

The trial court found that being a female was a BFOQ. Before discussing its findings in detail, however, it is necessary to set forth the framework within which we view this case.

Section 703(a) of the 1964 Civil Rights Act provides, in part:

(a) It shall be an unlawful employment practice for an employer—
(1) to fail or refuse to hire or to discharge any individual, or otherwise to discriminate against any individual with respect to his compensation, terms, condi-

tions, or privileges of employment, because of such individual's race, color, religion, sex or national origin . . . .

The scope of this section is qualified by § 703(e) which states:

(e) Notwithstanding any other provision of this subchapter,
(1) it shall not be an unlawful employment practice for an employer to hire and employ employees . . . on the basis of his religion, sex, or national origin in those certain instances where religion, sex, or national origin is a bona fide occupational qualification reasonably necessary to the normal operation of that particular business or enterprise . . . .

Since it has been admitted that appellee has discriminated on the basis of sex, the result in this case turns, in effect, on the construction given to this exception.

We note, at the outset, that there is little legislative history to guide our interpretation. The amendment adding the word "sex" to "race, color, religion and national origin" was adopted one day before House passage of the Civil Rights Act. It was added on the floor and engendered little relevant debate. In attempting to read Congress' intent in these circumstances, however, it is reasonable to assume, from a reading of the statute itself, that one of Congress' main goals was to provide equal access to the job market for both men and women. Indeed, as this court in *Weeks* v. *Southern Bell Telephone and Telegraph Co.*, 408 F.2d 228 at 235 clearly stated, the purpose of the Act was to provide a foundation in the law for the principle of nondiscrimination. Construing the statute as embodying such a principle is based on the assumption that Congress sought a formula that would not only achieve the optimum use of our labor resources but, and more importantly, would enable individuals to develop as individuals.

Attainment of this goal, however, is, as stated above, limited by the bona fide occupational qualification exception in section 703(e). In construing this provision, we feel, as did the court in *Weeks, supra,* that it would be totally anomalous to do so in a manner that would, in effect, permit the exception to swallow the rule. Thus, we adopt the EEOC guidelines which state that "the Commission believes that the bona fide occupational qualification as to sex should be interpreted narrowly." 29 CFR 1604.1(a). Indeed, close scrutiny of the language of this exception compels this result. As one commentator has noted:

"The sentence contains several restrictive adjectives and phrases: it applies only *'in those certain instances'* where there are *'bona fide'* qualifications *'reasonably necessary'* to the operation of that *'particular'* enterprise. The care with which Congress has chosen the words to emphasize the function and to limit the scope of the exception indicates that it had no intention of opening the kind of enormous gap in the law which would exist if [for example] an employer could legitimately discriminate against a group solely because his employees, customers, or clients discriminated against that group. Absent much more explicit language, such a broad exception should not be assumed for it would largely emasculate the act. (Emphasis added.) 65 Mich. L. Rev. (1967).

Thus, it is with this orientation that we now examine the trial court's decision. Its conclusion was based upon (1) its view of Pan Am's history of the use of flight attendants; (2) passenger preference; (3) basic psychological reasons for the preference; and (4) the actualities of the hiring process.

Having reviewed the evidence submitted by Pan American regarding its own experience with both female and male cabin attendants it had hired over the years, the trial court found that Pan Am's current hiring policy was the result of a pragmatic process, "representing a judgment made upon adequate evidence acquired through Pan Am's considerable experience, and designed to yield under Pan Am's current operating conditions better *average* performance for its passengers than would a policy of mixed male and female hiring." (Emphasis added.) The performance of female attendants was *better* in the sense that they were *superior* in such non-mechanical aspects of the job as "providing reassurance to anxious passengers, giving courteous personalized service and, in general, making flights as pleasurable as possible within the limitations imposed by aircraft operations."

The trial court also found that Pan Am's passengers overwhelmingly preferred to be served by female stewardesses. Moreover, on the basis of the expert testimony of a psychiatrist, the court found that an airplane cabin represents a unique environment in which an air carrier is required to take account of the special psychological needs of its passengers. These psychological needs are better attended to by females. This is not to say that there are no males who would not have the necessary qualities to perform these non-mechanical functions, but the trial court found that the actualities of the hiring process would make it more difficult to find these few males. Indeed, "the admission of men to the hiring process, in the present state of the art of employment selection, would have increased the number of unsatisfactory employees hired, and reduced the average levels of performance of Pan Am's complement of flight attendants. . . ." In what appears to be a summation of the difficulties which the trial court found would follow from admitting males to this job the court said "that to eliminate the female sex qualification would simply eliminate the *best* available tool for screening out applicants *likely* to be unsatisfactory and thus reduce the *average* level of performance." (Emphasis added.)

Because of the narrow reading we give to section 703(e), we do not feel that these findings justify the discrimination practiced by Pan Am.

We begin with the proposition that the use of the word "necessary" in section 703(e) requires that we apply a business *necessity* test, not a business *convenience* test. That is to say, discrimination based on sex is valid only when the *essence* of the business operation would be undermined by not hiring members of one sex exclusively.

The primary function of an airline is to transport passengers safely from one point to another. While a pleasant environment, enhanced by the obvious cosmetic effect that female stewardesses provide as well as, according to the finding of the trial court, their apparent ability to perform the non-mechanical functions of the job in a more effective manner than most men, may all be important, they are tangential to the essence of the business involved. No one has suggested that having male stewards will so seriously affect the operation of an airline as to jeopardize or even minimize its ability to provide safe transportation from one place to another. Indeed the record discloses that many airlines including Pan Am have utilized both men and women flight cabin attendants in the past and Pan Am, even at the time of this suit, has 283 male stewards employed on some of its foreign flights.

We do not mean to imply, of course, that Pan Am cannot take into consideration the ability of *individuals* to perform the non-mechanical functions of the job. What we hold is that because the non-mechanical aspects of the job of flight cabin attendant are not "reasonably necessary to the normal operation" of Pan Am's business, Pan Am cannot exclude *all* males simply because *most* males may not perform adequately.

Appellees argue, however, that in so doing they have complied with the rule in *Weeks*. In that case, the court stated:

> We conclude that the principle of nondiscrimination requires that we hold that in order to rely on the bona fide occupational qualification exception an employer has the burden of proving that he had reasonable cause to believe, that is, a factual basis for believing, that all or substantially all women would be unable to perform safely and efficiently the duties of the job involved. *Id.* at 235.

We do not agree that in this case "all or substantially all men" have been shown to be inadequate and, in any event, in *Weeks*, the job that most women supposedly could not do was necessary to the normal operation of the business. Indeed, the inability of switchman to perform his or her job could cause the telephone system to break down. This is of an entirely different magnitude than a male steward who is perhaps not as soothing on a flight as a female stewardess.

Appellees also argue, and the trial court found, that because of the actualities of the hiring process, "the *best* available initial test for determining whether a particular applicant for employment is likely to have the personality characteristics conducive to high-level performance of the flight attendant's job as currently defined is consequently the applicant's biological sex." Indeed, the trial court found that it was simply not practicable to find the few males that would perform properly.

We do not feel that this alone justifies discriminating against all males. Since, as stated above, the basis of exclusion is the ability to perform non-mechanical functions which we find to be tangential to what is "reasonably *necessary*" for the business involved, the exclusion of *all* males because this is the *best* way to select the kind of personnel Pan Am desires simply cannot be justified. Before sex discrimination can be practiced, it must not only be shown that it is impracticable to find the men that possess the abilities that most women possess, but that the abilities are *necessary* to the business, not merely tangential.

Similarly, we do not feel that the fact that Pan Am's passengers prefer female stewardesses should alter our judgment. On this subject, EEOC guidelines state that a BFOQ ought not be based on "the refusal to hire an individual because of the preferences of coworkers, the employer, clients or customers. . . ." 29 CFR § 1604.1(iii).

As the Supreme Court stated in *Griggs* v. *Duke Power Co.,* 401 U.S. 424 (1971), "the administration interpretation of the Act by the enforcing agency is entitled to great deference. . . . Indeed, while we recognize that the public's expectation of finding one sex in a particular role may cause some initial difficulty, it would be totally anomalous if we were to allow the preferences and prejudices of the customers to determine whether the sex discrimination was valid. Indeed, it was, to a large extent, these very prejudices the Act was meant to overcome. Thus, we feel that customer preference may be taken into account only when it is based on the company's inability to perform the primary function or service it offers.

Of course, Pan Am argues that the customers' preferences are not based on "stereotyped thinking," but the ability of women stewardesses to better provide the non-mechanical aspects of the job. Again, as stated above, since these aspects are tangential to the business, the fact that customers prefer them cannot justify sex discrimination.

The judgment is Reversed and the case is Remanded for proceedings not inconsistent with this opinion.

CASE QUESTIONS	1. What is the primary issue of the case?
	2. How does the court construe the BFOQ exception in Section 703(e)?
	3. When hiring flight cabin attendants may an airline take into consideration the ability of the individual males to perform the non-mechanical aspects of the job such as reassuring anxious passengers and making flights as pleasurable as possible?
	4. Was the court persuaded by the airline's argument that passengers prefer female stewardesses?

SECTION 102 / REMEDY OPTIONS

There are principally four procedures that may be followed to remedy discriminatory employment practices: (1) Title VII procedures, (2) district court action under the Civil Rights Act of 1866, (3) private grievances and arbitration proceedings and (4) NLRA unfair labor practice proceedings. This section provides selected information on each remedy and is not intended as an in-depth presentation on this obviously technical area of labor relations law.

Title VII Procedures

The Title VII procedures for remedying employment discrimination have been set out in the previous section of this chapter. These procedures provide a relatively inexpensive remedy for aggrieved parties. The use of conciliation before court action gives an employer an opportunity to support its actions or alter its practices without the public condemnation that might result from more formal proceedings. However, the EEOC case backlog is such that as of 1973 there is approximately a 20-month delay between the filing of a charge and the initiation of the EEOC investigation. This delay has caused some grievants to utilize the other remedies available to them.

The Civil Rights Act of 1866

The Supreme Court held in 1968, in the case of *James* v. *Alfred H. Mayer Co.,*[18] that Section 1 of the Civil Rights Act of 1866, and therefore its derivative, 42 U.S.C. § 1982 was an effective bar against private discrimination in the sale or rental of property. This interpretation laid the foundation for use of § 1981, also a derivative of the 1866 Act, as a jurisdictional basis for private employment discrimination cases. Using this jurisdictional device, a number of plaintiffs have intentionally bypassed the procedural requirements of Title VII in the hope of obtaining faster and more effective relief in the federal courts. The law is not well settled regarding this device, and decisions in judicial circuits recommend that the conciliatory processes of the EEOC be utilized after § 1981 jurisdiction is asserted: [19] thus the EEOC delays would not be avoided in these two circuits.

Grievance and Arbitration

An employee may seek a remedy against discriminatory employment practices through the grievance and arbitration procedures in an existing collective bargaining agreement. The advantage to the grievance and arbitration process is that it can be implemented with far less delay than the Title VII procedures, a suit under the Civil Rights Act of 1866 or NLRB proceedings. A difficulty with arbitration in employment discrimination cases is that the individual grievant is often left without adequate representation in the arbitration proceedings. The Supreme Court recognized in *Vaca* v. *Sipes* that because the remedies of grievance and arbitration are devised and controlled by the union and the employer, "they may very well prove unsatisfactory or unworkable for the individual grievant." [20] Indeed a union may often have an interest in perpetuating a discriminatory practice. A further difficulty with arbitration is that labor arbitrators are not as experienced in dealing with racial, sex or religious discrimination grievances as the EEOC or federal judges. Indeed an arbitrator may feel bound by the collective bargaining contract and thus may never reach the substantive legal questions inherent in racial, religious or sex discrimination charges. In *Alexander* v. *Gardner-Denver Company,*[21] the United States Supreme Court considered the question of whether or not an individual grievant's election to invoke grievance and arbitration machinery which resulted in an adverse arbitration award precludes the individual from filing a subsequent Title VII claim. The Court found that it did not. The Court held that Title VII was designed by Congress to supplement existing laws and institutions relating to employment discrimination; and that the doctrine of election of remedies is inapplicable in the present context, which

---

[18] 392 U.S. 409 (1968).
[19] *Cladwell* v. *National Brewing Co.,* 443 F.2d 1044 (5th Cir. 1971), *Young International Telephone and Telegraph Co.,* 438 F.2d 757, (3rd Cir. 1971).
[20] 386 U.S. 171, 185 (1967).
[21] 415 U.S. 147 (1974).

involves statutory rights distinctly separate from the employee's contractual rights, regardless of the fact that violation of both rights may have resulted from the same factual occurrence.

NLRA Remedies

An employer's racial discrimination is an unfair labor practice in violation of § 8(a)(1) of the NLRA if it is found that this discrimination interferes with the affected employees' Section 7 rights to act concertedly for their own protection.[22] In contrast, racial discrimination in employment is prohibited by Title VII without reference to the effect on the employees' Section 7 rights for concerted action. Hence certain discriminatory practices that are not violations under the NLRA may be violations under Title VII.

An example of NLRA action against a union for discriminatory practices is the *Business League of Gadsden* decision presented in Chapter 7, where the local union and the employer had entered into collective bargaining provisions discriminating against black union members. The employer had attempted to correct the situation under pressure from the Armed Services Ordinance Division and the President's Committee on Equal Opportunity. The Union's continuing policy resulted in the NLRB finding it in violation of Section 8(b)(1), (2) and (3), ordering it to cease and desist and to process the minority grievances over segregation and job opportunities and over losses in earnings. The order also required good faith bargaining by the union to obtain contract provisions prohibiting any racial discrimination in the future.

SECTION 103 / AFFIRMATIVE ACTION PROGRAMS

Executive Order 11246 authorizes the federal government to require bidders on government contracts to formulate and carry out affirmative action programs. An affirmative action program is a program that requires positive steps to be taken by employers and in some cases unions to achieve equal employment opportunity. Under the Executive Order, the Secretary of Labor is charged with supervising and coordinating the activities of the federal contracting agencies. The Secretary of Labor has established the Office of Federal Contract Compliance (OFCC) to administer the Order. In 1973 the OFCC issued entirely new regulations, referred to as "Order No. 4," to be used by nonconstruction contractors and government agencies for judging and developing affirmative action programs. Order No. 4 sets out the following requirements for an acceptable affirmative action program:

1. an analysis of all major job categories at a facility must be conducted with explanations if minority group members are being underutilized in job categories;

---

[22] *Tipler* v. *E. I. du Pont de Nemours & Co.,* 443 F.2d 125 (6th Cir., 1971). See also *Jubilee Manufacturing Co.,* 202 NLRB 2 (1973). In *Jubilee,* the Board majority stated that a finding of a violation of the NLRA would depend upon a showing of "the necessary direct relationship" between the alleged race or sex discrimination and interference with promotion of collective bargaining, protection of Section 7 rights and free representation elections. The Board pointed out that it was "by no means inevitable" that employer discrimination would set one group of employees against the other.

2. goals, timetables and affirmative action commitments must be designed to correct any identifiable deficiencies. When deficiencies exist, the regulations require the contractor to create specific goals and a timetable as a part of his written affirmative action program;
3. support data for the program and analysis shall be compiled and maintained as part of the contractor's affirmative action program; and
4. contractors shall direct special attention in their analysis and goal-setting to six categories identified by the government as most likely to show underutilization of minorities—officials and managers, professionals, technicians, sales workers, office and clerical workers and skilled craftsmen.[23]

The OFCC also has an affirmative action policy to achieve equal employment opportunity in federally-funded construction work. The OFCC favors voluntary area-wide affirmative action agreements entered into by local respresentatives of minority groups, construction unions and contractors. Such so called "home-town" plans have the advantages of being voluntary and covering all construction, including nonfederally assisted work. Home-town plans are in effect in Chicago, Pittsburgh, Boston and other major cities. The OFCC has indicated that where a hometown agreement cannot be reached, it is ready to install a Philadelphia-type plan. Such a plan is a government-imposed equal employment opportunity compliance program, issued under the authority of Executive Order 11246. The Philadelphia Plan *requires* bidders on all federal and federally assisted construction projects exceeding $500,000 to agree to meet specified goals and timetables to correct deficiencies in minority employment. The specifics of the Philadelphia Plan and arguments against its legality are presented in the *Contractors Association* decision reported below.

Contractors Association of Eastern Pennsylvania v. Shultz
United States Court of Appeals, Third Circuit, 1971. 442 F.2d 159

GIBBONS, C. J.: The original plaintiff, the Contractors Association of Eastern Pennsylvania (the Association) and the intervening plaintiffs, construction contractors doing business in the Philadelphia area (the Contractors), appeal from an order of the district court which denied their motion for summary judgment, granted the motion of the federal defendants to dismiss the Association complaint for lack of standing, and granted the cross-motion of the federal defendants for summary judgment. . . .

The complaint challenges the validity of the Philadelphia Plan, promulgated by the federal defendants under the authority of Executive Order No. 11246. That plan is embodied in two orders issued by officials of the United States Department of Labor, dated June 27, 1969 and September 23, 1969, respectively. . . . In summary, they require that bidders on any federal or federally assisted construction contracts for projects in a five-county area around Philadelphia, the estimated total cost of which exceeds $500,000, shall submit an acceptable affirmative action program which includes specific goals

---

[23] 38 F.R. 2970 (1973).

for the utilization of minority manpower in six skilled crafts: ironworkers, plumbers and pipefitters, steamfitters, sheetmetal workers, electrical workers, and elevator construction workers.

Executive Order No. 11246 requires all applicants for federal assistance to include in their construction contracts specific provisions respecting fair employment practices, including the provision:

> "The contractor will take affirmative action to ensure that applicants are employed, and that employees are treated during employment, without regard to their race, color, religion, sex or national origin."

The Executive Order empowers the Secretary of Labor to issue rules and regulations necessary and appropriate to achieve its purpose. On June 27, 1969 Assistant Secretary of Labor Fletcher issued an order implementing the Executive Order in the five-county Philadelphia area. The order required bidders, prior to the award of contracts, to submit "acceptable affirmative action" programs "which shall include specific goals of minority manpower utilization." The order contained a finding that enforcement of the "affirmative action" requirement of Executive Order No. 11246 had posed special problems in the construction trades.[24] Contractors and subcontractors must hire a new employee complement for each job, and they rely on craft unions as their prime or sole source for labor. The craft unions operate hiring halls. "Because of the exclusionary practices of labor organizations," the order finds "there traditionally has been only a small number of Negroes employed in these seven trades."[25] The June 27, 1969 order provided that the Area Coordinator of the Office of Federal Contract Compliance, in conjunction with the federal contracting and administering agencies in the Philadelphia area, would determine definite standards for specific goals in a contractor's affirmative action program. After such standards were determined, each bidder would be required to commit itself to specific goals for minority manpower utilization. The order set forth factors to be considered in determining definite standards, including:

> "(1) The current extent of minority group participation in the trade.
> (2) The availability of minority group persons for employment in such trade.
> (3) The need for training programs in the area and/or the need to assure demand for those in or from existing training programs.
> (4) The impact of the program upon the existing labor force."

Acting pursuant to the June 29, 1969 order, representatives of the Department of Labor held public hearings in Philadelphia on August 26, 27 and 28, 1969. On September 23, 1969, Assistant Secretary Fletcher made findings with respect to each of the listed factors and ordered that the following ranges be

---

[24] Recognition of this problem antedated the present Plan. Under the Philadelphia Pre-Award Plan, which was put into effect on November 30, 1967 by the Philadelphia Federal Executive Board, each apparent low bidder was required to submit a written affirmative action program assuring minority group representation in eight specified trades as a precondition to qualifying for a construction contract or subcontract. This predecessor Plan was suspended due to an Opinion letter by the Comptroller General stating that it violated the principles of competitive bidding. 48 Comp. Gen. 326 (1968).

[25] The order of June 27, 1969 listed "roofers and water proofers" among the trades underrepresented by minority craftsmen. The order of September 23, 1969 dropped this category from the list, leaving the six trades previously named.

established as the standards for minority manpower utilization for each of the designated trades in the Philadelphia area for the following four years:

Identification of Trade	Range of Minority Group Employment			
	Until 12/31/70	for 1971	for 1972	for 1973
Ironworkers............	5%–9%	11%–15%	16%–20%	22%–26%
Plumbers & Pipefitters	5%–8%	10%–14%	15%–19%	20%–24%
Steamfitters	5%–8%	11%–15%	15%–19%	20%–24%
Sheetmetal workers.......	4%–8%	9%–13%	14%–18%	19%–23%
Electrical workers........	4%–8%	9%–13%	14%–18%	19%–23%
Elevator construction workers..............	4%–8%	9%–13%	14%–18%	19%–23%

The order of September 23, 1969 specified that on each invitation to bid each bidder would be required to submit an affirmative action program. The order further provided:

"4. No bidder will be awarded a contract unless his affirmative action program contains goals falling within the range set forth . . . above.

* * *

6. The purpose of the contractor's commitment to specific goals as to minority manpower utilization is to meet his affirmative action obligations under the equal opportunity clause of the contract. This commitment is not intended and shall not be used to discriminate against any qualified applicant or employee. Whenever it comes to the bidder's attention that the goals are being used in a discriminatory manner, he must report it to the Area Coordinator of the Office of Federal Contract Compliance of the U. S. Department of Labor in order that appropriate sanction proceedings may be instituted.

* * *

8. The bidder agrees to keep such records and file such reports relating to the provisions of this order as shall be required by the contracting or administering agency."

In November, 1969, the General State Authority of the Commonwealth of Pennsylvania issued invitations to bid for the construction of an earth dam on Marsh Creek in Chester County, Pennsylvania. Although this dam is a Commonwealth project, part of the construction cost, estimated at over $3,000,000, is to be funded by federal monies under a program administered by the Department of Agriculture. The Secretary of Agriculture, one of the federal defendants, as a condition for payment of federal financial assistance for the project, required the inclusion in each bid of a Philadelphia Plan Commitment in compliance with the order of September 23, 1969. On November 14, 1969, the General State Authority issued an addendum to the original invitation for bids requiring all bidders to include such a commitment in their bids. It is alleged and not denied that except for the requirement by the Secretary of Agriculture that the Philadelphia Plan Commitment be included, the General State Authority would not have imposed such a requirement on bidders.

The Association consists of more than eighty contractors in the five-county Philadelphia area who regularly employ workers in the six specified crafts, and who collectively perform more that $150,000,000 of federal and federally assisted construction in that area annually. Each of the contractor plaintiffs is a regular bidder on federal and federally assisted construction projects. The complaint was filed prior to the opening of bids on the Marsh Creek dam. It sought injunctive relief against the inclusion of a Philadelphia Plan Commitment requirement in the invitation for bids. By virtue of a stipulation that the General State Authority would issue a new and superseding invitation for bids if the district court held the Plan to be unlawful, the parties agreed that bids could be received without affecting the justiciability of the controversy. Bids were received on January 7, 1970. One of the intervening contractor plaintiffs submitted a low bid and appeared at the time of the district court decision to be entitled to an award of the contract.

The complaints of the Association and the contractors refer to the fact that the Comptroller General of the United States has opined that the Philadelphia Plan Commitment is illegal and that disbursement of federal funds for the performance of a contract containing such a promise will be treated as unlawful. The plaintiffs point out that the withholding of funds after a contractor has commenced performance would have catastrophic consequences, since contractors depend upon progress payments, and are in no position to complete their contracts without such payments. They allege that the Philadelphia Plan is illegal and void for the following reasons:

1. It is action by the Executive branch not authorized by the constitution or any statute and beyond Executive power.
2. It is inconsistent with Title VII of the Civil Rights Act of 1964.
3. It is inconsistent with Title VI of the Civil Rights Act of 1964.
4. It is inconsistent with the National Labor Relations Act.
5. It is substantively inconsistent with and was not adopted in procedural accordance with Executive Order No. 11246.
6. It violates due process because
   (a) it requires contradictory conduct impossible of consistent attainment;
   (b) it unreasonably requires contractors to undertake to remedy an evil for which the craft unions, not they, are responsible;
   (c) it arbitrarily and without basis in fact singles out the five-county Philadelphia area for discriminatory treatment without adequate basis in fact or law; and
   (d) it requires quota hiring in violation of the Fifth Amendment. . . .

The plaintiffs contend that the Philadelphia Plan is social legislation of local application enacted by the Executive without the benefit of statutory or constitutional authority. . . .

The limitations of Executive power have rarely been considered by the courts. One of those rare instances is *Youngstown Sheet & Tube Co.* v. *Sawyer,* 343 U.S. 579 (1952). From the six concurring opinions and one dissenting opinion in that case, the most significant guidance for present purposes may be found in that of Justice Jackson:

". . . 1. When the President acts pursuant to an express or implied authorization of Congress, his authority is at its maximum, for it includes all that he possesses in his own right plus all that Congress can delegate. In these circumstances, and in these only, may he be said (for what it may be worth) to personify the federal sovereignty. If his act is held unconstitutional under these circumstances, it usually means that the Federal Government as an undivided whole lacks power. A seizure executed by the President pursuant to an Act of Congress would be supported by the strongest of presumptions and the widest latitude of judicial interpretation, and the burden of persuasion would rest heavily on any who might attack it.

2. When the President acts in absence of either a congressional grant or denial of authority, he can only rely upon his own independent powers, but there is a zone of twilight in which he and Congress may have concurrent authority, or in which its distribution is uncertain. Therefore, congressional inertia, indifference or quiescence may sometimes, at least as a practical matter, enable, if not invite, measures on independent presidential responsibility. In this area, any actual test of power is likely to depend on the imperatives of events and contemporary imponderables rather than on abstract theories of law. . . ."

While all federal procurement contracts must include an affirmative action covenant, the coverage on federally assisted contracts has been extended to construction contracts only. This choice is significant, for it demonstrates that the Presidents were not attempting by the Executive Order program merely to impose their notions of desirable social legislation on the states wholesale. Rather, they acted in the one area in which discrimination in employment was most likely to affect the cost and the progress of projects in which the federal government had both financial and completion interests. In direct procurement the federal goverment has a vital interest in assuring that the largest possible pool of qualified manpower be available for the accomplishment of its projects. It has the identical interest with respect to federally assisted construction projects. When the Congress authorizes an appropriation for a program of federal assistance, and authorizes the Executive branch to implement the program by arranging for assistance to specific projects, in the absence of specific statutory regulations it must be deemed to have granted to the President a general authority to act for the protection of federal interests. In the case of Executive Order Nos. 11246 and 11114 three Presidents have acted by analogizing federally assisted construction to direct federal procurement. If such action has not been authorized by Congress (Justice Jackson's first category), at the least it falls within the second category. If no congressional enactments prohibit what has been done, the Executive action is valid. Particularly is this so when Congress, aware of Presidential action with respect to federally assisted construction projects since June of 1963, has continued to make appropriations for such projects. We conclude, therefore, that unless the Philadelphia Plan is prohibited by some other congressional enactment, its inclusion as a pre-condition for federal assistance was within the implied authority of the President and his designees. We turn, then to a consideration of the statutes on which plaintiffs rely.

Plaintiffs suggest that by enacting Title VII of the Civil Rights Act of 1964, 42 U.S.C. § 2000e et seq., which deals comprehensively with discrimination in employment, Congress occupied the field. The express reference in that statute to Executive Order No. 10925 or any other Executive Order prescribing fair employment practices for Government contractors, 42 U.S.C. § 2000e-8(d), indicates, however, that Congress contemplated continuance of the Executive Order program. Moreover we have held that the remedies established by Title VII are not exclusive. *Young* v. *International Telephone & Telegraph Co.,*—F.2d—(3d Cir. 1971).

But while Congress has not prohibited Presidential action in the area of fair employment on federally assisted contracts, the Executive is bound by the express prohibitions of Title VII. The argument most strenuously advanced against the Philadelphia Plan is that it requires action by employers which violates the Act. Plaintiffs point to § 703(j), 42 U.S.C. § 2000e-2(j):

> "Nothing contained in this subchapter shall be interpreted to require any employer . . . [or] labor organization . . . to grant preferential treatment to any individual or to any group because of the race . . . of such individual or groups on account of an imbalance which may exist with respect to the total number of percentage of persons of any race . . . employed . . . in comparison with the total number or percentage of persons of such race . . . in the available work force in any community . . . or other area."

The Plan requires that the contractor establish specific goals for utilization of available minority manpower in six trades in the five-county area. Possibly an employer could not be compelled, under the authority of Title VII, to embrace such a program, although § 703(j) refers to percentages of minorities in an area work force rather than percentages of minority tradesmen in an available trade work force. We do not meet that issue here, however, for the source of the required contract provision is Executive Order No. 11246. Section 703(j) is a limitation only upon Title VII, not upon any other remedies, state or federal.

Plaintiffs, and more particularly the union amici, contend that the Plan violates Title VII because it interferes with a bona fide seniority system. Section 703(h), 42 U.S.C. § 2000(e)-2(h), provides:

> "Notwithstanding any other provision of this subchapter, it shall not be an unlawful employment practice for an employer to employ different standards of compensation, or different terms, conditions, or privileges of employment pursuant to a bona fide seniority or merit system . . ."

The unions, it is said, refer men from the hiring halls on the basis of seniority, and the Philadelphia Plan interferes with this arrangement since few minority tradesmen have high seniority. Just as with § 703(j), however, § 703(h) is a limitation only upon Title VII, not upon any other remedies.[26]

---

[26] This same subsection refers to ability tests. The Supreme Court recently in *Griggs* v. *Duke Power Co.,* 39 U.S.L.W. 4317 (U.S. Mar. 8, 1971) considered the extent to which such tests are permissible. The Court said:

"But Congress directed the thrust of the Act to the *consequences* of employment practices, not simply the motivation." 39 U.S.L.W. at 4319. It held that the tests must be job related. Nor can seniority make permanent the effects of past discrimination. *Local 189, United Papermakers & Paperworkers* v. *United States,* 416 F.2d 980 (5th Cir. 1969), *Quarlies* v. *Philip Morris, Inc.,* 279 F. Supp. 505 (E.D. Va. 1968).

Plaintiffs contend that the Plan, by imposing remedial quotas, requires them to violate the basic prohibitions of Section 703(a), 42 U.S.C. § 2000(e)-2(a):

"It shall be an unlawful employment practice for an employer—
(1) to fail or refuse to hire . . . any individual . . . because of such individual's race . . . or
(2) to . . . classify his employees in any way which would deprive . . . any individual of employment opportunities . . . because of such individual's race . . ."

Because the Plan requires that the contractor agree to specific goals for minority employment in each of the six trades and requires a good faith effort to achieve those goals, they argue, it requires (1) that they refuse to hire some white tradesmen, and (2) that they classify their employees by race, in violation of § 703(a). This argument rests on an overly simple reading both of the Plan and of the findings which led to its adoption.

The order of September 23, 1969 contained findings that although overall minority group representation in the construction industry in the five-county Philadelphia area was thirty percent, in the six trades representation was approximately one percent. It found, moreover, that this obvious underrepresentation was due to the exclusionary practices of the unions representing the six trades. It is the practice of building contractors to rely on union hiring halls as the prime source for employees. The order made further findings as to the availability of qualified minority tradesmen for employment in each trade, and as to the impact of an affirmative action program with specific goals upon the existing labor force. The Department of Labor found that contractors could commit to the specific employment goals "without adverse impact on the existing labor force." Some minority tradesmen could be recruited, in other words, without eliminating job opportunities for white tradesmen.

To read Section 703(a) in the manner suggested by the plaintiffs we would have to attribute to Congress the intention to freeze the status quo and to foreclose remedial action under other authority designed to overcome existing evils. We discern no such intention either from the language of the statute or from its legislative history. Clearly the Philadelphia Plan is color-conscious. Indeed the only meaning which can be attributed to the "affirmative action" language which since March of 1961 has been included in successive Executive Orders is that Government contractors must be color-conscious. Since 1941 the Executive Order program has recognized that discriminatory practices exclude available minority manpower from the labor pool. In other contexts color-consciousness has been deemed to be an appropriate remedial posture. *Porcelli* v. *Titus,* 302 F. Supp. 726 (D. N. J. 1969). It has been said respecting Title VII that "Congress did not intend to freeze an entire generation of Negro employees into discriminatory patterns that existed before the Act." *Quarles* v. *Philip Morris, Inc., supra,* 279 F. Supp. at 514. The *Quarles* case rejected the contention that existing nondiscriminatory seniority arrangements were so sanctified by Title VII that the effects of past discrimination in job assignments could not be overcome. We reject the contention that Title VII prevents the President acting through the Executive Order program from attempting to remedy the absence from the Philadelphia construction labor of minority tradesmen in key trades.

What we have said about Title VII applies with equal force to Title VI of the Civil Rights Act of 1964, 42 U.S.C. § 2000(d) et seq. That Title prohibits racial and other discrimination in any program or activity receiving federal financial assistance. This general prohibition against discrimination cannot be construed as limiting Executive authority in defining appropriate affirmative action on the part of a contractor.

We hold that the Philadelphia Plan does not violate the Civil Rights Act of 1964.

. . . The union amici vigorously contend that the Plan violates the National Labor Relations Act by interfering with the exclusive union referral systems to which the contractors have in collective bargaining agreements bound themselves. Exclusive hiring hall contracts in the building and construction industry are validated by Section 8(f) of the National Labor Relations Act, 29 U.S.C. § 158(f). In *Teamsters Local 357* v. *NLRB,* 365 U.S. 667 (1961), the Supreme Court held that the National Labor Relations Board could not proscribe exclusive hiring hall agreements as illegal per se since Congress had not chosen to prohibit hiring halls. It is argued that the President is attempting to do what the Supreme Court said the National Labor Relations Board could not do—prohibit a valid hiring hall agreement. . . .

It is clear that while hiring hall arrangements are permitted by federal law they are not required. Nothing in the National Labor Relations Act purports to place any limitation upon the contracting power of the federal government. We have said hereinabove that in imposing the affirmative action requirement on federally assisted construction contracts the President acted within his implied contracting authority. The assisted agency may either agree to do business with contractors who will comply with the affirmative action covenant, or forego assistance. The prospective contractors may either agree to undertake the affirmative action covenant, or forego bidding on federally assisted work. If the Plan violates neither the Constitution nor federal law, the fact that its contractual provisions may be at variance with other contractual undertakings of the contractor is legally irrelevant. Factually, of course, that variance is quite relevant. Factually it is entirely likely that the economics of the marketplace will produce an accommodation between the contract provisions desired by the unions and those desired by the source of the funds. Such an accommodation will be no violation of the National Labor Relations Act. . . .

The plaintiffs argue that the affirmative action mandate of § 202 of Executive Order No. 11246 is limited by the more general requirement in the same section. "The contractor will not discriminate against any employee or applicant for employment because of race, creed, color, or national origin." They contend that properly construed the affirmative action referred to means only policing against actual present discrimination, not action looking toward the employment of specific numbers of minority tradesmen.

Section 201 of the Executive Order provides:

"The Secretary of Labor shall be responsible for the administration of Parts II [government contracts] and III [Federal assistance] of this Order and shall adopt such rules and regulations and issue such orders as he deems necessary and appropriate to achieve the purposes thereof."

Acting under this broad delegation of authority the Labor Department in a series of orders of local application made it clear that it interpreted "affirmative action" to require more than mere policing against actual present discrimination. Administrative action pursuant to an Executive Order is invalid and subject to judicial review if beyond the scope of the Executive Order. *Peters* v. *Hobby,* 349 U.S. 331 (1955). But the courts should give more than ordinary deference to an administrative agency's interpretation of an Executive Order or regulation which it is charged to administer. *Udall* v. *Tallman,* 380 U.S. 1 (1965). . . . The Attorney General has issued an opinion that the Philadelphia Plan is valid, and the President has continued to acquiesce in the interpretation of the Executive Order made by his designee. The Labor Department interpretation of the affirmative action clause must, therefore, be deferred to by the courts. . . .

Plaintiffs urge that the Plan violates the Due Process Clause of the Fifth Amendment in several ways.

First, they allege that it imposes on the contractors contradictory duties impossible of attainment. This impossibility arises, they say, because the Plan requires both an undertaking to seek achievement of specific goals of minority employment and an undertaking not to discriminate against any qualified applicant or employee, and because a decision to hire any black employee necessarily involves a decision not to hire a qualified white employee. This is pure sophistry. The findings in the September 23, 1969 order disclose that the specific goals may be met, considering normal employee attrition and anticipated growth in the industry, without adverse effects on the existing labor force. According to the order the construction industry has an essentially transitory labor force and is often in short supply in key trades. The complaint does not allege that these findings misstate the underlying facts.

Next the plaintiffs urge that the Plan is arbitrary and capricious administrative action, in that it singles out the contractors and makes them take action to remedy the situation created by acts of past discrimination by the craft unions. They point to the absence of any proceedings under Title VII against the offending unions, and urge that they are being discriminated against. This argument misconceives the source of the authority for the affirmative action program. Plaintiffs are not being discriminated against. They are merely being invited to bid on a contract with terms imposed by the source of the funds. The affirmative action covenant is no different in kind than other covenants specified in the invitation to bid. The Plan does not impose a punishment for past misconduct. It exacts a covenant for present performance. . . .

Finally, the plaintiffs urge that the specific goals specified by the Plan are racial quotas prohibited by the equal protection aspect of the Fifth Amendment. See *Shapiro* v. *Thompson,* 394 U.S. 618, 641–42 (1969); *Schneider* v. *Rush,* 377 U.S. 163 (1964); *Bolling* v. *Sharpe,* 347 U.S. 497 (1954). The Philadelphia Plan is valid Executive action designed to remedy the perceived evil that minority tradesmen have not been included in the labor pool available for the performance of construction projects in which the federal government has a cost and performance interest. The Fifth Amendment does not prohibit such action. . . .

The judgment of the district court will be affirmed.

1. What is the purpose of the Philadelphia Plan and what action does it require of bidders?
2. How did the Court answer the plantiffs' arguments that the Plan required employers to violate Sections 703(j) and (h) of Title VII of the Civil Rights Act of 1964?
3. Does the Plan prohibit a valid hiring hall agreement which has been validated by § 8(f) of the NLRA?
4. What was the court's answer to the plaintiffs' argument that specific goals required by the Plan are racial quotas prohibited by the equal protection clause of the Fifth Amendment?

SECTION 104 / EQUAL PAY FOR EQUAL WORK

The Equal Pay Act of 1963 amended Section 6 of the Fair Labor Standards Act; it established a prohibition against discrimination in wages on account of sex. The Equal Pay Act is applicable to every employer having employees subject to a minimum wage under the Act. The employer may not discriminate on the basis of sex against employees in any establishment in which such employees are employed by paying them wages at rates lower than he pays employees of the opposite sex employed in the same establishment for work subject to the Equal Pay standards; that is, where equal work is performed by such employees and by employees of the opposite sex on jobs in the performance in which is required *equal skill, effort,* and *responsibility* and which are performed under similar working conditions.

The legislative history of the Equal Pay Act makes it clear that coverage under that Act is equal to that provided by the other provisions of Section 6 of the Fair Labor Standards Act. It is clear that wage classifications systems which designate certain jobs as "male jobs" and other jobs as "female jobs" frequently specify lower rates for the "female jobs." If such is the case, then this classification alone would raise a serious question as to whether the system itself inherently discriminated against the female employee who is classified in this manner.

Congress also realized that the jobs which were to be compared did not have to be identical. Minor insignificant differences in the job content will not render the Act inapplicable. Congress has stated that "equal" does not mean identical (*Daily Congressional Record,* Senate, May 28, 1963, p. 9219).

The *Wheaton Glass Company, Robert Hall Clothes,* and *Corning Glass Works* decisions presented in this section discuss many aspects of the problem of discrimination in wages because of sex.

Shultz v. Wheaton Glass Company

United States Court of Appeals, Third Circuit, 1970. 421 F.2d 259

FREEDMAN, C. J.: This appeal presents important problems in the construction of the Equal Pay Act of 1963 (29 U.S.C. § 206(d)), which was added as an amendment to the Fair Labor Standards Act of 1938. (29 U.S.C. §§ 201, et seq.).

The Equal Pay Act prohibits an employer from discriminating "between employees on the basis of sex by paying wages to employees . . . at a rate less than the rate at which he pays wages to employees of the opposite sex . . . for equal work on jobs the performance of which requires equal skill, effort, and responsibility, and which are performed under similar working conditions, except where such payment is made pursuant to . . . (iv) a differential based on any other factor other than sex. . . ."

Invoking the enforcement provisions of the Fair Labor Standards Act the Secretary of Labor brought this action against Wheaton Glass Co., claiming that it discriminated against its "female selector-packers" on the basis of sex by paying them at an hourly rate of $2.14, which is 10% less than the $2.355 rate it pays to its "male selector-packers." The Secretary sought an injunction against future violations and the recovery of back pay for past violations. The company denied that the female selector-packers perform equal work within the terms of the Act and claimed that in any event the 10% pay differential is within exception (iv) of the Act because it is based on a "factor other than sex."

After an extensive trial the district court entered judgment for the defendant, holding that the Secretary had failed to carry his burden of proving that the wage differential was based upon sex discrimination and that the company had discharged the burden of establishing the exception that the wage differential was based on a factor other than sex. *Wirtz* v. *Wheaton Glass Co.,* 284 F. Supp. 23 (D. N. J. 1968). The Secretary has appealed.

The company is one of the largest manufacturers of glass containers in the United States. Its plant at Millville, New Jersey, which is here involved, is called a "job shop" plant and manufactures glass containers to special order. Unlike the usual modern plants in the glass industry which make standard items in large quantities and employ automatic machinery, the company's job shop operation requires manual handling and visual inspection of the product.

Selector-packers are employed in the Bottle Inspection Department. They work at long tables and visually inspect the bottles for defects as they emerge on a conveyor from the oven, or "lehr." The defective products are discarded into waste containers. Those which meet the specifications are packed in cardboard cartons on a stand within arm's reach of the selector-packers and then lifted onto an adjacent conveyor or rollers and sent off to the Quality Control Department for further examination and processing. In the Bottle Inspection Department is another category of employees known as "snap-up boys," who crate and move bottles and generally function as handymen, sweeping and cleaning and performing other unskilled miscellaneous tasks. They are paid at the hourly rate of $2.16.

Prior to 1956, the company employed only male selector-packers. In that year, however, the shortage of available men in the Millville area forced the company to employ for the first time female selector-packers. On the insistence of the Glass Bottle Blowers Association of the United States and Canada, AFL-CIO, local 219, with which the company had a collective bargaining agreement, there was, in the language of the district court, "carved out of the total job of selector-packer . . . a new role of female selector-packer." This new classification was written into the collective bargaining agreement, and pursuant to it female selector-packers were not to lift bulky cartons or cartons weighing more than 35 pounds. At the union's insistence a provision was added to the collective bargaining agreement that no male selector-packer was to be replaced by a female selector-packer except to fill a vacancy resulting from retirement, resignation, or dismissal for just cause.

On its face the record presents the incongruity that because male selector-packers spend a relatively small portion of their time doing the work of snap-up boys whose hourly rate of pay is $2.16, they are paid $2.355 per hour for their own work, while female selector-packers receive only $2.14. This immediately casts doubt on any contention that the difference in the work done by male and female selector-packers, which amounts substantially to what the snap-up boys do, is of itself enough to explain the difference in the rate of pay for male and female selector-packers on grounds other than sex.

The district court explored this difference in some detail. The court found that while male and female selector-packers perform substantially identical work at the ovens, the work of the male selector-packers is substantially different because they perform sixteen additional tasks. These consist of lifting packages weighing more than 35 pounds; lifting cartons which, regardless of weight, are bulky or difficult to handle; stacking full cartons; tying stacks of cartons; moving wooden pallets fully loaded with stacks of cartons; . . .

The district court, . . . placed its conclusion on a factor of "flexibility." The company's job shop requires frequent shutdowns of the ovens when a customer's order is completed and before the run of a new order is begun. During such shutdowns the idled female selector-packers are assigned to what is known as the "Resort" area, where they inspect and pack glassware rejected by the Quality Control Inspection Department. Idled male selector-packers are similarly reassigned to the Resort area, but some of them are assigned to do work which otherwise would be done by snap-up boys.

The district court found that this availability of male selector-packers to perform the work of snap-up boys during shutdowns was an element of flexibility and deemed it to be of economic value to the company in the operation of its unique, customized plant. It is on this element of flexibility that the judgment of the district court ultimately rests.

Under the collective bargaining agreement the company could at any time assign selector-packers to perform the work of snap-up boys, although they would continue to receive their regular rate of pay. While this explains why male selector-packers would not have their pay reduced in performing work of snap-up boys, it does not run the other way and explain why their performance of the work of snap-up boys who receive only two cents per hour more than female selector-packers justifies their being paid 21½ cents per hour more than female selector-packers for performing selector-packer work. . . .

An even more serious imperfection in the claim of flexibility is the absence, as we have already indicated, of any finding or explanation why availability of men to perform work which pays two cents per hour more than women receive should result in overall payment to men of 21½ cents more than women for their common work. A 10% wage differential is not automatically justified by showing that some advantage exists to the employer because of a flexibility whose extent and economic value is neither measured nor determined and which is attained by the performance of work carrying a much lower rate of pay. In short, there is no finding of the economic value of the element of flexibility on which the district court justified the 10% discrimination in pay rate between male and female selector-packers. . . .

In adopting the Act, Congress chose to specify equal pay for "equal" work. In doing so, Congress was well aware of the experience of the National War Labor Board during World War II and its regulations requiring equal pay for "comparable" work. Under these regulations the National War Labor Board made job evaluations to determine whether inequities existed within a plant even between dissimilar occupations. Since Congress was aware of the Board's policy and chose to require equal pay for "equal" rather than "comparable" work, it is clear that the references in the legislative history to the Board's regulations were only to show the feasibility of administering a federal equal pay policy and do not warrant use of the Board's decisions as guiding principles for the construction of the Equal Pay Act.

On the other hand, Congress in prescribing "equal" work did not require that the jobs be identical, but only that they must be substantially equal. Any other interpretation would destroy the remedial purposes of the Act.

The Act was intended as a broad charter of women's rights in the economic field. It sought to overcome the age-old belief in women's inferiority and to eliminate the depressing effects on living standards of reduced wages for female workers and the economic and social consequences which flow from it.

Differences in job classifications were in general expected to be beyond the coverage of the Equal Pay Act. This was because in the case of genuine job classifications the differences in work necessarily would be substantial and the differences in compensation therefore would be based on the differences in work which justified them. Congress never intended, however, that an artificially created job classification which did not substantially differ from the genuine one could provide an escape for an employer from the operation of the Equal Pay Act. This would be too wide a door through which the content of the Act would disappear. . . .

The district court held that the Secretary failed to carry his burden of proof that the company's wage differential is based on sex discrimination. In view of the facts which the district court found, we hold this conclusion to be erroneous. The Secretary met his burden of proof when he showed that male selector-packers received a pay rate 10% higher than female selector-packers although both performed identical work and that the additional work of snap-up boys which male selector-packers also performed was work which carried virtually the same rate of pay as that done by women. When to these circumstances are added the origin of the classification of female selector-packers and their reduced pay even below that paid to snap-up boys, the Secretary clearly established his prima facie case that the wage differential was based on sex and therefore discriminated against women.

Under the statute, the burden of proof thereupon fell on the company to prove its claim that it came within exception (iv). This burden the district court held the company had successfully met.

There is no finding, nor indeed evidence in the record on which a finding could be based, of the economic value of the labor of snap-up boys performed by male selector-packers. Nor is there any finding or evidence from which adequate findings could be made to support the claim that flexibility justifies the 10% wage differential. There are no detailed studies, records or testimony showing the extent of the closing down of the ovens or of the amount of savings which the company effected by being able to use male selector-packers to help out in the work of snap-up boys. More significantly, there is nothing in the record to show the amount of any such savings or that the element of flexibility bore any relation to the 10% wage differential between male and female selector-packers. Nor are there any findings that all members of the class of male selector-packers were able and available to do the work of snap-up boys whereas no members of the class of female selector-packers were so available.

The burden of showing this properly rested on the company, for it invoked the defense that the differential was based on a factor other than sex. In cases such as this, where the justification for the differential rests on economic benefit, the company has peculiarly within its knowledge the means of proof, and the burden therefore is one which cannot be satisfied by general or conclusory assertions.

The district court held that the company met its burden of proving that it came within the exception because "the acceptable proof demonstrates that the defendant's disparity in wages is based upon factors other than sex. . . ." It also stated that "substantial differences exist, in fact, in the full job cycles between the sexes, thereby justifying the disparity in their wages." These, however, are statements of ultimate conclusions for which there is no adequate support either in findings of fact or in the record.

We are, of course, bound by findings of fact unless they are clearly erroneous. Federal Rule of Civil Procedure 52(a). See *Speyer, Inc.* v. *Humble Oil and Refining Co.,* 403 F.2d 766, 770 (3 Cir. 1968). We are not, however, bound by evidence which has not reached the status of a finding of fact, nor by conclusions which are but legal inferences from facts. *Baumgartner* v. *United States,* 322 U.S. 665, 670–71 (1944); *Lehmann* v. *Acheson,* 206 F.2d 592, 594 (3 Cir. 1953); and cases cited 2B Barron & Holtzoff, Federal Practice and Procedure § 1137, n. 12 (Wright ed. 1961).

Since the Secretary established his prima facie case and the company failed to prove that the discrimination in wages paid to female selector-packers was based on any factor other than sex, the claim of the Secretary was established and an appropriate judgment should have been entered in his favor.

The judgment of the district court, therefore, will be reversed with direction to enter an appropriate judgment in favor of plaintiff.

CASE QUESTIONS

1. What remedies did the Secretary of Labor seek in this case?
2. Is a wage differential automatically justified by a showing on behalf of the employer that an economic advantage exists because of "flexibility"?
3. What was the Congressional purpose of the Equal Pay Act of 1963?
4. Why is the burden of proof on the employer?

Hodgson v. Robert Hall Clothes, Inc.

United States Court of Appeals, Third Circuit, 1973. 473 F.2d 589

HUNTER, C. J.: This case involves the application of the Equal Pay Act of 1963, 29 U.S.C. § 206(d)(1) (1964). . . .

The Robert Hall Store in question is located in Wilmington, Delaware. It sells clothing, and contains a department for men's and boys' clothing and another department for women's and girls' clothing. The store is a one-floor building, and the departments are in separate portions of it.

The merchandise in the men's department was, on the average, of higher price and better quality than the merchandise in the women's department; and Robert Hall's profit margin on the men's clothing was higher than its margin on the women's clothing. Consequently, the men's department at all times showed a larger dollar volume in gross sales, and a greater gross profit.[27] Breaking this down, the salespeople in the men's department, on the average, sold more merchandise in terms of dollars and produced more gross profit than did the people in the women's department per hour of work.[28]

The departments are staffed by full and part-time sales personnel. At all times, only men were permitted to work in the men's department and only women were permitted to work in the women's department. The complaint is not addressed to the propriety of such segregated employment.

---

[27] The following table from the district court's opinion is instructive:

Re: Greenbank Road Store
SCHEDULE OF SALES AND GROSS PROFITS BY DEPARTMENT

Fiscal Year Ended June 30	Men's and Boys' Clothing Dept.			Ladies' and Girls' Clothing Dept.		
	Sales	Gross Profit	Gross Profit %	Sales	Gross Profit	Gross Profit %
1963	$210,639.48	$ 85,328.48	40.51	$177,742.17	$58,547.13	32.92
1964	178,867.50	73,608.08	41.16	142,788.22	44,612.12	31.24
1965	206,472.93	89,930.00	43.55	148,252.90	49,608.08	33.46
1966	217,765.79	97,447.54	44.74	166,479.47	55,463.29	33.31
1967	244,922.09	111,498.79	45.52	206,680.27	69,190.04	33.47
1968	263,663.53	123,681.60	46.90	230,156.63	79,846.92	34.69
1969	316,242.41	148,001.30	46.79	254,379.22	92,686.87	36.43

Hodgson v. *Robert Hall Clothes, Inc.,* 326 F. Supp. 1264, 1276 (Del. D.C. 1971).

[28] SCHEDULE OF HOURLY SALES, EARNINGS AND GROSS PROFIT

Year	Sales Per Hour	Excess M over F	Earnings Per Hour	Excess M over F	Gross Profit Per Hour	Excess M over F
MEN'S & BOYS'						
1963	38.31	40%	2.18	25%	15.52	72%
1964	40.22	32%	2.46	32%	16.55	74%
1965	54.77	64%	2.67	48%	23.85	114%
1966	59.58	73%	2.92	50%	26.66	134%
1967	63.14	71%	2.88	45%	28.74	133%
1968	62.27	70%	2.97	47%	29.21	127%
1969	73.00	77%	3.13	45%	34.16	127%
LADIES' & GIRLS'						
1963	27.31		1.75		9.00	
1964	30.36		1.86		9.49	
1965	33.30		1.80		11.14	
1966	34.31		1.95		11.43	
1967	36.92		1.98		12.36	
1968	37.20		2.02		12.91	
1969	41.26		2.16		15.03	

Hodgson v. *Robert Hall Clothes, Inc.,* 326 F. Supp. 1264, 1276 (Del. D.C. 1971).

The sales people receive a base salary and can earn additional incentive payments. Various factors relating to the garment sold determine the amount of incentive payments.[29] At all times, the salesmen received higher salaries than the saleswomen. Both starting salaries and periodic increases were higher for the males. The amount of incentive compensation was very slightly greater for the men.

The Secretary of Labor brought this action against Robert Hall in 1966, pursuant to 29 U.S.C. § 217, claiming that since June 13, 1964 Robert Hall had been discriminating against the saleswomen on the basis of sex because it compensated them less than it compensated salesmen even though the saleswomen and the salesmen were performing equal work. If proven, this was a violation of 29 U.S.C. § 206(d)(1).[30]

After a trial in late 1970, the district court filed its opinion on April 16, 1971. The court found that Robert Hall had a valid business reason for segregating its sales personnel, i.e, "the frequent necessity for physical contact between the sales persons and the customers which would embarrass both and would inhibit sales unless they were of the same sex." *Hodgson* v. *Robert Hall,* 326 F. Supp. 1264, 1269. However, it also found that this does not affect the application of the Equal Pay Act. It proceeded to hold that the sales personnel of each department performed equal work within the meaning of § 206(d)(1).

The question then facing it was whether Robert Hall could prove that the wage "differential was based on any other factor other than sex." 29 U.S.C. § 206(d)(iv). Robert Hall contended that its wage differentials were based on economic factors, i.e., the higher profitability of the men's department allowed it to pay the men more, and the lower profitability of the women's department forced Robert Hall to pay the workers in that department less. In support of this contention, Robert Hall introduced evidence of sales and profit margins from which the district court was able to make the findings in the tables previously quoted.

The district court accepted Robert Hall's contention that economic benefit to the employer could be a factor other than sex on which a wage differential could be based. But it decided that the figures for the average performance of each department were not sufficient to meet Robert Hall's burden of proof. The court held that the relevant figures were those relating to the economic benefit produced by each individual sales person. Although Robert Hall in the ordinary course of business retained no records from which such performance

---

[29] These factors included style, quality, price, mark-up, and ease of selling specific merchandise involved. *Hodgson* v. *Robert Hall, Inc., supra* at 1272, 1278.

[30] That section provides:

"No employer having employees subject to any provisions of this section shall discriminate, within any establishment in which such employees are employed, between employees on the basis of sex by paying wages to employees in such establishment at a rate less than the rate at which he pays wages to employees of the opposite sex in such establishment for equal work on jobs the performance of which requires equal skill, effort, and responsibility, and which are performed under similar working conditions, except where such payment is made pursuant to (i) a seniority system; (ii) a merit system; (iii) a system which measures earnings by quantity or quality of production; or (iv) a differential based on any other factor other than sex: *Provided,* That an employer who is paying a wage rate differential in violation of this subsection shall not, in order to comply with the provisions of this subsection, reduce the wage rate of any employee." 29 U.S.C. § 206(d)(1) 1964.

could be calculated, fortuitously there were records available for two ten-week periods out of the six years involved in this suit. Based on this evidence, the court compared the performances of the full-time male to the performances of the full-time female and compared the performances of the part-time males to those of the part-time females. It found that the full-time male was responsible for more dollar sales per hour of work than was the full-time female. In regard to the part-time personnel, the court found:

> "Two of Greenbank's part-time female employees, Alice Baker and C. Jarrell, were responsible for a higher per hour dollar volume of sales than three of the part-time male employees, McGonegal, Law and Layton, during the period from August 10, 1969 to October 18, 1969. A division of Jarrell's gross earnings (less incentive) by hours worked and a similar computation for the part-time salesmen discloses that Jarrell received a lower hourly rate than all three of these part-time salesmen, even though her gross sales per hour were more than that made by three of the five part-time salesmen." *Hodgson* v. *Robert Hall, supra* at 1278.

On the basis of these findings, the district court held that the wage differential in favor of the part-time salesmen was not "supported by any economic benefits which defendants received from the job performances of the salesmen." *Id.* at 1278. Accordingly, it found in favor of the secretary as to the part-time personnel (and awarded them back wages) and in favor of Robert Hall as to the full-time personnel. It also found that the incentive compensation system was based on the kind of item sold and that this was a "factor other than sex." Therefore, it held against the Secretary on this point. In addition, it denied interest on its award in favor of the part-time personnel.

This disposition left no one completely satisfied. The Secretary appeals from the decision adverse to the full-time female personnel and against the award of interest, and Robert Hall appeals from the decision in favor of the part-time female personnel. The Secretary decided not to appeal from the holding that the incentive system was based on a factor other than sex.

The initial question facing us is one raised by the Secretary. He contends that economic benefit to the employer cannot be used to justify a wage differential under § 206(d)(1)(iv).

He argues that "any other factor" does not mean *any* other factor. Instead he claims it means any other factor other than sex which "is related to job performance or is typically used in setting wage scales." He contends that economic benefits to an employer do not fall within this exception.

He recognizes that the men's department produces a greater profit for Robert Hall. His contention is that the salesmen have nothing to do with producing this benefit since the district court found that the salesmen and saleswomen performed equal work. Since the saleswomen cannot sell the higher-priced clothing sold in the men's department, this cannot be used as a factor on which to base a wage differential. Otherwise, "the exception could swallow the rule." *Schultz* v. *First Victoria National Bank*, 420 F.2d 648 (5th Cir. 1969).

Robert Hall does not argue that "any other" means "any other" either. It claims that a wage differential is permissible if based on a legitimate business reason. As the district court found, economic benefits could justify a wage differential. We need go no further than to say the district court was correct to hold in this case that economic benefits to an employer can justify a wage differential.

The Secretary's argument is incorrect for several reasons. It ignores the basic finding of the district court that Robert Hall's segregation of its work force was done for legitimate business purposes. It is also inconsistent with the wording of the statute.

In providing for exceptions, the statute states that they will apply when the males and females are doing equal work. Congress thus intended to allow wage differentials even though the contrasted employees were performing equal work. However, two of the examples given as exceptions, (§ 206(d)(1) (ii) and (iii)), may be read to say that the contrasted employees really are not performing equal work. If, for example, some employees produce a greater quantity of work than others, pursuant to § 206(d)(1)(iii), they may receive greater compensation.

The Secretary's test might be acceptable if §§ 206(d)(1)(ii) and (iii) stood alone. However, §§ 206(d)(1)(i) and (iv) indicate that there must be some factors upon which an employer may base a wage differential which are not related to job performance. We must point to the plain wording of the clause. It reads *"any* other factor. . . ." While the examples preceding § 206(d)(1)(iv) necessarily qualify it to some extent, they do not narrow it to the degree for which the Secretary contends.

The Secretary recognizes this reasoning in § 800.116(e) of his Wage-Hour Administrator's Interpretative Bulletin and § 34d07 of his Field Office Handbook. In both of these the Secretary approves a commission system in which the amount of compensation is determined by the type of article sold. The stated hypothesis is that the *sales people are performing equal work.* Since this is given, the only basis for approving such a system has to be that the economic benefit to the employer is greater. As the Field Office Handbook states, "Such a difference in commission rates might be based on many factors such as sales volume, markup, cost of the items sold, type of merchandise sold, turnover in merchandise, and the ease of selling merchandise in each particular department." These are all factors of value to the employer. It might take no more effort or skill to sell two different pairs of ten dollar shoes; but if the employer makes a four dollar profit on one pair as opposed to a two dollar profit on the other, the Secretary apparently allows a higher commission rate. That the salary in this case is a base salary rather than a commission is not a significant distinction. The principle remains the same: the compensation is based on economic benefit to the employer, and the work performed is equal.

This would make good business sense. The saleswomen are paid less because the commodities which they sell cannot bear the same selling costs that the commodities sold in the men's department can bear. Without a more definite indication from Congress, it would not seem wise to impose the economic burden of higher compensation on employers. It could serve to weaken their competitive position. If anything, the legislative history supports a broader reading of § 206(d)(iv) than that proposed by the Secretary. . . .

Our decision in *Schultz* v. *Wheaton Glass Co.,* 421 F.2d 259 (3d Cir. 1970), *cert. denied* 398 U.S. 905 (1970) also lends support to this result. In discussing whether the employer had met his burden of proving an exception to this act, we held against the employer partly because the record did not show that he had realized any greater economic benefits from certain additional activities allegedly performed by the male employees. While we did not specifically consider the issue of whether "economic benefit" falls under the act, the decision implicitly accepts the fact that it does. *Schultz* v. *Wheaton Glass Co., supra,* at 267. . . .

The next question is whether Robert Hall proved that it received the economic benefits upon which it claimed it based its salary differentials. It is well settled that the employer has the burden of proof on this issue. *E.g., Schultz* v. *Wheaton Glass Company, supra,* at 266.

Robert Hall introduced evidence to show that for every year of the store's operation, the men's department was substantially more profitable than the women's department.

Robert Hall contends that this greater profitability is a sufficient reason to justify paying the sales people in its men's department more than it pays the sales people in its women's department. It does not have to tie its compensation scheme into the performance of the individual sales person, and this is what the district court implicitly required.

We agree that the district court's opinion implies that such a correlation is necessary. It compared the individual performances of the full-time male and the full-time female. It also compared the individual performances of the part-time workers. *Hodgson* v. *Robert Hall Clothes, Inc., supra* at 1278, 1280. . . .

. . . The question is whether the Equal Pay Act requires the employer to justify his base salary by correlating it to individual performance.

The overwhelming evidence which showed that the men's department was more profitable than the women's was sufficient to justify the differences in base salary. These statistics proved that Robert Hall's wage differentials were not based on sex but instead fully supported the reasoned business judgment that the sellers of women's clothing could not be paid as much as the sellers of men's clothing. Robert Hall's executives testified that it was their practice to base their wage rates on these departmental figures.

While no business reason could justify a practice clearly prohibited by the act, the legislative history set forth above indicates a Congressional intent to allow reasonable business judgments to stand. It would be too great an economic and accounting hardship to impose upon Robert Hall the requirement that it correlate the wages of each individual with his or her performance. This could force it toward a system based totally upon commissions, and it seems unwise to read such a result into § 206(d)(iv). Robert Hall's method of determining salaries does not show the "clear pattern of discrimination," (Rep. Goodell, 109 Cong. Rec. 9203), that would be necessary for us to make it correlate more precisely the salary of each of its employees to the economic benefit which it receives from them. Robert Hall introduced substantial evidence. . . .

Since we have determined that Robert Hall has not violated § 206(d)(1), we find it unnecessary to reach the question of whether the district court was correct in not awarding interest in this case.

The decision of that court will be affirmed as to the full-time personnel and reversed as to the part-time personnel.

VAN DUSEN, Circuit Judge, dissenting: I respectfully dissent, since I believe the following findings of fact of the district court are not clearly erroneous:

> "After listening to voluminous nonexpert testimony for days on end concerning the differences and similarities between the jobs of salesmen and salesladies, the conclusion is warranted that such differences as existed were at best only incidental to the job of each when considered in its totality. The skill, effort and responsibility of each were substantially equal.
>
> "Plaintiff has borne the burden of proving by a preponderance of the evidence that defendants have discriminated between salesmen and salesladies by paying to the latter wages at a lesser rate than paid to the former for equal work on jobs that required equal skill, effort and responsibility. Plaintiff has thus made out a prima facie case against defendant for violating the Equal Pay Act. *Schultz* v. *Wheaton Glass Co., supra,* p. 266."

CASE QUESTIONS

1. Did the trial court find that Robert Hall had valid business reason for segregating its sales personnel?
2. Compare the "earnings per hour" of males and females for the year 1969.
3. May economic benefits to an employer be used to justify a wage differential under 206(d)(1)(iv)?
4. Does the Secretary of Labor have the burden of proving that the employer did not receive the economic benefits upon which the employer claimed it based its salary differentials?

Corning Glass Works v. Brennan

Supreme Court of the United States, 1974. 415 U.S. ___

MARSHALL, J.: These cases arise under the Equal Pay Act of 1963, 29 U.S.C. § 206(d)(1), which added to the Fair Labor Standards Act the principle of equal pay for equal work regardless of sex. The principal question posed is whether Corning Glass Works violated the Act by paying a higher base wage to male night shift inspectors than it paid to female inspectors performing the same tasks on the day shift, where the higher wage was paid in addition to a separate night shift differential paid to all employees for night work. In No. 73–29, the Court of Appeals for the Second Circuit, in a case involving several Corning plants in Corning, New York, held that this practice violated the Act. 474 F.2d 226 (1973). In No. 73–695, the Court of Appeals for the Third Circuit, in a case involving a Corning plant in Wellsboro, Pennsylvania, reached the opposite conclusion. 480 F.2d 1254 (1973). We granted certiorari and consolidated the cases to resolve this unusually direct conflict between two circuits.—U.S.—. Finding ourselves in substantial agreement with the analysis of the Second Circuit, we affirm in No. 73–29 and reverse in No. 73–695.

I

Prior to 1925, Corning operated its plants in Wellsboro and Corning only during the day, and all inspection work was performed by women. Between 1925 and 1930, the company began to introduce automatic production equipment which made it desirable to institute a night shift. During this period, however, both New York and Pennsylvania law prohibited women from working at night. As a result, in order to fill inspector positions on the new night shift, the company had to recruit male employees from among its male day workers. The male employees so transferred demanded and received wages substantially higher than those paid to women inspectors engaged on the two day shifts. During this same period, however, no plant-wide shift differential existed and male employees working at night, other than inspectors, received the same wages as their day shift counterparts. Thus a situation developed where the night inspectors were all male, the day inspectors all female, and the male inspectors received significantly higher wages.

In 1944, Corning plants at both locations were organized by a labor union and a collective-bargaining agreement was negotiated for all production and maintenance employees. This agreement for the first time established a plant-wide shift differential, but this change did not eliminate the higher base wage paid to male night inspectors. Rather, the shift differential was superimposed on the existing difference in base wages between male night inspectors and female day inspectors.

Prior to the June 11, 1964, effective date of the Equal Pay Act, the law in both Pennsylvania and New York was amended to permit women to work at night. It was not until some time after the effective date of the Act, however, that Corning initiated efforts to eliminate the differential rates for male and female inspectors. Beginning in June 1966, Corning started to open up jobs on the night shift to women. Previously separate male and female seniority lists were consolidated and women became eligible to exercise their seniority, on the same basis as men, to bid for the higher paid night inspection jobs as vacancies occurred.

On January 20, 1969, a new collective-bargaining agreement went into effect, establishing a new "job evaluation" system for setting wage rates. The new agreement abolished for the future the separate base wages for day and night shift inspectors and imposed a uniform base wage for inspectors exceeding the wage rate for the night shift previously in effect. All inspectors hired after January 20, 1969, were to receive the same base wage, whatever their sex or shift. The collective-bargaining agreement further provided, however, for a higher "red circle" rate for employees hired prior to January 20, 1969, when working as inspectors on the night shift. This "red circle" rate served essentially to perpetuate the differential in base wages between day and night inspectors.

The Secretary of Labor brought these cases to enjoin Corning from violating the Equal Pay Act and to collect back wages allegedly due female employees because of past violations. Three distinct questions are presented: (1) Did Corning ever violate the Equal Pay Act by paying male night shift inspectors more than female day shift inspectors? (2) If so, did Corning cure its violation of the Act in 1966 by permitting women to work as night shift inspectors? (3) Finally, if the violation was not remedied in 1966, did Corning cure its violation in 1969 by equalizing day and night inspector wage rates but establishing higher "red circle" rates for existing employees working on the night shift?

II

Congress' purpose in enacting the Equal Pay Act was to remedy what was perceived to be a serious and endemic problem of employment discrimination in private industry—the fact that the wage structure of "many segments of American industry has been based on an ancient but outmoded belief that a man, because of his role in society, should be paid more than a woman, even though his duties are the same." S. Rept. No. 176, 88th Cong., 1st Sess. (1963), at 1. The solution adopted was quite simple in principle: to require that "equal work be rewarded by equal wages." *Ibid.*

The Act's basic structure and operation are similarly straightforward. In order to make out a case under the Act; the Secretary must show that an employer pays different wages to employees of opposite sexes "for equal work on jobs the performance of which requires equal skill, effort, and responsibility, and which are performed under similar working conditions." Although the Act is silent on this point, its legislative history makes plain that the Secretary has the burden of proof on this issue, as both of the courts below recognized.

The Act also establishes four exceptions—three specific and one a general catch-all provision—where different payment to employees of opposite sexes "is made pursuant to (i) a seniority system; (ii) a merit system; (iii) a system which measures earnings by quantity or quality of production; or (iv) a differential based on any other factor other than sex." Again, while the Act is silent on this question, its structure and history also suggest that once the Secretary has carried his burden of showing that the employer pays workers of one sex more than workers of the opposite sex for equal work, the burden shifts to the employer to show that the differential is justified under one of the Act's four exceptions. All of the many lower courts that have considered this question have so held, and this view is consistent with the general rule that the application of an exemption under the Fair Labor Standards Act is a matter of affirmative defense on which the employer has the burden of proof.

The contentions of the parties in this case reflect the Act's underlying framework. Corning argues that the Secretary has failed to prove that Corning ever violated the Act because day shift work is not "performed under similar working conditions" as night shift work. The Secretary maintains that day shift and night shift work are performed under "similar working conditions" within the meaning of the Act. Although the Secretary recognizes that higher wages may be paid for night shift work, the Secretary contends that such a shift differential would be based upon a "factor other than sex" within the catch-all exception to the Act and that Corning has failed to carry its burden of proof that its higher base wage for male night inspectors was in fact based on any factor other than sex.

The courts below relied in part on conflicting statements in the legislative history having some bearing on this question of statutory construction. The Third Circuit found particularly significant a statement of Congressman Goodell, a sponsor of the Equal Pay bill, who, in the course of explaining the bill on the floor of the House, commented that "standing as opposed to sitting, pleasantness or unpleasantness of surroundings, periodic rest periods, hours of work, *differences in shift*, all would logically fall within the working conditions factor." 109 Cong. Rec. 9209 (1973) (emphasis added). The Second Circuit, in contrast, relied on a statement from the House Committee Report which, in describing the broad general exception for differentials "based on any other factor other than sex," stated:

"Thus, among other things, shift differentials . . . would also be excluded. . . ."

H. R. Rep. No. 309, 88th Cong., 1st Sess. (1963), at 3.

We agree with Judge Friendly, however, that in this case a better understanding of the phrase "performed under similar working conditions" can be obtained from a consideration of the way in which Congress arrived at the statutory language than from trying to reconcile or establish preferences between the conflicting interpretations of the Act by individual legislators or the committee reports. As Mr. Justice Frankfurter remarked in an earlier case involving interpretation of the Fair Labor Standards Act, "regard for the specific history of the legislative process that culminated in the Act now before us affords more solid ground for giving it appropriate meaning." *United States v. Universal C. I. T. Credit Corp.,* 344 U.S. 218, 222 (1952).

The most notable feature of the history of the Equal Pay Act is that Congress recognized early in the legislative process that the concept of equal pay for equal work was more readily stated in principle than reduced to statutory language which would be meaningful to employers and workable across the broad range of industries covered by the Act. As originally introduced, the Equal Pay bills required equal pay for "equal work on jobs the performance of which requires equal skills." There were only two exceptions— for differentials "made pursuant to a seniority or merit increase system which does not discriminate on the basis of sex. . . ."

In both the House and Senate committee hearings, witnesses were highly critical of the Act's definition of equal work and of its exemptions. Many noted that most of American industry used formal, systematic job evaluation plans to establish equitable wage structures in their plants. Such systems, as explained coincidentally by a representative of Corning Glass Works who testified at both hearings, took into consideration four separate factors in determining job value—skill, effort, responsibility and working conditions —and each of these four components was further systematically divided into various subcomponents. Under a job evaluation plan, point values are assigned to each of the subcomponents of a given job, resulting in a total point figure representing a relatively objective measure of the job's value.

In comparison to the rather complex job evaluation plans used by industry, the definition of equal work used in the first drafts of the Equal Pay Act was criticized as unduly vague and incomplete. . . .

We think it plain that in amending the Act's definition of equal work to its present form, the Congress acted in direct response to these pleas. Spokesmen for the amended bill stated, for example, during the House debates:

"The concept of equal pay for jobs demanding equal skill has been expanded to require also equal effort, responsibility, and similar working conditions. These factors are the core of all job classification systems. They form a legitimate basis for differentials in pay."

Indeed, the most telling evidence of congressional intent is the fact that the Act's amended definition of equal work incorporated the specific language of the job evaluation plan described at the hearings by Corning's own representative—that is, the concepts of "skill," "effort," "responsibility," and "working conditions."

Congress' intent, as manifested in this history, was to use these terms to incorporate into the new federal act the well-defined and well-accepted principles of job evaluation so as to ensure that wage differentials based upon bona fide job evaluation plans would be outside the purview of the Act. . . .

While a layman might well assume that time of day worked reflects one aspect of a job's "working conditions," the term has a different and much more specific meaning in the language of industrial relations. As Corning's own representative testified at the hearings, the element of working conditions encompasses two subfactors: "surroundings" and "hazards." "Surroundings" measure the elements, such as toxic chemicals or fumes, regularly encountered by a worker, their intensity, and their frequency. "Hazards" take into account the physical hazards regularly encountered, their frequency, and the severity of injury they can cause. This definition of "working conditions" is not only manifested in Corning's own job evaluation plans but is also well accepted across a wide range of American industry.

Nowhere in any of these definitions is time of day worked mentioned as a relevant criterion. The fact of the matter is that the concept of "working conditions," as used in the specialized language of job evaluation systems, simply does not encompass shift differentials. Indeed, while Corning now argues that night inspection work is not equal to day inspection work, all of its own job evaluation plans, including the one now in effect, have consistently treated them as equal in all respects, including working conditions. And Corning's Manager of Job Evaluation testified in No. 73–29 that time of day worked was not considered to be a "working condition." Significantly, it is not the Secretary in this case who is trying to look behind Corning's bona fide job evaluation system to require equal pay for jobs which Corning has historically viewed as unequal work. Rather, it is Corning which asks us to differentiate between jobs which the company itself has always equated. We agree with the Second Circuit that the inspection work at issue in this case, whether performed during the day or night, is "equal work" as that term is defined in the Act.

This does not mean, of course, that there is no room in the Equal Pay

Act for nondiscriminatory shift differentials. Work on a steady night shift no doubt has psychological and physiological impacts making it less attractive than work on a day shift. The Act contemplates that a male night worker may receive a higher wage than a female day worker, just as it contemplates that a male employee with 20 years seniority can receive a higher wage than a woman with two years seniority. Factors such as these play a role under the Act's four exceptions—the seniority differential under the specific seniority exception, the shift differential under the catch-all exception for differentials "based on any other factor other than sex."

The question remains, however, whether Corning carried its burden of proving that the higher rate paid for night inspection work, until 1966 performed solely by men, was in fact intended to serve as compensation for night work, or rather constituted an added payment based upon sex. We agree that the record amply supported the District Court's conclusion that Corning had not sustained its burden of proof. As its history revealed, "the higher night rate was in large part the product of the generally higher wage level of male workers and the need to compensate them for performing what were regarded as demeaning tasks." 474 F.2d, at 233. The differential in base wages originated at a time when no other night employees received higher pay than corresponding day workers and it was maintained long after the company instituted a separate plant-wide shift differential which was thought to compensate adequately for the additional burdens of night work. The differential arose simply because men would not work at the low rates paid women inspectors, and it reflected a job market in which Corning could pay women less than men for the same work. That the company took advantage of such a situation may be understandable as a matter of economics, but its differential nevertheless became illegal once Congress enacted into law the principle of equal pay for equal work.

III

We now must consider whether Corning continued to remain in violation of the Act after 1966 when, without changing the base wage rates for day and night inspectors, it began to permit women to bid for jobs on the night shift as vacancies occurred. . . .

. . . Congress required that employers pay equal pay for equal work and then specified:

"*Provided,* That an employer who is paying a wage differential in violation of this subsection shall not, in order to comply with the provisions of this subsection, reduce the wage rate of any employee."

The purpose of this proviso was to ensure that to remedy violations of the Act, "The lower wage rate must be increased to the level of the higher." H. R. Rep. No. 309, *supra,* at 3. . . .

By proving that after the effective date of the Equal Pay Act, Corning paid female day inspectors less than male night inspectors for equal work, the Secretary implicitly demonstrated that the wages of female day shift inspectors were unlawfully depressed and that the fair wage for inspection work was the base wage paid to male inspectors on the night shift. The whole purpose of the Act was to require that these depressed wages be raised, in part as a matter of simple justice to the employees themselves, but also as a matter of market economics, since Congress recognized as well that discrimination in wages on the basis of sex "constitutes an unfair method of competition." § 2(5).

We agree with Judge Friendly that

"In light of this apparent congressional understanding, we cannot hold that Corning, by allowing some—or even many—women to move into the higher paid night jobs, achieved full compliance with the Act. Corning's action still left the inspectors on the day shift—virtually all women—earning a lower base wage than the night shift inspectors because of a differential initially based on sex and still not justified by any other consideration; in effect, Corning was still taking advantage of the availability of female labor to fill its day shift at a differentially low wage rate not justified by any factor other than sex." 474 F.2d, at 235.

The Equal Pay Act is broadly remedial, and it should be construed and applied so as to fulfill the underlying purposes which Congress sought to achieve. If, as the Secretary proved, the work performed by women on the day shift was equal to that performed by men on the night shift, the company became obligated to pay the women the same base wage as their male counterparts on the effective date of the Act. To permit the company to escape that obligation by agreeing to allow some women to work on the night shift at a higher rate of pay as vacancies occurred would frustrate, not serve, Congress' ends. . . .

The company's final contention—that it cured its violation of the Act when a new collective-bargaining agreement went into effect on January 20, 1969—need not detain us long. While the new agreement provided for equal base wages for night or day inspectors hired after that date, it continued to provide unequal base wages for employees hired before that date, a discrimination likely to continue for some time into the future because of a large number of laid-off employees who had to be offered re-employment before new inspectors could be hired. After considering the rather complex method in which the new wage rates for employees hired prior to January 1969 were calculated and the company's stated purpose behind the provisions of the new agreement, the District Court in No. 73–29 concluded that the lower base wage for day inspectors was a direct product of the company's failure to equalize the base wages for male and female inspectors as of the effective date of the Act. We agree it is clear from the record that had the company equalized the base wage rates of male and female inspectors on the effective date of the Act, as the law required, the day inspectors in 1969 would have been entitled to the same higher "red circle" rate the company provided for night inspectors. We therefore conclude that on the facts of this case, the company's continued discrimination in base wages between night and day workers, though phrased in terms of a neutral factor other than sex, nevertheless operated to perpetuate the effects of the company's prior illegal practice of paying women less than men for equal work. Cf. *Griggs* v. *Duke Power Co.,* 401 U.S. 424, 430 (1971).

The judgment in No. 73–29 is affirmed. The judgment in No. 73–695 is reversed and the case remanded to the Court of Appeals for further proceedings consistent with this opinion.

It is so ordered.

MR. JUSTICE STEWART took no part in the consideration or decision of these cases.

THE CHIEF JUSTICE, MR. JUSTICE BLACKMUN, and MR. JUSTICE REHNQUIST dissented.

CASE
QUESTIONS

1. Summarize the facts of the case.
2. Who brought the two court actions against Corning Glass Works and what remedies were sought?
3. Does the statutory term "working conditions" encompass the time of day worked?
4. Did Corning cure its violation in June 1966 when it permitted women to work as night shift inspectors?

SECTION 105 / SELECTED CONSTITUTIONAL ARGUMENTS ON SEX DISCRIMINATION

In *Geduldig* v. *Aiello*,[31] the Supreme Court considered the Equal Protection Clause arguments of four women denied maternity benefits under a State of California disability insurance program for private employees, which program had an exclusion of benefits for normal pregnancies. The Court held that California's decision not to insure under its program the risk of disability resulting from normal pregnancy does not constitute an invidious discrimination violative of the Equal Protection Clause. The Court found that the program does not discriminate with respect to the persons or groups eligible for its protection; and that the State is not required by the Equal Protection Clause to sacrifice the self-supporting nature of the program.

The *La Fleur* decision, presented in this section, was initially successful in the Court of Appeals utilizing Equal Protection Clause arguments against mandatory maternity leave rules for pregnant teachers. However, the Supreme Court sustained the Court of Appeals on the basis of the Due Process Clause, finding the challenged maternity leave rules to be violative of due process since they create a conclusive presumption that every teacher who is four or five months pregnant is physically incapable of continuing her duties, whereas any such teacher's inability to continue past a fixed pregnancy is an individual matter.

Freedom of Press contentions relating to employment opportunities advertising were recently considered by the U.S. Supreme Court. In *Pittsburgh Press Company* v. *Pittsburgh Commission on Human Relations*,[32] the Supreme Court upheld an order of the Pittsburgh Commission on Human Relations that forbade placing help-wanted advertisements under the headings "Jobs—Male Interest" and "Jobs—Female Interest," the majority of the Court took the position that the order came under the "commercial speech" exception to the First Amendment, while the four dissenters viewed it as a prior restraint on the press. The commission had ordered the Pittsburgh Press to stop using the headings in

---

[31] 8 FEP 97 (1974).
[32] FEP 1141 (1973).

its help-wanted columns after the National Organization for Women, Inc. complained.

Speaking for the Supreme Court, Mr. Justice Powell held that the case came under the commercial speech doctrine of *Valentine* v. *Chrestensen,*[33] which sustained a city ordinance that banned the distribution of a handbill soliciting customers for a tour of a submarine. The Court distinguished the commercial speech cases from the holding of *New York Times* v. *Sullivan,*[34] a libel suit in which the Court held that paid political advertising was entitled to First Amendment protection. The help-wanted advertisements in *Pittsburgh Press,* the Court held, do not express a position on "Whether as a matter of social policy, certain positions ought to be filled by members of one or the other sex. . . . Each is no more than a proposal of possible employment. The advertisements are thus classic examples of commercial speech." The Court added that nothing in its holding prevented the Pittsburgh Press from publishing advertisements commenting on the ordinance and the commission or its enforcement practices or the propriety of sex preferences in employment.

In his dissent Chief Justice Burger called the decision "a disturbing enlargement of the 'commercial speech' doctrine." Mr. Justice Douglas argued that the newspaper could print whatever it pleased without censorship or restraint by government. The want ads express the preference of the employer for the kind of help he wants, Justice Douglas said, and the commission might issue an order against the employer if discrimination in employment was shown. Mr. Justice Stewart, whose dissent Justice Douglas joined, declared that the issue was whether government "can tell a newspaper in advance what it can print and what it cannot." Mr. Justice Blackmum also dissented substantially for the reasons stated by Mr. Justice Stewart.

The Appendix to the majority opinion contained the following information:

Among the advertisements carried in the Sunday Pittsburgh Press on January 4, 1970, was the following one, submitted by an employment agency and placed in the "JOBS—MALE INTEREST" column:

ACAD. INSTRUCTORS	$13,000
ACCOUNTANTS	10,000
ADM. ASS'T, CPA	15,000
ADVERTISING MGR.	10,000
BOOKKEEPER F-C.	9,000
FINANCIAL CONSULTANT	12,000
MARKETING MANAGER	15,000
MGMT. TRAINEE.	8,400
OFFICE MGR. TRAINEE	7,200
LAND DEVELOPMENT	30,000
PRODUCT. MANAGER.	18,000
PERSONNEL MANAGER.	OPEN
SALES-ADVERTISING	8,400
SALES-CONSUMER	9,600
SALES-INDUSTRIAL	12,000
SALES-MACHINERY	8,400
RETAIL MGR.	15,000

---

[33] 316 U.S. 52 (1942).
[34] 376 U.S. 254 (1964).

Most Positions Fee Paid
EMPLOYMENT SPECIALISTS
2248 Oliver Bldg. 261–2250
Employment Agency

On the same day, the same agency's advertisement in the "JOBS—FEMALE INTEREST" column was as follows:

ACAD. INSTRUCTORS	$13,000
ACCOUNTANTS	6,000
AUTO-INS. UNDERWRITER	OPEN
BOOKKEEPER-INS.	5,000
CLERK-TYPIST	4,200
DRAFTSMAN	6,000
KEYPUNCH D. T.	6,720
KEYPUNCH BEGINNER	4,500
PROOFREADER	4,900
RECEPTIONIST—Mature D. T.	OPEN
EXEC. SEC.	6,300
SECRETARY	4,800
SECRETARY, Equal Oppor.	6,000
SECRETARY D. T.	5,400
TEACHERS-Pt. Time	day 33.
TYPIST-Statistical	5,000

Most Positions Fee Paid
EMPLOYMENT SPECIALISTS
2248 Oliver Bldg. 261–2250
Employment Agency

Cleveland Board of Education v. LaFleur

Supreme Court of the United States, 1974. 414 U.S. __

STEWART, J.: The respondents in No. 72–777 and the petitioner in No. 72–1129 are female public school teachers. During the 1970–1971 school year, each informed her local school board that she was pregnant; each was compelled by a mandatory maternity leave rule to quit her job without pay several months before the expected birth of her child. These cases call upon us to decide the constitutionality of the school boards' rules.

I

Jo Carol LaFleur and Ann Elizabeth Nelson, the respondents in No. 72–777, are junior high school teachers employed by the Board of Education of Cleveland, Ohio. Pursuant to a rule first adopted in 1952, the school board requires every pregnant school teacher to take a maternity leave without pay, beginning five months before the expected birth of her child. Application for such leave must be made no later than two weeks prior to the date of departure. A teacher on maternity leave is not allowed to return to work until the beginning of the next regular school semester which follows the date when her child attains the age of three months. A doctor's certificate attesting to the health of the teacher is a prerequisite to return; an additional physical examination may be required. The teacher on maternity leave is not promised reemployment after the birth of the child; she is merely given priority in reassignment to a position for which she. is qualified. Failure to comply with the mandatory maternity leave provisions is grounds for dismissal.

Neither Mrs. LaFleur nor Mrs. Nelson wished to take an unpaid maternity leave; each wanted to continue teaching until the end of the school year. Because of the mandatory maternity leave rule, however, each was required to leave her job in March of 1971. The two women then filed separate suits in the United States District Court for the Northern District of Ohio under 42 U.S.C. § 1983, challenging the constitutionality of the maternity leave rule. The District Court tried the cases together, and rejected the plaintiffs' arguments. 326 F. Supp. 1208. A divided panel of the United States Court of Appeals for the Sixth Circuit reversed, finding the Cleveland rules in violation of the Equal Protection Clause of the Fourteenth Amendment. 465 F.2d 1184.

The petitioner in No. 72–1129, Susan Cohen, was employed by the School Board of Chesterfield County, Virginia. That school board's maternity leave regulation requires that a pregnant teacher leave work at least four months prior to the expected birth of her child. . . .

II

This Court has long recognized that freedom of personal choice in matters of marriage and family life is one of the liberties protected by the Due Process Clause of the Fourteenth Amendment. . . . As we noted in *Eisenstadt* v. *Baird,* 405 U.S. 438, 453, there is a right "to be free from unwarranted governmental intrusion into matters so fundamentally affecting a person as the decision whether to bear or beget a child."

By acting to penalize the pregnant teacher for deciding to bear a child, overly restrictive maternity leave regulations can constitute a heavy burden on the exercise of these protected freedoms. Because public school maternity leave rules directly affect "one of the basic civil rights of man," *Skinner* v. *Oklahoma, supra,* at 541, the Due Process Clause of the Fourteenth Amendment requires that such rules must not needlessly, arbitrarily, or capriciously impinge upon this vital area of a teacher's constitutional liberty. The question before us in these cases is whether the interests advanced in support of the rules of the Cleveland and Chesterfield County School Boards can justify the particular procedures they have adopted.

The school boards in these cases have offered two essentially overlapping explanations for their mandatory maternity leave rules. First, they contend that the firm cut-off dates are necessary to maintain continuity of classroom instruction, since advance knowledge of when a pregnant teacher must leave facilitates the finding and hiring of a qualified substitute. Secondly, the school boards seek to justify their maternity rules by arguing that at least some teachers become physically incapable of adequately performing certain of their duties during the latter part of pregnancy. By keeping the pregnant teacher out of the classroom during these final months, the maternity leave rules are said to protect the health of the teacher and her unborn child, while at the same time assuring that students have a physically capable instructor in the classroom at all times.

It cannot be denied that continuity of instruction is a significant and legitimate educational goal. Regulations requiring pregnant teachers to provide early notice of their condition to school authorities undoubtedly facilitate administrative planning toward the important objective of continuity. But, as the Court of Appeals for the Second Circuit noted in *Green* v. *Waterford Board of Education,* 472 F2d 629, 635:

"Where a pregnant teacher provides the Board with a date certain for commencement of leave, however, that value [continuity] is preserved; an arbitrary leave date set at the end of the fifth month is no more calculated to facilitate a planned and orderly transition between the teacher and a substitute than is a date fixed closer to confinement. Indeed, the latter . . . would afford the Board more, not less, time to procure a satisfactory long-term substitute." (Footnote omitted.).

Thus, while the advance notice provisions in the Cleveland and Chesterfield County rules are wholly rational and may well be necessary to serve the objective of continuity of instruction, the absolute requirements of termination at the end of the fourth or fifth month of pregnancy are not. Were continuity the only goal, cutoff dates much later during pregnancy would serve as well or better than the challenged rules, providing that ample advance notice requirements were retained. Indeed, continuity would seem just as well attained if the teacher herself were allowed to choose the date upon which to commence her leave, at least so long as the decision were required to be made and notice given of it well in advance of the date selected.

In fact, since the fifth or sixth months of pregnancy will obviously begin at different times in the school year for different teachers, the present Cleveland and Chesterfield County rules may serve to hinder attainment of the very continuity objectives that they are purportedly designed to promote. For example, the beginning of the fifth month of pregnancy for both Mrs. LeFleur and Mrs. Nelson occurred during March of 1971. Both were thus required to leave work with only a few months left in the school year, even though both were fully willing to serve through the end of the term. Similarly, if continuity were the only goal, it seems ironic that the Chesterfield County rule forced Mrs. Cohen to leave work in mid-December 1970 rather than at the end of the semester in January, as she requested.

We thus conclude that the arbitrary cutoff dates embodied in the mandatory leave rules before us have no rational relationship to the valid state interest of preserving continuity of instruction. As long as the teacher is required to give substantial advance notice of her condition, the choice of firm dates later in pregnancy would serve the boards' objectives just as well, while imposing a far lesser burden on the women's exercise of constitutionally protected freedom.

The question remains as to whether the fifth and sixth month cut-off dates can be justified on the other ground advanced by the school boards—the necessity of keeping physically unfit teachers out of the classroom. There can be no doubt that such an objective is perfectly legitimate, both on educational and safety grounds. And, despite the plethora of conflicting medical testimony in these cases, we can assume *arguendo* that at least some teachers become physically disabled from effectively performing their duties during the latter stages of pregnancy.

The mandatory termination provisions of the Cleveland and Chesterfield County rules surely operate to insulate the classroom from the presence of potentially incapacitated pregnant teachers. But the question is whether the rules sweep too broadly. See *Shelton* v. *Tucker*, 364 U.S. 479. That question must be answered in the affirmative, for the provisions amount to a conclusive presumption that every pregnant teacher who reaches the fifth or sixth month of pregnancy is physically incapable of continuing. There is no individualized determination by the teacher's doctor—or the school board's— as to any particular teacher's ability to continue at her job. The rules contain an irrebuttable presumption of physical incompetency, and that presumption applies even when the medical evidence as to an individual woman's physical status might be wholly to the contrary.

As the Court noted last Term in *Vlandis* v. *Kline*, 412 U.S. 441, 446, "permanent irrebuttable presumptions have long been disfavored under the Due Process Clauses of the Fifth and Fourteenth Amendments." . . .

Similarly, in *Stanley* v. *Illinois*, 405 U.S. 645, the Court held that an Illinois statute containing an irrebuttable presumption that unmarried fathers are incompetent to raise their children violated the Due Process Clause. Because of the statutory presumption, the State took custody of all illegitimate children upon the death of the mother, without allowing the father to attempt to prove his parental fitness. As the Court put the matter:

> "It may be, as the State insists, that most unmarried fathers are unsuitable and neglectful parents. It may also be that Stanley is such a parent and that his children should be placed in other hands. But all unmarried fathers are not in this category; some are wholly suited to have custody of their children." *Id.*, at 654 (footnotes omitted).

Hence, we held that the State could not conclusively presume that any particular unmarried father was unfit to raise his child; the Due Process Clause required a more individualized determination. . . .

These principles control our decision in the cases before us. While the medical experts in these cases differed on many points, they unanimously agreed on one—the ability of any particular pregnant woman to continue at work past any fixed time in her pregnancy is very much an individual matter. Even assuming *arguendo* that there are some women who would be physically unable to work past the particular cutoff dates embodied in the challenged rules, it is evident that there are large numbers of teachers who are fully capable of continuing work for longer than the Clevland and Chesterfield County regulations will allow. Thus, the conclusive presumption embodied in these rules, like that in *Vlandis*, is neither "necessarily nor universally true," and is violative of the Due Process Clause.

The school boards have argued that the mandatory termination dates serve the interest of administrative convenience, since there are many instances of teacher pregnancy, and the rules obviate the necessity for case-by-case determinations. Certainly, the boards have an interest in devising prompt and efficient procedures to achieve their legitimate objectives in this area. But, as the court stated in *Stanley* v. *Illinois, supra,* at 656:

> "[T]he Constitution recognizes higher values than speed and efficiency. Indeed, one might fairly say of the Bill of Rights in general, and the Due Process Clause in particular, that they were designed to protect the fragile values of a vulnerable citizenry from the overbearing concern for efficiency and efficacy that may characterize praiseworthy government officials no less and perhaps more, than mediocre ones." (Footnote omitted.)

While it might be easier for the school boards to conclusively presume that all pregnant women are unfit to teach past the fourth or fifth month or even the first month, of pregnancy, administrative convenience alone is insufficient to make valid what otherwise is a violation of due process of law. The Fourteenth Amendment requires the school boards to employ alternative administrative means, which do not so broadly infringe upon basic constitutional liberty, in support of their legitimate goals.

We conclude, therefore, that neither the necessity for continuity of instruction nor the state interest in keeping physically unfit teachers out of the classroom can justify the sweeping mandatory leave regulations that the Cleveland and Chesterfield County School Boards have adopted. While the regulations no doubt represent a good-faith attempt to achieve a laudable goal, they cannot pass muster under the Due Process Clause of the Fourteenth Amendment, because they employ irrebuttable presumptions that unduly penalize a female teacher for deciding to bear a child.

III

In addition to the mandatory termination provisions, both the Cleveland and Chesterfield County rules contain limitations upon a teacher's eligibility to return to work after giving birth. Again, the school boards offer two justifications for the return rules—continuity of instruction and the desire to be certain that the teacher is physically competent when she returns to work. As is the case with the leave provisions, the question is not whether the school board's goals are legitimate, but rather whether the particular means chosen to achieve those objectives unduly infringe upon the teachers' constitutional liberty.

Under the Cleveland rule, the teacher is not eligible to return to work until the beginning of the next regular school semester following the time when her child attains the age of three months. A doctor's certificate attesting to the teacher's health is required before return; an additional physical examination may be required at the option of the school board.

The respondents in No. 72–777 do not seriously challenge either the medical requirements of the Cleveland rule or the policy of limiting eligibility to return to the next semester following birth. The provisions concerning a medical certificate or supplemental physical examination are narrowly drawn methods of protecting the school board's interest in teacher fitness; these requirements allow an individualized decision as to teacher's condition, and thus avoid the pitfalls of the presumptions inherent in the leave rules. Similarly, the provision limiting eligibility to return to the semester following delivery is a precisely drawn means of serving the school board's interest in avoiding unnecessary changes in classroom personnel during any one school term.

The Cleveland rule, however, does not simply contain these reasonable medical and next-semester eligibility provisions. In addition, the school board requires the mother to wait until her child reaches the age of three months before the return rules begin to operate. The school boards have offered no reasonable justification for this supplemental limitation, and we can perceive none. To the extent that the three months provision reflects the school board's thinking that no mother is fit to return until that point in time, it suffers from the same constitutional deficiencies that plague the irrebuttable presumption in the termination rules. The presumption, moreover, is patently unnecessary, since the requirement of a physician's certificate or a medical examination fully protects the school's interests in this regard. And finally, the three month provision simply has nothing to do with continuity of instruction, since the precise point at which the child will reach the relevant age will obviously occur at a different point throughout the school year for each teacher.

Thus, we conclude that the Cleveland return rule, insofar as it embodies the three months age provision, is wholly arbitrary and irrational, and hence violates the Due Process Clause of the Fourteenth Amendment. The age limitation serves no legitimate state interest, and unnecessarily penalizes the female teacher for asserting her right to bear children. . . .

IV

For the reasons stated, we hold that the mandatory termination provisions of the Cleveland and Chesterfield County maternity regulations violate the Due Process Clause of the Fourteenth Amendment, because of their use of unwarranted conclusive presumptions that seriously burden the exercise of protected constitutional liberty. For similar reasons, we hold the three months' provision of the Cleveland return rule unconstitutional.

Accordingly, the judgment in No. 72–777 is affirmed; the judgment in No. 72–1129 is reversed, and the case is remanded to the Court of Appeals for the Fourth Circuit for further proceedings consistent with this opinion.

It is so ordered.

CASE QUESTIONS

1. Summarize the Cleveland School Board's mandatory maternity leave rule.
2. What are the principal purposes claimed to be served by the Cleveland Board of Education's mandatory maternity leave rule?

3. What is the gist of the Court's Due Process Clause position?
4. Did the Court allow to stand the part of the Cleveland School Board's rule that prevented reemployment earlier than three months after birth?

SECTION 106 / AGE DISCRIMINATION

The *Age Discrimination in Employment Act of 1967* forbids discrimination against older men and women by employers, unions and employment agencies. This law specifically protects individuals between the ages of 40 and 65 years of age. *Executive Order 11141* prohibits age discrimination by government contractors and the federal government staff. There are no age limits specified in this order. If reasonable factors other than age disqualify an individual for a job, an employer is not obligated to hire the individual merely because he or she is between the ages of 40 and 65.

The *Greyhound Lines* decision reported below, considers an employer's argument that its hiring policy, limiting new driver applicants to persons under age 35, was protected under the "bona fide occupational qualification" exception to the Age Discrimination Law. The trial judge, in the decision presented below, held that Greyhound failed to meet its "burden of demonstrating that its policy of age limitation is reasonably necessary to the normal and safe operation of its business." However, the trial judge's ruling was overturned by a three member panel of the United States Court of Appeals holding that Greyhound is not violating the Age Discrimination in Employment Act for its hiring age limitations policy, since the company has a rational basis in fact to believe that elimination of its hiring age policy will increase the likelihood of risk of harm to its passengers and others.[35] The Court of Appeals thus modified the burden of proof requirements on the company, finding that Greyhound need only demonstrate a minimal increase in the risk of harm to its passengers and the public; the Court said, "it is enough to show that elimination of the hiring policy might jeopardize the life of one more person than might otherwise occur under the present hiring practice." The Court of Appeals pointed out in support of its opinion that Greyhound had sustained its burden of proof, that in addition to the general testimony by transportation industry officials, the company presented evidence relating to the rigors of the extra-board work assignment system to which all new drivers between ages 40 and 65 would be assigned under its seniority system; evidence concerning the degenerative physical and sensory changes that a human being undergoes about age 35 that have detrimental impact upon driving skills and are not detectible by physical examinations; and statistical evidence reflecting, among other things, that the company's safest driver is one who has between 16 to 20 years of driving experience with the company and who is between 50 and 55 years of age, the optimum blend of age and experience with the company that could never be attained in hiring an applicant 40 years of age or older.

The U.S. District Court opinion is reported here for its extensive testimonial

---

[35] 7 FEP 817 (7th Cir. 1974)

content and, coupled with the Court of Appeals ruling, to demonstrate the process of issue resolution under our judicial system. It is submitted that final adjudication of the case will be made by the U.S. Supreme Court.

Hodgson v. Greyhound Lines, Inc.

United States District Court, Northern District of Illinois, 1973. 354 F. Supp. 230

PARSONS, D. J.: The proceedings upon which the following opinion is rendered are based upon a Complaint filed by the Secretary of Labor of the United States Department of Labor, requesting the restraining of alleged violations of Sections 4(a)(1), 4(a)(2) and 4(e) of the Age Discrimination in Employment Act of 1967 and for such further relief as is deemed appropriate, including the restraint of any further refusal by defendant to employ persons denied employment in the past because of their ages.

During the course of trial, I have had the benefit of the testimony of eminent witnesses, the arguments of counsel, written memoranda and a multitude of exhibits. This is a case of great moment and my decision has come only after deep deliberation and study.

The issue, herein, is whether defendant's policy of refusing to consider applications of individuals between the ages of 40 and 65 for initial employment as bus drivers is a bona fide occupational qualification reasonably necessary to the normal operation of its business. Section 4(f)(1) of the Act states as follows:

"It shall not be unlawful for an employer, employment agency, or labor organization—

"(1) to take any action otherwise prohibited under subsections (a), (b), (c), or (e) of this section where age is a bona fide occupational qualification reasonably necessary to the normal operation of the particular business, or where the differentiation is based on reasonable factors other than age;"

The plaintiff alleges that the defendant has failed to meet its burden of proving that its age limitation policy for bus driver position is a bona fide occupational qualification reasonably necessary to the normal operation of its business.

The defendant has admitted that it does not consider applicants for the position of interstate bus drivers persons who are between the age of 40 to 65 years and contends that it is entitled to an exception because of Section (f)(1), *supra,* of the Act.

Defendant contends that if it were required to hire beginning interstate bus operators up to the age of 65 an unacceptable risk to the safety of its passengers and other members of the motoring public would ensue.

The defendant has offered the following arguments for its allegation.

"1. The defendant is required by law and by the nature of its business to exercise the highest degree of care, not only in the operation of its buses but in the hiring of bus drivers.

"2. Although individuals up to the age of 65 may be able to pass the required physical examination and be otherwise qualified, such physical examination is incapable of discovering the physical and sensory changes common to all man, [sic], caused by aging, that make an interstate bus operator less safe in the normal operation of the defendant's business.

"3. That the normal operation of the defendant's business requires that a beginning interstate bus operator serve from 10 to 20 years on the "extra board" which service requires the highest degree of physical ability and use of the senses.

"4. That its experience of over 40 years proves that an interstate bus driver is most safe after acquiring 16 years of interstate bus driving experience which experience could not be acquired by newly-employed drivers up to the age of 65 years."

Through the centuries volumes have been written on the subject of aging. It is a process that intrigues not only the scientific and philosophic mind but the less learned one as well. Aging is a phenomenon in which all humanity shares. The volumes that have been written are doubtless merely a fraction of what is yet to be studied. There will be inquiry and research as long as man exists for there will be the fascination with himself that leads to such study. For a moment, however, I must rely for my decision on that which exists in the realm of learning and on what I believe is both justifiable and correct under the existing law.

Defendant's policy of not considering applicants over the age of 35 has been in effect since approximately 1929. This is true regardless of an applicant's prior experience. At least two of defendant's officers, Mr. Forman and Mr. Gocke testified that they did not know why age 35 was originally selected or why other ages were not selected. However, they and defendants other witnesses vigorously support the age limitation policy and maintain that since the policy has produced results from a safety standpoint it has never been deemed necessary to change the rule. The National Association of Motor Bus Owners (hereinafter referred to as NAMBO) was granted leave to participate as *amicus curiae* for the defendant. In its trial brief it stated the issue at bar succinctly:

"It is submitted that the essence of the motor carriage of passengers is safety and that if the employment of drivers over age 35 would undermine that safety, the maximum age standard utilized by defendant is 'reasonably necessary' within the meaning of the *bona fide* occupational qualification exception to the Act."

Thus, the battle lines have been drawn. The plaintiff contends that the Age Discrimination in Employment Act of 1967 was enacted for the express purpose of "promoting employment of older persons based on their ability rather than age" and prohibiting "arbitrary age discrimination." *Hodgson* v. *First Federal Savings and Loan Ass'n of Broward County, Fla.,* 455 F.2d 818, 820 (5th Cir, 1972). The defendant contends that it has established a "valid justification" for its hiring practices. *Hodgson* v. *First Federal, supra,* pg. 822.

"In discrimination cases the law with respect to burden of proof is well-settled. The plaintiff is required only to make out a prima facie case of unlawful discrimination at which point the burden shifts to the defendant to justify the existence of any disparities. . . . Once the plaintiff has made out his prima facie case we look to the defendant for an explanation since he is in a position to know whether he failed to hire a person for reasons which would exonerate him. *Hodgson v. First Fed. Sav. & L. Ass'n, supra,* pg. 822."

I find that the plaintiff has made a *prima facie* case of refusal by the defendant to hire on the basis of age. Thus, it is incumbent upon me to carefully examine defendant's position and each of its contentions in order to arrive at a decision as to whether or not the defendant's reasons do indeed "exonerate" it.

Defendant, Greyhound Lines, Inc., is the nation's largest inter-city bus carrier with 105,000 route miles within the continental United States. The defendant employs approximately 9,500 bus drivers all of whom must meet certain requirements that are set by the defendant in accordance with Federal Regulations, State Statutes and the defendant's own policies. The above mentioned requirements relate to an individual's character, age (minimum age is 24, maximum is 35), height, weight, education, health, driver training school and probationary period.

The purpose of the health examination is to detect the presence of any physical or mental defect that would affect the applicant's ability safely to operate a motor vehicle. Included in the instructions from the Department of Transportation and the defendant that the examining physicians receive is the following:

"The examining physician should be aware of the vigorous physical demands and mental and emotional responsibilities placed on the driver of a commercial motor vehicle. In the interest of public safety the examining physician is required to certify that the driver does not have any physical, mental, or organic defect of such a nature as to affect the driver's ability to operate safely a commercial motor vehicle. . . . History of certain defects may be cause for rejection or indicate the need for making certain laboratory tests or a further, and more stringent, examination. . . .

It is axiomatic that common carriers are held to an extremely high degree of care. Thus, it is the defendant's obligation to exercise the highest degree of care possible in all aspects of its business including, of course, the hiring of bus drivers.

When successfully completed the aforementioned qualifications and requirements merely constitute an entry into defendant's organization. Greyhound bus drivers must continue to meet standards set by the defendant in accordance with Federal Regulations. Those standards include a low accident rate, safe driving habits, good health, good driver attitude and courtesy to customers. Each driver's reaction time is checked periodically as is his driving ability under all weather conditions. A physical examination is required by Federal Regulations at two-year intervals up to age 50 and annually thereafter until age 65.

Thus, it may be seen, *a fortiori,* that defendant does exercise a high degree of care in the hiring of its bus drivers.

Defendant's next contention is that the required physical examination "is incapable of discovering those physical and sensory changes common to all men" that would cause an interstate bus driver to be less safe while in the operation of defendant's business. This premise is not as easily dealt with as was defendant's first contention. The expert testimony tendered at trial and in exhibits differs greatly and so I feel constrained to review certain portions of that material.

Defendant's witness, Dr. Harold Brandaleone, a physician specializing in internal medicine and a medical consultant to bus and trucking companies, testified that he did not believe a man past 40 should be employed in a new job of driving an intercity bus. Dr. Brandaleone testified that in general after a certain age, usually about 40, degenerative changes occur in the individual such as arteriosclerotic changes in the blood vessels, the heart, the blood vessels in the brain, the kidneys, the lungs, his lower extremities and his visual capacity or sensory changes including a decrease in his ability to see at night. In response to questions concerning physical examinations Dr. Brandaleone testified as follows:

> "Well, physical examination can find many of them but there are many things that cannot be deteted by physical examination, or even those that may be detected at a periodic examination that could occur every year or every two years in the interim, and this is the thing that concerns me. . . .

Further in the testimony the witness testified that the undetectable effects of aging in persons over age 40 are equally as likely to occur in defendant's present bus drivers over age 40 yet he did not consider them unsafe nor did he recommend that defendant retire its drivers at age 40. . . .

Professor Ross A. McFarland, Ph. D., a physiological psychologist and specialist in the field of aging was tendered as a witness by the plaintiff. Dr. McFarland testified that chronological age is not a reliable index of a person's physical or psychological condition and cannot be a basis to determine the ability of a person to drive. (tr. 1832; 1834; 1854). He emphasized that chronological age is not an accurate index of a person's physical condition, (tr. 1816; 1819), and stated that many physiological and emotional alterations which result from the aging process are not necessarily a cause for driver limitation or impairment. (tr. 1834).

Dr. McFarland testified as follows:

> ". . . I think the Greyhound data would show very little evidence that accidents have occurred because of physical defects. I think their medical screening is good and that they would pick up the physically ill or the markedly physically defective person, that would come out. . . .

Later in the trial in response to cross-examination, Dr. McFarland stated the following:

> ". . . I am saying that the physical examinations are poor and do not test functional ability, and I want a man judged on the basis of his functional ability, his capacity to do the work, and whenever you employ a man, you immediately put him through all of the functional tests of driving. . . ."

Thus, having read and listened to the various witnesses and drawn upon my own experience and knowledge I find one common thread throughout;

there is no agreement as to the reliability or the proper weight that ought to be placed on physical examinations. I find that a physical examination is no more valid a test of driving ability for a 25 year old than for a 45 year old. Therefore, I cannot utilize defendant's second reason as a criterion for deciding that a man of 25 would, merely by virtue of of being 25, be a safer driver than the man of 45. I cannot state with definitive certainty that such physical examinations as are given would be capable or incapable of discovering the physical and sensory changes common to all men nor that those changes are necessarily caused only by the aging process nor that such changes in and of themselves make an interstate bus operator less safe in the normal operation of defendant's business.

The third argument tendered by defendant in defense of its policy concerns itself with the "extra board" system. Within Greyhound's organization there are two general classifications of drivers; those who perform "regular runs" and those who perform "extra board." A regular run is one which is performed regularly and is a scheduled service between two given points. On the other hand, "extra board" runs vary and are performed on the basis of passenger demand and consist of special operations, tours, charters and extra sections of regular runs if there is a call for more than one bus on a regular run. Extra board drivers do not have scheduled routes and work off of the board on a first in, first out basis. On the average an extra board driver is called to perform about four driving runs in a seven day period. . . .

It is defendant's strong contention that the rigors of the extra board are such as to necessitate the imposition of an age limitation. Defendant asserts that persons between the ages of 40 and 65 simply do not have the stamina for the irregular work schedule of the extra board. Five of defendant's drivers appeared as witnesses and each testified that being an extra board driver is demanding and physically exhausting work.

However, after listening to the testimony concerning extra board *vis a vis* regular run driving, I am not convinced that the irregular hours and possible adverse driving conditions are any more difficult for those applicants over 40 years of age than for those under 40. I cannot accede to a contention which flatly states that all applicants over 40 are inflexible, unadaptable and untrainable and, in effect, that is what I am called upon to do. The defendant has not tendered the necessary statistical evidence to allow for such a finding. The defendant's policy is not based on personal experience or observations of new applicants age 40 or over.

"Speculation cannot supply the place of proof."
Galloway v. *U.S.,* 319 U.S. 372, 395; *Moore* v. *Chesapeake Ry. Co.,* 340 U.S. 573, 578.

In *Weeks* v. *Southern Bell Telephone and Telegraph Co.,* 408 F.2d 228, 235 (5th Cir. 1969), plaintiff's application for the position of switchman was refused consideration solely because of her sex. The court held in refusing to accept defendant's contention that the job was too strenuous for women:

"We conclude that the principle of non-discrimination requires that we hold that in order to rely on the bona fide occupational qualification exception an employer has the burden of proving that he had reasonable cause to believe, that is, a factual basis for believing, that all or substantially all women would be unable to perform safely and efficiently the duties of the job involved."

The question thus arises as to whether or not Greyhound has established a "factual basis" for its belief that applicants between the ages of 40 and 65 would be unable to perform safely the duties of an extra board driver. I find it has not established such a basis. It is true as the plaintiff has asserted that "the defendant is in a position to obtain the pertinent objective data simply by comparing the accident records of its extra board drivers who are over 39 years of age with the accident records of its extra board drivers who are under that age. Nor has the defendant compared the relationship between age and applicant failures at the training stages. It is also true as plaintiff states that the defendants instead combined its statistics for extra board drivers and regular run drivers. These statistics actually show that its drivers over age 40 have a better safety record that those under 40. Thus it may be assumed that the better safety record of Greyhound drivers over age 40 applies to those on the extra board as well as to those on the regular runs. . . .

Defendant's fourth argument for continuation of its policy is that an interstate bus driver is most safe after acquiring 16 years of interstate bus driving experience and such experience could not be acquired by newly-employed drivers between age 40 and 65. Numerous charts tendered by the defendant as evidence purported to show statistics which would support defendant's contention. For instance, during 1968–71 drivers between the ages of 24–40 had the highest number of accidents per driver, whereas drivers 41–60 had about the same low accident experience (the drivers between 56–60 showed a slight increase in accidents over the safest age group of 51–55 but substantially below the age group 24–40). . . .

. . . However, we are not in the realm of conjecture and I find that defendant has not satisfactorily proved that the safety record of those drivers with 16 years of interstate bus driving experience is due to the fact that these individuals were hired before reaching the age of 40.

Nor has defendant impressed me with a cogent reason for its refusal to hire drivers over the age of 40 even though those drivers have had other interstate bus driving experience including driving extra board runs for other companies. Defendant contends that applicants over the age of 40 cannot be "untrained" if they have had prior experience and that:

> "it has been our experience that it is easier to take someone who has never driven a large vehicle and teach him to drive it than to take someone who has learned to drive a large vehicle someplace else and then teach him to drive the way we want and expect him to drive our large vehicle."

Yet, all five of defendant's driver-witnesses had previous commercial driving experience driving buses or large trucks before being employed by Greyhound.

It is, I believe, inconsistent to maintain that those who have driven large vehicles and are under age 40 are able to be "untrained" where as those over age 40 cannot be "untrained." Defendant has offered no evidence that would satisfactorily prove such a contention. . . .

The following exchange between counsel for plaintiff and Mr. Forman, an officer of defendant, serves to buttress my decision that the defendant's policy is not founded on the "factual basis" for its belief that "all or substantially all (members of the protected class) would be unable to perform safely and efficiently the duties of the job involved" that is required under *Weeks, supra,* pg. 235:

> Q. "Is that right, you have in fact no personal experience in initially employing anyone 40 or over as a Greyhound driver?"
> A. "That is correct."
> Q. "Then you in fact cannot state, based on your own personal knowledge, that the consideration in employment of otherwise qualified individuals 40 or over for initial employment as a bus driver with Greyhound would adversely affect safety, isn't that right?"
> A. "You have to take into consideration the problem of the extra board, the rigors that it demands and what this man's life style will be at that time. Good basic common sense tells us that to begin his career as a Greyhound bus driver over age 40, go through the portion of his apprenticeship, when he has the highest number of accidents, and about the time he is getting to his stride the aging process catches up with him and he is right back into the upswing again without having a flattening out."

I must disagree. "Good basic common sense" does not suffice as "objective data" to satisfy the "factual basis" of the *Weeks* decision. Nor has defendant had any experience with applicants above age 40 so that it could factually state that such drivers would have the highest number of accidents during their apprenticeship.

Defendant need not hire all applicants; the rigid requirements and qualifications now in effect for those applicants under age 40 will continue to be in effect.

Employers are required to "consider" individuals on the basis of what they can contribute, not on the basis of chronological age (113 Cong. Daily Rec. 34744). If ever there were an opportunity for "individual consideration" surely this is one for through its screening process defendant has ample opportunity to exclude those individuals it finds unsuitable for interstate bus driving.

Safety is the foremost concern involved herein not only for defendant but for plaintiff and this Court as well, but I cannot accept the contention that persons over 40 cannot become safe bus drivers. I believe strongly that functional capacity and not chronological age ought to be the most important factor as to whether or not an individual can do a job safely. This determination must be made repeatedly throughout the employee's employment experience. The human variances involved are myriad; there is no way to generalize as to the physical capability and physiological make up of an individual. Nor is there a way to project how an individual will be affected by the aging process.

I thereby conclude that the data prepared by the defendant and the evidence it has presented have not met the burden of demonstrating that its policy of age limitation is reasonably necessary to the normal and safe operation of its business nor that age is a bona fide occupational qualification within the meaning of the Act. Therefore, it is adjudged, ordered and decreed that judgment for the plaintiff and against the defendant be and the same hereby is entered.

CASE QUESTIONS

1. What is the issue before the court?
2. On what section of the Age Discrimination in Employment Act of 1967 did the employer-defendant base its defense?
3. Who has the burden of proof in age discrimination cases?
4. Did the District Court decision require Greyhound to hire "older" men on a proportionate basis to younger men?
5. State the holding and rationale for the Court of Appeals decision.

QUESTIONS ON CHAPTER 12

1. What are the three major federal statutes dealing with the regulation of equal rights in employment?
2. State the general purpose of the Civil Rights Act of 1964.
3. What federal agency has the responsibility to achieve compliance with Title VII of the amended Civil Rights Act?
4. What remedies are available to grievants charging discriminatory employment practices?
5. On what authority does the federal government require bidders on government contracts to formulate and carry out affirmative action progress?

Chapter 13

Public Employment
and Labor Law

SECTION 107 / INTRODUCTION

This chapter will review the legislation and other legal aspects of labor relations in the public service. The increasing unionization and use of collective bargaining by government workers requires an understanding of the differences of doctrine and of legal premises that distinguish government as an employer from the nongovernment enterprise. The common law, the legislation and the economic environment that have influenced labor relations in what is commonly known as the private sector are largely inapplicable in the government area. Insofar as labor relations are concerned some significant differences exist also between national, state and local levels of government in regard to labor legislation, administration, and collective bargaining practices.

As a starting point, the first section of the chapter focuses on the right of government employees to strike. This topic is the dominant public-interest issue in the area of government employee collective bargaining; an overview of the philosophies of government employee bargaining may be gained from the cases in the section. The following sections contain materials on the legal framework for regulating and guiding collective negotiations and for dispute handling at each level of government. A final section presents an overall evaluation of progress and prospective problems.

SECTION 108 / STRIKES BY GOVERNMENT EMPLOYEES

In its definition of the term "employer," the National Labor Relations Act expressly excludes the United States, wholly owned government corporations, states, and municipal corporations. Thus, public employees have no rights under the Act. This does not mean, however, that the collective bargaining process is not afforded recognition by governing bodies. The federal government permits its employees to form, join, and assist labor organizations, as do generally the states. Municipal bodies are not uniform as to policy on this issue, as some of them prohibit their employees from affiliating with a labor union.

Section 19(b)(4) of Executive Order 11491 of 1969, which regulates Federal Service labor relations, makes it an unfair practice for a labor organization to:

"Call or engage in a strike, work stoppage, or slowdown, picket any agency in a labor-management dispute; or condone any such activity by failing to take affirmative action to prevent or stop it . . ."

The *Postal Clerks* v. *Blount* case reported in this section gives the judicial answers to the objections raised by the Postal Clerks concerning the right of public employees in the Federal Service to strike.

The right of public employees in state and municipal service to strike is prohibited by statute or court decision in most states.[1] However, despite these legal prohibitions, and in the face of severe penalties against unions, union officers and individual union members, many public employee labor organizations have engaged in strikes in recent years. The *Board of Education, Union Beach* case reported in this section gives New Jersey's view on the legality of a teachers' strike. The *DeLury* case that follows reports on the famous New York City sanitation strike. *DeLury* demonstrates the use of the injunctive and punitive powers given the judiciary under the Taylor Act, and gives the rationale for the State's policy in forbidding public employee strikes.

Postal Clerks v. Blount

United States District Court, District of Columbia, 1971. 325 F.Supp 879

Before WRIGHT, MACKINNON, Circuit Judges, and PRATT, District Judge.

PER CURIAM: This action was brought by the United Federation of Postal Clerks (hereafter sometimes referred to as "Clerks"), an unincorporated public employee labor organization which consists primarily of employees of the Post Office Department, and which is the exclusive bargaining representative of approximately 305,000 members of the clerk craft employed by defendant. Defendant Blount is the Postmaster General of the United States. The Clerks seek declaratory and injunctive relief invalidating portions of 5 U.S.C. § 7311, 18 U.S.C. § 1918, an affidavit required by 5 U.S.C. § 3333 to implement the above statutes, and Executive Order 11491, C.F.R., Chap. II, p. 191. The Government, in response, filed a motion to dismiss or in the alternative for summary judgment, and plaintiff filed its opposition thereto and cross motion for summary judgment. A three-judge court was convened pursuant to 28 U.S.C. § 2282 and § 2284 to consider this issue.

5 U.S.C. § 7311(3) prohibits an individual from accepting or holding a position in the federal government or in the District of Columbia if he

---

[1] Hawaii, Pennsylvania and Vermont prohibit strikes only if the public health, safety or welfare would be endangered; impasse resolution machinery must also be exhausted before going out on strike. Alaska law creates for strike-right purposes three employee categories, scaled to the degree to which an interruption in service can be tolerated: the right to strike is denied to protective services; is granted with limits to utility, sanitation and school employees; and is granted without limit to all others.

"(3) participates in a strike . . . against the Government of the United States or the government of the District of Columbia . . ."

Paragraph C of the appointment affidavit required by 5 U.S.C. § 3333, which all federal employees are required to execute under oath, states (POD Form 61):

"I am not participating in any strike against the Government of the United States or any agency thereof, and I will not so participate while an employee of the Government of the United States or any agency thereof."

18 U.S.C. § 1918, in making a violation of 5 U.S.C. § 7311 a crime, provides:

"Whoever violates the provision of section 7311 of title 5 that an individual may not accept or hold a position in the Government of the United States or the government of the District of Columbia if he . . .
"(3) participates in a strike, or asserts the right to strike, against the Government of the United States or the District of Columbia . . .
"shall be fined not more than $1,000 or imprisoned not more than one year and a day, or both."

Section 2(e)(2) of Executive Order 11491 exempts from the definition of a labor organization any group which:

"asserts the right to strike against the Government of the United States or any agency thereof, or to assist or participate in such strike, or imposes a duty or obligation to conduct, assist or participate in such a strike . . ."

Section 19(b)(4) of the same Executive Order makes it an unfair labor practice for a labor organization to:

"call or engage in a strike, work stoppage, or slowdown; picket any agency in a labor-management dispute; or condone any such activity by failing to take affirmative action to prevent or stop it; . . ."

Plaintiff contends that the right to strike is a fundamental right protected by the Constitution, and that the absolute prohibition of such activity by 5 U.S.C. § 7311(3) and the other provisions set out above thus constitutes an infringement of the employees' First Amendment rights of association and free speech and operates to deny them equal protection of the law. Plaintiff also argues that the language to "strike" and "participates in a strike" is vague and overbroad and therefore violative of both the First Amendment and the due process clause of the Fifth Amendment. For the purposes of this opinion, we will direct our attention to the attack on the constitutionality of 5 U.S.C. § 7311(3), the key provision being challenged. . . .

At common law no employee, whether public or private, had a constitutional right to strike in concert with his fellow workers. Indeed, such collective action on the part of employees was often held to be a conspiracy. When the right of private employees to strike finally received full protection, it was by statute, Section 7 of the National Labor Relations Act, which "took this conspiracy weapon away from the employer in employment relations which affect interstate commerce" and guaranteed to employees in the private sector the right to engage in concerted activities for the purpose of collective bargaining. See discussion in *Local 232* v. *Wisconsin Employment Relations Board,* 336 U.S. 245, 257–259 (1948). It seems clear that public employees stand on no stronger footing in this regard than private employees and that in the absence of a statute, they too do not possess the right to strike. The Supreme Court has spoken approvingly of such a restriction, see *Amell* v. *United States,* 384 U.S. 158, 161 (1965), and at least one federal district court has invoked the provisions of a predecessor statute, 5 U.S.C. § 118p-r, to enjoin a strike by government employees. *Tennessee Valley Authority* v. *Local Union No. 110 of Sheet Metal Workers,* 233 F. Supp. 997 (D.C.W.D. Ky. 1962). Likewise, scores of state cases have held that state employees do not have a right to engage in concerted work stoppages, in the absence of legislative authorization. See, e.g., *Los Angeles Metropolitan Transit Authority* v. *Brotherhood of R. R. Trainmen,* 54 Cal. 2nd 634, (1960); *Board of Education* v. *Redding,* 32 Ill. 2d 567, (1965). It is fair to conclude that, irrespective of the reasons given, there is a unanimity of opinion on the part of courts and legislatures that government employees do not have the right to strike. See Moberly, *The Strike and Its Alternative in Public Employment,* University of Wisconsin Law Review (1966) pp. 549–550, 554.

Congress has consistently treated public employees as being in a different category than private employees. The National Labor Relations Act of 1937 and the Labor Management Relations Act of 1947, (Taft-Hartley) both defined "employer" as not including any governmental or political subdivisions, and thereby indirectly withheld the protections of § 7 from governmental employees. Congress originally enacted the no-strike provision separately from other restrictions on employee activity, i.e., such as those struck down in *Stewart* v. *Washington,* 301 F. Supp. 610 (D.C. D.C 1969) and *NACL* v. *Blount,* 305 F. Supp. 546, (D.C. D.C. 1969), by attaching riders to appropriations bills which prohibited strikes by government employees. See for example the Third Urgent Deficiency Appropriation Act of 1946, which provided that no part of the appropriation could be used to pay the salary of anyone who engaged in a strike against the Government. Section 305 of the Taft-Hartley Act made it unlawful for a federal employee to participate in a strike, providing immediate discharge and forfeiture of civil service status for infractions. Section 305 was repealed in 1955 by Public Law 330, and re-enacted in 5 U.S.C. § 118p-r, the predecessor to the present statute.

Given the fact that there is no constitutional right to strike, it is not irrational or arbitrary for the Government to condition employment on a promise not to withhold labor collectively, and to prohibit strikes by those in public employment, whether because of the prerogatives of the sovereign, some sense of higher obligation associated with public service, to assure the continuing functioning of the Government without interruption, to protect public health and safety or for other reasons. Although plaintiff argues that the provisions in question are unconstitutionally broad in covering all Government employees regardless of the type or importance of the work they do, we hold that it makes no difference whether the jobs performed by certain public employees are regarded as "essential" or "non-essential," or whether similar jobs are performed by workers in private industry who do have the right to strike protected by statute. Nor is it relevant that some positions in private industry are arguably more affected with a public interest than are some positions in the Government service. While the Fifth Amendment contains no Equal Protection Clause similar to the one found in the Fourteenth Amendment, concepts of Equal Protection do inhere in Fifth Amendment Principles of Due Process. *Bolling* v. *Sharp,* 347 U.S. 497 (1954). The Equal Protection Clause, however, does not forbid all discrimination. Where fundamental rights are not involved, a particular classification does not violate the Equal Protection Clause if it is not "arbitrary" or "irrational," i.e., "if any state of facts reasonably may be conceived to justify it." *McGowan* v. *Maryland,* 366 U.S. 420, 426 (1961). Compare *Kramer* v. *Union Free School District,* 395 U.S. 621, 627–628 (1969). Since the right to strike cannot be considered a "fundamental" right, it is the test enunciated in *McGowan* which must be employed in this case. Thus, there is latitude for distinctions rooted in reason and practice, especially where the difficulty of drafting a no-strike statute which distinguishes among types and classes of employees is obvious.

Furthermore, it should be pointed out that the fact that public employees may not strike does not interfere with their rights which are fundamental and constitutionally protected. The right to organize collectively and to select representatives for the purposes of engaging in collective bargaining is such a fundamental right. *Thomas* v. *Collins,* 323 U.S. 516 (1945); *NLRB* v. *Jones & Laughlin,* 301 U.S. 1, 33 (1937). But, as the Supreme Court noted in *Local 232* v. *Wisconsin Employment Relations Board, supra,* "The right to strike, because of its more serious impact upon the public interest, is more vulnerable to regulation than the right to organize and select representatives for lawful purposes of collective bargaining which this Court has characterized as a 'fundamental right' and which, as the Court has pointed out, was recognized as such in its decisions long before it was given protection by the National Labor Relations Act." 336 U.S. at 259.

Executive Order 11491 recognizes the right of federal employees to join labor organizations for the purpose of dealing with grievances, but that Order clearly and expressly defines strikes, work stoppages and slowdowns as unfair labor practices. As discussed above, that Order is the culmination of a long-standing policy. There certainly is no compelling reason to imply the existence of the right to strike from the right to associate and bargain collectively. In the private sphere, the strike is used to equalize bargaining power, but this has universally been held not to be appropriate when its object and purpose can only be to influence the essentially political decisions of Government in the allocation of its resources. Congress has an obligation to ensure that the machinery of the Federal Government continues to function at all times without interference. Prohibition of strikes by its employees is a reasonable implementation of that obligation. . . .

Accordingly, we hold that the provisions of the statute, the appointment affidavit and the Executive Order, as construed above, do not violate any constitutional rights of those employees who are members of plaintiff's union. The Government's motion to dismiss the complaint is granted. Order to be presented.

WRIGHT, C. J., concurring: . . . My following comments are addressed to the main issue raised in Part I of the opinion—the validity of the flat ban on federal employees' strikes under the Fifth Amendment of the Constitution. This question is, in my view, a very difficult one, and I cannot concur fully in the majority's handling of it.

It is by no means clear to me that the right to strike is not fundamental. The right to strike seems intimately related to the right to form labor organizations, a right which the majority recognizes as fundamental and which, more importantly, is generally thought to be constitutionally protected under the First Amendment—even for public employees. See *Melton* v. *City of Atlanta,* 39 U.S.L.W. 2469 (N.D. Ga. 1971); *Atkins* v. *City of Charlotte,* 296 F. Supp. 1068 (W.D.N.C. 1969). If the inherent purpose of a labor organization is to bring the workers' interests to bear on management, the right to strike is, historically and practically, an important means of effectuating that purpose. A union that never strikes, or which can make no credible threat to strike, may wither away in ineffectiveness. That fact is not irrelevant to the constitutional calculations. Indeed, in several decisons, the Supreme Court has held that the First Amendment right of association is at least concerned with essential organizational activities which give the particular association life and promote its fundamental purposes. See *Williams* v. *Rhodes,* 393 U.S. 23 (1968); *United Mine Workers* v. *Illinois State Bar Assn.,* 389 U.S. 217 (1967). I do not suggest that the right to strike is co-equal with the right to form labor organizations. Nor do I equate striking with the organizational activities protected in *Williams* (access to the ballot) or *United Mine Workers* (group legal representation). But I do believe that the right to strike is, at least, within constitutional concern and should not be discriminatorily abridged without substantial or "compelling" justification.

Hence the real question here, as I see it, is to determine whether there is such justification for denying federal employees a right which is granted to other employees of private business. Plaintiff's arguments that not all federal services are "essential" and that some privately provided services are no less "essential" casts doubt on the validity of the flat ban on federal employees' strikes. In our mixed economic system of governmental and private enterprise, the line separating governmental from private functions may depend more on the accidents of history than on substantial differences in kind.

Nevertheless, I feel that I must concur in the result reached by the majority in Part I of its opinion. As the majority indicates, the asserted right of public employees to strike has often been litigated and, so far as I know, never recognized as a matter of law. The present state of the relevant jurisprudence offers almost no support for the proposition that the government lacks a "compelling" interest in prohibiting such strikes. No doubt, the line between "essential" and "non-essential" functions is very, very difficult to draw. For that reason, it may well be best to accept the demarcations resulting from the development of our political economy. If the right of public employees to strike—with all its political and social ramifications—is to be recognized and protected by the judiciary, it should be done by the Supreme Court which has the power to reject established jurisprudence and the authority to enforce such a sweeping rule.

1. What is the gist of the Postal Clerks arguments?
2. Under common law did public or private employees have a constitutional right to strike?
3. Does the court distinguish between the right of public employees to strike and the right to unionize?
4. What is the holding of the Court on the question of public employees' Constitutional right to strike?
5. In the concurring opinion, what is Judge Wright's position as to the proper judicial forum to consider the recognition of public employees' right to strike?

Board of Education, Borough of Union Beach v. New Jersey Education Association

New Jersey Supreme Court, 1968. 53 N.J. 29

WEINTRAUB, C. J.: Plaintiff Board of Education (herein Board) obtained a judgment, after a plenary trial, restraining certain activities by defendants and directing them, in effect, to undo actions already taken. The trial court's opinion is reported in 96 N.J. Super. 371 (Ch. Div. 1967). We certified defendants' appeal before argument in the Appellate Division.

The Board is a public body, N. J. S. 18A;10–1, charged with the conduct of the public school system in the Borough of Union Beach. Defendant New Jersey Education Association (NJEA), with a membership of about 57,000, represents teachers and administrators in public schools in New Jersey. Defendant Union Beach Teachers Association (UBTA) represented 46 of the 47 full-time teachers employed by the Board at the time of the events about to be related. It is affiliated with NJEA, and NJEA is affiliated with a national organization, the defendant National Education Association (NEA), with more than a million members. Defendant Haller was the president of UBTA, and the other individual defendants are officers or representatives of NJEA.

In February 1967 a dispute arose between the secretary of the Board and defendant Haller, president of UBTA. Haller was a teacher in plaintiff's system but had not yet acquired tenure. On March 14, 1967 the Board met to consider teacher contracts for the following school year and decided not to offer one to Haller and two other nontenure teachers who were active in UBTA. Haller was so notified on March 29. UBTA held a special meeting of its membership on March 31 at which a lengthy resolution was adopted listing 17 grievances.

The trial court found the resolution to be a sham in its assertion of alleged grievances, which finding is not, however, pivotal in the decision of the case. The grievances had not been presented before and no effort had been made to pursue established grievance procedures. The real controversy, which comes within the general terms of the 17th alleged grievance, involved the Board's decision not to reemploy Haller and the two other teachers. Indeed, at the meeting of March 31 representatives of NJEA scored the decision of the Board not to reemploy a nontenure teacher without giving a reason and on that basis urged the teachers to submit resignations *en masse*. At the Board's meeting of April 4 Haller presented the "grievance" resolution described above, and also the resignations of 36 of the 47 teachers, to be effective on June 3, about two weeks short of the end of the school term. The Board called upon the teachers to withdraw their resignations. A few did, and on April 17, the Board accepted the remaining 31 resignations.

Meanwhile, on April 12 UBTA resolved that "sanctions be imposed" against the Board and requested NJEA to follow suit. On April 21 the NJEA resolved to "impose sanctions" on the Board, and gave wide circulation to its resolution. . . .

> We interrupt the chronology to explain what defendants mean by "sanctions." In 1962 the NEA resolved:
>
> "The National Education Association believes that, as a means of preventing unethical or arbitrary policies or practices that have a deleterious effect on the welfare of the schools, professional sanctions should be invoked. These sanctions would provide for appropriate disciplinary action by the organized profession.
>
> The National Education Association calls upon its affiliated state associations to cooperate in developing guidelines which would define, organize, and definitely specify procedural steps for invoking sanctions by the teaching profession."

In its "Guidelines" NEA states:

> "As used by a professional education organization, sanctions mean censure, suspension or expulsion of a member; severance of relationship with an affiliated association or other agency; imposing of a deterrent against a board of education or other agency controlling the welfare of the schools; bringing into play forces that will enable the community to help the board or agency to realize its responsibility; or the application of one or more steps in the withholding of services."

With reference to "sanctions" imposed by NEA upon a school district, the "Guidelines" include the following "types of sanctions":

> "3. Notification to certification and placement services of unsatisfactory conditions of employment for educators.
>
> 4. Warning to members that acceptance of employment as a new teacher in the school district would be considered as unethical conduct and could lead to discharge from and future refusal of membership in the national professional association.
>
> 5. Advice to members presently employed that, if their private arrangements permit, they should seek employment elsewhere."

As to a member of NEA who is guilty of "unethical" conduct, the "sanctions" authorized are private or public censure, suspension from membership or expulsion from membership.

The "Guidelines" deal with the imposition of "sanctions" by a local education association and also by a state association. As to an offending member, the "sanctions" are those just listed, *i.e.,* private or public censure, suspension or expulsion. As to the school districts, the local education association and the state association also impose "sanctions," and we quote the following from the "Guidelines" with respect to such action at the state level:

"3. Notification to state and national accrediting agencies of professionally unsatisfactory conditions in a school district;

4. Withholding of placement services, when the state association maintains a placement office; notice to public and private placement agencies of unsatisfactory conditions in a school district and request to observe professional disapproval;

5. Notification to members of association of unacceptable conditions for employment in such district and the professional significance of accepting or refusing employment in a school district against which sanctions have been invoked."

In harmony with the "Guidelines," NJEA made wide distribution of its notice of imposition of "sanctions" on the school district, sending notices to its 57,000 members, to the presidents and placement directors of all teacher colleges in New Jersey, to like officials and other connected with state preparatory colleges in Pennsylvania, New York, West Virginia, Connecticut, Delaware and Maryland, and to all state association executive secretaries. It sent sanction notices to building representatives in selected key districts surrounding plaintiff school district. It also sent a letter to teachers considering employment by the Board, warning that "If a contract is signed by you while professional sanctions are in effect at Union Beach, you will be in violation of the professional code of ethics."

All of the notices referred to above quoted NEA Resolution 66–16, which reads:

"A violation of sanctions by a member of the profession is a violation of the 'Code of Ethics of the Education Profession.' Therefore, the offering or accepting of employment in areas where sanctions are in effect should be evaluated in terms of the Code, and local, state, and national associations should continue to develop procedures for disciplining members who violate sanctions."

NJEA proclaimed through the local press that it would be "a violation of the professional code of ethics for any teacher to accept employment in Union Beach or for any administrator to offer employment in Union Beach as long as the sanctions which had been invoked were in effect."

It has long been the rule in our State that public employees may not strike. We recently refused to hold that teachers are beyond that ban, saying in *In re Block,* 50 N.J. 494, 499–500 (1967):

". . . Nor can defendants claim a right to strike under the State Constitution, Art. I, ¶ 19, upon the thesis that they are in private employment because teaching can be pursued under private auspices. We rejected the relevancy here of the distinction between 'governmental' and 'proprietary' functions in *Delaware River and Bay Authority.* When government undertakes itself to meet a need, it necessarily decides the public interest requires the service, and its employees cannot reverse or frustrate that decision by a concerted refusal to meet that need. In any event, teachers are ill-situated to profit from the distinction we have rejected, since the maintenance of a free public school system is mandated by the State Constitution itself. Art. VIII, § 4, ¶ 1."

And we have rejected the notion that public employees may resort to strike because they think their cause is just or in the public good. So, in discussing the contempt sentences imposed in *In re Buehrer,* 50 N.J. 501, 508 (1967), we said:

. . . Defendants say the trial court gave no weight to their claim that they struck and defied the order because of a frustration born of an inability to obtain for the school system what they believed it had to have. The prosecution disputes this claim of high purpose. The trial court of course did not evaluate the teachers' demands upon the Board, and neither do we. The notion that some higher right justifies concerted defiance of law can have no role in the courtroom. It cannot excuse; on the contrary, it emphasizes the deliberate nature of the violation. Nor can it meliorate the wrong, especially when the plea comes from public servants who should set the good example."

Defendants deny there was a "strike." They seek to distinguish the usual concerted refusal to work from what transpired here. As to the teachers employed by the Board, defendants say they merely resigned as of a future date, and with respect to the interference with the Board's recruitment of replacements, defendants, as we understand them, say a refusal to accept employment is inherently different from a quit. But the subject is the public service, and the distinctions defendants advance are irrelevant to it, however arguable they may be in the context of private employment. Unlike the private employer, a public agency may not retire. The public demand for services which makes illegal a strike against government inveighs against any other concerted action designed to deny government the necessary manpower, whether by terminating existing employments in any mode or by obstructing access to the labor market. Government may not be brought to a halt. So our criminal statute, N. J. S. 2A:98–1, provides in simple but persuasive terms that any two or more persons who conspire "to commit any act" for the "obstruction of . . . the due administration of the laws" are guilty of a misdemeanor.

Hence, although the right of an individual to resign or to refuse public employment is undeniable, yet two or more may not agree to follow a common course to the end that an agency of government shall be unable to function. Here there was such collective action by agreement both as to the quitting and as to new employment. As to the mass resignations, an agreement to that end must be inferred from the very adoption by the members through their teachers union of the program of sanctions which, despite some verbal obscurity in this regard, quite plainly imports an understanding to withdraw services when the union officialdom "imposes sanctions" upon a school district. The use of "unethical" in condemning new employment because of working conditions must mean is it also "unethical" to continue an existing employment under the same conditions. The full understanding must be that upon the imposition of sanctions, all services will be withdrawn. We have no doubt that the agreement to strike was not articulated because of the established illegality of that course. In any event, if it should be thought the plan did not include the obligation to quit in connection with the imposition of sanctions, we think it clear that the teachers entered into an agreement to quit when they voted in favor of mass resignations and then executed 36 of them. Although the Board accepted the resignations and hence does not ask that that work stoppage be ended, we are satisfied the stoppage was concerted action to an illegal end.

And with respect to blacklisting of the school district and the scheme of "sanctions" upon teachers who offer or take employment with a "sanctioned" school board, it can escape no one that the purpose is to back up a refusal of others to continue to work. At a minimum the object is to withhold additional services a school district may need to discharge its public duty, which, as we have said, is no less illegal. Such an illegal agreement may come into being at the time of the strike or may antedate it. If individuals enter into a union or association on terms that upon the occurrence of some stipulated event or signal they will impede government in its recruitment of services, that very arrangement constitutes an agreement the law denounces. An agreement not to seek, accept, or solicit employment in government whenever the upper eschelon of the union makes a prescribed pronouncement is, no less than an accomplished shutdown, a thrust at the vitality of government, and comes within the same policy which denounces a concerted strike or quit or slowdown or other obstruction of the performance of official duties.

The several actions taken pursuant to the so-called "Guidelines" are thus illegal even if tested in isolation from each other. But of course the so-called imposition of "sanctions" upon the Board, the mass resignations, and the threat of "sanctions" upon teachers who offer or accept new employment, are all part and parcel of a single illegal plan to block government. That the conventional terminology of a "strike" nowhere appears is of no moment. The substance of a situation and not its shape must control. A doctrine designed to protect the public interest is equal to any demand upon it. It does not yield to guise or ingenuity. . . .

Finally, we see no basis for invoking the clean-hands doctrine. It is enough to say, as the opinion of the trial court adequately reveals, that the doctrine will not be invoked when to do so will injure the public. It would be absurd to subject the public to the wrongs of defendants merely because the Board too may have acted improperly. . . .

Affirmed.

CASE QUESTIONS

1. What action by the Board precipitated the controversy?
2. What was the UBTA's reaction?
3. Did the teachers admit that there was a "strike"?
4. Do public employees have a right to resign or to refuse public employment?
5. What argument could the teachers make in favor of the equitable defense of "unclean hands"?
6. Was the court right in not invoking the "clean-hands" doctrine?

City of New York v. DeLury

New York State Court of Appeals, 1968. 23 N.Y. 2d 175

FULD, Ch. J.: We recently decided, in *Rankin* v. *Shanker* (23 N.Y. 2d 111), that public employees and labor organizations representing them were not entitled to a trial by jury in a criminal contempt proceeding for the violation of section 210, subdivision 1, of the Taylor Law.[2] In so holding, we concluded that a legislative classification "which differentiates between strikes by public employees and employees in private industry" is reasonable and does not offend against the constitutional guarantee of equal protection of the law (23 N.Y. 2d, at p. 118). The case now before us calls upon the court to determine, primarily, whether the Taylor Law's mandate that public employees shall not strike and that labor oganizations representing them shall not cause or encourage a strike violates due process requirements of the State or Federal Constitution.

At about seven o'clock in the morning of February 2, 1968, virtually all of the santitation men in the City of New York—employees of the Department of Sanitation—failed, without excuse, to report for work. Later in the day, at a demonstration in front of City Hall, members of the Uniformed Sanitation-men's Association (referred to herein as the "Union") were addressed by their president, the defendant DeLury, in these words:

> "Your sentiments before was go-go-go. I'd accept a motion for go-go-go (cheers). All in favor signify by saying yes (cheers). All opposed (boos). I didn't come here to bargain, I took a firm position with the City, I gave the members a final offer of this union. Now I want to show discipline here this morning—or this afternoon—I don't want to show where there is confusion in the members—You got a job at the locations to see that this is effective 100% (cheers)."

A nine-day strike, ending on the night of February 10, resulted. During that period, few, if any, of the sanitation men reported for work, in consequence of which garbage and refuse accumulated on the city streets at the rate of 10,000 tons a day. This constituted a serious health and fire threat; indeed, the Commissioner of Health characterized the "garbage situation" as "a serious one to the health of the city" and the Fire Commissioner declared that the Fire Department "experienced a marked increase in the number of outside rubbish fires."

On February 2, the very day the work stoppage began, the City instituted the present action to enjoin the defendants from "striking" and moved for a preliminary injunction. A temporary restraining order was granted which

---

[2] The Taylor Law was enacted in 1967 (L. 1967, ch. 392: Civil Service Law, art. 14, §§ 200–212) to supersede the Condon-Wadlin Act (L. 1947. Ch. 391, adding Civil Service Law, former § 22-a renum. by L. 1958, ch. 790; former § 108 of Civil Service Law). Like its predecessor, the Taylor Law prohibits strikes by public employees (§ 210, subd. 1) but, unlike Condon-Wadlin, it does not mandate termination of employment for its violation. The Taylor Law grants to all public employees (which, broadly speaking, includes all employees in the service of the State or any subdivision thereof) rights which in the main they did not formerly possess, namely, the right to be represented by employee organizations of their own choosing and the right to negotiate collectively with public employers and, in addition, the right to require public employees to negotiate and to enter into collective agreements with them. It sets up a Public Employment Relations Board—known as PERB—to "resolve disputes concerning the representation status of employee organizations" and to assist in the "voluntary resolution" of disputes between public employers and employee organizations." It also authorizes under the so-called "home rule" section (Civil Service Law, § 212), the adoption by local governments of "provisions and procedures" which are "substantially equivalent" to those of the Taylor Law. The New York City equivalent of such law is Local Law No. 53 of 1967 but the parties did not utilize the machinery therein provided for resolving disputes between the city and municipal employee organizations. All public employees, whether or not covered by the "home rule" section (§ 212), are subject to the statutory mandate of section 210, subdivision 1, of the Civil Service Law prohibiting them from striking.

enjoined the carrying on of the strike and required the leaders of the Union to instruct the members to return to work. Three days later, on February 5, the court at Special Term granted a preliminary injunction which again contained a directive to DeLury that he shall "forthwith instruct all members [of the Union] not to engage or participate in any strike, concerted stoppage of work or concerted slowdown against the plaintiff." Although because of the health and fire hazards involved, immediate compliance with the orders was vital, the members of the Union, as previously noted, remained away from their jobs until February 10.

An application, brought on by order to show cause, to punish the Union and DeLury for criminal contempt for wilfully disobeying the restraining order, came on for hearing before the court; the testimony adduced concerning the strike and its effects, as well as the conduct of DeLury, was substantially as outlined above. . . .

At the conclusion of the hearings, the court, dismissing charges which had also been asserted against other officers, found DeLury and the Union guilty of criminal contempt for wilfully disobeying its lawful mandate. It sentenced DeLury to 15 days in jail and fined him $250 and it fined the Union $80,000. In addition, the court ordered that the Union's right to dues check-off be forfeited for a period of 18 months. The Appellate Division affirmed Special Term's orders and granted the defendants leave to appeal to our court on a certified question.

We consider, first, the defendants' contention that the Taylor Law is unconstitutional on the ground that, in prohibiting strikes by public employees, it deprives them of due process of law. Manifestly, neither the Fourteenth Amendment to the Federal Constitution nor the Bill of Rights of the State Constitution (art. 1) grants to any individual an absolute right to strike. . . .

Although acknowledging that the right to strike is not absolute, the defendants would have us read the opinion in the *Auto Workers* case to mean that a prohibition against strikes will be upheld only where workers strike in violation of a no-strike clause or where there is a secondary boycott, violence or a trespass such as a sitdown. There is no basis for so narrowly viewing that decision. The Supreme Court did not limit the doctrine there applied to instances of illegal strikes mentioned by it. Rather, it laid down a general rule, applicable in all cases involving illegal strikes, namely, that the State, in governing its internal affairs, had the power to prohibit *any* strike if the prohibition was reasonably calculated to achieve a valid state policy in an area which was open to state regulation. (Cf. *Teamsters Union* v. *Vogt, Inc.,* 354 U.S. 284, 294–295).

Our query must, therefore, be whether the condemnation of strikes by public employees, as provided in the Taylor Law, does effectuate a valid policy of our State.

For many years, strikes against the Government have been outlawed by special legislation and by common law. Today, no less than 20 States have statutes condemning strikes by some or all of its public employees and at least seven States have achieved the same result by the application of common law principles. (See Rubin, A Summary of State Collective Bargaining Law in

Public Employment, published by Cornell University in 1968.) In addition, a Federal statute specifically provides that strikes by Federal employees are illegal (U.S. Code, tit. 5, § 7311). Substantial reasons are at hand for this almost universal condemnation of strikes by public employees. As Professor George W. Taylor, an outstanding authority in the field of labor relations and one of the architects of the Taylor Law, put it (Public Employment: Strikes or Procedures?, 20 Industrial and Labor Relations Rev. 617, 619),

> "One of the vital interests of the public which should be considered in the government-employee relationship is the ability of representative government to perform the functions of levying taxes and, through the budgeting of governmental resources, of establishing priorities among the government services desired by the body politic."

Quite obviously, the ability of the Legislature to establish priorities among government services would be destroyed if public employees could, with impunity, engage in strikes which deprive the public of essential services. The striking employees, by paralyzing a city through the exercise of naked power, could obtain gains wholly disproportionate to the services rendered by them and at the expense of the public and other public employees. The consequence would be the destruction of democratic legislative processes because budgeting and the establishment of priorities would no longer result from the free choice of the electorate's representatives but from the coercive effect of paralyzing strikes of public employees. . . .

The defendants' argument—that they are entitled to a trial by jury—may be disposed of summarily. In our decision in *Rankin* v. *Shanker* (23 N.Y. 2d 119, *supra*), as the lines already quoted from the opinion in that case establish, we expressly held that a jury trial in a criminal contempt proceeding (under § 753-a of the Judiciary Law and § 808 of the Labor Law) is not available to public employees, or to officers of labor organizations representing them, charged with violation of the Taylor Law (Civil Service Law, §§ 200 *et seq.*). This, of course, applies equally to the present defendants. . . .

In conclusion, then—section 210, subdivision 1, of the Civil Service Law designed to prevent the paralysis of Government, offends against no constitutional guarantee or requirement. Self-interest of individual or organization may not be permitted to endanger the safety, health or public welfare of the State or any of its subdivisions. There was here indisputable proof not only of deliberate disobedience of the explicit provisions of the Taylor Law but wilful defiance of the court's lawful mandates as well. Such defiance, the more egregious when committed by employees in the public sector, is not to be tolerated.

The order appealed from should be affirmed, with costs, and the question certified answered in the affirmative.

CASE QUESTIONS

1. What is the primary question the New York State Court of Appeals is called upon to determine?
2. What was defendant DeLury's role in the dispute?

3. What action did the lower court take against the defendant and the Union for violating the preliminary injunction?

4. In Professor Taylor's view, does condemnation of
strikes by public employees effectuate a valid policy for
a state government?

SECTION 109 / THE FEDERAL EMPLOYEE SECTOR

The legal structure underlying collective activities of federal government
employees has developed slowly compared to that regulating nongovernment
unionization and bargaining. For a great many years the influence of law was
negative toward union activity in both areas, injuring rather than protecting it.
We have seen how the common law, the equity powers and the anti-trust laws
were used to discourage all organizing tactics of labor in the period before the
legal revolution of the 1930's.

In the early part of the twentieth century the executive power of the President had been used to preclude even the lobbying activities by federal employee
representatives seeking to improve government employment conditions. President Theodore Roosevelt in the 1900's issued executive orders to prevent lobbying
efforts by prohibiting federal officers, employees or their associations from soliciting pay increases or legislation in Congress under the penalty of dismissal. In
the next administration President William Howard Taft repeated these restrictive
executive orders. Congress had moderated this restraint as to postal employees
by enacting the Lloyd-LaFollette Act to allow unaffiliated organizations to present their grievances to Congress without retaliation. Unionization of blue collar
employees in the Post Office Department, the Government Printing Office, the
Tennessee Valley Authority and U. S. Navy Yards had thereafter developed.
Unionization of the workers on railroads and later of industrial workers in the
mass production industries also increased after the Congress had enacted the
legislation to guarantee workers the right to engage in collective activities. The
National Labor Relations Act explicitly excluded all government agencies and
their employees from coverage and when it was amended in the effort to impose
restrictions on unions and their representatives in 1947, the Congress did not
entirely overlook the federal employees. It then included as Section 305 of the
new Labor Management Relations Act an absolute strike prohibition for any
U.S. government employee with violation to be subject to immediate discharge,
and reemployment barred in the civil service for three years.

Soon after John Kennedy became President in 1961, a task force on employer-employee relations in the federal service was appointed to investigate labor
relations in the federal government. It was then reported that one third of the
federal Civil Service employees already belonged to labor organizations, approx-
imating the percentage of unionization among all nongovernment, nonagricul-
tural employees. The study resulted in the proposal that the government should
respond affirmatively to organization by any considerable group of employees for
"collective dealing." The recommendations resulted in the signing of Executive
Order 10988 by President Kennedy. The Order provided that civilian employees

could organize and that organized employee groups in appropriate limits would be recognized. Excluded were any organizations asserting against the government the right to strike or advocating the overthrow of the government. Also excluded from recognition were organizations discriminating with regard to membership conditions because of race, color, creed or national origin.

Under Order 10988, a bureau or office of government primarily performing intelligence, investigative or security functions, including the FBI and the CIA, could be excluded from the Order by the determination of the head of the agency, if he believed it inconsistent with national security considerations. Like the National Labor Relations Act policy, units would not be accorded exclusive recognition if they included supervisory, managerial, executives or persons with special personnel responsibilities; professionals could be recognized separately or in a larger unit but only after a self-determination vote for such representation.

Management rights to direct and to discipline employees were specifically reserved by the Order, subject to all other applicable laws and regulations. The rules and regulations for implementing the Order were to be worked out after consultation with the representatives of the several existing employee organizations. Each agency management was itself to be responsible for determining appropriate bargaining units, and also deciding whether a majority of the employees in such a unit had designated a labor organization as their representative. A panel of qualified arbitrators was made available, however, for assisting in determining disputes over such issues by investigating the facts and then rendering advisory opinions, subject to management's acceptance or rejection.

The Civil Service Commission was authorized to assist in the carrying out of Order 10988 by providing technical advice to agencies as to employee-employer relations, and also by training management officials in such matters. It was also instructed to prepare jointly with the Department of Labor proposed standards of conduct for employee organizations as well as a code of fair labor practices for the federal service. The Secretary of Labor, the Secretary of Defense, the Civil Service Commission Chairman and the Postmaster General were to act as an advisory group to the President concerning the proposed codes and standards as well as to implement the program initially in other respects.

The substance of the Executive Order defined informal recognition for groups or organizations seeking to communicate with management; also formal recognition was to be accorded for those groups representing at least 10 percent of an appropriate unit; "exclusive representation recognition" was further provided for any organization selected by a majority. Although group recognition was thus to be implemented, the procedures for establishing appropriate bargaining units and for determination of majority choice disputes were clearly management oriented with management's authority emphasized throughout the Order. Explicitly stated also was the right of employees to refrain from joining any organization.

Deficiencies to sound improvement of labor relations lay in: (1) no provision for a central review or for impartial determinations of disputes concerning conditions of employment; (2) no substitute for no union rights to use economic action was provided; (3) the Order permitted no final and binding arbitration of grievances since arbitration could be advisory with only non-binding recommendations. Thus everything was left subject to the agency head's approval or disapproval. No provision was made to resolve disputed changes proposed for agreements or for agency policy except by determination of the department head, whose final decision could be subjected to no appeal. Executive Order 10988 was an improvement, but it created much confusion and dissent by reason of the management authority orientation, the lack of machinery for impartial review, and the failure to provide for good faith genuine bargaining. The concepts of informal and formal recognition were also to cause resentment, since it offered management a way to play one minority unit off against another, or indeed for several units to make management face dilemmas by making contradictory and inconsistent requests.

On May 21, 1963 the Standards of Conduct for Employee Organizations and a Code of Fair Labor Practices in the Federal Service were published as a Presidential document pursuant to Executive Order 10988.[3] To summarize the standards of conduct for employee organizations, recognition under the Executive Order required them to have internal democratic procedures and practices, to conduct periodic elections, to apply equal treatment to members and a fair process in disciplinary proceedings. Also, excluded from office were any persons identified with "corrupt influences" or affiliated with "Communist or other totalitarian moments," or engaging in interests conflicting with their duty to the employee organization and its members. It was mandatory further to provide accounting and financial controls and regular financial reports to be available to members, with the intent to maintain "fiscal integrity in the conduct of the affairs of the organization."

In addition to these Standards of Conduct, a Code of Fair Labor Practices was also adopted. The code prohibited agency management from engaging in the practices prohibited for private management similar to what is specified in the National Labor Relations Act's Section 8(a) unfair labor practices. Employee organizations were likewise prohibited from engaging in practices such as are included in the National Labor Relations Act in Section 8(b)(1) and (2)—but not the remaining unfair practice paragraphs. Also included, however, were prohibitions against coercing or taking reprisal against members to hinder or to impede the discharge of government, against denying membership or discriminating as to membership for race, color, creed or national origin. Enforcement methods for alleged violations of the code of Fair Labor Practices were left to each agency, subject to general procedures that were included in the Code.

The introduction of this new status for labor organizations in the Federal government under Executive Order 10988 gave much impetus to unionization of the public sector employees, similar to what the enactments of 1926 legislation had given to railroad workers, and the 1933 and 1935 legislation had provided for workers in manufacturing, mining, trucking and water transportation. With all its limitations, including the absence of real collective bargaining enforcement and no substitutes for the lack of economic power, it did nevertheless provide the stimulus for Federal and also indirectly for state and local employees to organize for bargaining directly with their government employers. In addition to the use of lobbying tactics that had been effectively applied in Congress by the Post Office workers and other organizations, the endorsement of union recog-

---

[3] Presidential Documents: Title 3—Memorandum of May 21, 1963.

nition for direct dealing induced also some state legislation for organizing and bargaining rights by the municipal, county and state employees.

But the limitations of Executive Order 10988 concerning good faith bargaining rights and the inadequate union power to compel genuine bargaining, where the last step was the department head with no external appeal, made the system unsatisfactory to the employees and to their representatives. These factors added to the fundamental difficulty that compensation and benefits, seniority rules and promotions, retirement and annual leave were set by a combination of legislation and civil service regulations that were largely non-negotiable.

Although at best collective action by government employees can never be as effective as in the private sector, the signing of the Executive Order developed considerable enthusiasm for union membership and hopes for action. Frustrations caused subsequent disillusionment, with threats of strike action and actual stoppages occuring among Air Traffic Controllers and Postal Workers.

To improve the program, President Nixon in 1969 signed Executive Order 11491, clarifying the responsibilities of employees, their representatives and government officials. Under the new system final authority no longer rests with the department concerned, since a permanent Federal Labor Relations Council has been created to interpret this Order, to make major policy decisions, and to hear appeals on various matters.

After an assistant Labor Secretary for labor-management relations has made judgments on allegations of violations of the unfair labor practices or the standards of conduct now incorporated into Executive Order 11491, he or she has authority to issue cease and desist orders against the government agency or against the labor organization (including orders for appropriate affirmative action similar to NLRB actions). The decisions may be appealed to the Labor Relations Council. The Council is composed of the Civil Service Commission Chairman as Council Chairman, the Secretary of Labor, an official of the President's Executive Office, and any other Executive Department officials whom the President selects to appoint. Also reviewable by the Council are any other decisions made by an assistant Secretary of Labor, regarding units for recognition or resulting from elections to determine majority choice within a unit.

Other changes include grievance procedures, with final arbitration of grievances allowed over disputed applications and interpretations of existing agreements, subject to exceptions that can be reviewed by the Federal Labor Relations Council. Additional detailed regulations on negotiating an agreement between an exclusively recognized organization and a Federal agency also define what may be covered in bargaining, the elements of good faith bargaining, the right to appeal to the Council, and the steps to take if negotiation impasses should occur. A further improvement added by Executive Order 11491 is a Federal Service Impasses Panel, an agency within the Council, appointed by the President, authorized by the Order "to take any action it considers necessary to settle an impasse." This may meet the major problem of the old system—the problem of management always having the final say.

Executive Order 11491, further amended in 1971 in a few minor details, has reduced if not eliminated most of the inconsistencies and confusions that existed previously over the duties and obligations of management as well as of the labor organization. With the clarification and substantive improvement of procedures, an interesting period in federal employee labor relations now exists. If the participants will utilize this carefully worked out system for due process in collective relations between federal employees and their managers, it will be an example to be used by other governmental jurisdictions for handling labor relations. Since Executive Orders have no permanence when a new President takes office, the provisions of #11491 might well be incorporated into a Congressional enactment after further experience indicates the pros and cons in practical terms.

SECTION 110 / **STATE AND LOCAL EMPLOYMENT**

Before the issuance of Executive Order 10899 in 1962, labor associations at all levels of government had lobbied for improvements in benefits and conditions rather than participating in formal collective bargaining or direct negotiation. After 1962, with the encouragement of organizing at the national level, state and local government workers renewed their efforts to get collective bargaining agreements. These efforts were accepted by the electorate, by local government officials, and by management. State legislation was enacted to prescribe standards and procedures for state and local government employer-employee consultation or negotiation for agreements.

Legislation for collective negotiations also came out of studies by a task force which was established by the National Governors' Conference. A number of state studies were undertaken by legislative or by tripartite committees or by a combination of legislative and bipartisan representatives in the industrialized and urbanized states where public sector bargaining problems had developed, including New York, New Jersey, Michigan, Illinois, Pennsylvania, Rhode Island, Minnesota and Connecticut. In a few states with restrictive employee relations legislation, the laws were revised. Some of the states undertook to draft and enact collective bargaining laws for the first time.

A complicated pattern has resulted. The legislative coverage of some state laws includes both state and municipal employment; in some states the law covers only municipal employees, often excluding policemen, and firemen and sometimes teachers. Special statutes for teachers exist in eleven states: California, Connecticut, Delaware, Maryland, Minnesota, Nebraska, North Dakota, Oregon, Rhode Island, Vermont, and Washington. Other local employees are covered by a separate statute in twelve states, while state employees only are covered in 13 jurisdictions. A single law that is identical for both state and local employees (distinguishing teachers or police or firefighters in some) exists in a few states.

The state laws differ not only in their jurisdiction or coverage but also in their substantive provisions. For example a number of these statutes require the government agency whose employees are represented by an employee organization to recognize it and to negotiate; some states provide only for the right to organize and "to meet and confer" with the management of the agency. Some state laws make bargaining mandatory with all state and local employees who are organized, except that teachers are to be accorded only the mandatory right to meet and to confer with the school officials representing the school board.

Many of the special teacher statutes allow the local school board to decide such important matters as the method for determination of majority representation or the extent that third party mediation will be employed; several of the states provide for proportional representation by employee organization councils where more than one organization may speak for the teachers.

A few states completely restrict unionization, having adopted laws that prohibit bargaining with organizations of public employees. In Texas a union, if not claiming the right to strike as to public employee members, is permitted to present grievances but not to bargain. North Carolina state and local employees were prohibited from being members of any nationally affiliated organization until a Federal Court held this to be an unconstitutional restriction; the court sustained, however, a provision forbidding state or local authorities from negotiating agreements.[4]

Where the law permits or requires collective bargaining negotiations and an impasse develops with inability to agree, usually the laws provide for mediation. A few states provide for fact-finding with recommendations by neutrals on the disputed issues (e.g. Connecticut, Massachusetts, Michigan, Minnesota, and Wisconsin).

In New York State the Conlin-Wadlin Law was revised in 1967 when the legislature enacted the Public Employees Fair Employment Law, following recommendations of a study committee. The Taylor Act, as it is called, continued the prohibition of strikes, but requires the public employer to negotiate with any recognized or certified organizations in an effort to reach agreement concerning wages and conditions of employment and grievance administration. A Public Employment Relations Board is established to resolve disputes over representation, with power to certify bargaining units and a majority choice, to institute mediation and fact finding if a bargaining impasse necessitates such steps, to impose penalties for strikes by termination of any union check-off privileges or by suspension of the union's certification. Other judicially imposed penalties may also be applied. A subsequent amendment in 1969 added "improper labor practices" that were prohibited for employers and for employee organizations, usually designated unfair practices.

The New York law makes no exclusion or special provision for any categories of employees such as police, firefighting, or teaching. The New York State Board has jurisdiction over all public employees, state and local; the statute allows establishment, through local legislation, of local public employment relations agencies, but subject to the State Board's exclusive jurisdiction over the "improper labor practice" administration and enforcement.

Since the effective date of the Taylor Act in September, 1967, over 90 percent of the New York state and local employees have exercised their rights in some 2,500 bargaining units with 1100 public employers.[5] The bulk of the reported disputes involved school districts. All costs of mediation and fact finding are borne by the State of New York, with the fact finding step comprising a compulsory submission of disagreements and the presentation of positions by both parties to a dispute.

Fact finding results in a report on the facts, accompanied by recommendations or advisory proposals for settling the remaining issues that have not been

---

[4] *Atkins* v. *City of Charlotte*, 70 LRRM 2732.
[5] Robert D. Helsby and Thomas E. Joyner, *Collective Bargaining in Government* (Englewood Cliffs: Prentice-Hall, Inc., 1972) p. 104.

resolved by agreement. Under the New York State legislation, however, final recourse, whenever the fact finding is not effective and a stalemate continues, consists of referring the matter to the legislature for a further hearing and action the legislature concludes necessary and appropriate. The possibility of partisan politics becoming a consideration in the final disposition of a matter may induce more effort of the parties to settle the problem themselves to avoid such political intervention. On the other hand, it may discourage bargaining concessions from a group believing the legislature would favor its position.

To accomplish final determination of public bargaining disputes and still avoid strikes, Rhode Island enacted legislation for compulsory collective bargaining with compulsory arbitration for all public employees at the state or local level. If the bargaining over the terms for an agreement results in a deadlock on issues other than wage and benefits, the parties must use arbitration which results in final and binding decisions made by an *ad hoc* tripartite board. Moreover, for disputes that involve fire or police departments, all matters including the economic issues are subject to binding awards. The appointment of the neutral chairman for each tripartite board follows his selection and agreement by the two nominees of the parties, subject to the rules and procedures of the American Arbitration Association. The latter is a nongovernment public service organization.

The unanimous award of a board in a Providence, Rhode Island, police dispute is printed below.[6] In addition to deciding the numerous issues in dispute, it expresses the critical opinion of the board as to the impact of the statutory process on the collective bargaining that preceded the arbitration.

Municipal labor relations usually come under the preemptive jurisdiction of the state legislation, a pattern which originated with enactment of a Wisconsin Municipal Employee Relations Act in 1959. As stated above, the New York State Taylor Law allows municipalities also to establish local labor relations agencies through local legislation. With New York City dealing with over 100 local unions affiliated with over 50 parent organizations, the City has enacted an ordinance establishing an Office of Collective Bargaining. Since it started to function in 1968, through 1971, it has handled over 300 bargaining unit negotiations, appointing impasse panels for deadlocked situations. After the garbage collectors' illegal strike in 1968 and a teachers' strike a year earlier, serious debate arose as to whether the public interest could be protected adequately by public dispute procedures that allow the union or the employer to reject the proposals of mediators and fact finders. As a result of discussions between the leaders of several major unions with which the city had agreements and the city officials with whom they negotiate, the City officials proposed an amendment to the City ordinance whereby the Office of Collective Bargaining could invoke compulsory arbitration if a threat of public injury through a strike warranted such a step. In March, 1972, the amendment was enacted with the assent of several of the city's major labor spokesmen.

The majority of all government employment is performed at municipal, county or other local levels of government. Most of the strikes occuring in government service are local; according to the Bureau of Labor Statistics data,

---

[6] *Fraternal Order of Police* and *City of Providence* (July, 1971).

in recent years local government stoppages were 15 times as frequent as state government stoppages in the three year period 1966 to 1968.[7] In addition to such work as garbage and waste collection and other trucking work performed directly by municipal or county employees, similar duties are extensively performed by private contractors. It has been argued that the law should provide equal rights and restrictions for all employed on similar public duties, regardless of the employer, since essentiality of the services is no different.

To meet the argument for equal treatment it has been suggested that legislation establish three categories of employment depending on the importance to the health and safety of the community. Police, fire fighting and prison work, for example, would be subject to full no-strike legislation with compulsory arbitration as the alternative terminal point for stalemated negotiations. For public hospital, or school and sanitation services workers as the next category, a limited right to strike would be incorporated into the legislation, subject to judicial review and injunctive prohibition upon a showing of a serious threat to the community. Other activities of government would be in a low priority class, to be handled like any private employment as far as bargaining and striking are involved. Unlike the present legal situation, such proposals place the emphasis on practical expediency with more concern for equity than for doctrinal absolutes or legal theory.

Whether to hold all strikes of public workers illegal or to allow some use of economic action not seriously imperiling the health, safety or welfare of the community is a question of public policy. The line between public inconvenience and public health or safety is a difficult one to draw except in relation to the facts of a specific situation. Secondary effects of interrupted public services may be as important as the immediate and obvious effects. Government clerks frequently perform work less related to community health or safety than services performed by private utility workers. Teachers strikes may be inconvenient but are usually less serious than those by drivers of food distributors, workers on railroads, milk companies or gasoline suppliers.

The essential problem of law is not whether to prohibit the use of the strike, but how to devise law that can effectively provide enforcement of strike prohibitions and provide at the same time acceptable substitutes to the use of strikes in essential services.

Fraternal Order of Police, Lodge #3 and City of Providence

Arbitration Board Decision

Pursuant to the Policeman's Arbitration Act of the General Laws of Rhode Island, Chapter 9.2 of Title 28, this Board consisting of Joseph Coleman, Arthur Novogroski, and A. Howard Myers as chairman, was named to decide the unresolved issues for an agreement to run from July 1, 1971.

At hearings conducted on June 14, June 30, and July 13, 1971, the parties

---

[7] Sheila C. White, "Work Stoppages of Government Employees," *Monthly Labor Review,* Vol. 92, No. 12 (December, 1969), p. 30.

were given full opportunity to present witnesses, documentary evidence, factual data, and arguments relative to the issues submitted for determination by the Board.

There remained for our decision at the conclusion of the hearings the following fifteen F.O.P. and seven City proposals: the coverage of transfers to other divisions, residence requirements, hours of work, overtime, call back pay, vacations, paid holidays, clothing allowance, clothing maintenance, severance pay, night shift differential, sick leave, group life insurance, salaries, hospital and physician cost protection, seniority definition, seniority loss, reduction of work force, renegotiation clause, union security indemnification, employment security clause, duration of agreement.

At the conclusion of the hearing on July 12, the members of the Arbitration Board held an executive session at which unanimity of opinion was reached on the award and on general points of view which needed to be stated clearly in this opinion. As the parties know, this is the third consecutive year in which they have failed to settle numerous differences over the terms for a new agreement. In addition to twenty-three separate issues left for our determination this year, an arbitration board last year was required to decide twenty-two issues. In the year before, fifteen issues were left for decision by that board.

This board has serious doubts as to the adequacy of the effort and good faith brought to the collective bargaining process, or the will of the parties to reach an agreement, or their willingness to give and take either on any particular item or in an exchange of one item for another. Without such willingness and flexibility on the part of both the City and the Lodge, a bargaining impasse is inevitable.

Little improvement appears from one year to the next in the direction of the parties themselves arriving at agreement; it might be said that the opposite of progress is shown in the increasing number of issues on which the parties rely on outsiders for determination. With mediation in addition to the negotiation, one would expect something more than behavior conditioned toward its impact on subsequent arbitration. In fact, we doubt whether that type of discussion can be called bargaining. It does not indicate the attitudes needed for reaching do-it-yourself settlements.

This dicta is relevant to our decision because it is our impression that elaborate presentations of data and argument on very complex issues would have been made to one another in bargaining if more effective results had been sought. The impasses that cause arbitration with the imposition of a contract by an arbitration board cannot improve collective bargaining; nor is maturity in the bargaining relations accomplished by contract awards of third parties who have neither the direct experience nor the omniscience to take over the responsibility of the parties in establishing the rules and terms to govern their future relations.

For these reasons we are of the unanimous opinion that we must reject some proposals as not having been sufficiently considered by the parties themselves. We have also endorsed several proposals that may meet constructively the problem raised, even though the counter-proposal requires more joint discussion between the parties.

On the basis of these considerations, we make these unanimous findings and award as follows: . . .

12) Article XII, Section 1   Salaries

A major disputed issue concerns revision of salaries. The present weekly salary scale, the City's proposal made during negotiations, the F.O.P. proposal (for 37 ½ hours) and the new salary scale are as follows:

	Current	*City*	*F.O.P.*	*Award*
Patrolman (appt.)........	$155	$167	$205	$155
Patrolman (12 mos.)......	159	171	215	171
Patrolman (18 mos.)......	162	174	225	175
Sergeant...............	178	190	250	196
Lieutenant.............	190	202	275	209
Captain	205	217	300	226

Because the evidence shows no pattern to support the requests and because of the additional cost of the new salary scale, the following proposed changes are rejected:
a) A 10% night relief differential
b) Longevity compensation

13) Article XIV, Section 1   Blue Cross-Blue Shield and Life Insurance

The proposals of F.O.P. have been reviewed. The evidence submitted does not support the request for Plan B Blue Cross but it does sustain the requested major medical family insurance (80% up to $10,000) as provided by 10 of the 15 cities and by 16 Rhode Island towns. The data also shows 9 of 15 cities and 7 of the towns now provide life insurance, the amount approximating $5,000. We therefore find as part of the award that the parties shall negotiate a plan for $10,000 of family major medical protection and $5,000 life insurance coverage, or the equivalent, to be effective January 1, 1972, at the latest.

14) Article XX, Section 1   Duration

The F.O.P. requests a one-year term while the City proposes a three-year term with a cost of living adjustment for the second and third years. We are restricted by the fact that the statute limits us to a one-year agreement unless a longer term is mutually accepted. Since the arbitrators have no discretion to award more than the Union proposal, the period from July 1, 1971, to June 30, 1972, with retroactivity from July 1, 1971, we are awarding accordingly.

CASE QUESTIONS

1. Does the decision indicate that compulsory arbitration encourages the bargaining process?
2. Why was there "doubt that that type of discussion can be called bargaining"?
3. Why would the statute prevent the board of arbitration from awarding a contract term longer than one year?
4. What appears to be the statutory standard applied by the Board in reaching its decision on the economic impasse?

SECTION 111 / EVALUATION OF PROGRESS AND PROBLEMS

The legal foundation created by the executive orders and the legislative enactments in the 1960's underwrote the permanence of public employee unionization and collective bargaining at the local, state and national levels. Much of the development stemmed from the extension into public service of the private industry practices and the public policies that were implemented by the National Labor Relations Act. But a number of legal questions and complications are unique to the public sector and require some further consideration.

The federal program for bargaining rights and procedures, as revised and improved by the 1969 Executive Order, No. 11491, established a constructive basis for meeting the limitations and the deficiencies of the 1962 Executive Order. A major difficulty remains in the fact of the impermanent authority of an executive order as compared to Congressional legislation. What a President can create by order, another President may terminate or emasculate by another order. Although it would arouse vehement opposition, disestablishment of the collective bargaining process in the national government by a President hostile to its continuance remains a legal possibility until Congress enacts a more permanent long-range legislative foundation.

As a byproduct of the 1962 Executive order the state and local legislative pattern changed considerably, as has been indicated. The variety of the enactments in different states, the total lack of laws in many of the states, and the existence of conflicts between the existing law and other unrelated legal requirements on public management have created confusion and frustrations. This lack of clarity and the lack of law in some jurisdictions of government has caused the unions operating in state, county and local collective bargaining to suggest the adoption by Congressional preemption of at least minimum local standards for union-government relations which would be mandatory in all states.

Some of the legal difficulties to collective negotiations at the level of local government arise, as previously discussed, from the extent of management authority and the limitations imposed by civil service laws and regulations. Wages, leave of absence proposals, job specifications, rate differentials based on job specifications, and merit pay programs are frequently outside of the scope of collective bargaining because legally they are beyond the discretion of the bargaining negotiators. In many local governments the state has preempted all authority over such personnel matters by legislative action. The bargaining process in such states becomes secondary, with primary attention and effort turned by labor to lobbying activity at the state capital.

A separate but related obstacle to public service negotiating arises from the fiscal restraints imposed by law. The need for state approval of local tax programs, and the inability to raise funds by other than a real property tax also can interfere with bargaining. The resultant lack of income or of new sources of funds can be like a straight jacket imposed on the management of a local department or a district. Faced with the statutory duty to bargain, and such a legal obstacle to making any reasonable counterproposal, the public official is in an unyielding legal trap.

Another problem in the fiscal aspects of public bargaining, the law usually requires the filing of a budget based on estimated future needs. Bargaining, mediation and fact finding are time-consuming processes; the management representatives may be obliged to take a rigid position on economic issues based on earlier budget estimates previously submitted under statutory requirements. Further, when additional funds are needed for retroactive wage payments under an agreement or an arbitration award, more budgetary difficulties are created. Some laws preclude such payments unless provided for in the budget for the calendar period involved. The problem of coordinating collective bargaining and budget making requirements under the local or state laws often requires statutory revisions. Alteration of the time of bargaining to an earlier date might eliminate this inconsistency between the two functions of government administration.

Other legal restrictions on the bargaining process arise from constitutional questions as to the legality of conceding demands for union shop membership requirements in agreements, for dues check-off provisions, or for compulsory grievance arbitration provisions where different internal appeal procedures are written into a state law. These problems and similar conflicts usually exist when the state mandates collective bargaining. If a state legislates terms of employment conditions, or fiscal administration requirements that create obstacles for the bargainers, it defeats its own policy at the level where most of the bargaining takes place, in the local communities. Failure of public sector collective bargaining to function may eventually result from such restraints imposed by law on the bargaining representatives of local public management.

QUESTIONS ON CHAPTER 13

1. Should employees covered by civil service regulations have legal protection for bargaining representation? Give reasons.
2. What contradictions may exist between the two systems of government working-condition regulation, civil service and collective bargaining?
3. How has the federal government provided for bargaining rights?
4. How has the federal government provided for dispute resolution in bargaining?
5. Do state employees all have equal rights to unionize?
6. What is the relation of municipal labor relations to state legislation?
7. Is the right of local employees to bargain impeded by having taken away the legal right to strike? What substitutes do the laws provide?

Appendix

The National Labor Relations Act and the Labor Management Relations Act, 1947, as Amended by the Reporting and Disclosure Act of 1959 *

[PUBLIC LAW 101—80TH CONGRESS]

AN ACT to amend the National Labor Relations Act, to provide additional facilities for the mediation of labor disputes affecting commerce, to equalize legal responsibilities of labor organizations and employers, and for other purposes.

Be it enacted by the Senate and House of Representatives of the United States of America in Congress assembled,

Short Title and Declaration of Policy

Sec. 1. (a) This Act may be cited as the "Labor Management Relations Act, 1947."

(b) Industrial strife which interferes with the normal flow of commerce and with the full production of articles and commodities for commerce, can be avoided or substantially minimized if employers, employees, and labor organizations each

---

* Section 201(d) and (e) of the Labor-Management Reporting and Disclosure Act of 1959 which repealed Section 9(f), (g), and (h) of the Labor Management Relations Act, 1947, and Section 505 amending Section 302(a), (b), and (c) of the Labor Management Relations Act, 1947, took effect upon enactment of Public Law 86–257, September 14, 1959. As to the other amendments of the Labor Management Relations Act, 1947, Section 707 of the Labor-Management Reporting and Disclosure Act provides:

The amendments made by this title shall take effect sixty days after the date of the enactment of this Act and no provision of this title shall be deemed to make an unfair labor practice, any act which is performed prior to such effective date which did not constitute an unfair labor practice prior thereto.

recognize under law one another's legitimate rights in their relations with each other, and above all recognize under law that neither party has any right in its relations with any other to engage in acts or practices which jeopardize the public health, safety, or interest.

It is the purpose and policy of this Act, in order to promote the full flow of commerce, to prescribe the legitimate rights of both employees and employers in their relations affecting commerce, to provide orderly and peaceful procedures for preventing the interference by either with the legitimate rights of the other, to protect the rights of individual employees in their relations with labor organizations whose activities affect commerce, to define and proscribe practices on the part of labor and management which affect commerce and are inimical to the general welfare, and to protect the rights of the public in connection with labor disputes affecting commerce.

TITLE I
Amendment of National Labor Relations Act

Sec. 101. The National Labor Relations Act is hereby amended to read as follows:

Findings and Policies

Sec. 1. The denial by some employers of the right of employees to organize and the refusal by some employers to accept the procedure of collective bargaining lead to strikes and other forms of industrial strife or unrest, which have the intent or the necessary effect of burdening or obstructing commerce by (a) impairing the efficiency, safety, or operation of the instrumentalities of commerce; (b) occurring in the current of commerce; (c) materially affecting, restraining, or controlling the flow of raw materials or manufactured or processed goods from or into the channels of commerce, or the prices of such materials or goods in commerce; or (d) causing diminution of employment and wages in such volume as substantially to impair or disrupt the market for goods flowing from or into the channels of commerce.

The inequality of bargaining power between employees who do not possess full freedom of association or actual liberty of contract, and employers who are organized in the corporate or other forms of ownership association substantially burdens and affects the flow of commerce, and tends to aggravate recurrent business depressions, by depressing wage rates and the purchasing power of wage earners in industry and by preventing the stabilization of competitive wage rates and working conditions within and between industries.

Experience has proved that protection by law of the right of employees to organize and bargain collectively safeguards commerce from injury, impairment, or interruption, and promotes the flow of commerce by removing certain recognized sources of industrial strife and unrest, by encouraging practices fundamental to the friendly adjustment of industrial disputes arising out of differences as to wages, hours, or other working conditions, and by restoring equality of bargaining power between employers and employees.

Experience has further demonstrated that certain practices by some labor organizations, their officers, and members have the intent or the necessary effect of burdening or obstructing commerce by preventing the free flow of goods in such commerce through strikes and other forms of industrial unrest or through concerted activities which impair the interest of the public in the free flow of such commerce. The elimination of such practices is a necessary condition to the assurance of the rights herein guaranteed.

It is hereby declared to be the policy of the United States to eliminate the causes of certain substantial obstructions to the free flow of commerce and to mitigate and eliminate these obstructions when they have occurred by encouraging the practice and procedure of collective bargaining and by protecting the exercise by workers of full freedom of association, self-organization, and designation of representatives of their own choosing, for the purpose of negotiating the terms and conditions of their employment or other mutual aid or protection.

Definitions

Sec. 2. When used in this Act—

(1) The term "person" includes one or more individuals, labor organizations, partnerships, associations, corporations, legal representatives, trustees, trustees in bankruptcy, or receivers.

(2) The term "employer" includes any person acting as an agent of an employer, directly or indirectly, but shall not include the United States or any wholly owned Government corporation, or any Federal Reserve Bank, or any State or political subdivision thereof, or any corporation or association operating a hospital, if no part of the net earnings inures to the benefit of any private shareholder or individual, or any person subject to the Railway Labor Act, as amended from time to time, or any labor organization (other than when acting as an employer), or anyone acting in the capacity of officer or agent of such labor organization.

(3) The term "employee" shall include any employee, and shall not be limited to the employees of a particular employer, unless the Act explicitly states otherwise, and shall include any individual whose work has ceased as a consequence of, or in connection with, any current labor dispute or because of any unfair labor practice, and who has not obtained any other regular and

substantially equivalent employment, but shall not include any individual employed as an agricultural laborer, or in the domestic service of any family or person at his home, or any individual employed by his parent or spouse, or any individual having the status of an independent contractor, or any individual employed as a supervisor, or any individual employed by an employer subject to the Railway Labor Act, as amended from time to time, or by any other person who is not an employer as herein defined.

(4) The term "representatives" includes any individual or labor organization.

(5) The term "labor organization" means any organization of any kind, or any agency or employee representation committee or plan, in which employees participate and which exists for the purpose, in whole or in part, of dealing with employers concerning grievances, labor disputes, wages, rates of pay, hours of employment, or conditions of work.

(6) The term "commerce" means trade, traffic, commerce, transportation, or communication among the several States, or between the District of Columbia or any Territory of the United States and any State or other Territory, or between any foreign country and any State, Territory, or the District of Columbia, or within the District of Columbia or any Territory, or between points in the same State but through any other State or any Territory or the District of Columbia or any foreign country.

(7) The term "affecting commerce" means in commerce, or burdening or obstructing commerce or the free flow of commerce, or having led or tending to lead to a labor dispute burdening or obstructing commerce or the free flow of commerce.

(8) The term "unfair labor practice" means any unfair labor practice listed in section 8.

(9) The term "labor dispute" includes any controversy concerning terms, tenure or conditions of employment, or concerning the association or representation of persons in negotiating, fixing, maintaining, changing, or seeking to arrange terms or conditions of employment, regardless of whether the disputants stand in the proximate relation of employer and employee.

(10) The term "National Labor Relations Board" means the National Labor Relations Board provided for in section 3 of this Act.

(11) The term "supervisor" means any individual having authority, in the interest of the employer, to hire, transfer, suspend, lay off, recall, promote, discharge, assign, reward, or discipline other employees, or responsibly to direct them, or to adjust their grievances, or effectively to recommend such action, if in connection with the foregoing the exercise of such authority is not of a merely routine or clerical nature, but requires the use of independent judgment.

(12) The term "professional employee" means—

(a) any employee engaged in work (i) predominantly intellectual and varied in character as opposed to routine mental, manual, mechanical, or physical work; (ii) involving the consistent exercise of discretion and judgment in its performance; (iii) of such a character that the output produced or the result accomplished cannot be standardized in relation to a given period of time; (iv) requiring knowledge of an advanced type in a field of science or learning customarily acquired by a prolonged course of specialized intellectual instruction and study in an institution of higher learning or a hospital, as distinguished from a general academic education or from an apprenticeship or from training in the performance of routine mental, manual, or physical processes; or

(b) any employee, who (i) has completed the courses of specialized intellectual instruction and study described in clause (iv) of paragraph (a), and (ii) is performing related work under the supervision of a professional person to qualify himself to become a professional employee as defined in paragraph (a).

(13) In determining whether any person is acting as an "agent" of another person so as to make such other person responsible for his acts, the question of whether the specific acts performed were actually authorized or subsequently ratified shall not be controlling.

National Labor Relations Board

Sec. 3. (a) The National Labor Relations Board (hereinafter called the "Board") created by this Act prior to its amendment by the Labor Management Relations Act, 1947, is hereby continued as an agency of the United States, except that the Board shall consist of five instead of three members, appointed by the President by and with the advice and consent of the Senate. Of the two additional members so provided for, one shall be appointed for a term of five years and the other for a term of two years. Their successors, and the successors of the other members, shall be appointed for terms of five years each, excepting that any individual chosen to fill a vacancy shall be appointed only for the unexpired term of the member whom he shall succeed. The President shall designate one member to serve as Chairman of the Board. Any member of the Board may be removed by the President, upon notice and hearing, for neglect of duty or malfeasance in office, but for no other cause.

(b) The Board is authorized to delegate to any group of three or more members any or all of the powers which it may itself exercise. The Board is also authorized to delegate to its regional directors its powers under section 9 to determine the unit appropriate for the purpose of collective bargaining, to investigate and provide for hearings, and determine whether a question of representation exists, and to direct an election or take a secret ballot under subsection (c) or (e) of Section 9 and certify the results thereof, except that upon the filing of a request therefor with the Board by any interested person, the Board may review any action of a regional director delegated to him under this paragraph, but such a review shall not, unless specifically ordered by the Board, operate as a stay of any action taken by the regional director. A vacancy in the Board shall not impair the right of the remaining members to exercise all of the powers of the Board, and three members of the Board shall, at all times, constitute a quorum of the Board, except that two members shall constitute a quorum of any group designated pursuant to the first sentence hereof. The Board shall have

an official seal which shall be judicially noticed.

(c) The Board shall at the close of each fiscal year make a report in writing to Congress and to the President stating in detail the cases it has heard, the decisions it has rendered, the names, salaries, and duties of all employees and officers in the employ or under the supervision of the Board, and an account of all moneys it has disbursed.

(d) There shall be a General Counsel of the Board who shall be appointed by the President, by and with the advice and consent of the Senate, for a term of four years. The General Counsel of the Board shall exercise general supervision over all attorneys employed by the Board (other than trial examiners and legal assistants to Board members) and over the officers and employees in the regional offices. He shall have final authority, on behalf of the Board, in respect of the investigation of charges and issuance of complaints under section 10, and in respect of the prosecution of such complaints before the Board, and shall have such other duties as the Board may prescribe or as may be provided by law. In case of a vacancy in the office of the General Counsel the President is authorized to designate the officer or employee who shall act as General Counsel during such vacancy, but no person or persons so designated shall so act (1) for more than forty days when the Congress is in session unless a nomination to fill such vacancy shall have been submitted to the Senate, or (2) after the adjournment *sine die* of the session of the Senate in which such nomination was submitted.

Sec. 4. (a) Each member of the Board and the General Counsel of the Board shall receive a salary of $12,000 * a year, shall be eligible for reappointment, and shall not engage in any other business, vocation, or employment. The Board shall appoint an

---

* Pursuant to Public Law 90–206, 90th Congress, 81 Stat. 644, approved December 16, 1967, and in accordance with Section 225(f)(ii) thereof, effective in 1969, the salary of the Chairman of the Board shall be $40,000 per year and the salaries of the General Counsel and each Board member shall be $38,000 per year.

executive secretary, and such attorneys, examiners, and regional directors, and such other employees as it may from time to time find necessary for the proper performance of its duties. The Board may not employ any attorneys for the purpose of reviewing transcripts of hearings or preparing drafts of opinions except that any attorney employed for assignment as a legal assistant to any Board member may for such Board member review such transcripts and prepare such drafts. No trial examiner's report shall be reviewed, either before or after its publication, by any person other than a member of the Board or his legal assistant, and no trial examiner shall advise or consult with the Board with respect to exceptions taken to his findings, rulings, or recommendations. The Board may establish or utilize such regional, local, or other agencies, and utilize such voluntary and uncompensated services, as may from time to time be needed. Attorneys appointed under this section may, at the direction of the Board, appear for and represent the Board in any case in court. Nothing in this Act shall be construed to authorize the Board to appoint individuals for the purpose of conciliation or mediation, or for economic analysis.

(b) All of the expenses of the Board, including all necessary traveling and subsistence expenses outside the District of Columbia incurred by the members or employees of the Board under its orders, shall be allowed and paid on the presentation of itemized vouchers therefor approved by the Board or by any individual it designates for that purpose.

Sec. 5. The principal office of the Board shall be in the District of Columbia, but it may meet and exercise any or all of its powers at any other place. The Board may, by one or more of its members or by such agents or agencies as it may designate, prosecute any inquiry necessary to its functions in any part of the United States. A member who participates in such an inquiry shall not be disqualified from subsequently participating in a decision of the Board in the same case.

Sec. 6. The Board shall have authority from time to time to make, amend, and rescind, in the manner prescribed by the Administrative Procedure Act, such rules and regulations as may be necessary to carry out the provisions of this Act.

Rights of Employees

Sec. 7. Employees shall have the right to self-organization, to form, join, or assist labor organizations, to bargain collectively through representatives of their own choosing, and to engage in other concerted activities for the purpose of collective bargaining or other mutual aid or protection, and shall also have the right to refrain from any or all of such activities except to the extent that such right may be affected by an agreement requiring membership in a labor organization as a condition of employment as authorized in section 8(a)(3).

Unfair Labor Practices

Sec. 8. (a) It shall be an unfair labor practice for an employer—

(1) to interfere with, restrain, or coerce employees in the exercise of the rights guaranteed in section 7;

(2) to dominate or interfere with the formation or administration of any labor organization or contribute financial or other support to it: *Provided,* That subject to rules and regulations made and published by the Board pursuant to section 6, an employer shall not be prohibited from permitting employees to confer with him during working hours without loss of time or pay;

(3) by discrimination in regard to hire or tenure of employment or any term or condition of employment to encourage or discourage membership in any labor organization: *Provided,* That nothing in this Act, or in any other statute of the United States, shall preclude an employer from making an agreement with a labor organization (not established, maintained, or assisted by any action defined in section 8(a) of this Act as an unfair labor practice) to require as a condition of employment membership therein on or after the thirtieth day following the beginning of such employment or the effective date of such

agreement, whichever is the later, (i) if such labor organization is the representative of the employees as provided in section 9(a), in the appropriate collective-bargaining unit covered by such agreement when made; and (ii) unless following an election held as provided in section 9(e) within one year preceding the effective date of such agreement, the Board shall have certified that at least a majority of the employees eligible to vote in such election have voted to rescind the authority of such labor organization to make such an agreement: *Provided further,* That no employer shall justify any discrimination against an employee for nonmembership in a labor organization (A) if he has reasonable grounds for believing that such membership was not available to the employee on the same terms and conditions generally applicable to other members, or (B) if he has reasonable grounds for believing that membership was denied or terminated for reasons other than the failure of the employee to tender the periodic dues and the initiation fees uniformly required as a condition of acquiring or retaining membership;

(4) to discharge or otherwise discriminate against an employee because he has filed charges or given testimony under this Act;

(5) to refuse to bargain collectively with the representatives of his employees, subject to the provisions of section 9(a).

(b) It shall be an unfair labor practice for a labor organization or its agents—

(1) to restrain or coerce (A) employees in the exercise of the rights guaranteed in section 7: *Provided,* That this paragraph shall not impair the right of a labor organization to prescribe its own rules with respect to the acquisition or retention of membership therein; or (B) an employer in the selection of his representatives for the purposes of collective bargaining or the adjustment of grievances;

(2) to cause or attempt to cause an employer to discriminate against an employee in violation of subsection (a)(3) or to discriminate against an employee with

respect to whom membership in such organization has been denied or terminated on some ground other than his failure to tender the periodic dues and the initiation fees uniformly required as a condition of acquiring or retaining membership;

(3) to refuse to bargain collectively with an employer, provided it is the representative of his employees subject to the provisions of section 9(a);

(4) (i) to engage in, or to induce or encourage any individual employed by any person engaged in commerce or in an industry affecting commerce to engage in, a strike or a refusal in the course of his employment to use, manufacture, process, transport, or otherwise handle or work on any goods, articles, materials, or commodities or to perform any services; or (ii) to threaten, coerce, or restrain any person engaged in commerce or in an industry affecting commerce, where in either case an object thereof is:

(A) forcing or requiring any employer or self-employed person to join any labor or employer organization or to enter into any agreement which is prohibited by section 8(e);

(B) forcing or requiring any person to cease using, selling, handling, transporting, or otherwise dealing in the products of any other producer, processor, or manufacturer, or to cease doing business with any other person, or forcing or requiring any other employer to recognize or bargain with a labor organization as the representative of his employees unless such labor organization has been certified as the representative of such employees under the provisions of section 9: *Provided,* That nothing contained in this clause (B) shall be construed to make unlawful, where not otherwise unlawful, any primary strike or primary picketing;

(C) forcing or requiring any employer to recognize or bargain with a particular labor organization as the representative of his employees if another labor organization has been certified as the representative of such employees under the provisions of section 9;

(D) forcing or requiring any employer to assign particular work to employees in a particular labor organization or in a particular trade, craft, or class rather than to employees in another labor organization or in another trade, craft, or class, unless such employer is failing to conform to an order or certification of the Board determining the bargaining representative for employees performing such work:

Provided, That nothing contained in this subsection (b) shall be construed to make unlawful a refusal by any person to enter upon the premises of any employer (other than his own employer), if the employees of such employer are engaged in a strike ratified or approved by a representative of such employees whom such employer is required to recognize under this Act: *Provided further,* That for the purposes of this paragraph (4) only, nothing contained in such paragraph shall be construed to prohibit publicity, other than picketing, for the purpose of truthfully advising the public, including consumers and members of a labor organization, that a product or products are produced by an employer with whom the labor organization has a primary dispute and are distributed by another employer, as long as such publicity does not have an effect of inducing any individual employed by any person other than the primary employer in the course of his employment to refuse to pick up, deliver, or transport any goods, or not to perform any services, at the establishment of the employer engaged in such distribution;

(5) to require of employees covered by an agreement authorized under subsection (a)(3) the payment, as a condition precedent to becoming a member of such organization, of a fee in an amount which the Board finds excessive or discriminatory under all the circumstances. In making such a finding, the Board shall consider, among other relevant factors, the practices and customs of labor organizations in the particular industry, and the wages currently paid to the employees affected;

(6) to cause or attempt to cause an employer to pay or deliver or agree to pay or deliver any money or other thing of value, in the nature of an exaction, for services which are not performed or not to be performed; and

(7) to picket or cause to be picketed, or threaten to picket or cause to be picketed, any employer where an object thereof is forcing or requiring an employer to recognize or bargain with a labor organization as the representative of his employees, or forcing or requiring the employees of an employer to accept or select such labor organization as their collective bargaining representative, unless such labor organization is currently certified as the representative of such employees:

(A) where the employer has lawfully recognized in accordance with this Act any other labor organization and a question concerning representation may not appropriately be raised under section 9(c) of this Act,

(B) where within the preceding twelve months a valid election under section 9(c) of this Act has been conducted, or

(C) where such picketing has been conducted without a petition under section 9(c) being filed within a reasonable period of time not to exceed thirty days from the commencement of such picketing: *Provided,* That when such a petition has been filed the Board shall forthwith, without regard to the provisions of section 9(c)(1) or the absence of a showing of a substantial interest on the part of the labor organization, direct an election in such unit as the Board finds to be appropriate and shall certify the results thereof: *Provided further,* That nothing in this subparagraph (C) shall be construed to prohibit any picketing or other publicity for the purpose of truthfully advising the public (including consumers) that an employer does not employ members of, or have a contract with, a labor organization, unless an effect of such picketing is to induce any individual employed by any other person in the course of his employment, not to pick up, deliver or transport any goods or not to perform any services.

Nothing in this paragraph (7) shall be construed to permit any act which would otherwise be an unfair labor practice under this section 8(b).

(c) The expressing of any views, argument, or opinion, or the dissemination thereof, whether in written, printed, graphic, or visual form, shall not constitute or be evidence of an unfair labor practice under any of the provisions of this Act, if such expression contains no threat of reprisal or force or promise of benefit.

(d) For the purposes of this section, to bargain collectively is the performance of the mutual obligation of the employer and the representative of the employees to meet at reasonable times and confer in good faith with respect to wages, hours, and other terms and conditions of employment, or the negotiation of an agreement, or any question arising thereunder, and the execution of a written contract incorporating any agreement reached if requested by either party, but such obligation does not compel either party to agree to a proposal or require the making of a concession: *Provided,* That where there is in effect a collective-bargaining contract covering employees in an industry affecting commerce, the duty to bargain collectively shall also mean that no party to such contract shall terminate or modify such contract, unless the party desiring such termination or modification—

(1) serves a written notice upon the other party to the contract of the proposed termination or modification sixty days prior to the expiration date thereof, or in the event such contract contains no expiration date, sixty days prior to the time it is proposed to make such termination or modification;

(2) offers to meet and confer with the other party for the purpose of negotiating a new contract or a contract containing the proposed modifications;

(3) notifies the Federal Mediation and Conciliation Service within thirty days after such notice of the existence of a dispute, and simultaneously therewith notifies any State or Territorial agency established to mediate and conciliate disputes within the State or Territory where the dispute occurred, provided no agreement has been reached by that time; and

(4) continues in full force and effect, without resorting to strike or lockout, all the terms and conditions of the existing contract for a period of sixty days after such notice is given or until the expiration date of such contract, whichever occurs later;

The duties imposed upon employers, employees, and labor organizations by paragraphs (2), (3), and (4) shall become inapplicable upon an intervening certification of the Board, under which the labor organization or individual, which is a party to the contract, has been superseded as or ceased to be the representative of the employees subject to the provisions of section 9(a), and the duties so imposed shall not be construed as requiring either party to discuss or agree to any modification of the terms and conditions contained in a contract for a fixed period, if such modification is to become effective before such terms and conditions can be reopened under the provisions of the contract. Any employee who engages in a strike within the sixty-day period specified in this subsection shall lose his status as an employee of the employer engaged in the particular labor dispute, for the purposes of sections 8, 9, and 10 of this Act, as amended, but such loss of status for such employee shall terminate if and when he is reemployed by such employer.

(e) It shall be an unfair labor practice for any labor organization and any employer to enter into any contract or agreement, express or implied, whereby such employer ceases or refrains or agrees to cease or refrain from handling, using, selling, transporting or otherwise dealing in any of the products of any other employer, or to cease doing business with any other person, and any contract or agreement entered into heretofore or hereafter containing such an agreement shall be to such extent unenforcible and void: *Provided,* That nothing in this subsection (e) shall apply to an agreement between a labor organization and an employer in the construction industry relating to the contracting or subcontracting of work to be done at the site of the construction, alteration, painting, or repair of a building, structure, or other work: *Provided further,* That for the purposes of this subsection (e) and section 8(b)(4)(B) the terms "any employer," "any person engaged in commerce or an industry affecting commerce," and "any person" when used in relation to the terms "any other producer, processor, or manufacturer," "any other employer," or "any other person" shall not include persons in the relation of a jobber, manufacturer, contractor, or subcontractor working on the goods or premises of the jobber or manufacturer or performing parts of an integrated process of production in the apparel and clothing industry: *Provided further,* That nothing in this Act shall prohibit the enforcement of any agreement which is within the foregoing exception.

(f) It shall not be unfair labor practice under subsections (a) and (b) of this section for an employer engaged primarily in the building and construction industry to make an agreement covering employees engaged (or who, upon their employment, will be engaged) in the building and construction industry with a labor organization of which building and construction employees are members (not established, maintained, or assisted by any action defined in section 8(a) of this Act as an unfair labor practice) because (1) the majority status of such labor organization has not been established under the provisions of section 9 of this Act prior to the making of such agreement, or (2) such agreement requires as a condition of employment, membership in such labor organization after the seventh day following the beginning of such employment or the effective date of the agreement, whichever is later, or (3) such agreement requires the employer to notify such labor organization of opportunities for employment with such employer, or gives such labor organization an opportunity to refer qualified applicants for such employment, or (4) such agreement specifies minimum training or experience qualifications for employment or provides for priority in opportunities for employment based upon length of service with such employer, in the industry or in the particular geographical area: *Provided,* That nothing in this subsection shall set aside the final proviso to section 8(a)(3) of this Act: *Provided further,* That any agreement which would be invalid, but for clause (1) of this subsection, shall not be a bar to a petition filed pursuant to section 9(c) or 9(e).*

Representatives and Elections

Sec. 9. (a) Representatives designated or selected for the purposes of collective bargaining by the majority of the employees in a unit appropriate for such purposes, shall be the exclusive representatives of all the employees in such unit for the purposes of collective bargaining in respect to rates of pay, wages, hours of employment, or other conditions of employment: *Provided,* That any individual employee or a group of employees shall have the right at any time to present grievances to their employer and to have such grievances adjusted, without the intervention of the bargaining representative, as long as the adjustment is not inconsistent with the terms of a collective-bargaining contract or agreement then in effect: *Provided further,* That the bargaining representative has been given opportunity to be present at such adjustment.

(b) The Board shall decide in each case whether, in order to assure to employees the fullest freedom in exercising the rights guaranteed by this Act, the unit appropri-

---

* Section 8(f) is inserted in the Act by subsection (a) of Section 705 of Public Law 86–257. Section 705(b) provides:

Nothing contained in the amendment made by subsection (a) shall be construed as authorizing the execution or application of agreements requiring membership in a labor organization as a condition of employment in any State or Territory in which such execution or application is prohibited by State or Territorial law.

ate for the purposes of collective bargaining shall be the employer unit, craft unit, plant unit, or subdivision thereof: *Provided,* That the Board shall not (1) decide that any unit is appropriate for such purposes if such unit includes both professional employees and employees who are not professional employees unless a majority of such professional employees vote for inclusion in such unit; or (2) decide that any craft unit is inappropriate for such purposes on the ground that a different unit has been established by a prior Board determination, unless a majority of the employees in the proposed craft unit vote against separate representation or (3) decide that any unit is appropriate for such purposes if it includes, together with other employees, any individual employed as a guard to enforce against employees and other persons rules to protect property of the employer or to protect the safety of persons on the employer's premises; but no labor organization shall be certified as the representative of employees in a bargaining unit of guards if such organization admits to membership, or is affiliated directly or indirectly with an organization which admits to membership, employees other than guards.

(c) (1) Whenever a petition shall have been filed, in accordance with such regulations as may be prescribed by the Board—

(A) by an employee or group of employees or any individual or labor organization acting in their behalf alleging that a substantial number of employees (i) wish to be represented for collective bargaining and that their employer declines to recognize their representative as the representative defined in section 9(a), or (ii) assert that the individual or labor organization, which has been certified or is being currently recognized by their employer as the bargaining representative, is no longer a representative as defined in section 9(a); or

(B) by an employer, alleging that one or more individuals or labor organizations have presented to him a claim to be recognized as the representative defined in section 9(a);

the Board shall investigate such petition and if it has reasonable cause to believe that a question of representation affecting commerce exists shall provide for an appropriate hearing upon due notice. Such hearing may be conducted by an officer or employee of the regional office, who shall not make any recommendations with respect thereto. If the Board finds upon the record of such hearing that such a question of representation exists, it shall direct an election by secret ballot and shall certify the results thereof.

(2) In determining whether or not a question of representation affecting commerce exists, the same regulations and rules of decision shall apply irrespective of the identity of the persons filing the petition or the kind of relief sought and in no case shall the Board deny a labor organization a place on the ballot by reason of an order with respect to such labor organization or its predecessor not issued in conformity with section 10(c).

(3) No election shall be directed in any bargaining unit or any subdivision within which, in the preceding twelve-month period, a valid election shall have been held. Employees engaged in an economic strike who are not entitled to reinstatement shall be eligible to vote under such regulations as the Board shall find are consistent with the purposes and provisions of this Act in any election conducted within twelve months after the commencement of the strike. In any election where none of the choices on the ballot receives a majority, a run-off shall be conducted, the ballot providing for a selection between the two choices receiving the largest and second largest number of valid votes cast in the election.

(4) Nothing in this section shall be construed to prohibit the waiving of hearings by stipulation for the purpose of a consent election in conformity with regulations and rules of decision of the Board.

(5) In determining whether a unit is appropriate for the purposes specified in subsection (b) the extent to which the employees have organized shall not be controlling.

(d) Whenever an order of the Board made pursuant to section 10(c) is based in whole or in part upon facts certified following an investigation pursuant to subsection (c) of this section there is a petition for the enforcement or review of such order, such certification and the record of such investigation shall be included in the transcript of the entire record required to be filed under section 10(e) or 10(f), and thereupon the decree of the court enforcing, modifying, or setting aside in whole or in part the order of the Board shall be made and entered upon the pleadings, testimony, and proceedings set forth in such transcript.

(e) (1) Upon the filing with the Board, by 30 per centum or more of the employees in a bargaining unit covered by an agreement between their employer and a labor organization made pursuant to section 8(a) (3), of a petition alleging they desire that such authority be rescinded, the Board shall take a secret ballot of the employees in such unit, and shall certify the results thereof to such labor organization and to the employer.

(2) No election shall be conducted pursuant to this subsection in any bargaining unit or any subdivision within which, in the preceding twelve-month period, a valid election shall have been held.

Prevention of Unfair Labor Practices

Sec. 10. (a) The Board is empowered, as hereinafter provided, to prevent any person from engaging in any unfair labor practice (listed in section 8) affecting commerce. This power shall not be affected by any other means of adjustment or prevention that has been or may be established by agreement, law, or otherwise: *Provided,* That the Board is empowered by agreement with any agency of any State or Territory to cede to such agency jurisdiction over any cases in any industry (other than mining, manufacturing, communications, and transportation except where predominantly local in character) even though such cases may involve labor disputes affecting commerce, unless the provision of the State or Territorial statute applicable to the determination of such cases by such agency is inconsistent with the corresponding provision of this Act or has received a construction inconsistent therewith.

(b) Whenever it is charged that any person has engaged in or is engaging in any unfair labor practice, the Board, or any agent or agency designated by the Board for such purposes, shall have power to issue and cause to be served upon such person a complaint stating the charges in that respect, and containing a notice of hearing before the Board or a member thereof, or before a designated agent or agency, at a place therein fixed, not less than five days after the serving of said complaint: *Provided,* That no complaint shall issue based upon any unfair labor practice occurring more than six months prior to the filing of the charge with the Board and the service of a copy thereof upon the person against whom such charge is made, unless the person aggrieved thereby was prevented from filing such charge by reason of service in the armed forces, in which event the six-month period shall be computed from the day of his discharge. Any such complaint may be amended by the member, agent, or agency conducting the hearing or the Board in its discretion at any time prior to the issuance of an order based thereon. The person so complained of shall have the right to file an answer to the original or amended complaint and to appear in person or otherwise and give testimony at the place and time fixed in the complaint. In the discretion of the member, agent, or agency conducting the hearing or the Board, any other person may be allowed to intervene in the said proceeding and to present testimony. Any such proceeding shall, so far as practicable, be conducted in accordance with the rules of evidence applicable in the district courts of the United States under the rules of civil procedure for the district courts of the United States, adopted by the Supreme Court of the United States pursuant to the Act of June 19, 1934 (U.S.C., title 28, secs. 723-B, 723-C).

(c) The testimony taken by such member, agent, or agency or the Board shall be reduced to writing and filed with the Board. Thereafter, in its discretion, the Board upon notice may take further testimony or hear argument. If upon the preponderance of the testimony taken the Board shall be of the opinion that any person named in the complaint has engaged in or is engaging in any such unfair labor practice, then the Board shall state its findings of fact and shall issue and cause to be served on such person an order requiring such person to cease and desist from such unfair labor practice, and to take such affirmative action including reinstatement of employees with or without back pay, as will effectuate the policies of this Act: *Provided,* That where an order directs reinstatement of an employee, back pay may be required of the employer or labor organization, as the case may be, responsible for the discrimination suffered by him: *And provided further,* That in determining whether a complaint shall issue alleging a violation of section 8(a)(1) or section 8(a)(2), and in deciding such cases, the same regulations and rules of decision shall apply irrespective of whether or not the labor organization affected is affiliated with a labor organization national or international in scope. Such order may further require such person to make reports from time to time showing the extent to which it has complied with the order. If upon the preponderance of the testimony taken the Board shall not be of the opinion that a person named in the complaint has engaged in or is engaging in any such unfair labor practice, then the Board shall state its findings of fact and shall issue an order dismissing the said complaint. No order of the Board shall require the reinstatement of any individual as an employee who has been suspended or discharged, or the payment to him of any back pay, if such individual was suspended or discharged for cause. In case the evidence is presented before a member of the Board, or before an examiner or examiners thereof, such member, or such examiner or examiners, as the case may be, shall issue and cause to be served on the parties to the proceeding a proposed report, together with a recommended order, which shall be filed with the Board, and if no exceptions are filed within twenty days after service thereof upon such parties, or within such further period as the Board may authorize, such recommended order shall become the order of the Board and become effective as therein prescribed.

(d) Until the record in a case shall have been filed in a court, as hereinafter provided, the Board may at any time, upon reasonable notice and in such manner as it shall deem proper, modify or set aside, in whole or in part, any finding or order made or issued by it.

(e) The Board shall have power to petition any court of appeals of the United States, or if all the courts of appeals to which application may be made are in vacation, any district court of the United States, within any circuit or district, respectively, wherein the unfair labor practice in question occurred or wherein such person resides or transacts business, for the enforcement of such order and for appropriate temporary relief or restraining order, and shall file in the court the record in the proceedings, as provided in section 2112 of title 28, United States Code. Upon the filing of such petition, the court shall cause notice thereof to be served upon such person, and thereupon shall have jurisdiction of the proceeding and of the question determined therein, and shall have power to grant such temporary relief or restraining order as it deems just and proper, and to make and enter a decree enforcing, modifying, and enforcing as so modified, or setting aside in whole or in part the order of the Board. No objection that has not been urged before the Board, its member, agent, or agency, shall be considered by the court, unless the failure or neglect to urge such objection shall be excused because of extraordinary circumstances. The findings of the Board with respect to questions of fact if supported by substantial evidence on the record considered as a whole shall be conclusive. If either party shall apply to the court for leave to adduce additional evidence and shall show to the satisfaction of the court that such additional evidence is material and that there were reasonable grounds for the failure to adduce such evidence in the hearing before the Board, its member, agent, or agency, the court may order such additional evidence to be taken before the Board, its member, agent, or agency, and to be made a part of the record. The Board may modify its findings as to the facts, or make new findings, by reason of additional evidence so taken and filed, and it shall file such modified or new findings, which findings with respect to questions of fact if supported by substantial evidence on the record considered as a whole shall be conclusive, and shall file its recommendations, if any, for the modification or setting aside of its original order. Upon the filing of the record with it the jurisdiction of the court shall be exclusive and its judgment and decree shall be final, except that the same shall be subject to review by the appropriate United States court of appeals if application was made to the district court as hereinabove provided, and by the Supreme Court of the United States upon writ of certiorari or certification as provided in section 1254 of title 28.

(f) Any person aggrieved by a final order of the Board granting or denying in whole or in part the relief sought may obtain a review of such order in any circuit court of appeals of the United States in the circuit wherein the unfair labor practice in question was alleged to have been engaged in or wherein such person resides or transacts business, or in the United States Court of Appeals for the District of Columbia, by filing in such court a written petition praying that the order of the Board be modified or set aside. A copy of such petition shall be forthwith transmitted by the clerk of the court to the Board, and thereupon the aggrieved party shall file in the court the record in the proceeding, certified by the Board, as provided in section 2112 of title 28, United States Code. Upon the filing of such petition, the court shall proceed in the same manner as in the case of an application by the Board under subsection (e) of this section, and shall have the same jurisdiction to grant to the Board such temporary relief or restraining order as it deems just and proper, and in like manner to make and enter a decree enforcing, modifying, and enforcing as so modified, or setting aside in whole or in part the order of the Board; the findings of the Board with respect to questions of fact if supported by substantial evidence on the record considered as a whole shall in like manner be conclusive.

(g) The commencement of proceedings under subsection (e) or (f) of this section shall not, unless specifically ordered by the court, operate as a stay of the Board's order.

(h) When granting appropriate temporary relief or a restraining order, or making and entering a decree enforcing, modifying, and enforcing as so modified, or setting aside in whole or in part an order of the Board, as provided in this section, the jurisdiction of courts sitting in equity shall not be limited by the Act entitled "An Act to amend the Judicial Code and to define and limit the jurisdiction of courts sitting in equity, and for other purposes," approved March 23, 1932 (U.S.C., Supp. VII, title 29, secs. 101–115).

(i) Petitions filed under this Act shall be heard expeditiously, and if possible within ten days after they have been docketed.

(j) The Board shall have power, upon issuance of a complaint as provided in subsection (b) charging that any person has engaged in or is engaging in an unfair labor practice, to petition any district court of the United States (including the District Court of the United States for the District of Columbia), within any district wherein the unfair labor practice in question is alleged to have occurred or wherein such person resides or transacts business, for appropriate temporary relief or restraining order. Upon the filing of any such petition the court shall cause notice thereof to be served upon such person, and thereupon shall have jurisdiction to grant to the Board such temporary relief or restraining order as it deems just and proper.

(k) Whenever it is charged that any person has engaged in an unfair labor practice within the meaning of paragraph (4)(D) of section 8(b), the Board is empowered and directed to hear and determine the dispute out of which such unfair labor practice shall have arisen, unless, within ten days after notice that such charge has been filed, the parties to such dispute submit to the Board satisfactory evidence that they have adjusted, or agreed upon methods for the voluntary adjustment of, the dispute. Upon compliance by the parties to the dispute with the decision of the Board or upon such voluntary adjustment of the dispute, such charge shall be dismissed.

(1) Whenever it is charged that any person has engaged in an unfair labor practice within the meaning of paragraph (4)(A), (B), or (C) of section 8(b), or section 8(e) or section 8(b)(7), the preliminary investigation of such charge shall be made forthwith and given priority over all other cases except cases of like character in the office where it is filed or to which it is referred. If, after such investigation, the officer or regional attorney to whom the matter may be referred has reasonable cause to believe such charge is true and that a complaint should issue, he shall, on behalf of the Board, petition any district court of the United States (including the District Court of the United States for the District of Columbia) within any district where the unfair labor practice in question has occurred, is alleged to have occurred, or wherein such person resides or transacts business, for appropriate injunctive relief pending the final adjudication of the Board with respect to such matter. Upon the filing of any such petition the district court shall have jurisdiction to grant such injunctive relief or temporary restraining order as it deems just and proper, notwithstanding any other provision of law: *Provided further,* That no temporary restraining order shall be issued without notice unless a petition alleges that substantial and irreparable injury to the charging party will be unavoidable and such temporary restraining order shall be effective for no longer than five days and will become void at the expiration of such period. *Provided further,* That such officer or regional attorney shall not apply for any restraining order under section 8(b)(7) if a charge against the employer under section 8(a)(2) has been filed and after the preliminary investigation, he has reasonable cause to believe that such charge is true and that a complaint should issue. Upon filing of any such petition the courts shall cause notice thereof to be served upon any person involved in the charge and such person, including the charging party, shall be given an opportunity to appear by counsel and present any relevant testimony: *Provided further,* That for the purposes of this sub-

section district courts shall be deemed to have jurisdiction of a labor organization (1) in the district in which such organization maintains its principal office, or (2) in any district in which its duly authorized officers or agents are engaged in promoting or protecting the interests of employee members. The service of legal process upon such officer or agent shall constitute service upon the labor organization and make such organization a party to the suit. In situations where such relief is appropriate the procedure specified herein shall apply to charges with respect to section 8(b)(4)(D).

(m) Whenever it is charged that any person has engaged in an unfair labor practice within the meaning of subsection (a)(3) or (b)(2) of section 8, such charge shall be given priority over all other cases except cases of like character in the office where it is filed or to which it is referred and cases given priority under subsection (1).

Investigatory Powers

Sec. 11. For the purpose of all hearings and investigations, which, in the opinion of the Board, are necessary and proper for the exercise of the powers vested in it by section 9 and section 10—

(1) The Board, or its duly authorized agents or agencies, shall at all reasonable times have access to, for the purpose of examination, and the right to copy any evidence of any person being investigated or proceeded against that relates to any matter under investigation or in question. The Board, or any member thereof, shall upon application of any party to such proceedings, forthwith issue to such party subpenas requiring the attendance and testimony of witnesses or the production of any evidence in such proceeding or investigation requested in such application. Within five days after the service of a subpena on any person requiring the production of any evidence in his possession or under his control, such person may petition the Board to revoke, and the Board shall revoke, such subpena if in its opinion the evidence whose production is required does not relate to any matter under investigation, or any matter in question in such proceedings, or if in

its opinion such subpena does not describe with sufficient particularity the evidence whose production is required. Any member of the Board, or any agent or agency designated by the Board for such purposes, may administer oaths and affirmations, examine witnesses, and receive evidence. Such attendance of witnesses and the production of such evidence may be required from any place in the United States or any Territory or possession thereof, at any designated place of hearing.

(2) In case of contumacy or refusal to obey a subpena issued to any person, any district court of the United States or the United States courts of any Territory or possession, or the District Court of the United States for the District of Columbia, within the jurisdiction of which the inquiry is carried on or within the jurisdiction of which said person guilty of contumacy or refusal to obey is found or resides or transacts business, upon application by the Board shall have jurisdiction to issue to such person an order requiring such person to appear before the Board, its member, agent, or agency, there to produce evidence if so ordered, or there to give testimony touching the matter under investigation or in question; and any failure to obey such order of the court may be punished by said court as a contempt thereof.

(3) *

(4) Complaints, orders, and other process and papers of the Board, its member, agent, and agency, may be served either personally or by registered mail or by telegraph or by leaving a copy thereof at the principal office or place of business of the person required to be served. The verified return by the individual so serving the same setting forth the manner of such service shall be proof of the same, and the return post office receipt or telegraph receipt therefor when registered and mailed or telegraphed as aforesaid shall be proof of service of the same. Witnesses summoned before the Board, its member, agent, or

---

* Section 11(3) is repealed by Sec. 234, Public Law 91–452, 91st Congress, S. 30, 84 Stat. 926, October 15, 1970. See Title 18, U.S.C. Sec 6001, et seq.

agency, shall be paid the same fees and mileage that are paid witnesses in the courts of the United States, and witnesses whose depositions are taken and the persons taking the same shall severally be entitled to the same fees as are paid for like services in the courts of the United States.

(5) All process of any court to which application may be made under this Act may be served in the judicial district wherein the defendant or other person required to be served resides or may be found.

(6) The several departments and agencies of the Government, when directed by the President, shall furnish the Board, upon its request, all records, papers, and information in their possession relating to any matter before the Board.

Sec. 12. Any person who shall willfully resist, prevent, impede, or interfere with any member of the Board or any of its agents or agencies in the performance of duties pursuant to this Act shall be punished by a fine of not more than $5,000 or by imprisonment for not more than one year, or both.

Limitations

Sec. 13. Nothing in this Act, except as specifically provided for herein, shall be construed so as either to interfere with or impede or diminish in any way the right to strike, or to affect the limitations or qualifications on that right.

Sec. 14. (a) Nothing herein shall prohibit any individual employed as a supervisor from becoming or remaining a member of a labor organization, but no employer subject to this Act shall be compelled to deem individuals defined herein as supervisors as employees for the purpose of any law, either national or local, relating to collective bargaining.

(b) Nothing in this Act shall be construed as authorizing the execution or application of agreements requiring membership in a labor organization as a condition of employment in any State or Territory in which such execution or application is prohibited by State or Territorial law.

(c) (1) The Board, in its discretion, may, by rule of decision or by published rules adopted pursuant to the Administrative Procedure Act, decline to assert jurisdiction over any labor dispute involving any class or category of employers, where, in the opinion of the Board, the effect of such labor dispute on commerce is not sufficiently substantial to warrant the exercise of its jurisdiction: *Provided,* That the Board shall not decline to assert jurisdiction over any labor dispute over which it would assert jurisdiction under the standards prevailing upon August 1, 1959.

(2) Nothing in this Act shall be deemed to prevent or bar any agency or the courts of any State or Territory (including the Commonwealth of Puerto Rico, Guam, and the Virgin Islands), from assuming and asserting jurisdiction over labor disputes over which the Board declines, pursuant to paragraph (1) of this subsection, to assert jurisdiction.

Sec. 15. Wherever the application of the provisions of section 272 of chapter 10 of the Act entitled "An Act to establish a uniform system of bankruptcy throughout the United States," approved July 1, 1898, and Acts amendatory thereof and supplementary thereto (U.S.C., title 11, sec. 672), conflicts with the application of the provisions of this Act, this Act shall prevail: *Provided,* That in any situation where the provisions of this Act cannot be validly enforced, the provisions of such other Acts shall remain in full force and effect.

Sec. 16. If any provision of this Act, or the application of such provision to any person or circumstances, shall be held invalid, the remainder of this Act, or the application of such provision to persons or circumstances other than those as to which it is held invalid, shall not be affected thereby.

Sec. 17. This Act may be cited as the "National Labor Relations Act."

Sec. 18. No petition entertained, no investigation made, no election held, and no certification issued by the National Labor Relations Board, under any of the provisions of section 9 of the National Labor Relations Act, as amended, shall be invalid by reason of the failure of the Congress of Industrial Organizations to have complied with the requirements of section 9(f), (g),

or (h) of the aforesaid Act prior to December 22, 1949, or by reason of the failure of the American Federation of Labor to have complied with the provisions of section 9(f), (g), or (h) of the aforesaid Act prior to November 7, 1947: *Provided,* That no liability shall be imposed under any provision of this Act upon any person for failure to honor any election or certificate referred to above, prior to the effective date of this amendment: *Provided, however,* That this proviso shall not have the effect of setting aside or in any way affecting judgments or decrees heretofore entered under section 10(e) or (f) and which have become final.

Effective Date of Certain Changes *

Sec. 102. No provision of this title shall be deemed to make an unfair labor practice any act which was performed prior to the date of the enactment of this Act which did not constitute an unfair labor practice prior thereto, and the provisions of section 8(a)(3) and section 8(b)(2) of the National Labor Relations Act as amended by this title shall not make an unfair labor practice the performance of any obligation under a collective-bargaining agreement entered into prior to the date of the enactment of this Act, or (in the case of an agreement for a period of not more than one year) entered into on or after such date of enactment, but prior to the effective date of this title, if the performance of such obligation would not have constituted an unfair labor practice under section 8(3) of the National Labor Relations Act prior to the effective date of this title, unless such agreement was renewed or extended subsequent thereto.

Sec. 103. No provisions of this title shall affect any certification or representatives or any determination as to the appropriate collective-bargaining unit, which was made under section 9 of the National Labor Relations Act prior to the effective date of this title until one year after the date of such certification or if, in respect of any such certification, a collective-bargaining

---

* The effective date referred to in Sections 102, 103, and 104 is August 22, 1947.

contract was entered into prior to the effective date of this title, until the end of the contract period or until one year after such date, whichever first occurs.

Sec. 104. The amendments made by this title shall take effect sixty days after the date of the enactment of this Act, except that the authority of the President to appoint certain officers conferred upon him by section 3 of the National Labor Relations Act as amended by this title may be exercised forthwith.

TITLE II
Conciliation of Labor Disputes in Industries Affecting Commerce; National Emergencies

Sec. 201. That it is the policy of the United States that—

(a) sound and stable industrial peace and the advancement of the general welfare, health, and safety of the Nation and of the best interests of employers and employees can most satisfactorily be secured by the settlement of issues between employers and employees through the processes of conference and collective bargaining between employers and the representatives of their employees;

(b) the settlement of issues between employers and employees through collective bargaining may be advanced by making available full and adequate governmental facilities for conciliation, mediation, and voluntary arbitration to aid and encourage employers and the representatives of their employees to reach and maintain agreements concerning rates of pay, hours, and working conditions, and to make all reasonable efforts to settle their differences by mutual agreement reached through conferences and collective bargaining or by such methods as may be provided for in any applicable agreement for the settlement of disputes; and

(c) certain controversies which arise between parties to collective-bargaining agreements may be avoided or minimized by making available full and adequate governmental facilities for furnishing assistance to employers and the representatives of their employees in formulating for inclusion with such agreements provision for adequate notice of any proposed changes in the terms of such agreements, for the final adjustment of grievances or questions regarding the application or interpretation of such agreements, and other provisions designed to prevent the subsequent arising of such controversies.

Sec. 202. (a) There is hereby created an independent agency to be known as the Federal Mediation and Conciliation Service (herein referred to as the "Service," except that for sixty days after the date of the enactment of this Act such term shall refer to the Conciliation Service of the Department of Labor). The Service shall be under the direction of a Federal Mediation and Conciliation Director (hereinafter referred to as the "Director"), who shall be appointed by the President by and with the advice and consent of the Senate. The Director shall receive compensation at the rate of 12,000 * per annum. The Director shall not engage in any other business, vocation, or employment.

(b) The Director is authorized, subject to the civil-service laws, to appoint such clerical and other personnel as may be necessary for the execution of the functions of the Service, and shall fix their compensation in accordance with the Classification Act of 1923, as amended, and may, without regard to the provisions of the civil-service laws and the Classification Act of 1923, as amended, appoint and fix the compensation of such conciliators and mediators as may be necessary to carry out the functions of the Service. The Director is authorized to make such expenditures for supplies, facilities, and services as he deems necessary. Such expenditures shall be allowed and paid upon presentation of itemized vouchers therefor approved by the Director or by any employee designated by him for that purpose.

(c) The principal office of the Service

---

* Pursuant to Public Law 90–206, 90th Congress, 81 Stat. 644, approved December 16, 1967, in accordance with Sec 225(f)(ii) thereof, effective in 1969, the salary of the Director shall be $40,000 per year.

shall be in the District of Columbia, but the Director may establish regional offices convenient to localities in which labor controversies are likely to arise. The Director may by order, subject to revocation at any time, delegate any authority and discretion conferred upon him by this Act to any regional director, or other officer or employee of the Service. The Director may establish suitable procedures for cooperation with State and local mediation agencies. The Director shall make an annual report in writing to Congress at the end of the fiscal year.

(d) All mediation and conciliation functions of the Secretary of Labor or the United States Conciliation Service under section 8 of the Act entitled "An Act to create a Department of Labor," approved March 4, 1913 (U.S.C., title 29, sec. 51), and all functions of the United States Conciliation Service under any other law are hereby transferred to the Federal Mediation and Conciliation Service, together with the personnel and records of the United States Conciliation Service. Such transfer shall take effect upon the sixtieth day after the date of enactment of this Act. Such transfer shall not affect any proceedings pending before the United States Conciliation Service or any certification, order, rule, or regulation theretofore made by it or the Secretary of Labor. The Director and the Service shall not be subject in any way to the jurisdiction or authority of the Secretary of Labor or any official or division of the Department of Labor.

Functions of the Service

Sec. 203. (a) It shall be the duty of the Service, in order to prevent or minimize interruptions of the free flow of commerce growing out of labor disputes, to assist parties to labor disputes in industries affecting commerce to settle such disputes through conciliation and mediation.

(b) The Service may proffer its services in any labor dispute in any industry affecting commerce, either upon its own motion or upon the request of one or more of the parties to the dispute, whenever in its judgment such dispute threatens to cause a substantial interruption of commerce. The Director and the Service are directed to avoid attempting to mediate disputes which would have only a minor effect on interstate commerce if State or other conciliation services are available to the parties. Whenever the Service does proffer its services in any dispute, it shall be the duty of the Service promptly to put itself in communication with the parties and to use its best efforts, by mediation and conciliation, to bring them to agreement.

(c) If the Director is not able to bring the parties to agreement by conciliation within a reasonable time, he shall seek to induce the parties voluntarily to seek other means of settling the dispute without resort to strike, lock-out, or other coercion, including submission to the employees in the bargaining unit of the employer's last offer of settlement for approval or rejection in a secret ballot. The failure or refusal of either party to agree to any procedure suggested by the Director shall not be deemed a violation of any duty or obligation imposed by this Act.

(d) Final adjustment by a method agreed upon by the parties is hereby declared to be the desirable method for settlement of grievance disputes arising over the application or interpretation of an existing collective-bargaining agreement. The Service is directed to make its conciliation and mediation services available in the settlement of such grievance disputes only as a last resort and in exceptional cases.

Sec. 204 (a) In order to prevent or minimize interruptions of the free flow of commerce growing out of labor disputes, employers and employees and their representatives, in any industry affecting commerce, shall—

(1) exert every reasonable effort to make and maintain agreements concerning rates of pay, hours, and working conditions, including provision for adequate notice of any proposed change in the terms of such agreements;

(2) whenever a dispute arises over the terms or application of a collective-bargaining agreement and a conference is requested by a party or prospective party thereto, arrange promptly for such a conference to be held and endeavor in such conference to settle such dispute expeditiously; and

(3) in case such dispute is not settled by conference, participate fully and promptly in such meetings as may be undertaken by the Service under this Act for the purpose of aiding in a settlement of the dispute.

Sec. 205. (a) There is hereby created a National Labor-Management Panel which shall be composed of twelve members appointed by the President, six of whom shall be selected from among persons outstanding in the field of management and six of whom shall be selected from among persons outstanding in the field of labor. . . .

(b) It shall be the duty of the panel, at the request of the Director, to advise in the avoidance of industrial controversies and the manner in which mediation and voluntary adjustment shall be administered, particularly with reference to controversies affecting the general welfare of the country.

National Emergencies

Sec. 206. Whenever in the opinion of the President of the United States, a threatened or actual strike or lock-out affecting an entire industry or a substantial part thereof engaged in trade, commerce, transportation, transmission, or communication among the several States or with foreign nations, or engaged in the production of goods for commerce, will, if permitted to occur or to continue, imperil the national health or safety, he may appoint a board of inquiry to inquire into the issues involved in the dispute and to make a written report to him within such time as he shall prescribe. Such report shall include a statement of the facts with respect to the dispute, including each party's statement of its position but shall not contain any recommendations. The President shall file a copy of such report with the Service and shall make its contents available to the public.

Sec. 207. (a) A board of inquiry shall be composed of a chairman and such other members as the President shall determine, and shall have power to sit and act in any place within the United States and to conduct such hearings either in public or in private, as it may deem necessary or proper, to ascertain the facts with respect to the causes and circumstances of the dispute.

(b) Members of a board of inquiry shall receive compensation at the rate of $50 for each day actually spent by them in the work of the board, together with necessary travel and subsistence expenses.

(c) For the purpose of any hearing or inquiry conducted by any board appointed under this title, the provisions of sections 9 and 10 (relating to the attendance of witnesses and the production of books, papers, and documents) of the Federal Trade Commission Act of September 16, 1914, as amended (U.S.C. 19, title 15, secs. 49 and 50, as amended), are hereby made applicable to the powers and duties of such board.

Sec. 208. (a) Upon receiving a report from a board of inquiry the President may direct the Attorney General to petition any district court of the United States having jurisdiction of the parties to enjoin such strike or lock-out or the continuing thereof, and if the court finds that such threatened or actual strike or lock-out—

(i) affects an entire industry or a substantial part thereof engaged in trade, commerce, transportation, transmission, or communication among the several States or with foreign nations, or engaged in the production of goods for commerce; and

(ii) if permitted to occur or to continue, will imperil the national health or safety, it shall have jurisdiction to enjoin any such strike or lock-out, or the continuing thereof, and to make such other orders as may be appropriate.

(b) In any case, the provisions of the Act of March 23, 1932, entitled "An Act to amend the Judicial Code and to define and limit the jurisdiction of courts sitting in equity, and for other purposes," shall not be applicable.

(c) The order or orders of the court shall be subject to review by the appropriate circuit court of appeals and by the Supreme Court upon writ of certiorari or certification as provided in sections 239 and 240 of the Judicial Code, as amended (U.S.C., title 29, secs. 346 and 347).

Sec. 209. (a) Whenever a district court has issued an order under section 208 enjoining acts or practices which imperil or threaten to imperil the national health or safety, it shall be the duty of the parties to the labor dispute giving rise to such order to make every effort to adjust and settle their differences, with the assistance of the Service created by this Act. Neither party shall be under any duty to accept, in whole or in part, any proposal of settlement made by the Service.

(b) Upon the issuance of such order, the President shall reconvene the board of inquiry which has previously reported with respect to the dispute. At the end of a sixty-day period (unless the dispute has been settled by that time), the board of inquiry shall report to the President the current position of the parties and the efforts which have been made for settlement, and shall include a statement by each party of its position and a statement of the employer's last offer of settlement. The President shall make such report available to the public. The National Labor Relations Board, within the succeeding fifteen days, shall take a secret ballot of the employees of each employer involved in the dispute on the question of whether they wish to accept the final offer of settlement made by their employer as stated by him and shall certify the results thereof to the Attorney General within five days thereafter.

Sec. 210. Upon the certification of the results of such ballot or upon a settlement being reached, whichever happens sooner, the Attorney General shall move the court to discharge the injunction, which motion shall then be granted and the injunction discharged. When such motion is granted, the President shall submit to the Congress a full and comprehensive report of the proceedings, including the findings of the board of inquiry and the ballot taken by the National Labor Relations Board, together with such recommendations as he may see fit to make for consideration and appropriate action.

Compilation of Collective Bargaining Agreements, etc.

Sec. 211. (a) For the guidance and information of interested representatives of employers, employees, and the general public, the Bureau of Labor Statistics of the Department of Labor shall maintain a file of copies of all available collective bargaining agreements and other available agreements and actions thereunder settling or adjusting labor disputes. Such file shall be open to inspection under appropriate conditions prescribed by the Secretary of Labor, except that no specific information submitted in confidence shall be disclosed.

(b) The Bureau of Labor Statistics in the Department of Labor is authorized to furnish upon request of the Service, or employers, employees, or their representatives, all available data and factual information which may aid in the settlement of any labor dispute, except that no specific information submitted in confidence shall be disclosed.

Exemption of Railway Labor Act

Sec. 212. The provisions of this title shall not be applicable with respect to any matter which is subject to the provisions of the Railway Labor Act, as amended from time to time.

TITLE III
Suits by and against Labor Organizations

Sec. 301. (a) Suits for violation of contracts between an employer and a labor organization representing employees in an industry affecting commerce as defined in this Act, or between any such labor organizations, may be brought in any district court of the United States having jurisdiction of the parties, without respect to the amount in controversy or without regard to the citizenship of the parties.

(b) Any labor organization which represents employees in an industry affecting commerce as defined in this Act and any employer whose activities affect commerce as defined in this Act shall be bound by the acts of its agents. Any such labor organization may sue or be sued as an entity and in behalf of the employees whom it represents in the courts of the United States. Any money judgment against a labor organization in a district court of the United States shall be enforceable only against the organization as an entity and against its assets, and shall not be enforceable against any individual member or his assets.

(c) For the purposes of actions and proceedings by or against labor organizations in the district courts of the United States, district courts shall be deemed to have jurisdiction of a labor organization (1) in the district in which such organization maintains its principal office, or (2) in any district in which its duly authorized officers or agents are engaged in representing or acting for employee members.

(d) The service of summons, subpena, or other legal process of any court of the United States upon an officer or agent of a labor organization, in his capacity as such, shall constitute service upon the labor organization.

(e) For the purposes of this section, in determining whether any person is acting as an "agent" of another person so as to make such other person responsible for his acts, the question of whether the specific acts performed were actually authorized or subsequently ratified shall not be controlling.

Restrictions on Payments to Employee Representatives

Sec. 302. (a) It shall be unlawful for any employer or association of employers or any person who acts as a labor relations expert, adviser, or consultant to an employer or who acts in the interest of an employer to pay, lend, or deliver, or agree to pay, lend, or deliver, any money or other thing of value—

(1) to any representative of any of his employees who are employed in an industry affecting commerce; or

(2) to any labor organization, or any officer or employee thereof, which represents, seeks to represent, or would admit to membership, any of the employees of such employer who are employed in an industry affecting commerce; or

(3) to any employee or group or committee of employees of such employer employed in an industry affecting commerce in excess of their normal compensation for the purpose of causing such employee or group or committee directly or indirectly to influence any other employees in the exercise of the right to organize and bargain collectively through representatives of their own choosing; or

(4) to any officer or employee of a labor organization engaged in an industry affecting commerce with intent to influence him in respect to any of his actions, decisions, or duties as a representative of employees or as such officer or employee of such labor organization.

(b)(1) It shall be unlawful for any person to request, demand, receive, or accept, or agree to receive or accept, any payment, loan, or delivery of any money or other thing of value prohibited by subsection (a).

(2) It shall be unlawful for any labor organization, or for any person acting as an officer, agent, representative, or employee of such labor organization, to demand or accept from the operator of any motor vehicle (as defined in part II of the Interstate Commerce Act) employed in the transportation of property in commerce, or the employer of any such operator, any money or other thing of value payable to such organization or to an officer, agent, representative or employee thereof as a fee or charge for the unloading, or in connection with the unloading, of the cargo of such vehicle: *Provided,* That nothing in this paragraph shall be construed to make unlawful any payment by an employer to any of his employees as compensation for their services as employees.

(c) The provisions of this section shall not be applicable (1) in respect to any money or other thing of value payable by an employer to any of his employees whose established duties include acting openly for such employer in matters of labor relations or personnel administration or to any representative of his employees, or to any officer or employee of a labor organization, who is also an employee or former employee of such employer, as compensation for, or by reason of, his service as an employee of such employer; (2) with respect to the payment or delivery of any money or other thing of value in satisfaction of a judgment of any court or a decision or award of an arbitrator or impartial chairman or in compromise, adjustment, settlement or release of any claim, complaint, grievance, or dispute in the absence of fraud or duress; (3) with respect to the sale or purchase of an article or commodity at the prevailing market price in the regular course of business; (4) with respect to money deducted from the wages of employees in payment of membership dues in a labor organization: *Provided,* That the employer has received from each employee, on whose account such deductions are made, a written assignment which shall not be irrevocable for a period of more than one year, or beyond the termination date of the applicable collective agreement, whichever occurs sooner; (5) with respect to money or other thing of value paid to a trust fund established by such representative, for the sole and exclusive benefit of the employees of such employer, and their families and dependents (or of such employees, families, and dependents jointly with the employees of other employers making similar payments, and their families and dependents): *Provided,* That (A) such payments are held in trust for the purpose of paying, either from principal or income or both, for the benefit of employees, their families and dependents, for medical or hospital care, pensions on retirement or death of employees, compensation for injuries or illness resulting from occupational activity or insurance to provide any of the foregoing, or unemployment benefits or life insurance, disability and sickness insurance, or accident insurance; (B) the detailed basis on which such payments are to be made is specified in a written agreement with the employer, and employees and employers are equally represented in the administration of such fund, together with such neutral persons as the representatives of the employers and the representatives of employees may agree upon and in the event the employer and the employee groups deadlock on the administration of such fund and there are no neutral persons empowered to break such deadlock, such agreement provides that the two groups shall agree on an impartial umpire to decide

such dispute, or in event of their failure to agree within a reasonable length of time, an impartial umpire to decide such dispute shall, on petition of either group, be appointed by the district court of the United States for the district where the trust fund has its principal office, and shall also contain provisions for an annual audit of the trust fund, a statement of the results of which shall be available for inspection by interested persons at the principal office of the trust fund and at such other places as may be designated in such written agreement; and (C) such payments as are intended to be used for the purpose of providing pensions or annuities for employees are made to a separate trust which provides that the funds held therein cannot be used for any purpose other than paying such pensions or annuities; (6) with respect to money or other thing of value paid by any employer to a trust fund established by such representative for the purpose of pooled vacation, holiday, severance or similar benefits, or defraying costs of apprenticeship or other training programs: *Provided,* That the requirements of clause (B) of the proviso to clause (5) of this subsection shall apply to such trust funds; (7) with respect to money or other thing of value paid by any employer to a pooled or individual trust fund established by such representative for the purpose of (A) scholarships for the benefit of employees, their families, and dependents for study at educational institutions, or (B) child care centers for pre-school and school age dependents of employees: *Provided,* That no labor organization or employer shall be required to bargain on the establishment of any such trust fund, and refusal to do so shall not constitute an unfair labor practice: *Provided further,* That the requirements of clause (B) of the proviso to clause (5) of this subsection shall apply to such trust fund; or (8) with respect to money or any other thing of value paid by any employer to a trust fund established by such representative for the purpose of defraying the costs of legal services for employees, their families, and dependents for counsel or plan of their choice: *Provided,* That the requirements of clause (B) of the proviso to clause (5) of this subsection shall apply to such trust funds: *Provided further,* That no such legal services shall be furnished: (A) to initiate any proceeding directed (i) against any such employer or its officers or agents except in workman's compensation cases, or (ii) against such labor organization, or its parent or subordinate bodies, or their officers or agents, or (iii) against any other employer or labor organization, or their officers or agents, in any matter arising under the National Labor Relations Act, as amended, or this Act; and (B) in any proceeding where a labor organization would be prohibited from defraying the costs of legal services by the provisions of the Labor-Management Reporting and Disclosure Act of 1959.*

(d) Any person who willfully violates any of the provisions of this section shall, upon conviction thereof, be guilty of a misdemeanor and be subject to a fine of not more than $10,000 or to imprisonment for not more than one year, or both.

(e) The district courts of the United States and the United States courts of the Territories and possessions shall have jurisdiction, for cause shown, and subject to the provisions of section 17 (relating to notice to opposite party) of the Act entitled "An Act to supplement existing laws against unlawful restraints and monopolies, and for other purposes," approved October 15, 1914, as amended (U.S.C., title 28, sec. 381), to restrain violations of this section, without regard to the provisions of sections 6 and 20 of such Act of October 15, 1914, as amended (U.S.C., title 15, sec. 17, and title 29, sec. 52), and the provisions of the Act entitled "An Act to amend the Judicial Code and to define and limit the jurisdiction of courts sitting in equity, and for other purposes," approved March 23, 1932 (U.S.C., title 29, secs. 101–115).

(f) This section shall not apply to any contract in force on the date of enactment of this Act, until the expiration of such con-

---

* Section 302(c)(7) has been added by Public Law 91–86, 91st Congress, S. 2068, 83 Stat. 133, approved October 14, 1969. Section 302(c)(8) was added by Public Law 93–95, 93rd Congress, 87 Stat. 314, approved August 15, 1973.

tract, or until July 1, 1948, whichever first occurs.

(g) Compliance with the restrictions contained in subsection (c)(5)(B) upon contributions to trust funds, otherwise lawful, shall not be applicable to contributions to such trust funds established by collective agreement prior to January 1, 1946, nor shall subsection (c)(5)(A) be construed as prohibiting contributions to such trust funds if prior to January 1, 1947, such funds contained provisions for pooled vacation benefits.

Boycotts and Other Unlawful Combinations

Sec. 303. (a) It shall be unlawful, for the purpose of this section only, in an industry or activity affecting commerce, for any labor organization to engage in any activity or conduct defined as an unfair labor practice in section 8(b)(4) of the National Labor Relations Act, as amended.

(b) Whoever shall be injured in his business or property by reason of any violation of subsection (a) may sue therefor in any district court of the United States subject to the limitations and provisions of section 301 hereof without respect to the amount in controversy, or in any other court having jurisdiction of the parties, and shall recover the damages by him sustained and the cost of the suit.

Restriction on Political Contributions

Sec. 304. Section 313 of the Federal Corrupt Practices Act, 1925 (U.S.C., 1940 edition, title 2, sec. 251; Supp. V, title 50, App., sec. 1509), as amended, is amended to read as follows:

SEC. 313. It is unlawful for any national bank, or any corporation organized by authority of any law of Congress, to make a contribution or expenditure in connection with any election to any political office, or in connection with any primary election or political convention or caucus held to select candidates for any political office, or for any corporation whatever, or any labor organization to make a contribution or expenditure in connection with any election at which Presidential and Vice

Presidential electors or a Senator or Representative in, or a Delegate or Resident Commissioner to Congress are to be voted for, or in connection with any primary election or political convention or caucus held to select candidates for any of the foregoing offices, or for any candidate, political committee, or other person to accept or receive any contribution prohibited by this section. Every corporation or labor organization which makes any contribution or expenditure in violation of this section shall be fined not more than $5,000; and every officer or director of any corporation, or officer of any labor organization, who consents to any contribution or expenditure by the corporation or labor organization, as the case may be, in violation of this section shall be fined not more than $1,000 or imprisoned for not more than one year, or both. For the purposes of this section 'labor organization' means any organization of any kind, or any agency or employee representation committee or plan, in which employees participate and which exists for the purpose, in whole or in part, of dealing with employers concerning grievances, labor disputes, wages, rates of pay, hours of employment, or conditions of work.

TITLE IV

Creation of Joint Committee to Study and Report on Basic Problems Affecting Friendly Labor Relations and Productivity

Sec. 401. There is hereby established a joint congressional committee to be known as the Joint Committee on Labor-Management Relations. . . .

TITLE V

Definitions

Sec. 501. When used in this Act—

(1) The term "industry affecting commerce" means any industry or activity in commerce or in which a labor dispute would burden or obstruct commerce or tend to burden or obstruct commerce or the free flow of commerce.

(2) The term "strike" includes any strike or other concerted stoppage of work by employees (including a stoppage by reason of the expiration of a collective-bargaining agreement) and any concerted slowdown or other concerted interruption of operations by employees.

(3) The terms "commerce," "labor disputes," "employer," "employee," "labor organization," "representative," "person," and "supervisor" shall have the same meaning as when used in the National Labor Relations Act as amended by this Act.

Saving Provision

Sec. 502. Nothing in this Act shall be construed to require an individual employee to render labor or service without his consent, nor shall anything in this Act be construed to make the quitting of his labor by an individual employee an illegal act; nor shall any court issue any process to compel the performance by an individual employee of such labor or service, without his consent; nor shall the quitting of labor by an employee or employees in good faith because of abnormally dangerous conditions for work at the place of employment of such employee or employees be deemed a strike under this Act.

Separability

Sec. 503. If any provision of this Act, or the application of such provision to any person or circumstance, shall be held invalid, the remainder of this Act, or the application of such provision to persons or circumstances other than those as to which it is held invalid, shall not be affected thereby.

Labor-Management Reporting and Disclosure Act of 1959

[PUBLIC LAW 86–257—86TH CONGRESS, S. 1555 SEPTEMBER 14, 1959]

AN ACT to provide for the reporting and disclosure of certain financial transactions and administrative practices of labor organizations and employers, to prevent abuses in the administration of trusteeships by labor organizations, to provide standards with respect to the election of officers of labor organizations, and for other purposes.

Be it enacted by the Senate and House of Representatives of the United States of America in Congress assembled,

SHORT TITLE

Section 1. This Act may be cited as the "Labor-Management Reporting and Disclosure Act of 1959."

Declaration of Findings, Purposes, and Policy

Sec. 2. (a) The Congress finds that, in the public interest, it continues to be the responsibility of the Federal Government to protect employees' rights to organize, choose their own representatives, bargain collectively, and otherwise engage in concerted activities for their mutual aid or protection; that the relations between employers and labor organizations and the millions of workers they represent have a substantial impact on the commerce of the Nation; and that in order to accomplish the objective of a free flow of commerce it is essential that labor organizations, employers, and their officials adhere to the highest standards of responsibility and ethical conduct in administering the affairs of their organizations, particularly as they affect labor-management relations.

(b) The Congress further finds, from recent investigations in the labor and management fields, that there have been a number of instances of breach of trust, corruption, disregard of the rights of individual employees, and other failures to observe high standards of responsibility and ethical conduct which require further and supplementary legislation that will afford necessary protection of the rights and interests of employees and the public generally as they relate to the activities of labor organizations, employers, labor relations consultants, and their officers and representatives.

(c) The Congress, therefore, further finds and declares that the enactment of this Act is necessary to eliminate or prevent improper practices on the part of labor organizations, employers, labor relations consultants, and their officers and representatives which distort and defeat the policies of the Labor Management Relations Act, 1947, as amended, and the Railway Labor Act, as amended, and have the tendency or necessary effect of burdening or obstructing commerce by (1) impairing the efficiency, safety, or operation of the instrumentalities of commerce; (2) occurring in the current of commerce; (3) materially affecting, restraining, or controlling the flow of raw materials or manufactured or processed goods into or from the channels of commerce, or the prices of such materials or goods in commerce; or (4) causing diminution of employment and wages in such volume as substantially to impair or disrupt the market for goods flowing into or from the channels of commerce.

Definitions

Sec. 3. For the purposes of titles I, II, III, IV, V (except section 505), and VI of this Act—

(a) "Commerce" means trade, traffic, commerce, transportation, transmission, or communication among the several States or between any State and any place outside thereof.

(b) "State" includes any State of the United States, the District of Columbia,

533

Puerto Rico, the Virgin Islands, American Samoa, Guam, Wake Island, the Canal Zone, and Outer Continental Shelf lands defined in the Outer Continental Shelf Lands Act (43 U.S.C. 1331–1343).

(c) "Industry affecting commerce" means any activity, business, or industry in commerce or in which a labor dispute would hinder or obstruct commerce or the free flow of commerce and includes any activity or industry "affecting commerce" within the meaning of the Labor Management Relations Act, 1947, as amended, or the Railway Labor Act, as amended.

(d) "Person" includes one or more individuals, labor organizations, partnerships, associations, corporations, legal representatives, mutual companies, joint-stock companies, trusts, unincorporated organizations, trustees, trustees in bankruptcy, or receivers.

(e) "Employer" means any employer or any group or association of employers engaged in an industry affecting commerce (1) which is, with respect to employees engaged in an industry affecting commerce, an employer within the meaning of any law of the United States relating to the employment of any employees or (2) which may deal with any labor organization concerning grievances, labor disputes, wages, rates of pay, hours of employment, or conditions of work, and includes any person acting directly or indirectly as an employer or as an agent of an employer in relation to an employee but does not include the United States or any corporation wholly owned by the Government of the United States or any State or political subdivision thereof.

(f) "Employee" means any individual employed by an employer, and includes any individual whose work has ceased as a consequence of, or in connection with, any current labor dispute or because of any unfair labor practice or because of exclusion or expulsion from a labor organization in any manner or for any reason inconsistent with the requirements of this Act.

(g) "Labor dispute" includes any controversy concerning terms, tenure, or conditions of employment, or concerning the association or representation of persons in negotiating, fixing, maintaining, changing, or seeking to arrange terms or conditions of employment, regardless of whether the disputants stand in the proximate relation of employer and employee.

(h) "Trusteeship" means any receivership, trusteeship, or other method of supervision or control whereby a labor organization suspends the autonomy otherwise available to a subordinate body under its constitution or bylaws.

(i) "Labor organization" means a labor organization engaged in an industry affecting commerce and includes any organization of any kind, any agency, or employee representation committee, group, association, or plan so engaged in which employees participate and which exists for the purpose, in whole or in part, of dealing with employers concerning grievances, labor disputes, wages, rates of pay, hours, or other terms or conditions of employment, and any conference, general committee, joint or system board, or joint council so engaged which is subordinate to a national or international labor organization, other than a State or local central body.

(j) A labor organization shall be deemed to be engaged in an industry affecting commerce if it—

(1) is the certified representative of employees under the provisions of the National Labor Relations Act, as amended, or the Railway Labor Act, as amended; or

(2) although not certified, is a national or international labor organization or a local labor organization recognized or acting as the representative of employees of an employer or employers engaged in an industry affecting commerce; or

(3) has chartered a local labor organization or subsidiary body which is representing or actively seeking to represent employees of employers within the meaning of paragraph (1) or (2); or

(4) has been chartered by a labor organization representing or actively seeking to represent employees within the meaning of paragraph (1) or (2) as the local or subordinate body through which such employees may enjoy membership or become affiliated with such labor organization; or

(5) is a conference, general committee, joint or system board, or joint council, subordinate to a national or international labor organization, which includes a labor organization engaged in an industry affecting commerce within the meaning of any of the preceding paragraphs of this subsection, other than a State or local central body.

(k)"Secret ballot" means the expression by ballot, voting machine, or otherwise, but in no event by proxy, of a choice with respect to any election or vote taken upon any matter, which is cast in such a manner that the person expressing such choice cannot be identified with the choice expressed.

(1) "Trust in which a labor organization is interested" means a trust or other fund or organization (1) which was created or established by a labor organization, or one or more of the trustees or one or more members of the governing body of which is selected or appointed by a labor organization, and (2) a primary purpose of which is to provide benefits for the members of such labor organization or their beneficiaries.

(m) "Labor relations consultant" means any person who, for compensation, advises or represents an employer, employer organization, or labor organization concerning employee organizing, concerted activities, or collective bargaining activities.

(n) "Officer" means any constitutional officer, any person authorized to perform the functions of president, vice president, secretary, treasurer, or other executive functions of a labor organization, and any member of its executive board or similar governing body.

(o) "Member" or "member in good standing," when used in reference to a labor organization, includes any person who has fulfilled the requirements for membership in such organization, and who neither has voluntarily withdrawn from membership nor has been expelled or suspended from membership after appropriate proceedings consistent with lawful provisions of the constitution and bylaws of such organization.

(p) "Secretary" means the Secretary of Labor.

(q) "Officer, agent, shop steward, or other representatives," when used with respect to a labor organization, includes elected officials and key administrative personnel, whether elected or appointed (such as business agents, heads of departments or major units, and organizers who exercise substantial independent authority), but does not include salaried nonsupervisory professional staff, stenographic, and service personnel.

(r) "District court of the United States" means a United States district court and a United States court of any place subject to the jurisdiction of the United States.

TITLE I—BILL OF RIGHTS OF MEMBERS OF LABOR ORGANIZATIONS

Bill of Rights

Sec. 101. (a) (1) EQUAL RIGHTS.— Every member of a labor organization shall have equal rights and privileges within such organization to nominate candidates, to vote in elections or referendums of the labor organization, to attend membership meetings, and to participate in the deliberations and voting upon the business of such meetings, subject to reasonable rules and regulations in such organization's constitution and bylaws.

(2) FREEDOM OF SPEECH AND ASSEMBLY.—Every member of any labor organization shall have the right to meet and assemble freely with other members; and to express any views, arguments, or opinions; and to express at meetings of the labor organization his views, upon candidates in an election of the labor organization or upon any business properly before the meeting, subject to the organization's established and reasonable rules pertaining to the conduct of meetings: *Provided,* That nothing herein shall be construed to impair the right of a labor organization to adopt and enforce reasonable rules as to the responsibility of every member toward the organization as an institution and to his refraining from conduct that would interfere with its

performance of its legal or contractual obligations.

(3) DUES, INITIATION FEES, AND ASSESSMENTS.—Except in the case of a federation of national or international labor organizations, the rates of dues and initiation fees payable by members of any labor organization in effect on the date of enactment of this Act shall not be increased, and no general or special assessment shall be levied upon such members, except—

(A) in the case of a local labor organization, (i) by majority vote by secret ballot of the members in good standing voting at a general or special membership meeting, after reasonable notice of the intention to vote upon such question, or (ii) by majority vote of the members in good standing voting in a membership referendum conducted by secret ballot; or

(B) in the case of a labor organization, other than a local labor organization or a federation of national or international labor organizations, (i) by majority vote of the delegates voting at a regular convention, or at a special convention of such labor organization held upon not less than thirty days' written notice to the principal office of each local or constituent labor organization entitled to such notice, or (ii) by majority vote of the members in good standing of such labor organization voting in a membership referendum conducted by secret ballot, or (iii) by majority vote of the members of the executive board or similar governing body of such labor organization, pursuant to express authority contained in the constitution and bylaws of such labor organization: *Provided,* That such action on the part of the executive board or similar governing body shall be effective only until the next regular convention of such labor organization.

(4) PROTECTION OF THE RIGHT TO SUE.—No labor organization shall limit the right of any member thereof to institute an action in any court, or in a proceeding before any administrative agency, irrespective of whether or not the labor organization or its officers are named as defendants or respondents in such action or proceeding, or the right of any member of a labor

organization to appear as a witness in any judicial, administrative, or legislative proceeding, or to petition any legislature or to communicate with any legislator: *Provided,* That any such member may be required to exhaust reasonable hearing procedures (but not to exceed a four-month lapse of time) within such organization, before instituting legal or administrative proceedings against such organizations or any officer thereof: *And provided further,* That no interested employer or employer association shall directly or indirectly finance, encourage, or participate in, except as a party, any such action, proceeding, appearance, or petition.

(5) SAFEGUARDS AGAINST IMPROPER DISCIPLINARY ACTION.—No member of any labor organization may be fined, suspended, expelled, or otherwise disciplined except for nonpayment of dues by such organization or by any officer thereof unless such member has been (A) served with written specific charges; (B) given a reasonable time to prepare his defense; (C) afforded a full and fair hearing.

(b) Any provision of the constitution and bylaws of any labor organization which is inconsistent with the provisions of this section shall be of no force or effect.

Civil Enforcement

Sec. 102. Any person whose rights secured by the provisions of this title have been infringed by any violation of this title may bring a civil action in a district court of the United States for such relief (including injunctions) as may be appropriate. Any such action against a labor organization shall be brought in the district court of the United States for the district where the alleged violation occurred, or where the principal office of such labor organization is located.

Retention of Existing Rights

Sec. 103. Nothing contained in this title shall limit the rights and remedies of any member of a labor organization under any State or Federal law or before any court or other tribunal, or under the constitution and bylaws of any labor organization.

Right to Copies of Collective Bargaining Agreements

Sec. 104. It shall be the duty of the secretary or corresponding principal officer of each labor organization, in the case of a local labor organization, to forward a copy of each collective bargaining agreement made by such labor organization with an employer to any employee who requests such a copy and whose rights as such employee are directly affected by such agreement, and in the case of a labor organization other than a local labor organization, to forward a copy of any such agreement to each constituent unit which has members directly affected by such agreement; and such officer shall maintain at the principal office of the labor organization of which he is an officer copies of any such agreement made or received by such labor organization, which copies shall be available for inspection by any member or by any employee whose rights are affected by such agreement. The provisions of section 210 shall be applicable in the enforcement of this section.

Information As To Act

Sec. 105. Every labor organization shall inform its members concerning the provisions of this Act.

TITLE II—REPORTING BY LABOR ORGANIZATIONS, OFFICERS AND EMPLOYEES OF LABOR ORGANIZATIONS, AND EMPLOYERS

Report of Labor Organizations

Sec. 201. (a) Every labor organization shall adopt a constitution and bylaws and shall file a copy thereof with the Secretary, together with a report, signed by its president and secretary or corresponding principal officers, containing the following information—

(1) the name of the labor organization, its mailing address, and any other address at which it maintains its principal office or at which it keeps the records referred to in this title;

(2) the name and title of each of its officers;

(3) the initiation fee or fees required from a new or transferred member and fees for work permits required by the reporting labor organization;

(4) the regular dues or fees or other periodic payments required to remain a member of the reporting labor organization; and

(5) detailed statements, or references to specific provisions of documents filed under this subsection which contain such statements, showing the provision made and procedures followed with respect to each of the following: (A) qualifications for or restrictions on membership, (B) levying of assessments, (C) participation in insurance or other benefit plans, (D) authorization for disbursement of funds of the labor organization, (E) audit of financial transactions of the labor organization, (F) the calling of regular and special meetings, (G) the selection of officers and stewards and of any representatives to other bodies composed of labor organizations' representatives, with a specific statement of the manner in which each officer was elected, appointed, or otherwise selected, (H) discipline or removal of officers or agents for breaches of their trust, (I) imposition of fines, suspensions, and expulsions of members, including the grounds for such action and any provision made for notice, hearing, judgment on the evidence, and appeal procedures, (J) authorization for bargaining demands, (K) ratification of contract terms, (L) authorization for strikes, and (M) issuance of work permits. Any change in the information required by this subsection shall be reported to the Secretary at the time the reporting labor organization files with the Secretary the annual financial report required by subsection (b).

(b) Every labor organization shall file annually with the Secretary a financial report signed by its president and treasurer or corresponding principal officers containing the following information in such detail as may be necessary accurately to disclose its financial condition and operations for its preceding fiscal year—

(1) assets and liabilities at the beginning and end of the fiscal year;

(2) receipts of any kind and the sources thereof;

(3) salary, allowances, and other direct or indirect disbursements (including reimbursed expenses) to each officer and also to each employee who, during such fiscal year, received more than $10,000 in the aggregate from such labor organization and any other labor organization affiliated with it or with which it is affiliated, or which is affiliated with the same national or international labor organization;

(4) direct and indirect loans made to any officer, employee, or member, which aggregated more than $250 during the fiscal year, together with a statement of the purpose, security, if any, and arrangements for repayment;

(5) direct or indirect loans to any business enterprise, together with a statement of the purpose, security, if any, and arrangements for repayment; and

(6) other disbursements made by it including the purposes thereof;

all in such categories as the Secretary may prescribe.

(c) Every labor organization required to submit a report under this title shall make available the information required to be contained in such report to all of its members, and every such labor organization and its officers shall be under a duty enforceable at the suit of any member of such organization in any State court of competent jurisdiction or in the district court of the United States for the district in which such labor organization maintains its principal office, to permit such member for just cause to examine any books, records, and accounts necessary to verify such report. The court in such action may, in its discretion, in addition to any judgment awarded to the plaintiff or plaintiffs, allow a reasonable attorney's fee to be paid by the defendant, and cost of the action.

Report of Officers and Employees of Labor Organizations

Sec. 202. (a) Every officer of a labor organization and every employee of a labor organization (other than an employee performing exclusively clerical or custodial services) shall file with the Secretary a signed report listing and describing for his preceding fiscal year—

(1) any stock, bond, security, or other interest, legal or equitable, which he or his spouse or minor child directly or indirectly held in, and any income or any other benefit with monetary value (including reimbursed expenses) which he or his spouse or minor child derived directly or indirectly from, an employer whose employees such labor organization represents or is actively seeking to represent, except payments and other benefits received as a bona fide employee of such employer;

(2) any transaction in which he or his spouse or minor child engaged, directly or indirectly, involving any stock, bond, security, or loan to or from, or other legal or equitable interest in the business of an employer whose employees such labor organization represents or is actively seeking to represent;

(3) any stock, bond, security, or other interest, legal or equitable, which he or his spouse or minor child directly or indirectly held in, and any income or any other benefit with monetary value (including reimbursed expenses) which he or his spouse or minor child directly or indirectly derived from, any business a substantial part of which consists of buying from, selling or leasing to, or otherwise dealing with, the business of an employer whose employees such labor organization represents or is actively seeking to represent;

(4) any stock, bond, security, or other interest, legal or equitable, which he or his spouse or minor child directly or indirectly held in, and any income or any other benefit with monetary value (including reimbursed expenses) which he or his spouse or minor child directly or indirectly derived from, a business any part of which consists of buying from, or selling or leasing directly or indirectly to, or otherwise dealing with such labor organization;

(5) any direct or indirect business transaction or arrangement between him

or his spouse or minor child and any employer whose employees his organization represents or is actively seeking to represent, except work performed and payments and benefits received as a bona fide employee of such employer and except purchases and sales of goods or services in the regular course of business at prices generally available to any employee of such employer; and

(6) any payment of money or other thing of value (including reimbursed expenses) which he or his spouse or minor child received directly or indirectly from any employer or any persons who acts as a labor relations consultant to an employer, except payments of the kinds referred to in section 302(c) of the Labor Management Relations Act, 1947, as amended.

(b) The provisions of paragraphs (1), (2), (3), (4), and (5) of subsection (a) shall not be construed to require any such officer or employee to report his bona fide investments in securities traded on a securities exchange under the Securities Exchange Act of 1934, in shares in an investment company registered under the Investment Company Act of 1940, or in securities of a public utility holding company registered under the Public Utility Holding Company Act of 1935, or to report any income derived therefrom.

(c) Nothing contained in this section shall be construed to require any officer or employee of a labor organization to file a report under subsection (a) unless he or his spouse or minor child holds or has held an interest, has received income or any other benefit with monetary value or a loan, or has engaged in a transaction described therein.

Report of Employers

Sec. 203. (a) Every employer who in any fiscal years made—

(1) any payment or loan, direct or indirect of money or other thing of value (including reimbursed expenses), or any promise or agreement therefor, to any labor organization or officer, agent, shop steward, or other representative of a labor organization, or employee of any labor organization, except (A) payments or loans made by any national or State bank, credit union, insurance company, savings and loan association or other credit institution and (B) payments of the kind referred to in section 302 (c) of the Labor Management Relations Act, 1947, as amended;

(2) any payment (including reimbursed expenses) to any of his employees, or any group or committee of such employees, for the purpose of causing such employee or group or committee of employees to persuade other employees to exercise or not to exercise, or as the manner of exercising, the right to organize and bargain collectively through representatives of their own choosing unless such payments were contemporaneously or previously disclosed to such other employees;

(3) any expenditure, during the fiscal year, where an object thereof, directly or indirectly, is to interfere with, restrain, or coerce employees in the exercise of the right to organize and bargain collectively through representatives of their own choosing, or is to obtain information concering the activities of employees or a labor organization in connection with a labor dispute involving such employer, except for use solely in conjunction with an administrative or arbitral proceeding or a criminal or civil judicial proceeding;

(4) any agreement or arrangement with a labor relations consultant or other independent contractor or organization pursuant to which such person undertakes activities where an object thereof, directly or indirectly, is to persuade employees to exercise or not to exercise, or persuade employees as to the manner of exercising, the right to organize and bargain collectively through representatives of their own choosing, or undertakes to supply such employer with information concerning the activities of employees or a labor organization in connection with a labor dispute involving such employer, except information for use solely in conjunction with an administrative or arbitral proceeding or a criminal or civil judicial proceeding; or

(5) any payment (including reimbursed expenses) pursuant to an agreement or arrangement described in subdivision (4);

shall file with the Secretary a report, in a form prescribed by him, signed by its president and treasurer or corresponding principal officers showing in detail the date and amount of each such payment, loan, promise, agreement, or arrangement and the name, address, and position, if any, in any firm or labor organization of the person to whom it was made and a full explanation of the circumstances of all such payments, including the terms of any agreement or understanding pursuant to which they were made.

(b) Every person who pursuant to any agreement or arrangement with an employer undertakes activities where an object thereof is, directly or indirectly—

(1) to persuade employees to exercise or not to exercise, or persuade employees as to the manner of exercising, the right to organize and bargain collectively through representatives of their own choosing; or

(2) to supply an employer with information concerning the activities of employees or a labor organization in connection with a labor dispute involving such employer, except information for use solely in conjunction with an administrative or arbitral proceeding or a criminal or civil judicial proceeding;

shall file within thirty days after entering into such agreement or arrangement a report with the Secretary, signed by its president and treasurer or corresponding principal officers, containing the name under which such person is engaged in doing business and the address of its principal office, and a detailed statement of the terms and conditions of such agreement or arrangement. Every such person shall file annually, with respect to each fiscal year during which payments were made as a result of such an agreement or arrangement, a report with the Secretary, signed by its president and treasurer or corresponding principal officers, containing a statement (A) of its receipts of any kind from employers on account of labor relations advice or services,

designating the sources thereof, and (B) of its disbursements of any kind, in connection with such services and the purposes thereof. In each such case such information shall be set forth in such categories as the Secretary may prescribe.

(c) Nothing in this section shall be construed to require any employer or other person to file a report covering the services of such person by reason of his giving or agreeing to give advice to such employer or representing or agreeing to represent such employer before any court, administrative agency, or tribunal of arbitration or engaging or agreeing to engage in collective bargaining on behalf of such employer with respect to wages, hours, or other terms or conditions of employment or the negotiation of an agreement or any question arising thereunder.

(d) Nothing contained in this section shall be construed to require an employer to file a report under subsection (a) unless he has made an expenditure, payment, loan, agreement, or arrangement of the kind described therein. Nothing contained in this section shall be construed to require any other person to file a report under subsection (b) unless he was a party to an agreement or arrangement of the kind described therein.

(e) Nothing contained in this section shall be construed to require any regular officer, supervisor, or employee of an employer to file a report in connection with services rendered to such employer nor shall any employer be required to file a report covering expenditures made to any regular officer, supervisor, or employee of an employer as compensation for service as a regular officer, supervisor, or employee of such employer.

(f) Nothing contained in this section shall be construed as an amendment to, or modification of the rights protected by, section 8(c) of the National Labor Relations Act, as amended.

(g) The term "interfere with, restrain, or coerce" as used in this section means interference, restraint, and coercion which, if done with respect to the exercise of rights guaranteed in section 7 of the National Labor Relations Act, as amended, would, under section 8(a) of such Act, constitute an unfair labor practice.

Attorney-Client Communications Exempted

Sec. 204. Nothing contained in this Act shall be construed to require an attorney who is a member in good standing of the bar of any State, to include in any report required to be filed pursuant to the provisions of this Act any information which was lawfully communicated to such attorney by any of his clients in the course of a legitimate attorney-client relationship.

Reports Made Public Information

Sec. 205. (a) The contents of the reports and documents filed with the Secretary pursuant to sections 201, 202, and 203 shall be public information, and the Secretary may publish any information and data which he obtains pursuant to the provisions of this title. The Secretary may use the information and data for statistical and research purposes, and compile and publish such studies, analyses, reports, and surveys based thereon as he may deem appropriate.

(b) The Secretary shall by regulation make reasonable provision for the inspection and examination, on the request of any person, of the information and data contained in any report or other document filed with him pursuant to section 201, 202, or 203.

(c) The Secretary shall by regulation provide for the furnishing by the Department of Labor of copies of reports or other documents filed with the Secretary pursuant to this title, upon payment of a charge based upon the cost of the service. The Secretary shall make available without payment of a charge, or require any person to furnish, to such State agency as is designated by law or by the Governor of the State in which such person has his principal place of business or headquarters, upon request of the Governor of such State, copies of any reports and documents filed by such person with the Secretary pursuant to section 201, 202, or 203, or of information and data contained therein. No person shall be required by reason of any law of any State to furnish to any officer or agency of such State any information included in a report filed by such person with the Secretary pursuant to the provisions of this title, if a copy of such report, or of the portion thereof containing such information, is furnished to such officer or agency. All moneys received in payment of such charges fixed by the Secretary pursuant to this subsection shall be deposited in the general fund of the Treasury.

Retention of Records

Sec. 206. Every person required to file any report under this title shall maintain records on the matters required to be reported which will provide in sufficient detail the necessary basic information and data from which the documents filed with the Secretary may be verified, explained or clarified, and checked for accuracy and completeness, and shall include vouchers, worksheets, receipts, and applicable resolutions, and shall keep such records available for examination for a period of not less than five years after the filing of the documents based on the information which they contain.

Effective Date

Sec. 207. (a) Each labor organization shall file the initial report required under section 201(a) within ninety days after the date on which it first becomes subject to this Act.

(b) Each person required to file a report under section 201(b), 202, 203(a), or the second sentence of 203(b) shall file such report within ninety days after the end of each of its fiscal years; except that where such person is subject to section 201(b), 202, 203(a), or the second sentence of 203(b), as the case may be, for only a portion of such a fiscal year (because the date of enactment of this Act occurs during such person's fiscal year or such person becomes subject to this Act during its fiscal year) such person may consider that portion as the entire fiscal year in making such report.

Rules and Regulations

Sec. 208. The Secretary shall have authority to issue, amend, and rescind rules and regulations prescribing the form and publication of reports required to be filed under this title and such other reasonable rules and regulations (including rules prescribing reports concerning trusts in which a labor organization is interested) as he may find necessary to prevent the circumvention or evasion of such reporting requirements. In exercising his power under this section the Secretary shall prescribe by general rule simplified reports for labor organizations or employers for whom he finds that by virtue of their size a detailed report would be unduly burdensome, but the Secretary may revoke such provision for simplified forms of any labor organization or employer if he determines, after such investigation as he deems proper and due notice and opportunity for a hearing, that the purposes of this section would be served thereby.

Criminal Provisions

Sec. 209. (a) Any person who willfully violates this title shall be fined not more than $10,000 or imprisoned for not more than one year, or both.

(b) Any person who makes a false statement or representation of a material fact, knowing it to be false, or who knowingly fails to disclose a material fact, in any document, report, or other information required under the provisions of this title shall be fined not more than $10,000 or imprisoned for not more than one year, or both.

(c) Any person who willfully makes a false entry in or willfully conceals, withholds, or destroys any books, records, reports, or statements required to be kept by any provision of this title shall be fined not more than $10,000 or imprisoned for not more than one year, or both.

(d) Each individual required to sign reports under sections 201 and 203 shall be personally responsible for the filing of such reports and for any statement contained therein which he knows to be false.

Civil Enforcement

Sec. 210. Whenever it shall appear that any person has violated or is about to violate any of the provisions of this title, the Secretary may bring a civil action for such relief (including injunctions) as may be appropriate. Any such action may be brought in the district court of the United States where the violation occurred or, at the option of the parties, in the United States District Court for the District of Columbia.

TITLE III—TRUSTEESHIPS
Reports

Sec. 301. (a) Every labor organization which has or assumes trusteeship over any subordinate labor organization shall file with the Secretary within thirty days after the date of the enactment of this Act or the imposition of any such trusteeship, and semiannually thereafter, a report, signed by its president and treasurer or corresponding principal officers, as well as the trustees of such subordinate labor organization, containing the following information: (1) the name and address of the subordinate organization; (2) the date of establishing the trusteeship; (3) a detailed statement of the reason or reasons for establishing or continuing the trusteeship; and (4) the nature and extent of participation by the membership of the subordinate organization in the selection of delegates to represent such organization in regular or special conventions or other policy-determining bodies and in the election of officers of the labor organization which has assumed trusteeship over such subordinate organization. The initial report shall also include a full and complete account of the financial condition of such subordinate organization as of the time trusteeship was assumed over it. During the continuance of a trusteeship the labor organization which has assumed trusteeship over a subordinate labor organization shall file on behalf of the subordinate labor organization the annual financial report required by section 201(b) signed by the president and treasurer or corresponding principal officers of the labor organization which has assumed such trusteeship and the trustees of the subordinate labor organization.

(b) The provisions of section 201(c), 205, 206, 208, and 210 shall be applicable to reports filed under this title.

(c) Any person who willfully violates this section shall be fined not more than $10,000 or imprisoned for not more than one year, or both.

(d) Any person who makes a false statement or representation of a material fact, knowing it to be false, or who knowingly fails to disclose a material fact, in any report required under the provisions of this section or willfully makes any false entry in or willfully withholds, conceals, or destroys any documents, books, records, reports, or statements upon which such report is based, shall be fined not more than $10,000 or imprisoned for not more than one year, or both.

(e) Each individual required to sign a report under this section shall be personally responsible for the filing of such report and for any statement contained therein which he knows to be false.

Purposes for Which a Trusteeship May Be Established

Sec. 302. Trusteeships shall be established and administered by a labor organization over a subordinate body only in accordance with the constitution and bylaws of the organization which has assumed trusteeship over the subordinate body and for the purpose of correcting corruption of financial malpractice, assuring the performance of collective bargaining agreements or other duties of a bargaining representative, restoring democratic procedures, or otherwise carrying out the legitimate objects of such labor organization.

Unlawful Acts Relating to Labor Organization Under Trusteeship

Sec. 303. (a) During any period when a subordinate body of a labor organization is in trusteeship, it shall be unlawful (1) to count the vote of delegates from such body

in any convention or election of officers of the labor organization unless the delegates have been chosen by secret ballot in an election in which all the members in good standing of such subordinate body were eligible to participate, or (2) to transfer to such organization any current receipts or other funds of the subordinate body except the normal per capita tax and assessments payable by subordinate bodies not in trusteeship: *Provided,* That nothing herein contained shall prevent the distribution of the assets of a labor organization in accordance with its constitution and bylaws upon the bona fide dissolution thereof.

(b) Any person who willfully violates this section shall be fined not more than $10,000 or imprisoned for not more than one year, or both.

Enforcement

Sec. 304. (a) Upon the written complaint of any member or subordinate body of a labor organization alleging that such organization has violated the provisions of this title (except section 301) the Secretary shall investigate the complaint and if the Secretary finds probable cause to believe that such violation has occurred and has not been remedied he shall, without disclosing the identity of the complainant, bring a civil action in any district court of the United States having jurisdiction of the labor organization for such relief (including injunctions) as may be appropriate. Any member or subordinate body of a labor organization affected by any violation of this title (except section 301) may bring a civil action in any district court of the United States having jurisdiction of the labor organization for such relief (including injunctions) as may be appropriate.

(b) For the purpose of actions under this section, district courts of the United States shall be deemed to have jurisdiction of a labor organization (1) in the district in which the principal office of such labor organization is located, or (2) in any district in which its duly authorized officers or agents are engaged in conducting the affairs of the trusteeship.

(c) In any proceeding pursuant to this section a trusteeship established by a labor organization in conformity with the procedural requirements of its constitution and bylaws and authorized or ratified after a fair hearing either before the executive board or before such other body as may be provided in accordance with its constitution or bylaws shall be presumed valid for a period of eighteen months from the date of its establishment and shall not be subject to attack during such period except upon clear and convincing proof that the trusteeship was not established or maintained in good faith for a purpose allowable under section 302. After the expiration of eighteen months the trusteeship shall be presumed invalid in any such proceeding and its discontinuance shall be decreed unless the labor organization shall show by clear and convincing proof that the continuation of the trusteeship is necessary for a purpose allowable under section 302. In the latter event the court may dismiss the complaint or retain jurisdiction of the cause on such conditions and for such period as it deems appropriate.

Report to Congress

Sec. 305. The Secretary shall submit to the Congress at the expiration of three years from the date of enactment of this Act a report upon the operation of this title.

Complaint by Secretary

Sec. 306. The rights and remedies provided by this title shall be in addition to any and all other rights and remedies at law or in equity: *Provided,* That upon the filing of a complaint by the Secretary the jurisdiction of the district court over such trusteeship shall be exclusive and the final judgment shall be res judicata.

TITLE IV—ELECTIONS
Terms of Office; Election Procedures

Sec. 401. (a) Every national or international labor organization, except a federation of national or international labor organizations, shall elect its officers not less often than once every five years either by secret ballot among the members in good standing or at a convention of delegates chosen by secret ballot.

(b) Every local labor organization shall elect its officers not less often than once every three years by secret ballot among the members in good standing.

(c) Every national or international labor organization, except a federation of national or international labor organizations, and every local labor organization, and its officers, shall be under a duty, enforceable at the suit of any bona fide candidate for office in such labor organization in the district court of the United States in which such labor organization maintains its principal office, to comply with all reasonable requests of any candidate to distribute by mail or otherwise at the candidate's expense campaign literature in aid of such person's candidacy to all members in good standing of such labor organization and to refrain from discrimination in favor of or against any candidate with respect to the use of lists of members, and whenever such labor organizations or its officers authorize the distribution by mail or otherwise to members of campaign literature on behalf of any candidate or of the labor organization itself with reference to such election, similar distribution at the request of any other bona fide candidate shall be made by such labor organization and its officers, with equal treatment as to the expense of such distribution. Every bona fide candidate shall have the right, once within 30 days prior to an election of a labor organization in which he is a candidate, to inspect a list containing the names and last known addresses of all members of the labor organization who are subject to a collective bargaining agreement requiring membership therein as a condition of employment, which list shall be maintained and kept at the principal office of such labor organization by a designated official thereof. Adequate safeguards to insure a fair election shall be provided, including the right of any candidate to have an observer at the polls and at the counting of the ballots.

(d) Officers of intermediate bodies, such as general committees, system boards, joint boards, or joint councils, shall be elected not less often than once every four years by secret ballot among the members in good standing or by labor organization officers representative of such members who have been elected by secret ballot.

(e) In any election required by this section which is to be held by secret ballot a reasonable opportunity shall be given for the nomination of candidates and every member in good standing shall be eligible to be a candidate and to hold office (subject to section 504 and to reasonable qualifications uniformly imposed) and shall have the right to vote for or otherwise support the candidate or candidates of his choice, without being subject to penalty, discipline, or improper interference or reprisal of any kind by such organization or any member thereof. Not less than fifteen days prior to the election notice thereof shall be mailed to each member at his last known home address. Each member in good standing shall be entitled to one vote. No member whose dues have been withheld by his employer for payment to such organization pursuant to his voluntary authorization provided for in a collective bargaining agreement shall be declared ineligible to vote or be a candidate for office in such organization by reason of alleged delay or default in the payment of dues. The votes cast by members of each local labor organization shall be counted, and the results published, separately. The election officials designated in the constitution and bylaws or the secretary, if no other official is designated, shall preserve for one year the ballots and all other records pertaining to the election. The election shall be conducted in accordance with the constitution and bylaws of such organization insofar as they are not inconsistent with the provisions of this title.

(f) When officers are chosen by a convention of delegates elected by secret ballot, the convention shall be conducted in accordance with the constitution and bylaws of the labor organization insofar as they are not inconsistent with the provisions of this title. The officials designated in the constitution and bylaws or the secretary, if no other is designated, shall preserve for one year the credentials of the delegates and all minutes and other records of the convention pertaining to the election of officers.

(g) No moneys received by any labor organization by way of dues, assessment, or similar levy, and no moneys of an employer shall be contributed or applied to promote the candidacy of any person in an election subject to the provisions of this title. Such moneys of a labor organization may be utilized for notices, factual statements of issues not involving candidates, and other expenses necessary for the holding of an election.

(h) If the Secretary, upon application of any member of a local labor organization, finds after hearing in accordance with the Administrative Procedure Act that the constitution and bylaws of such labor organization do not provide an adequate procedure for the removal of an elected officer guilty of serious misconduct, such officer may be removed, for cause shown and after notice and hearing, by the members in good standing voting in a secret ballot conducted by the officers of such labor organization in accordance with its constitution and bylaws insofar as they are not inconsistent with the provisions of this title.

(i) The Secretary shall promulgate rules and regulations prescribing minimum standards and procedures for determining the adequacy of the removal procedures to which reference is made in subsection (h).

Enforcement

Sec. 402. (a) A member of a labor organization—

(1) who has exhausted the remedies available under the constitution and bylaws of such organization and of any parent body, or

(2) who had invoked such available remedies without obtaining a final decision within three calendar months after their invocation,

may file a complaint with the Secretary within one calendar month thereafter alleging the violation of any provision of section 401 (including violation of the constitution and bylaws of the labor organization pertaining to the election and removal of officers). The challenged election shall be presumed valid pending a final decision thereon (as hereinafter provided) and in the interim the affairs of the organization shall be conducted by the officers elected or in such other manner as its constitution and bylaws may provide.

(b) The Secretary shall investigate such complaint and, if he finds probable cause to believe that a violation of this title has occurred and has not been remedied, he shall, within sixty days after the filing of such complaint, bring a civil action against the labor organization as an entity in the district court of the United States in which such labor organization maintains its principal office to set aside the invalid election, if any, and to direct the conduct of an election or hearing and vote upon the removal of officers under the supervision of the Secretary and in accordance with the provisions of this title and such rules and regulations as the Secretary may prescribe. The court shall have power to take such action as it deems proper to preserve the assets of the labor organization.

(c) If, upon a preponderance of the evidence after a trial upon the merits, the court finds—

(1) that an election has not been held within the time prescribed by section 401, or

(2) that the violation of section 401 may have affected the outcome of an election,

the court shall declare the election, if any, to be void and direct the conduct of a new election under supervision of the Secretary and, so far as lawful and practicable, in conformity with the constitution and bylaws of the labor organization. The Secretary shall promptly certify to the court the names of the persons elected, and the court shall thereupon enter a decree declaring such persons to be the officers of the labor organization. If the proceeding is for the removal of officers pursuant to subsection (h) of section 401, the Secretary shall certify the results of the vote and the court shall enter a decree declaring whether such persons have been removed as officers of the labor organization.

(d) An order directing an election, dismissing a complaint, or designating elected officers of a labor organization shall be ap-pealable in the same manner as the final judgment in a civil action, but an order directing an election shall not be stayed pending appeal.

Application of Other Laws

Sec. 403. No labor organization shall be required by law to conduct elections of officers with greater frequency or in a different form or manner than is required by its own constitution or bylaws, except as otherwise provided by this title. Existing rights and remedies to enforce the constitution and bylaws of a labor organization with respect to elections prior to the conduct thereof shall not be affected by the provisions of this title. The remedy provided by this title for challenging an election already conducted shall be exclusive.

Effective Data

Sec. 404. The provision of this title shall become applicable—

(1) ninety days after the date of enactment of this Act in the case of a labor organization whose constitution and bylaws can lawfully be modified or amended by action of its constitutional officers or governing body, or

(2) where such modification can only be made by a constitutional convention of the labor organization, not later than the next constitutional convention of such labor organization after the date of enactment of this Act, or one year after such date, whichever is sooner. If no such convention is held within such one-year period, the executive board or similar governing body empowered to act for such labor organization between conventions is empowered to make such interim constitutional changes as are necessary to carry out the provisions of this title.

TITLE V—SAFEGUARDS FOR LABOR ORGANIZATIONS

Fiduciary Responsibility of Officers of Labor Organizations

Sec. 501. (a) The officers, agents, shop stewards, and other representatives of a labor organization occupy positions of trust in relation to such organization and its members as a group. It is, therefore, the duty of each such person, taking into account the special problems and functions of a labor organization, to hold its money and property solely for the benefit of the organization and its members and to manage, invest, and expend the same in accordance with its constitution and bylaws and any resolutions of the governing bodies adopted thereunder, to refrain from dealing with such organization as an adverse party or in behalf of an adverse party in any matter connected with his duties and from holding or acquiring any pecuniary or personal interest which conflicts with the interests of such organization, and to account to the organization for any profit received by him in whatever capacity in connection with transactions conducted by him or under his direction on behalf of the organization. A general exculpatory provision in the constitution and bylaws of such a labor organization or a general exculpatory resolution of a governing body purporting to relieve any such person of liability for breach of the duties declared by this section shall be void as against public policy.

(b) When an officer, agent, shop steward, or representative or any labor organization is alleged to have violated the duties declared in subsection (a) and the labor organization or its governing board or officers refuse or fail to sue or recover damages or secure an accounting or other appropriate relief within a reasonable time after being requested to do so by any member of the labor organization, such member may sue such officer, agent, shop steward, or representative in any district court of the United States or in any State court of competent jurisdiction to recover damages or secure an accounting or other appropriate relief for the benefit of the labor organization. No such proceeding shall be brought except upon leave of the court obtained upon verified application and for good cause shown, which application may be made ex parte. The trial judge may allot a reasonable part of the recovery in any action under this subsection to pay the fees of counsel prosecuting the suit at the instance of the member of the labor organization and to compensate such member for any expenses necessarily paid or incurred by him in connection with the litigation.

(c) Any person who embezzles, steals, or unlawfully and willfully abstracts or converts to his own use, or the use of another, any of the moneys, funds, securities, property, or other assets of a labor organization of which he is an officer, or by which he is employed, directly or indirectly, shall be fined not more than $10,000 or imprisoned for not more than five years, or both.

Bonding

Sec. 502. (a) Every officer, agent, shop steward, or other representative or employee or any labor organization (other than a labor organization whose property and annual financial receipts do not exceed $5,000 in value), or of a trust in which a labor organization is interested, who handles funds or other property thereof shall be bonded for the faithful discharge of his duties. The bond of each such person shall be fixed at the beginning of the organization's fiscal year and shall be in an amount not less than 10 per centum of the funds handled by him and his predecessor or predecessors, if any, during the preceding fiscal year, but in no case more than $500,-000. If the labor organization or the trust in which a labor organization is interested does not have a preceding fiscal year, the amount of the bond shall be, in the case of a local labor organization, not less than $1,-000, and in the case of any other labor organization or of a trust in which a labor organization is interested, not less than $10,000. Such bonds shall be individual or schedule in form, and shall have a corporate surety company as surety thereon. Any person who is not covered by such bonds shall not be permitted to receive, handle, disburse, or otherwise exercise custody or control of the funds or other property of a labor organization or of a trust in which a labor organization is interested. No such bond shall be placed through an agent or broker or with a surety company in which any labor organization or any officer, agent, shop steward, or other representative of a labor organization has any direct or indirect interest. Such surety company shall be a corporate surety which holds a grant of authority from the Secretary of the Treasury under the Act of July 30, 1947 (6 U.S.C. 6–13), as a acceptable surety on Federal bonds.

(b) Any person who willfully violates this section shall be fined not more than $10,000 or imprisoned for not more than one year, or both.

Making of Loans; Payment of Fines

Sec. 503. (a) No labor organization shall make directly or indirectly any loan or loans to any officer or employee of such organization which results in a total indebtedness on the part of such officer or employee to the labor organization in excess of $2,000.

(b) No labor organization or employer shall directly or indirectly pay the fine of any officer or employee convicted of any willful violation of this Act.

(c) Any person who willfully violates this section shall be fined not more than $5,000 or imprisoned for not more than one year, or both.

Prohibition Against Certain Persons Holding Office

Sec. 504. (a) No person who is or has been a member of the Communist Party or who has been convicted of, or served any part of a prison term resulting from his conviction of, robbery, bribery, extortion, embezzlement, grand larceny, burglary, arson, violation of narcotics laws, murder, rape, assault with intent to kill, assault which inflicts grievous bodily injury, or a violation of title II or III of this Act, or conspiracy to commit any such crimes, shall serve—

(1) as an officer, director, trustee, member of any executive board or similar governing body, business agent, manager, organizer, or other employee (other than as an employee performing exclusively clerical or custodial duties) of any labor organization, or

(2) as a labor relations consultant to a person engaged in an industry or activity

affecting commerce, or as an officer, director, agent, or employee (other than as an employee performing exclusively clerical or custodial duties) of any group or association of employers dealing with any labor organization,

during or for five years after the termination of his membership in the Communist Party, or for five years after such conviction or after the end of such imprisonment, unless prior to the end of such five-year period, in the case of a person so convicted or imprisoned, (A) his citizenship rights, having been revoked as a result of such conviction, have been fully restored, or (B) the Board of Parole of the United States Department of Justice determines that such person's service in any capacity referred to in clause (1) or (2) would not be contrary to the purposes of this Act. Prior to making any such determination the Board shall hold an administrative hearing and shall give notice of such proceeding by certified mail to the State, county, and Federal prosecuting officials in the jurisdiction or jurisdictions in which such person was convicted. The Board's determination in any such proceeding shall be final. No labor organization or officer thereof shall knowingly permit any person to assume or hold any office or paid position in violation of this subsection.

(b) Any person who willfully violates this section shall be fined not more than $10,000 or imprisoned for not more than one year, or both.

(c) For the purposes of this section, any person shall be deemed to have been "convicted" and under the disability of "conviction" from the date of the judgment of the trial court or the date of the final sustaining of such judgment on appeal, whichever is the later event, regardless of whether such conviction occurred before or after the date of enactment of this Act.

TITLE VI—MISCELLANEOUS PROVISIONS

Investigations

Sec. 601. (a) The Secretary shall have power when he believes it necessary in order to determine whether any person has violated or is about to violate any provision of this Act (except title I or amendments made by this Act to other statutes) to make an investigation and in connection therewith he may enter such places and inspect such records and accounts and question such persons as he may deem necessary to enable him to determine the facts relative thereto. The Secretary may report to interested persons or officials concerning the facts required to be shown in any report required by this Act and concerning the reasons for failure or refusal to file such a report or any other matter which he deems to be appropriate as a result of such an investigation.

(b) For the purpose of any investigation provided for in this Act, the provisions of sections 9 and 10 (relating to the attendance of witnesses and the production of books, papers, and documents) of the Federal Trade Commission Act of September 16, 1914, as amended (15 U.S.C. 49, 50), are hereby made applicable to the jurisdiction, powers, and duties of the Secretary or any officers designated by him.

Extortionate Picketing

Sec. 602. (a) It shall be unlawful to carry on picketing on or about the premises of any employer for the purpose of, or as part of any conspiracy or in furtherance of any plan or purpose for, the personal profit or enrichment of any individual (except a bona fide increase in wages or other employee benefits) by taking or obtaining any money or other thing of value from such employer against his will or with his consent.

(b) Any person who willfully violates this section shall be fined not more than $10,000 or imprisoned not more than twenty years, or both.

Retention of Rights Under Other Federal and State Laws

Sec. 603. (a) Except as explicitly provided to the contrary, nothing in this Act shall reduce or limit the responsibilities of any labor organization or any officer, agent, shop steward, or other representative of a labor organization, or of any trust in which a labor organization is interested, under any other Federal law or under the laws of any State, and, except as explicitly provided to the contrary, nothing in this Act shall take away any right or bar any remedy to which members of a labor organization are entitled under such other Federal law or law of any State.

(b) Nothing contained in titles I, II, III, IV, V, or VI of this Act shall be construed to supersede or impair or otherwise affect the provisions of the Railway Labor Act, as amended, or any of the obligations, rights, benefits, privileges, or immunities of any carrier, employee, organization, representative, or person subject thereto; nor shall anything contained in said titles (except section 505) of this Act be construed to confer any rights, privileges, immunities, or defenses upon employers, or to impair or otherwise affect the rights of any person under the National Labor Relations Act, as amended.

Effect on State Laws

Sec. 604. Nothing in this Act shall be construed to impair or diminish the authority of any State to enact and enforce general criminal laws with respect to robbery, bribery, extortion, embezzlement, grand larceny, burglary, arson, violation of narcotics laws, murder, rape, assault with intent to kill, or assault which inflicts grievous bodily injury, or conspiracy to commit any of such crimes.

Service of Process

Sec. 605. For the purposes of this Act, service of summons, subpena, or other legal process of a court of the United States upon an officer or agent of a labor organization in his capacity as such shall constitute service upon the labor organization.

Administrative Procedure Act

Sec. 606. The provisions of the Administrative Procedure Act shall be applicable to the issuance, amendment, or rescision of any rules or regulations, or any adjudication, authorized or required pursuant to the provisions of this Act.

Other Agencies and Departments

Sec. 607. In order to avoid unnecessary expense and duplication of functions among Government agencies, the Secretary may make such arrangements or agreements for cooperation or mutual assistance in the performance of his functions under this Act and the functions of any such agency as he may find to be practicable and consistent with law. The Secretary may utilize the facilities or services of any department, agency, or establishment of the United States or of any State or political subdivision of a State, including the services of any of its employees, with the lawful consent of such department, agency, or establishment; and each department, agency or establishment of the United States is authorized and directed to cooperate with the Secretary and, to the extent permitted by law, to provide such information and facilities as he may request for his assistance in the performance of his functions under this Act. The Attorney General or his representative shall receive from the Secretary for appropriate action such evidence developed in the performance of his functions under this Act as may be found to warrant consideration for criminal prosecution under the provisions of this Act or other Federal law.

Criminal Contempt

Sec. 608. No person shall be punished for any criminal contempt allegedly committed outside the immediate presence of the court in connection with any civil action prosecuted by the Secretary or any other person in any court of the United States under the provisions of this Act unless the facts constituting such criminal contempt are established by the verdict of the jury in a proceeding in the district court of the United States, which jury shall be chosen and empaneled in the manner prescribed by the law governing trial juries in criminal prosecutions in the district courts of the United States.

Prohibition On Certain Discipline By Labor Organization

Sec. 609. It shall be unlawful for any labor organization, or any officer, agent, shop steward, or other representative of a labor organization, or any employee thereof to fine, suspend, expel, or otherwise discipline any of its members for exercising any right to which he is entitled under the provisions of this Act. The provisions of section 102 shall be applicable in the enforcement of this section.

Deprivation of Rights Under Act By Violence

Sec. 610. It shall be unlawful for any person through the use of force or violence, or threat of the use of force or violence, to restrain, coerce, or intimidate, or attempt to restrain, coerce, or intimidate any member of a labor organization for the purpose of interfering with or preventing the exercise of any right to which he is entitled under the provisions of this Act. Any person who willfully violates this section shall be fined not more than $1,000 or imprisoned for not more than one year, or both.

Separability Provisions

Sec. 611. If any provision of this Act, or the application of such provision to any person or circumstances, shall be held invalid, the remainder of this Act or the application of such provision to persons or circumstances other than those as to which it is held invalid, shall not be affected thereby.

Text of Title VII of the Civil Rights Act of 1964 as Amended by the Equal Employment Opportunity Act of 1972

Definitions

Sec. 701. For the purposes of this title—

(a) The term "person" includes one or more individuals, governments, governmental agencies, political subdivisions, labor unions, partnerships, associations, corporations, legal representatives, mutual companies, joint-stock companies, trusts, unincorporated organizations, trustees, trustees in bankruptcy, or receivers. (As amended by P.L. No. 92–261, eff. March 24, 1972.)

(b) The term 'employer' means a person engaged in an industry affecting commerce who has fifteen or more employees for each working day in each of twenty or more calendar weeks in the current or preceding calendar year, and any agent of such a person, but such term does not include (1) the United States, a corporation wholly owned by the Government of the United States, an Indian tribe, or any department or agency of the District of Columbia subject by statute to procedures of the competitive service (as defined in section 2102 of title 5 of the United States Code), or (2) a bona fide private membership club (other than a labor organization) which is exempt from taxation under section 501(c) of the Internal Revenue Code of 1954, except that during the first year after the date of enactment of the Equal Employment Opportunity Act of 1972, persons having fewer than twenty-five employees (and their agents) shall not be considered employers. (As amended by P.L. No. 92–261, eff. March 24, 1972.)

(c) The term "employment agency" means any person regularly undertaking with or without compensation to procure employees for an employer or to procure for employees opportunities to work for an employer and includes an agent of such a person. (As amended by P.L. No. 92–261, eff. March 24, 1972.)

(d) The term "labor organization" means a labor organization engaged in an industry affecting commerce, and any agent of such an organization, and includes any organization of any kind, any agency, or employee representation committee, group, association, or plan so engaged in which employees participate and which exists for the purpose, in whole or in part, of dealing with employers concerning grievances, labor disputes, wages, rates of pay, hours, or other terms or conditions of employment, and any conference, general committee, joint or system board, or joint council so engaged which is subordinate to a national or international labor organization.

(e) A labor organization shall be deemed to be engaged in an industry affecting commerce if (1) it maintains or operates a hiring hall or hiring office which procures employees for an employer or procures for employees opportunities to work for an employer, or (2) the number of its members (or, where it is a labor organization composed of other labor organizations or their representatives, if the aggregate number of the members of such labor organization) is (A) twenty-five or more during the first year after the date of enactment of the Equal Employment Opportunity Act of 1972, or (B) fifteen or more thereafter. (As amended by P.L. No. 92–261, eff. March 24, 1972)

(1) is the certified representative of employees under the provisions of the National Labor Relations Act, as amended, or the Railway Labor Act, as amended;

(2) although not certified, is a national or international labor organization or a local labor organization recognized or acting as the representative of employees of an employer or employers engaged in an industry affecting commerce; or

(3) has chartered a local labor organization or subsidiary body which is representing or actively seeking to represent employees of employers within the meaning of paragraph (1) or (2); or

(4) has been chartered by a labor

organization representing or actively seeking to represent employees within the meaning of paragraph (1) or (2) as the local or subordinate body through which such employees may enjoy membership or become affiliated with such labor organization; or

(5) is a conference, general committee, joint or system board, or joint council subordinate to a national or international labor organization, which includes a labor organization engaged in an industry affecting commerce within the meaning of any of the preceding paragraphs of this subsection.

(f) The term "employee" means an individual employed by an employer, except that the term "employee" shall not include any person elected to public office in any State or political subdivision of any State by the qualified voters thereof, or any person chosen by such officer to be on such officer's personal staff, or an appointee on the policy making level or an immediate adviser with respect to the exercise of the constitutional or legal powers of the office. The exemption set forth in the preceding sentence shall not include employees subject to the civil service laws of a State government, governmental agency or political subdivision. (As amended by P.L. 92–161, eff. March 24, 1972)

(g) The term "commerce" means trade, traffic, commerce, transportation, transmission, or communication among the several States; or between a State and any place outside thereof; or within the District of Columbia, or a possession of the United States; or between points in the same State but through a point outside thereof.

(h) The term "industry affecting commerce" means any activity, business, or industry in commerce or in which a labor dispute would hinder or obstruct commerce or the free flow of commerce and includes any activity or industry "affecting commerce" within the meaning of the Labor-Management Reporting and Disclosure Act of 1959, and further includes any governmental industry, business, or activity. (As amended by P.L. No. 92–261, eff. March 24, 1972)

(i) The term "State" includes a State of the United States, the District of Columbia, Puerto Rico, the Virgin Islands, American Samoa, Guam, Wake Island, the Canal Zone, and Outer Continental Shelf lands defined in the Outer Continental Shelf Lands Act.

(j) The term 'religion' includes all aspects of religious observance and practice, as well as belief, unless an employer demonstrates that he is unable to reasonably accommodate to an employee's or prospective employee's religious observance or practice without undue hardship on the conduct of the employer's business. (As amended by P.L. 92–261, eff. March 24, 1972)

Exemption

Sec. 702. This title shall not apply to an employer with respect to the employment of aliens outside any State, or to a religious corporation, association, educational institution, or society with respect to the employment of individuals of a particular religion to perform work connected with the carrying on by such corporation, association, educational institution, or society of its activities. (As amended by P.L. 92–261, eff. March 24, 1972)

Discrimination Because of Race, Color, Religion, Sex, or National Origin

Sec. 703. (a) It shall be an unlawful employment practice for an employer—

(1) to fail or refuse to hire or to discharge any individual, or otherwise to discriminate against any individual with respect to his compensation, terms, conditions, or privileges of employment, because of such individual's race, color, religion, sex, or national origin; or

(2) to limit, segregate, or classify his employees or applicants for employment in any way which would deprive or tend to deprive any individual of employment opportunities or otherwise adversely affect his status as an employee, because of such individual's race, color, religion, sex, or national origin. (As amended by P.L. 92–261, eff. March 24, 1972)

(b) It shall be an unlawful employment practice for an employment agency to fail or refuse to refer for employment, or otherwise to discriminate against, any individual because of his race, color, religion, sex, or national origin, or to classify or refer for employment any individual on the basis of his race, color, religion, sex or national origin.

(c) It shall be an unlawful employment practice for a labor organization—

(1) to exclude or to expel from its membership, or otherwise to discriminate against, any individual because of his race, color, religion, sex, or national origin;

(2) to limit, segregate, or classify its membership or applicants for membership or to classify or fail or refuse to refer for employment any individual, in any way which would deprive or tend to deprive any individual of employment opportunities, or would limit such employment opportunities or otherwise adversely affect his status and an employee or as an applicant for employment, because of such individual's race, color, religion, sex, or national origin; or

(3) to cause or attempt to cause an employer to discriminate against an individual in violation of this section.

(d) It shall be an unlawful employment practice for any employer, labor organization, or joint labor-management committee controlling apprenticeship or other training or retraining, including on-the-job training programs to discriminate against any individual because of his race, color, religion, sex, or national origin in admission to, or employment in, any program established to provide apprenticeship or other training.

(e) Notwithstanding any other provision of this title, (1) it shall not be an unlawful employment practice for an employer to hire and employ employees, for an employment agency to classify, or refer for employment any individual, for a labor organization to classify its membership or to classify or refer for employment any individual, or for an employer, labor organization, or joint labor-management committee controlling apprenticeship or other training or retraining programs to admit or employ any individual in any such program, on the basis of his religion, sex, or national origin in those certain instances where religion, sex, or national origin is a bona fide occupational qualification reasonably necessary to the normal operation of that particular

business or enterprise, and (2) it shall not be an unlawful employment practice for a school, college, university, or other educational institution or institution of learning to hire and employ employees of a particular religion if such school, college, university, or other educational institution or institution of learning is, in whole or in substantial part, owned, supported, controlled, or managed by a particular religion or by a particular religious corporation, association, or society, or if the curriculum of such school, college, university, or other educational institution or institution of learning is directed toward the propagation of a particular religion.

(f) As used in this title, the phrase "unlawful employment practice" shall not be deemed to include any action or measure taken by an employer, labor organization, joint labor-management committee, or employment agency with respect to an individual who is a member of the Communist Party of the United States or of any other organization required to register as a Communist-action or Communist-front organization by final order of the Subversive Activities Control Board pursuant to the Subversive Activities Control Act of 1950.

(g) Notwithstanding any other provision of this title, it shall not be an unlawful employment practice for an employer to fail or refuse to hire and employ any individual for any position, for an employer to discharge an individual from any position, or for an employment agency to fail or refuse to refer any individual for employment in any position, or for a labor organization to fail or refuse to refer any individual for employment in any position, if—

(1) the occupancy of such position, or access to the premises in or upon which any part of the duties of such position is performed or is to be performed, is subject to any requirement imposed in the interest of the national security of the United States under any security program in effect pursuant to or administered under any statute of the United States or any Executive order of the President; and

(2) such individual has not fulfilled or has ceased to fulfill that requirement.

(h) Notwithstanding any other provision of this title, it shall not be an unlawful employment practice for an employer to apply different standards of compensation, or different terms, conditions, or privileges of employment pursuant to a bona fide seniority or merit system, or a system which measures earnings by quantity or quality of production or to employees who work in different locations, provided that such differences are not the result of an intention to discriminate because of race, color, religion, sex, or national origin; nor shall it be an unlawful employment practice for an employer to give and to act upon the results of any professionally developed ability test provided that such test, its administration or action upon the results is not designed, intended, or used to discriminate because of race, color, religion, sex, or national origin. It shall not be an unlawful employment practice under this title for any employer to differentiate upon the basis of sex in determining the amount of the wages or compensation paid to employees of such employer if such differentiation is authorized by the provisions of Section 6(d) of the Fair Labor Standards Act of 1938 as amended (29 USC 206(d)).

(i) Nothing contained in this title shall apply to any business or enterprise on or near an Indian reservation with respect to any publicly announced employment practice of such business or enterprise under which a preferential treatment is given to any individual because he is an Indian living on or near a reservation.

(j) Nothing contained in this title shall be interpreted to require any employer, employment agency, labor organization, or joint labor-management committee subject to this title to grant preferential treatment to any individual or to any group because of the race, color, religion, sex, or national origin of such individual or group on account of an imbalance which may exist with respect to the total number or precentage of persons of any race, color, religion, sex, or national origin employed by any employer, referred or classified for employment by any employment agency or labor organization, admitted to membership or classified by any labor organization, or admitted to, or employed in, any apprentice-

ship or other training program, in comparison with the total number or percentage of persons of such race, color, religion, sex, or national origin in any community, State, section, or other area, or in the available work force in any community, State, section, or other area. (As amended by P.L. 92–261, eff. March 24, 1972)

Other Unlawful Employment Practices

Sec. 704. (a) It shall be an unlawful employment practice for an employer to discriminate against any of his employees or applicants for employment, for an employment agency or joint labor-management committee controlling apprenticeship or other training or retraining, including on-the-job training programs, to discriminate against any individual, or for a labor organization to discriminate against any member thereof or applicant for membership, because he has opposed any practice, made an unlawful employment practice by this title, or because he has made a charge, testified, assisted, or participated in any manner in an investigation, proceeding, or hearing under this title. (As amended by P.L. No. 92–261, eff. March 24, 1972)

(b) It shall be an unlawful employment practice for an employer, labor organization, employment agency, or joint labor-management committee controlling apprenticeship or other training or retraining, including on-the-job training programs, to print or cause to be printed or published any notice or advertisement relating to employment by such an employer or membership in or any classification or referral for employment by such a labor organization, or relating to any classification or referral for employment by such an employment agency, or relating to admission to, or employment in, any program established to provide apprenticeship or other training by such a joint labor-management committee indicating any preference, limitation, specification, or discrimination, based on race, color, religion, sex, or national origin, except that such a notice or advertisement may indicate a preference, limitation, specification or discrimination based on religion, sex or national origin when religion, sex, or national origin is a bona fide occupational qualification for employment. (As amended by P.L. No. 92–216, eff. March 24, 1972)

Equal Employment Opportunity Commission

Sec. 705. (a) There is hereby created a Commission to be known as the Equal Employment Opportunity Commission, which shall be composed of five members, not more than three of whom shall be members of the same political party. Members of the Commission shall be appointed by the President by and with the advice and consent of the Senate for a term of five years. Any individual chosen to fill a vacancy shall be appointed only for the unexpired term of the member whom he shall succeed, and all members of the Commission shall continue to serve until their successors are appointed and qualified, except that no such member of the Commission shall continue to serve (1) for more than sixty days when the Congress is in session unless a nomination to fill such vacancy shall have been submitted to the Senate, or (2) after the adjournment *sine die* of the session of the Senate in which such nomination was submitted. The President shall designate one member to serve as Chairman of the Commission, and one member to serve as Vice Chairman. The Chairman shall be responsible on behalf of the Commission for the administrative operations of the Commission, and, except as provided in subsection (b), shall appoint, in accordance with the provisions of title 5, United States Code, governing appointments in the competitive service, such officers, agents, attorneys, hearing examiners, and employees as he deems necessary to assist it in the performance of its functions and to fix their compensation in accordance with the provisions of chapter 51 and subchapter III of chapter 53 of title 5, United States Code, relating to classification and General Schedule pay rates: *Provided,* That assignment, removal, and compensation of hearing examiners shall be in accordance with sections 3105, 3344, 5362, and 7521 of title 5, United States Code.

(b)(1) There shall be a General Counsel of the Commission appointed by the President, by and with the advice and consent of the Senate, for a term of four years. The General Counsel shall have responsibility for the conduct of litigation as provided in sections 706 and 707 of this title. The General Counsel shall have such other duties as the Commission may prescribe or as may be provided by law and shall concur with the Chairman of the Commission on the appointment and supervision of regional attorneys. The General Counsel of the Commission on the effective date of this Act shall continue in such position and perform the functions specified in this subsection until a successor is appointed and qualified.

(2) Attorneys appointed under this section may, at the direction of the Commission, appear for and represent the Commission in any case in court, provided that the Attorney General shall conduct all litigation to which the Commission is a party in the Supreme Court pursuant to this title. (As amended by P.L. No. 92–261, eff. March 24, 1972)

(c) A vacancy in the Commission shall not impair the right of the remaining members to exercise all the powers of the Commission and three members thereof shall constitute a quorum.

(d) The Commission shall have an official seal which shall be judicially noticed.

(e) The Commission shall at the middle and at the close of each fiscal year report to the Congress and to the President concerning the action it has taken; the names, salaries, and duties of all individuals in its employ and the moneys it has disbursed; and shall make such further reports on the cause of and means of eliminating discrimination and such recommendations for further legislation as may appear desirable.

(f) The principal office of the Commission shall be in or near the District of Columbia, but it may meet or exercise any or all its powers at any other place. The Commission may establish such regional or State offices as it deems necessary to accomplish the purpose of this title.

(g) The Commission shall have power—

(1) to cooperate with and, with their

consent, utilize regional, State, local, and other agencies, both public and private, and individuals;

(2) to pay to witnesses whose depositions are taken or who are summoned before the Commission or any of its agents the same witness and mileage fees as are paid to witnesses in the courts of the United States;

(3) to furnish to persons subject to this title such technical assistance as they may request to further their compliance with this title or an order issued thereunder;

(4) upon the request of (i) any employer, whose employees or some of them, or (ii) any labor organization, whose members or some of them, refuse or threaten to refuse to cooperate in effectuating the provisions of this title, to assist in such effectuation by conciliation or such other remedial action as it is provided by this title:

(5) to make such technical studies as are appropriate to effectuate the purposes and policies of this title and to make the results of such studies available to the public;

(6) to intervene in a civil action brought under section 706 by an aggrieved party against a respondent other than a government, governmental agency or political subdivision. (As amended by P.L. No. 92–261, eff. March 24, 1972)

(h) The Commission shall, in any of its educational or promotional activities, cooperate with other departments and agencies in the performance of such educational and promotional activities.

(i) All officers, agents, attorneys and employees of the Commission, including the members of the Commission, shall be subject to the provisions of section 9 of the act of August 2, 1939, as amended (Hatch Act), notwithstanding any exemption contained in such section.

Prevention of Unlawful Employment Practices

Sec. 706. (a) The Commission is empowered, as hereinafter provided, to prevent any person from engaging in any unlawful employment practice as set forth in section 703 or 704 of this title.

(b) Whenever a charge is filed by or on behalf of a person claiming to be aggrieved, or by a member of the Commission, alleging that an employer, employment agency, labor organization, or joint labor-management committee controlling apprenticeship or other training or retraining including on-the-job training programs, has engaged in an unlawful employment practice, the Commission shall serve a notice of the charge (including the date, place and circumstances of the alleged unlawful employment practice) on such employer, employment agency, labor organization, or joint labor-management committee (hereinafter referred to as the 'respondent') within ten days and shall make an investigation thereof. Charges shall be in writing under oath or affirmation and shall contain such information and be in such form as the Commission requires. Charges shall not be made public by the Commission. If the Commission determines after such investigation that there is not reasonable cause to believe that the charge is true, it shall dismiss the charge and promptly notify the person claiming to be aggrieved and the respondent of its action. In determining whether reasonable cause exists, the Commission shall accord substantial weight to final findings and orders made by State or local authorities in proceedings commenced under State or local law pursuant to the requirements of subsections (c) and (d). If the Commission determines after such investigation that there is reasonable cause to believe that the charge is true, the Commission shall endeavor to eliminate any such alleged unlawful employment practice by informal methods of conference, conciliation, and persuasion. Nothing said or done during and as a part of such informal endeavors may be made public by the Commission, its officers or employees, or used as evidence in a subsequent proceeding without the written consent of the persons concerned. Any person who makes public information in violation of this subsection shall be fined not more than $1,000 or imprisoned for not more than one year, or both. The Commission shall make its determination on reasonable cause as promptly as possible and, so far as practicable, not later than one hundred and twenty days from the filing of the charge or, where applicable under subsection (c) or (d), from the date upon which the Commission is authorized to take action with respect to the charge.

(c) In the case of an alleged unlawful employment practice occurring in a State, or political subdivision of a State, which has a State or local law prohibiting the unlawful employment practice alleged and establishing or authorizing a State or local authority to grant or seek relief from such practice or to institute criminal proceedings with respect thereto upon receiving notice thereof, no charge may be filed under subsection (a) by the person aggrieved before the expiration of sixty days after proceedings have been commenced under the State or local law, unless such proceedings have been earlier terminated, provided that such sixty-day period shall be extended to one hundred and twenty days during the first year after the effective date of such State or local law. If any requirement for the commencement of such proceedings is imposed by a State or local authority other than a requirement of the filing of a written and signed statement of the facts upon which the proceeding is based, the proceeding shall be deemed to have been commenced for the purposes of this subsection at the time such statement is sent by registered mail to the appropriate State or local authority.

(d) In the case of any charge filed by a member of the Commission alleging an unlawful employment practice occurring in a State or political subdivision of a State which has a State or local law prohibiting the practice alleged and establishing or authorizing a State or local authority to grant or seek relief from such practice or to institute criminal proceedings with respect thereto upon receiving notice thereof, the Commission shall, before taking any action with respect to such charge, notify the appropriate State or local officials and, upon request, afford them a reasonable time, but not less than sixty days (provided that such sixty-day period shall be extended to one hundred and twenty days during the first

year after the effective day of such State or local law), unless a shorter period is requested, to act under such State or local law to remedy the practice alleged.

(e) A charge under this section shall be filed within one hundred and eighty days after the alleged unlawful employment practice occurred and notice of the charge (including the date, place and circumstances of the alleged unlawful employment practice) shall be served upon the person against whom such charge is made within ten days thereafter, except that in a case of an unlawful employment practice with respect to which the person aggrieved has initially instituted proceedings with a State or local agency with authority to grant or seek relief from such practice or to institute criminal proceedings with respect thereto upon receiving notice thereof, such charge shall be filed by or on behalf of the person aggrieved within three hundred days after the alleged unlawful employment practice occurred, or within thirty days after receiving notice that the State or local agency has terminated the proceedings under the State or local law, whichever is earlier, and a copy of such charge shall be filed by the Commission with the State or local agency.

(f) (1) If within thirty days after a charge is filed with the Commission or within thirty days after expiration of any period of reference under subsection (c) or (d), the Commission has been unable to secure from the respondent a conciliation agreement acceptable to the Commission, the Commission may bring a civil action against any respondent not a government, governmental agency, or political subdivision named in the charge. In the case of a respondent which is a government, governmental agency, or political subdivision, if the Commission has been unable to secure from the respondent a conciliation agreement acceptable to the Commission, the Commission shall take no further action and shall refer the case to the Attorney General who may bring a civil action against such respondent in the appropriate United States district court. The person or persons aggrieved shall have the right to intervene in a civil action brought by the Commission or the Attorney General in a case involving a government, governmental agency, or political subdivision. If a charge filed with the Commission pursuant to subsection (b) is dismissed by the Commission, or if within one hundred and eighty days from the filing of such charge or the expiration of any period of reference under subsection (c) or (d), whichever is later, the Commission has not filed a civil action under this section or the Attorney General has not filed a civil action in a case involving a government, governmental agency, or political subdivision, or the Commission has not entered into a conciliation agreement to which the person aggrieved is a party, the Commission, or the Attorney General in a case involving a government, governmental agency, or political subdivision, shall so notify the person aggrieved and within ninety days after the giving of such notice a civil action may be brought against the respondent named in the charge (A) by the person claiming to be aggrieved or (B) if such charge was filed by a member of the Commission, by any person whom the charge alleges was aggrieved by the alleged unlawful employment practice. Upon application by the complainant and in such circumstances as the court may deem just, the court may appoint an attorney for such complainant and may authorize the commencement of the action without the payment of fees, costs, or security. Upon timely application, the court may, in its discretion, permit the Commission, or the Attorney General in a case involving a government, governmental agency, or political subdivision, to intervene in such civil action upon certification that the case is of general public importance. Upon request, the court may, in its discretion, stay further proceedings for not more than sixty days pending the termination of State or local proceedings described in subsections (c) or (d) of this section or further efforts of the Commission to obtain voluntary compliance.

(2) Whenever a charge is filed with the Commission and the Commission concludes on the basis of a preliminary investigation that prompt judicial action is necessary to carry out the purpose of this Act, the Commission, or the Attorney General in a case involving a government, govern-

mental agency, or political subdivision, may bring an action for appropriate temporary or preliminary relief pending final disposition of such charge. Any temporary restraining order or other order granting preliminary or temporary relief shall be issued in accordance with rule 65 of the Federal Rules of Civil Procedure. It shall be the duty of a court having jurisdiction over proceedings under this section to assign cases for hearing at the earliest practicable date and to cause such cases to be in every way expedited.

(3) Each United States district court and each United States court of a place subject to the jurisdiction of the United States shall have jurisdiction of actions brought under this title. Such an action may be brought in any judicial district in the State in which the unlawful employment practice is alleged to have been committed, in the judicial district in which the employment records relevant to such practice are maintained and administered, or in the judicial district in which the aggrieved person would have worked but for the alleged unlawful employment practice, but if the respondent is not found within any such district, such an action may be brought within the judicial district in which the respondent has his principal office. For purposes of sections 1404 and 1406 of title 28 of the United States Code, the judicial district in which the respondent has his principal office shall in all cases be considered a district in which the action might have been brought.

(4) It shall be the duty of the chief judge of the district (or in his absence, the acting chief judge) in which the case is pending immediately to designate a judge in such district to hear and determine the case. In the event that no judge in the district is available to hear and determine the case, the chief judge of the district, or the acting chief judge, as the case may be, shall certify this fact to the chief judge of the circuit (or in his absence, the acting chief judge) who shall then designate a district or circuit judge of the circuit to hear and determine the case.

(5) It shall be the duty of the judge designated pursuant to this subsection to assign the case for hearing at the earliest

practicable date and to cause the case to be in every way expedited. If such judge has not scheduled the case for trial within one hundred and twenty days after issue has been joined that judge may appoint a master pursuant to rule 53 of the Federal Rules of Civil Procedure.

(g) If the court finds that the respondent has intentionally engaged in or is intentionally engaging in an unlawful employment practice charged in the complaint, the court may enjoin the respondent from engaging in such unlawful employment practice, and order such affirmative action as may be appropriate, which may include, but is not limited to, reinstatement or hiring of employees, with or without back pay (payable by the employer, employment agency, or labor organization, as the case may be, responsible for the unlawful employment practice), or any other equitable relief as the court deems appropriate. Back pay liability shall not accrue from a date more than two years prior to the filing of a charge with the Commission. Interim earnings or amounts earnable with reasonable diligence by the person or persons discriminated against shall operate to reduce the back pay otherwise allowable. No order of the court shall require the admission or reinstatement of an individual as a member of a union, or the hiring, reinstatement, or promotion of an individual as an employee, or the payment to him of any back pay, if such individual was refused admission, suspended, or expelled, or was refused employment or advancement or was suspended or discharged for any reason other than discrimination on account of race, color, religion, sex, or national origin or in violation of section 704(a). (As amended by P.L. No. 92–261, eff. March 24, 1972)

(h) The provisions of the Act entitled "An Act to amend the Judicial Code and to define and limit the jurisdiction of courts sitting in equity, and for other purposes," approved March 23, 1932 (29 U.S.C. 101–115), shall not apply with respect to civil actions brought under this section.

(i) In any case in which an employer, employment agency, or labor organization fails to comply with an order of a court issued in a civil action brought under this section the Commission may commence proceedings to compel compliance with such order. (As amended)

(j) Any civil action brought under this section and any proceedings brought under subsection (j) shall be subject to appeal as provided in sections 1291 and 1292, title 28, United States Code. (As amended by P.L. 92–261, eff. March 24, 1972)

(k) In any action or proceeding under this title the court, in its discretion, may allow the prevailing party, other than the Commission or the United States, a reasonable attorney's fee as part of the costs, and the Commission and the United States shall be liable for costs the same as a private person.

Sec. 707. (a) Whenever the Attorney General has reasonable cause to believe that any person or group of persons is engaged in a pattern or practice of resistance to the full enjoyment of any of the rights secured by this title, and that the pattern or practice is of such a nature and is intended to deny the full exercise of the rights herein described, the Attorney General may bring a civil action in the appropriate district court of the United States by filing with it a complaint (1) signed by him (or in his absence the Acting Attorney General), (2) setting forth facts pertaining to such pattern or practice, and (3) requesting such relief, including an application for a permanent or temporary injunction, restraining order or other order against the person or persons responsible for such pattern or practice, as he deems necessary to insure the full enjoyment of the rights herein described.

(b) The district courts of the United States shall have and shall exercise jurisdiction of proceedings instituted pursuant to this section, and in any such proceeding the Attorney General may file with the clerk of such court a request that a court of three judges be convened to hear and determine the case. Such request by the Attorney General shall be accompanied by a certificate that, in his opinion, the case is of general public importance. A copy of the certificate and request for a three-judge court shall be immediately furnished by such clerk to the chief judge of the circuit (or in his absence, the presiding circuit judge of the circuit) in which the case is pending. Upon receipt of such request it shall be the duty of the chief judge of the circuit or the presiding circuit judge, as the case may be, to designate immediately three judges in such circuit, of whom at least one shall be a circuit judge and another of whom shall be a district judge of the court in which the proceeding was instituted, to hear and determine such case, and it shall be the duty of the judges so designated to assign the case for hearing at the earliest practicable date, to participate in the hearing and determination thereof, and to cause the case to be in every way expedited. An appeal from the final judgment of such court will lie to the Supreme Court.

In the event the Attorney General fails to file such a request in any such proceeding, it shall be the duty of the chief judge of the district (or in his absence, the acting chief judge) in which the case is pending immediately to designate a judge in such district to hear and determine the case. In the event that no judge in the district is available to hear and determine the case, the chief judge of the district, or the acting chief judge, as the case may be, shall certify this fact to the chief judge of the circuit (or in his absence, the acting chief judge) who shall then designate a district or circuit judge of the circuit to hear and determine the case.

It shall be the duty of the judge designated pursuant to this section to assign the case for hearing at the earliest practicable date and to cause the case to be in every way expedited.

(c) Effective two years after the date of enactment of the Equal Employment Opportunity Act of 1972, the functions of the Attorney General under this section shall be transferred to the Commission, together with such personnel, property, records, and unexpended balances of appropriations, allocations, and other funds employed, used, held, available, or to be made available in connection with such functions unless the President submits, and neither House of Congress vetoes, a reorganization plan pursuant to chapter 9 of title 5, United States Code, inconsistent with the provisions of this subsection. The Commission shall carry out such functions in accordance with subsections (d) and (e) of this section.

(d) Upon the transfer of functions provided for in subsection (c) of this section, in all suits commenced pursuant to this section prior to the date of such transfer, proceedings shall continue without abatement, all court orders and decrees shall remain in effect, and the Commission shall be substituted as a party for the United States of America, the Attorney General, or the Acting Attorney General, as appropriate.

(e) Subsequent to the date of enactment of the Equal Employment Opportunity Act of 1972, the Commission shall have authority to investigate and act on a charge of a pattern or practice of discrimination, whether filed by or on behalf of a person claiming to be aggrieved or by a member of the Commission. All such actions shall be conducted in accordance with the procedures set forth in section 706 of this Act. (As last amended by P.L. No. 92–261, eff. March 24, 1972)

Effect of State Laws

Sec. 708. Nothing in this title shall be deemed to exempt or relieve any person from any liability, duty, penalty, or punishment provided by any present or future law of any State or political subdivision of a State, other than any such law which purports to require or permit the doing of any act which would be an unlawful employment practice under this title.

Investigations, Inspections, Records, State Agencies

Sec. 709. (a) In connection with any investigation of a charge filed under section 706, the Commission or its designated representative shall at all reasonable times have access to, for the purposes of examination, and the right to copy any evidence of any person being investigated or proceeded against that relates to unlawful employment practices covered by this title and is relevant to the charge under investigation.

(b) The Commission may cooperate with State and local agencies charged with the administration of State fair employment practices laws and, with the consent of such agencies, may, for the purpose of carrying out its functions and duties under this title and within the limitation of funds appropriated specifically for such purpose, engage in and contribute to the cost of research and other projects of mutual interest undertaken by such agencies, and utilize the services of such agencies and their employees, and, notwithstanding any other provision of law, pay by advance or reimbursement such agencies and their employees for services rendered to assist the Commission in carrying out this title. In furtherance of such cooperative efforts, the Commission may enter into written agreements with such State or local agencies and such agreements may include provisions under which the Commission shall refrain from processing a charge in any cases or class of cases specified in such agreements or under which the Commission shall relieve any person or class of persons in such State or locality from requirements imposed under this section. The Commission shall rescind any such agreement whenever it determines that the agreement no longer serves the interest of effective enforcement of this title.

(c) Every employer, employment agency, and labor organization subject to this title shall (1) make and keep such records relevant to the determinations of whether unlawful employment practices have been or are being committed, (2) preserve such records for such periods, and (3) make such reports therefrom as the Commission shall prescribe by regulation or order, after public hearing, as reasonable, necessary, or appropriate for the enforcement of this title or the regulations or orders thereunder. The Commission shall, by regulation, require each employer, labor organization, and joint labor-management committee subject to this title which controls an apprenticeship or other training program to maintain such records as are reasonably necessary to carry out the purposes of this title, including, but not limited to, a list of applicants who wish to participate in such program, including the chronological order in which applications were received, and to furnish to the Commission upon request, a detailed description of the manner in which persons are selected to participate in the apprenticeship or other training program. Any employer, employment agency, labor organization, or joint labor-management committee which believes that the application to it of any regulation or order issued under this section would result in undue hardship may apply to the Commission for an exemption from the application of such regulation or order, and, if such application for an exemption is denied, bring a civil action in the United States district court for the district where such records are kept. If the Commission or the court, as the case may be, finds that the application of the regulation or order to the employer, employment agency, or labor organization in question would impose an undue hardship, the Commission or the court, as the case may be, may grant appropriate relief. If any person required to comply with the provisions of this subsection fails or refuses to do so, the United States district court for the district in which such person is found, resides, or transacts business, shall, upon application of the Commission, or the Attorney General in a case involving a governmental agency or political subdivision, have jurisdiction to issue to such person an order requiring him to comply.

(d) In prescribing requirements pursuant to subsection (c) of this section, the Commission shall consult with other interested State and Federal agencies and shall endeavor to coordinate its requirements with those adopted by such agencies. The Commission shall furnish upon request and without cost to any State or local agency charged with the administration of a fair employment practice law information obtained pursuant to subsection (c) of this section from any employer, employment agency, labor organization, or joint labor-management committee subject to the jurisdiction of such agency. Such information shall be furnished on condition that it not be made public by the recipient agency prior to the institution of a proceeding under State or local law involving such information. If this condition is violated by a recipient agency, the Commission may decline to honor subsequent requests pursuant to this subsection. (As amended by P.L. 92–261, eff. March 24, 1972)

(e) It shall be unlawful for any officer or employee of the Commission to make public in any manner whatever any information obtained by the Commission pursuant to its authority under this section prior to the institution of any proceeding under this title involving such information. Any officer or employee of the Commission who shall make public in any manner whatever any information in violation of this subsection shall be guilty of a misdemeanor and upon conviction thereof, shall be fined not more than $1,000, or imprisoned not more than one year.

Investigatory Powers

Sec. 710. For the purpose of all hearings and investigations conducted by the Commission or its duly authorized agents or agencies, section 11 of the National Labor Relations Act (49 Stat. 455; 29 U.S.C. 161) shall apply. (As amended by P.L. 92–261, eff. March 24, 1972)

Notices to Be Posted

Sec. 711. (a) Every employer, employment agency and labor organization, as the case may be, shall post and keep posted in conspicuous places upon its premises where notices to employees, applicants for employment and members are customarily posted a notice to be prepared or approved by the Commission setting forth excerpts from or, summaries of, the pertinent provisions of this title and information pertinent to the filing of a complaint.

(b) A willful violation of this section shall be punishable by a fine of not more than $100 for each separate offense.

Veterans' Preference

Sec. 712. Nothing contained in this title shall be construed to repeal or modify any Federal, State, territorial, or local law creating special rights or preference for veterans.

Rules and Regulations

Sec. 713. (a) The Commission shall have authority from time to time to issue, amend, or rescind suitable procedural regulations to carry out the provisions of this title. Regulations issued under this section shall be in conformity with the standards and limitations of the Administrative Procedure Act.

(b) In any action or proceeding based on any alleged unlawful employment practice, no person shall be subject to any liability or punishment for or on account of (1) the commission by such person of an unlawful employment practice if he pleads and proves that the act of omission complained of was in good faith, in conformity with, and in reliance on any written interpretation or opinion of the Commission, or (2) the failure of such person to publish and file any information required by any provision of this title if he pleads and proves that he failed to publish and file such information in good faith, in conformity with the instructions of the Commission issued under this title regarding the filing of such information. Such a defense, if established, shall be a bar to the action or proceeding, notwithstanding that (A) after such act or omission, such interpretation or opinion is modified or rescinded or is determined by judicial authority to be invalid or of no legal effect, or (B) after publishing or filing the description and annual reports, such publication or filing is determined by judicial authority not to be in conformity with the requirements of this title.

Forcibly Resisting the Commission or Its Representatives

Sec. 714. The provisions of sections 111 and 1114, title 18, United States Code, shall apply to officers, agents, and employees of the Commission in the performance of their official duties. Notwithstanding the provisions of sections 111 and 1114 of title 18, United States Code, whoever in violation of the provisions of section 1114 of such title kills a person while engaged in or on account of the performance of his official functions under this Act shall be punished by imprisonment for any term of years or for life. (As amended by P.L. 92–261, eff. March 24, 1972)

Special Study by Secretary of Labor

Sec. 715. There shall be established an Equal Employment Opportunity Coordinating Council (hereinafter referred to in this section as the Council) composed of the Secretary of Labor, the Chairman of the Equal Employment Opportunity Commission, the Attorney General, the Chairman of the United States Civil Service Commission, and the Chairman of the United States Civil Rights Commission, or their respective delegates. The Council shall have the responsibility for developing and implementing agreements, policies and practices designed to maximize effort, promote efficiency, and eliminate conflict, competition, duplication and inconsistency among the operations, functions and jurisdictions of the various departments, agencies and branches of the Federal Government responsible for the implementation and enforcement of equal employment opportunity legislation, orders, and policies. On or before July 1 of each year, the Council shall transmit to the President and to the Congress a report of its activities, together with such recommendations for legislative or administrative changes as it concludes are desirable to further promote the purposes of this section. (As amended by P.L. No. 92–261, eff. March 24, 1972)

Effective Date

Sec. 716. (a) This title shall become effective one year after the date of its enactment. (The effective date thus is July 2, 1965.)

(b) Notwithstanding subsection (a), sections of this title other than sections 703, 704, 706, and 707 shall become effective immediately.

(c) The President shall, as soon as feasible after the enactment of this title, convene one or more conferences for the purpose of enabling the leaders of groups whose members will be affected by this title to become familiar with the rights afforded and obligations imposed by its provisions, and for the purpose of making plans which will result in the fair and effective administration of this title when all of its provisions become effective. The President shall invite the participation in such conference or conferences of (1) the members of the President's Committee on Equal Employment Opportunity, (2) the members of the Commission on Civil Rights, (3) representatives of State and local agencies engaged in furthering equal employment opportunity, (4) representatives of private agencies engaged in furthering equal employment opportunity, and (5) representatives of employers, labor organizations, and employment agencies who will be subject to this title.

Non Discrimination in Federal Government Employment

Sec. 717. (a) All personnel actions affecting employees or applicants for employment (except with regard to aliens employed outside the limits of the United States) in military departments as defined in section 102 of title 5, United States Code in executive agencies (other than the General Accounting Office) as defined in section 105 of title 5, United States Code (including employees and applicants for employment who are paid from nonappropriated funds), in the United States Postal Service and the Postal Rate Commission, in those units of the Government of the District of Columbia having positions in the competitive service, and in those units of the legislative and judicial branches of the Federal Government having positions in the competitive service, and in the Library of Congress shall be made free from any discrimination based on race, color, religion, sex, or national origin.

(b) Except as otherwise provided in this subsection, the Civil Service Commission shall have authority to enforce the provisions of subsection (a) through appropriate remedies, including reinstatement or hiring of employees with or without back pay, as will effectuate the policies of this section, and shall issue such rules, regulations, orders and instructions as it deems necessary and appropriate to carry out its responsibilities under this section. The Civil Service Commission shall—

(1) be responsible for the annual review and approval of a national and regional equal employment opportunity plan which each department and agency and each appropriate unit referred to in subsection (a) of this section shall submit in order to maintain an affirmative program of equal employment opportunity for all such employees and applicants for employment;

(2) be responsible for the review and evaluation of the operation of all agency equal employment opportunity programs, periodically obtaining and publishing (on at least a semi-annual basis) progress reports from each such department, agency, or unit; and

(3) consult with and solicit the recommendations of interested individuals, groups, and organizations relating to equal employment opportunity.

The head of each such department, agency, or unit shall comply with such rules, regulations, orders, and instructions which shall include a provision that an employee or applicant for employment shall be notified of any final action taken on any complaint of discrimination filed by him thereunder. The plan submitted by each department, agency, and unit shall include, but not be limited to—

(1) provision for the establishment of training and education programs designed to provide a maximum opportunity for employees to advance so as to perform at their highest potential; and

(2) a description of the qualifications in terms of training and experience relating to equal employment opportunity for the principal and operating officials of each such department, agency, or unit responsible for carrying out the equal employment opportunity program and of the allocation of personnel and resources proposed by such department, agency, or unit to carry out its equal employment opportunity program.

With respect to employment in the Library of Congress, authorities granted in this subsection to the Civil Service Commission shall be exercised by the Librarian of Congress.

(c) Within thirty days of receipt of notice of final action taken by a department, agency, or unit referred to in subsection 717(a), or by the Civil Service Commission upon an appeal from a decision or order of such department, agency, or unit on a complaint of discrimination based on race, color, religion, sex or national origin, brought pursuant to subsection (a) of this section, Executive Order 11478 or any succeeding executive orders, or after one hundred and eighty days from the filing of the initial charge with the department, agency, or unit or with the Civil Service Commission on appeal from a decision or order of such department, agency, or unit until such time as final action may be taken by a department, agency, or unit, an employee or applicant for employment, if aggrieved by the final disposition of his complaint, or by the failure to take final action on his complaint, may file a civil action as provided in section 706, in which civil action the head of the department, agency, or unit, as appropriate, shall be the defendant.

(d) The provisions of section 706 (f) through (k), as applicable, shall govern civil actions brought hereunder.

(e) Nothing contained in this Act shall relieve any Government agency or official of its or his primary responsibility to assure nondiscrimination in employment as required by the Constitution and statutes or of its or his responsibilities under Executive Order 11478 relating to equal employment opportunity in the Federal Government. (As amended by 92–261, eff. March 24, 1972)

Special Provision with Respect to Denial, Termination and Suspension of Government Contracts

Sec. 718. No Government contract, or portion thereof, with any employer, shall be denied, withheld, terminated, or suspended, by any agency or officer of the United States under any equal employment opportunity law or order, where such employer has an affirmative action plan which has previously been accepted by the Government for the same facility within the past twelve months without first according such employer full hearing and adjudication under the provisions of title 5, United States Code, section 554, and the following pertinent sections: Provided, That if such employer has deviated substantially from such previously agreed to affirmative action plan, this section shall not apply: Provided further, That for the purposes of this section an affirmative action plan shall be deemed to have been accepted by the Government at the time the appropriate compliance agency has accepted such plan unless within forty-five days thereafter the Office of Federal Contract Compliance has disapproved such plan. (As added by P.L. 92–261, eff. March 24, 1972)

Index